FV

BLACK CHILD DEVELOPMENT IN AMERICA 1927-1977

compiled by HECTOR F. MYERS,
PHYLLIS G. RANA,
MARCIA HARRIS

BLACK CHILD DEVELOPMENT IN AMERICA 1927-1977

An Annotated Bibliography

GREENWOOD PRESS
Westport, Connecticut • London, England

Library of Congress Cataloging in Publication Data

Myers, Hector F
  Black child development in America, 1927-1977.

  Includes index.
  1. Afro-American children—Bibliography. 2. Child
development—United States—Bibliography. I. Rana,
Phyllis G., joint author. II. Harris, Marcia, joint
author. III. Title.
Z1361.N39M94   [E185.86]   016.30143'14'0973   78-20028
ISBN 0-313-20719-4

Library of Congress Catalog Card Number: 78-20028
ISBN: 0-313-20719-4

First published in 1979

Greenwood Press, Inc.
51 Riverside Avenue, Westport, Connecticut 06880

Printed in the United States of America

10 9 8 7 6 5 4 3 2 1

CONTENTS

PREFACE

This bibliography represents a comprehensive compilation and catalogue of the social science literature on the Black child in America. Although not exhaustive in its coverage, this document includes most of the literature published on the subject in the major social science journals and periodicals during the past five decades. The motivation for this book emerged from the need of the compilers and their colleagues to have available the full range of published material on the development of the Black child in one simple-to-use reference source. As the size and number of entries in this document suggest, Black child development has been an area of considerable interest and research activity over the past years. Currently, however, there is no single organized source in which this voluminous literature can be accessed. Consequently, students and scholars in the field must engage in the exhausting and often frustrating task of searching the literature on their topic of interest without any reasonable sense of what the available literature on the topic might be, what the major trends in that body of research are, or how the literature on their topic fits historically with the trends in the general area of Black child development. Consequently, there is a certain redundancy and repetition of theoretical and methodological errors throughout this literature.

The compilers in no way endorse the assumptions or findings of the studies listed. Rather, the intent of this document is simply to provide the serious scholar, professional, and student a well-organized, annotated reference document covering almost all of the available literature on Black child development. It is hoped that this document will encourage many critical review articles as well as stimulate empirical studies that will clarify many of the issues and questions about the Black child that the current literature either ignores, distorts, or fails to clarify.

The scope of the work included in this document covers a span of fifty years: 1927 to 1977. The articles are organized into five major areas of emphasis: language development, physical development, cognitive development, personality development, and social development. These categories are generally representative of the focus of attention in the developmental literature. However, the content of many of the articles actually covered several of these areas. Nevertheless, the authors grouped the articles according to their major emphasis as suggested in the titles or abstracts of the studies.

Due to the wide range of issues that have been addressed in Black child development over the past decades and the many diverse sources in which this literature has been published, there is great variability in the quality, content, and organization of the abstracts. A full notation of the abstract sources used is included on page xix. The articles selected for inclusion in the bibliography were not chosen at random, nor were any articles including a sample of Black children excluded, regardless of the quality of the study or the theoretical persuasion of the author. All identified articles that addressed any of the five areas of Black child development from birth through adolescence were included. In a few instances where Black children were part of a sample with adults, these studies were also included. Furthermore, due to the nature of most research on the Black child, he/she is usually studied in comparison to White children and/or to other non-White ethnic groups. As a result, a substantial number of the studies listed include samples of White, Latino (for example, Mexican-American or Puerto Rican), and Native American children. The compilers do not consider this to be detracting from the major theme of Black child development. Rather, it reflects the predominant practice in social science research to study the Black child primarily as he or she compares to or differs from White or other non-Black ethnic minority children.

Although comprehensive, this bibliography includes only the social science literature on the Black child published in the professional journals. Omitted from this document are the many important works on the Black child that are part of the popular literature. This literature includes such important works as Ralph Ellison, *Invisible Man* (1952); Richard Wright, *Black Boy* (1945); Claude Brown, *Manchild in the Promised Land* (1965); Anne Moody, *Growing Up In Mississippi* (1968); Maya Angelou, *I Know Why the Caged Bird Sings* (1969); Toni Morrison, *Bluest Eye* (1970), *Sula* (1973), and *The Song of Solomon* (1977); Zora Neale Hurston, *Their Eyes Were Watching God* (1939); Rosa Guy, *The Friends* (1973) and *Ruby* (1976); Kristin Hunter, *Survivors* (1975) and *Soul Brothers and Sister Lou* (1968); Mildred Taylor, *Roll of Thunder Hear My Cry* (1976); Frankcina Glass, *Marvin and Tige* (1977); Phyllis Harrison and Barbara Wyden, *The Black Child—A Parents' Guide* (1973); and James P. Comer and Alvin Poussaint, *Black Child Care* (1975).

It is important that serious students become familiar with this body of knowledge and use it to supplement the scientific literature. This folk literature represents the primary literary vehicle that looks at the Black child within his/her phenomenal reality. The authors as participant-observers and experiential authorities convey the theme of the child as actor engaged in the struggle for survival and mastery in an essentially hostile and ungiving world. Although the scientific literature concentrates on measuring the characteristics and abilities of the child relative to standardized norms, the popular literature describes the transaction of environmental demands and the development of personal characteristics and coping strategies in Black children.

Except for a select few, all abstracts were quoted directly from the original abstract sources. Those that were created or modified by the compilers are so identified. In addition, a limited number of articles were not annotated. This is due to the fact that they were not annotated in the original abstract source. Generally, these references represent earlier research on the Black child.

Each abstract is listed numerically throughout the bibliography. The Author and Subject indexes provide an easy method of locating citations by referring to these numbers. The format of each reference follows the American Psychological Association (APA) style: The name of the article is in lowercase with capitalization of the first letter of all proper names and capitalization of the first letter after major punctuations. If citation is from a journal, the volume is underlined and the number of the journal is in parentheses. In addition, there are several common abbreviations used throughout the bibliography in the abstracts. The abbreviations that were in the original abstract source were retained for the purposes of this document. A list of these abbreviations with their full meaning can be found on page xxi.

The authors are deeply indebted to the Center for Minority Group Mental Health Programs, National Institute of Mental Health, for their faith, continued support, and funding of the Frantz Fanon Research and Development Center. We further acknowledge Dr. John Peterson, who as a staff member of the Fanon Center initiated the formal organization and preparation of the first draft of the manuscript and contributed to the writing of the introduction. A special note of appreciation is also due to Dr. Lewis M. King, director of the Fanon Center, and to the entire staff of the center for their forebearance and continued encouragement of this project. We thank Bonnie Goss for her typing and editorial services throughout the various phases of the project, and we appreciate the contributions of Jean Collins and the many Black students at UCLA and the other colleges and universities in southern California. Their curiosity and continued struggle with the treatment of the Black child in the social science literature stimulated this bibliography.

Special acknowledgments and thanks are given to the following organizations for permission to reprint abstracts in this document: Society for Research in Child Development for *Child Development Abstracts & Bibliography*; National Institute of Education for *ERIC Abstracts*—Education Resources Information Center; National Institute of Mental Health, Alcohol, Drug Abuse, and Mental

Health Administration, U.S. Department of Health, Education and Welfare for the National Institute of Mental Health Clearinghouse; American Psychological Association for *Psychological Abstracts,* copyright 1979, reprinted by permission; Sage Publications, Inc., for *Sage Race Relations Abstracts* and *Human Resources Abstracts*; and Sociological Abstracts, Inc., by special permission for *Sociological Abstracts* and *Language and Language Behavior Abstracts.*

This bibliography was supported by Public Health Service Grant MH 25580-03 from the Center for Minority Group Mental Health Programs, National Institute of Mental Health.

Hector F. Myers
Phyllis G. Rana
Marcia Harris

INTRODUCTION

A civilization that proves incapable of solving the problems it creates is a decadent civilization. A civilization that chooses to close its eyes to its most crucial problems is a stricken civilization. A civilization that uses its principles for trickery and deceit is a dying civilization.

—Aime Cesaire, *Discourse on Colonialism*, 1972.

   The American scientific community has been engaging in a continuous struggle to identify and define the factors that account for the relative status and functioning of the Black child in American society. As the length and breadth of this bibliography clearly reflect, this has been a very active research area fraught with many conflicts and controversies. Despite the many divergent views on the issues, this voluminous literature consistently describes the Black American child as comparatively less equipped and endowed than his White counterpart. The various controversies that are evident among the investigations emerge not from any questions of the assumptions, paradigms, or methodologies used in addressing the Black child, but rather from the attempt to make causal attributions of the findings to discrete psychobiological processes. Therefore, the major question consistently asked is whether the Black child's "deficits" relative to the normative White child are due to "a faulty gene pool" or to "a depriving environment." This essentially negative-comparative perspective does not allow for the exploration of more generic and less value-laden questions about the nature of the Black child as a developmental and transacting being within particular phenomenal contexts and historical realities. Instead, there is a voluminous body of research that essentially defines the Black child as an inadequate version of the White child. He or she has no functional being except as he/she is similar to or different from the "idealized White norm." The nature of the phenomena—that is, the Black child—is lost due to the negative comparative reductionism of the process and method of study.

The investigation of Black child development in America involves a number of stages that reflect general societal concerns. As a result of mass immigration, the major interest in the 1920s was the differential assimilation of the non-White racial subgroups into the population. In the field of psychology, considerable attention was devoted to comparative analyses of physical characteristics between Blacks and Whites. The beginning of massive internal migration by Black Americans to northern urban centers in the 1930s was reflected in studies of eugenics and the nature-nurture controversy of minority intellectual performance. Subsequently, the rise of Hitler, World War II, and the Civil Rights Movement focused concern on studies of the irrational and psychodynamic aspects of prejudice toward minority Blacks. Somewhat later, the trend in empirical studies changed to represent the positive psychological consequences of minority group membership and racial identity associated with the Black Power and nationalist Pan-African movements. Finally, a related but less fully explored concern involved systematic attempts to study the attitudinal and psychological effects of desegregation on Black children, an interest sparked by the Supreme Court Decision of 1954.

The general results of these studies suggest that the behavioral development of Black children is impaired in comparison to Whites by a number of factors. Some studies of physical development of Black infants point to a specific acceleration of gross motor function, while other suggest a more global precocity. Other investigators have not confirmed these findings. For a number of years, it has been found that analgesics and anesthetics employed during labor and delivery, as well as deprived nutritional diets, affect the physical behavior of the minority newborn infant. It has also been found that the feeding patterns of the newborn are altered by the level of obstetric medication used during labor and delivery. Although the child may not need to be taught most of the basic motor patterns, in recent years a number of studies have documented the differential effects of caregiver practices on the development of exploratory behavior in Black and White children. Evidence has been reported to suggest that the restricted range of exploratory behaviors of Black children may be attributable to Black mothers being more restrictive, disapproving, and controlling toward their children.

During the past few decades, similar evidence has been marshaled to support the view that minority children are deficient in verbal expressiveness, a deficiency largely attributed to cultural deprivation. Many Black children in the United States have been reported to speak an English dialect often considered an ungrammatical approximation to standard English. Further, the academic failure of Black children has been attributed, at least in part, to this presumed deficiency in language. Many of the studies argue that lower-class mothers tend to use more impoverished language models with their children. Conversely, some investigators have provided data that minority children are not verbally inexpressive. These investigators have questioned situations in which spontaneous, culturally congruent speech was not examined within its cultural context. Although it is highly probable that infants are capable of thought before the development of formal speech, evidence suggests that once language begins, it becomes a major factor influencing the pattern and rate of cognitive development. Therefore, it is important that the question of richness versus restrictiveness of Black language be clarified.

A major theoretical issue in the study of Black-White differences in cognitive development is the nature versus nurture question. The contemporary genetic-environmental debate about IQ relates to two types of general learning ability that are differentially exhibited by children of various socioeconomic status and racial groups. The data appear to suggest racial differences as measured by conventional intelligence tests in conceptual and problem-solving abilities. On the other hand, no differences in associative learning are generally reported. Enormous disagreement continues, however, about the relative contribution of inheritance versus environmental determinants of this intellectual performance. Essentially, the studies that involve research with twins provide the greatest support for the genetically derived basis of intelligence. Intervention studies have indicated, in comparison, that phenotypic differences in IQ can be changed given appropriate and timely environmental manipulations.

Finally, the personality and social development of behavior among Black American children has been found to generally parallel the trends reported for physical and cognitive development. The more recent studies strongly suggest that the major political upheaval of the 1960s and early 1970s had some marked positive effects on these areas of Black child development. Studies performed in the late 1940s and early 1950s report that Blacks perceive the contradiction between the American ideals of equality and freedom and justice for all and their roles as subjugated members of a racially segregated society. Further, the data report a pattern of aggressive behavior manifested among Blacks that is attributed to the presence of deleterious racial and personal attitudes—low self-esteem. Noteworthy among these results were findings that preschool Black children tended to reject and devalue their own ethnic group and to select White identity models. This configuration of self-devaluation, ingroup rejection, and outgroup preference was consistently replicated for over two decades. In contrast, however, recent evidence suggests that the attitudes of Blacks have changed radically since the emergence of the Black Power and Black consciousness movements of the 1960s. In studies on self-esteem, for example, Black children have no longer been found to reject their own racial group but rather tend to prefer and embrace it. Further, several longitudinal studies have supported these results regarding the personality and social development of Blacks during adolescence and adulthood.

From even this cursory review of this literature, several themes that are offshoots of and contribute to the elaboration of the more general theme of the deficient Black child can be identified. These themes are developed and elaborated upon to varying degrees depending on the quality of the studies. By and large, the earlier studies of the 1920s to 1950s were of poor quality both theoretically and methodologically. Simplistic questions were generally asked, and poorly structured and control studies were conducted; yet broad sweeping conclusions applicable to all Black children were often drawn. Although they continued to elaborate on the same deficit theme, the studies of more recent vintage—the 1960s to 1970s— have been better designed, asked more complex questions, and been somewhat more cautious in their conclusions. Despite the variance in overall quality of the studies cited, however, these compilers contend that the vast majority of the studies on the Black child consistently commit certain thematic errors. Most salient among these are:

1. *The Black-White comparison paradigm.* Researchers argue, somewhat legitimately, that the scientific pursuit of knowledge requires points of reference that are used and assumed to be normative. They also argue that an important objective in the research on minority group children is the need to determine what factors in these groups account for their relative failure to develop the "normative" skills for performance at the expected levels within society. The appropriate statistical theory and technology has been developed to define the parameters guiding the process by which norms are "objectively determined." Unfortunately, however, social scientists have begun to reify the concept of norms. They have lost sight of the fact that despite all objective statistical principles and procedures, norms are convenient and pragmatic points of reference that represent particular societal values, ideologies, and social praxes. Norms are not objective, immutable facts in the real world. Therefore, their pragmatic utility does not justify their use as the primary and only model for research on the Black child.

The research on Black child development with its consistent practice of defining Black behavior exclusively in terms of White normative behavior perpetuates the mystification and idealization of the White norm. In so doing, very little can be said about variation among Black children within the phenomenal Black reality. What, for example, is normative Black development? What factors seem to account for deviations from this norm, both positive and negative, among Black children? Is the environment different, not only quantitatively but also qualitatively, for Blacks? Questions such as these are not currently being asked by researchers, nor are they likely to be explored as long as a Black-White comparison model of inquiry is used exclusively.

2. *The utility of "standardized" measures as primary tools of investigations.* This error represents a specialized form of the Black-White comparison paradigm. In many studies, White comparison groups are not actually included. Instead, only standardized tests are used to measure the variables of interest. The rationale

given is the need for comparability of results and the need for a standard reference in order to insure consistency and meaningfulness in interpretation of the findings. Furthermore, the assumption is made that most of these instruments were normed on a sample that was representative of the entire U.S. population. The assumption is, in fact, not tenable for the majority of the tests popularly used.

A further and even more serious error is committed when these tests are not either replaced or at least supplemented by other methods of assessment that are sensitive to the phenomenal realities of Black children. The arguments pro and con on this issue are legion. Suffice it to say that the fundamental question is not whether the tests are valid for Black children, or whether the tests have been used inappropriately as tools of oppression. The answers to these questions rest on value premises that are not consensually shared. The fundamental scientific question remains how to accurately and sensitively assess the Black child and for what purpose such an assessment would be made. If the goal is to know the child, then measures normed on non-Black children are not likely to be the best tools to achieve this end. One runs the risk of committing the error of scientific arrogance when the phenomena are forced to fit the tools rather than having the tools fit the phenomena. As Fanon sensitively remarks:

I, the man of color, want only this: that the tool never possess the man.[1]

3. *The assumption that Difference = Deficiency.* This theoretical weakness consistent throughout the literature is related to issues 1 and 2 above. Consistent with the assumptions of the appropriateness of the White norm as the referent for Black behavior and of standardized tests as valid measures of the same, researchers, by logical extension, have interpreted deviations in Black performance on these tests as indicative of Black deficiencies. The historical experiences of the oppression of Blacks in the United States make it reasonable to expect that deficiencies are likely to exist in Blacks as a group. The same should be expected for all oppressed individuals and groups, including the poor, other ethnic minorities, women, and gays. We may even logically expect group deficiencies to be evident among White males, the group generally acknowledged as the ruling class of American society, because even the oppressor suffers from the system of oppression.

The problem rests, therefore, not in whether deficiencies actually exist in Black children as a group, but whether all of the assessed Black-White differences are truly reflective of deficiencies. The unquestioning tendency of many investigations to make this assumption makes them both victims and agents of cultural ethnocentric arrogance. Groups differ in culturally defined and culturally consistent ways. These differences are generic to the groups and are legitimate ways of being in the world. There is a tendency to ignore the legitimacy of these differences as normative and to recognize only one normative cultural behavior pattern. Thus, despite the vastness of the literature on the Black child, there are no defined, reliable, and acceptable criteria for distinguishing what is a legitimate Black-White difference from what is a true deficiency.

Furthermore, the possibility that many of the assessed Black-White differences may actually represent legitimate strengths in the Black child has not been considered. An excellent example of this is the often-reported physical precocity of the Black child. Investigations reluctantly acknowledge this group difference in physical development and note quickly that the difference disappears somewhere between the ages of thirteen months and two years. This consistent preoccupation with deficit labeling along with the total absence of any consideration of strengths in the Black child seriously questions the ideal of scientific impartiality and objectivity.

4. *The myth of Black homogeneity and the normativeness of the Black poor.* A chronic methodological weakness in the studies included in this bibliography is the consistent practice of comparing the behavior of low-income Black children to that of middle-income White children. This design commits two major errors. First, it confounds social class with race; and second, it perpetuates the implicit assumption that the behavior and characteristics of the Black lower class are normative and representative of all Black behavior.

With few exceptions, most of the early studies failed to account for the variable of social class in the study of Black behavior. Thus, characteristics that were attributed to the factor of race may very well have been more a function of the social class and geographic location of the sample. Later studies began to note the important effect of social class on many of the behavioral characteristics previously attributed to race.

An additional criticism is also warranted, particularly of the psychological literature. The variable of social class has consistently been used as a structural, demographic variable. Typically two or more social classes are identified using criteria that are presumably free of cross-ethnic variability (for example, the Hollingshead and Redlick categories). Such an approach assumes, without verification, that the state of being lower class or middle class is the same for Blacks and for Whites. Thus, these are essentially homogeneous and comparable categories. The classical sociological studies by Frazier in the 1940s and 1950s noted several important quantitative and qualitative differences between the Black and White middle class despite similarities in such standard SES criteria as parental education and/or income. Sociologists have also noted significant qualitative differences between subgroups among the poor. Several investigations distinguish, for example, three categories within the lower classes: the working poor, the stable or integrated poor, and the disinherited. It is reasonable to suspect from the characteristics attributed to these groups that important psychological and behavioral differences exist between them, both within and across ethnic lines. Unfortunately, research on the Black child fails to make these distinctions.

Finally, the research perpetuates the myth of homogeneity among Black children by consistently sampling mainly from low-income groups, by failing to study the Black population as a distinct group with its unique within-group variations, and by generally excluding middle-class samples from their designs. The psychological study of human development may very well be characterized as the study of the development of the White, middle-class American child. Black child development, on the other hand, is essentially the product of the study of the Black child from the lower classes. The middle-class Black child and the lower-class White child are comparatively invisible in our scientific literature.

In summary, a major theme consistent throughout the social science literature is the inferiorization of the Black child, both in terms of the assumptions made, the assessment tools and the sampling designs used, and the results reported and interpreted. If it can be assumed that the literature compiled in this comprehensive volume is accurately reflective of the norm of American social sciences, then our assumption of scientific objectivity and unbiased inquiry is untenable. What is found here is a body of literature fraught with ideological and theoretical biases, methodological imprecisions, and conclusions with questionable generalizability. It would be unfair and unwise, however, to discard all of this research as inadequate. The more recent studies are qualitatively superior and less subject to the criticisms discussed. We hope that making this document available will serve to stimulate greater commitment by the most sophisticated scientific talent available to tackle the complex issues in Black child development. As Frantz Fanon noted,

There comes a time when silence is dishonest. What matters is not (simply) to know the world, but to change it.[2]

NOTES

1. Frantz Fanon, *Black Skin, White Masks* (New York: Grove Press, 1967), p. 231.
2. Frantz Fanon, *Towards the African Revolution* (New York: Grove Press, 1969), p. 54.

ABSTRACT SOURCES

1. *Child Development Abstracts and Bibliography: 1927-1977.* Society for Child Development, University of Chicago Press, 5801 Ellis Avenue, Chicago, Illinois 60637.
2. *ERIC Abstracts (Education Resources Information Center): 1975-1977.* Central ERIC, National Institute of Education, Office of Dissemination, 1200 19th Street N.W., Washington, D.C. 20208.
3. *Human Resources Abstracts: 1966-1977.* Sage Publications, Inc., Publishers of Professional Social Sciences, 275 South Beverly Drive, Beverly Hills, California 90212.
4. *Language and Language Behavior Abstracts: 1968-1977.* Sociological Abstracts (Cosponsored by the International Sociological Association), Post Office Box 22206, San Diego, California 92122.
5. *NIMH (National Institute of Mental Health) Clearinghouse: 1927-1977.* National Institute of Mental Health, Alcohol, Drug Abuse, and Mental Health Administration, U. S. Department of Health, Education and Welfare, 5600 Fishers Lane, Rockville, Maryland 20857.
6. *Psychological Abstracts: 1927-1977.* American Psychological Association, 1200 17th Street N.W., Washington, D.C. 20036.
7. *Sage Race Relations Abstracts: 1975-1977.* Sage Publications, Inc., Publishers of Professional Social Sciences, 275 South Beverly Drive, Beverly Hills, California 90212.
8. *Sociological Abstracts: 1959-1977.* Sociological Abstracts (Cosponsored by the International Sociological Association), Post Office Box 22206, San Diego, California 92122.

ABBREVIATIONS

This list includes only those abbreviations whose definitions are *not* provided in the text of the document.

CA	Chronological age
df	Degrees of freedom in Chi-square
EQ	Abstract from the *Eugenics Quarterly*
f	Frequency
F ratio	Analysis of variance (F statistic)
F-test	Analysis of variance
FR	Fixed ratio
Gm	Grams
IQ	Intelligence quotient
LF	Labor force
LMc	Lower middle class
LLc	Lower lower class
LSc	Lower social class
MA	Mental age
MMPI	Minnesota Multiphasic Personality Inventory
Ms	Middle status
Md	Median
msec.	Millisecond

N	Number of cases
n.d.	No date
O, O's	Observer, observers
PA	Abstract from *Psychological Abstracts*
R, R's	Respondent, respondents
r, r'ed	Correlation, correlated
Rc	Ruling class
r.p.m.	Revolutions per minute
RT	Reaction time
S, Ss	Subject, subjects
SC	Social class
SD	Social distance
SES	Socioeconomic status
TAT	Thematic Apperception Test
VR	Variable ratio
WAIS	Wechsler Adult Intelligence Scale
Wc	Working class
WISC	Wechsler Intelligence Scale for Children
$\bar{x}$	Mean, average
X^2	Chi-square
$\leqq$	Total

BLACK CHILD DEVELOPMENT IN AMERICA 1927-1977

1

LANGUAGE DEVELOPMENT

1. Ammon, P. R. and Ammon, M. S. Effects of training black preschool children in vocabulary vs. sentence construction. Journal of Educational Psychiatry, 1971, 62 (5), 421-426.

Assigned 36 male and 36 black lower class preschoolers to vocabulary training, sentence training, and control groups. Each subject was tested before and after a six-week training period with the Peabody Picture Vocabulary Test (PPVI), a sentence imitation test (SIT), and a picture interview (PI). Vocabulary training involved practice in recognizing and applying words from the PPVI and the PI. Sentence training consisted of imitating sentences similar to those in the SIT and constructing new instances of the same sentence types. Analyses of variance show that vocabulary training had a positive effect on recognition and production of the words taught (p<.025), but did not transfer to sentence training. Results suggest that vocabulary is more amenable to early training with disadvantaged children.

2. Anastasi, A. and D'Angelo, R. Y. A comparison of Negro and white preschool children in language development and Goodenough Draw-A-Man IQ. Journal of Genetic Psychology, 1952, 81, 147-165.

Goodenough's IQs and linguistic data were obtained on 5-year-old Negro and white children. Socioeconomic factors were uniform for the two groups. No significant race differences were found in Goodenough scores, but girls excelled in all subgroups. Mean sentence length yielded a significant Race x Sex interaction. In the white groups the girls surpassed the boys, while in the Negro groups, the boys excelled. 32 references.

3. Anastasiow, N. J. and Stayroah, N. G. Miscue language patterns
of mildly retarded and nonretarded students. American Journal of
Mental Deficiency, 1973, 77 (4), 431-434.

Investigated the differences and similarities in the language
miscues of 10 black educable mental retardates (EMRs) and three
nonretarded black groups: 27 kindergartners; 13 first graders;
and 33 fourth and sixth graders (CA peers of the EMR groups).
Responses to a variation of P. Menyuk's repeated sentence task
were analyzed. The sentences employed a wide variety of basic
sentence types and syntactic structures. It was found that EMRs
were similar to their CA peers on concrete word errors, and similar to kindergartners on function-word errors. These results
lend support for the hypothesis that EMRs have a slower rate of
language development, and suggest that existing language programs for EMRs should concentrate on function words.

4. Asbury, C. A. Some effects of training on verbal mental functioning in Negro preschool children: A research note. Journal of Negro
Education, 1970, 39 (1), 100-103.

The present experiment was undertaken to investigate the effects
of a selected training procedure on the verbal development of
Negro preschool children, as measured by a standardized test of
verbal aptitude. More specifically, the study sought to explore
differences which might result from a defined period of structured intervention in a learning situation through use of published materials and outline of procedure. It is concluded that
specialized training of Negro preschool children for a short
period of time does not result in a significant improvement of
their mental functioning in the area of verbal ability. Apparently,
substantial gains in this ability are influenced in no small way
by factors which await further investigation to determine their
nature and the extent to which they come to bear. This is an
area which should be subjected to more intensive exploration.
Reprinted by permission.

5. Bachmann, J. K. Field techniques in an urban language study.
TESOL Quarterly, 1970, 4 (3), 255-260.

To examine differences in nonstandard grammatical usage among and
between Negro and white working class informants a sample of 24
individuals was selected. It was thought that the speech of
kindergarten children would show greater differences than that of
adults. Accordingly, Negro and white children and their parents
were interviewed in Alexandria, Virginia, a southern dialect
area. Four tasks involving free conversation, description of
pictures, repetition and direct eliciting were presented to each
informant. The expectation that the amount of nonstandard usage
would vary according to the type of task administered was confirmed, especially among the adults. Four of the five statistically significant differences involved the Negro children. The
two significant differences between Negro children and white children (use of zero copula and the uninflected present tense verb
with third person singular subject) were no longer significant
between the adult groups, suggesting that the differences become

less pronounced with age. No significant differences were found between the adult informant groups. Negro children had significantly greater usage of the form "hisself" and of zero copula than did their parents, and the white children had greater usage of the form "was" with plural subject. The size of the sample was limited by the number of available white and Negro children with comparable family backgrounds. It was possible, however, to construct a model for in-depth analysis using different eliciting techniques which might be helpful for future studies. Reprinted by permission.

6. Baldwin, T.L., McFarlane, P. T., and Garvey, C. J. Children's communication accuracy related to race and socioeconomic status. Child Development, 1971, 42 (2), 345-357.

Arranged 96 fifth graders in dyads of peers of the same sex, socioeconomic status (SES) and race. Male and female, low- and middle-SES, and black and white dyads were observed working on a task which required accurate communication of descriptive information. Results show that middle-SES dyads were significantly more accurate than low-SES dyads, and white dyads were significantly more accurate than black dyads. Observed differences could not be attributed to differences in the: (a) mean dyad IQ, or (b) amount of verbal production. Differences between SES groups are partly explained by differences in the number of critical descriptive attributes communicated.

7. Baratz, J. C. A bi-dialectal task for determining language proficiency in economically disadvantaged Negro children. Child Development, 1969, 40 (3), 889-902.

Administered to disadvantaged Negro and lower middle class white children a repetition task involving standard and nonstandard English sentences. Results indicated Negroes performed significantly better than whites on the nonstandard stimuli. The converse was true for the standard sentences. The interaction of age and grammatical features was also significant for both groups. Results indicate that: (a) there are two dialects involved in the educational complex of black subjects; (b) black subjects are generally not bi-dialectal; (c) there is evidence of interference from their dialect when blacks attempt to use standard English; and (d) language assessment of disadvantaged Negroes must involve measures of their knowledge of nonstandard English, as well as additional measures of their knowledge of standard English.

8. Baratz, J. C. Language and cognitive assessment of Negro children: Assumptions and research needs. Journal of the American Speech and Hearing Association, 1969, 11 (3), 87-91.

Differences between standard English and Negro nonstandard English occur in varying degrees in regard to the sound system, grammar and vocabulary. The psychologist has viewed these differences in terms of "underdevelopment." Nonstandard English should be viewed from a linguistic perspective. A linguist makes three basic assumptions: (1) All humans develop language. The linguist assumes that any verbal system used by a community is a language, and that no language is structurally better than any other language. (2) That children learn language in the context of their total environment. (3) That by the time the child is five, he has developed language -- he has learned the rules of his linguistic environment.

9. Baratz, J. C. Language in the economically disadvantaged child: A perspective. Journal of the American Speech and Hearing Association, 1968, 10, 143-145.

A review of the literature suggests that the economically deprived child has learned a language which differs from standard English. Therefore, the speech pathologist must view these children differently from those having language pathologies stemming from physical or emotional difficulties. The language of the disadvantaged child is different but not pathological. Instead of being remediated, he needs to be taught standard English.

10. Baratz, J. C. Should black children learn white dialect? Journal of the American Speech and Hearing Association, 1970, 12 (9), 415-417.

Standardization is a sociolinguistic fact, and black children should be taught standard English. Standard English is the dialect which uses a set of grammatical patterns in oral pronunciation similar to those used in written form. Negro nonstandard dialect uses a set of distinctive grammar patterns not in conformity with the written forms of English. The opposition to such a program involves the parents and those who feel that "the black man always is the one who has to change." Others contend that Negro nonstandard dialect and standard English are compatible, therefore a nonstandard speaker need not learn standard English. All of these oppositions cannot stand up to linguistic and social reality. It is concluded that the black child is automatically excluded if he does not learn standard English, and therefore, the child should be taught the reading and writing skills of standard English so that he will be able to speak standard English. Reprinted by permission.

11. Baratz, S. S. and Baratz, J. C. Negro ghetto children and urban education: A cultural solution. Florida FL Reporter, 1969, 7 (1), 13-14 and 151.

The failure of urban education to educate Negro ghetto children is examined and the present means of dealing with the problem are viewed as clearly inadequate. The difficulty a Negro child has in acquiring reading skills (an important measure of educational success) is due to a cultural variable: the Negro ghetto child has a different language system which is part of his culture and which interferes with his learning to read. Unless and until this variable is considered, and specific educational innovation based upon it, the majority of the inner city Negro children will continue to fail despite the introduction of social improvements to the educational setting. Three reasons are given why the Negro dialect has not received recognition: (a) it is superfi-

cially similar to standard English; (b) it poses a threat to
the middle class Negro who has acquired standard English; and
(c) there is a confusion of equality with sameness. It is
stressed that to say a Negro is different is not to say that
he is inferior. One should not confuse a political and moral
position with a cultural fact. Reprinted by permission.

12. Bartel, N. R., Grill, J. J., and Bryen, D. N. Language characteristics of black children: Implications for assessment. Journal
of School Psychology, 1973, 11 (4), 351-364.

After delineating a number of phonological and syntactic characteristics of black English, a review of recent comparative
studies is presented. While evidence is mixed concerning the
question of whether a language deficit exists among lower
class black children along with a dialect difference, there
is clear evidence of the existence of a dialect. The problem
facing educators is that no standardized tests have been
developed for use with speakers of the dialect. The use
of available tests with dialect speaking children may result
in gross errors in educational placement of these children.
Reprinted by permission.

13. Bell, P., et. al. Children's attitudes toward speakers of
standard and nonstandard English. 22 pp. See ERIC Abstracts, No.
ED-130-546, 1974.

There has been disagreement among linguists and psychologists
concerning the age at which children develop social perceptions of others on the basis of difference in speech. The
purpose of the present study was to determine in what ways
8- and 9-year-old children from different socioeconomic
backgrounds might react to dialect differences. The 92
subjects came from three schools: 32 from a school in a
lower- and working-class neighborhood in New York City; 30
from a public school in a middle class suburban area near
Albany, New York; and 30 from a high-tuition suburban private
school for upper middle class children, also near Albany.
The children were randomly chosen 8- and 9-year-olds of both
sexes. The study was designed to explore their reactions
to "standard" and "nonstandard" black American English and
to determine the extent to which such children could verbally
conceptualize their attitudes using a simplified version of
the Osgood Semantic Differential Scale. The scale included
the five categories of intelligence (smart-dumb), appearance
(pretty-ugly), personality (nice-mean), economic background
(rich-poor), and race (black-white). The results show that
8- and 9-year-olds are sensitive to speech differences and,
moreover, have absorbed many of the attitudes of society
toward standard and nonstandard speech. They are also able
to conceptualize verbally their attitudes toward speech
differences. They have not yet, however, formulated a complete
racial stereotype matching the adult model.

14.   Berdan, R. Have/got in the speech of Anglo and black children.
Southwest Regional Laboratory (SWRL) Professional Papers, 1973, 22,
1-15. (SWRL Educational Research and Development, 4665 Lampson Avenue,
Los Alamitos, California 90720.)

   A report of a study in which the use of "have/got" and its alternate surface realizations were investigated in the speech of
   Anglo and black grade-school children from lower and middle
   income neighborhoods. Techniques were devised to elicit
   multiple occurrences of the construction in a range of diagnostic environments, including questions and negatives. The
   use of "have/got" by Anglo children results from a transforma-
   tional Got-Insertion rule. No such rule exists for the black
   children: "have" and "got" are independent lexical items.
   Some of the forms used by younger children appear to represent
   developmental stages rather than ethnic dialects. Reprinted by
   permission.

15.   Berdan, R. The use of linguistically determined groups in
sociolinguistic research. Southwest Regional Laboratory (SWRL) Professional Papers, 1973, 26, 1-20. (SWRL Educational Research and
Development, 4665 Lampson Avenue, Los Alamitos, California 90720.)

   The established unit for reporting sociolinguistic data has
   been the sociologically determined group. Characteristically,
   only the mean rate of nonstandard usage for the group is reported for any linguistic feature. Such reporting obscures
   the possibility of linguistic heterogeneity within the group.
   Data from some published studies suggest that, for both Anglo
   and black adults, sociologically determined groups are in fact
   linguistically heterogeneous. Data from Los Angeles school
   children indicate that school classrooms are heterogeneous
   with respect to different forms of agreement usage. An
   alternative analysis is proposed in which children are grouped
   on the basis of linguistic criteria. Members of these groups
   share a common grammar. There is an implicational relationship among the grammars employed by such linguistically determined groups. The linguistically determined groups do not
   map exactly onto traditional sociologically determined groups.
   This relation may be expressed as the probability that a member
   of a sociologically determined group is a member of some linguistically determined group. This interpersonal variation may
   be distinguished from intrapersonal variation or the probability
   that a rule of a particular grammar will apply. Reprinted by
   permission.

16.   Berdan, R. and Pfaff, C. W. Sociolinguistic variation in the
speech of young children: An experimental study. Southwest Regional
Laboratory (SWRL) Professional Papers, 1972, 21, 1-16. (SWRL Educational Research and Development, 4665 Lampson Avenue, Los Alamitos,
California 90720.)

   Thirty Anglo and black kindergarten children responded to three
   types of elicitation procedure: production tasks, repetition
   tasks, and a storytelling task. Seven phonological and syntactic
   features known to be characteristic of black English were investigated. In general, black children responded with more

nonstandard forms than did Anglo children. Within each group, there was considerable variation in the proportion of nonstandard usage. Repetition tasks produced fewer nonstandard responses than did production tasks. Responses to the production tasks were found to form an implicational scale with a high coefficient of reproducibility. Reprinted by permission.

17. Bereiter, C. and Engelmann, S. Teaching Disadvantaged Children in the Preschool. Englewood Cliffs, N.J.: Prentice-Hall, Inc., 1966.

A new kind of preschool, emphasizing directed language learning, is necessary for disadvantaged children. "Cultural deprivation is basically and primarily language deprivation. These children need direct and intensive language learning to catch up to normally advantaged children." This book presents in detail the procedures for achieving the desired verbal ability. It also touches effectively upon general management of the preschool, and music, arithmetic, and reading activities consonant with the verbal language program.

18. Blue, C. M. and Vergason, G. A. Echoic responses of standard English features by culturally deprived black and white children. Perceptual and Motor Skills, 1973, 37 (2), 575-581.

Investigated echoic responses to 24 sentences, each containing a critical feature of the standard English language. Subjects were 20 black and 20 white lower socioeconomic status children randomly selected from each of grades 1, 3, and 5, of two southern public schools with five-year histories of stability and equality of racial composition. The performance of whites was significantly superior to that of blacks. Grade level was also critical. Both racial groups improved in their echoic performance with advancing age and/or education.

19. Boone, S. L. and Montare, A. Test of the language-aggression hypothesis. Psychological Reports, 1976, 39 (3, Part 1), 851-857.

Tested two hypotheses concerning the role of language in aggression: (a) that relatively low levels of proficiency in the use of language are associated with relatively high levels of observable aggression; and (b) that high levels of language proficiency are associated with low levels of aggression. The Vocabulary subtest of the WISC, the Metropolitan Achievement Test in Reading, the total number of words spoken during a free speech session, and the number of different words used during that session constituted the language measures for the 55 black, 25 Puerto Rican, and 52 white male 9- to 13-year-old subjects. Aggression was measured using an adaptation of the physical and verbal aggression categories used by J. Walters, et. al. (1957). Results support both predictions for the comparisons between black and Puerto Rican subjects but not for the white subjects.

20. Bouchard, E. L. Psycholinguistic attitude study. Studies of Language and Language Behavior, 1969, 8, 437-450.

Fifth and sixth graders were asked to listen to a tape recording with excerpts of conversations by speakers of three dialects: middle class white, lower class white, and lower class Negro. Subjects were asked to rate the personality of each speaker by voice cues alone. In addition, the children listened to the tape again in order to determine race and probable occupation. It was predicted and confirmed that this technique would elicit stereotypes based upon the dialects. The middle class white speakers were judged significantly higher than the lower class white speakers who in turn were rated significantly higher than the lower class Negro speakers. Thus, it was found that children of 10 and 11 years of age are indeed aware of the social significance of language differences. Reprinted by permission.

21. Brottman, M. A. Language remediation for the disadvantaged preschool child. Monographs of the Society for Research in Child Development, 1968, Serial No. 124.

Five papers representing divergent views of language programs for disadvantaged preschool children are presented. They describe three positions on a continuum of structure in language instruction: (a) unstructured, emphasizing social-emotional development including language usage; (b) semi-structured, through a materials and games approach; and (c) highly structured, through language pattern-drill. Rationale as a basis for evaluation of language competence are examined and several experimental instruments are described. The various approaches to teaching language presented here are compared in a study of preschool children. The results demonstrate no clear advantage of one approach over any other and raise questions of the efficacy of language programs, problems of research design, and problems of evaluation. Some future directions in language programs are indicated through a review of current programs.

22. Brown, D., et. al. Developmental aspects of pupil performance on bidialectal tests. Research and Development Memorandum No. 137. Washington, D. C.: National Institute of Education (DHEW), May 1975, 53 pp. Also, see ERIC Abstracts, No. ED-106-867, 1975.

The purposes of this study were to redefine, through further experimentation, previously developed instruments measuring bidialectal proficiency; to measure any possible developmental trends in bidialectal proficiency; and to establish the relation of proficiency in black standard English (BSE) and black nonstandard English (BNSE) to other measurements of reading and/or language ability. In order to assess developmental trends, the experiment was conducted with kindergartners (20 subjects), first graders (23 subjects), third graders (24 subjects), and sixth graders (24 subjects). The results of the study are presented in both narrative and table form.

23. Broyer, J. A. Review: Teaching Black Children to Read, edited by
J. C. Baratz and R. W. Shuy, Washington, D. C.: Center for Applied Linguistics, 1969. Educational Theory, 1971, 21 (2), 226-228.

A favorable review. The book presents research sponsored by the
Center for Applied Linguistics, and contains a collection of eight
recent essays by linguists concerned with the problem of teaching
black ghetto children to read. It is usually assumed that there
is one "standard" or "ordinary" language which constitutes the norm
of correct communication. The relation to the "standard" or "ordinary" English, different dialects, such as black nonstandard English, are assumed to be deficient forms needing remediation. It is
the joint aim of the authors to show that both of these assumptions
are false. The book argues that: (a) language is as plural as
culture is diverse, and that "all languages are approximately
equally adequate for the needs of the culture of which they are a
part"; and (b) with no single normative standard of ordinary language, varied forms of the language, such as black ghetto English,
must be accepted as valid; as different but not deficient. The
thesis that an empirical study of the use of various languages and
language dialects will establish their functional equality when
judged from the perspective of the language user is defended.
Reprinted by permission.

24. Carson, A. S. and Rabin, A. I. Verbal comprehension and communication in Negro and white children. Journal of Educational Psychology,
1960, 51, 47-51.

Three groups (30 in each group) of children were matched for age,
sex, grade placement, and level of verbal comprehension of two
vocabulary tests -- Full-Range Picture Vocabulary Test, and WISC.
The three groups were: northern Negroes migrated to Lansing,
Michigan; northern whites; and southern Negroes. When these children were tested in terms of the level of communication based on
meaning, the white children were superior to the northern Negro
children, and in turn, the northern Negroes were superior to the
southern Negroes. Results are discussed in relation to possible
racial and cultural geographic factors.

25. Carver, R. P. Use of a recently developed listening comprehension
test to investigate the effect of disadvantagement upon verbal proficiency. American Education Research Journal, 1969, 6, 263-270.

It was hypothesized that the effect of disadvantagement is more
associated with the development of reading proficiency rather than
verbal proficiency in general. In order to test this hypothesis,
a test designed especially for disadvantaged Negro boys was
administered to 1,084 eighth grade boys in different ethnic and
income level groups. Although the test appears to be reliable,
valid, and preferred by low-income Negroes in comparison to middle-
income whites, the low-income Negroes showed a deficit on this
test comparable to that shown by other standardized measures of
aptitude and listening comprehension.

26. Caskie, P. G. Predictability of the position of the deleted
auxiliary verb in the speech of black and white children at two age
levels. Southeastern Conference on Linguistics, 1970, 12-13.

> This paper is concerned with the child's acquisition of the Eng-
> lish auxiliary verb system, and in particular, with the child's
> use of the auxiliary verb in information (WH) questions. Failure
> to invert the tense marked aux. in WH questions is characteristic
> of both potential Standard English (SE) speakers and Negro Non-
> standard English (NNE) speakers aged 4 to 5 years. This failure
> to apply the question inversion transformation results in such
> sentences as, "Where it is?" and "Who you are?". Such sentences
> are also found, however, in the speech of adolescent NNE speakers,
> while not at all in the speech of SE speakers of comparable age.
> To attempt to account for the similarity in performance in interro-
> gative sentences by groups differing in both age and dialect
> group membership, an instrument containing auxiliary verbs used
> in both declarative and interrogative sentences was designed and
> administered to 58 NNE and SE speaking children. Based on the
> systematicity of the test results, it was possible to predict the
> position of the auxiliary verb, even when seemingly omitted in
> sentences like, "Why she here?". As a result, a special Deletion
> Rule was written to account for this phenomenon. Reprinted by
> permission.

27. Chen, H. P. Speech sound status of newborn Negro and white
infants. Proceedings of the Iowa Academy of Science, 1942, 49, 447.

28. Cicirelli, V. G., et. al. Performance of disadvantaged primary
grade children on the revised Illinois Test of Psycholinguistic Abilities. Psychology in the Schools, 1971, 8 (3), 240-246.

> Presents data based on the Illinois Test of Psycholinguistic
> Abilities (ITPA) on the performance of disadvantaged first, second
> and third graders who were subdivided into Caucasian, Negro and
> Mexican-American groups. Intercorrelations among the subscores
> of ITPA and correlations between ITPA and the Metropolitan Readi-
> ness Test and the Stanford Achievement Test are given. Variations
> in the ITPA profiles for the various subgroups are described. It
> is concluded that the strongest abilities of the children correlate
> the least with achievement and readiness.

29. Cohen, S. A. and Kornfeld, G. S. Oral vocabulary and beginning
reading in disadvantaged black children. Reading Teacher, 1970, 24
(1), 33-38.

> A report of a study of existing analyses of urban black children's
> functional vocabularies compared to vocabulary demands of basal
> readers. The theoretical hypothesis was: Urban ghetto children
> have sufficient conceptual vocabulary to handle the reading mate-
> rials used for beginning reading instruction. Operationally stated,
> the hypothesis reads: The vocabularies of urban ghetto children
> as defined and measured in the Thomas (1962) study will match 80
> percent of the vocabulary demands in (1) five different first grade
> readers, (2) a vocabulary list drawn from major basal readers,

(3) Bank Street Readers, and (4) Chandler Language Experience Readers. In the light of subsequent research, it appears that the technique Thomas used to measure his population and the setting in which it was done could not tap the full conceptual vocabularies of his disadvantaged children. Yet, when one does not confuse conceptual vocabulary with verbal output or articulation, one finds that urban disadvantaged black children can handle most of the conceptual vocabulary in beginning readers. This is based on the most conservative measure of conceptual vocabulary. It is recognized that Thomas' population was limited to the greater Detroit area. One would not generalize these findings to rural disadvantaged children. However, one could feel confident that the findings apply generally to disadvantaged blacks in large northern urban areas. The important point is that paucity of conceptual vocabulary in these populations cannot be used as an excuse for reading retardation in the primary grades. The fact is, these children do have most of the vocabulary demanded of them in their basal readers. School people cannot continue to pass the buck of failure in first grade reading to the black child's verbal deficiencies and lack of necessary vocabulary. Reprinted by permission.

30. Copple, C. E. and Suci, G. J. The comparative ease of processing standard English and black nonstandard English by lower class black children. Child Development, 1974, 45 (4), 1048-1053.

Assessed the speed with which children who were speakers of black nonstandard English responded appropriately to sentences presented in their dialect as compared to standard English. Also investigated two grammatical features that differ in standard and nonstandard dialect. Subjects were 96, 5- and 7-year-olds.

31. Cullinan, B. E., Jaggar, A. M., and Strickland, D. S. Language expansion for black children in the primary grades: A research report. Young Children, 1974, 29 (2), 98-112.

Discusses data that indicate that the greatest gains in language occur during the first grade. Black children are asked to learn two language skills at that time: competence in understanding and reading. Experimental kindergarten children taught spontaneous and creative types of language activities expanded their oral language. It is concluded that use of the English language in realistic situations at the kindergarten level improves the black child's linguistic competence, and, in turn, his productive control over standard English.

32. DeStafano, J. S. Register: Social variation in language use. Elementary School Journal, 1972, 72 (4), 189-194.

The contributions by linguists to the study of language include study of its structure and social variations. The variation of language forms with respect to phonology, syntax and lexicon to fit different situations, constitutes register -- change or switching of a language. It is postulated that by the time black ghetto children enter school they control several language-registers in keeping with different social situations. School

experiences increase the range of language-registers among the
pupils, as well as among alert teachers.

33. Drennan, M. and Hansen, H. P. The child who doesn't speak standard
English. Acta Symbolica, 1970, 1 (2), 3-15.

An attempt to show that the Afro-American has an organized language
system in all three component areas -- structural, grammatical, and
phonological -- demonstrating that this language system as it
evolved in America truly contains the order to be rated as its
own language or dialect of English rather than a poor approximation of another dialect. The majority in America speak dialects
of Standard Network and School English. Due to the historical
development of the Afro-American language, it does not have all
of the components of standard English. Children coming to school
need to use the standard English presented in the texts and by the
teachers. Not all Afro-American children need an intensive language program, many speak a standard English. Nevertheless, many
others have within their heritage a different language pattern.
Since public schools are presently geared to one dialect of English
and since many children enter school speaking a second dialect
as a primary language system, it is hoped that eventually educators
will consider it equally acceptable and not "second rate." It is
concluded that only after the educational system ceases trying to
eradicate Afro-American and rather supplements it with another
dialect for greater social mobility, will the schools be helping
all children. Reprinted by permission.

34. Edwards, J. and Stern, C. A comparison of 3 intervention programs with disadvantaged preschool children. Journal of Special Education, 1970, 4, 205-214.

Three groups of 40 Head Start children participated in three preschool intervention programs: the U C L A Preschool Language Program, the BRL Readiness for Language Arts Program, and the placebo
program. Compared to both the placebo group and a regular control
group, children in the two structured language programs were
superior on a number of academic performance measures. Although
the language programs were quite different in terms of their instructional content, activities and materials, there were few
measurable differences between the test performances of the two
groups. Irrespective of the instructional treatment, Anglo-
American and Mexican-American children tended to perform better
than Afro-American children. Most of the significant differences were noted between the latter two groups. The Head Start
site which employed the teacher with the most preschool teaching
experience tended to have higher mean scores than the other three
sites, which employed paraprofessional teachers. The results
indicate that: (1) the more task-oriented a structured preschool
intervention program is, the greater will be the gains in specific
cognitive and linguistic skills, and (2) given a specific program,
children taught by experienced preschool teachers will tend to
evidence the greatest gains.

35. Eisenberg, L., Berlin, C. I., Dill, A., and Frank, S. Class and race effects on the intelligibility of monosyllables. Child Development, 1968, 39 (4), 1077-1089.

160 Negro and white school children of low and middle socioeconomic class families listened to female representatives of both uneducated and educated white and Negro groups read lists of monosyllables. The most intelligible speech was generated by the educated speakers, regardless of the race of the speaker or the listeners. Negro children showed generally poorer listening scores than whites, and Negro speakers generated slightly poorer intelligibility scores than whites, independent of the race and class of the listeners with one exception: uneducated speakers were understood better by members of their own race. A second exception showed a small but significant relation between the listening scores that the children obtained and their ability to re-articulate the lists to 40 teachers. Great variability within subjects probably overcame the effects of race and class.

36. Elenbogen, E.M. and Thompson, G. R. A comparison of social class effects in two tests of auditory discrimination. Journal of Learning Disabilities, 1972, 5 (4), 209-212.

Investigated the relatively poor performance of lower class children on tests of auditory discrimination. Each of 30 white middle- and 15 black lower-class kindergartners was individually administered two tests of auditory discrimination: the Wepman Auditory Discrimination Test, and a modified Wepman in which phonemes were exchanged between word pairs to create nonsense syllables. Social class differences in error scores disappeared with the use of the distorted form of the Wepman. Results suggest that the Wepman may measure a vocabulary factor in addition to auditory discrimination.

37. Entwisle, D. R. Developmental sociolinguistics: Inner city children. In Allan C. Ornstein (Ed.), Educating the Disadvantaged: School Year 1968-1969., 123-136. New York: AMS Press, 1970.

The major development of language and verbal concepts occurs before age eight, probably without much influence from formal schooling. Thus, the child's subculture may be the only substantial environmental influence on his language development. However, little data exists concerning the influence of personal and community beliefs and values on the use of language, especially as related to the language acquisition of children. Cultural differences are assumed to be important in language and cognitive development, yet there is little documentation to support these assumptions. In attempting to gather data on the relationship of language to social context, free associations to work stimuli were used to study the comparative language development of inner city and middle class children. Inner city children -- of low and medium intelligence, black and white -- responded to stimulus words from several form classes -- such as nouns and adverbs -- with free associations. Results were compared with previously gathered data on white

middle class children. Paradigmatic responses to adjectives,
verbs, pronouns, and adverbs, as well as primary responses to
nouns, suggested that first grade white ghetto children are
more advanced in linguistic development than suburban children
of the same intelligence level. Although the black ghetto
children are less advanced than the white ghetto children, their
responses to all form classes were as high, if not higher, than
those of the white suburban children when median IQ was held
constant. Rates of linguistic development differed according
to social class; for certain form classes, the relative advantage of the ghetto children disappeared by fifth grade. Optimum
exposure for language development might include simple and
limited choice verbalization, that found in the verbalization
between black mothers and their preschool children. Middle
class first grade children may be temporarily disadvantaged in
this respect because their exposure involves more complicated
models. The study, indicating the lack of retardation in slum
children of low level verbal functions, indicates the need for
the examination of smaller cognitive areas in respect to social
class and subcultural variation.

38. Entwisle, D. R. Semantic Systems of Minority Groups. Baltimore,
Maryland: The Center for the Study of Social Organization of Schools,
The Johns Hopkins University, June 1969. 15 pp.

This report concerns the acquisition of semantics, with emphasis
on the differences among minority groups. Semantic structure
has repercussions in wide areas in children's grammatical development. A child in an impoverished environment may find it most
difficult to expand his semantic system. Data concerning
blacks versus whites show little difference at first grade
level; however, with advancing age, the differences increase.
By third grade the blacks show a slowed pace of development compared with suburban whites. Income, and not simply membership in
a minority, has a great deal to do with development in this area.
One specific deficit is related to problems with verbs and adverbs. The progress in the semantic system of suburban children
is quite orderly, whereas slum children make only limited progress in conceptualizing. It is interesting to note that inner
city youngsters progress relatively well before starting school,
probably because of television's effects, but they begin a de-
celeration of development once in school, especially where reading skills are concerned. Remedies range from games to drill
skills to the more complicated one of integration.

39. Everhart, R. W. A study of growth and development in Negro and
white children with dyslalia. Exceptional Children, 1957, 23, 168-
170.

A group of 30 Negro boys and 17 Negro girls with articulation
handicaps were compared with 48 white boys and 15 white girls
with articulation problems in grades 1 thru 6 upon a number of
developmental processes. No differences were found between white
and Negro boys on onset of holding head up, crawling, walking,
talking, height, weight, intelligence, reading, or arithmetic.

Significant differences were found between Negro and white boys,
favoring Negroes with respect to the onset of sitting alone, and
favoring white boys on voluntary control of bladder. There were
no significant differences on any of the above variables for
Negro and white girls with dyslalia.

40. Fader, D. The Naked Children. New York: Macmillan, 1971. 254 pp.

This is a passionate story about the author's experience during
one school year in a black ghetto junior high school in Washington,
D. C. where he introduced his "English in Every Classroom" experiment. This experiment is an attempt to promote literary interests
of the students by massive infusion of "real" and pertinent materials, such as newspapers, magazines, and paperback books in
every classroom. (The program was first conducted at Maxey
Boys Training School in Whitmore Lake, Michigan, which is described in the author's earlier work, Hooked on Books: Program
and Proof, Putnam, 1968.) The story revolves primarily around
five eighth- and ninth-grade students. It encompasses events,
dialogues, and the author's philosophy of education. Interpretations and qualifications of the events are interspersed
throughout the work. The major part of the book describes the
five children, their feelings, their ways of dealing with the
everyday encounters and the development of friendships between
the author and the children which have helped him to obtain some
knowledge concerning children's failure to succeed in school. In
the concluding part, the "linguistic impoverishment" of these
disadvantaged children is analyzed. The implications are made
that schools on every level have failed to teach a great percentage of children how to read or use standard English. The
author, however, concludes ". . . that most children will not
learn in school what their family and community do not value
outside of school . . . it has no place in their lives" (p. 119).
He is particularly critical of the use of standard textbooks
in ghetto schools as they do not stimulate the children to
literacy because their contents are not relevant to the students' environmental experiences. The book is very readable,
the author's arguments are convincing, and especially his perceptive observations about the symptoms of "linguistic impoverishment" deserve to be considered by anyone interested in teaching
children in disadvantaged environments.

41. Foreit, K. G. and Donaldson, P. L. Dialect, race and language
proficiency: Another dead heat on the merry-go-round. Child Development, 1971, 42 (5), 1572-1574.

Presents a detailed review of J. Baratz's (see PA, Vol. 44:217A)
study comparing sentence imitation of standard and nonstandard
English by Negro and Caucasian children. Critical flaws in
methodology and data analysis, which obscure the significance
of the author's conclusions, are pointed out. Suggestions for
re-analysis of the data and replication of the experiment are
presented.

42. Fox, G. T. Jr. A test used to determine the extent to which
the Whorf Hypothesis and the Bernstein Thesis are applicable to
either black dialect or to standard English. Paper presented at the
Annual Meeting of the American Educational Research Association, Chicago, April 1974. Also, see ERIC Abstracts, No. ED-095-541, 1974.

Syntactical rule differences in black dialect that can be more
helpful to young adolescents' perceptions than the corresponding
rules in standard English were studied. The syntactical rule
in black dialect that was identified as being more explicit
than the corresponding rule in standard English was the invariant
"be" verb form (as in "I be honest"). The perception studied
was young adolescents' recognition of apparent contradictions;
for example, in a given situation, a person can be honest and
lying. Results suggest that more emphasis be placed upon young
adolescents as rule-makers and rule-users. Theories such as
the Whorf Hypothesis and the Bernstein Thesis did not satis-
factorily explain the decision-making processes used by the
children when deciding to use or not to use two contradictory
words to describe the same person or object.

43. Frasure, N. E. and Entwisle, D. R. Semantic and syntactic
development in children. Developmental Psychology, 1973, 9 (2),
236-245.

Administered a sentence recall task using either meaningful,
anomalous, or random work groups to 36 lower class black, 36
middle class white, and 37 lower class white kindergartners,
first and third graders. Data suggest substantial development
in ability to make use of syntactic and semantic cues over
this age range. White middle class children make more use of
such cues than white or black lower class subjects at every
age level. Semantic cues facilitated performance at early
ages for all groups, while syntactic cues facilitated performance somewhat later, especially for lower class groups.

44. Gantt, W. N., Wilson, R. M., and Dayton, C. M. An initial
investigation of the relationship between syntactical divergency
and the listening comprehension of black children. Reading Research
Quarterly, 1975, 10 (2), 193-211.

To determine the relationship between measures of oral language
production and measures of listening skill, two groups of 48
black pupils each were randomly selected from the third grade
in two schools. One was a lower class (Title I) school, and
the other a low middle class (Non-Title I) school. The subjects
in each school were randomly assigned to three subgroups of
16 each. A black and white adult male educator and several
black peers administered the tests. For the combined sample,
all correlations were significant (p<.05). A Newman-Keuls
test applied post-hoc to the means for the three testers revealed that the black adult tester elicited significantly
more divergent English than either the white adult tester (p<.05)
or the black peer tester (p<.05). Results of the six Bonferini
tests on total word production indicated that the testers were

homogeneous within the Non-Title I school, but that the black
adults and black peer testers elicited significantly more words
(p<.01) in the Title I school than the white adult testers.
(Modified.)

45. Garmiza, C. and Anisfeld, M. Factors reducing the efficiency of
reference-communication in children. Merrill-Palmer Quarterly, 1976,
22 (2), 125-136.

Describes a study which evaluated the level of communication of
first- and second-grade children in three tasks. Resistance to
shifting of perspectives was seen as a contributant to ineffi-
cient communication.

46. Garvey, C. and Dickstein, E. Levels of analysis and special
class differences in language. Language and Speech (Teddington),
1972, 15 (4), 375-384.

Examined the effect of level of linguistic analysis on correlations observed between language variables and status variables.
Three levels of analysis of a linguistic construction were
selected for study: (a) grammatical form; (b) lexical choice;
and (c) use of a prediction type. The corpus was the speech of
48 dyads of fifth grade children (male, female; low, middle
socioeconomic status; and Negro, white) performing three problem
solving tasks. The grammatical form of the construction differentiated between social groups, sexes, and races. Lexical choice
within the construction differentiated between social groups.
Use of the prediction type, however, seemed to depend primarily
on the task itself. Findings demonstrate that status differences
in speech behavior at one level of linguistic analysis cannot
be taken as evidence that similar status differences exist at
another level. (Modified.)

47. Gay, J. and Tweney, R. D. Comprehension and production of standard
and black English by lower class black children. Developmental Psychology, 1976, 12, 262-268.

72 lower class black kindergartners, third, and sixth graders had
to comprehend stimulus sentences with contrasting grammatical
characteristics in black English and standard English and had to
produce sentences spontaneously when shown stimulus pictures.
It was hypothesized that comprehension of easy standard English
contrasts would increase with age, and comprehension of hard
contrasts in both black and standard English would change with
age. Results indicated that comprehension of both easy and hard
contrasts in both black and standard English increased with age
in parallel fashion.

48. Genshaft, J. L. and Hirt, M. Language differences between black
children and white children. Developmental Psychology, 1974, 10 (3),
451-456.

Examined 48 black and 48 white children, matched for social
class and·nonverbal intelligence in a free-recall situation on

vocabulary words and sentences presented in black dialect and
standard English. On standard English sentences, both groups
performed equally well. On sentences in black dialect, the
white subjects performed significantly worse. Findings are
interpreted as support for bilingual language development in
black ghetto children and emphasize the importance of social
class and intelligence when comparing white and black subjects
on language tasks.

49. Golub, L. S. English syntax of black, white, Indian and Spanish-
American children. Elementary School Journal, 1975, 75 (5), 323-334.

Compared linguistic ability (LA) and linguistic performance (LP)
among the children of four ethnic groups: black, white, Spanish-
American, and Indian. The LA of the 268 intermediate grade
subjects (47% male and 53% female) was measured by 12 variables
of I. G. Mattingly and J. F. Kavanagh's Linguistic Abilities
Test (LAT). The LP of the subjects was measured on 11 variables
from L. S. Golub and W. C. Frederick's study (LPS). Two hypotheses were tested: (a) There are no differences among the groups
in LA as indicated by the mean scores on the LAT; and (b) There
are no differences among the groups in LP as measured by the LPS.
The LAT scores indicated significant differences (p<.05) between
whites and the other groups on 11 of the 12 variables, the
exception being the ability to distinguish probable English
grapheme clusters. Black subjects resembled the Mexican-
American and Indian subjects more than they resembled the white
subjects. The first hypothesis is rejected. The LPS, syntactic
density, was measured by the subjects' writing about pictures
and tape-presented materials. No significant differences were
found among the groups, and the second hypothesis is accepted.
(Modified.)

50. Golub, L. S. Reading, writing and black English. Elementary
School Journal, 1972, 72 (4), 195-202.

Quantitative, rather than qualitative, differences denote the
variations between the languages of black and white school children. The greatest difference is phonological rather than syntactical. Children have learned by the time they enter school
that the environment determines the language-register to be
employed. Techniques in the use of tape recorders are described
which teachers can utilize in teaching various language-registers
of black and white pupils in order to appropriate adult language-
registers. (Modified.)

51. Gottesman, R. L. Auditory discrimination ability in Negro
dialect-speaking children. Journal of Learning Disabilities, 1972,
5 (2), 94-101.

Selected three groups of 40 first grade boys: Negro dialect-
speaking, Negro standard English-speaking, and Caucasian standard
English-speaking. Subjects were given an auditory discrimination test composed of word pairs pronounced as (a) homonyms in
Negro dialect but as contrasting words in standard English; and

(b) contrasting words by all subjects. The word pairs were
presented on tape by both Negro dialect and standard English
speakers. Results indicate that there were no significant
group differences in auditory discrimination performance on
those word pairs which could be commonly differentiated in speech
of all subjects. However, both groups of standard English-
speaking subjects scored significantly higher than the group
of Negro dialect-speaking subjects on those word pairs pronounced
as homonyms in Negro dialect when they were presented contrast-
ingly by standard English speakers.

52. Gruson, L. E. and Jacobson, L. I. Effects of modeling language
units of differing complexity on the language acquisition of preschool
black children. Proceedings of the Annual Convention of the American
Psychological Association, 1971, 6 (1), 197-198.

Investigated the effects of the modeling of five linguistic
response classes and information complexity on language usage
in preschool Negro children from poverty backgrounds. It was
found that the modeling of simple language units, comprised of
single sentences, resulted in more effective language acquisition than the modeling of complex language units, comprised of
groups of sentences. In addition, particular categories of
language usage were influenced significantly more than others
as a result of the simple language units treatment. Thus, the
effects of information complexity and the specific characteristics of modeled stimuli significantly influence the effectiveness of modeling as a method of language learning.

53. Gupta, W. and Stern, C. Comparative effectiveness of speaking
vs. listening in improving spoken language of disadvantaged young
children. Journal of Exceptional Education, 1969, 38 (1), 54-57.

The hypothesis that children who repeat sentences aloud will
acquire greater facility in forming similar sentences on their
own than those who only listen to the spoken sentences was
tested with 40 disadvantaged Negro children, 43 to 55 months
old. Identical sequences of 5- to 15-minute daily lessons plus
two days of testing were presented under two treatment conditions, speaking and not-speaking. By analysis of covariance a
significant difference was found (.01 level) favoring the speaking
group. This difference was attributable to scores on the verbalization subtest, as both groups demonstrated equal facility
in identification. A transfer task with verbalization to entirely
different pictures produced similar significant treatment effects
(p<.01). Reprinted by permission.

54. Gussett, J. C. The use of nonstandard English to improve communications in mathematics. See ERIC Abstracts, No. ED-128-537, 1969.

In order to test whether ghetto children would respond to a
set of instructional materials that incorporate the language,
the customs, and the general background of the disadvantaged
student, a six-week long course of study for seventh grade general mathematics is developed. This course of study is then

used in an experiment that employs nonstandard English to
improve communications in mathematics. Subjects are members of
two seventh grade general mathematics classes. Sixty-two
students participated in the study -- 35 females and 27 males.
Control and experimental groups are statistically the same
for intelligence quotient scores, reading scores, and pretest
scores on a standardized mathematics achievement test. The
experimental group uses the 30 mathematics lessons developed
for the study, while the control group uses a mathematics text-
book. Both the experimental and the control group receive the
Metropolitan Achievement Test -- Advanced Arithmetic as the
posttest. After the posttest has been administered, the mean
gain score for the experimental group is found to be 2.20
higher than the mean gain score of the control group. One
of the major conclusions made from an analysis of the data
is that a set of general mathematics problems designed specifically for the disadvantaged student can be written in nonstandard English if suitable precautions are taken.

55. Guthrie, J. T. and Baldwin, T. L. Effects of discrimination,
grammatical rules, and application of rules on the acquisition of
grammatical concepts. Journal of Educational Psychology, 1970, 61
(5), 358-364.

Shows the occurrence of the indefinite article to be a concept
similar to those studied in the general concept-formation paradigm. The acquisition of this grammatical concept was examined
using 80 inner city, Negro fifth graders. Learning an auditory
discrimination of instances and noninstances of the concept did
not affect the acquisition of the ability to produce instances
of the concept orally. Likewise, learning to verbalize the
grammatical rule which governs the concept did not facilitate
concept-formation. However, training on the application of
the verbalized rule strongly facilitated concept-formation
(p<.001). The application training was superior to rule learning for low- but not high-IQ subjects. Performance on a concept-
transfer task was not facilitated by the acquisition of the concept.

56. Hall, V. C., Turner, R. R., and Russell, W. Ability of children
from four subcultures and two grade levels to imitate and comprehend
crucial aspects of standard English: A test of the different language
exploration. Journal of Educational Psychology, 1973, 64 (2), 147-158.

Administered an instrument measuring imitation and comprehension
of four omissions of black nonstandard English dialect from
standard English (possessive "s", past "-ed", critical phrase
marker, (and) third person singular "-s") and the Raven Coloured
Progressive Matrices to 16 boys from each of four subcultures
(urban lower class white, urban lower class black, rural lower
class white, suburban middle class white) from first and fourth
grades. The black first and fourth graders exhibited significantly more dialect imitations on two types of omission (p<.01).
There were no significant differences among the first graders or
among the three lower class fourth grade groups on comprehension

scores. Both middle class groups performed significantly better
on the Raven than the other groups (p<.05), but there were no
significant differences among the three lower class groups.
The hypothesis that black dialect interferes with standard
English comprehension received little support. (Modified.)

57. Hall, W. S. and Freedle, R. O. A developmental investigation
of standard and nonstandard English among black and white children.
Human Development, 1973, 16 (6), 440-464.

Studied language imitation, comprehension, and free production
of standard and nonstandard English in two experiments with a
total of 420 black and white 5-, 8-, and 10-year-olds from low
and middle socioeconomic backgrounds. Rate of improvement measures indicate that blacks improved at the same rate as whites
in responding to standard English sentences. According to
correlational results, the two dialect systems functioned
behaviorally as separate cognitive systems. In a communication
task, blacks and whites produced and comprehended messages of
about the same quality.

58. Hausman, R. M. and Apffel, J. A. Differential effects on the
ITPA Illinois Test of Psycholinguistic Abilities profile of the final
version of the Peabody Language Development Kits (Levels #1 and #2)
with young disadvantaged Negro children. IMRID Papers and Reports,
1968, 5 (24), 20 pp.

The differential effects of the final revision of Levels 1 and
2 of the Peabody Language Development Kits (PLDK) on the Illinois
Test of Psycholinguistic Abilities (ITPA) profiles of young
disadvantaged black chilren were studied. Contrasted with 90
control subjects were 90 experimental subjects who received a
daily 30-minute oral language stimulation exercise from the
PLDK throughout the school year. The pretesting and interim
testing were spread by eight months, while the pretests and
posttests were administered 20 months apart. The study took
place in elementary schools in a southern inner city where over
three-quarters of the pupils were black. The program was
differentially effective only in the vocal expressive and auditory vocal sequential components of the ITPA as measured by
the Vocal Encoding and Auditory-Vocal Sequencing subtests.
This suggests that PLDK lessons should be coordinated with
other grammatical exercises in order to achieve maximum improvement in the major oral language defects of the disadvantaged
children of the type studied in this investigation.

59. Heider, E. R. Style and accuracy of verbal communication within
and between social classes. Journal of Personality and Social Psychology, 1971, 18 (1), 33-47.

Reports two experiments in isolating social class differences in
language which actually affect interpersonal communication.
143 10-year-old middle class white, lower class white, and
lower class Negro boys and girls encoded (described) abstract
and face stimuli from sets of 6 similar items, so that "another

child" could pick out that item at a later time. Consistent
class differences of encoding style were found. Subjects were
recalled and asked to decode examples of the different styles
of description given by each class and sex of subject. For
each class, the most successfully decoded style was the class'
preferred encoding style. Overall, middle class subjects were
superior encoders and decoders. There was no evidence of overall
greater within- than between-class accuracy. There were no
consistent sex or race differences.

60. Henning, J. J. and Levy, R. H. Verbal-performance IQ differences
of white and Negro delinquents on the WISC and WAIS. Journal of
Clinical Psychology, 1967, 23 (2), 164-168.

The verbal minus performance IQ difference was examined separately
at 15 age levels, for white and Negro subjects, and for subjects
tested with the "WISC" and those tested with the "WAIS." The
"WISC" samples produced performance IQs in excess of verbal
IQs more often than did the "WAIS" samples. The white subjects
also produced higher performance IQs in relation to verbal IQs
than did the Negroes. When the pattern of subtest rankings
from this study was compared with the subtest pattern of delinquent poor readers and non-delinquent poor readers from two
studies reported in the literature, the "WISC-W" and "WAIS-W"
samples showed consistently significant correlations with both
poor reader patterns, while the "WISC-N" and "WAIS-N" groups
lacked this relationship. This was interpreted by the authors
as support for the idea that a reading disability pattern
rather than sociopathic personality as such is what is being
seen in the intra-subtest Wechsler pattern of white, male delinquents. However, inferiority of the verbal to performance
IQ was not seen as a function of this poor reader subtest pattern.
Reprinted by permission.

61. Hockman, C. H. Black dialect reading tests in the urban elementary school. Reading Teacher, 1973, 26 (6), 581-583.

The effects of specific dialectal changes in upper primary
reading comprehension tests are investigated to test the hypothesis that black children would do better on nonstandard English sections of the instrument. Two alternate forms of the
California Reading Test were administered to 128 black and 138
white third, fourth and fifth graders from a mid-western city.
Results indicate no significant differences in test scores on
black dialect items for either blacks or whites as had been
hypothesized. It is concluded that there is a need for research
on the influence of black dialect on children beginning school
and on the influence of programs and teachers using black dialect with these children.

62. Houston, S. H. A sociolinguistic consideration of the black
English of children in northern Florida. Language, 1969, 45 (3),
599-607.

Although nonstandard dialects and their implications for education are receiving much current attention, most treatments of

child dialect, when not pure linguistic description, concentrate
on analysis of supposed verbal and conceptual deficience of the
children. The present paper, in contrast to such studies, com-
bines linguistic and sociolinguistic approaches to dialect investigation: it is an examination of a subset of black English,
namely that spoken by children of a county in Florida. The
paper discusses the linguistic composition of Florida Child Black
English, as well as such sociolinguistic topics as bidialectism,
reading problems, and reasons behind reports of the children's
non-fluency. Reprinted by permission.

63. Houston, S. H. Syntactic complexity and information transmission
in first graders: A cross-cultural study. Journal of Psycholinguistic
Research, 1973, 2 (2), 99-114.

Notes that within a specific language, certain syntactic items
may fail to mature in children at the expected rate, because of
structural oddities of the constructions (e.g., the conflict
between surface- and deep-structure subject of the main verb).
It is predictable that a syncretistic child attempting to deal
with such items in a text will analyze them according to the
surface-structure analogic method which defines verbal syncretism, and so will fail to make sense of them. The communication
of the disadvantaged black child has been described by some
researchers as less efficient and slower to mature than that of
others. The dual hypothesis of syncretism and faulty mastery
of difficult syntax was examined in 172 black and white lower
and upper socioeconomic status first graders by means of an
experimental story-repeating format. Hypotheses are examined
for the cause of children's distinctive communication technique, and the whole question of the significance of black-white
differences in communicative style and verbal maturity is discussed.

64. Hunt, B. C. Black dialect and third and fourth graders' performance on the Gray oral reading test. Reading Research Quarterly,
1974, 10 (1), 103-123.

Analyzed errors made by 65 inner city third and fourth graders
in the Gray Oral Reading Test. Tests were first scored according to the manual (Score I) and then rescored not counting
errors attributable to the use of black dialect (Score II).
For the total group, the mean difference between the two scorings
was about 3 points in raw score; this difference was statistically significant. The mean Score I for the total group yielded
a grade equivalent of 1.8; mean Score II was equivalent to a
grade level of 1.9. There was no significant difference between
third and fourth graders in the mean differences between scores;
however, the mean difference for the girls was significantly
greater than that for the boys (p<.01). There was also a significant difference between the mean differences of better and
poorer readers when the group was divided in half on the basis
of the test scores (p<.001). The mean difference of the better
readers was equivalent to 1/2 year in grade level; a few of
them scored differences of a year or more. When errors were

counted on score passages only, 46 percent of the errors made
by the total group were attributable to the dialect. (Modified.)

65. Jeruchimowicz, R., Costello, J., and Bagur, S. Knowledge of
action and object words: A comparison of lower and middle class
Negro preschoolers. Child Development, 1971, 42 (2), 455-464.

To investigate whether preschoolers of different social classes
find action and object words (i.e., verbs and nouns) equal in
difficulty, 39 lower (SES) and 40 middle (SES) black children
were tested on the Peabody Picture Vocabulary Test. Proportions
of errors on action and object words were compard with and between groups. Subjects were also compared on proportion of action
concepts in their storytelling to pictures. LSES subjects made
a significantly higher proportion of errors on action concepts
than on object words, whereas MSES subjects showed no difference. Both on verbs and nouns, the proportion of errors made
by LSES subjects was significantly higher than by MSES subjects.
However, there were no social class differences in the proportion
of action concepts in the speech sampled. It is concluded that
LSES and MSES subjects may not be significantly different in
their tendency to use dynamic concepts or in having experienced
them, but may be deficient in labels for many action concepts
which they already have.

66. John, V. P. The intellectual development of slum children:
Some preliminary findings. American Journal of Orthopsychiatry, 1963,
33 (5), 813-822.

This study examines patterns of linguistic and cognitive behavior
in a sample of Negro children from various social classes. Three
major levels of language behavior -- labeling, relating, categorizing, were analyzed. Consistent class differences in language
skills were shown to emerge between groups of Negro children of
different socioeconomic classes.

67. Johnson, K. and Simons, H. D. Black children and reading: What
teachers need to know. Phi Delta Kappan, 1972, 53 (5), 288-290.

To work effectively with black children, teachers must understand black culture and black dialect and adapt their teaching
strategies accordingly. Most teachers believe that standard
English is the one correct form of the English language. Many
black children, however, speak a variety of English that linguists have labeled black dialect. Teachers must understand
that black dialect is a legitimate linguistic system, that
standard English is not better than black dialect, and that
black dialect is systematic. The relation between black dialect and learning to read is not yet clear, and much more research needs to be done before it can be determined that the use
of beginning readers in dialect would be justified, but it is
important for teachers to be flexible and try new ideas.

68. Johnson, K. R. Black dialect shift in oral reading. Journal of
Reading Behavior, 1975, 18 (7), 535.

The grammar of the black dialect is analyzed to aid teachers in
distinguishing errors from "translation" in black dialect
speakers. Three types of miscues are discussed: the substitution miscue, the omission miscue, and the insertion miscue.
Examples of each type are included. Teachers of dialect children
must understand the features of the dialect to work properly with
these children.

69. Karlsen, B. and Blocker, M. Black children and final consonant
blends. The Reading Teacher, 1974, 27 (5), 462-463.

A report of an attempt to determine the extent to which a group
of black students can perceive final consonant blends auditorily.
The test employed consists of five items from each of five forms
of the experimental edition of the 1973 Stanford Achievement
Test, Primary I, Word Study Skills. Sixty-eight black children completed the test and obtained a mean score of 22.94, a
score practically identical to the national average. Results
verify that black children generally do have problems pronouncing
final consonant blends. However, the generalization that this
problem carries over to the auditory discrimination of such
blends is in error; black children do perceive them, and they can
differentiate between words that they pronounce the same, both
from the standpoint of sound and meaning. Reprinted by permission.

70. Katz, P. A. Verbal discrimination performance of disadvantaged
children: Stimulus and subject variables. Child Development, 1967,
38 (1), 233-242.

The present study investigated the effects of stimulus modality
and familiarity upon the discrimination performance of 72 normal
and retarded readers at three age levels. The subjects were
Negro males from lower socioeconomic backgrounds. Significant
differences in discrimination performance were obtained between
good and poor readers of the second, fourth and sixth grades,
with the magnitude of differences decreasing with age. For
all groups, poorest performance was associated with unfamiliar
visual stimuli, whereas the best discrimination was evident on
familiar visual stimuli. Although the performance of the older
children and better readers was superior in all tasks, the difference between reading groups was smallest with the most unfamiliar stimuli, thus suggesting that both perceptual skills
and stimulus familiarity factors play a role in children's discrimination performance. Reprinted by permission.

71. Kirk, S. A. Ethnic differences in psycholinguistic abilities.
Exceptional Children, 1972, 39 (2), 112-118.

Summarizes the results of several research studies on the psycholinguistic abilities of blacks, Indians and Mexican-Americans,
as measured by the Illinois Test of Psycholinguistic Abilities.
Black subjects appeared to have superior ability (as compared to

their other abilities and to other ethnic groups) in short-term
auditory sequential memory, while Indian and Mexican-American
subjects had superior ability in short-term visual sequential
memory. It is hypothesized that ethnic group differences may
be accounted for by different child rearing practices among the
ethnic groups.

72. Kofsky, E. The effect of verbal training on concept identification in disadvantaged groups. Psychonomic Science, 1967, 7 (10),
365-366.

Training disadvantaged children in labeing and discriminating
component stimulus attributes resulted in greater attention to
these attributes in inductive concept attainment, but in no
greater success in solving concept tasks.

73. Leventhal, D. S. and Stedman, D. J. A factor analytic study of
the Illinois Test of Psycholinguistic Abilities. Journal of Clinical
Psychology, 1970, 26 (4), 473-477.

The Illinois Test of Psycholinguistic Abilities: Experimental
Edition (ITPA) is a psychodiagnostic instrument devised to
assess theoretically discrete and basic cognitive skills. In
its genesis the ITPA, comprising nine subtests, was designed to
provide independent estimates of a child's level of functioning
in each of the nine abilities theoretically addressed. Factor
analyses of the ITPA subtest intercorrelations resulting from
scores generated by 285 white and 55 Negro 6-year-old children
cast doubt upon the independence of the abilities assessed. Significant racial-socioeconomic differences in ITPA performance
were found. Issues relating to the practical use and future
experimental work with the ITPA were discussed. Reprinted by
permission.

74. Levine, M.A. and Hanes, M. L. Dialect usage as a factor in
developmental language performance of primary grade school children.
19 pp. See ERIC Abstracts, No. ED-131-936, 1976.

This study investigated the relationship between dialect usage
and performance on four language tasks designed to reflect
features developmental in nature: articulation, grammatical
closure, auditory discrimination, and sentence comprehension.
Predictor and criterion language tasks were administered to
90 kindergarten, first, and second grade children randomly
selected from a Northcentral Florida elementary school with a
racial group ratio of 40 percent black and 60 percent white.
All children were from rural families of low and lower-middle
socioeconomic status backgrounds. When the variance attributed to cognitive development and language facility scores was
systematically covaried, results indicated that dialect usage
was significantly related to receptive performance but not
significantly related to expressive performance. This finding
bears two interpretations: (1) the basilect speaking child is
deficient in comprehending developmental language forms; and
(2) he is in addition demonstrating a basic deficiency in comprehending standard dialect. The later interpretation would

contend that the kindergarten through second grade basilect-speaking children examined in this study have not as yet acquired the skill of bi-dialectic comprehension, i.e., the ability to translate standard English into their own dialect for processing. The question of dialect interference, then, appears to be a localizing phenomenon. The amount of basilect used seemingly interferes with some specific language skills, and not with others.

75. Levy, B. B. and Cook, H. Dialect proficiency and auditory comprehension in standard and black nonstandard English. Journal of Speech and Hearing Research, 1973, 16 (4), 642-649.

Administered two tasks (dialect proficiency and auditory comprehension) to 32 black second graders. Sixteen subjects received the auditory comprehension task in black nonstandard English; the others received the task in standard English. Subjects were asked to identify the race of the speakers and how well they liked the stories and speakers. Performance was significantly better on the questions in the standard treatment. Within treatments, there was a positive correlation between dialect proficiency and auditory comprehension. Subjects correctly identified black speakers but tended to misidentify standard speakers. Results are discussed in terms of a "difference" vs. a "bicultural" model of dialect proficiency and achievement.

76. Light, R. L. Social factors and speech variation: Some observations in Albany, New York. The English Record, 1974, 26 (1), 15-25.

Twenty-five interviews with five white and seven black children, ages 10 to 12, were conducted to determine the extent to which nonstandard forms of four grammatical features were used (i.e., plural, possessive, third person singular, and absence of multiple negation). In addition, the data obtained from the interviews were analyzed to determine how social factors of race of the interviewer and race and sex of the child affects the use of these forms. Comparison of this study to the Washington and Detroit studies indicates that for the plural and possessive suffixes, the percentage of omission of the third person singular was lower for Albany black children. There were quantitative differences between white and black speakers' use of multiple negation, but this was demonstrated to be a feature of nonstandard white dialect and black dialect. In conversation, for the most part, the race of the interviewer and sex of the child had little influence upon the usage of nonstandard forms of the above features as compared with the race of the child. All the white children used the nonstandard forms. Two possible conclusions are suggested: incorporation by white children of nonstandard black dialect, or support for Shy's idea of a "linguistic continuum" (see: "The Sociolinguists and urban language problems," in Williams, Frederick (Ed.), Language and Poverty: Perspectives on a Theme. Chicago: Markham Publishing Company, 1970).

77. Lewit, D. W. and Abner, E. V. Black-white semantic differences
and interracial communication. Journal of Applied Social Psychology,
1971, 1 (3), 263-277.

In Phase I, black and white adolescent males made semantic differential ratings of 14 concepts representing a wide range of
values. Mother, father, girls, TV, God, police, and "next year"
yielded profiles significantly different for the two racial
groups. In Phase II, 28 blacks and 28 whites each attempted to
decode the profiles of 1 black and 1 white other. For combined
racial groups, accuracy was greater when the other was similarity.
Disregarding semantic similarity, accuracy was greater than when
the other was of the same race. Semantic similarity made little
difference, however, when both encoder and decoder were black.
Whites excelled in decoding the profiles of other whites where
concepts were commonly encoded by both racial groups, while blacks
were more accurate interracially where concepts were differentially encoded by the two racial groups. Results are related to
the assumption of a standard set of meanings for whites and a
standard-nonstandard dual system for blacks.

78. Loman, B. (Ed. and Transcriber). Conversations in a Negro American Dialect. Washington, D. C.: Center for Applied Linguistics, 1967.
164 pp.

The present volume is based on data which were collected and
analyzed during research investigations conducted by the "Urban
Language and Materials Development Project" of the Center for
Applied Linguistics. One of the objectives of this project is
to analyze the nonstandard dialect of English spoken by school
age Negro children of a lower socioeconomic stratum in the District of Columbia with the aim of producing scientific information on which a sound approach to the teaching of standard
English to these children can ultimately be based. A series of
free conversations with children 10 years old was recorded.
The primary purpose of the recording program was to provide
texts for a study of intonation and stress patterns. Four children were selected as the main informants for the study and
each was to participate in four types of speech events: (a) to
talk with another boy or another girl of approximately the same
age; (b) to talk with an adult from their own family or from a
family in the neighborhood; (c) to talk with a member of the
UL staff; and (d) to talk alone, e.g., tell a story in front
of a small, mixed audience. This arrangement was planned to
provide a varied corpus from which it would be possible to describe general tendencies in the prosodic system of the dialect,
and also to discover characteristic variations correlated with
age, sex, and status of the interlocutor. For various reasons,
it was not possible to carry out this program in all its details.
As a rule, the choice of topics for the conversations was acci-
dental; often a sequence of utterances developed spontaneously
after a period of silence. In other cases the topics were suggested to the participants. From the recordings, shorter
passages were selected for analysis and description; in general
these passages concentrate on a single family group and are

characterized by natural, spontaneous speech. Some brief bio-
graphic data on the informants is presented. Selected passages
from the recordings are transcribed in a modified standard
orthography. The transcription includes notation of consonant
reduction, substitution, and assimilation, as well as certain
other characteristic phenomena of the consonant system. Inter-
jections are written in phonetic transcription. A modified
version of the Trager-Smith system is used to transcribe the
prosodic aspects of the texts. In all, 14 conversations are
presented. Reprinted by permission.

79. Manzer, C. W. The uniformity and variety of word associations
of Negro boys and girls. Psychology Bulletin, 1934, 31, 627.

80. Marsh, J. and Fitch, J. The effect of singing on the speech
articulation of Negro disadvantaged children. Journal of Music
Therapy, 1970, 7 (3), 88-94.

> "One of the greatest deficits of the culturally de-
> prived child is in the area of communication and
> language skills. . . . This deficit becomes a
> crucial barrier when the child is to be educated
> outside his usual environment, as in the plight
> of the Southern Negro child newly placed in an
> integrated educational situation. . . . Although
> much attention has been given to the language defi-
> cits of the culturally disadvantaged child by
> various socially-oriented professions, the field
> of music therapy has not yet developed its poten-
> tial in this area. It is conceivable that any
> language program for the disadvantaged would
> greatly stress oral language skills . . . and
> singing would seem to be a valuable tool in teach-
> ing such skills to children. Few references can
> be found in the use of music in the improvement
> of speech patterns."

An attempt was made to determine the effect of singing specially
composed music on: (a) the articulation of ending "s" consonants
as pronounced in continuous speech by Southern Negro children,
and (b) the syllabic frequency in continuous speech of Southern
Negro children. Subjects were 30 fourth, fifth and sixth graders.
Although the results were not statistically significant, it is
felt that there was enough improvement in certain areas to warrant
further research.

81. Marwit, S. J. Black and white children's use of standard English
at 7, 9, and 12 years of age. Developmental Psychology, 1977, 13 (1),
81-82.

A Berko-type task, requiring a subject to derive the present,
plural, possessive, and time extension forms of nonsense syllables,
was re-administered to 64 black and white 7th graders previously
tested in Grades 2 and 4. Results indicate (a) linguistic convergence for all subjects between 4th and 7th grades on possessive,

time extension, and plural tasks; and (b) linguistic divergence
between black and white subjects over time on the present tense
task. It is emphasized that findings be interpreted with caution
because of the effect of nonrandom attribution (44%) on the longitudinally collected data.

82. Marwit, S. J. and Marwit, K. L. Black children's use of nonstandard grammar: Two years later. Developmental Psychology, 1976,
12, 33-38.

A Berko-type task requiring subjects to derive the present,
plural, possessive, and time-extension forms of nonsense syllables
was administered to both black and white second graders and re-
administered to a subsample of these same children upon their
reaching the fourth grade. At both second- and fourth-grade
levels, white subjects supplied significantly more standard
English responses and black subjects significantly more hypothesized nonstandard English responses to each of the four tasks.

83. Marwit, S. J. and Marwit, K. L. Grammatical responses of Negro
and Caucasian second graders as a function of standard and nonstandard
English presentation. Journal of Educational Psychology, 1973, 65 (2),
187-191.

Two black and two white examiners tested 176 black and 164 white
second graders on tasks requiring subjects to derive the present,
plural, possessive and time extension forms of nonsense syllables.
Half of each group received instructions and stimuli in standard
English, and half in black nonstandard English. White subjects
gave significantly more standard English and black subjects
gave significantly more nonstandard English endings to present,
plural, possessive, and time extension words, and these differences were obtained regardless of type of presentation. Findings indicate that racial differences in language functioning
are greater when subjects are tested by a black examiner than
when tested by a white examiner. The internal consistency of
nonstandard English responses by black subjects supports the
linguistic difference hypothesis. (Modified.)

84. Marwit, S. J., Marwit, K. L., and Boswell, J. J. Negro children's
use of nonstandard grammar. Journal of Educational Psychology, 1972,
63 (3), 218-224.

Describes an experiment in which two black and two white examiners presented 93 black and 108 white second graders with the
task of deriving the present plural, possessive, and time-
extension forms of nonsense syllables. The hypothesis that
white subjects would supply more standard English forms and
black subjects more nonstandard forms was supported. The
hypothesized characteristics of black nonstandard English
were upheld in all but one category. The possibility of black
nonstandard English being a distinct "quasi-foreign" language
system and its implications are discussed. (Modified.)

85. Marwit, S. J. and Neumann, G. Black and white children's comprehension of standard and nonstandard English passages. Journal of
Educational Psychology, 1974, 66 (3), 329-332.

Two black and two white examiners administered standard English
and nonstandard English forms of the Reading Comprehension section of the California Reading Test to 60 black and 53 white
second graders. The hypothesis that black subjects comprehend nonstandard English materials better than those in standard English was not supported. Within each form, white subjects
generally obtained higher scores than nonstandard English presentations. Black subjects performed as well as white subjects
under the white examiner-standard English condition only. Results are discussed in relation to other studies of the linguistic
interference hypothesis.

86. Mathewson, G. C. Relationship between ethnic group attitudes
toward dialect and comprehension of dialect folktales. Journal of
Educational Research, 1974, 68 (1), 15-18.

The effects of ethnic group attitudes toward dialect upon comprehension of dialect folktales were studied in third graders. It
was predicted that black third graders would like folktales in
black English (BE) better than the same folktales in standard
English (SE), and better than other folktales in Hawaiian,
Pidgin, or Cajun dialect. A result of this preference was
predicted to be heightened comprehension of black English tales.
Children with other ethnic backgrounds were expected to favor
folktales in SE over those in Pidgin, Cajun, or BE. Results
supported the predictions in both listening and reading conditions with the exception that black children did not show elevated liking or comprehension in response to reading BE.

87. Mattleman, M. S. and Robert, L. E. The language of the inner
city child: A comparison of Puerto Rican and Negro third grade girls.
Journal of Negro Education, 1969, 38 (2), 173-176.

This investigation compared the oral language of two groups of
inner city girls, Negro and Puerto Rican. It was an attempt to
study in depth a small number of children from both quantitative and descriptive aspects. The sample was composed of 5 Negro
and 6 Puerto Rican girls from the third grade who were identified as highly verbal in English on the basis of teacher judgment. Each child was asked to respond individually in an interview to a series of three pictures from the Daily Language Facility Test. Each of the resulting oral language protocols was
analyzed for facility as measured by the test itself, for
fluency as determined by word count, and for syntactic structure using a category system developed by one of the investigators. The results of this study indicated that the Negro
children tended to score higher on the Daily Language Facility
Test and were more fluent than Puerto Rican children. An analysis of the syntactic structure showed that Negro children
used more prepositional phrases, more transformations, greater
variety in sentence pattern, and more linking verb construction

than Puerto Rican children -- suggesting more sophisticated
speech. The results of this investigation indicate replication
is warranted. The Puerto Rican children in this study appeared
to possess less language proficiency than Negro children. If
the results of this study are supported by additional research,
Puerto Rican children would seem to require a different type of
instructional situation or perhaps curricular objective (e.g.,
reading) than Negro children at the third grade level.

88. Newton, E. S. Verbal destitution: The pivotal barrier to
learning. Journal of Negro Education, 1960, 24, 497-499.

A study of 69 of the most "verbally destitute" students in a
reading-skills center revealed: (a) all subjects were South-
easterners; (b) all had been culturally limited to church or
school experiences; (c) the language patterns were those of
their parents, teachers and ministers; and (d) they came from
high schools that graduated less than 50 students annually.

89. Nolen, P. S. Reading nonstandard dialect materials: A study
at grades two and four. Child Development, 1972, 43 (3), 1092-1097.

Explored differences in the recall of printed language patterns
with 156 Negro and Caucasian low-socioeconomic-status second and
fourth graders. Standardized reading passages in standard English with equivalent forms rewritten in Negro dialect and nonstandardized reading passages in Negro dialect were used. Negro
subjects showed no reliable differences in performance related to
language patterns. Second grade Negro subjects reading recall
from both standardized passages was not significantly different from that of Caucasians. Only at grade four did Caucasian
subjects recall significantly more than their Negro counterparts.
There was no significant interaction between the dialect variable
and race or grade of reader.

90. Nurss, J. R. and Day, D. E. Imitating comprehension and production of grammatical structure. Journal of Verbal Learning and Verbal
Behavior, 1971, 10 (1), 68-74.

Gathered baseline data from 147 Southern urban higher status
white and lower status white and black 4-year-old boys and girls
on measures of their ability to imitate, comprehend, and produce
selected grammatical structures. Subjects were given the Brown,
Fraser, Bellugi Test of Grammatical Contrasts. The higher status
white group performed significantly better on all three tasks
than either of the lower status groups. The task ordered in
difficulty: Comprehension = Imitation > Production. An alternate
scoring system was devised to account for possible dialect differences between the test and the lower status children. Status
effects on language development are discussed.

91. Oakland, T. D., Williams, F. C., and Harmer, W. R. A longitudinal study of auditory perception and reading instructions with first grade Negro children. Journal of Special Education, 1973, 7 (2), 141-154.

Briefly reviews previous research which shows that children of lower socioeconomic status (SES) are deficient in auditory-perception abilities and reading achievement and suggests that deficits in auditory abilities may attenuate development of reading skills. In 1968-1969, two strategies were implemented in an attempt to increase the reading achievement of 31 black lower-socioeconomic status first graders (with 31 others serving as controls) through (a) auditory-perception training, and (b) supplemental reading instruction that did not rely heavily upon auditory perception abilities. Two-year follow-up data on the subjects indicated that auditory-perception training alone did not increase reading achievement. It is concluded that reading instruction designed to circumvent perceptual deficits may prove effective and deserves further research.

92. Osser, H., Wang, M. D., and Zaid, F. The young child's ability to imitate and comprehend speech: A comparison of two subcultural groups. Child Development, 1969, 40 (4), 1063-1075.

Administered two psycholinguistic tasks, designed to assess speech imitation and speech comprehension abilities, to 16 lower class Negro and 16 middle class white children. Average age for subjects was five years. The study attempted to discover whether gross environmental differences between the two groups would be reflected in their verbal performances. Subjects were tested for their control of 13 common syntactic structures. Results indicate that the white subjects' performance was superior to that of the Negro subjects, even when differences between their dialect and standard English were taken into consideration. Several sources of the group differences are examined.

93. Pasamanick, B. and Knoblock, H. Early language behavior in Negro children and the testing of intelligence. Journal of Abnormal and Social Psychology, 1955, 50, 401-402.

Forty (40) Negro children examined by a white examiner were found to have lowered language scores on third examinations at two years of age. This was apparently due to lack of verbal responsiveness, rather than poor comprehension of language. This apparent early awareness of racial differences and loss of rapport has serious implications in the field of ethnic group psychology, particularly in the use of verbal items on intelligence tests.

94. Politzer, R. L. Auditory discrimination and the "disadvantaged": Deficit or difference? The English Record, 1971, 21 (4), 174-179.

The suggestion that dialect difference may be responsible for the consistently lower auditory discrimination performance of blacks and lower socioeconomic status groups is never thought

through to its logical conclusion: the so-called "deficit
phenomenon" in auditory discrimination may be a mirage created
by a misunderstanding of the task involved in the auditory discrimination test. The Wepman Test involves an individual's
decision whether a pair like dim/din is made up of identical
or different items. The task is not as simple as it seems
to non-native speakers of English. Most errors in perception
caused by native language backgrounds are simply errors in
categorization. Much of the literature dealing with the disadvantaged, however, continues to classify and treat their
auditory discrimination problems as related to "hearing",
"auditory memory span", or "faulty perception". Obviously,
the auditory discrimination problem is only a small but
very concrete instance in which the language "deficit" of the
disadvantaged turns out to be a simple "difference". The major
distinction between the two approaches is that "deficit" puts
the blame on one party -- "difference" implies no such judgment; it takes two to make a difference. Reprinted by permission.

95. Porterfield, C. L. Adaptive mechanisms of young disadvantaged
stutterers and non-stutterers. Journal of Projective Techniques and
Personality Assessment, 1969, 33 (4), 371-375.

Administered the Human Form of the Children's Apperception
Test (CAT-H) and the Bender Gestalt Test to a group of Negro
preschool stutterers and like age and ability groups of non-
stuttering classmates (adaptive group) and non-stutterers
referred for negative attention-getting behavior (maladaptive
group). Utilizing Haworth's Schedule of Adaptive Mechanisms
to evaluate CAT-H protocols, it was found that the categories
of repression-denial, symbolization, and projection-introjection
differentiated stutterers from their non-stuttering peers.
A similar comparison of stutterers and maladaptive non-
stutterers indicated no significant differences between groups.
Differences were found between stutterer and maladaptive
groups on Bender Gestalt scores, suggesting the Bender's
relevance to overt behavior.

96. Quay, L. C. Language dialect, reinforcement, and the intelligence-
test performance of Negro children. Child Development, 1971, 42 (1),
5-15.

Administered the Stanford-Binet to 100 4-year-old Negro children
from Project Head Start under two conditions of language (standard English and Negro dialect), and two conditions of reinforcement (praise and candy). No reliable IQ differences among the
groups and no significant interactions occurred. Differences
in performance on individual Stanford-Binet items were negligible.
Findings raised questions concerning the existence of motivational and language differences in young Negro children who are
provided experiences designed to bring them into the mainstream
culture.

97. Quay, L. C. Negro dialect and Binet performance in severely disadvantaged black four-year-olds. Child Development, 1972, 43 (1), 245-250.

Administered the Stanford-Binet Test of Intelligence, Form L-M, to two groups of 25 black 4-year-olds selected from an extremely deprived, physically and socially isolated community, under two conditions of language (standard English and Negro dialect). No reliable IQ differences between the groups were found, and comparisons of item difficulty yielded no differences in performance on individual Binet items. The findings, confirming the results of an earlier study using a less deprived population, indicate that young black children did not benefit from having the Binet administered in Negro dialect.

98. Ralph, J. B. Language development in socially disadvantaged children. Review of Educational Research, 1965, 35 (5), 389-400.

Deficits in language and speech are a frequent handicap of socially disadvantaged children. In the process of language acquisition, they are more subject to a lack of vocal stimulation during infancy, to a paucity of conversational experiences in the first 3 or 4 years of life with verbally mature adults, and to severe limitations in opportunities to develop mature cognitive behavior. He suggests developing procedures which will allow investigation in the various modes of verbal functioning and adaptation used by the child, including his language in context with his activities with peers.

99. Ramer, A. L. and Rees, N. S. Selected aspects of the development of English morphology in black American children of low socioeconomic background. Journal of Speech and Hearing Research, 1973, 16 (4), 569-577.

Used a modification of J. Berko's test (1958) to explore the use of six morphological rules, as a function of age, by 90 black children in the Head Start Program. For each of the six morphological rules tested, black English and standard American English take different forms. Five age groups were tested: preschool, kindergarten, and first, fifth and eighth grades. Results indicate that, in the presence of the white examiner, the occurrence of basilect (black English forms) responses decreased while the occurrence of standard English responses increased as the age of the subjects increased. In no case, however, did even the oldest subjects use standard English responses to the exclusion of the alternate black English forms. (Modified.)

100. Ratusnik, D. L., Koenigsknecht, R. A., and Friedman, P. Ethnic and social class comparisons of standard and nonstandard grammatical usage by preschool children. Proceedings of the 81st Annual Convention of the American Psychological Association, Montreal, 1973, 8, 853-854.

Investigated the use of selected phonological and grammatical structures among low and middle socioeconomic preschoolers.

The lower class group was equally divided by race (black and
white), while the middle class group was made up of all white
subjects. Four speech elicitation tasks emphasizing different
modes of speech stimulus presentation were employed. The four
modes of presentation represented different degrees of sponta-
neity ranging from imitation to spontaneous formulation. For
lower class subjects, the generative nature of grammar was
observed to be consistent across different stimulus presentation modes on the phonological and grammatical structures which
were characteristic of the lower socioeconomic black groups
observed. Some of the results support previous empirical
observations of significant overlapping among lower class children in English language behavior, regardless of race.

101. Ratusnik, D. L. and Koenigsknecht, R. A. Influence of age on
black preschoolers' nonstandard performance of certain phonological
and grammatical forms. Perceptual and Motor Skills, 1976, 42, 199-206.
(See ERIC Abstracts, 1976.)

102. Risley, T. R. and Hart, B. Developing correspondence between
the nonverbal and verbal behaviors of preschool children. Journal of
Applied Behavior Analysis, 1968, 1 (4), 267-281.

Correspondence was developed between children's nonverbal and
verbal behavior such that their nonverbal behavior could be
altered simply by reinforcing related verbal behavior. Two
groups of 6 children each were given a food snack at the end
of the day for reporting use of a specific preschool material
during free play (Procedure A); and then only for reports for
use which corresponded to actual use of that material earlier
that day (Procedure B). Initially, Procedure A alone had little
or no effect on the subjects' use of materials. Procedure B
resulted in all of the subjects in one group actually using a
specific material, and after repeating Procedures A and B with
this group across a series of different materials, Procedure A
alone was sufficient to significantly increase use of a specific material. Correspondence between verbal and nonverbal
behavior was produced such that, in this group of 4-year-old
disadvantaged Negro children, "saying" controlled "doing" 22
or more hours later. In the second group, Procedure B initially did not increase the use of a specific material; rather,
subjects' reports decreased to correspond to the intermittent
use of the material. It appeared from subsequent procedures
with this group that maintenance of a high level of reporting
was crucial to the saying-then-doing correspondence seen in
the first group.

103. Rowe, F. B., Brooks, S., and Watson, B. Communication through
gesture. American Annals of the Deaf, 1960, 105, 232-237.

Thirty (30) pictures of American Indian sign language gestures
were matched with word meanings by 238 college and 259 high
school students, including both sexes, white and Negro races,
deaf and non-deaf persons. All groups scored above chance.
White students scored higher than Negro students. Scores of
deaf students tended to exceed those of non-deaf students.

104. Ryan, E., Bouchard, E., and Carranza, M. A. Evaluative reactions
of adolescents toward speakers of standard English and Mexican-American
accented English. Journal of Personality and Social Psychology, 1975,
31 (5), 855-863.

> Sixty-three Mexican-American, black and Anglo adolescent female
> subjects rated the personalities of male speakers of standard
> English and Mexican-American accented English. To demonstrate
> that the functional separation of speech styles is reflected
> in these evaluative reactions, two speech contexts (home and
> school) and two sets of rating scales (status stressing and
> solidarity stressing) were employed. Although standard English
> speakers received more favorable ratings in every case, the
> differences were significantly greater in the school context
> than in the home context, and for status ratings than for soli-
> darity ratings. Mexican-Americans did not prefer accented
> English in the home context or on solidarity scales.

105. Rystrom, R. Dialect training and reading: A further look.
Reading Research Quarterly, 1970, 5 (4), 581-599.

> A presentation of the results of a dialect training project
> conducted in a rural Georgia Negro school. Several reading
> experts have written that the dialect spoken by many Negro
> children may interfere with the acquisition of decoding skills.
> In order to confirm or reject this position two determinations
> must be made: the extent to which these children can be taught
> to speak an approximation of standard white speech; the effects
> of the dialect training upon reading achievement. All four
> first grades at the school where the research was conducted
> were divided in such a way that interactive effects could be
> identified. Two groups were given dialect training while the
> control groups received a language placebo. In order to examine
> effects between phoneme-grapheme controlled readers and dialect
> training, the four classes were also divided into two groups
> taught to read using basal series and two groups which used a
> linguistic series. At the conclusion of the treatment period
> no significant results between groups were obtained which would
> confirm the assumption that dialect has a causative effect
> upon reading achievement. Reprinted by permission.

106. Rystrom, R. Perceptions of vowel letter-sound relationships by
first grade children. Reading Research Quarterly, 1973-1974, 9 (2),
170-185.

> Studied the processing strategies used by ordinary children in
> regular classrooms when they learn to connect letters with
> sounds. Black and white children were asked to write either
> an a, an e, or an i in a number of words. First graders did
> not appear to have strong preconceptions of letter-sound rela-
> tionships when they entered school, but their year-end responses
> were significantly more like adult responses. No significant
> differences were found between the responses of speakers of
> black English and white English. (French and Spanish abstracts.)

107. Schotta, S. G. Differentiation of dialects by Black children
in the rural South. Southeastern Conference on Linguistics, 1970, 24.

   This paper is part of a series of studies on the socio-linguistic
   setting of Prince Edward County, Virginia. An earlier study
   showed that: (a) there is considerable linguistic separatism
   between the Black and White communities despite long-time resi-
   dency of both groups, and (b) Black students have a capability
   in writing standard English although they are not motivated to
   use SE verbally. The purposes of this particular phase of the
   series are: (a) to examine the linguistic features identified
   as black and white by Black students; (b) to determine the limits
   of capability of Black speakers for the white features and the
   White speakers for the black features; and (c) to study the
   chronological development of bi-dialectalism in selected individuals of different ages. Finally, these (and other) data
   are used to study possible correlations between verbal ability
   (specifically, bi-dialectalism among Black students) and academic
   achievement and delinquency. Although Prince Edward County is
   unique in that it provided the only instance in American history
   in which a locality faced with the choice of complying with the
   federal court order or terminating public education, decided to
   close its schools in 1959, in many respects it is characteristic
   of rural Southern communities which have not developed an export
   economy. Because Prince Edward County typifies such areas, it
   is compared with similarly-situated localities of almost total
   White population. Reprinted by permission.

108. Semmel, M. I. and Herzog, B. G. The effects of grammatical
form-class on the verbal recall of Negro and Caucasian educable
mentally-retarded children. Studies in Language and Language Behavior, 1966, 3, 1-19.

   Content form-class is investigated as a variable in verbal
   recall of Negro and Caucasian educable mentally-retarded (EMR)
   children. Subjects for the first study were 10 Negro and 10
   Caucasian EMR boys, aged 9-1 to 12-6, with similar IQ and
   socioeconomic background. Subjects were administered a verbal-
   recall task composed of 20 words, controlled for frequency,
   including: 5 nouns, 5 verbs, 5 adjectives and 5 adverbs.
   Stimuli were randomly presented by tape recordings over three
   trials. Form-class was found to be a significant variable;
   nouns were recalled most often and adverbs least often. There
   was no significant difference between adjectives and verbs.
   Negro subjects had higher recall scores than Caucasian subjects.
   Subjects recalled significantly more words on the second and
   third trials than the first. Interaction effects were not
   significant. The second study tested older EMR boys aged 12-2
   to 14-8, of similar characteristics to those in the first
   study. The same procedure was used. The effects of form-
   class and trials were significant; however, interactions and
   differences between racial subgroups were not significant.
   Nouns were recalled most frequently, followed by adjectives.
   Differences between adverbs and verbs were not significant.
   Trials 2 and 3 had significantly higher recall scores than

Trial 1. Comparison of data from Studies I and II revealed that older subjects recalled more stimuli than younger subjects. The significant main effect differences in form-class were qualified by an interaction between form-class and age. The older subjects recalled significantly more adjectives and adverbs. Reprinted by permission.

109. Sigel, I. E. and Perry, C. Psycholinguistic diversity among "culturally deprived" children. American Journal of Orthopsychiatry, 1968, 38 (1), 122-126.

It is often implied that that segment of the population called "culturally deprived" is a homogeneous group. Analysis of the scores of 25 Negro children given the Illinois Test of Psycholinguistics reveals sufficient variability to cast doubt on the utility of the concept. Implications for education are discussed.

110. Simons, H. D. Black dialect phonology and word recognition. Journal of Educational Research, 1974, 68 (2), 67-70.

Examined the hypothesis that black children can read words that are closer to their black-dialect (BD) pronunciation better than words that are further away. This hypothesis was tested by administering to a total of 76 second, third and fourth grade blacks two lists of BD real word homophones, e.g., "dold"-"doal". It was predicted that the second member in each pair would be easier to read than the first because it is closer to BD phonology. A multivariate and univariate analysis of variance of the differences between the closer and further homophones failed to support the prediction. (Modified.)

111. Simons, H. D. and Johnson, K. R. Black English syntax and reading interference. Research in the Teaching of English, 1974, 8 (3), 339-358.

A report of a study that attempted to demonstrate that the mismatch between the grammatical features of black dialect and standard English grammar used in children's reading materials is a source of reading interference. Sixty-seven second and third grade black dialect speaking children were selected on the basis of the number of dialect features produced on a sentence repetition task. In a repeated measure design, each subject read orally a text written in black dialect and a parallel text written in standard English. Subjects also retold the contents of the texts and answered multiple choice comprehension questions. The analysis of oral reading miscues and the measures of comprehension formed the dependent variables for the study. The hypothesis of reading interference led to the prediction that the dialect text, because it reduced the mismatch between the children's language and the printed language would produce greater comprehension, more effective use of contextual and graphophonic information, and fewer dialect related miscues than the standard English text. The results fail to support the predictions of the reading interference hypothesis. Reprinted by permission.

112. Smith, H. W. and May, W. T.   Influence of the examiner on the
ITPA scores of Negro children.   Psychological Reports, 1967, 20, 499-
502.

To establish local normative data for 6-year-old southern Negro
children from low socioeconomic backgrounds on the Illinois
Test of Psycholinguistic Abilities and to evaluate the effects
of examiner differences, 2 Negro and 4 Caucasian examiners with
little experience tested 171 subjects.   The overall language
score and 5 subscales reflected significant examiner differences;
thus the normative value of the scores is questionable.

113. Somervill, M. A.   Dialect and reading: A review of alternative
solutions.   Review of Educational Research, 1975, 45, 247-262.

The focus of the report was the disadvantaged children, particularly the urban ghetto black child.   The primary question was
whether it is possible to improve the academic achievements of
these children by teaching them in their own dialect rather than
in standard English.   The review cites a number of studies in
which training through dialect has not been efficient.   Somervill takes the position that most investigations of the problem
have been remarkably inadequate.   The best that can be said to
date is that the investigations have been inconclusive.   The
review calls for more empirical investigations of the phenomenon
of nonstandard language among minority groups.

114. Stephenson, B. L. and Gay, W. O.   Psycholinguistic abilities
of black and white children from four socioeconomic status levels.
Exceptional Children, 1972, 38 (9), 705-709.

Administered the Illinois Test of Psycholinguistic Abilities,
Revised Edition, to 160 black and white first graders of average
mental ability from the lower-lower, upper-lower, lower-middle,
and upper-middle socioeconomic status (SES) levels as determined
by the McGuire-White Index of Socioeconomic Status.   Results
indicate that the level of performance and pattern of psycholinguistic abilities of black subjects were relatively free
of a systematic influence from SES, but the performance of white
subjects was related to SES.   The lower SES levels and black
subjects showed less variability than the middle SES and white
subjects.   The reported lower SES visual-motor orientation and
middle SES auditory vocal orientation were not supported in
this study.

115. Stern, C. and Keislar, E.   Comparative effectiveness of echoic
and modeling procedures in language instruction with culturally-
disadvantaged children.   Journal of Special Education, 1969, 3, 177-
185.

The comparative effectiveness of echoic and modeling procedures
for language instruction was investigated with 48 Head Start
children, randomly assigned to the following treatments:
echoic prompting (listening to and echoing each sentence in
every lesson); parallel prompting (listening to a sentence for
the first picture and, using this as a model, producing a sen-

tence for the second picture); listening only; and control. The
hypothesis that children required to produce sentences by
modeling would be superior in producing new sentences in a
similar situation was supported.

116. Terrell, F. Dialectal differences between middle class black
and white children who do and do not associate with lower class black
children. Language and Speech, 1975, 18 (1), 65-73.

117. Williams, F. and Naremore, R. C. Language attitudes: Analysis
of teacher differences. Speech Monographs, 1974, 41 (4), 391-396.

Analyzed differences among teachers in their attitude toward
the speech of different ethnic groups. A Q-type factor analysis
was carried out to group teachers according to their patterns
of rating videotaped speech samples of black, Anglo and Mexican-
American children. 130 teachers did the rating using 10 semantic
differential scales. In support of previous research, ratings
reflected global judgments of confidence-eagerness and ethnicity-
nonstandardness. General corroboration was found among speech
ratings, teachers' stereotype ratings of different ethnic groups,
and the teachers' academic expectations of children representing
such groups. Implications for the assumption that teachers are
a relatively homogeneous group are discussed.

118. Williams, F. and Wood, B. S. Negro children's speech: Some
social class differences in word predictability. Language and Speech,
1970, 13 (3), 141-150.

Language samples of junior high school aged Negro girls of low
and middle socioeconomic classes were subjected to word predictability procedures undertaken by additional students from the
same two populations. Results indicated that the middle class
students could readily approximate the language of the middle
and low class samples, but the lower class students did significantly more poorly in approximating the language of the
middle class students, although they performed as well as the
middle class students in approximating language in samples
from students of their same social status. Reprinted by permission.

119. Wolfram, W. Sociolinguistic alternatives in teaching reading
to nonstandard speakers. Reading Research Quarterly, 1970, 6 (1), 9-33.

A critical review of the alternative strategies in teaching
reading to lower class black children, based on current research
in the field of sociolinguistics. The two main strategies
discussed are the retention of extant materials with adjustments in teaching procedures and the revision of basic materials.
If no change is made in materials, then the options are to
teach children Standard English prior to reading or allow the
students to read materials with dialectally appropriate render-
ings. If the revision of materials is undertaken, the alternative strategies include the neutralization of grammatical
differences in materials or the use of dialect primers. The

review of these alternatives deals with both the linguistic
and socio-cultural factors that contribute to a sociolinguistic
perspective. It is concluded that the acceptance of dialectally
appropriate reading of extant material should be initiated while
further experimentation takes place with the revision of current
materials and the use of dialect primers. Reprinted by permission.

2
PHYSICAL DEVELOPMENT

120. Altemus, L. A. A comparison of cephalofacial relationships.
Angle Orthodontry, 1960, 30, 223-240.

> The author presents roentgenographic standards of the growth
> pattern of head, face, jaws, and teeth of American Negro chil-
> dren, i.e., 40 boys, 40 girls in Dental Stage IV A (permanent
> teeth all erupted up to and including M2). The standards are
> compared to those of white children of a similar Dental Stage.
> The absolute cephalofacial dimensions are greater in Negro
> children; specifically lower facial height exceeds upper in
> the Negro and corpal length of mandible exceeds length of
> anterior cranial base; the teeth are anterior to the anterior
> facial arc (through nasion, nasal spine, pogonion). It is
> pointed out that intraracial variability is so great that in
> some cases Negro and white standards are interchangeable.

121. Altemus, L. A. Frequency of the incidence of malocclusion in
American Negro children aged 12-16. Angle Orthodontry, 1959, 29,
189-200.

> Based on 3,289 children in four junior and senior high schools
> in Washington, D. C., with permanent dentitions and who had
> received no orthodontic care. Malocclusion was assessed in
> two ways: (1) counting of teeth out of normal occlusal align-
> ment; (2) classification via the Angle system. It was found
> that 83% had malocclusion, 4% had "ideal" occlusion, 13% had
> "normal" occlusion. This compares with white children: 80%,
> 3%, 17%, respectively. There are fewer maloccluded teeth per
> child in whites. In the Angle classification Negro children
> have fewer Normal, Class II, Division I, and Class III maloc-
> clusions.

122. Altemus, L. A. and Ferguson, A. D. Comparative incidence of
birth defects in Negro and white children. Pediatrics, 1965, 36,
56-61.

> From a review of the literature, the authors conclude that
> total incidence of birth defects among North American children

varies from 1 to 6%. The authors conclude that from analysis
of records of two District of Columbia hospitals (representing
60% of all Negro children born in the area) approximately 6%
of Negro children have birth defects as compared with 2-3% Caucasian children. Incidence of clubfoot and mongolism was
similar in both groups. Socioeconomic status seems to have
an influence on total incidence of birth defects; Negro children
from the lower socioeconomic group had three times as many birth
defects as children from a somewhat higher socioeconomic group.
Multiple defects observed in North American Negro children are
tabulated.

123. Anderson, N. A., Brown, E. W., and Lyon, R. A. Causes of pre-
maturity. III. Influence of race and sex on duration of gestation and
weight at birth. American Journal of the Disabled Child, 1943, 65,
523-534.

A group of live-born single infants which included 1,731 white
male, 1,658 white female, 1,144 Negro male, and 1,153 Negro
female infants, was studied. The mean birth weight of the
white boys was 7 pounds, 6 ounces; of the white girls, 7
pounds, 2 ounces, of the Negro boys, 6 pounds, 15 ounces,
and of the Negro girls, 6 pounds, 11 ounces. The mean gestation periods of the groups were: white boys, 279 days; white
girls 279.9 days; Negro boys 274.7 days; and Negro girls, 273.3
days. A significant race and sex difference in average birth
weight and significant race differences in average gestation
period were found also in three groups as follows: (a) infants
of at least 210 days gestation period; (b) infants whose birth
weight was at least 5 pounds, 8 ounces; and (c) infants whose
gestation period was at least 238 days and whose birth weight
was 5 pounds, 8 ounces.

124. Bain, K. Racial aspects of maternal and child health. The
Child, 1941, 5, 273-279.

The author first discusses the apparent differences in susceptibility to certain diseases, differences in incidence
rates and mortality rates from these conditions, and differences in maternal and infant mortality rates, birth and
stillbirth rates among the Negroes, Indians, Orientals, and
Mexicans as compared with the whites. She then attempts to
explain how economic status, in terms of low income and bad
living conditions, affect the health of the minority groups.
In view of the increase in the number of public health and
welfare organizations that are including in their programs
aid and care to the colored peoples in this country the author
concludes that the picture will not be as dark in the future.

125. Bakwin, H. The Negro infant. Human Biology, 1932, 4, 1-33.

A review of the literature on the Negro infant under the following headings: geographical distribution, economic status,
types of feeding, illegitimacy, body build, physiological
and developmental differences, motor tests, blood grouping,

prenatal environment, and birth, death and morbidity rates.
The only differences are connected with the skin. The darker
skin absorbs less ultraviolet light, so that rickets and tetany
are more common in temperate climates. The body temperature
is regulated better in the Negro when the environment temperature is high, and the dark skin is more resistant to skin
infections.

126. Bakwin, H. and Patrick, T. W. Jr. The weight of Negro infants.
Journal of Pediatrics, 1944, 24, 405-407.

A study was made of the weight during the first year of life
of 114 Negro infants seen in private practice. No significant
differences between the weight gain of these infants and those
of white infants were observed. It is postulated that the
slower growth of Negro infants observed in earlier studies
was due to differences in socioeconomic status of the Negro
and white groups compared.

127. Barabasz, A. F., Dodd, J. M., Smith, M., and Carter, D. E.
Focal point dependency in inversion perception among Negro, urban
Caucasian and rural Caucasian children. Perceptual and Motor
Skills, 1970, 31 (1), 136-138.

21 deprived Negro, 41 deprived rural Caucasian and 23 nondeprived Caucasian preschool children viewed 12 figure pairs
and indicated which figure of each pair was upside down.
Analysis of variance results demonstrate significant differences in focal point dependency between nondeprived urban
Caucasians and deprived urban Negroes, and between deprived
urban Negroes and deprived rural Caucasians. No significant
differences were found between nondeprived urban Caucasians
and deprived rural Caucasians.

128. Barr, G. E., Allen, C. M., and Shinefield, H. R. Height and
weight of 7,500 children of three skin colors. American Journal
of Diseases of Children, 1972, 124, 866-872.

Height and weight were determined in 7,500 children aged 5-
14 years who participated in the Pediatric Multiphasic Program at Kaiser-Permanente Medical Center in San Francisco
from 1967 to 1970. In general, the black children were
somewhat taller and heavier, and those of yellow skin color
markedly shorter and lighter, than the white children.
Development and use of separate standards for height and
weight in children of white, black and yellow skin color
are recommended.

129. Bayley, N. Comparisons of mental and motor test scores for
ages 1-15 months by sex, birth order, race, geographical location,
and education of parents. Child Development, 1965, 36 (2), 379-412.

Revised forms of Bayley's Scales of Mental and Motor Development were administered to 1,409 infants, ages 1-15 months.
The study population was found to be representative of the U. S.

No differences in scores were found for either scale between
boys and girls, first-born and later-born, education of either
father or mother, or geographic residence. No differences were
found between Negroes and whites on the mental scale, but
the Negro subjects tended consistently to score above the
whites on the Motor Scale. Scores for a small sample of
Puerto Rican babies were the same as for the total white sample.
Emphasis was placed on the need to study carefully the development of mental processes in the second year of life. Within
this period evidently will be found the explanation of the
SES and ethnic differences in mental functioning that are
repeatedly found for children 4 years and older.

130. Beasley, W. C. Visual pursuit in 109 white and 142 Negro
newborn infants. Child Development, 1933, 4, 106-120.

Concerned with problems in the vision of newborn infants.
The infants were examined in a special experimental cabinet
measuring 30 inches wide by 42 inches long by 40 inches high
inside. Pursuit tests were given to 109 white infants and
142 Negro infants. Negro infants showed a slightly higher
proportion of Type A ("excellent") pursuit. In vertical
pursuit, the Negroes exhibit a greater proportion of pursuit
responses and the difference is significant. Also, in the
case of ability to pursue an object traversing in a circular
path in the visual field, Negroes show a striking superiority
to whites.

131. Berlin, C. I. and Dill, A. C. The effects of feedback and
positive reinforcement on the Wepman Auditory Discrimination Test
scores of lower class Negro and white children. Journal of Speech
and Hearing Research, 1967, 10 (2), 384-389.

Twenty-four Negro and 21 white lower class children, 8 to 9
years old, received the Wepman Auditory Discrimination Test
in two forms. The experimental group of 10 whites and 12
Negroes received special feedback and reinforcement, while
the control group of 11 whites and 12 Negroes simply received
a second trial. The special instructions and feedback improved
the discrimination scores of the Negro experimental subjects
only. No change was observed in the control group subjects
who received an unadorned second trial.

132. Bikshapathi, A. C. Health and the Urban Poor: A Bibliography.
Washington, D. C.: National Institute of Education (DHEW), 1975.
(See ERIC-CUE Urban Disadvantaged Series, No. 45.) 62 pp. Available
from: Institute for Urban and Minority Education, Box 40, Teachers
College, New York, New York 10027. ERIC Abstracts, No. ED-114-445.

526 journal articles, monographs, books and reports dating
from 1970 to 1974 comprise this bibliography on issues relating to and attempted solutions of the health problems of
minority urban youth. Documents are classified under the
following headings: health problems and behavior of ethnic
and racial minority groups, health problems realted to growth

and development, health and environment, learning disabilities, school and community health delivery systems, services and policies, school and community health care personnel, educating health consumers, physical fitness, and recreation and health. The following observations are made: (a) societal health problems can often be identified early in a person's life; (b) school is a critical factor and force in prevention of and treatment of health problems; (c) school personnel are not adequately trained to deal with health problems, and health workers in the community are not aware of health problems and programs in the schools; and (4) ethnic minority children are most vulnerable to health problems and least likely to receive remedial services.

133. Blumenthal, F. Racial differences in resistance to respiratory infection. Human Biology, 1942, 14, 104-109.

Two waves of respiratory infection among Negro and white boys (12-17 years old) at the New York Training School for Boys, Warwick, were subjected to statistical and clinical comparison. The two groups lived under identical conditions. During the first wave, the rate of infection among the Negro boys was 11.6% and among the white boys 2.3%. "This would seem to indicate that the resistance against the particular infective agent responsible is lower in the Negro race than in the white race." The second wave, which immediately followed the first, affected both races in almost equal proportion. The majority of the cases of the first epidemic presented symptoms of tracheo-bronchial infection; the cases of the second were mostly affected with frontal sinusitis.

134. Braine, M. D. S., Heimer, C. B., Wortis, H., and Freedman, A. M. Factors associated with impairment of the early development of prematures. Monographs of the Society for Research in Child Development, 1966, 31 (4), Serial No. 106.

The relationships were investigated between impairment in the early development of 351 Negro, single birth, premature infants of birth weight up to 2,100 grams and various complications of the maternal and neonatal course, as well as birth weight, sex, and social class, examined five times prior to 13-1/2 months of age with respect to reflex behavior, visual, "mental", and gross motor development. The premature of both sexes scored significantly lower than the full-term infants on the standardized test of gross motor development at 13-1/2 months. . . . Within the sample of prematures, test scores tended to be linearly related to birth weight. . . . Socio-environmental differences within this group of premature infants . . . only contributed to the impairment found in the less intact groups. Significant impairment in development was found to be independently associated with five of the complications of the maternal and neonatal course: toxemia of pregnancy, hyperbilirubinemia, hypoxia, high neonatal weight loss, and neonatal infections. . . . Male prematures were found to have significantly greater impairment than

female prematures of comparable birth weight, despite there
being no sex difference in the severity of complications. It
appeared that there is a greater vulnerability of the male
premature which was most apparent in relation to toxemia and
hyperbilirubinemia. . . . Finally, the relationship between
low birth weight and the complications to the degree of impairment was evaluated. There was no clear evidence for the existence of substantial impairment correlated with birth weight
which was not also correlated with the complications.

135. Caccamo, J. and Yater, A. C. The ITPA and Negro children with
Down's syndrome. Exceptional Children, 1972, 38 (8), 642-643.

Results of studies investigating the psycholinguistic abilities
of Negro children, Kirk and Kirk (1971) show that "in auditory
sequential memory (short-term auditory memory) both the lower-
and middle-class Negro children show superiority over their
other abilities and over that of the Caucasian standardization (p. 34)." The superiority of the Negro child in auditory
sequential memory raised the question as to whether or not
this superiority would be observed in Negro children with
exceptionalities. The revised edition of the ITPA was administered to a sample of Negro children with Down's syndrome. A
comparison of profile of abilities for the sample of Negro
children with Down's syndrome was made with the profile abilities of Caucasian children with Down's syndrome (Strank, 1964;
McCarthy, 1965). Results indicated Negro children with Down's
syndrome do not differ significantly from their Caucasian
counterparts, in patterns of psycholinguistic abilities as
tested by the ITPA.

136. Carlson, J. S. Some relationships between class inclusion,
perceptual capabilities, verbal capabilities and race. Human Development, 1971, 14 (1), 30-38.

Assessed the development of the concept of class inclusion as
related to order of presentation of materials, type of question, and relationships between perceptual and verbal capabilities and race. Subjects were 113 white and 98 black 5.6- to
9.6-year-old children from an integrated school serving a
middle class community. For purposes of analysis, the sample
was divided into eight 1/2-year groupings. Results indicated
that for the age classifications used: (a) order of presentation of materials was not a significant variable; (b) questions
which mentioned the class last were generally easier to solve;
(c) white subjects showed a clear developmental trend whereas
black subjects did not; (d) the Raven Progressive Matrices
Test was a significant predictor for white but not for black
subjects; and (e) the Peabody Picture Vocabulary Test was not
significantly related to class inclusion for either group.

137. Carpenter, G. C. Visual regard of moving and stationary faces
in early infancy. Merrill-Palmer Quarterly of Behavior and Development, 1974, 20 (3), 181-194.

The effect of stimulus movement on the visual behavior of
young infants using a horizontal movement was explored; and
changes in visual response to stimulus movement over the early
weeks of life by use of a repeated measures design were observed.
Further, the possibility that in an earlier study with Negro
mothers, stimulus brightness might have influenced the differential response, is examined. Results indicate three independent, additive effects contributing to visual response of
young infants: (a) greater attention to horizontally moving
or stationary faces; (b) differential attention among the
particular stimulus faces used, with least attention to the
mother; and (c) increasing attention from 2 to 7 weeks of age.
These results, together with those of previous studies, indicate that discrimination of stimulus movement can be demonstrated at a younger age for some kinds of spatial displacement
than for others.

138. Carpenter, G. C., Tecce, J. J., Stechler, G., and Friedman, S.
Differential visual behavior to human and humanoid faces in early
infancy. Merrill-Palmer Quarterly of Behavior and Development, 1970,
16 (1), 91-108.

From a sample of 18 normal full-term Negro females, findings
indicate active regulation of visual input differentially related to the experimental stimuli; the observed discriminative
visual behavior of infants in the first two months of life
does not appear to be determined solely on the basis of stimulus properties but seem to reflect a more complex level of
information processing, including association from past experience with the stimulus object.

139. Cherry, F. F., Bancroft, H., and Newsom, W. T. Growth of
Negro premature infants. Pediatrics, 1959, 24, 13-22.

Weight, length and head and chest circumferences were measured
at intervals from birth to one year in premature Negro infants,
417 at the beginning of the study. They were given a mixture
of 1 part evaporated milk to 2 parts water with dextrimaltose
added to give an energy value of 67 Cal. per 100 ml. Three
months after discharge from hospital the mixture was changed
to one of equal parts evaporated milk and water without added
carbohydrate. All babies were given vitamins A, D, and C. Results are tabulated for two birthweight groups, and for each
group the sexes are considered separately. Additional tables
show time at which birthweight was regained and multiplied
from 2- to 6-fold, and average daily energy intake per kg.
bodyweight during the first 4 to 10 weeks of life. Sex differences are discussed. They were not considered sufficiently
great to warrant presentation of separate graphs of measurements according to age of boys and girls. On the average head
circumference exceeded chest circumference, but the difference

decreased with increasing age. No infant had larger chest
than head circumference before 6 weeks of age.

140. Christie, A. Prevalence and distribution of ossification centers
in the newborn infant. American Journal of Diseases of Children, 1949,
77, 355-361.

The patterns for development of the centers of ossification
found in newborn infants are presented in tabular form. This
study was based on 1,112 single-born newborn infants (298 white
boys, 267 white girls, 271 Negro boys and 276 Negro girls).
Their osseous development was studied according to weight
at birth, sex and race. It would appear that the order of
appearance of the centers is as follows: calcaneous, talus,
distal epiphysis of the femur, proximal epiphysis of the tibia,
cuboid bone, head of the humerus, capitatum, hamate bone,
third cuneiform bone and head of the femur. In general, all
centers were found to be farther advanced in infants who were
judged to be more mature when weight at birth was used as
the criterion. On the whole, the Negro infants had a greater
prevalence of any one center than the white infants. In
general, the female infants had a greater prevalence of each
center than the male infants in both races in the various
weight groups. The possible research and clinical significance of these findings is discussed.

141. Codwell, J. E. Motor function and the hybridity of the American Negro. Journal of Negro Education, 1949, 18, 452-464.

505 Negro high school boys were classified into three groups
on a Negroid-white continuum using skin color, hair form, eye
color, lip thickness and nasal width as criteria. The McColoy
Motor Capacity and Motor Ability Tests, the Otis Self-Administered
Test of Mental Ability, and the Bernreuter Personality Inventory
were administered to the group. It was found that generally,
motor function is not related to hybridity and that Negroes
tend to preserve Negroid characteristics even when a white
mixture is evident. Motor function is slightly influenced by
intelligence, socioeconomic status or personality. However,
weight, stature, sitting height, leg length and total span as
a composite showed little association to motor function.

142. Crump. P. E., Horton, C. P., Masuoka, J., and Ryan, D. Growth
and development. I. Relation of birth weight in Negro infants to
sex, maternal age, parity, prenatal care, and socioeconomic status.
Journal of Pediatrics, 1957, 51, 678-697.

A study of the relation of birth weight of 2,081 Negro infants
finds them smaller than white infants. Data from the study
show a relationship between small babies at birth and certain
conditions more common to the Negro mother, e.g., younger age
at conception and less prenatal care and supervision.

143. Dickens, D. and Ford, R. N. Geophagy (dirt eating) among Mississippi Negro school children. American Sociological Review, 1942, 7, 59-65.

There are at least four hypotheses whereby dirt eating may be explained. First, dirt eating may be related to hookworm. A second hypothesis is that dirt fills a deficiency in the diets of those who eat it. The third hypothesis is that dirt eating is a cultural trait, the origin of which is lost. The fourth hypothesis is that dirt is eaten to relieve hunger pains. This study was confined to the prevalence of dirt eating among rural Negro school children in Oktibbela County, Mississippi. Data were secured from all children above the third grade who were present at the time of the survey in the 11 Negro schools having three or more teachers. The conclusions were: First, 25% of the Negro boys and girls in this study had eaten dirt within the 10- to 16-day interval previous to the study and it seems likely that others ate dirt at some time during the year. Second, the method employed in the testing technique, of hiding critical words in a list of words lacking emotional tone, yielded reliable and valid results. Third, there was no evidence that the hookworm hypothesis could be supported. Fourth, there was some eivdence that Negro boys and girls ate dirt because of an iron deficiency. Further investigation is indicated. Fifth, if the hypothesis of dirt eating to make up a diet deficiency should fail to be supported by further investigation, then we may have to conclude, as do most of the Negroes themselves, that dirt eating is simply a culture trait like dipping snuff or smoking.

144. Dorman, M. F. and Geffner, D. S. Hemispheric specialization fc᷊ speech perceptions in 6-year-old black and white children from low and middle socioeconomic classes. Cortex, 1974, 10 (2), 171-176.

Hemispheric specialization for speech perception in 6-year-old black and white children from low and middle socioeconomic classes (SEC) is reported. Subjects were presented a dichotic listening task composed of·syllable pairs. All groups evidenced a significant right ear advantage (REA) at recall. The magnitude of the REA did not differ as a function of race or SEC. The outcome suggests that earlier results, which indicated smaller REAs for low SEC subjects, may have been due to a floor effect resulting from task difficulty and motivational variables.

145. Emory, E. K., et. al. Brazelton Scale performance of infants of varying birth weight. Paper presented at the Biennial Southeastern Conference on Human Development (4th), (Nashville, Tennessee, April 15-17, 1976). Also, see ERIC Abstracts, No. ED-128-072, 1976.

The effects of low, full (normal) and high birth weights on the broad range of neonatal behaviors measured by the Brazelton Neonatal Assessment Scale were investigated in a study which also attempted to replicate results of the authors' earlier study of the Brazelton Scale. Data from the original

sample of 52 infants were included in the later study to make
a total sample of 140 clinically normal newborns of over 37
weeks' gestational age. The infants' behaviors were scored
on the 27-item Brazelton Scale. The principal component
factor analysis of the second study yielded three main factors:
attention-orientation, arousal and temperament. Results for
the attention-orientation factor showed a significant main
effect for birth weight, in that the mean score for the full-
weight or normal group was higher than that for either the low
or high groups. With low-weight neonates rated as a high-risk
group for later developmental problems, it is hypothesized
that a similar potential may exist for high-weight infants of
normal gestational age. There were also some sex-birthweight
interactions for the arousal and temperament factors, but
these data are given a cautious interpretation because of
certain characteristics of the sample.

146. Emrich, R., Brodie, A. G., and Blayney, J. R. Prevalence of
Class I, Class II, and Class III malocclusions (angle) in an urban
population: An epidemiological study. Journal of Dental Research,
1965, 44, 947-953.

Samples were from Evanston-Oak Park, Illinois, 11,036 children
6 to 8 years old, 14,951 children 12 to 14 years old, both
sexes, white and Negro; 7,654 children were seen at both ages.
In the 6-8 year group 69% were classed as normal, 54% in the
12-14 year group. For Class I the result was 19% at 6-8 years,
30% at 12-14 years. For Class II the result was 11% and 14%,
respectively. For Class III the result was 1% in both groups.
In the children seen twice 27% classed as normal at first
examination were Class I at the second; 43% with Class I at
6-8 years, were normal at 12-14 years. The prevalence of
Classes I, II, III, at 12-14 years, was 30%, 14%, 1%, respectively.

147. Erhardt, C. L. and Chase, H. C. Part 2, Ethnic group education of mother and birth weight. American Journal of Public Health,
1973, 63 (Supplement), 17-26.

Weight distributions of infants from 142,017 live births in
New York City in 1968 are analyzed according to ethnic origin
and education of mothers. Weight distributions of babies differed among four specified ethnic groups. Although there were
inconsistencies in the data, the proportion of low-weight babies
generally decreased with advancing educational attainment of
the mother. Only the white foreign born group exhibited
comparatively stable proportions of low birth weight infants
over the entire educational range. The proportion of low birth
weight infants among Negro native borns was markedly reduced
with increased education of the mother. Results reflect the
role of education in fostering understanding of the determinants
of low birth weight: short duration of gestation, limited
prenatal weight, and existence of medical problems.

148. Espenschade, A. A note on the comparative motor ability of Negro and white tenth grade girls. Child Development, 1946, 17, 245-248.

Results of the Brace Test of Motor Ability for 35 Negro girls matched with an equal number of white girls on the basis of age, weight and height, are reported. The average total scores for the two groups do not differ significantly, but the white girls do tend to be superior to the Negro girls on two parts of the tests involving a sense of balance.

149. Espenschade, A. Fitness of fourth grade children. Research Quarterly of the American Association for Health, Physical Education and Recreation, 1958, 29, 274-278.

The purpose of this study was to compare performances of fourth grade children on the Kraus-Weber Test of Minimum Muscular Fitness with those on the California Physical Performance Test. The subjects were fourth grade children in 7 of the 15 elementary schools of Berkeley, California. The results showed that children who failed on strength test item or any two or more items on the K-W test make lower scores on the average in running, jumping, throwing, and sit-ups than do those who pass all K-W items; the difference was significant in all events for boys but only in the throw for girls. Significantly more Negro boys and both Negro and white girls passed the K-W test than did white boys; however, if the floor-touch test is omitted, no significant sex or race differences were found.

150. Ferguson, A. D., Cutter, F. F., and Scott, R. B. Growth and development of Negro infants. VI. Relationships of certain environmental factors to neuromuscular development during the first year of life. Journal of Pediatrics, 1956, 48, 308-313.

The neuromuscular development of 708 healthy full-term Negro infants from different socioeconomic classes was studied during the first year of life. The age of "walking alone" was not related to the number of siblings or education of parents. The greater the infant's weight the slower the development of "sitting" and "walking alone". No relationship was found between intelligence at 13 months and age of "walking alone".

151. Ferguson, A. D., Scott, R. B., and Bakwin, H. Growth and development of Negro infants: Comparison of the deciduous dentition of Negro and white infants. Journal of Pediatrics, 1957, 50, 327-331.

The first tooth erupts earlier in Negro infants than in white infants. White infants from private practice had more teeth at the age of one year than did Negro infants seen in clinics.

152. Fillmer, H. T. and Linder, R. Comparison of auditory and visual modalities. Education Milwaukee, 1970, 91 (2), 110-113.

108 lower class southern Negro second grade boys were tested for purposes of assessing comparative recall strengths of

auditory, visual, and simultaneous auditory-visual presentations.
Each subject was asked to recall one auditory, one visual, and
one auditory-visual set of stimuli in the exact sequences they
were heard or seen by the subject. The sets of stimuli were
presented in exactly the same manner again and again until one
perfect repetition or ten trials were completed, whichever came
first. Scoring was accomplished by recording checks for each
correct response. The most essential finding of this study is
that the auditory channel proved to be distinctly inferior to
the visual and the auditory-visual channels for two of the
three tasks.

153. Finlaysen, A. B. Social and economic background of retarded
children. Journal of Educational Sociology, 1941, 15, 38-45.

36 educationally retarded Negro children in Washington, D. C.
were studied in an effort to analyze their socioeconomic background and its relationship to retardation. Each child furnished a detailed account of his home life and general environment. The child and the parents or guardians were also visited
in their homes. "The problem of Negro retardation is a serious
one and can be solved in America only by democratic problem-
solving educational programs conducted through the school."

154. Frankenburg, W. K., Dick, N. P., and Carland, J. Development
of preschool aged children of different social and ethnic groups:
Implications for developmental screening. Journal of Pediatrics,
1975, 87 (1), 125-132.

The developmental status of 1,180 children representing a
cross section of Denver's ethnic and parental occupational
groups was compared with that of 1,055 children (349 Anglo,
354 Spanish surname, and 352 blacks) whose parents were unskilled workers. The children varied in age from 2 weeks to
6.4 years and were evaluated with the Denver developmental
screening test. Comparisons were made in developmental
achievements as reflected by individual item differences for
Anglo children from unskilled families with Anglos from
cross sectional families. A second comparison of Anglo,
Spanish, and black children of the unskilled sample was
also made. The first analysis comparing 910 Anglo children
from the cross sectional sample with 349 Anglo children from
the unskilled families demonstrated significant differences
(p<0.05) for 39 of the 105 items. Below 20 months of age,
children of the unskilled sample were more advanced, whereas
after 20 months of age, the children of the cross sectional
sample were advanced in all test sectors except for items
in the personal social sector. Comparisons of Anglo, black
and Spanish surname children from the unskilled families
showed fewer differences in rates of development.

155. Freeman, H., Kathryn, B., and Vander Zwaag, R. Nutritional deficiencies in disadvantaged preschool children. American Journal of Diseases of Children, 1971, 121, 455-463.

 The nutritional status of 100 preschool children from the
 economic depressed area of Nashville was evaluated and correlated with Stanford-Binet test scores. Findings included
 mild growth retardation, nonspecific physical abnormalities,
 and goiter (the latter in 8.7%). Laboratory studies revealed
 decreased body stores of vitamin A (96%), iron (35%), folic
 acid (17%), and thiamine (13%) in a high proportion of the
 children. Results of hospital oriented biochemical screening
 tests were normal. Significant correlations were found
 between initial intelligence quotient, final IQ, and IQ difference following language education, all of which related inversely to age. Biochemical indices and IQ did not correlate.
 Anthropometric measurements revealed correlation between height
 and serum vitamin A and iron, and an inverse correlation between head:chest ratio and erythrocyte transketolase activity.
 Relevant ecologic factors included a marginal family income,
 a lack of parental understanding about nutrition, and a lack
 of parental supervision, particularly at mealtime.

156. Fry, P. C., Howard, J. E. Sr., and Logan, B. C. Body weight and skinfold thickness in black, Mexican-American and white infants. Nutrition Reports International, 1975, 11 (2), 155-160.

 1,811 black and Mexican-American Dallas infants were found to
 grow in weight in a manner virtually identical to that of white
 infants measured in Boston some 30 to 40 years ago. Subcutaneous
 fat in the triceps and subscapular areas and circumference of
 the mid upper arm were measured on 394 well nourished infants
 ranging in age from newborn to three years. They were equally
 distributed between three ethnic groups of black, white and
 Mexican-American. In general, Dallas subjects had less subcutaneous fat in the triceps area than Northern European
 children with whom they were compared. Also, Dallas subjects
 were found to have smaller mid upper arm circumferences than
 Northern European children and black and Puerto Rican children in New York City.

157. Gatewood, M. C. and Weiss, A. P. Race and sex differences in newborn infants. Journal of Genetic Psychology, 1930, 38, 31-49.

 78 infants were observed under experimentally controlled conditions, including periods of no stimulation and periods of
 stimulation by light, sound, temperature, odor, holding arms,
 and holding nose. Some 65 different kinds of movements were
 noted. Negro infants appeared less active than white, and
 males less active than females. The sexes of the Negroes
 differed more from each other than those of the whites. The
 increases of number of movements observed during the stimulation periods over the number during no stimulation are in the
 following ratios: white female 148%, white male 364%, Negro
 female 122%, Negro male 331%. Whether such sex and race

differences are significant for subsequent development requires
investigation over longer periods.

158. German, P. S., Skinner, E. A., Shapiro, S., and Salkever, D. S.
Preventive and episodic health care of inner city children. Journal
of Community Health, 1976, 2 (2), 92-106.

Children in low income, inner city households who used different
sources of ambulatory care were analyzed with regard to their
experiences in securing preventive and episodic illness care.
An examination of preventive health care revealed that while
the majority of children of school age were immunized, only
about half of the children under age 6 were. Among children
in the 3 to 5 age group, those attending day care centers
were more likely to be immunized than those not in such programs. There was no relationship between source of care or
day care participation and whether a child received care for
an episode of illness. Age and usual source of care made a
difference in determining whether a child sought care for
earaches or received regular care for asthma.

159. Gibson, C. B. Tuberculosis in Negro children. American Review
of Tuberculosis, 1934, 29 (April), 430.

160. Gill, N. and Herdtner, L. L. Perceptual and socioeconomic
variables, instruction in body-orientation, and predicted academic
success in young children. Perceptual and Motor Skills, 1968, 26,
1175-1184.

Perceptual differences were investigated at the first grade
level among Negro and white lower class children and middle
class white children; and nursery, kindergarten and first
grade middle class white children. Half of the nursery
school children had been given special exercises to enhance
body awareness. A rod-and-frame test, the Frostig test, and
the Metropolitan Achievement test were the criterion measures.
Lower class children were less effective; race was not a significant factor, special exercises were beneficial; and perceptual performance was more highly correlated with predicted
academic success for girls.

161. Gover, M. Negro mortality. II. The birth rate and infant
and maternal mortality. Public Health Reporter, 1946, 61, 1529-1538.

Analysis of Census data is presented for the birth registra-
tion states, 1920-1943. While infant and maternal mortality
rates have declined, the acceleration in decline is not as
great for Negroes as for whites. The Negro birth rate in
1940 was higher than the white in the North and lower in the
South. Infant and maternal mortality is higher among Negroes
than among whites and higher in the South than in the North.

162. Greenberg, J. W. and Alshan, L. M. Perceptual-motor functioning and school achievement in lower class black children. Perceptual and Motor Skills, 1974, 38 (1), 60-62.

Perceptual-motor functioning was studied in 160 lower class, black fifth grade children, 80 achieving at or above grade level and 80 achieving at least two years below grade level. On the Bender Motor Gestalt Test, the lower achievers made significantly more errors than high achievers, including both rotation and non-rotation errors. Sex differences were minimal and, where observed, stemmed from a particularly high frequency of non-rotation errors among the low achieving girls. Performance of the high achievers was close to published norms, for the Bender; but lower achievers fell substantially below the norms.

163. Guttentag, M. Negro-white differences in children's movements. Perceptual and Motor Skills, 1972, 35 (2), 435-436.

Describes an experiment in which the spontaneous movement responses of a total of 46 black lower class and white lower-middle class 4-year-olds were recorded on videotape under several controlled conditions. Tapes were coded for total movement and for gross movement responses. Results show that blacks emitted a significantly greater number of movement responses and a greater variety of movement responses than did both white groups.

164. Hammill, D., Goodman, L., and Wiederholt, J. L. Use of the Frostig DTVP with economically disadvantaged children. Journal of School Psychology, 1971, 9 (4), 430-435.

Considered the reliability and validity of the Developmental Test of Visual Perception when used with a sample of economically disadvantaged, predominantly Negro kindergartners (N=88), and first graders (N=74), from a large Eastern city. Regarding reliability, test-retest and split-half procedures were employed; for validity, the test was correlated with the Slosson Intelligence Test, the Metropolitan Readiness Test, and the Metropolitan Achievement Test. It is concluded that: (a) the total test values alone evidence the necessary reliability to be used with confidence for diagnostic purposes; and (b) the validity of the measure has not been sufficiently demonstrated.

165. Hammonds, K. E. The health status of urban black preschool children. Journal of the National Medical Association, 1975, 67 (1), 36-40.

The black preschool child from an urban low income family is caught in a 3-way crossfire by being black, poor, and preschool age. Many of his physical, mental and emotional problems result from circumstances affecting the family (i.e., survival) and community. Coping with daily necessities of food, clothing and shelter, along with social stigmata and low income lowers

the priority of preventive health care for the children. The
result is rampant poor health among the children. Many traditional health institutions have failed to solve the problem
and newer comprehensive ideas and programs are being tried.
Black-white and rich-poor inequities still exist in health
care, though some advances have been made. Therefore, such
ideas and programs, particularly in urban settings, deserve
careful evaluation and development.

166. Hansley, C. and Busse, T. V. Perceptual explorations in Negro
children. Developmental Psychology, 1969, 1 (4), 446.

Examined and attempted to generalize from the hypothesis of
D. Elkind and J. Weiss that, "perceptual performance
is determined both by the level of the subject's perceptual
development and by the nature of the stimulus configuration."
12 Negro boys and 12 Negro girls at each of four age levels
(5, 6, 7 and 8 years), were subjects. Results indicate,
contrary to previous findings, that "exploration of an array
is primarily a function of the child's level of perception
and only very secondarily a function of the configuration of
the stimulus array."

167. Hardy, M. C. Socioeconomic background of children with impaired
hearing. Child Development, 1954, 25, 295-308.

Results from pure-tone audiometric tests followed by otological
examination of all substandard cases failed to support the
generalization by Fiedler that children with hearing defects
are "underprivileged in every sense of the word." Findings
from 37,000 elementary school children of sharply contrasting
socioeconomic backgrounds show, neither in consistent trends
nor statistically significant differences, evidence suggestive of higher incidence of impaired hearing where living
conditions are poor. Even where entire neighborhoods are
characterized as blighted, frequency of hearing impairment
was no greater than in the best residential sections. By
diagnosis 3.0% were found in favored neighborhoods, 2.1% in
average, and 1.9% in poor. According to population character,
frequency of impairment was highest in white neighborhoods
and lowest in Negro areas -- 2.5% in exclusively white, 1.9%
in mixed population neighborhoods, and 1.6% in non-white where
at least 80% were Negro. What was done about the child's
hearing difficulty, however, was directly associated with
socioeconomic status but was unrelated to previous awareness
of the problem. Loss had not been expected by the parents
of 70% of those with impaired hearing.

168. Harmon, C. Racial differences in reaction time at the preschool
level. Child Development, 1937, 8, 279-281.

169. Henderson, N. B. and Engel, R. Neonatal visual evoked potentials as predictors of psychoeducational tests at age seven. Developmental Psychology, 1974, 10 (2), 269-276.

The effectiveness of neonatal visual evoked responses for predicting total and subtest IQ scores, sensorimotor, perceptual-motor, and achievement test scores at age 7, was determined. The most reliable visual evoked response was used. The children represented a cross section of county hospital births. Visual evoked response and test outcomes were obtained between narrow age ranges. In a simple correlation matrix of visual evoked response with 12 independent measures for 4 race and sex groups, only one correlation (arithmetic for black girls) reached significance.

170. Henton, C. L. A comparative study of the onset of menarche among Negro and white children. Journal of Psychology, 1958, 46, 65-73.

Subjects were 133 white and 801 Negro girls in school in Montgomery, Alabama. Hypothesis was tested that Negroes matured earlier. Mean ages of menstruation were approximately equal, with insignificant critical ratios.

171. Henton, C. L. The effect of socioeconomic and emotional factors on the onset of menarche among Negro and white girls. Journal of Genetic Psychology, 1961, 98, 255-264.

Subjects were 133 white and 801 Negro girls. A comparison of SES and emotional factors was not significant. Differences in socioeconomic factors were manifested in degrees. Negro girls experienced more emotion than did white girls from the onset of their menses.

172. Horton, C. P. and Crump, E. P. Growth and development: II. Skin color in Negro infants and parents: Its relationship to birth weight, reflex maturity, socioeconomic status, length of gestation and parity. Journal of Pediatrics, 1958, 53, 547-558.

The subjects were 661 children included in a five-year longitudinal study. Skin color is rated on a 9-point scale. Darker skin color is related to lower SES. Factors such as length of gestation and birth weight appear unrelated to skin color.

173. Horton, C. P. and Crump, E. P. Growth and development. III. Skin color in Negro infants and parents: Its relationship to birth weight, reflex maturity, socioeconomic status, length of gestation and parity. Journal of Pediatrics, 1958, 53, 547-558.

The subjects are 661 children included in a five-year longitudinal growth study and as many of their parents as possible. Darker skin color, as determined on a 9-position color chart, is related to lower socioeconomic status. Factors such as length of gestation and birth weight appear unrelated to skin color.

174. Howard, R. G. and Brown, A. M. Twinning: A marker for biological insults. Child Development, 1970, 41 (2), 519-530.

     Analyzed birth records of 314 consecutive twin births with
     respect to race, sex, birth weight, gestational age, present-
     ation, and type of delivery, Apgar ratings, socioeconomic
     ratings, time lapsed between delivery of first and second twin,
     use of oxytocic drugs during labor, and frequency of diagnosis
     of multiple births. Twin neonates were found to be a nonrepre-
     sentative sample of newborns with respect to birth weight and
     gestation, with male pairs and same-sex pairs the least repre-
     sentative. Significant differences were found between Negro
     and Caucasian twins -- Negroes having shorter gestation, lower
     birth weight and socioeconomic ratings, but higher parity. One-
     third of the twins were delivered from breech presentation,
     and had lower Apgar and socioeconomic ratings, shorter gesta-
     tion, and lower birth weight. Twins recruited into a longi-
     tudinal study had more favorable perinatal conditions than
     the larger twin sample.

175. Hurley, R. Poverty and organic impairment. Poverty and Mental
Retardation: A Causal Relationship, pp. 53-70. New York: Vintage
Books, 1969.

     The deadening influence of poverty on mental ability begins at
     the moment of conception. Damage done to the child during the
     reproductive cycle is likely to be permanent because it is
     organic. Apart from the greater biomedical risks a poor child
     encounters before birth, he also suffers from the cumulative
     ill effects of poverty upon his mother. Poor prenatal care,
     overwork, undernourishment, and the other physical and emotional
     stresses of poverty cause higher rates of fetal death and more
     premature births among low-income women. The mortality rate
     for nonwhite infants in the U. S. in 1964 was 41.1 per one
     thousand, or nearly twice the white infant mortality rate of
     21.6 per one thousand. Among premature children, those at
     the lower social levels perform more poorly than those in the
     more privileged groups. The prematurity rate varies directly
     with the lack of prenatal care and poor women most frequently
     cannot afford proper care. The poor also cannot afford private
     maternity care and so give birth in overcrowded general delivery
     clinics, often without an attending physician. These conditions
     make it more likely that their children will, by accident or
     professional inattention, suffer the brain injuries possible
     when delivery is difficult. Organic damage due to disease and
     poor nutrition, both during the reproductive cycle and after
     the child is born, occurs among the poor much more often than
     among other classes. Poor nutrition can also impair intelli-
     gence, sometimes causing permanent damage to the central nervous
     system. Lead poisoning caused by eating chips of lead-based
     paint also may result in permanent mental retardation. Its
     usual victims are poor children, since they live in the sort
     of housing where such paint is still a danger. Poor children
     also get less frequent pediatric care. In 1963, 9.6% of children
     under 15 from families with income under $2,000 visited a

pediatrician, while nearly 30% of those from families with income over $7,000 made such visits.

176. Johnston, F. E. and Beller, A. Anthropometric evaluation of the body composition of black, white and Puerto Rican newborns. American Journal of Clinical Nutrition, 1976, 29 (1), 61-65.

194 white, black and Puerto Rican infants to 5 days old were measured in the ward nurseries of two Philadelphia city hospitals. In addition to birth weight and length, triceps and subscapular skinfolds and upper arm circumference were obtained. Upper arm muscle circumference was calculated. Females had greater skinfold thickness than males but significant differences were found only for the triceps. Whites and blacks did not differ in skinfold thickness, but Puerto Rican infants had significantly smaller triceps skinfolds. Differences in nutritional status are attributed to environmental factors.

177. Kessler, A. and Scott, R. B. Growth and development of Negro infants. II. Relation of birth weight, body length and epiphysial maturation to economic status. American Journal of Diseases of Children, 1950, 80, 370-378.

Roentgenograms were taken of the knees of 300 newborn Negro infants, and the diameters of the distal femoral and proximal tibial epiphyses were measured. We have confirmed previous observations of the relation of epiphysial maturation to birth weight, body length and sex. We have not been able to demonstrate any relation between economic status or milk intake during pregnancy and the size of these centers.

178. Kiil, V. Frontal hair direction. Journal of Heredity, 1952, 43, 247-248.

The frontal hair direction of 812 persons of different races was noted. Of 348 Chinese-American pupils in San Francisco schools, 90.2% had type I direction, 4.6%, type II and 5.2% type III. Of 304 Indian school children from Albuquerque, 84.6% showed type I direction, 4.6% type II and 10.8% type III. Of 160 Negro patients, mostly children, in Charity Hospital, New Orleans, 30.6% showed type I, 19.4% type II and 50.0% type III. This last group was the most mixed. The geographical distribution of different types of frontal hair direction may be used as a means of tracing migration and intermixture of racial groups.

179. Knoblock, H. and Pasamanick, B. Further observations on the behavioral development of Negro children. Journal of Genetic Psychology, 1953, 83, 137-157.

44 of an original group of 53 Negro infants were examined for a third time and their developmental progress studied and correlated with various individual and environmental factors. No evidence for a downward trend in development is found.

180. Knoblock, H. and Pasamanick, B. The relationship of race and
socioeconomic status to the development of motor behavior patterns
in infancy. Psychiatric Research Reports, 1958, (10), 123-133.

Subjects were 992 infants born in Boston in 1952. There were
no significant Negro-white differences in developmental evaluation of motor behavior. The differences which exist in motor
behavior in premature infants can be the result of greater
brain damage in the more premature infants and this in turn
can be related to lower socioeconomic status.

181. Krogman, W. Growth of head, face, trunk and limbs in Philadelphia white and Negro children of elementary and high school age.
Monographs of the Society for Research in Child Development, 1970,
35 (3), 80.

Reviews anthropometric findings from a population of white
and Negro children.

182. Lanbeth, M. and Lanier, L. H. Race differences in speed of
reaction. Journal of Genetic Psychology, 1933, 42, 255-297.

It has been held that the racial differences found on many
psychological tests are essentially differences of speed;
which view, especially as stated by Klineberg, is here critically and experimentally analyzed. The Stanford-Binet Scale,
a rational learning test, and six tests of rate of response
were applied to 30 white and to 30 Negro 12-year-old boys.
Comparisons show that the more complex the test, the higher
the relative score made by the whites; and since there is
roughly a parallel increase of speed differences in their
favor, it follows that the theory of a general speed difference between the races is untenable. Intercorrelations between the various tests are found to be higher for the Negroes,
possibly indicative of a more primitive and less differentiated
type of mental organization.

183. Lee, J. W. A study of certain tongue characteristics in 72
pairs of Negro twins. Journal of Heredity, 1956, 47, 17-19.

This is a study of 72 pairs of twins 6 to 16 years old in
East Baton Rough Parish in Louisiana. All the twins were
Negroes; 22 of them were identical and of the nonidentical
32 were of like sex, 18 of unlike sex. Determination of
identity was made using Newman's criteria plus similarity
of blood grouping. In tongue-rolling, 95.5% of the identical
twins, 84.4 of the nonidentical like-sex pairs and 88.9 of
the unlike sex pairs were concordant. In tongue-folding, the
percentages were respectively 95.5, 90.7 and 89.3; and in
tasting of phenyl thiocarbonide the percentages of concordance
were 91.0, 84.4 and 77.8 respectively. The differences between
the three sets of twins as to height, weight, head width and
head breadth are also shown in another table.

184. Lewis, J. H. The Biology of the Negro. Chicago: University of Chicago Press, 1942.

This volume represents a start toward a systematic anthropology, comparative racial pathology. It compares Caucasians and Negroes, using the latter designation loosely, with respect to the expressions of disease among them. The first quarter of the book considers basic description in terms of population and vital statistics, the anatomy of the Negro, biochemical and physiological characteristics. The extensive, scattered literature is then organized into chapters on medical diseases; surgical diseases; obstetrics and gynecology; diseases of the skin; diseases of the eye, ear, nose and throat; and dental diseases. Specific bibliographic references are provided throughout.

185. Lueth, H. C. and Sutton, D. C. Chorea in the Negro race. Journal of Pediatrics, 1933, 3, 775.

Of 165 children studied in the clinic for the follow-up of patients with cardiac disease of the Cook County Hospital, 131 were white and 34 were Negroes. Chorea was observed in 37% of the white children and 26% of the colored children. Chorea showed the same characteristics in both races. These figures are published to refute the common statement that chorea is rarely seen in the Negro race.

186. Mack, R. W. and Ipsen, J. The height-weight relationship in early childhood: Birth to 48-month correlations in an urban, low income Negro population. Human Biology, 1974, 46 (1), 21-32.

A knowledge of the maternal variables studied contributed very little to a prediction of the relative weight either at birth or at subsequent intervals. Likewise, the relative weight at birth accounted for only 3% of the observed deviations at four months. In contrast, 25% to 30% of the observed deviations at 12 months could be attributed to the four-month deviations. This relationship persisted to a significant degree through the 48 months of measurement. The implications of this strong correlation between the relative weight at four months and the relative weights at 12 and 48 months are discussed in relationship to the possibility of earlier intervention in the course of early childhood obesity.

187. Malina, R. M. Patterns of development in skinfolds of Negro and white Philadelphia children. Human Biology, 1966, 38, 89-103.

A cross sectional study was made upon a sample of 1,092 clinically normal Philadelphia white and Negro school children 6 - 12 years of age. Skinfold measurements were taken at the triceps, subscapular, and midaxillary (xiphoid level) sites. All thicknesses were recorded to the nearest half-millimeter with a Lange skinfold caliper and converted to logarithmic transforms for the analysis. All skinfold sites showed a progressive increase in thickness from 6 - 10 years

of age. From 10 to 12 years, the pattern of increase and/or
decrease was variable. White females had the largest skinfolds
at all sites. White males had greater skinfolds at the triceps
and midaxillary sites than Negro females, while the latter
showed greater skinfolds than Negro males at all ages and at
all sites. Comparisons were also made with other samples of
a similar age range.

188. Malina, R. M., Mueller, W. H., and Holman, J. D. Parent-child
correlations and heritability of stature in Philadelphia black and
white children 6 to 12 years of age. Human Biology, 1976, 48 (3),
475-486.

Parent-child correlations for stature and midparent-child
regression for stature were considered in a cross sectional
sample of 422 black and 384 white 6- to 12-year-olds. Children's
statures were measured, while parental heights were reported
on questionnaires. Parent-child correlations for the white
sample were consistently higher than those for blacks, and the
differences reached significance for father-daughter, father-
child, and all midparent relationships. Heritabilities of
stature in the two samples, as given by the midparent-child
regression, were 37% for blacks and 49% for whites (p< 0.001).
Absence of assortative mating among blacks and diminished
parent-child environmental similarity are considered as
possible factors contributing to decreased similarity of
black parents and their children, although the possibility
of greater step-parentage among black fathers (i.e., social
rather than biological father) must also be considered.

189. Malina, R. M., et al. Body dimensions and proportions, white
and Negro children, 6 to 11 years. United States: National Health
Survey Series 11, No. 143. Available from: Superintendent of Docu-
ments, U. S. Government Printing Office, Washington, D. C. 20402,
Order Publication No. DHEW (HRA) 75-1625. Also, see ERIC Abstracts,
No. ED-117-284, 1974.

The fifth in a series of reports presenting analyses and discussions of data on height, weight, and 28 other body measurements taken from a probability sample of noninstitutionalized
children in the United States aged 6 to 11 years, this document
compares the growth patterns of white and Negro children for 20
body measurements. Emphasis is placed on comparisons of age
and sex specific means and medians for Negro and white children.
These national estimates are based on cross sectional data,
which are said to limit the analyses to attained size rather
than velocities of growth. All dimensions are said to increase
almost linearly with age from 6 through 11 years in Negro and
white children, both males and females. Conclusions derived
from these data are considered to agree generally with most
other anthropometric comparisons of American white and Negro
children with these statistics providing figures held to be
current, comprehensive, and reliable national estimates. 26
detailed tables of statistical material are provided.

190. McCormack, M. K., Dicker, L., Katz, S. H., et al. Growth patterns of children with sickle cell disease. Human Biology, 1976, 48 (3), 429-437.

> The growth status of 46 American black children with sickle cell anemia (SS) and 26 children with sickle cell trait (AS) were compared with that of normal black children from Philadelphia. As a group, the children with SS were shown to have lower heights, weights, sitting heights, biacromial breadths, bicondylar femur breadths, upper arm circumferences, and calf circumferences, but not triceps skinfold (girls only), than normal children of comparable chronological ages. They showed a considerable delay in skeletal maturation at all ages compared with normals. Log$_{10}$ weight/height ratios indicated that the SS boys were thinner for their heights than the SS girls, as well as the AS boys or girls, and normal boys or girls. This was especially true at the taller heights. The SS girls were shown to be slightly thinner for their heights than normals at lower heights, but equal to normals at taller heights. Sickle cell trait children showed delays in skeletal maturation when compared with normal children. Sickle cell trait males additionally showed decreased biacromial breadth and females with sickle cell trait showed decreased values on all measures except sitting height and triceps skinfold thickness.

191. Meenes, M. Eidetic phenomena in Negro school children. Psychology Bulletin, 1933, 30, 688-689.

192. Meenes, M. The incidence of the eidetic imagery in Negro school children. Journal of Negro Education, 1937, 6, 592-595.

> The author opens the article with a critical discussion of techniques of experimentation and explanations which have been proposed to account for the greater incidence of eidetic imagery in Negro subjects. Data are presented from the studies of various investigators to show the frequency of eidetic imagery of white and Mexican children. These data are compared with those obtained in studies by Gill and Hicks, graduate students at Howard University. The conclusion is drawn that "Negro school children show a smaller percentage of eidetic ability than is usually reported in investigations on white school children." While there was some indication of a higher incidence of eidetic imagery in lighter than in darker Negro children, the author concludes that as yet there is no evidence of racial differences.

193. Meredith, H. V. North American Negro infants: Size at birth and growth during the first postnatal year. Human Biology, 1952, 24, 290-308.

> This paper reviews the literature on comparative size of North American Negro and white infants with respect to eight anthropometric measures. The material is handled in two sections -- one dealing with the period from birth to 8 postnatal weeks, the other with the period from 3 months to 1 year.

194. Meredith, H. V. Physical growth from birth to two years: I. Stature. A review and synthesis of North American research for the period 1850-1941. University of Iowa Studies in Child Welfare, 1943, 19, 407.

This is a comprehensive review and synthesis of the research situation prior to 1942 in infant stature in North America. Part I supplies a synthesis of the information. Closely related findings are gathered together, organized and exhibited in a manner to portray the degree of association between stature in infancy and such variables as sex, race, time, SES, geographic region, stature of parents, order of birth, prematurity, disease and diet. Special consideration is given to individual differences and to gain over designated age intervals.

Part II presents an annotated bibliography on infant stature which draws upon 130 different studies executed in North America prior to 1942. Numerical values are reproduced for central tendency and variability of stature at selected ages, for central tendency and variability of increase of stature between certain ages, for seriation measurements on individual infants, and for correlation of stature with other variables.

195. Michelson, N. Investigations in the physical development of Negroes. I. Stature. American Journal of Physical Anthropology, 1943, 1, n.s., 191-213.

The author collected 4,745 stature measurements on Negro girls between 21 days and 17.9 years of age from Riverdale Orphanage, Harlem Clinics and a public school in New York City, and 316 measurements on Negro males between 21 days and 33.9 months of age from Harlem Clinics. The correlation between the rhythm of growth and the onset of puberty of Negro females was found to be in conformity with similar observations made on white girls by other investigators. The children measured in the Riverdale Orphanage in 1940 were taller than children of corresponding ages measured there in 1900. However, the Negro children are smaller than whites of the same generation. Negro infants who had been under the dietary regime of the New York City Department of Health showed an increase in stature as compared with corresponding age groups studied two decades earlier by Woodbury.

196. Michelson, N. Studies in the physical development of Negroes. III. Cephalic index. American Journal of Physical Anthropology, 1943, 1, n.s., 417-424.

The data on which this study is based were obtained on whites and Negroes in New York in 1935 and on Negroes in 1941. The latter group included only individuals who had been under the dietary regimen employed by the New York City Health Department, from birth to 4 years of age or over. A decrease in the cephalic index from birth to adult age is shown for the Negro groups. The excess of the female over the male cephalic index was about the same for the whites and Negroes. A possible

tendency toward a change in the head form toward the brachy-
cephalic type was detected among a group of Negro children
who had been on the Health Department dietary regimen.

197. Michelson, N. Studies in the physical development of Negroes.
IV. Onset of puberty. American Journal of Physical Anthropology,
1944, 2, n.s., 151-166.

Data concerning time of first menstruation were obtained by
interview from 1,397 Negro adolescent girls in New York City
from 1935 to 1940 and, for purposes of comparison, from 2,449
white girls in a Brooklyn high school in 1938. Corrected as
well as uncorrected values showed the following: (a) the
Negro groups as a whole have a later onset of puberty than
whites; (b) Negro girls who lived in the South until beyond the
age of onset of puberty have a later onset than girls who were
born in the North or those who were born in the South but
came to the North before puberty. West Indian Negroes matured
later than any of the other groups in the study. The relation
between the premenarcheal acceleration in growth and time of
onset of menstruation was the same in the Negro and white
groups. The question of the relationship between socioeconomic
status and type of nutrition is discussed.

198. Milne, C., Seefeldt, V., and Reuschlein, P. Relationship between
grade, sex, race, and motor performance in young children. Research
Quarterly, 1976, 47 (4), 726-730.

553 black and white children in kindergarten, grade 1, and
grade 2, as part of a total test battery, were tested on items
of agility, speed, power, flexibility, and endurance. Analysis
of variance was used to determine the effects of grade, sex,
and race on gross motor performance. Significant improvements were found at each grade for speed, power, and endurance
items; males had significantly better performances than females
on all items with the exception of flexibility; black children
had significantly lower values than white children on the speed
item at each grade level.

199. Mitchell, A. G. and Cook, W. C. Mongolism in the Negro.
Journal of the American Medical Association, 1932, 99, 2105-2106.

The authors report four cases of Mongolism occurring in the
Negro. They have seen others having typical features of this
type of idiocy. They have found only 11 other such cases
reported in the literature.

200. Moore, J. E. A comparison of Negro and white children in speed
of reaction on an eye-hand coordination test. Journal of Genetic
Psychology, 1941, 59, 225-228.

White children (43 boys, 49 girls) and Negroes (39 boys and
42 girls), all 6 years to 7 years and 5 months old, took a
simple eye-hand coordination test. Comparisons of total group
and of single sex groups showed the whites always faster, but
no differences approached statistical significance.

201. Moore, J. E. A comparison of Negro and white preschool children
on a vocabulary test and eye-hand coordination test. Child Development, 1942, 13, 247-252.

     82 white and 78 Negro subjects, ranging in age from 2 to 7 years,
     were given the Van Alstyne Picture Vocabulary Test for Preschool
     Children, and the Preschool Form of the Moore Eye-Hand Coordina-
     tion Test. Of the nine groups, the white children were superior
     to the Negro children on the Van Alstyne Test in 8 age groups,
     and on the Moore Test in 5 age groups. The difference in culture
     is related to these findings.

202. Moore, J. E. A comparison of white and Negro children on a
simple eye-hand coordination test. Psychological Bulletin, 1940,
37, 555.

203. Morgan, H. Neonatal precocity and the black experience. The
Negro Educational Review, 1976, 27 (2), 129-134.

     "Black children who find themselves too often among unwelcoming
     and uncaring adults and hostile institutions need all the
     developmental freedom they can muster to build muscle neces-
     sary for encountering the very white society in which we all
     live." The brainwashing effect of white society (which really
     ultimately controls our schools) and sterile schools, unwelcoming
     adults and peers, help drastically to diminish self-worth by
     reinforcing a punitive approach to the child's motor excite-
     ment. The problem begins at birth and continues through the
     early years of growth, as black mothers are encouraged to re-
     ject their child's motor achievements. A constant selling
     job is done to black parents to make them believe that their
     children are defective and the system is perfect. A large per-
     centage of black children are labeled as hyperactive in the
     schools. Drugs, particularly amphetamines and Ritalin, are
     the prescribed therapy.

204. Munday, B., Shepherd, M. L., Emerson, L., Hamil, B. M., Poole,
M. W., Macy, I. G., and Raiford, T. E. Hemoglobin Differences in
Healthy White and Negro Infants. (No reference cited.)

     There is no racial difference for hemoglobin values during the
     first three months of life, but from the fourth to twelfth
     months the average value for Negro infants is from .5 to 1.0
     grams per 100 cubic centimeters of blood less than that for
     white. During this latter period, hemoglobin determinations
     on Negroes show greater variations than do those in white in-
     fants. There is no corresponding difference in arythrocyte
     counts.

205. Osborne, R. T. and Gregor, A. J. Racial differences in heritability estimates for tests of spatial ability. Perceptual and Motor
Skills, 1968, 27 (3, Part 1), 735-739.

     172 pairs of identical (monozygotic, MZ) twins and 112 pairs
     of like-sexed fraternal (dizygotic, DZ) twins were given a

battery of psychological tests which included Surface Development Test, Porteus Mazes, Newcastle Spatial Test, Paper Folding
Test, Identical Picture Test, Perceptual Speed, Object-Aperture
Test, Form B, and Cube Comparisons. 242 were boys and 326 girls,
of whom 482 were white and 86 Negro. Ages ranged from 13 to
18 years. Using four different heritability ratios the relative intrapair similarity of MZ and like-sexed DZ twins on
selected spatial tests was determined. Although the MZ and
DZ intraclass r's are generally higher for the white than for
Negro children, the heritability estimates which are determined
by rMZ-rDZ differences are higher for the Negro pupils. Environment does not play a more significant role in the development
of spatial ability of Negro subjects than white subjects.

206. Paige, D. M., Davis, L., and Cordova, A. Growth in the disadvantaged. Journal of School Health, 1975, 45 (3), 161.

Many individual black children show a poor nutritional profile,
the overall growth pattern of the surveyed population parallels
that commonly used and accepted Boston-Stuart growth standards.
Despite the apparent adequacy of growth, utilization of growth
standards generated by a white suburban population generations
ago may inadequately express the current growth potential of
black children.

207. Pasamanick, B. A comparative study of the behavioral development
of Negro infants. Journal of Genetic Psychology, 1946, 69, 3-44.

"The development of a group of 53 Negro infants (28
male, 25 female) living with their own families,
was studied and compared with that of three groups
of white infants; 57 infants (25 male and 32 female),
who were living in boarding homes; 22 infants (7 male
and 15 female), living in a child caring institution; and 20 infants (8 male, 12 female) from superior families and living at home."

The following was concluded:

"The average New Haven Negro infant of this study
is fully equal in behavioral development to the
average New Haven white baby. No outstanding
characteristic was found which could be called a
'racial' difference, with the possible exception
of the definite acceleration in gross motor behavior displayed by the Negroes. . . ."

There are no significant correlations of development with depth
of pigmentation, number of years of parental schooling, and
regional origin of the parents. The onset of the depressing influence of exogenous factors upon Negro development might be
construed as beginning during the third half-year of life.

208. Peck, L. and Hodges, A. B. A study of the eidetic imagery of
young Negro children. Journal of Negro Education, 1937, 6, 601-610.

209. Perino, J. and Ernhart, C. B. The relation of subclinical lead
level to cognitive and sensorimotor impairment in black preschoolers.
Journal of Learning Disabilities, 1974, 7 (10), 616-620.

> The relation of subclinical lead levels to cognitive and sensori-
> motor impairment in black preschoolers is discussed. Findings
> indicate that the lead levels of 80 black preschool children
> were below the criteria set up for lead poisoning, but a re-
> gressive formula reveals that the relationship was significant,
> and, as lead level increases, general cognitive, verbal, and
> perceptual abilities decrease. Results reveal that lead levels
> are not related significantly to parental intelligence, birth
> order, birth weight, or number of siblings. Lead level is,
> however, related to the educational level of the parents. It
> is concluded that the criteria set for lead poisoning warrant
> reexamination.

210. Pierce-Jones, J. and King, F. J. Perceptual differences between
Negro and white adolescents of similar symbolic brightness. Perceptual
and Motor Skills, 1960, 11, 191-194.

> Subjects were 84 Negro and 84 white children. Hypothesis is
> that Negro and white children selected to be similar in average
> levels of symbolic (verbal-quantitative) abilities, do not
> differ significantly in certain perceptual closure factors
> measured by four tests using verbal and figural stimulus.
> Negro-white means were significantly different in 3 of 4
> comparisons. The pattern of differences on the test using
> verbal stimuli tended to favor the hypothesis tested, but this
> was not true of the nonverbal closure measures. Failure to
> use "performance intelligence" as a control variable might
> account for the results disagreeing with the hypothesis.

211. Poindexter, H. A. Handicaps in the normal growth and development of rural Negro children. American Journal of Public Health,
1938, 28, 1048-1052.

212. Rambar, A. C. Mongoloid imbecility in the Negro. Archives of
Pediatrics, 1935, 52, 58ff.

> The writer reports two cases of Mongoloid imbecility in the
> Negro and calls attention to the infrequent reference to this
> condition in the literature. He finds that nine authors have
> reported a total of only 22 instances of Mongoloid idiocy
> occurring in the Negro race.

213. Ramsey, G. V. Sexual growth of Negro and white boys. Human
Biology, 1950, 22, 146-149.

> The median age reported for first ejaculation by 37 Negroes
> was 13.8 years, and for 286 whites, was also 13.8. The median
> age for first appearance of pubic hair for the Negro was 13.3,
> for the white group, was 13.6. The median age for the first
> recognition of voice change was 13.7 for the Negro males and
> 13.4 for the white males.

214. Rhoads, T. F., Rapoport, M., Kennedy, R., and Stokes, J.
Studies in the growth and development of male children receiving
evaporated milk. II. Physical growth, dentition and intelligence
of white and Negro children through the first four years as influenced
by vitamin supplements. Journal of Pediatrics, 1945, 26, 415-454.

A total of 233 male children, of whom 42% were Negro and all
from low income groups, were given supplementary feedings (in
addition to the home diet) of evaporated milk. The children
were divided into four groups. Each group received vitamin
supplementation of differing amounts and kind. Anthropometric
measurements were made at regular intervals, and at the age of
three years all children were given the revised Stanford-Binet
Test. No relationship to vitamin intake was found for either
the physical or the mental measurements, but racial differences
both in body build and intelligence quotients were present.
The mean IQ of the white children was 103.9; of the Negroes,
96.3.

215. Rhodes, A. A comparative study of motor abilities of Negroes
and whites. Child Development, 1937, 8, 369-371.

In this investigation 80 Negro children, 20 in each age group
between 2 and 5 years old; and two groups of adults, 24
Negroes and 20 whites, all university students, were given
four of the motor ability tests used in the study of Goodenough
and Smart. Results compared with those previously reported
by Goodenough and Smart for white children indicate "that as
far as motor abilities of the kind measured by these tests
are concerned, there is little, if any, difference between
Negroes and whites at any level of development."

216. Roberts, F. L. Vital capacity of Negro children. Journal of
the Tennessee Academy of Science, 1926, 1 (4), 18.

In 1564 white and 1254 Negro children, the vital capacity of
the former exceeded that of the Negroes by 7-12%.

217. Robinson, H. B. and Robinson, N. M. Longitudinal development
of very young children in a comprehensive day care program: The
first two years. Child Development, 1971, 42 (6), 1673-1683.

Reports intelligence test results for 19 infants and 12
2-1/2- to 4-1/2-year-old children given stimulating day care
for up to 2-1/2 years. Tests included the Bayley Mental Scale,
the Bayley Motor Scale, and the Bayley Behavior Profile, which
were administered every three months. Older subjects were
given several language assessment measures, along with the
Stanford-Binet and Peabody Picture Vocabulary Test. Four-
year-old subjects were given three additional tests designed
to measure various mental abilities. Comparisons with test
scores of two groups of control children suggest that comprehensive group care, if of high quality, may enhance development at a crucial period when verbal abilities are beginning
to emerge. A much greater positive effect of the program

was found with culturally deprived, preschool Negro subjects
than with more advantaged Caucasian subjects. Consistently
higher scores on verbal tasks than sensorimotor tasks were
found for Graham Center preschool groups.

218. Robischon, P. Pica practice and other hand-mouth behavior and
children's development level. Nursing Research, 1971, 20 (1), 4-16.

Tested the hypothesis that children who practice pica, and
those who show other persistent hand-mouth behavior, have a
lower level of development than children who do not exhibit
these behaviors. Well 19- to 24-month-old children with no
history of deviation from health, whose parents were Negroes
born in the United States of the lower socioeconomic class,
served as subjects. Parents of 130 children were interviewed
to select children for three study groups: pica; Hand-mouth;
and control. Each group was matched for age. Two testers who
had no knowledge of the children's group assignment examined
the children using the Denver Development Screening Test,
which assesses four areas of behavior: gross motor, fine
motor-adaptive, language, and personal-social. Children prac-
ticing pica and children in the hand-mouth group both had
significantly lower gross motor scores than children in the
control group, but the differences in the other areas of behavior were not significant.

219. Robson, J. R. K., Larkin, F. A., Bursick, J. H., and Perri,
K. P. Growth standards for infants and children: A cross sectional
study. Pediatrics, 1975, 56 (6), 1014-1020.

Measurements of height and weight were collected on 1,233
black and white infants and children attending a Child Health
Clinic in Washtenaw County, Michigan. Polynomial curves were
fitted to each race and sex group and, from these estimates
were made of the 3rd, 50th, and 97th percentiles for height
and weight. Blacks tended to be lighter and shorter than
whites in early infancy. In the second year of life, blacks
tended to exceed whites in height and weight achievement. For
infants and children in the 97th percentile this change in
status occurred earlier. The differences in weight and height
achievement were statistically significant in the two race
groups, but not between sexes. The percentile estimates differed significantly from the percentiles of local as well
as the Iowa, Harvard, and Tanner (United Kingdom) standards.
Differences in the racial and environmental background of the
clinic population and the samples used in the development of
the national standards probably account for the variations
in the percentile estimates. It is concluded that race and
sex specific standards are required before growth achievements
in infants and children can be properly evaluated.

220. Rosenblith, J. F. Relations between neonatal behaviors and those at eight months. Developmental Psychology, 1974, 10 (6), 779-792.

A replication sample design with four samples of a nearly randomly chosen clinic population of newborns was used to determine whether newborn behavioral assessments are related to those at 8 months. Neonatal behavior was assessed by the Graham/Rosenblith Scales and 8-month behavior by the Collaborative Project (Bayley) Examination. In addition to analyses within replication samples, relations were examined separately for males and females, blacks and whites, and within each of four gestational age categories. Many relations between scores on the neonatal examination and performance at 8 months are significant. Most of those found for the total were found in Sample 1, which was used to generate hypotheses for checking against final results. Fewer relations between ratings and 8-month performance were significant.

221. Royster, L. T. Body type of Negro children. Archives of Pediatrics, 1936, 53, 259-266.

From a study of 9,700 Negro children, males and females, aged 6 to 15 years, it is shown that the standards of Lucas and Pryor for body build of white children (mean bi-iliac height index) do not apply to Negro children, the index in the latter being much smaller at each age.

222. Schachter, J., Kerr, J. L., and Wimberly, F. C. Racial differences in newborn heart rate level. Psychophysiology, 1974, 11 (2), 220.

In a paper presented at the Thirteenth Annual Meeting of the Society for Psychophysiological Research, racial differences in heart rate (HR) of newborn infants were studied. Swaddled newborns were presented with repeated auditory clicks for a 3-1/2-hour interfeeding period on the second, and again on the third, postnatal day. During each 20 minutes of the session, the average R-R interval was calculated to ten 20-second epochs during which no effective stimulus occurred. For one group of 33 white and 35 black newborns, data from five 20-minute periods indicated that the average R-R interval for white subjects was 37 msec. longer than for blacks on the second postnatal day, and 47 msec. longer on the third postnatal day. This race effect was also significant for a second group of 19 white and 12 black subjects, based upon data from ten 20-minute periods. The difference remained essentially the same among those subjects selected from the above two groups who had neither complications of pregnancy nor complications of labor or delivery. Hour level for the first 20 minutes of each session showed no association with: (a) level of maternal depression or anxiety during pregnancy; (b) parity; (b) gestational age; (d) birthweight; or (e) level of maternal medication for delivery.

223. Schachter, J., Kerr, J. L., Wimberly, F. C., and Lachin, J. M.
Heart rate levels of black and white newborns. Psychosomatic Medicine, 1974, 36 (6), 513-524.

Among a low socioeconomic class urban population in Northeastern
U. S., black newborns had higher heart rate levels during sleep
than white newborns. This difference could be accounted for
by none of the perinatal variables studied, including proportion of rapid eye movement sleep, degree of motor activity,
amount of crying, birthweight or gestational age. The specu-
lative possibility that the elevated heart rate in these black
newborns is one precursor of hypertension is discussed.

224. Schlutz, F. W., Morse, M., Cassels, D. E., and Iob, L. V. A
study of the nutritional and physical status and the response to
exercise of 16 Negro boys 13 to 17 years of age. Journal of Pediatrics,
1940, 17, 466-480.

Sixteen Negro boys, 13 to 17 years of age, have been studied
as to nutritional status, physical status, including lung
volume and its subdivisions, blood and "available fluid"
volumes, basal oxygen consumption, heart rate, and blood
pressure, and response to exercise, including both cardio-
vascular and blood changes.

225. Scott, R. B., Crawford, R. P., and Jenkins, M. E. Incidence of
sicklemia in the newborn Negro infant. American Journal of the
Diseases of Children, 1948, 75, 842-849.

Of 262 newborn Negro infants tested for the sickling r trait
on the first, third and fifth days of life, the reactions of
9 or 3.4% were positive. No cases of active sickle cell
anemia were detected. Of 209 older children tested for the
sickling trait the reactions of 16, or 7.6%, were positive.
There is apparently a lower incidence of expression of the
sickle cell trait in early life than in later life. Factors
responsible for this difference are unknown at present. There
is an indication that newborn infants who exhibit the sickling
trait in the first few days of life experience a potentiation
of the sickling phenomenon in later infancy and childhood.

226. Scott, R. B., Jenkins, M. E., and Crawford, R. P. Growth and
development of Negro infants. I. Analysis of birth weights of 11,818
newly born infants. Pediatrics, 1950, 6, 425-431.

The hypothesis investigated was that the smaller weight at
birth in the older reports for Negro infants was really due
to economic and other extrinsic causes. Average birth weight
for over 5,000 males at Freedmen's Hospital, Washington, D. C.
(1939-1947), was 3378 Gm. and for over 5,000 females, 3269 Gm.
This series ranks fifth among 12 reports studied. Some association with increasing income is noted, to which the authors
are inclined to attribute the relatively higher birth weights.

227. Scott, R. B., Ferguson, A. D., Jenkins, M. E., and Cutter, F. E. Growth and development of Negro infants: III. Growth during the first year of life as observed in private pediatric practice. Journal of Pediatrics, 1950, 37, 885-893.

Three physicians reported the weight each month, and the body length every three months, of 634 Negro infants from the lower middle income level. The mean birth weight of the boys was 7.66 pounds and the girls 7.20 pounds. At one year, the mean weight of the boys was 22.59 pounds and the girls' was 21.33 pounds. The mean length at one month was 21.1 inches for boys and 20.9 inches for girls. At one year, it was 29.8 inches for the boys and 29.5 inches for the girls. No significant differences were found between the growth curves of Negro and white children from comparable socioeconomic levels.

228. Scott, R. B., et al. Growth and development of Negro infants: V. Neuromuscular patterns of behavior during the first year of life. Pediatrics, 1955, 16, 24-30.

Subjects were 708 Negro infants from two different SES back-grounds. Their 12 neuromuscular patterns of behavior were contrasted with a similar study of white infants. After 35 weeks, there were no differences between the two Negro groups; however, with the exception of smiling and vocalizing, the Negro group was accelerated over the white group. The differences were attributed to environmental factors.

229. Seegmiller, B. R. and King, W. L. Relations between behavioral characteristics of infants, their mothers' behaviors, and performance on the Bayley Mental and Motor Scales. Journal of Psychology, 1975, 90 (First Half), 99-111.

The relations between infant test room behaviors as measured by the infant behavior record, the mother's (or mother surro-gate's) responses to her infant in the testing situation, and the infant's test performance on the Bayley Mental and Psycho-motor Scales, were studied at 14, 18, and 22 months in a sample of firstborn, black male infants in the Harlem area. With increasing age, social responsiveness played a relatively less important role in successful performance, while object respon-siveness became increasingly important. Bayley Motor scores were related to many fewer ratings than the Mental scores. Gross muscle coordination was related to performance at all three ages, and energy ratings at two of the three ages. For both the Mental and Motor scores, fewer relationships were observed at the 18-month testing as compared to the 14-month and 22-month testings. By 22 months, infants scoring higher on the Bayley Mental Scales had mothers who were more highly involved with their child's achievement as judged by test room behaviors.

230. Shin, E. H. Black-white differentials in infant mortality in
the South, 1940-1970. Demography, (n.d.), 12 (1), 1-19.

The article examines black-white differentials in infant
mortality in 10 selected southern states during the period
1940-70. To measure the extent of black-white differentials
the author used Fein's "time lag" statistics and the ratios
of black-white mortality rates. In both neonatal and post-
neonatal mortality rates the gap between blacks and whites
has widened in the period 1940-70 in the southern states.
Compared with the northern states sampled no significant differences were observed in the extent of black-white differentials. Neonatal mortality differentials had a weak inverse
relationship with income inequality while a positive association between variations among the southern states in post-
neonatal mortality and income differentials was found. The
influence of artifacts of the data upon the trends and variations was noted through a detailed methodology.

231. Solomon, P. Narcolepsy in Negroes. Diseases of the Nervous
System, 1945, 6, 179-183.

Neuropsychiatric screening of Negro recruits detected narcolepsy in 19 of 10,000 men, an incidence 60 times that found
in white recruits. 18 of these were from the Deep South.
Three had a family history of narcolepsy; one case seemed
organic; two probably organic; and 16 appeared to be "idio-
pathic" in etiology. Only two cases showed symptoms in early
childhood. "A study of the data suggests that the Southern
Negro may have a constitutional predisposition toward the
development of narcolepsy and that this predisposition
may be related in some Negroes to a faulty resistance toward
sleep or increased readiness for sleep."

232. Steggerda, M. Growth of Racial Characteristics. Cold Spring
Harbor, Long Island, N.Y.: Carnegie Institution of Washington,
Department of Genetics, n.d.

The investigation concerns approximately 75 boys and 75 girls
in each of the following racial groups: Maya Indians (Yucatan),
Navajo Indians (Arizona), American Negroes (Alabama), and
Dutch whites (Michigan). These groups are measured yearly,
beginning each child at approximately 5 years of age. It is
hoped to measure the children until they reach maturity. The
Yucatan Indians have already been observed for three successive
years, the others once or twice. Sixty physical measurements
are taken on each child. The measurements include height,
weight, body segments, dimensions of the head and face, erup-
tion of teeth, change in eye and hair color, and others. (This
resume received in Washington, D. C. on August 4, 1933.)

233. Sterling, E. B. The physical status of the urban Negro child -- Health studies of Negro children. Public Health Reports, 1928, Reprint No. 1251, Washington, 57-60.

An intensive study of a group of more than 5,000 Negro school children from 6 to 14 years of age in Atlanta, Georgia.

234. Stigler, R. Comparisons of capacity to perceive minute movements in the visual periphery, in whites and Negroes. Biological Review, 1940, 30, 114-126.

With a simple attachment (kinestemeter) to a perimeter, peripheral acuity for movement was studied in two whites and two Negroes. The values obtained were 4-1/2 times as great in one, and 2-1/2 times as great in the other Negro, than in the two whites. Whether this superiority of the Negroes is due to practice or innate ability remains an open question which might well be settled by investigation on North American city-bred Negroes.

235. Stone, D. B. and Kudla, K. J. An analysis of health needs and problems as revealed by a selected sample of Project Head Start children. Journal of School Health, 1967, 37, 470-476.

The article is based on a study to "identify and analyze common health needs and problems of the socially disadvantaged pre-school child as revealed in a selected sample of Operation Head Start children from a community of approximately 50,000 people in a central Mid-western state." A sample of 100 subjects was drawn from a population of 180 children. Information was taken from three standard government forms regarding seven areas of concern: medical history, immunization history, eye examination, dental examination, general information, diagnosis and impressions, and family history. The findings are presented in two sections: (a) percentage of total responses as revealed in the seven content areas, and (b) significant findings when age, sex and race are compared to a particular item or question. The most significant findings resulted from comparison of hospitalizations, immunizations, eye examinations, dental examinations, tuberculin testing, family structure, and other minor conditions by age, sex and racial group. Suggestions are made regarding home, school and community action for improving care to this age group.

236. Strandskov, H. H. and Ondina, D. A comparison of the percentages of stillbirths among single and plural births in the total, the "white" and the "colored" U. S. populations. American Journal of Physical Anthropology, 1947, 5, 41-49.

The stillbirth percentages among single and plural births in the U. S. population from 1922 to 1936 are here presented. It is demonstrated that stillbirth percentages increase significantly with each increase in number of embryos per pregnancy, e.g., in the total population: 3.504% among stillbirths, 7.533% among twins, 14.281% among triplets, 19.922%

among quadruplets. The probable causes of the increase are
discussed. The percentage of stillbirths among the males is
shown to be significantly higher than among the females, a
condition attributed to gene factors. Finally, the percentage of stillbirths is significantly higher among the single
and plural births of the "colored" population than among
corresponding births of the "whites," a phenomenon due primarily
to environmental factors, according to the authors, although
genetic factors could also be partly responsible.

237. Sweeney, D. R., Zegers, R., and Collins, W. E. Color blindness
in male Negro children. Journal of Social Psychology, 1964, 62 (1),
85-91.

Subjects were 1,137 Negro males between the ages of 6 and 15.
The H-R-R Pseudoisochromatic Plate Test was used as a preliminary screening device. All subjects failing the plates were
tested with an anomaloscope. 2.99% of the total sample failed
both tests. Screening plate failures at the lower age levels
accounted for some lack of agreement between the two tests.
It was concluded that Negro populations may be a more fruit-
ful source of blue-yellow color vision defect, and that an
age factor could be of importance in color vision screening
tests.

238. Tandy, E. C. Infant and maternal mortality among Negroes.
Children's Bureau Publication, 1937, No. 243, Washington, D. C., 34 pp.

This report is a statistical study of the present situation and
the trend of infant and maternal mortality among the Negroes.
It includes some preliminary findings from the Children's
Bureau study of causes of stillbirth. The material is reprinted,
with the addition of some 1935 figures, from the Journal of
Negro Education for July, 1937.

239. Thompson, W. H. A study of the frequency of Mongoloidism in
Negro children in the United States. Proceedings of the American
Association of Mental Deficiency, 1939, 44 (1), 91-94.

A questionnaire was sent to both state and private institutions
for the feeble minded, and to public school systems in over 100
large cities, concerning the number of Mongoloids in their populations. No school system reported any Mongolism of the colored
race. Returns from Southern schools, as well as from Southern
institutions, failed to reveal any Mongolism of the colored
race. Of the 1,777 Mongoloids in 45 institutions, 21 were
colored. Of 139 cases of the mixed type with Mongolism tendencies, only one was colored. Comparisons among age, sex and
mental level of colored and whites are made.

240. Truong, T. B., Ferguson, A. D., Booker, C. R., and Scott, R. B. Growth and development of Negro infants: X. Fetal hemoblogin in sicklers and nonsicklers during the first two years of life. American Journal of the Diseases of Children, 1964, 107, 25-29.

Fetal hemoglobin concentrations were determined in corresponding age groups of (a) 299 nonsickling infants from 1 day to 24 months of age, (b) 6 infants with sickle cell anemia, and (c) 15 infants with sickle cell trait. All of the infants in the study group were Negro. In the normal nonsickling Negro infants the fetal hemoglobin concentration was not unlike that previously described by Singer and co-workers, for Negro and white infants. It appears that race may not be a significant factor in fetal hemoglobin persistence and disappearance in the normal infant. Infants with sickle cell anemia did have higher amounts of fetal hemoglobin than nonsicklers. When the infants with sickle cell trait were compared with normal infants there was some variation in regard to concentration of fetal hemoglobin; however, employing the Singer technique, we did not find a consistently higher concentration of hemoglobin F in the trait subjects at corresponding age periods.

241. Van Alstyne, D. and Osborne, E. Rhythmic responses of Negro and white children two to six: With a special focus on regulated and free rhythm situations. Monographs of Social Research in Child Child Development, 1937, 2 (4), iv-64. (Washington, D. C.: National Research Council.)

483 5-1/2- to 6-1/2-year-old Negro and white children were given an adaptation of the Seashore test for motor rhythm performance and a new type of free rhythm or rhythm-memory test. Scoring was done by counting on the recording appartus clap markings that fell within a $\pm$.05 seconds tolerance. Negroes were about 50% better than whites in simple "slow" and "fast" rhythms, and more so among the younger children. The difference decreased markedly with increased complexity of rhythm pattern, and with increase in age. Negroes were much superior in following a set pace than in reproducing remembered patterns. All children were about 250% better in the free rhythm than in the regulated series. Girls were slightly superior, and a positive but insignificant relation to intelligence was found. Teachers' ratings showed low predictive ability. A slight relationship to amount of pigmentation was demonstrated. Little relation between musical background and rhythm score was found. The effect of practice was very small. It is suggested that the Negro child is more naturally adaptable to a 45 r.p.m. rhythm than the white. Genetically, it is shown that ability to maintain a pattern appears earlier than ability to maintain a set pace. The apparatus is described, and some additional theoretical implications are discussed.

242. Voors, A. W., Foster, T. A., Frerichs, R. R., et. al. Studies
of blood pressures in children, ages 5 to 14 years, in a total biracial community. The Bogalusa heart study. Circulation, 1976, 54
(2), 319-327.

> Blood pressure, height, weight, maturation, triceps skinfold
> thickness, serum lipids, and hemoglobin were measured as risk
> factors for coronary artery disease in 3,524 children (93% of
> the eligible population) in Bogalusa, Louisiana. Nine blood
> pressures were taken on each child by trained observers with
> mercury sphygomomanometers (Baumanometer) and Physiometrics
> automatic recorders in a rigid randomized design in a relaxed
> atmosphere with other children present. The pressures observed
> were low compared to reported data. Black children had signi-
> ficantly higher blood pressures than white children. This
> difference, starting before age 10, was largest in the children
> in the upper 5% of the pressure ranks. Stepwise multiple
> regression analysis revealed that this racial difference was
> significant when measured by an automatic recorder. Body
> size, expressed by height and by weight/height index, was a
> strong determinant of blood pressure level. Other positive
> determinants were blood hemoglobin and external maturation.

243. Wakefield, E. G. and Dellinger, S. C. A report of identical
Albino twins of Negro parents. Annals of Internal Medicine, 1936,
9, 1149.

> Total albinism in identical Negro twins is reported. Their
> physical and mental state is recorded, along with remarks con-
> cerning the etiology of albinism and twinning. The scarcity
> of the condition in identical twins is pointed out.

244. Walters, C. E. Comparative development of Negro and white
infants. Journal of Genetic Psychology, 1967, 110 (2), 243-251.

> 51 Negro and 57 white babies were equated for socioeconomic
> status and tested at 12, 24, and 36 weeks on the Gesell Devel-
> opmental Schedules. When comparisons were made on the Gesell
> Test and its component subdivisions, the only significant dif-
> ference found was in motor behavior at 12 weeks in favor of
> the Negro infants. The groups were divided into socioeconomic
> subgroups and compared for development. The results of all
> comparisons suggest that factors, other than racial, probably
> account for the few differences found between the two races.

245. Whitney, K. M. A case of Mongolian idiocy in a Negro boy.
Eugenics News, 1936, 21, 2-9.

> History of the name "Mongolian" idiocy or imbecility, and
> theories regarding etiology of the type and its absence among
> Negroes, are reviewed. The general clinical picture is sum-
> marized with respect to physical anomalies, life age, mental
> age, speech, personality and general behavior patterns. The
> case history of a 12-year-old Mongol Negro boy is presented.
> Though the positive findings are mentioned as worthy of comment:

a possible venereal disease in the father, admixture of blood
of three races, tuberculosis on one side of the family, and
miscarriage on the other. It is concluded that analysis of
overt physical signs in hereditary background has shed little
light on the cause of this type of defect and the search for
the factor or factors that are responsible.

246. Whitten, C. F. Growth status of children with sickle cell
anemia. American Journal of the Diseases of Children, 1961, 102,
355-364.

The growth status of 48 children with sickle cell anemia from
2-13 years of age has been compared with their normal siblings
(79) and with standards for normal white children. On these
bases, children with sickle cell anemia, as a group, weigh
less, are shorter, and are of thinner body build. Their spans
are normal. Their upper-to-lower segment ratios are similar
to the normal siblings, but, consistently, they are smaller
than the ratios of normal white children. Skeletal maturation
does not appear to be affected, with the exception of the possibility of a delay occurring in early adolescence. We were
unable to uncover a factor in the clinical course of these
patients which would differentiate those children with sickle
cell anemia who are underweight and those who are of normal
weight. Peripheral arterial oxygen saturations were below
normal in 18 of 27 patients, but no correlation was found
between the weight status and degree of peripheral arterial
oxygen unsaturation. Two children had their hemoglobin concentrations maintained at normal levels for three months, with
the result that one showed a marked increase in weight and
the other's weight remained stationary.

247. Williams, J. R. and Scott, R. B. Growth and development of
Negro infants: IV. Motor development and its relationship to child
rearing practices in two groups of Negro infants. Child Development,
1953, 24 (2), 103-121.

Gross motor acceleration in Negro children, a "stereotype often
applied", is shown to be a function of socioeconomic level
rather than a "rational" characteristic. Children from a
lower socioeconomic level showed "significant gross motor
acceleration" compared to those from a higher group.

248. Wingerd, J., Solomon, I. L., and Schoen, E. J. Parent-specific
height standards for preadolescent children of three racial groups,
with method for rapid determination. Pediatrics, 1973, 52 (4),
555-560.

Parent-specific height standards for preadolescent children of
three racial groups were determined, and a method for rapid
determination is presented. Since parent-specific height
standards are important in evaluating abnormalities of childhood growth, such standards have been determined from 59,000
height measurements of 11,233 California children, aged 1 to
9 years, of white, black and other racial groups. Mean heights

or the three groups diverged increasingly with age after one
year: blacks were the tallest, the mixed group the shortest.
Positive correlation between midparent height and child height
increased with age. Non-white children, especially blacks,
were taller for parental height than were whites. The discrepancy may reflect differing growth patterns; or the non-white
children may become taller than their parents. A convenient
"slide rule" is presented, which makes the determination of
the parent-specific height centile for any kind of either sex
in each racial group clinically feasible.

249. Yarrow, L. J., Rubenstein, J. L., Pedersen, F. A., and Jankowki,
J. J. Dimensions of early stimulation and their differential effects
on infant development. Merrill-Palmer Quarterly, 1972, 18 (3),
205-218.

Analyzed time sampling observations of 21 male and 20 female
5-month-old black infants under the care of a stable "primary
caretaker", in terms of environmental and infant variables.
Among the social variables, level, variety, and positive affect
were interrelated; there was a relatively low relationship
between the frequency measure, contingent response to positive
vocalization, and the latency measure, with contingent response
to distress suggesting that maternal responsiveness is not a
highly general trait. A cluster-social responsiveness, including vocalizing to sound stimulus, anticipatory adjustment
to lifting, enjoying frolic play, and smiling to a mirror
image, was significantly correlated to instigating stimuli
(level, variety and expression of positive affect), but unrelated to soothing stimuli, contingent response to distress.
The strongest grouping of significant relationships was the
cognitive-motivational set called "goal directed behaviors".
Variety, responsiveness, and complexity showed no significant
relationships with the cognitive-motivational and fine motor
variables, all measures which involve responses to inanimate
objects. It is suggested that the infant's orientation to
objects and to people very early becomes part of a feedback
system with the environment. His smiling, vocalizing, and
reaching out to people; his visually attending to and manipulating objects, tend to be self-reinforcing and, to some
extent, self-perpetuating.

3

COGNITIVE DEVELOPMENT

250. Abramson, T. The influence of examiner race on first grade and kindergarten subjects' Peabody Picture Vocabulary Test scores. Journal of Educational Measurement, 1969, 6 (4), 241-245.

The tests administered by two white and two Negro examiners to 88 and 113 white and Negro first graders and Kindergartners, respectively, in an integrated urban school, found a small but statistically significant interaction of examiner's race and subject's race on test performance for the first grade but not for the kindergarten. These findings are limited to young children who were in an urban school setting for at least five months and who were given an encoding-type task by an adult whom they had usually seen at least once a day in their school environment.

251. Adams, J. and Lieb, J. J. Canter-BIP and Draw-A-Person Test performance of Negro and Caucasian Head Start children. Psychology in the Schools, 1973, 10 (3), 299-304.

The Canter Background Interference Procedure (BIP) and the Draw-A-Person (DAP) performance of Negro and Caucasian Head Start children were studied. Results reveal a lack of ethnic group differences. The notion that increased structure in a drawing task enhances the likelihood of bias against subcultural groups is partially supported. The capacity to perform a graphomotor task in the context of irrelevant stimuli does not differ as a function of ethnic group. The data offers further evidence that the Canter BIP represents an instrument free of sex, intelligence level, emotional status, maturational, and ethnic group effects that add to error variance in the application of the Bender-Gestalt Test.

252. Adams, J., McIntosh, E. I., and Weade, B. L. Ethnic background, measured intelligence and adaptive behavior scores in mentally retarded children. American Journal of Mental Deficiency, 1973, 78 (1), 1-6.

The degree to which classification of levels of mental retardation based upon a measure of adaptive behavior (the Vineland

Social Maturity Scale) differed from the classification based
upon I.Q., for Negro and Caucasian children, was assessed.
The Negro group scored lower on IQ, but the groups did not
differ on deviation social quotient (DSQ). The distribution
of levels of impairment differed as a function of race for classification based upon IQ but not for that based upon DSQ. On
the basis of IQ, more Negro than Caucasian children were classified as "borderline" or above. This effect was not found for
DSQ. The relative utility of the two types of classification,
which may well vary as a function of ethnic background and the
purpose of the classification, awaits further research.

253. Adler, M. Intelligence testing of the culturally disadvantaged:
Some pitfalls. Journal of Negro Education, 1968, 37 (4), 364-369.

A review of the literature of research on gifted children
shows that some ethnic groups are mentioned more frequently
than one would expect, given their proportional number in
the total population. With other groups, the reverse is true.
The Negro is most consistently mentioned in the latter group.
The majority of these studies have relied upon intelligence
tests as the method of selection. Research on intelligence
tests have shown them to be influenced by such factors as
speed, schooling, environment-language facility, motor coordination, physical factors such as hearing and sight, socioeconomic class, sampling, and race of examiner. The method of identification will structure the resultant group of gifted children. A selection method relying solely on intelligence
tests as a criterion will work against the selection of
children coming from the group that is now known as the culturally disadvantaged. Since Negro children make up such
a large percentage of this group, extreme caution must be
exercised in the use of intelligence tests as the sole criterion
of giftedness, or mental retardation for that matter.

254. Albott, W. L. and Gunn, H. E. Bender-Gestalt performance by
culturally disadvantaged first graders. Perceptual and Motor Skills,
1971, 33 (1), 247-250.

Obtained Bender-Gestalt Test error profiles from 35 black,
culturally deprived, first graders. The profiles, scored by
E. Koppitz' method (see PA, Vol. 39, 1970), were compared with
the Koppitz norms and with data published by N. Henderson,
B. Butler, and G. Goffeney (see PA, Vol. 44, 4246). Results
indicate that the current sample was significantly different
in mean performance when compared with the norms (p<.001) but
not when compared with the Henderson, et. al., data. Additional analyses showed a Sex x Error type interaction, with
males making more errors on four of the six possible error
types. Subjects were also found to have the most difficulty
with Designs 4, 7 and 8. Error type and difficulty with particular designs are discussed and related. Areas of confound-
ing are noted.

255. Ali, F. Dimensions of competence in young children. Genetic
Psychology Monographs, 1973, 88 (2), 305-328.

    Defined competence in terms of individual-environmental inter-
    action, with an emphasis on exploration and manipulation as
    the two major components. To study this concept, 50 disadvan-
    taged Negro 4- to 5-year-olds were tested individually in pre-
    determined, semi-controlled situations on exploratory and
    manipulatory tasks. The examiner and one observer made rat-
    ings and observations simultaneously, obtained moderate to
    high reliabilities. Factor analysis revealed three factors:
    General Competence, Emotional Freedom, and Intellectual Com-
    petence, each of which accounted, respectively, for 47.68,
    12.81, and 6.92 of the total variance. Only Factors I and III
    were significantly correlated (r=.65). Results are discussed
    in terms of theoretical notions of R. W. White and others
    concerning competence.

256. Allen, M. E. A comparative study of Negro and white children
in melodic and harmonic sensitivity. Journal of Negro Education,
1942, 11, 158-164.

    The findings of 16 earlier tests of Negroes and whites for
    musical talent are summarized. Kwalavosser tests were used
    in Allen's own study of 1,000 Negro children and 1,000 white
    children between the ages of 12 and 18 years. On the whole,
    scores earned by the whites show them to be superior to the
    Negroes in both melodic and harmonic sensitivity, but the
    size of the difference in means does not always support an
    unqualified statement of superiority.

257. Allen, S. S., Dubanoski, R. A., and Stevenson, H. W. Children's
performance as a function of race of E, race of S, and type of verbal
reinforcement. Journal of Experimental Child Psychology, 1966, 4,
248-256.

    White boys (N=108) and Negro boys (N=108) from grades 1-2 and
    4-6, were tested by white or Negro women in a simple perfor-
    mance task under one of three conditions: praise, control, or
    criticism. Differences in base-rate of response were asso-
    ciated with Race of S, Race of E, and the interaction between
    Race of E and Race of S and between Race of E and Age of S.
    In the analysis of change in rate of response after the intro-
    duction of the experimental condition, a same-race effect was
    found, with Es of the same race as S producing the greater
    increments in response. In general, Negro Es were more effec-
    tive as reinforcing agents than were white Es. Separate ana-
    lysis of performance in each of the experimental conditions
    are presented. Reprinted by permission.

258. Ames, L. B. and August, J. Comparison of mosaic response of
Negro and white primary-school children. Journal of Genetic Psychology,
1966, 109, 123-129.

    Comparison of Mosaic response of 217 Negro elementary-school
    children with products of several groups of same-age white

children reveals that the product of the 5- and 6-year-old
Negro is considerably less mature than that of the same-age
white child. However, the discrepancy in performance decreases
at later ages. This is in contrast to the Rorschach response
that in the Negro at all ages from 5 to 10 is less adequate
than that of the white child but most closely resembles it
at 5 years of age, becoming increasingly less adequate in the
years that follow. The conspicuous difference in response to
these two tests -- the Mosaic response improving markedly with
age, the Rorschach failing to do so -- suggests the importance
of testing the Negro child on a wide variety of tests.

259. Ames, L. B. and Ilg, F. L. Search for children showing academic
promise in a predominantly Negro school. Journal of Genetic Psychology, 1967, 110 (2), 217-231.

Responses of 388 Negro elementary school children compared
with those of white children of similar age and socioeconomic
status on the Gesell School Readiness Tests, plus the Rorschach and the Lowenfeld Mosaic, show that for most tests
Negro children develop in the same way but at a slower rate
than do white children. Except for Rorschach Test responses,
the course and stages of development were similar for the
two groups. About one-third of the Negro children showed
"academic promise". Responses of Negro children fall on a
rectilinear rather than a normal curve.

260. Anastasiow, N. J. and Hanes, M. L. Cognitive development and
the acquisition of language in three subcultural groups. Developmental
Psychology, 1974, 10 (5), 703-709.

Investigated the relationship between cognitive development
and language acquisition by administering a sentence repetition
task and a discrimination, seriation and numeration Piagetian
task to a total of 67 black inner, white middle class, and white
rural children. Within each subcultural group, samples were
drawn from each of three grade levels: kindergarten, first
grade, and second grade. Results indicate that when valid
reconstructions from standard English to Negro nonstandard
English forms were considered correct, the performances of
black inner city and white middle class children were non-
significantly different. However, significant differences
between the three groups were found on function-word omission
scores and Piagetian task scores. Analyses of covariance were
performed using Piagetian task scores. Analyses of covariance
and function support D. I. Slobin's (1973) proposition that
the acquisition of semantic notions in language is predictable
for cognitive development.

261. Anttonen, R. G. and Fleming, E. S. Standardized test information: Does it make a difference in black student performance? Journal of Educational Research, 1976, 70 (1), 26-31.

Assessed the effect upon pupil performance of providing elementary level teachers various types of standardized test

information. Results of an analysis of covariance model revealed no significant differences in standardized achievement
or intelligence between 106 second-sixth grade low socioeconomic
level children whose teacher had one of four types of test information (randomly assigned) for each child in her class.
The four test information groups were: (a) Stanford Achievement Test scores; (b) Kuhlman-Anderson Intelligence Test scores;
(c) a combination of Stanford Achievement and Kuhlman-Anderson
IQ; and (d) nonstandardized test information. The usefulness
of providing standardized test scores to teachers is questioned,
and the importance of examining and assessing alternative evaluation models is stressed.

262. Asbury, C. A. Cognitive correlates of discrepant achievement
in reading. Journal of Negro Education, 1973, 42 (2), 123-133.

98 black and 127 white first grade students in rural North
Carolina were administered the Peabody Picture Vocabulary Test
(PPVT), the Primary Mental Abilities Test (PMA), the Preschool
Inventory and the Metropolitan Readiness Test (MRT) at the beginning of the school year. The Metropolitan Achievement Test
was administered at the end of the school year. Analyses of
variance show that: (a) in reading achievement, there were
no specific cognitive differences between under- or overachievers or between boys and girls; (b) whites were significantly superior to blacks on all cognitive variables except
PMA perceptual ability; and (c) black males were superior to
black females on the PPVT and readiness (MRT), while white
females were superior to white males on the same variables.

263. Asbury, C. A. Maturity factors related to discrepant achievement of white and black first graders. Journal of Negro Education,
1975, 44 (4), 493-501.

Tested seven hypotheses on relationships between deviation from
expected school achievement and social, emotional, and physical maturity factors. Subjects (Ss) were 98 black and 127
white first graders in eight randomly chosen classes of a rural
North Carolina public school system. Regression equations with
Primary Mental Ability Test total as predictor and scores
from four subtests of the Metropolitan Achievement Test (primary Battery) as criteria were based on a random subsample of
50. For each subtest, 3-way analyses of variance were made of
Preschool Attainment Record maturity quotients for any of the
remaining 175 Ss classified as under- or overachievers. Significant maturity differences occured: (a) between races for
arithmetic, reading and word knowledge; (b) between sexes for
word discrimination; and (c) between achievement levels for
reading achievement. It is concluded that maturity differences
appear inconsequential for certain kinds of achievement at a
given developmental point.

264. Asbury, C. A. Some selected problems involved in assessing the
intelligence and achievement of disadvantaged groups: With emphasis
on the Negro. Quarterly Review of Higher Education Among Negroes,
1968, 36, 133-144.

265. Atchison, C. O. Use of the Wechsler Intelligence Scale for
Children with eighty mentally defective Negro children. American
Journal of Mental Deficiency, 1955, 60, 378-379.

> IQ test records of 80 mentally defective Negro children aged
> 6-8 to 13 years, mean 9-6, were analyzed to determine whether
> a significant discrepancy occurred between verbal and perfor-
> mance scores. Subjects scoring low on verbal tended to score
> low on performance but high verbal scorers did not tend to
> score high on performance. Mean verbal score for the group
> was significantly higher than the mean performance score.
> Author suggests that the V-P relationship may be different
> for defective Negro children than for defective whites as
> reported in the literature.

266. Bean, K. L. Negro responses to verbal and nonverbal test
materials. Journal of Psychology, 1942, 13, 343-353.

> 49 eighth grade pupils of both sexes from a Baton Rouge, Loui-
> siana high school were given the Otis Self Administration
> Intermediate Examination, Form A, and the revised Minnesota
> Paper Form Board, Series BB. A small reliable difference
> in favor of the non-language material was found. The author
> concludes that "these Negroes do not fail on intelligence
> test items merely because of lack of vocabulary or compre-
> hension of complex sentence structure. Fundamental capacity
> to reason is probably low in most of the members of this
> group." Other factors, such as efficiency of visual imagery
> and reading ability, may leave affected the scores on the
> Otis Test. The author warns against generalizing at present
> about the type of intelligence test most fair to Negroes in
> this section of the South.

267. Beard, J. G., et. al. Relative achievement levels of white
and black children before and after desegregation. Paper presented
at the Annual Meeting of the American Educational Research Association Annual Meeting, Washington, D. C., April 1975. Also, see ERIC
Abstracts, No. 113-414, 1975.

> Changes in the relative academic achievement of Florida's
> black and white children over the last 13 years during which
> desegregation was taking place are investigated. The avail-
> ability of achievement data for the entire black and white
> population, along with the 13-year time span between observa-
> tions, are seen as principal advantages. Data show that the
> academic achievement gap between white and black children
> was smaller in 1974 than in 1961. The amount of decrease in
> the gap is stated to be small, yet of practical significance
> for the four subject areas examined: reading, vocabulary,
> math computation, and math problem solving. Of these areas,

convergence in the black and white distribution was greater
for math computation than for the other subtest areas examined.
The use of different tests in 1961 and 1974 is held to make
assessment of changes in the absolute performance level of
black or white children difficult. It is suggested that the
study be viewed as an evaluation of a social action program
rather than a scientific experiment.

268. Beckham, A. S. The intelligence of a Negro high school population in a northern city. Journal of Genetic Psychology, 1939, 54,
326-327.

The Herman-Nelson tests of mental ability were given to 284
freshmen, 264 sophomores, 187 juniors, and 177 seniors in a
Chicago Negro high school, selected by taking every 10th
name (every 5th name for seniors) from an alphabetical list.
Each group included a CA range of 7 or 8 years, and each was
average in intelligence, including scholastically retarded,
normally placed and advanced students. Tables showing IQ
range and mean IQ for each age level, as well as age distribution with each group, are included.

269. Beckham, A. S. Race and intelligence. Opportunity, August 1932,
10 (8), 240-242.

It is almost impossible for a white psychologist to get the
true IQ of a Negro child in the South, where racial barriers
and differences are ubiquitous. Among such handicaps to the
white tester are timidity or fear in the child, unfamiliar
pronunciation or enunciation of the examiner, use of a
vocabulary with which the rural Negro child has had too little
experience, inability to rouse the child's enthusiasm.

270. Beckham, A. S. Social background and art aptitude of superior
Negro children. Psychological Bulletin, 1941, 38, 565.

271. Beckham, A. S. A study of the intelligence of colored adolescents of different social-economic status in typical metropolitan
areas. Journal of Social Psychology, 1933, 4, 70-91.

The results of Stanford-Binet Tests on 1,100 Negro children 12
to 17 years of age are given. The majority of the group were
from Washington; smaller portions were from Baltimore and New
York. The distribution and IQ ratings according to school,
grade, age, occupation of parents, and family size, are reported. The mean IQ increases steadily with school grade,
and with occupational class, with the exception of the highest,
i.e., the professional class. It appears to decrease slightly
with increasing size of family. Comparative results from 100
delinquents are included. An extreme lack of correspondence
between vocational aspirations and ability indicates the need
for vocational guidance.

272. Beckham, A. S. A study of social background and art aptitude of superior Negro children. <u>Journal of Applied Psychology</u>, 1942, <u>26</u>, 777-784.

The Lewerenz Test in Fundamental Abilities of Visual Art was given to 100 intellectual superior school children, 100 art pupils, and 100 randomly selected pupils. The results indicate that intelligence is an important factor in many of the art test items. A few of the items showed significant age differences. "The girls were superior in two important test items, while the boys showed a superiority in four." Boys surpassed girls in line drawings; the superior girls excelled in recognition and placing of colors. Children of laborers achieved high scores about as often as did children of semi-professional or professional parents.

273. Beckham, A. S. A study of social background and music ability of superior Negro children. <u>Journal of Applied Psychology</u>, 1942, <u>26</u>, 210-217.

This study is concerned with interracial differences. 100 intellectually superior, 100 unselected, and 30 musically superior Negro children were given the Kwalwasser-Dyekema Music Tests. The data were analyzed in terms of the IQ differences between groups, music ability and age, and music instructions vs. no instructions. The author summarized: "The teachers' opinions of musically superior children corroborate test results. The musically superior picked by teachers outrank the intellectually superior. Intelligence was not an important factor in making high musical aptitude scores. Age as a factor was only slight."

274. Bennett, J. E. The effects of integration on achievement in a large elementary school. <u>Florida Journal of Educational Research</u>, 1974, <u>16</u>, 12-15.

Reports on the effects of integration in two large elementary schools, based on analysis of students' Stanford Achievement Test scores. In the first year, blacks showed severe drops in reading and in mathematics; whites showed less overall decline. The subsequent year scores for both black and white pupils showed a rebound. Integration appeared to be more disruptive to blacks than to whites.

275. Berry, F. M. and Jones, Q. R. Stimulus encoding in paired associate learning by illiterate children: A methodological demonstration of a picture-redundancy paradigm. <u>Journal of General Psychology</u>, 1973, <u>88</u> (1), 55-63.

Describes and tests a picture-redundancy paried-associate (PA) paradigm for use in studies of stimulus selection among illiterate populations. The picture-redundancy task was given to 21 illiterate, preschool black children (mean age = 4 years) attending Project Head Start. During PA learning, subjects were observed to employ both multiple- and single-cue stimulus

encoding strategies. It is concluded that the picture-
redundancy analogue to the traditional redundant-stimulus PA
task should prove useful in other investigations of stimulus
encoding strategies which are based on illiterate subjects.

276. Bianchini, J. C. and Vale, C. A. Investigation of the appropriateness of the Anchor Test Study equating results for selected
subgroups. Final report. Washington, D. C.: U. S. Office of Education (DHEW), March 1975. Also, see ERIC Abstracts, No. ED-121-814.

The Anchor Test Study (ATS) yielded equating tables for vocabulary, reading comprehension, and total reading scores for
eight commonly used reading tests at the 4th, 5th and 6th
grade levels. Because of the original ATS sampling design
which resulted in a nationally representative sample of school
children at those grades, the equating tables might not be
considered equally applicable for selected subgroups of the
population -- specifically, for black and Spanish-surnamed
subgroups. The present study was done to determine whether
use of the ATS equating tables for these two ethnic subgroups
is warranted. Essentially, the analysis focused upon detecting interaction between test interrelationships and ethnic
affiliation in a way most relevant to the expected uses of
the ATS equating tables -- average differences between equivalent and obtained scores for each ethnic group, in various
parts of the score range, were tested for significance. The
detailed procedures for accomplishing the implied statistical
tests are described. The analyses appear in Appendices A, B
and C (for grades 4, 5 and 6, respectively) organized by vocabulary, reading comprehension, and total reading scores within
grade level. The results did not indicate any systematic
ethnic bias. The few isolated instances which did exist might
be attributed largely to the sampling procedure used in the
ATS: i.e., maximizing representation of the total population,
rather than that of any specific subgroup.

277. Biller, H. B. Parental and sex role factors in cognitive and
academic functioning. Nebraska Symposium on Motivation, 1973, 83-123.

The relationship between qualitative and quantitative variations
in paternal behavior and the child's cognitive functioning and
classroom adjustment are discussed. Data are reviewed which
suggest that achievement, quality of child's paternal relationship and absence or presence of fathers are functionally related.
Underachieving boys seem to have inadequate relationships with
their fathers, with underachievement often related to fathers
who are insecure in their masculinity. High achieving boys
perceive themselves as closer to and more similar to their
fathers. The absence of a father is more of a handicap in
lower class than in middle class children. Different children
suffer differentially from father absence, with girls less
affected than boys and black children most severely affected.

278. Birns, B. and Golden, M. Prediction of intellectual performance
at 3 years from infant tests and personality measures. Merrill-Palmer
Quarterly, 1972, 18 (1), 53-58.

> Reports a cross-sectional study of social class and cognitive
> development in infancy, and a longitudinal follow-up study of
> 89 to 126 of the same black children at 3 years of age. The
> testing of the 18- and 24-month-old infants included the Cattell
> Infant Intelligence Scale, the Piaget Object Scale, and seven
> Personality Rating scales; while at 3 years old, subjects were
> given only the Stanford-Binet. The most significant finding
> was that the amount of pleasure manifested by infants on the
> Cattell and Piaget Scales was predictive of their later intel-
> lectual performance on the Stanford-Binet. The 18-month Cattell
> and Piaget Scale scores did not correlate with the 36-month
> Binet scores, whereas Pleasure in Task was significantly cor-
> related with performance on both the Cattell at 18 months and
> the Binet at 3 years old. Results support the hypothesis that
> while there may be discontinuity between perceptual-motor
> development and later problem solving ability on the verbal
> level, there may be continuity in terms of certain personality
> traits as related to both pre-verbal and verbal intelligence.

279. Blackstock, E. C. and King, W. L. Recognition and reconstruction
memory for seriation in 4- and 5-year-olds. Developmental Psychology,
1973, 9 (2), 255-259.

> Determined whether preoperational children can recognize a
> regularly seriated configuration of rods before they are able
> to reconstruct one from the disarranged elements. Thirty-two
> 4-year-old, and thirty-two 5-year-old black Head Start children
> were given six recognition and six reconstruction tasks. Re-
> sults show that the ability to recognize a seriated configura-
> tion clearly precedes in development the ability to reconstruct
> one. Regular variations in the perceptual qualities of the
> nonseriated configurations which facilitated recognition per-
> formance made reconstruction more difficult, and vice versa.

280. Blank, M. and Frank, S. M. Story recall in kindergarten children: Effect of method of presentation on psycholinguistic performance. Child Development, 1971, 42 (1), 299-312.

> Devised a story-retelling task as a means of testing syntactic
> and semantic aspects of language performance in 34 kindergart-
> ners. Two groups of subjects were matched for age, IQ, and
> ethnic background (Negro, Puerto Rican, and white subjects in
> each group). Syntactic recall was reduced in amount and varied
> in pattern from the commonly used single sentence imitation
> task. Several factors appeared to be responsible, including
> such variables as semantic content and "stress" (the need to
> retain large amounts of information). Linguistic performance,
> including both semantic and syntactic recall, was enhanced by
> varying the method of presentation so that subjects were re-
> quired to play a more active role in the situation. In addi-

tion to the method of presentation, intelligence was found to
influence performance in that subjects with higher MAs showed
significantly better recall.

281. Blank, M. and Solomon, F. A tutorial language program to
develop abstract thinking in socially disadvantaged preschool children. Child Development, 1968, 39, 378-389.

A specialized language program was developed to facilitate
abstract thinking in young deprived children through short,
individual tutoring sessions on a daily basis. The role of
individual attention in the experiment was controlled through
the use of a comparison group which had daily individual sessions without the specialized tutoring. A second comparison
group was included which consisted of children who received
their usual training in the regular nursery school program.
The results show a marked gain in IQ for the group who received
the specialized tutoring and no significant gains for the control groups.

282. Blatt, B. and Garfunkel, F. Educating intelligence: Determinants of school behavior of disadvantaged children. Exceptional
Children, 1967, 33, 601-608.

The study was concerned with the effect of educational intervention activites upon the intellectual performance of lower
class deprived preschool children. A total of 69 subjects
met the criteria established and by stratified random assignment were placed into two experimental groups and one nonexperi-
mental group. The study began in 1962 and the intervention
phase lasted two years; follow-up evaluations were completed
during one additional year. A number of cognitive (e.g.,
Binet, ITPA), noncognitive (e.g., Rorschach, Vineland), and
environmental (e.g., Warner Index of Status Characteristics)
measures were used. In the end, "Analyses of the data led to
the inequivocal inference that there was no more difference
between the groups at the conclusion of the study than there
had been at the beginning."

283. Bloom, R. Effects of racial and expressive cues in probability
learning in children. Psychological Reports, 1969, 24 (3), 791-794.

Exposed 120 white 11- to 12-year-old children, divided into
four groups, to a probability-learning task in which they
were to guess which of two stimuli would appear. The stimuli
were either pictures of angry or smiling faces which were
either white or Negro in appearance. When the input ratio
was 70% angry to 30% smiling faces, subjects underestimated
the dominant input. When the input was reversed, expectancies
for dominant stimulus more closely approximated the input
ratio. Racial cues were not a determinant for choice responses
even though such cues were apparently highly visible for most
subjects.

284. Bogart, C. and Houk, A. S. What is the next step? Journal of
Reading, 1971, 14 (8), 531-536 & 582.

> A first person account of problems and attempted solutions in
> teaching reading to black ghetto junior high students. Over
> half the students had below average intelligence, and discipline
> was nearly nonexistent. The teacher had to diagnose reading
> problems long hidden behind misbehavior. As these students
> were identified and encouraged, others with less severe prob-
> lems came forward for help. Whenever possible, special mate-
> rials were obtained. In spite of hopeful signs from the students,
> this individualized program was severely limited by a lack of
> funds and man hours. It is concluded that, given small classes
> and proper materials and more time for teachers, such children
> all can learn to read. However, only a national funding commit-
> ment to reading and a curriculum reform can achieve that goal.
> Reprinted by permission.

285. Bogatz, G. A. and Ball, S. A summary of the major findings in
"The second year of Sesame Street: A continuing evaluation." New York:
Children's Television workshop. Princeton, N. J.: Educational Test-
ing Service. For related documents see IR 003 418-419.   See ERIC
Abstracts, No. ED-122-802, November 1971.

> To determine the effectiveness of Sesame Street in imparting
> basic facts and skills to children aged 3 to 5, data from the
> first year study was reanalyzed, and a second-year research
> study was undertaken. The second-year study included a new
> study of 283 disadvantaged children and a follow-up study of
> 283 disadvantaged children from the first-year study. Results
> showed significant gains in many basic skills, such as naming
> letters, matching by form, sight reading, recognizing numbers,
> naming numbers, and counting. The follow-up study findings
> showed that Sesame Street "graduates" who were frequent viewers
> and who entered school during the show's second year were,
> according to teacher rankings, better prepared than their non-
> or low-viewing classmates and adapted well to school. Regard-
> less of racial, ethnic, or socioeconomic background, the chil-
> dren who viewed Sesame Street learned the most.

286. Boney, J. D. Predicting the academic achievement of secondary
school Negro students. The Personnel and Guidance Journal, 1966, 44,
700-703.

> The efficiency of aptitude and mental ability measures to pre-
> dict high school grade-point average for Negro students in
> secondary school was studied. The total sample of 222 stu-
> dents was randomly divided into two samples in order to deter-
> mine the consistency with which the variables predicted the
> criteria. The predictor variables were: The Differential Apti-
> tude Tests, the California Test of Mental Maturity, the Coopera-
> tive Ability Tests, the Sequential Tests of Educational Pro-
> gress, Junior High School Grade-Point Average, and Social Status
> Ratings. The data were analyzed by multiple linear regression.
> The instruments consistently yielded substantial correlations

with High School Grade-Point Average. Negro students appeared
to be as predictable as other groups.

287. Bonner, M. W. and Belden, B. R. A comparative study of the
performance of Negro seniors of Oklahoma City high schools on the
Wechsler Adult Intelligence Scale and the Peabody Picture Vocabulary
Test. Journal of Negro Education, 1970, 39 (4), 354-358.

A presentation of the comparative results of performance of
60 Negro high school seniors on the Wechsler Adult Intelligence
Scale (WAIS) and the Peabody Picture Vocabulary Test (PPVT).
Subjects were tested individually on the WAIS followed immediately by the PPVT. Briefly, the main findings of the study
are: (a) There is a positive significant correlation between
the WAIS and the PPVT. Each coefficient of correlation was
significant at the .05 level except those which were calculated between the WAIS Digit Span, Picture Arrangement, and
Object Assembly, and the PPVT. (b) The IQ estimated by use
of the PPVT is somewhat lower than that estimated by the WAIS.
(c) A possibility of using PPVT to predict or to estimate
WAIS scores for this population of Negro seniors does exist.
The standard error of estimate is so large, however, that
such use must ultimately depend upon how the knowledge of the
predicted score is to be used. Reprinted by permission.

288. Bordeaux, E. A. and Shope, N. H. An evaluation of three
approaches to teaching reading in first grade. Reading Teacher,
1966, 20 (1), 6-11.

Three approaches to teaching first-grade reading were compared:
(a) a basal reader approach (BR) (the control group); (b) a
basal reader plus intensive phonics (P); and (c) a basal reader
plus intensive phonics and sensory experience (SE). Subjects
were 751 children, 385 white and 366 Negro, in 28 classrooms
of about 30 each. The test period ran for 140 school days.
Results indicated that if only the BR and P methods were considered, it would make no difference which one was used with
whites, but it would benefit Negroes more to use the P method.
However, SE appears most beneficial overall, for whites and
Negroes. Reprinted by permission.

289. Bornstein, H. and Chamberlain, K. An investigation of the
effects of "verbal load" in achievement tests. American Educational
Research Journal, 1970, 7 (4), 597-604.

It was argued that the language used in multiple choice achievement test items should be no more complex than is necessary to
test the examinee's knowledge of the subject matter. Excessive
complexity might constitute a source of bias against people
with limited verbal skills. A test of this hypothesis was
made by comparing a simplified language version of STEP social
studies test items against an "original language form" with
junior and senior high school students in Oakland, California.
About two-thirds of the students were Negro. Mean reading
comprehension scores fell at about the 30th percentile on

national norms. Test results on both forms appeared to be
internally consistent and in accord with general expectations
for this student sample. There was, however, no support for
the notion that the simplified language test version would yield
different results. Test difficulty and relationships with reading comprehension scores and social studies grades were essentially the same for both forms. Reprinted by permission.

290. Bousfield, M. B. The intelligence and school achievement of
Negro children. Journal of Negro Education, 1932, 1, 388-395.

Colored children who had resided at least three years in Chicago
were used in this research. The questionnaire evaluating economic and environmental conditions revealed them to be an underprivileged group. The Otis Self-Administering Test of Mental
Ability, the Pintner Non-Language, and the McCall Multi-Mental
Scale were given them. In addition, the New Stanford Reading
and Arithmetic Achievement Tests were administered. On the
non-language tests the group tested normal. On the McCall,
which required vocabulary knowledge, but did not require
reading knowledge to the extent of the Otis, 68% of the cases
fell between 36.8 and 53.5, i.e., from nearly 14 points below
to 3.3 above the norm. On the Otis test, the group median
was 87.15, with a standard deviation of 12.82. The correlations between Otis and arithmetic and Pintner and arithmetic
were low. Correlations of Otis and Pintner with age were
negative. Reading and arithmetic correlations with age were
low. When age was partialled out of correlations between
Otis and reading, Otis and arithmetic, Pintner and reading,
and Pintner and arithmetic, the partial correlations were
higher than the total ones. Age was a definite but not a
powerful factor.

291. Bradbury, P. J., Wright, S. D., Walker, C. E., and Ross, J. M.
Performance on the WISC as a function of sex of examiner, sex of
subject, and age of subject. Journal of Psychology, 1975, 90 (First
Half), 51-55.

A completely randomized factorial analysis was used in assessing the effect of sex of the experimenter, sex of subject, and
age of subject on Wechsler Intelligence Scale for Children
(WISC) performance. The subjects were 511 male and female,
black and white public school children who were referred for
possible mental retardation or learning disability. Results
indicate that for white subjects, female experimenters obtained
significantly higher scores for the youngest (6 years old to
9 years old) age group, while male experimenters obtained
higher scores for the intermediate (9 years old to 12 years
old) age group. Children 12 years old to 15 years old seem
to perform equally well with either male or female experimenters.
Performance decreased with age, and males generally performed
better than females. Implications of the study include increasing sophistication in interpreting test results and avoid-
ing experimenter-subject combinations that increase the chance
of poor results.

292. Brazziel, W. F. Quality school programs. In Quality Education for All Americans. Washington, D. C.: Howard University Press, 1974, pp. 21-72.

Diverse programming is as necessary for the many types of black children as it is for the many types of white children. Middle class black children must have mental rigor at every point in the school program, and teachers must demand much from these children and confer with their parents if they fail to progress. Quality education for poor children will often simply be unavailable because of unfortunate school practices. Readiness tests must be substituted for IQ and criterion-referenced tests for achievement tests, and a high-impact program must be applied to move the children along. Perhaps the most powerful teaching system for black children mangled by poverty is the DISTAR program of Science Research Associates. This program has been refined over the past 15 years to help overcome several hazards poor black children encounter in their schools. A home-start program to assist parents in the home and family curriculum is desirable for poor black children; the program may be either teacher-based or parent-based. Some of the more effective programs to spur achievement in depressed areas have involved strong leadership by black superintendents who rallied parental energies. Reading summers, district competition, parents as homework supervisors, and a vast array of other projects are possible under hard-driving black administrators. To increase high school graduation rates, a wide variety of work-study opportunities for students might be introduced; cooperative education presents an alternative to traditional forms of education that are turning kids off. A final area is special education which must be reserved for truly retarded children; children improperly tested and misplaced must be returned to the regular classroom.

293. Bresnahan, J. L. and Shapiro, M. M. Learning strategies in children from different socioeconomic levels. In H. W. Reese (Ed.), Advances in Child Development and Behavior: VII. New York: Academic Press, 1972, XIV. 221 pp.

Conducted eight experiments in concept acquisition with 4- to 9-year-old black and white preschool children and first and third graders chosen from lower class groups (e.g., Head Start participants), middle, and higher classes. Results show that lower class subjects did not adopt the win-stay-lose-shift strategy used by higher class subjects but perseverated on an incorrect hypothesis and chose consistency more often.

294. Bridgeman, B. and Burbach, H. J. Effects of black vs. white peer models on academic expectations and actual performance of fifth grade students. Journal of Experimental Education, 1976, 45 (1), 9-12.

274 black and white fifth graders of both sexes were shown one of two videotapes of 12 other students working on an academic

task (reading a paragraph and answering questions about it).
On one tape, two black students were congratulated by the
teacher for having gotten the best scores, while on the other
tape two white sutdents were congratulated. Comparisons indicated that black males who viewed the videotape of blacks
succeeding expected to, and actually did, score higher than
black males who observed white students succeeding. All other
comparisons were not significant.

295. Bridgeman, B. and Buttram, J. Race differences on nonverbal
analogy test performance as a function of verbal strategy training.
Journal of Educational Psychology, 1975, 67 (4), 586-590.

Hypothesized that the relatively poor performance of black
students on nominally nonverbal reasoning tests (A. R. Jensen's
Level II) may be due to their failure to use verbal problem-
solving strategies efficiently and spontaneously. 200 fourth
and fifth graders, both black and white, showed no race differences on Level I ability (digit span memory). Half of the
subjects of each race were then trained to use a verbal strategy on nonverbal analogies. For subjects who received no
special training there were significant race differences on
the analogies test (p<.001), but for those who received the
training, there were not (p<.05). Results suggest that a
significant proportion of observed race differences on Level II
tasks may be attributable to a failure of many blacks to use
spontaneously an efficient verbal strategy rather than a
genetic reasoning deficit.

296. Brown, F. An experimental and critical study of the intelligence of Negro and white kindergarten children. Journal of Genetic
Psychology, 1944, 65, 161-175.

Second generation native white kindergarten children (341)
were compared for Stanford-Binet, Form L, intelligence with
91 Negro kindergarten children of the same CA. Mean white IQ
was 107.1 and mean Negro IQ was 100.8 with practically identical variance. All children were divided into six groups on
the basis of parent's occupation. Groups ranged in mean IQ
from high to low; white female, white male, Negro male, Negro
female. Variance for white and Negro IQs were homogeneous
at all occupational levels. The total Negro group resembled
the white semiskilled and unskilled occupational group. The
findings are related to a theory of developmental construction
based on cultural factors.

297. Brown, N. W. Non-cognitive characteristics in the prediction
of reading readiness. Educational and Psychological Measurement,
1976, 36 (2), 537-542.

Compared the Lowenfeld Mosaic Test (LMT) with the Metropolitan
Readiness Test (MRT) and with teachers' ratings to predict
school readiness. Subjects were 6-year-olds in three groups:
10 children in a Federally funded neighborhood center, 10 middle
class blacks, and 10 middle class whites. Subjects were pre-

tested with the Slosson Intelligence Test (SIT), the LMT,
and the MRT. The teachers and examiner made their predictions
of each subject's readiness; the teachers' predictions were
based on observation and MRT scores, and those of the examiner,
only on the LMT. At the end of the first semester subjects
were administered the Slosson Oral Reading Test (SORT) and
their grades compiled. An analysis of results revealed the
single best predictor of reading success to be the examiner's
rating based on the LMT.

298. Bruce, M. Factors affecting intelligence test performance of
whites and Negroes in the rural South. Archives in Psychology, New
York, 1940, (252), 99.

Three intelligence tests -- the Kuhlmann-Anderson Group Test,
the Grace Arthur Point Performance Scale, and the 1916 Stanford-
Binet -- were administered to 521 white and 432 black children
aged 6 to 12.9 years in a county in the Piedmont Region of
Virginia in an attempt to isolate factors which "differentiate between white and Negro groups" and which "are responsible for the subnormal intelligence quotients in the rural
South." The major findings showed both whites and Negroes
below national averages, and whites superior to Negroes.
Distributions of total scores showed skewness in the Negro
sample and absence of skew in the white sample. This lends
itself to interpretation in the light of selective migration
among Negroes but not among whites. "The investigator is
inclined to believe that there is an innate difference between
the particular white and Negro groups studied," though the
demonstrated difference in the shapes of the distribution
curves "prevents this study from being used as evidence of
the superiority of the white race." The author attributes
the general inferiority of rural samples of the South either
to innate inferiority or to the failure of psychologists
to develop tests free from cultural influence.

299. Bruner, J. S. Poverty and childhood. Oxford Review of Education, n.d., 1, 31-50.

I should like to consider what we know about the education
of the very young, about what may be formative influences
during infancy and early childhood upon later intellectual
competence, and how these influences may be more compassion-
ately deployed. Our focus will be upon the manner in which
social and cultural background affects upbringing and thereby
affects intellectual functioning. Within that wide compass,
we shall limit ourselves further by concentrating principally
upon the impact of poverty and dispossession.

300. Buck, M. R. and Austrin, H. R. Factors related to school achievement in an economically disadvantaged group. Child Development,
1971, 42 (6), 1813-1826.

50 matched pairs of eighth grade, economically disadvantaged,
Afro-American students, categorized as adequate achievers or

underachievers, were administered a measure of internal-
external control of reinforcements and rated by teachers.
Maternal attitudes were ascertained from questionnaires and
interviews. Adequate achievers were found to be more internal
than underachievers, and rated as more positive and less
deviant in classroom behavior. Mothers of adequate achievers
tended to report fewer negative responses and to rate their
children as more competent. The mothers did not differ in
minimal standard, or in attainment of values. Findings are
discussed in the light of social-learning theory.

301. Bucky, S. F. and Banta, T. J. Racial factors in test performance. Developmental Psychology, 1972, 6 (1), 7-13.

Conducted individual 10-minute interviews of 36 Negro and 36
Caucasian preschool children, using Negro and Caucasian
examiners. Subjects were then given tests of motor impulse
control, reflectivity, innovative behavior, and curiosity.
The warm-up interview was video-taped and later evaluated by
two clinical psychologists along 13 social interaction dimensions. Caucasian subjects generally scored higher on the
tests though the race of the examiner was critical. Caucasian and Negro subjects obtained higher scores with Caucasian
examiners than with Negroe examiners. Caucasian examiners
were rated as providing a more positive social atmosphere
than Negro examiners for both groups.

302. Burke, A. A. Placement of black and white children in educable
mentally handicapped classes and learning disabilities classes.
Exceptional Children, 1975, 41 (6), 438-439.

Data from the WISC and WAIS scores (used for placement) of
107 educable mentally handicapped students and 73 learning
disabled students in middle and high school suggest that
there is a trend toward increased placement in learning disability classes of blacks with learning problems. Findings
on the overall and separate racial composition of each
placement category are also presented.

303. Burnes, K. Clinical assumptions about WISC subtest scores
and test behavior relationships. Journal of Consulting and Clinical
Psychology, 1971, 36 (2), 299.

Administered the WISC to 40 white and 38 Negro 8-year-old
boys. The examiner and an observer independently scored the
subjects' behavior for attention, energy level, social skills,
task persistence, and concern about performance. Thirteen
clinical psychologists completed a questionnaire ranking
behaviors considered important to performance on each of the
WISC subtests. Fifteen hypotheses resulted, eight involving
attention, and none involving concern about performance.
Analysis of scores and ratings produced eight significant
relationships, three involving concern about performance.
Emphasis on attention was found to be greatly overestimated.
Sixteen correlations were significant for race and socio-

economic status. "Results indicate that: (a) most of the clinically assumed relationships do not exist; and (b) the importance of test behavior to performance may vary among groups of children and tasks."

304. Burnes, K. Patterns of WISC scores for children of two socio-economic classes and races. Child Development, 1970, 41 (2), 493-499.

Negro and white 8-year-old boys from lower and upper middle class homes were given the WISC in order to determine group patterns of intellectual abilities. Results show lower class subjects of both races obtaining the lower scores, but config-urations of scores for each group are similar. A few differ-ences are found between socioeconomic groups, but not between races.

305. Busse, T. V. Child rearing antecedents of flexible thinking. Developmental Psychology, 1969, 1 (5), 585-591.

Related the behavior, attitudes, and social class of 48 Negro mothers and 48 Negro fathers to the development of their fifth grade boys' flexible thinking, defined as the ability to con-sider alternative means to a given end. Linear relationships were found linking flexible thinking with mother commands, father love, father total words, social class, and two father factors -- "powerlessness vs. powerfulness", and "rigid-absolute vs. warm sympathetic standards". Quadratic relation-ships were found linking flexible thinking with mother mani-pulation and three father factors -- "active vs. ignoring role with children", "discouraging vs. tolerating physical aggression in children", and "powerlessness vs. powerfulness".

306. Busse, T. V., Blum, P., and Gutride, M. Testing conditions and the measurement of creative abilities in lower class preschool children. Multivariate Behavioral Research, 1972, 7 (3), 287-298.

Tested the effects of playlike verbal- and nonverbal-feedback testing conditions on three creative ability measures (Con-struction Test, Pattern Meanings Test, Starkweather Test) using 87 black and 88 white lower class 4-year-olds. Most of the creativity measures used were unaffected by variations in testing conditions. In addition, different forms of the creativity measures hypothesized to be parallel proved to have only weak relationships with each other. However, split-half reliabilities of the individual measures were fairly high.

307. Caldwell, M. B. and Smith, T. A. Intellectual structure of southern Negro children. Psychological Reports, 1968, 23, 63-71.

In the 1950's, the WISC was given by the same examiner to 48 Negro children in each of five southern states. Ages which ranged from 5 years, 7 months to 12 years, 6 months, and sexes were equally distributed within each state. Analysis of the data showed that the verbal IQ was significantly higher than

the performance IQ for both sexes, all ages, and all but one
location. There were few sex differences, except for its
influence on the factor structure of the 12 verbal and performance tests. Age was not an interesting classification
of the data. Geographical groups differed much more in WISC
performance than did age or sex groups. This is consistent
with strong regional differences in Negro intellectual performance apparent from a review of previous studies.

308. Canady, H. G. The effect of "rapport" on the IQ: A new
approach to the problem of racial psychology. Journal of Negro
Education, 1936, 5, 209-219.

In this study 418 Negro children and 25 white children were
compared to determine the degree of loss or gain in Stanford-
Binet IQ when tested by a Negro. 23 Negro subjects and 18
white subjects were tested first by a Negro examiner (N) and
second by a white examiner (W). The remaining 25 Negroes and
7 white subjects were tested first by W and second by N. The
intervals between tests ranged from one day to one year. In
the combined Negro group only 4 gained more than 10 points
under N, and only 5 of the combined white group lost more than
10 points. Under N an average increase of 6 points in IQ
was found for Negroes and an average decrease of 6 points for
whites. The change in individuals was not systematically
upward or downward, but rather haphazard. It is noted that
retests of many children by the same examiner show a change
of about 5 points up or down.

309. Canady, H. G. The problem of equating the environment of
Negro-white groups for intelligence testing in comparative studies.
Journal of Social Psychology, 1943, 17, 3-15.

The writer emphasizes the difficulty, if not impossibility,
of equating Negroes and whites by reference to similarity
of environment. It is difficult to secure data on intelligence "which will be unaffected by differences in environmental influences without a more widespread and radical
control of social and economic conditions than a mere scientific experiment can provide." Further, the application to
both racial groups of a test standardized on northern whites
is a questionable procedure: "The mental reactions which
make an individual atypical in one culture may fit him perfectly for another."

310. Canady, H. G. A study of sex differences in intelligence-
test scores among 1,306 Negro college freshmen. Journal of Negro
Education, 1943, 12, 167-172.

An analysis of the ACE test scores of 637 men and 669 women
reveal a significant sex difference for gross scores, but
does indicate male superiority on the numerical parts of the
test. The results do not support a theory of greater male
variability.

311. Case R. and Pascual-Leone, J. Failure of conservative training
of disadvantaged black teenagers: A neo-Piagetian interpretation.
Perceptual and Motor Skills, 1975, 40 (2), 545-546.

   Results which interpret the failure of some black teenagers
   to learn conservation of area, weight, and volume, as due to
   right hemispheric processing and sensitivity to misleading
   visual cues, are rebutted. From a structural point of view,
   conservation tasks resemble Witkin's field-dependence situations. Based on neo-Piagetian theory, it is proposed that
   the failure of certain disadvantaged black teenagers to profit
   from conservation training is related to their field-dependence.

312. Cerbus, G. and Oziel, L. J. Correlation of the Bender-Gestalt
and the WISC for Negro children. Perceptual and Motor Skills, 1971,
32 (1), 276.

   A significant correlation (-.44, p<.01) of the Bender-Gestalt
   as scored by the Koppitz system with the WISC Full Scale IQ
   in a sample of 40 Negro school children is attributable mainly
   to the association between the Bender and the Performance
   subtests. The Bender-Performance IQ correlation (-.72) is
   significantly higher in a "referral" subgroup (-.89) than in
   the normal subjects' (-.58).

313. Clarke, D. P. Stanford-Binet Scale "L" response patterns in
matched racial groups. Journal of Negro Education, 1941, 10, 230-238.

   Two groups of 116 boys 14 to 16 years of age, were matched in
   every respect except race. The problem was to determine
   whether groups matched for amount of intelligence would respond differently to individual items of the Revised Stanford-
   Binet Intelligence Scale, Form L. No significant differences
   were found. However, Negro superiority in reasoning and number
   functions was strongly indicated for these groups and was
   explained on a basis of cultural rather than racial differences.

314. Cohen, R. Language and the structure of poverty. Sociological Focus on Language and Conduct, 1969-1970, 3 (2), 53-56.

   In this synthesis of relevant research, it is suggested that
   individuals act in response to definable, internally consistent,
   integrated rule-sets, and that individuals vary systematically
   in their patterns of cognitive and social organization more
   than do the formal criteria used to select persons for social
   participation. Student behavior requirements are relatively
   standardized. Many children from low-income homes exhibit
   conceptual styles other than the "analytic" style required by
   the educational system. Hence, these children may appear to
   be cognitively and socially inadequate. Three analytic
   styles have been identified, each of which is internally
   consistent. The two basic modes of cognitive organization,
   relational and analytic, are mutually incompatible. Each of
   these conceptual styles, or rule-sets for the selection and
   organization of sense data, has specific characteristics. The

analytic style exhibits analytic abstraction and field independence. There are two derivational styles as well: the
flexible, exhibiting analytic abstraction and selective field
dependence; and the conflictual style exhibiting descriptive
abstraction and field independence. The relational style is
characterized by descriptive abstraction and total field dependence. Inability to function in formal settings because of non-
analytic conceptual styles may contribute to generational
poverty.

315. Cole, M. and Bruner, J. S. Cultural differences and inferences
about psychological processes. American Psychologist, 1971, 26 (10),
867-876.

It has been demonstrated that culturally deprived black children tested appropriately for optimum performance, have the
same grammatical competence as middle class whites, but it
may be expressed in different settings. The psychological
status of the concept of competence is brought deeply into
question when one examines conclusions based on standard
experiments. If performance is treated only as a shallow
expression of deeper competence, then one inevitably loses
sight of the ecological problem of performance. The significance of a particular situation for the person's ability
to cope with life in his own milieu must be realized. Cultural differences reside more in differences in the situations
to which different cultural groups apply their skills than
to differences in the skills possessed by the groups in question. In the present social context of the United States,
the middle class has rendered differences into deficits
because middle class behavior is the yardstick of success.
The teacher of culturally disadvantaged children should
recognize educational difficulties as a difference rather
than an intellectual disease, and concentrate on how to
get the child to transfer skills he already possesses to the
task at hand.

316. Cole, N. S. and Fowler, W. R. Pattern analysis of WISC scores
achieved by culturally disadvantaged southern blacks. Psychological Reports, 1974, 36 (1, Part 1), 305-306.

An analysis of the pattern of WISC scores for 54 black children from northeast Georgia and southwest South Carolina
was performed to determine whether there was any reliable
difference in their performance on the various subtests.
Results indicate that highest scores are obtained in picture
completion, similarities, and comprehension; lowest scores
are on picture arrangement, information, coding, block design,
and object assembly. It is contended that such data do not
support the view that southern black culture has a less detrimental effect on performance than on verbal subtests of the
WISC. It is suggested that if replicated, implications should
be examined.

317. Conklin, K. R. Why compensatory schooling seems to make "no difference". Journal of Education, Boston, 1974, 156 (2), 34-42.

Presents an analysis of why traditional compensatory education has failed to help disadvantaged or black children improve their standing on measures of academic achievement and post school success in relation to the standing of middle class or white children. Linguistic and cultural characteristics are cited as deeply influencing the manner of perceiving the world at an early age, and this is reflected in IQ evaluation and the problems of compensatory education. Compensatory education is seen as a method to help minority groups learn how to "succeed" as well as possible according to the standards of a different group.

318. Cooke, D. H. Reaction of white and Negro pupils in learning multiplication combinations. Peabody Reflector, 1935, 8, 11-12.

24 white and 29 Negro third grade children (ages not given) in a city of about 200,000 population in which whites and Negroes had separate schools were practiced under similar conditions on the multiplication of 64 digit-pairs (4 x 5, 5 x 4, 2 x 9, etc.). Combinations involving 0 or 1 were omitted. Mean IQ as determined by Haggerty Intelligence Examination, Delta 2, was 82.3 for whites and 81.3 for Negroes. After "considerable drill" in addition and subtraction, the children were drilled and tested by their respective teachers 30 minutes daily for (apparently) 49 days. The author concludes that: "In the final analysis, it appears that there is very little difference in the reactions of white and Negro pupils in learning the multiplication combinations." He also finds that the number of drill periods required to learn any combination increases with magnitude of the combination, combinations containing 6 thru 9 requiring "more than twice as much time, on the average," for learning as those containing 2 thru 9 requiring "more than twice as much time on the average," for learning as those containing 2 thru 5.

319. Coppinger, N. W. and Ammons, R. B. The Full Range Picture Vocabulary Test: VIII. A normative study of Negro children. Journal of Clinical Psychology, 1952, 8, 136-140.

80 Negro children in grades 1 thru 8 were tested with both forms of the Full Range Picture Vocabulary Test and the vocabulary test from Form L of the 1937 Stanford-Binet. The sample was stratified with respect to grade placement, age, sex and parental occupation. Scores on the two forms correlated +.96 with each other and +.81 and +.84 with Binet vocabulary scores. There was no detectable practice effect. On the basis of these findings and the results of various analyses of items difficulty, the authors conclude that the Full Range Vocabulary Test is suitable for use with Negro children. Negro norms are given, based on the scores of the children in the present sample.

320. Corley, G. B. and Lewis, C. W. The impact of individualized instruction on low achieving youth. Urban Education, 1975, 10 (3), 321-326.

The impact of individualized instruction on the academic achievement of low performing inner city youth was explored by studying 30 seventh grade pupils from a self-contained classroom. The children were heterogeneously grouped, but as a class were average with respect to scholastic aptitude. However, they had developed patterns of low motivation, and achievement test scores averaged approximately two years below the expectation for their grade level. Results of this study indicate that performances in problem solving and vocabulary development increased dramatically during individualized instruction. Achievement was less than might typically be expected during a period of traditional teaching, but the overall gain was at least as much as might be expected of children over a year's time. Educators with limited budgets and instructional resources might consider incorporating temporary individualized programs to validate the conclusions found here.

321. Costello, J. and Ali, F. Reliability and validity of Peabody Picture Vocabulary Test scores of disadvantaged preschool children. Psychological Reports, 1971, 28 (3), 755-760.

Test-retest correlations over a two-week period for 36 black preschoolers was 0.77 for the standard Peabody test; values of 0.87 and 0.80 were obtained for a modified format with similar samples. Quite modest validity was suggested by correlations of the standard Peabody test with two other psychological tests assessing intellectual behaviors and with teachers' ratings of several classroom verbal behaviors. While Form A of the Peabody could be used as a first approximation in a continuing assessment program, scores cannot be considered alone for either intellectual or language evaluation. Reprinted by permission.

322. Costello, J. and Dickie, J. Leiter and Stanford-Binet IQs of preschool disadvantaged children. Developmental Psychology, 1970, 2 (2), 314.

Administered the Leiter International Performance Scale, Arthur Revision, and the Stanford-Binet to 17 Negro children in an urban Head Start program to assess their usefulness in "evaluating intellectual gains resulting from preschool programs for disadvantaged children." Results indicate: (a) no sex differences, and (b) greater variation for Leiter scores. It is concluded that the Leiter was not as useful as the Stanford-Binet. A discussion of the differences between the tests is included.

323. Covin, T. M. and Hatch, G. WISC Full Scale IQ mean differences of black children and white children aged 6 through 15 and having problems in school. Psychological Reports, 1977, 40 (1), 281-282.

Reports differences in Full Scale WISC IQ for 300 black and 300 white southern 6- to 15-year-olds, from families of low income, who were referred for psychometric assessment. The difference between IQs of these blacks and whites tended to increase from ages 6 through 15 years. The blacks tended generally to decrease in IQ from ages 6-15, while the whites tended to increase in IQ from ages 6-12 and then decrease through age 15.

324. Criner, B. H. (Ed.). Programmed Tutoring in reading, Lenoir County, North Carolina: A program using paraprofessionals for the individual tutoring of disadvantaged children in reading. Washington, D. C.: Office of Education (DHEW), 1974. 18 pp. Also, see ERIC Abstracts, No. ED-106-417, 1974.

This report is based upon one component of an Elementary Secondary Education Act Title I project in the Lenoir County, North Carolina, public schools for the 1973-74 school term. Programmed Tutoring was developed as a supplement to classroom teaching. The three basic skills of reading (sight reading, word analysis, and comprehension) are broken down into subskills which are taught by nine item programs. Each of the programs has a series of test and teaching steps which must be followed. The tutoring procedures are simple. They are systematically programmed and are specified in great detail so that tutors with limited education and work experience can be trained to a high degree of effectiveness. Of the 461 students enrolled in Programmed Tutoring, 228 were first graders, 194 were second graders, and 40 were third graders. Approximately 57% of the students were boys and 43% were girls; 63% were black and 37% were white. In 1972-73, through the help of a Home-School-Community Coordinator in each school, a parental visitation program for programmed tutorial was expanded. Evaluation reports for the six years during which this component has been in operation show that this activity significantly improved the educational attainment of disadvantaged children in the area of reading.

325. Croake, J. W., Keller, J. F., and Catlin, N. WPPSI, Rutgers, Goodenough, Goodenough-Harris IQs for lower socioeconomic black preschool children. Psychology, 1973, 10 (2), 58-65.

Administered the Rutgers Drawing Test (RDT), the Wechsler Preschool and Primary Scale of Intelligence (WPPSI), the Draw-A-Man Test (DAMT), and the Goodenough-Harris Drawing Test (GHDT) to 63 3- to 5-year-old lower socioeconomic black boys and girls. Thirty-eight subjects were tested again one year later. Mean IQs were consistently higher for girls, post-tests, and the performance scale, and decreased with age. Highest scores were found for the WPPSI, followed in order by the DAMT, GHDT, and RDT. Correlations indicated that the

WPPSI had the highest temporal stability followed by the
GHDT, RDT, and the DAMT. Interest correlations were higher
for girls, the younger age groups, and for performance scales.
WPPSI IQs correlated highest with the GHDT.

326. D'Angelo, R., Walsh, J., and Lomanzino, L.   IQs of Negro Head
Start children in the Vane Kindergarten Test. Journal of Clinical
Psychology, 1971, 27 (1), 82-83.

The Vane Kindergarten Test (VKT) was administered to 225 48-
to 71-month-old Negro children enrolled in a Head Start program. Negro girls tended to score higher than boys on all
measures in the two youngest age groups. Other sex and age
findings were noted. Use of the VKT with children below
the age of 54 months is questioned. "Further study is suggested to determine whether absence of expected findings is
due to limitations in the Vane's discriminatory value or to
general change in the mode of Negro functioning."

327. Davis, R. A. Jr.   Some relations between amount of school
training and intelligence among Negroes. Journal of Educational
Psychology, 1928, 19, 127-130.

The Terman Group Intelligence Examination, Form A, was given
to 222 students in a Negro normal and industrial school located
in the South. The school is a state accredited school of good
standing. The intelligence quotients ranged from 55 to 105,
with a median at 78. The number of months the students had
previously attended school was computed. It was found that
there was an enormous difference in the number of months
which these students had attended school in comparison with
what the standards were for the various grades. For example,
the standard number of months for completing Grade VIII is
72, while the Negroes in that grade had attended 53.5 months.
For this reason, it is impossible to use the scores obtained
on an ordinary intelligence test unless the number of months
of schooling is also taken into consideration. There is
positive correlation between the number of months in school
and the IQ.

328. Deitz, S. and Johnson, J. W.   Performance of lower and middle
class children on a discrimination reversal task. Psychonomic
Science, 1968, 11 (6), 191-192.

Investigated a discrimination reversal learning task, which
form the relevant and color the irrelevant dimension, using
a counterbalancing of order of positive form. Although no
differences were found in acquisition, children took more
trials reversing to squares than to circles. No differences
were found between lower and middle class white and Negro
children in average trials to acquisition or reversal.

329. Denmark, F. L. and Guttentag, M. Effect of integrated and
nonintegrated programs on cognitive change in preschool children.
Perceptual and Motor Skills, 1969, 29, 375-380.

Cognitively disadvantaged, Negro, preschool children (N-63) in
four different intervention programs were compared with controls
before and after treatments. Neither differences in program
content nor the presence of white, middle class children were
significant in determining cognitive improvement. Duration of
program alone was related to cognitive change.

330. Deutsch, C. P. Some effects of poverty on children. In Milly
Cowles (Ed.), Perspectives in the Education of Disadvantaged Children,
pp. 83-95. Cleveland: The World Publishing Company, 1967.

The principles that underlie the compensatory education or
enrichment programs at the Institute for Developmental Studies
(New York Medical School) state that the disadvantaged child's
deficits in skills necessary for effective school learning are
reversible. The reversal can be achieved with carefully planned
preschool programs. Before such programs can be developed
it is necessary to understand the child's deficits. The
author divides them into physical, social, emotional, and cognitive types, and gives a brief overview of each. Physically,
slum dwellers are more prone to malnutrition, disease, disability, premature births and other paranatal disorders, and
physical difficulties arising from lack of early diagnosis
and treatment of minor ailments. Social effects of poverty
include a high percentage of broken homes, lack of adequate
male role models at home, and alienation from society. Emotional problems of concern among school children are motivation
and self-concept. It is necessary to change teachers' attitudes toward these children and to raise the teachers' concept
of what the child can accomplish with their help. There has
been little research into the effects of deprivation on cognition. However, what research has been done shows that
absence of early stimulation is extremely detrimental. Emphasis is being placed on identification of those environmental
aspects which contribute to this effect.

331. Dill, J. R., Bradford, C., and Grossett, M. Comparative
indices of school achievement by black children from different preschool programs. Psychological Reports, 1975, 37 (3, Part 1), 871-877.

Categorized 728 black first, second and third graders according to their preschool experience (developmental day care,
custodial day care, Head Start, and none). Subjects' school
records were used to obtain four indices of school achievement: demographic-family variables, class ranking and attendance, personal-social behavior ratings, and academic achievement. Analyses showed subjects from developmental day care
programs were more likely to be born in the North, were enrolled in higher ranked classes, and had higher levels of
reading performance. Results suggest that the type of pre-

school program an urban child attends can influence his early
school achievement. Also, it is important to include additional dimensions of achievement for these children.

332. Di Lorenzo, L. T. and Salter, R. An evaluative study of pre-
kindergarten programs for educationally disadvantaged children:
Follow-up and replication. Exceptional Children, 1968, 35, 111-119.

Starting in 1964, eight school districts in New York State
cooperated with the State Education Department to test the
effects of prekindergarten programs. A total of 1,235 subjects were involved with experimental and control groups measured on social status, IQ, language development, and reading
readiness. Data were analyzed after one and two years on sex,
race, and type of program. Results indicated that the pre-
kindergarten experience was beneficial for the disadvantaged
and the nondisadvantaged as measured by the Stanford-Binet
(IQ), the Peabody Picture Vocabulary Test, and the Illinois
Test of Psycholinguistic Abilities. The programs with the
most specific and structured cognitive activities showed the
most gain; one program employing the Edison Responsive Environments' "talking typewriter" showed no gains. Other results
are described and discussed.

333. Doke, L. A. and Risley, T. R. Stimulus generalization across
individuals along dimensions of sex and race: Findings with children from an all-Negro neighborhood. Proceedings of the American
Psychological Association, 1970, 5 (part 2), 735-736.

Negro children in two age groups (5- to 8-, and 9- to 12-
year-olds) served in an experimental comparison of the discriminative control exerted by sex and race of a Negro girl
and a Caucasian boy differentially controlled responding on
two push buttons. Responses during test probes picturing children from each race-sex grouping indicated predominant control
by the stimulus dimension of sex for younger subjects, and
less predictable stimulus control for older subjects. Subsequent racial discrimination training was not sufficient
in transferring stimulus control on later generalization tests
to a dimension of race. Additional results suggest that this
failure may have been partially a function of discrimination
training histories.

334. Dyer, H. S. School factors and equal educational opportunity.
Harvard Educational Review, 1968, 38 (1), 38-56.

The Coleman Report investigated the relationship between pupil
achievement and pupil background. Separate regression analyses were performed on each of ten groups: Mexican-Americans,
Puerto Ricans, Indian-Americans, Oriental-Americans, Northern
Negroes, Southern Negroes, Northern whites, Southern whites,
all Negroes, and all whites. The author then surveys three
earlier studies of the effects of schooling on achievement
and cognitive development in which the conclusions differ
from those of the Coleman Report: The Mollenkopf and Melville

study in 1953, Samuel Goodman's Quality Measurement Project in
1957-1958, and Marion F. Shaycoft's study in 1960. These
studies ran contrary to the finding of the Coleman Report that
the differential effects of schools on pupil achievement
arise, not princiaplly from factors that the school system
controls, but from factors outside the school. The author
criticizes the Coleman Report for giving the school systems
the false impression that there is not much they can do to
improve pupils' achievement. School characteristics which
influence achievement are determined by sorting the 45 school
characteristic variables into correlates and noncorrelates
of pupil achievement. Zero order correlations tables of the
Supplemental Appendix to the Coleman Report are inspected,
and on this basis 19 correlates and 26 noncorrelates are found.
A comparison of the correlates and noncorrelates shows (a) a
relatively large number of correlates in some of the minority
groups as compared with the small number in the white majority;
(b) a majority of the items have to do with the characteristics of the pupils and the teachers; and (c) functional school
characteristics are for the most part hard to change, while
those that are nonfunctional are the easy-to-change characteristics.

335. Eagle, N. and Harris, A. S. Interaction of race and test on
reading performance scores. Journal of Educational Measurement, 1969,
6 (3), 131-135.

    This study examines the relationship between race and perfor-
    mance on two nationally standardized reading tests. The appro-
    priate reading tests of the Iowa Test of Basic Skills and
    Metropolitan Achievement Battery were administered to all
    fourth and sixth grade students in all elementary schools of
    an urban school district near New York City. Although white
    pupils earned higher scores than nonwhite pupils on both
    tests, the Metropolitan produced significantly greater differ-
    ences between the races than the Iowa, at both grade levels.
    Factorial analysis of variance confirmed the statistical
    significance of these differences. Implications of Race x Test
    (suggesting SES x Test) interaction effects for program evalua-
    tion and instruction are briefly discussed. Reprinted by permission.

336. Eisenberg, L., Berlin, C. I., Dill, A., and Frank, S. Class
and race effects on the intelligibility of monosyllables. Child
Development, 1968, 39 (4), 1077-1089.

    160 Negro and white school children of low and middle socio-
    economic class families listened to female representatives
    of both uneducated and educated white and Negro groups read
    lists of monosyllables. The most intelligible speech was
    generated by the educated speakers, regardless of the race
    of the speaker or the listeners. Negro children showed gener-
    ally poorer listening scores than whites, and Negro speakers
    generated slightly poorer intelligibility scores than whites,
    independent of the race and class of the listeners with one
    exception: uneducated speakers were understood better by

members of their own race. Experiment II showed a small but
significant relation between the listening scores the children
obtained and their ability to rearticulate the lists to 40
teachers. Great variability within subjects probably overcame
the effects of race and class.

337. Elkind, D. and Deblinger, J. A. Perceptual training and reading achievement in disadvantaged children. Child Development, 1969,
40, 11-19.

Matched two groups of second grade inner city children for
reading achievement and perceptual ability. Twenty-five subjects were trained with a series of nonverbal perceptual exercises for 1/2 hour three times a week for 15 weeks. Twenty-
one control subjects met for a comparable time but were trained
with a commercial reading program, "The Bank Street Readers".
Results showed that the experimental group made significantly
greater improvement on word form and word recognition than the
control groups. The results are interpreted as supporting a
perceptual activity analysis of the perceptual process in
reading.

338. Emanuel, J. M. and Sagan, E. L. The intelligence, reading
achievement, and arithmetic achievement scores of Head Start attendees
compared to Head Start non-attendees in the first, second and third
grades. Training School Bulletin, 1974, 71 (2), 119-132.

Intelligence, reading achievement and arithmetic achievement
scores for children who attended a Head Start program in either
the summer of 1967, 1968, or 1969, were compared with the children who did not attend. The Culture Fair Intelligence Test,
Scale One or Two, and the reading and arithmetic test section
of the Stanford Achievement Test, Form W, were administered
to all students in grades one, two and three in two predominantly Negro elementary schools. The analysis of variance
technique was used to analyze the data. Significant differences were found in the intelligence scores and arithmetic
achievement scores of Head Start attendees and the Head Start
non-attendees.

339. Erickson, M. T. Intelligence: Prenatal and preconception
environmental influences. Science, 1967, 157 (3793), 1210.

Comments on W. A. Kennedy's article suggesting a study of the
role of environmental variables by placing illegitimate Negro
children into middle class Negro homes at birth, later comparing IQ and achievement scores with lower class Negro and white
children. This is criticized on the basis that heredity cannot
be attributed as the cause of test score differences. The
reasons for this conclusion are listed. W. A. Kennedy's reply
follows, suggesting that practical solutions exist to answer
Erickson's criticisms.

340. Fagan, J., Broughton, E., Allen, M., Clark, B., and Emerson, P.
Comparison of the Binet and WPPSI with lower class 5-year-olds. Journal of Consulting and Clinical Psychology, 1969, 33, 6607-6609.

> The Stanford-Binet and WPPSI were administered to 32 5-year-old
> lower class children, 16 of whom were Negro and 16 white. A
> correlation coeficient of .80 was found between the Binet and
> WPPSI. Contrary to previous research, significant differences
> were found in the IQ scores obtained from the measures, with
> the Binet mean of 95.2 being 8 points higher than the WPPSI.
> No significant sex or race differences were found in IQs. A
> decided preference for the Binet was reported by the examiners
> on the basis of ease of administration, greater scoring clarity,
> and subjective assessment of accuracy.

341. Farnham-Diggory, S. Cognitive synthesis in Negro and white
children. Monographs of the Society for Research in Child Development, 1970, 35 (2), 84 pp.

> Explored symbolic abilities, and their development, with a
> view toward the technology of pedagogy. It was found that
> racial differences in symbolic abilities, while present,
> might be remediable through various cognitive training tech-
> niques.

342. Federici, L., et. al. Use of the Meeting Street School Screening Test and the Myklebust Pupil Rating Scale with first grade black
urban children. Psychology in the Schools, 1976, 13 (4), 386-389.

> This study examines the use of two diagnostic instruments in
> identifying children with a high risk of learning problems.
> The Meeting Street School Screening Test (MSSST) and the
> Myklebust Pupil Rating Scale are compared as educational
> screening devices for black children from urban areas.

343. Feldman, D. H. and Markwalder, W. Systematic scoring of ranked
distractors for the assessment of Piagetian reasoning levels. Educational and Psychological Measurement, 1971, 31 (2), 347-362.

> Attempted to determine if a map reading test could be used
> to assess both a child's map reading skill and his level of
> reasoning ability according to Piaget's theory of cognitive
> development. The latter would be assessed by the analysis
> of the child's choice of distractors. A new instrument for
> measuring spatial reasoning was designed and validated based
> on conceptual analysis of a geographic map. All 25 items
> were designed to induce response indicative of the four reason-
> ing levels suggested by Piaget. The sample included 270 fifth,
> seventh and ninth graders evenly distributed across three
> different ethnic groups (black, white and Chinese). The re-
> sults tend to indicate that the instrument devised may be
> capable of measuring reasoning stage levels as well as map
> achievement. Results also show that children of different

ethnic backgrounds tend to go through the same set of developmental stages and that children of specific developmental levels
tend to select distractor indications of that level.

344. Ferrell, G. V.   Comparative study of sex differences in school
achievement of white and Negro children.   Journal of Educational Research, 1949, 43, 116-121.

Four subtests of the Stanford Achievement Test -- language usage,
arithmetic computation, social studies, and elementary science
-- were given to 300 white and 300 Negro children in grades 4,
5 and 6. There was an equal number with each sex. Among the
white children, girls were superior to boys in language usage,
arithmetic, and general science, and boys were superior in
social studies. Among the Negroes, girls were superior in
language usage and general science, and boys were superior in
arithmetic and social studies. Only the differences in language usage were certainly significant. Reprinted by permission.

345. Feshbach, N. D.   Cross-cultural studies of teaching styles in
4-year-olds and their mothers.   In A. D. Pick (Ed.), Minnesota Sym-
posia on Child Psychology: VII.   Minneapolis, Minnesota: University
of Minnesota Press, 1973.

Investigated individual differences in the responses of black
and white English and Israeli 4-year-olds to various reinforcement styles used by mothers in teaching their children.
A study of maternal reinforcement styles and learning problems is also presented.

346. Feshbach, N. D. and Devor, G.   Teaching styles in 4-year-olds.
Child Development, 1969, 40 (1), 183-190.

Hypothesized that middle class Caucasian children would spontaneously use more positive reinforcements and lower class
children more negative reinforcements when interacting with
peers. Data bearing on this hypothesis were obtained by having
102 4-year-old boys and girls of different race and social
class backgrounds instruct 102 3-year-old subjects of the same
social class and race. The prediction for positive reinforcement was confirmed for middle class Caucasians. While lower
class children did make greater use of negative reinforcement,
for most of the social class comparisons, the differences were
not statistically significant. Middle class Negro children
displayed the least number of reinforcements, positive or
negative, of all the groups.

347. Figurelli, J. C. and Keller, H. R.   The effects of training and
socioeconomic class upon the acquisition of conservation concepts.
Child Development, 1972, 43 (1), 293-298.

Investigated a simple short-term training procedure with 48
middle and lower class black 6- to 8-year-olds. Subject's
performance on each of the three forms of the Concept Assessment Kit Conservation was the primary dependent variable in a

2 x 2 factorial design, combining socioeconomic level (lower vs. middle), and presence or absence of training upon the acquisition of conservation concepts. Middle class subjects scored significantly higher than lower class subjects on both the pretest and transfer test. Training resulted in significantly higher post-test performance for both groups, regardless of class. Finally, lower class subjects required significantly more training task repetitions to learn a conservation task than did middle class subjects.

348. Findley, W. G. Grouping for instruction. In L. P. Miller (Ed.), The Testing of Black Students: A Symposium. Englewood Cliffs, N.J.: Prentice Hall, 1974. 113 pp.

Discusses theoretical, empirical, and practical reasons for the unsoundness of the ability grouping system in schools, especially as it affects black children. The effects of ability grouping programs on academic performance and self-concepts in black children and more profitable alternatives to this system (e.g., peer tutoring) are discussed).

349. Fishman, J. A. Review: "Intelligence and cultural environment" by P. E. Vernon (London: Methuen, 1969); and "Teaching black children to read" edited by C. Baratz and R. W. Shuy (Washington: Center for Applied Linguistics, 1969). Science, 1969, 165 (3898), 1108-1109.

The two books are reviewed together since (a) both are concerned with black children in particular and with other socially disadvantaged populations more generally, and (b) both regard language as being crucially involved in the lower performance of many black children on intelligence tests and in reading. The reviewer contrasts the two schools of thought and practice represented by these two works. One approach is based on the traditional research tradition of intergroup differences in intelligence and cognitive development. The other stresses the intracommunal sophistication and organization of the language and behavior of disadvantaged individuals.

350. Fitz-Gibbon, C. T. Improving practices in inner city schools: Two contributions. Paper presented at the American Educational Research Association Annual Meeting (Washington, D. C.: April, 1975). Also, see ERIC Abstracts, No. ED-107-746, 1975.) 18 pp.

Two studies are briefly reported here, one concerned with a method for locating high ability inner city students, and the other dealing with a method of motivating low achieving inner city students. Both studies drew on a population of black junior high school students, eighth and ninth graders, 14, 15, and 16 years of age. In the first study, four potential screening measures were applied to the eighth grade of an inner city junior high school. For each measure, those students in the top 2% on that measure were given the Advanced Progressive Matrices test and then the Wechsler Intelligence Scale for Children (WISC). The WISC performance scores were

taken as the criterion identifying the top nine students
(approximately 2%), who were to be designated "mentally gifted"
within this population. The second study investigated a method
of motivating low-achieving junior high school students to
learn mathematics by using them as tutors for fourth graders.
Before each tutoring session, the tutors were coached on the
material they were to teach. At the end of this brief pilot
study, arithmetic tests were given in the fourth and ninth
grade classrooms. Results showed significant gains for the
ninth grade tutors.

351.   Forrester, B. and Klaus, R.   The effect of race of the examiner
on intelligence test scores of Negro kindergarten children.   Peabody
Papers in Human Development, 1964, 2, 1-7.

352.   Furby, L.   Implications of within-group heritabilities for
sources of between-group differences: IQ and racial differences.
Developmental Psychology, 1973, 9 (1), 28-37.

Examines within-group heritabilities to determine the sources
of between-group differences.   The four logically possible
combinations of within-group heritabilities were examined,
along with their implications for the sources of between-
group differences.   In all cases, it was found that relative
heritabilities alone do not suggest the nature of the between-
group differences.   However, when the shapes of the empirical
distributions are examined along with the relative heritabilities, then the sources of between-group differences are at
least strongly suggested.   In particular, the present knowledge
of the relative shapes and heritabilities of the IQ distribution for blacks and whites suggests, but does not prove,
that blacks and whites have similar genotypes for IQ but
differ on IQ-determining environmental factors.

353.   Garfunkel, F. and Blatt, B.   The standardization of intelligence tests on southern Negro schools.   Training School Bulletin,
1963, 60 (2), 94-99.

The authors state that the task of predicting the academic
success of southern Negro school children is complicated
because the school and its relationship to vocational accomplishment represent, in general, a different set of values for
southern Negroes than for other cultural groups.   Tests like
the Stanford-Binet, cannot be indiscriminately used with all
cultural groups.   The authors criticize a recent study that
applied the Stanford-Binet Test to develop a set of norms for
southern Negro school children in that it assumes that the Test
is appropriate and that only norms are needed.   Criteria for
success and means to attain it must be reevaluated simultaneously with the development of predictive instruments.

354. Garrett, H. E. Negro-white differences in mental ability in the United States. Science Monitor, New York, 1947, 65, 329-333.

An analysis of the available data indicates that the American Negro on the average ranks consistently lower than American whites on tests of mental ability, and the "regularity of this result from babyhood to adulthood makes it extremely unlikely, in the present writer's opinion, that environmental opportunities can possibly explain all the differences found." The differences between American Negroes and northern and southern whites is not completely explained by the selective migration hypothesis nor the environmental theory. "The point may be stressed again that the differences between American Negroes and American whites are not true racial differences."

355. Garth, T. R., Lovelady, B. E., and Smith, H. W. The intelligence and achievement of southern Negro children. School and Society, 1930, 32, 431-435.

The Otis Classification Test was given to 2,006 Negro children in Oklahoma and Texas. It is asserted on the basis of the data gathered that the mental growth of the Negroes, while starting at practically the same point as that of the whites, lags increasingly with increasing years. The average IQ and EQ of the Negroes were, respectively, 77.9 and 76.6. The accomplishment ratio for the group (103), however, was above that for the whites. The educational retardation of the 2,006 cases was on the average 61.1%, the retardation being relatively less among those in the upper grades than among those in the lower.

356. Gaudia, G. Race, social class, and age of achievement of conservation on Piaget's tasks. Developmental Psychology, 1972, 6 (1), 158-165.

Administered a series of standardized conservation tasks to 126 lower socioeconomic status Indian, Negro and Caucasian children in the first three grades. The tasks included the conservation of area, number, continuous and discontinuous quantity, weight, and mass. Significant differences were found between the groups on age of acquisition of conservation. The entire research sample differed significantly from the racially and socially homogeneous norming group. Age of acquisition of conservation was at least a year retarded in the Negro sample and in the lower socioeconomic status children, with older children showing the most retardation. There were significant correlations between conservation and CA and IQ within all groups at every age level.

357. Gay, G. and Abrahams, R. D. Does the pot melt, boil, or brew? Black children and white assignment procedures. Journal of School Psychology, 1973, 11 (4), 330-340.

The cultural conditioning of black chilren which affects their performance on psychological tests is discussed. It is felt

that the distinctive attitudes, perceptions and behavioral
patterns of blacks must be considered. Included in the discussion are blacks' attitudes toward whites, sytems of time
allocations, expressions of identity, attitudes toward learning, dissemination of information among blacks, black learning
styles and maturation processes. Each topic is discussed in
terms of its manifestation in a testing or assessment situation;
how it conflicts with assessors' orientations and expectations;
and how distorted, unreliable evaluations result from the
failure of assessors to consider implications of cultural
relativism in interpreting black behavior.

358. Gerstein, A. I., Brodzinsky, D. M., and Reiskind, N. Perceptual integration on the Rorschach as an indicator of cognitive
capacity: A developmental study of racial differences in a clinic
population. Journal of Consulting and Clinical Psychology, 1976,
44 (5), 760-765.

Rorschach protocols of 173 7- to 14-year-old blacks and whites
who had been evaluated at a child guidance clinic were rescored with respect to developmental level of perceptual
integration. Blacks had higher perceptual-integration scores
in comparison to whites. This finding, however, was accounted
for by the higher performance of low-IQ (70-89) blacks as
compared to low-IQ whites. No differences were obtained
between average-IQ (90-109) blacks or whites. It is suggested
that standard IQ tests may not adequately tap the cognitive
capacity of some black children and that use of the Rorschach
from a developmental/structural perspective may provide a
useful adjunctive measure of intelligence that would more
realistically assess children's cognitive competence.

359. Gilliland, A. R. Socioeconomic status and race as factors in
infant intelligence test scores. Child Development, 1951, 22,
271-273.

Babies 6 to 12 weeks of age, and of similar socioeconomic
backgrounds, were compared on the basis of their being reared
at home or in an institution; home babies were superior in IQ
by 5 points. Three studies compared infants rated high versus
low or mid parent socioeconomic status. All three studies
showed the mean IQ for Negroes to be a high or slightly
higher than that of white children of the same age. The author
concludes that below 36 weeks of age, the SES of parents has
no demonstrable influence in the intelligence test scores of
the infants in this study.

360. Glover, J. A. Comparative levels of creative ability among
elementary school children. Journal of Genetic Psychology, 1976,
129 (1), 131-135. Also, see ERIC Abstracts, No. EJ-155-501.

A total of 86 black fourth grade children and 111 white fourth
grade children randomly selected from normal classrooms in a
rural county school system in Tennessee were compared on
Torrance's Unusual Uses and Ask and Guess activities. No

differences were found on the frequency or flexibility measures for either activity.

361. Goffeney, B., Henderson, N. B., and Butler, B. V. Negro-white,
male-female, eight-month developmental scores compared with seven-
year WISC and Bender test scores. Child Development, 1971, 42 (2),
595-604.

   A total of 626 Bayley Scale of infant tests scores at about
   8 months significantly correlated (r=.11-.21) with WISC Full,
   Verbal and Performance and Bender-Gestalt scores at 7 years.
   For black boys, no 8-month measure correlated significantly
   with any 7-year measure. Mental and fine motor scores of
   girls correlated significantly with Full, Verbal, Performance
   and Bender scores, but gross motor did not. Except for gross
   motor, female scores contributed most to total group relationships. Generally, mental and fine motor measurements had
   significant but low predictive value for girls of both races
   and white boys, but nonsignificant value for black boys.

362. Golden, M. and Birns, B. Social class and cognitive development in infancy. Merrill-Palmer Quarterly, 1968, 14 (2), 139-149.

   Using a cross sectional approach, 192 12-, 18-, and 24-month-
   old Negro children representing three socioeconomic status
   groups were compared on the Piaget Object Scale and the
   Cattell Infant Intelligence Scale. No social class differences were found in intellectual performance during the first
   two years of life.

363. Golden, M., Birns, B., and Bridger, W. A. Social class differentiation in cognitive development among black preschool children.
Child Development, 1971, 42 (1), 37-45.

   Reports a longitudinal study of 89 Negro children from different social classes. While there were no significant SES differences on the Cattell Infant Intelligence Scale at 18 and
   24 months of age, there was a high 23-point mean IQ difference
   on the Stanford-Binet at three years of age between subjects
   from welfare and middle class Negro families. The range in
   mean IQs of the Negro subjects in the extreme SES groups
   (93-116) was almost identical to that obtained by L. M.
   Terman and M. A. Merrill in their standardization sample of
   831 white children between 2-1/2 and 5 years of age.

364. Goldman, R. D. and Hartig, L. K. The WISC may not be a valid
predictor of school performance for primary-grade minority children.
American Journal of Mental Deficiency, 1976, 80 (6), 583-587.

   Tested the validity of the WISC for predicting several criterial
   teachers' ratings for primary-grade children: 320 black, 430
   Anglo-American, and 201 Mexican-American. Validities for the
   combined groups were good, but validities for the separate
   groups differed markedly. Validities were good for the
   Anglo-American, but near zero for the blacks and Mexican-

Americans. These results suggest that the WISC may be of
little value in the assessment of the educability of minority
children. The implications for educational placement and the
heredity-environment controversy are discussed.

365. Goldstein, H. S. and Peck, R. Cognitive functions in Negro
and white children in a child guidance clinic. Psychological Reports,
1971, 28, 379-384.

The IQs of Negro and white children attending an inner city
child guidance clinic were examined. The tests employed were
the WISC and the Harris modification of the Goodenough Draw-
A-Man test. The white males (N=22) scored significantly higher
than the Negro males (N=34) only on the Verbal part of the
WISC. The Similarities score of Negro males with low Vocabulary scores was significantly higher than their Vocabulary
scores. White females (N=18), however, achieved significantly
higher scores than Negro females (N=17) on Verbal, Performance,
and Full Scale IQs as well as on Harris scores. The differences in presenting symptomatology of Negro and white girls
is seen as a determinant of these cognitive differences.

366. Goodlet, C. B. and Greene, V. R. The mental abilities of
twenty-nine deaf and partially deaf Negro children. West Virginia
State College Bulletin, June 1940, 1-23.

The results of the administration of five non-language tests
to 29 deaf and partially deaf students at the West Virginia
State School for the Colored Deaf and Blind reveal varying
degrees of retardation among the subjects depending upon the
type of test used. A comparison of mental and educational ages
indicated that these pupils are not accomplishing as much as
even their retarded mentality would allow. Recommendations as
to the type of instruction and training of teachers are made.

367. Green, D. R. Racial and ethnic bias in test construction.
Washington, D. C.: Office of Education (DHEW), 1971. 104 pp.   Also,
see ERIC Abstracts, No. ED-056-090, 1971.

To determine if tryout samples typically used for item selection contribute to test bias against minority groups, item
analyses were made of the California Achievement Test using
seven subgroups of the standardization sample: Northern White
Suburban, Northern Black Urban, Southern White Suburban,
Southern Black Rural, Southern White Rural, Southwestern Mexican Urban and Southwestern Anglo-American Suburban. The
best half of the items in each test were selected for each
group. Typically about 30% of the items in the upper half of
the distribution of item-test correlations for a group on a
test did not meet this criterion with another group. By this
criterion minority groups were relatively similar as were the
three suburban groups. The resulting unique item tests did
not correlate well with each other. Scores of minority groups
were relatively better on the selected items. Thus, standard
item selection procedures produce tests best suited to groups

like the majority of the tryout sample and are therefore
biased against other groups to some degree. This degree
varies. Ways to minimize this bias need to be developed.

368. Green, D. R. and Roudabush, G. E. An investigation of bias in
a criterion-referenced test. See ERIC Abstracts, No. ED-113-379,
n.d., 49 pp.

Scores on the Prescriptive Reading Inventory, the California
Achievement Tests, 1970 Edition, the Short Form Tests of
Academic Aptitude were obtained for black pupils and representative samples of pupils in grades 1-3. These scores were
compared in an attempt to assess bias in the Prescriptive
Reading Inventory, a criterion-referenced achievement test.
Using factor analyses, contingency analyses, and regression
analyses, interrelationships among the reading scores on the
two tests were compared. It was hypothesized that the norm-
referenced test would show more bias as indicated by differential relationships among scores. The regression analyses
indicated some bias in all the tests used. The contingency
analyses, made of the CRT only, suggested little bias. The
factor analyses suggested parts of the CRT were not biased
but the remaining parts and the NRT measures were. In all
cases, the amount of bias appeared small.

369. Green, R. B. and Rohwer, W. D. Jr. SES differences on learning
and ability tests in black children. American Educational Research
Journal, 1971, 8, 601-609.

A sample of 60 fourth grade black children was stratified with
respect to socioeconomic status (SES) into three groups corresponding to the categories of low, lower-middle, and middle SES.
Three tasks were administered individually to each subject:
Raven Coloured Progressive Matrices; digit-span series; and a
pictorial paired-associate learning task. Scores were also
available for all subjects on the Lorge-Thorndike Intelligence
Test, on the reading portion of the SAT and on performance
in school courses. The proportion of SES-related variation
in performance on the paired-associate task was negligible
whereas for all other measures that proportion was substantial, especially on the digit-span task. The results were
discussed in relation to two different accounts of SES differences in performance on intellectual tasks.

370. Greenberg, J. W. and Davidson, H. H. Home background and school
achievement of black urban ghetto children. American Journal of
Orthopsychiatry, 1972, 42 (5), 803-810.

Investigated home and family variables for 80 high and 80 low
achieving black fifth graders from lower class urban families.
Parents of high achievers were rated significantly (p<.001-.01)
higher in concern for education, awareness, use of rationale
discipline, and structure and orderliness in the home. High
achievers seemed to come from somewhat better socioeconomic
circumstances within the working class. Absence of the father,

working mother, number of siblings, number of schools attended,
and nursery-kindergarten experience, were not related to achievement.

371. Greenberg, J. W., Shore, M. S., and Davidson, H. H. Caution
and creativity as correlates of achievement in disparate social
racial groups. Journal of Negro Education, 1972, 41 (4), 377-382.

Studied "caution" as measured by a 30-item multiple choice test
and a 12-item semantic differential scale, and "creativity", as
measured by a nonverbal drawing test, in relation to 40 upper
middle class white fifth graders in a suburban school, and
40 lower class blacks in urban ghetto schools in central Harlem.
Each group was equally divided by sex. Scores on standardized
reading achievement indicated that male and female means at both
schools were at the seventh grade level. A two-way analysis
of variance by social class and sex was performed for two
caution scores and three creativity scores. Significance
(p<.05) was obtained on only two interactions and no main
effects. It is concluded that high achieving students from
different social classes may be similar.

372. Grimmett, S. A. Black and white children's free recall of
unorganized and organized lists: Jensen's Level I and Level II.
Journal of Negro Education, 1975, 44 (1), 24-33.

Tested A. Jensen's theory of differences among blacks and whites
in conceptual (Level II) and associative (Level I) learning
abilities. Subjects were 60 lower class first graders divided
equally by sex and ethnic background. Tape-recorded lists
-- organized (List 2) and unorganized (List 1) -- from the AA
and A Thorndike-Lorge frequencies, and a digit span test (considered a Level I measure) were used. List 2 was used with
pictures under three learning conditions. Analysis of variance
and the chi-square analyses were made of recall scores. There
were no race, sex or condition effects on clustering-type recall. List 1 (a Level I task), and List 2 (a Level II task),
were significantly related for both blacks and whites, especially for blacks. The digit span mean for blacks was significantly higher than that for whites. These and other
findings largely contradict Jensen's theory. Possible explanations are suggested. Teaching first grade black children
by rote seems unwarranted.

373. Guinagh, B. J. An experimental study of basic learning ability
and intelligence in low socioeconomic status children. Child Development, 1971, 42 (1), 27-36.

Examined two constructs, basic learning ability and intelligence, as proposed by A. Jensen to explain the different
patterns of ability found in middle and low socioeconomic
status (SES) levels. Basic learning ability was measured by
Raven's Progressive Matrices (RPM). 40 low SES Negro and 40
low SES white third graders were tested. Training on the RPM
had different effects on the two races. In the low SES white

sample, both the high and low digit span groups had scores on the RPM posttest significantly greater than their respective control groups. In the low SES Negro group, only the high digit span experimental group had RPM posttest scores larger than its control group. The low digit span group did not gain from the experimental treatment.

374. Gustafson, L. Relationship between ethnic group membership and the retention of selected facts pertaining to American history and culture. Journal of Educational Sociology, 1951, 31, 49-56.

Subjects were 41 Negro and Jewish and WASP tenth graders from Akron. They were matched for IQ, age and sex. There were differences among the Jewish and Negro groups as to expected and observed choices of facts relating to American history and culture.

375. Gutelius, M. F. and Kirsch, A. D. Factors promoting success in infant education. American Journal of Public Health, 1975, 65 (4), 384-387.

In a study of factors contributing to infant educational success, frequent personal contacts and close friendly relations between staff and mothers in an infant stimulation program are shown to result in significantly more favorable intelligence quotient scores in comparison with those in a group of mothers given less attention and support. The program involved the mothers of black infants who were given prenatal care and counseling on postnatal needs for physical, mental and emotional development; intervention for the experimental mothers began by the seventh month of pregnancy and lasted until the child's third birthday. Implications for childhood education techniques and orientations are discussed.

376. Hall, V. C. and Kaye, D. B. Patterns of early cognitive development among boys in four subcultural groups. Journal of Educational Psychology, 1977, 69 (1), 66-87. Also, see ERIC Abstracts, No. EJ-156-126, 1977.

600 boys divided by age (6-8), race (black and white) and social class (middle and lower) were given tests for memory, intelligence, learning, and transfer. Findings indicated social class differences on learning and intelligence tests, with racial differences on intelligence, digit span, and paired-associate learning.

377. Hall, W. S., Reder, S., and Cole, M. Story recall in young black and white children: Effects of racial group membership, race of experimenter, and dialect. Developmental Psychology, 1975, 11, 628-634.

The experiment reported here tested the effects of racial group membership, race of experimenter, and dialect on unstructured and probed recall. Subjects were aged 4, 6 years. 16 were black, and an equal number were white. Subgroups of 4 children

within each racial group were randomly assigned to the experimental conditions so that order of exposure to experimenter
(black and white) and dialects (Standard English vs. Black
English vernacular) were counterbalanced. We found that whites
performed better than blacks in Standard English, blacks performed better than whites in Black English vernacular, blacks
tested in Black English vernacular were equivalent to whites
tested in Standard English, and whites performed better in
Standard English than in Black English vernacular.

378. Halpin, Glennelle, Halpin, Gerald, and Torrance, E. P. Comparisons of creative thinking abilities of blind and deaf children. Perceptual and Motor Skills, 1973, 37 (1), 154.

> The creative thinking abilities of 34 blind and 34 deaf chil-
> dren matched for sex (male-female), race (Caucasian-Negro),
> and age (9 to 12 years) were compared. The Torrance Test,
> Thinking Creatively With Words, was administered to all sub-
> jects. Since Activities 1, 2 and 3 contain a visual stimulus
> which the blind could not see, only scores from Activities 4,
> 5, 6 and 7 were used. These activities were scored for ver-
> bal fluency, verbal flexibility, and verbal originality.
> Results of the two-way analysis of variance, with type of
> deprivation and sex as the independent variables, indicated
> that the means of verbal fluency, verbal flexibility, and
> verbal originality did not differ significantly for the blind
> and deaf or for the males and females. Blindness and deaf-
> ness did not differentially affect scores on Torrance's test
> for children.

379. Halpin, Glennelle, Halpin, Gerald, and Torrance, E. P. Effects
of sex, race and age on creative thinking abilities of blind children. Perceptual and Motor Skills, 1973, 37 (2), 389-390.

> The influences of sex, race and age on the creative thinking
> abilities of blind children were studied. Scores on the
> creativity measures for 61 blind children did not generally
> vary greatly as a function of age, sex and race, but the
> 11- to 12-year-old Caucasians did score significantly higher
> on verbal flexibility than did any of the other groups in
> the race-age analysis. Results for the blind were not unlike
> results reported for the sighted.

380. Hammer, E. F. Comparison of the performance of Negro children
and adolescents on two tests of intelligence, one an emergency
scale. Journal of Genetic Psychology, 1954, 84, 85-93.

> "The California Test of Mental Maturity and H-T-P were adminis-
> tered to 207 students at . . . a Negro school, a representative
> semi-urban, semi-rural school in Virginia. The Time Apprecia-
> tion Test, an emergency intelligence scale, was administered
> to all students 10 years of age or above." The author con-
> cludes the baseline IQ should be 75. He considers it likely
> that there is greater emotional maladjustment of the Negro
> subjects in comparison with white subjects.

381. Hammill, D., Iano, R., McGettigan, J., and Wiederholt, J. L.
Retardates' reading achievement in the resource room model: The
first year. Training School Bulletin, 1972, 69, 104-107.

> The purpose of this study was to determine whether integrating
> EMR children into regular grades and providing them with support-
> ive help in a resource room would improve their achievement.
> 22 EMR children in an elementary school were removed from
> a special class and placed into the integrative program.
> Reading achievement tests were administered at the beginning
> and end of the school year. The gains in the children's
> reading scores indicated that their progress in reading was
> accelerated during the time they participated in the inte-
> grative program.

382. Harcum, P. M. and Harcum, E. R. Tempo modification in visual
perception of EMR children. Perceptual and Motor Skills, 1973, 37
(1), 179-188.

> Primary and intermediate educable mentally retarded (EMR)
> children in urban schools given non-intellectual tasks which
> involved visual perception of spatial relationships were studied
> to determine effects of tempo modification on performance.
> Subjects copied visible patterns and also reproduced patterns
> from memory after tachistoscopic exposure. The major variable
> was perceptual tempo, manipulated by instructions to adopt a
> reflective rather than impulsive style of responding. Other
> variables were sex and race. Perceptual accuracy was in-
> creased by instructions to adopt a reflective attitude, pre-
> sumable because the latency of responding was increased.
> Of particular interest is the finding that black children
> improved more than white children with reflective instructions
> showing superior performance afterward.

383. Harris, A. J. and Lovinger, R. J. Longitudinal measures of
the intelligence of disadvantaged Negro adolescents. School Review,
1968, 76 (1), 60-66.

> A report on a survey designed to test the intelligence of a
> group of disadvantaged adolescents, first read as a paper at
> the October 1965 convention of the Educative Research Associa-
> tion of New York State at Albany. A group of 80 young Negro
> adolescents from Queens was located; they had taken the same
> IQ tests from the first grade through the ninth. The measures
> included administration of the Wechsler Intelligence Scale
> for Children (WISC) in the 7th and 9th grades and group tests
> in the 1st, 3rd, 6th and 8th grades, with the following re-
> sults: (a) the 80 subjects were not a completely representa-
> tive sample of students entering the 7th grade; they scored
> about 4 points higher in $\overline{X}$ IQ and about a half year higher
> in achievement than the Σ group of 196 pupils; (b) there is
> no evidence of declining IQ in this group; (c) the WISC seemed
> in general to be more satisfactory than any of the group
> tests; and (d) the Cattell-Culture-Fair test seems to be quite
> promising as a measure of the intellectual potential of dis-
> advantaged young adolescents. Reprinted by permission.

384. Harris, D. B. and Roberts, J. Intellectual maturity of children: Demographic and socioeconomic factors. Vital and Health
Statistics, Series II, 1972, (116), 74.

Presents the findings of a 1963-1965 survey of a probability
sample of 6- to 11-year-old U. S. children which measured the
intellectual maturity of 7,119 subjects based on the results
of a modified Goodenough-Harris Drawing Test (GHDT). Findings
are presented in relation to key demographic and socioeconomic
factors. (An earlier report gave the results by age and sex.)
Caucasian children performed better than Negro children, but
when variation in parents' education and family income were
controlled, the difference was negligible. Scores in the
Northeast, Midwest and West were approximately the same, but
scores in the South tended to be lower. The size of the
urban or rural community of residence showed no marked relationship to test scores, but children from communities which
were growing during the 1950's made slightly but consistently
better scores than those from communities which lost population. There was a consistent association between higher
test scores and the level of family income and parents'
education, factors which clearly favor the development of
the abilities measured by the GHDT.

385. Harrison, A. and Nadelman, L. Conceptual tempo and inhibition
of movement in black preschool children. Child Development, 1972,
43 (2), 657-668.

Studied the relationships among the impulsivity-reflection
dimension of conceptual tempo and the ability to inhibit
movement and intelligence in 50 black middle class preschool
children. The error and time scores on Kagan's Matching
Familiar Figures Test were used to categorize subjects as
reflective or impulsive. The Draw-A-Line Slowly and Walk
Slowly Tests, scored several ways, measured the subject's
ability to inhibit motor movement on request. The predicted
relation between conceptual tempo and inhibition of movement
was supported, more reflective subjects being significantly
able to inhibit motor movement upon request than impulsive
subjects. Ability to inhibit movement correlated positively
and significantly with response latency and negatively and
significantly with errors. Girls were more reflective and
better inhibitors than boys.

386. Harvey, F. A., et al. Evaluation of eight "Infinity Factory"
programs: Part I. Analysis of the eight-show series. See ERIC
Abstracts, No. ED-129-330, June 1976. 61 pp.

The "Infinity Factory" television series was developed to
help children ages 8 through 11 to understand the usefulness
of some basic mathematics skills for everyday life. Aimed
primarily at black and Latino children, the series concentrates
on: the decimal number system; measurement, especially the
metric system; estimation; mapping and scaling; and graphing.
Throughout the series there is emphasis on creative problem

solving techniques and on a positive student self-image. An
evaluation of eight of the programs was conducted using 1,000
students and their teachers in 39 third-sixth grade classes
in four cities as subjects. The evaluation measured student
attention, appeal of the overall programs and major segments
of each program, student comprehension of story line and gains
in math skills, attitudes toward math, social attitudes, and
teachers' opinions of the effectiveness and usefulness of the
series. This report gives a detailed analysis of the evaluation of the series taken as a whole.

387. Harvey, F. A., et. al. Evaluation of eight "Infinity Factory"
programs. Part II: Show-by-show analysis. See ERIC Abstracts,
No. ED 129-331, June 1976. 82 pp.

"Infinity Factory" is a television series which presents
mathematics in a common-sense way to help children to understand the usefulness of mathematics in their own lives. The
programs are for children ages 8 through 11, especially black
and Latino children. Along with mathematics, the programs
present a positive approach to the cultural and ethnic identity
of minority group children. Major segments of eight programs
and the series as a whole were evaluated. This report contains descriptions of each program and gives data on student
attention, student appeal, teachers' opinions of the programs,
and the number of kinds of related classroom activities.
For each show the report presents: an abstract of its evaluation, a description of the show, a summary of evaluation procedures, and a discussion of the results of the evaluation.

388. Harvey, F. A., et al. Evaluation of eight "Infinity Factory"
programs: Executive Summary. See ERIC Abstracts, No. ED-129-329,
June 1976. 18 pp.

"Infinity Factory" is a television series which presents mathematics in a common-sense way to help children understand the
usefulness of mathematics in their own lives. The 52 programs
in the series are for children ages 8 through 11, especially
black and Latino children. While covering decimal systems,
measurement, estimation, mapping and scaling, graphing, and
problem solving, the series also stresses positive self-images
for minority children and other humanistic goals. An evaluation study was conducted of eight programs, using over 1,000
students, grades three-six, as subjects. The study examined
the programs' effectiveness as a whole and individually. Results showed that the series was effective in imparting math
knowledge, holding student attention, and that teachers considered the programs to be effective and useful.

389. Heitzman, A. J. Effects of a token reinforcement system on
the reading behavior of black migrant primary school pupils. Journal of Educational Research, 1974, 67 (7), 299-302.

A black migrant family school population was investigated
to test the effects of a token reinforcement system on reading

behavior. Subjects were 70 black and 24 white primary school
pupils (token N=55; and no-token N=39). The receipt of tokens
was contingent upon a subject's emitting any response designated by the teacher as reading behavior. When a summer school
reading program was augmented by a token reinforcement system,
positive effects accrued. A token reinforcement system had
varying effects on the learning of black and white primary
school pupils. No relationship was established between the
number of tokens received per pupil and reading skills gains.

390. Henderson, N. B., Fay, W. H., Lindemann, S. J., and Clarkson,
Q. D. Will the IQ test ban decrease the effectiveness of reading
prediction? Journal of Educational Psychology, 1973, 65 (3), 345-355.

Achievement, IQ, and other tests were compared for effectiveness in predicting reading. For pooled subjects and each
separate group, the 7-year-olds' reading test predicted 8-year-
olds' oral reading better than any other test. The battery
and the reading test predicted: (a) not significantly differently for the pooled blacks and whites; (b) best for black
females; (c) poorest for black males; and (d) better for
pooled females than pooled males. Rank of IQ test means for
a group were not directly related to predictive effectiveness.
Alone, the IQ test contributed to no group as much as 27%
of the 8-year reading test variance and accounted in the
multiple regression for less than .04% of added variance.
The IQ score contributed as much to the reading prediction
for blacks as whites.

391. Hess, R. D. and Shipman, V. C. Early experience and the
socialization of cognitive modes in children. Child Development,
1965, 36, 869-886.

This paper deals with the question: What is cultural deprivation and how does it act to shape and depress the resources
of the human mind? The arguments presented are: first, that
the behavior which leads to social, educational, and economic
poverty is socialized in early childhood; second, that the
central quality involved in the effects of cultural deprivation is a lack of cognitive meaning in the mother-child
communication system; and, third, that the growth of cognitive
processes is fostered in family control systems which offer
and permit a wide range of alternatives of action and thought
and that such growth is constricted by systems of control
which offer predetermined solutions and few alternatives for
consideration and choice. The research group was composed
of 160 Negro mothers and their 4-year-old children selected
from four different social status levels. The data are presented to show social status differences among the four groups
with respect to cognitive functioning and linguistic codes and
to offer examples of relations between maternal and child
behavior that are congruent with the general lines of argument laid out.

392. Higgins, C. and Sivers, C. H. A comparison of Stanford-Binet and Colored Raven Progressive Matrices IQs for children with low socioeconomic status. Journal of Consulting Psychology, 1958, 22, 465-468.

393. Hilliard, A. G. The intellectual strengths of black children and adolescents: A challenge to pseudo-science. Journal of Non-White Concerns in Personnel Guidance, 1974, 2 (4), 178-190.

Genetic explanations for discovered differences between racial groups on tests of aptitude and achievement are reviewed. A sample of research pertaining to the black child and adolescent is presented with an extended set of references, and directions for future research are suggested. While primary focus is on blacks, the points developed are relevant to any ethnic or racial minority or any economically powerless group.

394. Hollingworth, L. S. and Witty, P. Intelligence as related to race. National Society for the Study of Education Yearbook, 1940, 39, 257-269.

The senior author discusses the problem of comparing races, outlining the position of anthropology, the present status of the concept of race, and the concept of census groups. Witty reviews the research dealing with the American Negro, with particular reference to one recent study. Conclusions from this investigation prove the falsity of the belief in the "lack of educability and the general constitutional inferiority of Negro children." "Superior Negro children resemble other groups of American children who are superior in test-intelligence." Suggested research topics in the field of race intelligence are listed.

395. Hollowinsky, I. Z. and Pascale, P. J. Performance on selected WISC subtests of subjects referred for psychological evaluation because of educational difficulties. Journal of Special Education, 1972, 6 (3), 231-235.

Investigated race and sex differences in the WISC performance of 50 male and 27 female black children, and 39 male and 18 female white children, referred for psychological evaluation. Subjects had a mean IQ of 79.55, a standard deviation of 12.52, and an IQ range of 57-129. Significant race differences occurred on only the Vocabulary subtest, with white children performing better than black children (p<.01). Boys performed significantly better than girls on the Picture Completion, Information, Vocabulary, and Block Design subtests (p<.05). The smallest F ratio for race differences occurred on the Block Design subtest. Subjects performed better on the Picture Completion subtest than on any other subtest. Findings do not support the hypothesis of racial differences in intelligence.

396. Horton, C. P. and Crump, E. P.   Growth and development: XI.
Description analysis of the backgrounds of 76 Negro children whose
scores are above or below average on the Merrill-Palmer Scale of
Mental Tests at three years of age. Journal of Genetic Psychology,
1962, 100 (2), 255-265.

    Subjects were 76 Negro children whose percentile scores on
    the Merrill-Palmer Scale of Mental Tests fell within 1-19 and
    80-99 at 36 months of age. Characteristics of both the child
    and his family were analyzed descriptively in relation to test
    performance, and included sex, birth weight, height and weight
    at 36 months, SES, education of parents, employment of mother,
    number of siblings, parents' marital status, and occupation
    of father.

397. Houtz, J. C. and Feldhusen, J. F. Problem solving ability of
disadvantaged elementary school children under four testing formats:
A replicated experiment. Psychology in the Schools, 1975, 12 (1),
26-33.

    Four forms of the Purdue Elementary Problem Solving Inventory,
    a test designed to measure the emerging problem solving skills
    of "disadvantaged" children, were developed. The four forms
    were designed to represent four levels of a continuum from
    abstract to concrete modes of representation of the problem
    stimuli. One form presented subjects with stories of people,
    objects and actions in a problem situation; a second form pre-
    sented cartoon black and white line drawings of the scenes;
    a third form presented the drawings life size as slides
    projected in front of the classroom; and a fourth form pre-
    sented full color, two-dimensional and three-dimensional
    models of the scenes. Two studies were conducted. In both,
    nondisadvantaged and disadvantaged second and fourth grade
    children participated. Results demonstrated that subjects
    on the models, slides, and picture forms significantly out-
    performed subjects on the stories form, regardless of grade
    or socioeconomic status.

398. Hughes, R. B. and Lessler, K. A comparison of WISC and Peabody scores of Negro and white rural school children. American
Journal of Mental Deficiency, 1965, 69 (6), 877-880.

    137 Negro and white culturally deprived from a rural county,
    and who were suspected of being mentally retarded, were given
    the WISC and PPVT to see if the PPVT could be substituted
    for the WISC as an individual test of intelligence. The WISC
    and PPVT were positively correlated with predictable race
    and sex differences occurring. It was concluded that even
    though standard error of estimates were relatively large,
    the PPVT could be substituted for the WISC as a screening
    instrument for use in the schools or by mental health per-
    sonnel.

399. Iscoe, I. and Pierce-Jones, J. Divergent thinking, age and
intelligence in white and Negro children. Child Development, 1964,
35 (3), 785-797.

    Ideational-fluency and ideational-flexibility scores were
    obtained from an unusual Uses Test given to 267 Texas white
    and Negro school children aged 5 to 9. Overall, these
    divergent-thinking scores were significantly higher for
    Negroes and showed low, significant r's with WISC for both
    races. Fluency scores were not dependent upon age as such,
    but upon race as such and in interaction with age. Flexibi-
    lity scores showed no overall relations with age or race.
    Certain interesting comparisons by WISC subtests, flexibility
    categories, and five age levels, are discussed and inter-
    preted. Doubts are raised concerning the notion of creative
    thinking as a simple function of age or of intelligence --
    there is need for more developmental studies of originality
    in varied social and cultural contexts.

400. Jackson, J. and Ayrer, J. Sickle cell trait and scholastic
achievement. Journal of Negro Education, 1974, 43 (4), 452-456.

    A longitudinal study of the scholastic achievement of black
    children from grades 4 thru 7 tested the hypothesis that there
    is no significant interaction effect between scholastic
    achievement and sickle cell trait. 29 students with reading
    comprehension, total arithmetic and composite grade equiva-
    lent, as determined by the Iowa Test of Basic Skills, were
    used as dependent variables and compared with the scores of
    29 control subjects. The results indicate that the sickle
    cell trait does not affect scholastic achievement. Implica-
    tions for further research in this area are discussed.

401. Jackson, T. S. Racial inferiority among Negro children. Crisis,
1940, 47, 241-266.

402. Jantz, R. K. and Sciara, F. J. Does living with a female
head-of-household affect the arithmetic achievement of black fourth
grade pupils? Psychology in the Schools, 1975, 12 (4), 468-472.

    Studied the records of 1,073 black fourth graders, of whom 300
    were living with a female head-of-household and 773 with a
    male head-of-household. No significant differences were found
    in mean scores between male and female subjects on the Metro-
    politan Achievement Test. Significant differences were found
    favoring those subjects living with male heads-of-household,
    particulary for females and for subjects with Lorge-Thorndike
    IQs over 100. It is noted that findings should not be con-
    sidered as simple cause and effect relationships but rather
    as indicative of potential difficulty for some pupils.

403. Jencks, C. and Brown, M. The effects of desegregation on student achievement: Some new evidence from the Equality of Educational Opportunity Survey. Sociology of Education, 1975, 48 (1),
126-140.

     Re-analysis of the 1966 Equality of Educational Opportunity
     Survey, using a quasilongitudinal design, suggests that the
     test performance of students in 51-75% white schools improved
     relative to national norms between first and sixth grade.
     Both black and white students in such schools showed improve-
     ment. Black students' performance relative to national norms
     seemed to decline slightly if they were in 76-100% white
     schools and seemed to remain constant if they were in 0-50%
     white schools. The racial composition of a high school did
     not appear to have had any appreciable effect on either black
     or white students' test scores between ninth and twelfth
     grades.

404. Jenkins, M. D. Case studies of Negro children of Binet IQ at
160 and above. Journal of Negro Education, 1943, 12, 159-166.

     Case studies of 14 Negro children of IQ 160 and above are
     summarized. On the basis of this material, the conclusions
     are reached that there is an appreciable number of Negro
     children of extremely high IQ, suggesting that Negroes are
     as variable as other racial groups; that extreme deviates
     in psychometric intelligence may remain unrecognized and
     thus denied the type of educational experience necessary
     for them; and that society limits the development of these
     gifted children.

405. Jenkins, M. D. Intellectually superior Negro youth: Problems
and needs. Journal of Negro Education, 1950, 19, 322-332.

     Negroes with Binet IQs above 160 are not as rare as supposed.
     The case records of 18 were assembled and studied. They were
     found not to differ essentially from bright white children of
     their intellectual level. However, the Negro child has less
     chance of being identified, has less attention paid to his
     special needs, receives less adequate guidance, has less
     chance of achievement because of a non-stimulating environ-
     ment, has greater financial difficulty in getting through
     school, and expends a greater proportion of his energy and
     intelligence on racial problems.

406. Jenkins, M. D. The intelligence of Negro children. Educational Methods, 1939, 19, 106-112. (Also, see Educational Abstract,
V:201.)

407. Jenkins, M. D. A socio-psychological study of Negro children
of superior intelligence. Journal of Negro Education, 1936, 5, 175-190.

     Subjects of this study were taken from grades three through
     eight of the public schools of Chicago. 103 children of
     Stanford-Binet IQ 120 or above were selected. Each child was

rated by one teacher on traits such as leadership, originality, etc. Interviews with parents furnished information relative to heredity, environment, developmental history and interests. The following tests were administered: New Stanford Achievement Test, Advanced Examination, Form W; Personality Index; pupil report and Sims Score Card for socioeconomic status. The data assembled suggest that "intelligence, as well as educability, are matters of individual difference rather than racial differences." Relatively large numbers of Negro children of very superior intelligence have been reported by other investigators. Girls with superior intelligence are found with more frequency than boys; on the basis of Stanford-Binet IQ, the ratio is 233:100. Throughout the several grade and age levels, superior Negro children are evenly spread. The IQ 200 of one Negro girl shows that Negro children are found in the very highest level of test performance. Negro ancestry is not a limiting factor in intelligence-test performance. Superior Negro children do not differ from other superior children.

408. Jenkins, M.D. The upper limit of ability among American Negroes. Science Monitor - New York, 1948, 66, 399-401.

Examination of a variety of studies leads to the conclusion that: "In some population groups there is to be found a 'normal' proportion of Negro subjects of very superior psychometric intelligence, and the extreme deviates reach the upper limits attained by white subjects. Although the incidence of superior cases is much lower among Negroes than whites, a phenomenon which might well be accounted for by differential environmental factors, we conclude that race per se (at least as it is represented in the American Negro) is not a limiting factor in psychometric intelligence."

409. Jensen, A. R. Cumulative deficit: A testable hypothesis. Developmental Psychology, 1974, 10 (6), 996-1019.

Discusses theoretical issues and the methodological problems involved in establishing the progressive decrement phenomenon in relation to the relevant research on disadvantaged groups, especially American blacks. In this group in particular there is no methodologically adequate evidence in the literature for a progressive decrement in IQ or other mental measurements. The present study with over 8,000 black and white elementary school children used differences between younger and older siblings, which satisfies more rigorous methodological requirements for the detection of progressive decrement than have existed in previous studies. A significant age decrement was found in Lorge-Thorndike Verbal IQ, but not in Nonverbal IQ, among blacks, although the mean white-black difference was similar for Nonverbal and Verbal IQ.

410. Jensen, A. R. The effect of race of examiner on the mental
test scores of white and black pupils. Journal of Educational Measurement, 1974, 11 (1), 1-14.

The effect of race of examiner on the mental test scores of
white and black pupils was investigated in one elementary
school system with 60% white and 40% black students, who were
given several ability tests by 12 white and 8 black examiners.
The test measured verbal and nonverbal IQ, perceptual-motor
cognitive development, speed and persistence under neutral
and motivating instructions, listening attention, and short-
term rote memory for numbers. With the exception of the speed
and persistence test, on which white examiners yielded significantly and consistently higher mean scores than black
examiners for both white and black pupils across grades one
to six, the results for the various cognitive ability tests
showed that race of examiner did not produce large or consistent effects in pupil testing.

411. Jensen, A. R. Ethnicity and scholastic achievement. Psychological Reports, 1974, 34 (2), 659-668.

Predicted scores on eight tests of scholastic achievement
(e.g., Stanford Achievement Test) by multiple regression
techniques from seven nonscholastic tests of ability (e.g.,
Lorge-Thorndike Intelligence Test and Raven's Progressive
Matrices), the Junior Eysenck Personality Inventory, and items
of personal background data, from 2,237 Anglo, 1,694 averaged
over grade level, the multiple correlation (R) between the
predictor variables and achievement scores was .60-.80 for
various school subjects. Ethnicity made no significant
contribution to the multiple (R) independently of the several
predictor variables.

412. Jensen, A. R. How biased are culture loaded tests? Genetic
Psychology Monographs, 1974, 90 (2), 185-244.

Conducted three studies in which the culture-loaded Peabody
Picture Vocabulary Test (PPVT) and the culture-reduced Raven's
Progressive Matrices (Colored and Standard forms) were compared on various internal criteria of culture bais. Subjects
were a total of 6,170 Anglo-American, black, and Mexican-
American school children, from kindergarten through eighth
grade, in three California school districts. On both the
PPVT and the Raven, the three ethnic groups (which showed
large mean differences) showed little difference in the rank
order of item difficulties, the relative difficulty of adjacent
items, the loadings of items on the first principal component,
and the choice of distractors for incorrect responses. Analysis
of variance (ANOVA) revealed very small Ethnic Group x Items
interaction, but an index of item bias derived from ANOVA
indicates that the Raven was considerably less biased than
the PPVT, especially in the Mexican-American group. The
Group x Items interaction was shown to be attributable
largely to differences in mental maturity. On both test

groups of culturally homogeneous younger and older white children (separated by two years) perfectly simulated the white-black differences in Group x Item interactions and choice of error distractors in the Raven. Certain expectations from a culture bias hypothesis were borne out only for the PPVT in the Mexican group. It is suggested that unless the empirically unsubstantiated assumption is made that culture bias affects all kinds of test items equally, the various item analyses of the present studies lend no support to the proposition that either the PPVT or the Raven is a culturally biased test for blacks.

413. Jensen, A. R. How much can we boost IQ and scholastic achievement? Harvard Educational Review, 1969, 39, 1-123.

Supports the contention that environmental influences are not as important in determining I.Q. or genetic factors. It is argued that prenatal factors are the most relevant environmental influences and that social class and social variables in intelligence cannot be accounted for in terms of environmental differences alone. Changes in IQ produced by compensatory education programs are generally small. The environment acts as a "threshold" variable. While environmental deprivation can prevent a child from performing up to his genetic potential. Environmental methods based on specific skills and mental abilities other than the IQ need to be developed. Diversity rather than uniformity of approaches and aim is suggested as the key to effective education programs.

414. Jensen, A. R. Intelligence, learning ability and socioeconomic status. Journal of Special Education, 1969, 3 (1), 23-35.

Compared two groups of 4- to 14-year-old Caucasian, Negro and Mexican-American children, one group of low socioeconomic status (SES) and one of middle and upper middle SES, on associative learning tests (free recall, serial learning, paired-associate learning, and digit span) and standardized intelligence tests (Stanford-Binet, Peabody Picture Vocabulary, Progressive Matrices). Subjects from a low SES background with IQs of 60 to 80 performed, in general, much better on the associative learning tasks than did middle SES subjects in the same IQ range. However, the learning performance of low SES subjects of above average IQ were not significantly different from those of middle SES subjects of the same IQ. Results are interpreted in terms of a two-level hierarchical model of mental abilities, going from associative learning to cognitive or conceptual learning and problem solving, in which the development of the lower-level associative abilities is necessary but not sufficient for the development of higher level conceptual abilities.

415.   Jensen, A. R.   Interaction of Level I and Level II abilities
with race and socioeconomic status. <u>Journal of Psychology</u>, 1974, <u>66</u>
(1), 99-111.

Two levels of mental abilities were hypothesized, based on
Jensen's Level I - Level II Theory to interact with socioeconomic
status (SES) and/or race, such that: (a) SES differences were
greater for Level II than for Level I abilities; (b) the correlation between Levels I and II, and the regression of Level I
upon Level II, were greater in upper than in lower SES populations. These hypotheses were borne out by the present data,
consisting of Level I measures (Digit Span Memory) and Level II
measures (Lorge-Thorndike Intelligence Tests, Verbal and Nonverbal) obtained on all white and black pupils in grades four
to six in one school district. The largest effects were attributable to differences between the white population and the
low SES black group.

416.   Jensen, A. R.   Jensen's theory of intelligence: A reply.
<u>Journal of Educational Psychology</u>, 1969, <u>60</u> (6), 427-433.

The criticism of A. R. Jensen's "theory of intelligence" by
L. G. Humphreys and P. Dackler lacks cogency because it: (a)
takes account of a limited portion of the evidence, and (b)
tests the theory by using data from Project TALENT based on
mental tests which are unsuited for this purpose.

417.   Jensen, A. R.   Level I and Level II abilities in three ethnic
groups. <u>American Educational Research Journal</u>, 1973, <u>10</u> (4), 263-
276.

A large battery of various tests of intelligence, scholastic
achievement, and short-term memory, was given to 2,000 white,
Negro and Mexican-American pupils in grades four, five and six
in a largely agricultural school district. The grades were
used as separate replications. Factor analysis with oblique
rotation yielded three main factors, identified as fluid and
crystallized intelligence (both being aspects of Level II
ability in Jensen's theory) and a memory factor (a Level I
ability). Mean factor scores for the three ethnic groups
differed significantly and showed Jensen's two-level theory
of abilities. Whites and Negroes differed markedly in fluid
and crystallized IQ, but not in memory. White and Mexican
groups differed markedly in crystallized intelligence, but
much less in fluid intelligence and memory. Negroes and
Mexicans differed most in fluid intelligence, but only
slightly in crystallized intelligence. Systematic ethnic
group differences occurred in the pattern of intercorrelations among factor scores, and in the correlations of the
factor scores with an index of socioeconomic status. Results are discussed in relation to Jensen's two-level theory
and Cattell's theory of fluid and crystallized intelligence.

418.   Jensen, A. R.   Social class, race and genetics: Implications
for education.   American Educational Research Journal, 1968, 5 (1),
1-42.

Present educational practices have proved unsuccessful in providing a segment of our population with the knowledge and
skills needed for economic self-sufficiency in a technological
society.   Literal equality of educational opportunity will not
solve this problem.   Failure to give due weight to the biological basis of individual and group differences in educationally relevant traits and abilities, and social environment factors, may hinder our efforts to discover optimal
instructional procedures suited to a diversity of abilities.
Inappropriate instruction procedures, often based on the
notion that all children learn in essentially the same way
except for easily changed environmental influences, can
alienate many children from ever entering upon any path of
educational fulfillment.

419.   Jensen, A. R.   A statistical note on racial differences in
the progressive matrices.   Journal of Consulting Psychology, 1959, 23,
273-274.

420.   Jensen, A. R.   Test bias and construct validity.   Paper presented
at the Annual Meeting of the American Psychological Association, 83rd,
Chicago, Illinois, September 1975.   31 pp.   Also, see ERIC Abstracts,
No. ED-114-415, 1975.

The several statistical methods described for detecting test
bias in terms of various internal features of a person's test
performances and the test's construct validity can be applied
to any groups in the population.   But the evidence regarding
groups other than U.S. blacks and whites is either lacking or
is still too sketchy to permit any strong conclusions.   The
evidence regarding black-white comparisons, however, is based
on a number of well-known, widely used, and quite diverse
standardized individual and group tests of intelligence given
to a large representative sample of whites and blacks.   The
results are unequivocal: none of the several subjective
indices of cultural bias shows any significant indication of
bias in any of these tests when they are used with blacks and
whites.   Correlation of raw scores with age, internal consistency reliability, rank order of item difficulty, relative
difficulty of adjacent items, item correlation with total
score, loadings of items or tests on the general factor, and
relative frequencies in choice of error distractors -- all
are substantially the same in black and white groups.   It is
concluded that these standardized tests of intelligence -- the
Peabody Picture Vocabulary, Raven's Progressive Matrices,
Wechsler Intelligence Scale for Children, Stanford-Binet,
Wonderlic Personnel Test, and most likely other similar tests
-- are not at all culturally biased for blacks and whites.
They behave statistically the same in both racial groups and
do essentially the same job in both groups.

421.   Jensen, A. R. and Figueroa, R. A.   Forward and backward digit
span interaction with race and IQ: Predictions from Jensen's theory.
Journal of Educational Psychology, 1975, 67, 882-893.

   It was predicted that forward digit span (FDS) should correlate
   less with IQ than backward digit span (BDS), and age and race
   should interact with FDS-BDS, with the FDS-BDS difference
   decreasing as a function of age and a greater white-black
   difference in BDS than in FDS. The predictions were substantiated in white and black subjects of ages 5-12 years who
   were given the WISC.

422.   Jensen, A. R. and Fredericksen, J.   Free recall of categorized
and uncategorized lists: A test of the Jensen hypothesis. Journal
of Educational Psychology, 1973, 65 (3), 304-312.

   Examined A. R. Jensen's two-level theory of mental abilities
   (Level I - rote learning and memory; and Level II - abstrac-
   tions and conceptual learning) in terms of Level I and Level II
   learning tasks (free recall of uncategorized and categorized
   lists, respectively) administered to Caucasian and Negro
   second and fourth graders (N=120). Performance measures
   were amount recalled and amount of clustering in recall of
   the categorized list. Results accord with previous studies
   based on other Level I - Level II tests given to children of
   low and middle socioeconomic status (both Caucasian and Negro)
   in different age groups, i.e., a larger socioeconomic status
   (or Negro-Caucasian) difference on Level II than on Level I
   measures, the difference increasing with age.

423.   John, V. P.   The intellectual development of slum children:
Some preliminary findings. American Journal of Orthopsychiatry,
1963, 33 (5), 813-822.

   This study examines certain patterns of linguistic and cognitive behavior in a sample of Negro children from various
   social classes. Three major levels of language behavior --
   labeling, relating, categorizing -- were analyzed. Consistent
   class differences in language skills were shown to emerge
   between groups of Negro children of different socioeconomic
   class.

424.   Johnson, G.   A comparison of two evaluation instruments for
the analyses of academic potential of Negro children. Phylon, 1959,
20, 44-47.

425.   Johnson, J. C. II and Jacobson, M. D.   Operation Summer-Thrust:
A study of the conceptual and verbal development of the culturally
and educationally disadvantaged primary grade pupil. Journal of
Negro Education, 1970, 39 (2), 171-176.

   A report of an investigation into the efficacy of a course of
   study developed to enhance the conceptualization and verbal
   proficiencies of primary grade Negro children who had been
   categorized as both educationally and culturally disadvan-

taged. 45 elementary school children, 15 each from kindergarten, first and second grade, who were ill-prepared to begin formal reading activities, were participants in a summer instructional program dedicated to the enhancement of functioning conceptual ability and verbal proficiency. The subjects were administered the Peabody Picture Vocabulary Test, the Metropolitan Reading Readiness Test and the Johnson Readiness Test during the first week of the program. In addition, the kindergarten children received the Johnson Listening Test while the older children received the Dolch Sight Vocabulary Test. The analysis comparing pre- and post-test measures demonstrated that the experimental program brought about an average gain for all three grades of 15.1 IQ points in verbal conceptual ability as measured by the Peabody Picture Vocabulary Test. This gain is statistically significant and educationally important. It also demonstrated that gains in overall verbal ability were limited to the kindergarten and first grade groups. It was also helpful at the second grade in developing reading readiness. Reprinted by permission.

426. Johnson, P. C. The intellectual growth of Virginia State College students. Virginia State College State Gazette, 1947, 53, 51-61.

The study sought to determine whether there was any evidence of intellectual growth in a group of students at a Negro college. In September 1943, 145 freshmen were given the Otis Quick Scoring Mental Abilities Test, Form Gamma A.M., and they took the test again in January 1946 as juniors. The means of the first and second tests were 96.3 and 102.0 respectively, and the difference was significant. A positive change was shown by 121 students, a negative change by 17, and no change by 7 students. The change decreases with an increase in the IQ and is negative with those with IQs over 120. Fifteeen students who showed increases in IQ of more than 12 were interviewed, and included the following factors in their explanation of their poorer results on the first test: unsatisfactory adjustment to college life; lack of familiarity with standard tests; general nervousness; poor study habits; and poor educational background.

427. Jones, F. N. The exploration of physical phenomena given by white and Negro school children. Psychological Bulletin, 1944, 41, 588.

428. Jones, F. N. and Arrington, M. G. The explanations of physical phenomena given by white and Negro children. Comparative Psychology Monograph, 1945, 18 (5), 43.

Closely following Deutsch's procedures for studying concepts of causal relations, these investigators made a qualitative and quantitative study of the study of the explanations of physical phenomena given by 161 Negro and 134 white children in grades 3 through 8. The aim was to discover whether there is justification for the claim that Negroes are more superstitious than whites. Results do not support this claim. Very

few answers in either group could be classified as supernatural
or superstititious, and it is concluded that: (1) "in view
of the inequalities in scholastic and other opportunities for
our two groups, the differences obtained were (a) less striking than the similarities, and (b) readily attributable to
environmental causes." (2) "The Negro children do not tend
to be superstitious or supernatural in their approach to
concrete situations, either as compared to the white sample
or in absolute number of responses."

429. Justman, J. Academic aptitude and reading test scores of
disadvantaged children showing varying degrees of mobility. Journal
of Educational Measurement, 1965, 2 (2), 151-155.

Otis IQs and Metropolitan Reading test scores of 934 pupils
from 16 schools in disadvantaged areas of New York City were
found to be negatively associated with degree of mobility.
Pupils who had attended only one school showed near average
functioning, whereas progressively poorer performance was
associated with number of schools attended.

430. Kaltsounis, B. Differences in creative thinking of black and
white deaf children. Perceptual and Motor Skills, 1971, 32 (1),
243-248.

Fluency, flexibility, originality, and elaboration scores were
obtained from Thinking Creatively With Pictures, Form A, given
to 233 white and black deaf children in grades 1, 2, 3, and 4.
Fluency scores were not dependent upon race as such but upon
grade level as such and in interaction with race. Flexibility
scores showed an overall relation with race and grade level
but not with sex. Originality scores were independent of
grade level, race, and sex. Elaboration scores were dependent
upon race and grade level and upon interaction of race with
grade level. Reprinted by permission.

431. Kaplan, H. and Matkom, A. Peer status and intellectual functioning of Negro children. Psychology in the Schools, 1967, 4 (2),
181-184.

372 children in each of 14 classes, grades two through eight,
were placed in rank order by sociometric techniques. It was
concluded that: (a) when Negro and white children of similar
sociometric status were compared, the white children tended
to have higher intelligence and reading scores; (b) rejections
were based on sex rather than racial factors; and (c) sociometric choices were not a reflection of the Negro-white feelings of the community.

432. Katz, I. Review of evidence relating to effects of desegregation on the intellectual performance of Negroes. American Psychology,
1964, 19 (6), 381-399.

A summary of the evidence regarding the effect of school desegregation on the academic performance of young Negroes.

Where the discrepancy of educational standards of Negro and white schools is marked, or where feelings of inferiority are acquired by Negro children outside the school, the minority groups in integrated classrooms are prone to have a low expectancy of academic success, with a lowering of achievement motivation. Rejection by white classmates of teachers should tend to elicit emotional responses (e.g., fear, anger, etc.) that are detrimental to intellectual functioning. When academic failure involves disapproval by significant others, emotional responses detrimental to performance are elicited by low expectancy of success. Acceptance by white peers should have a social facilitation effect on learning ability, and the anticipation of white approval should give scholastic success high-incentive value. Experimentally-created verbal-task situations low in social and failure threat, resulted in better performance by Negroes in the presence of whites than in the presence of other Negroes, suggesting that the white environment had greater incentive value of success. Suppression of hostile impulses occurred in Negro subjects tested by a white adult but not those tested by a Negro. Implications for educational practice are noted. Reprinted by permission.

433. Katz, I. Some motivational determinants of racial differences in intellectual achievement. International Journal of Psychology, 1967, 2 (1), 1-12.

Motivational studies of conditions that affect hope for success, kinds of social reinforcement as they affect achievement, and attitudes related to achievement, clarify the achievement gap existing between white and Negro students. The motivational formulation of Atkinson, Crandall and Rotter can help to integrate factors known about performance of minority group students. Future research could consider these factors in one- and two-race performance situations. Study of children in socially integrated (as opposed to simply desegregated) classrooms is particularly needed.

434. Katz, I, Henchy, T., and Allen, H. Effects of race of tester, approval-disapproval, and need on Negro children's learning. Journal of Personality and Social Psychology, 1968, 8 (1, Part 1), 38-42.

148 northern Negro boys of elementary school age were first administered a social desirability questionnaire, and then a verbal learning task, by white and Negro male examiners. Every subject received either approval or disapproval on the learning task. Performance was better with Negro testers, and when approval was given. Also, there was an interaction of the two variables with need for approval, as measured by the social desirability questionnaire. The race-of-the-examiner effects were predicted from an assumption that subjects would perceive Negro adults as more nurturant than white adults.

435.   Katz, P. A.   Role of irrelevant cues in the formation of
concepts in low class children.   Journal of Educational Psychology,
1968, 59 (4), 233-238.

Attempted to assess differences in concept formation abilities
of children at varying developmental stages.   The concept task
employed was a perceptual oriented one, with stimulus dimensions verbalized in advance and positive exemplars of the
concepts continuously visible to the children.   Results
obtained on 72 first, third and fifth grade Negro lower class
males revealed differences in concept ability associated with
both CA and IQ scores.   Increasing the amount of irrelevant
stimulus information elicited more errors in all age groups
but this variable did not interact significantly with developmental level.   The response latencies of the older and bright-
est subjects increased with the number of irrelevant cues,
whereas those of the less intelligent subjects did not.   This
finding was interpreted as suggestive of possible developmental
differences in information processing.

436.   Katz, P. A. and Seavey, C.   Labels and children's perception
of faces.   Child Development, 1973, 44 (4), 770-775.

The relation between type of label and perception of faces
was assessed.   64 second and sixth grade subjects were randomly assigned to four experimental conditions in which various
kinds of labeling training were associated with four purple
and green smiling and frowning faces.   All subjects then
judged the similarity of pairs of the faces.   Results reveal
the predicted effects of labeling only for white children.
Labels associated with color cues augmented the perception
of color differences, whereas labels based on expression
increased differentiation of expression variations, but not
of color cues.

437.   Kaufman, A. S.   Comparison of the performance of matched
groups of black children and white children on the Wechsler Preschool and Primary Scale of Intelligence.   Journal of Consulting
and Clinical Psychology, 1973, 41 (2), 186-191.

The intellectual ability of matched groups of black and white
children, 4 to 6-1/2 years old, were compared based on the
Wechsler Preschool and Primary Scale of Intelligence Verbal,
Performance and Full Scale IQs.   Subjects were matched on
age, sex, geographic region, father's occupation, and urban-
rural residence.   The whites had significantly higher verbal
and full scale IQs at all age levels.   Performance IQ, however,
was significantly higher for the whites in the youngest group,
but not for those aged 5 to 5-1/2, and 6 to 6-1/2, years.
Results were compared with previous findings, and the implications are discussed in terms of perceptual experiences.

438. Kaufman, A. S. Comparisons of WPPSI IQs obtained by matched
groups of black and white children. Proceedings of the Annual Convention of the American Psychological Association, 1972, 7 (1), 39-40.

> Compared the Wechsler Preschool and Primary Scale of Intelli-
> gence Verbal (V), Performance (P), and Full Scale (FS) IQs
> of blacks and whites who were matched on five variables in-
> cluding father's occupation. 132 matched pairs (4- to 4-1/2-
> year-olds) were obtained from the standardization sample. The
> whites had significantly higher V and FS IQs at all age
> levels, but the differences were about 10 points, rather
> than the 15 usually reported. P, however, was not signifi-
> cantly higher in the 5- to 6-1/2-year-olds, and the differences
> in P scores decreased almost linearly with increasing age.
> Implications of the results in relation to school experiences
> are discussed.

439. Kaufman, A. S. and DiCuio, R. F. Separate factor analyses of
the McCarthy scales for groups of black and white children. Journal
of School Psychology, 1975 (Spring), 13 (1), 10-18.

> Performed factor analyses of the McCarthy Scales of Children's
> Abilities (MSCA) on separate groups of black (N=124) and white
> (N=688) 3- to 7-year-olds to assess the comparability of the
> underlying structures and to evaluate the construct validity
> of the MSCA for each racial group. Little Jiffy I (principal
> components) solutions produced four factors for the blacks
> and three for the whites. Each white factor had a coefficient
> of congruence of .85-.93 with one black factor, indicating
> the close similarity of the solutions. In addition, the
> factors which emerged for the blacks and whites corresponded
> to several of the scales constituting the MSCA, offering evi-
> dence of the instrument's construct validity for each racial
> group.

440. Kaufman, A. S. and Hollenbeck, G. P. Comparative structure
of the WPPSI for blacks and whites. Journal of Clinical Psychology,
1974, 30 (3), 316-319.

> The Wechsler Preschool and Primary Scales of Intelligence
> (WPPSI) standardization sample was divided into black and white
> groups, and the comparative structure of the WPPSI was ex-
> plored. Each correlation matrix was subjected to three factor
> analytic techniques to assess the stability of the structures.
> Each analysis for the blacks and whites produced two factors:
> verbal and performance. The black and white verbal factors
> were found to be highly congruent, as were the performance
> factors. It is concluded that the abilities assessed by the
> WPPSI are the same, and correspond closely to Wechsler's
> designated scales, for both black and white children.

441. Kaufman, A. S. and Kaufman, N. I. Black-white differences at
ages 2-1/2 to 8-1/2 on the McCarthy Scale of Children's Abilities.
Journal of School Psychology, 1973, 11 (3), 196-206.

> Compared matched groups of black and white children on the new
> McCarthy Scales of Children's Abilities. Using the standard-
> ization sample as the data source, 148 matched pairs were
> obtained. These were grouped as follows: ages 2-1/2 to 3-1/2
> (N=43); 4 to 5-1/2 (N=60); 6-1/2 to 8-1/2 (N=45). Blacks and
> whites did not differ significantly on any of the cognitive
> scales at ages 2-1/2 to 3-1/2 and 4 to 5-1/2, although at ages
> 6-1/2 to 8-1/2 the whites scored slightly higher. The blacks
> scored significantly higher on the Motor Scale at ages 4 to
> 5-1/2, but there were no differences at other ages.

442. Kee, D. W. and Rohwer, W. D. Jr. Noun-pair learning in four
ethnic groups: Conditions of presentation and response. Journal of
Educational Psychology, 1973, 65 (2), 226-232.

> Noun-pair learning efficiency was assessed within four low
> socioeconomic status ethnic groups (blacks, Chinese-Americans,
> Spanish-Americans, and whites) as a function of presentation
> conditions and method of measurement (verbal recall vs. pictoral
> recognition). A mixed list paired-associate task was adminis-
> tered individually to 40 second grade children from each group.
> Results revealed substantial effects for presentation condi-
> tions but not for ethnic groups. Similar patterns of condi-
> tion effects emerged across response modes for all ethnic
> groups. Findings were taken as evidence of the generality
> of presentation condition effects in noun-pair learning as
> an empirical demonstration of parity in learning ability for
> children from different ethnic backgrounds.

443. Kennedy, W. A. A follow-up normative study of Negro intelligence and achievement. Monographs of the Society for Research in
Child Development, 1969, 34 (2), 40.

> Presents "a reassessment of a representative sample of strati-
> fied, random sample of 1,800 Negro elementary school children
> who were tested in the Fall of 1960 academic year. The mean
> of the Stanford-Binet, Form L-M, in 1960 was 79.2; in 1965 it
> was 79.4, a nonsignificant change. The standard deviation in
> the sample increased from 12.6 in 1960 to 14.3 in 1965, and
> the range in scores increased slightly. Although there was
> a tendency for the IQs to remain constant across grade level,
> as had been observed in 1960, there was again the obvious
> decline in IQ associated with chronological age. . . . The
> California Achievement Test data revealed a continuation of
> the trend, so clearly noticed in 1960, for Negro children to
> continue to fall behind academically, such that the amount
> of retardation at the tenth grade level is severe. Although
> the number of dropouts in the sample thus far has been small,
> nevertheless the children are clearly in serious academic
> difficulty when compared with the national normative sample."

444. Kennedy, W. A. and Lindner, R. S. A normative study of the Goodenough Draw-A-Man Test on Southeastern Negro elementary school children. Child Development, 1964, 35, 33-67.

To obtain test performance masures for a large representative sample of Negroes in the Southweastern United States to examine certain cultural variable effects, and to determine the effectiveness of the Goodenough in relation to other IQ scores, achievement test scores, and teacher ratings. A stratified random sampling of 1,800 Negro elementary school children was used in a study designed not to defend the Goodenough as an intelligence test, but to add to its precision as an intellectual screening device. By computing new weights for this population, a correlation of .67 was obtained with the Stanford-Binet, Form L-M.

445. Kennedy, W. A., Van de Riet, V., and White, J. C. Jr. A normative sample of intelligence and achievement of Negro elementary school children in the Southeastern United States. Monographs of the Society for Research in Child Development, 1963, 28 (6).

To provide normative data on a large, homogeneous sample upon which there were no previous normative data on intelligence to individual psychologists and educators who perform diagnostic evaluations on Negro school children, a sample from five southeastern states of 1,800 Negro elementary school children evenly distributed by grade and between rural, urban, and metropolitan counties was used to standardize the 1960 revision, Form L-M, of the Stanford-Binet Intelligence Test and the California Achievement Test. The sample had a mean IQ of 80.7, a SD of 12.4. There was a high correlation between the Binet IQ and the CAT. This research uncovered few surprises. That Negro elementary school children score significantly lower on intelligence tests was expected from a review of previous research. That the achievement scores would be significantly lower than the standardization sample follows logically, as they also depend upon cultural and socioeconomic factors. That the intelligence and achievement test scores would vary positively with socioeconomic levels and negatively with age could be deduced. That there was no significant difference in intelligence scores from grade level to grade level or from rural to metropolitan counties is surprising and difficult to explain, but probably relates to promotional and migrational characteristics.

446. Kennedy, W. A., Van de Riet, V., and White, J. C. Jr. Use of the Terman-Merrill Abbreviated Scale over the 1960 Stanford-Binet, Form L-M, on the Negro elementary school children of the Southeastern United States. Journal of Consulting Psychology, 1963, 27 (5), 456-457.

Consideration was given to the degree of precision which would have been lost had the Abbreviated Scale only been administered in a normative study of the 1960 Stanford-Binet, Form L-M, on 1,800 Negro elementary school children from five Southeastern

states (Kennedy, Van de Riet, and White, 1961). A Pearson
product-moment correlation of .99 was obtained between the
mental age scores on the full and abbreviated scales for the
1,800 subjects stratified according to age, grade, sex,
socioeconomic status and community size, and randomized
within these limits. There was little variation from grades
1 to 6, with a mean IQ of 80.7, a standard deviation of 12.4.
This low IQ in a homogeneous population is one explanation
for the high correlation. With these subjects little precision is gained from the use of the full scale over the
abbreviated scale of the 1960 Stanford-Binet, Form L-M.

447. Kennedy, W. A. and Vega, M. Negro children's performance on
a discrimination task as a function of examiner race and verbal
incentive. Journal of Personality and Social Psychology, 1965, 2,
839-843.

The differential effect of Negro and white examiners on the
performance of 324 rural Negro school children was the subject of this investigation. Each child was presented with
a task consisting of 24 oddity problems. Other experimental
variables were grade level (2, 6, 10), intelligence level
(high, medium, low), and a verbal incentive condition (praise,
blame, control). A significant interaction was found to exist
between examiner race, verbal incentive, and grade level. The
only significant difference between Negro subjects working
with Negro or white examiners was in the incentive condition.

448. King, W. L. and Siegmiller, B. Performance of 14- to 22-
month-old first-born male infants on two tests of cognitive development: The Bayley Scales, and the Infant Psychological Development
Scale. Developmental Psychology, 1973, 8 (3), 317-326.

Tested 51, 44- to 22-month-old black infants living in Harlem
(unselected for socioeconomic status) at three ages. The
mean Bayley mental score was elevated at 14 months but fell
to a level similar to the standardization sample at 18
months and remained stable at 22 months. The mean Bayley
psychomotor score was significantly greater than that of
the standardization sample at all three age levels. Variability on both the Bayley Mental and Psychomotor Scales was
small at 14 months and increased significantly with age
to equal the standardization sample at 22 months. The mental
scale showed good predictive validity, while the psychomotor
scale showed almost none. The Infant Psychological Developmental Scale appears to measure specific abilities and to
be most applicable below 18 months of age. Individually,
the scales showed almost no predictive validity. The
Bayley Mental Scale showed the greatest number of intercorrelations with other scales at all age levels. With
increasing age, vocalization and verbal ability became
more important determinants of test performance.

449. Klineberg, O. Negro Intelligence and Selective Migration. New
York: Columbia University Press, 1935.

A report of a research planned by the author and carried out
by several M.A. candidates under his direction. By investigation
of the school records in Nashville, Birmingham and Charleston,
it was determined that the children of parents who had migrated
were not, on the average, significantly different in school
abilities from those of parents who had not migrated. Then,
by a series of intelligence-test studies of Negro children of
10 and 12 years in New York City, it was established that in
general the intelligence level is positively correlated with
the duration of residence in the City; possible alternative
factors, like race mixture, are suitably controlled. Additional problems, such as sex differences, are touched upon,
and orienting chapters, bibliography and index are provided.

450. Klineberg, O. Negro-white differences in intelligence test
performance: A new look at an old problem. American Psychologist,
1963, 18 (4), 198-203.

Negro-white differences on mental tests are evaluated in this
paper, which was prepared at the suggestion of the Society for
the Psychology Study of Social Issues (Division 9 of the American Psychological Association). "The evidence against the
assumption of native differences in intelligence test performance between Negroes and whites still seems to me to be very
convincing." There is "no scientifically acceptable evidence
for the view that ethnic groups differ in innate abilities.
This is not the same as saying that there are no ethnic differences in such abilities. . . . The science of psychology can
offer no support to those who see in the accident of inherited
skin color or other physical characteristics any excuse for
denying to individuals the right to full participation in
American democracy."

451. Klineberg, O. On race and intelligence: A joint statement.
American Journal of Orthopsychiatry, 1957, 27, 420-422.

Statement by 18 social scientists.

452. Klineberg, O. The question of Negro intelligence. Opportunity,
1931, 9 (12), 366-367.

Comparison made of the school records of about 500 Negro children
in Nashville and Birmingham who moved north between 1915 and 1930
with school records of the total Negro school population of these
cities showed that those who went away had marks slightly below
the average of all the Negro children in those cities. There is
no evidence, so far as school marks are concerned, that it is the
more intelligent Negro families who migrate to the North. In
another study tests were given to Negro children born in the
South but then living in New York. Length of residence in the
North varied from one to twelve years. Over 1,500 children were
tested. There was on the whole a marked improvement in the test
scores, the longer the children had lived in New York.

453. Knoblock, H. and Pasamanick, B. Further observations on the
behavioral development of Negro children. Journal of Genetic Psychology, 1953, 83, 137-157.

   "Forty-four of an original group of 53 Negro infants were
   examined for the third time, and their developmental progress
   studied and correlated with various individual and environmental factors. . . . No evidence for a downward trend in
   development is found."

454. Knox, E. O. The Negro as a subject of research in 1935. II.
Journal of Negro Education, 1936, 5, 612-635.

   A study by O. W. Eagleson at Indiana indicates that white
   adolescents learn to discriminate visual magnitude better
   than do Negroes. One by M. D. Jenkins at Northwestern shows
   that Negro children over 124 IQ constitue 6.5% of the Chicago
   Negro school population and are found at all age and grade
   levels; girls of this level exceed boys 2.3 to 1. The superior
   Negroes are best in language subjects and poorest in arithmetic. An investigation by S. D. Scruggs at Kansas indicated
   that improvement in reading ability as measured by reading
   tests was associated in fifth grade Negro children with
   improvement in intelligence as measured by intelligence tests
   given at the same time and also by teacher ratings a year
   later, which suggests that mental test score is not a trustworthy measure of any fixed capacity. The change in intelligence was markedly constant.

455. Kohn, M. and Rosman, B. L. Cognitive functioning in five-year-
old boys as related to social-emotional and background-demographic
variables. Developmental Psychology, 1973, 8 (2), 277-294.

   Applied hierarchical multiple regression analysis to determine the extent to which cognitive functioning at the preschool
   level is a function of two major classes of variables, background-
   demographic variables, and measures of social-emotional functioning. 287 male kindergartners, 1/2 black and 1/2 white,
   served as subjects. Background variables as a group accounted
   for 6%-22% of the variance in 7 measures of cognitive functioning; social-emotional variables as a group accounted for
   4.8%-20.6% of the variance in these measures; jointly they
   accounted for 12.7%-34.5% of the variance. The most potent
   background variables were social class and race. The most
   potent social-emotional variables were interest-participation
   and task orientation; a third social-emotional variable,
   cooperation-compliance, was not related to cognitive functioning.

456. Kohn, M. and Rosman, B. L. Social-emotional, cognitive, and
demographic determinants of poor school achievement: Implications
for a strategy of intervention. Journal of Educational Psychology,
1974, 66 (2), 267-276.

   The effect of three classes of variables -- preschool cognitive
   functioning, preschool social-emotional functioning, and back-

demographic variables -- on early elementary school achievement
was examined. 209 black and white boys from lower class and
middle class backgrounds were evaluated during the preschool
period and received achievement tests during the second year
of elementary school. Each of the three classes of variables
accounted for a significant proportion of the variance of the
criterion measures. When the classes of variables were examined by means of hierarchical regression techniques, the
social-emotional and cognitive variables yielded the most
information for programs of psychological intervention.
Intervention directed at the social-emotional components of
cognitive performance is discussed.

457. Kresheck, J. D. and Nicolosi, L. A comparison of black and
white children's scores on the Peabody Picture Vocabulary Test.
Language, Speech and Hearing Services in Schools, 1973, 4 (1), 37-40.

Studied differences in performance on the Peabody Picture
Vocabulary Test (PPVT) between 50 black and 50 white 5-1/2- to
6-1/2-year-old children. Form A of the PPVT was administered
by the school speech clinician. Results show that white
children scored significantly (p<.001) higher than black
children. Black subjects scored about 1 year and 10 months
lower than white subjects with regard to mental age. It is
concluded that the PPVT appears to be unsuitable for testing
black children's receptive vocabulary.

458. Kugel, R. B., M.D. Familial retardation -- Fact or fancy?
In Jerome Helmuth (Ed.), Disadvantaged Child, Volume I, pp. 43-63.
Seattle, Washington: Special Child Publications, Seattle Seguin
School, Inc., 1967.

This study is based on analysis of 16 lower class families
with mentally retarded children. These low income families
had many more medical ills than a comparable group of middle
class families. Prenatal disorders, perinatal complications,
and postnatal disorders were more numerous than in the general
population. A high proportion of these children were encepha-
lopathic. It seems likely, therefore, that central nervous
system aberrations contributed to subnormal functioning in
at least half of the cases. As a group, these youngsters
came from families where social ills such as poor housing,
poor diets, and poor environment were rampant. It is therefore postulated that familial mental retardation may be produced by a biological disorder, a psychosocial disorder, or
a combination of both. The data suggest that the combination
is especially pernicious. While this type of mental retardation is familial, it is not necessarily hereditary. If subsequent studies corroborate this, significant help can be
given to this group. Efforts to rehabilitate lower socioeconomic class children at three to five years of age may
modify the deleterious effects of poor environment on their
intellectual functioning.

459. Lanier, L. H. An analysis of thinking reactions of white and
Negro children. Journal of Comparative Psychology, 1930, 10, 207-220.

The author tested, by means of the Peterson Rational Learning
Test, samplings of 12-year-old Negro and white children in
Nashville, Chicago and New York. The responses were analyzed
in terms of time, trials, unclassified errors, logical errors,
perseverative errors, and rate. The results show that Nashville whites excel Nashville Negroes reliably in time, perseverative errors and rate of response. Approximately 80% of
the whites surpassed the Negro averages in each case. The
whites also excelled in unclassified and logical errors, but
the differences were not large. There was no appreciable difference in trials. The Chicago results showed no reliable
race differences, although the whites excelled in every criterion except rate of response. The New York Negroes were
markedly superior to the whites of that city in trials, unclassified errors and logical errors. Correlations of test
factors with the skin color ratings of Negro children were
positive, but low and unreliable.

460. Lark-Horovitz, B. On art appreciation of children: IV. Comparative study of white and Negro children, 13 to 15 years old.
Journal of Educational Research, 1939, 30, 258-285.

Analysis is made of the results for the white and Negro
groups from the already published results on subject preference and portrait preference for pictures and preference for
textiles. The analysis indicates that Negro and white children differ widely in their picture choices made for subject
preference. They also differ as to the most preferred portrait
in that study, but show similar interests as to the whole
group of preferred portraits. They show great similarity
in their choices of textile patterns. The reasons for the
difference in preferences in the subject study are indicated
as the result of a questionnaire given all of the children;
color is more important for the Negro group.

461. Lawson, A. E. and Nordland, F. H. Training and generalization
of conservation in disadvantaged black teenagers: A neo-Piagetian
approach. Perceptual and Motor Skills, 1975, 40 (2), 503-513.

A program to train conservation of area, weight and volume to
a group of nonconserving black teenagers is reported. The
neo-Piagetian model of intellectual development proposed by
Pascual-Leone formed the basis of training procedures. Significant training effect was demonstrated for area and weight
conservation, while volume proved harder to train. No significant differences were found between experimental and control
group on volume task posttests. The effects of training did
not generalize to a conservation of length task. Overall gains
in conservation were demonstrated.

462. Lee, E. S. Negro intelligence and selective migration: A
Philadelphia test of the Klineberg hypothesis. American Sociological Review, 1951, 16, 227-233.

> "Klineberg's hypothesis that there is an increase in the in-
> telligence scores of southern Negro migrants to New York with
> increasing length of residence in New York is in the main sub-
> stantiated by independent evidence in Philadelphia." This
> study departed from Klineberg's by using data from retests
> of the same subject. A breakdown of the Primary Mental Abili-
> ties scores indicated consistent increases with length of
> residence for all categories except memory.

463. Leifer, A. Ethnic patterns in cognitive tasks. Proceedings of
the Annual Convention of the American Psychological Association, 1972,
7 (1), 73-74.

> Assessed culturally reinforced cognitive abilities in economi-
> cally disadvantaged preliterate children. Capabilities of 80
> disadvantaged preschoolers (20 each from Chinese, Italian,
> Negro and Puerto Rican backgrounds) were assessed in a con-
> structional task, body understanding, copying geometric forms,
> and in verbal ideational fluency. Chinese subjects signifi-
> cantly exceeded all other groups in constructional ability
> and in body understanding. Italian, Negro and Puerto Rican
> subjects significantly exceeded the Chinese group in verbal
> ideational fluency. There were no differences in the ability
> to copy geometric shapes. Using these strengths for further
> cognitive growth was the primary application of the findings.

464. Leifer, A. Mosaics of disadvantaged Negro and white preschoolers.
Journal of Genetic Psychology, 1972, 121 (1), 59-63.

> Compared the responses of 43 disadvantaged black preschoolers
> with 46 equally disadvantaged white preschoolers on the Lowen-
> feld Mosaic Test. The products of both groups were found to
> be approximately 1-1/2 years below their CAs. This slower rate
> of psychological development leaves both black and white econ-
> omically deprived children ill-equipped for formal school in-
> struction. Interaction of poor environmental conditions with
> the genotypic potential of children of both races appears to
> have the same unfavorable consequences for academic success.
> Criticism is directed at comparative statements about race
> differences in psychological development based on studies
> wherein race and socioeconomic status are confounded.

465. Levin, T. Preschool education and the communities of the poor.
In J. Hellmuth (Ed.), Disadvantaged Child, Volume I, pp. 349-406.
Seattle, Washington: Special Child Publications, Seattle Seguin
School, Inc., 1967.

> In 1965, 84 preschool centers existed in 60 impoverished urban
> and rural Negro communities throughout Mississippi. The plan-
> ning and administration of these centers was undertaken by the
> Child Development Group of Mississippi (CDGM), an organization
> interested in establishing a cooperative community-based

preschool program in poor Mississippi Negro communities. In
1965, CDGM was offered as a statewide program rather than a
small demonstration project, Federal funding was accepted,
and the program was developed with a community base. CDGM
is upholding goals in common with the civil rights movement --
the goals of social, political, and economic justice -- rather
than evading alliances in an attempt to appease local politicians
and allay Federal concerns. This article includes many photographs, and quotes from newsletters, teachers, parents, and
children. Four concepts underlie the program of the CDGM.
They have wide application to Head Start programs, to education, and to other Federal poverty programs. (1) Preconceived
concepts of child development cannot be imposed on poor communities. (2) Any community program will be regarded as an external agent unless it is run by the poor themselves. (3) The
nonprofessional community aides must be given dignified work
and full educational opportunity to achieve professional
status. (4) Head Start must be an instrument for social
change; that is, the child cannot be redeemed without redeem-
ing the community.

466. Lightfoot, S. L. Politics and reasoning: Through the eyes of
teachers and children. Harvard Educational Review, 1973, 43 (2),
197-244.

Evaluated the relationship between levels of political consciousness in black teachers and social and cognitive development in black children.

467. Little, W. B., Kenny, C. T., and Middleton, M. H. Differences
in intelligence among low socioeconomic class Negro children as a
function of sex, age, educational level of parents, and home stability.
Journal of Genetic Psychology, 1973, 123 (2), 241-250.

Used the WISC and Stanford-Binet Intelligence Scale in a longitudinal study which examined changes in intelligence among 118
low socioeconomic class black children at ages 4 and 7 as a
function of sex, home stability, and educational level of their
parents. Subjects whose parents had high school educations
obtained significantly higher IQs than subjects whose parents
did not have high school educations at age 4 but not at age 7.
These results support an interaction hypothesis concerning
the relative effects of heredity and environment on intelligence. Home stability and age interacted in such a manner
that subjects from unstable homes obtained significantly higher
IQ at age 4 than subjects from stable homes, but at age 7 obtained significantly lower IQs than subjects from stable
homes. (Modified.)

468. Long, H. H. The intelligence of colored elementary pupils in
Washington, D. C. Journal of Negro Education, 1934, 3, 205-222.

This study has for its aim the determination of the average
IQ of Negro children in Washington, D. C. by grade cross
sections of the school population, as well as determining
the relation between IQ and number of years a child has

resided in Washington. The effect of the socioeconomic
factor upon the IQ is stressed. As the Negro child becomes
older, the IQ decreases. It drops about three points between the fifth and sixth grades. The author found that
the average IQ varied only slightly after 8-1/2 years of
residence. It is pointed out that the influence of the
Washington environment is rather marked, inasmuch as there
is a general tendency for IQ to decrease with age. The average
IQ of colored elementary pupils born in Washington is only
4.76 points below that of the average white elementary pupil.
The author concludes that this difference is to be accounted
for by other than native factors.

469. Long, H. H. Test results of third grade children selected on
the basis of socioeconomic status: I. Journal of Negro Education,
1935, 4, 192-212.

This investigation attempts to study a twofold problem: First,
a comparison of test results from eight different intelligence
and achievement tests given to the same pupils; second, comparison of test results between two groups of pupils whose backgrounds are different, in order "to discover differential
behavior with respect to these tests." The first part of
the study describes the socioeconomic background. The second
part is devoted to the analysis of test results. Third grade
colored children in Washington, D. C. were used as subjects.
A homogeneous grouping was sought. 100 children were included
in each group. Group I averages several months older chrono-
logically than Group II. Differences in averages among four
intelligence tests are not marked, but differences in variability are large between the pair of numerical-verbal and the
pair of performance tests. The urban influence upon the
Pintner-Paterson Scale agrees with Klineberg's findings. In
Group I, differences on the Pintner-Paterson and Dearborn Tests
favor boys. The differences were 8 and 7 months respectively.
In Group II, there is no difference between sexes on the Pintner-
Paterson, and it is reduced to four months on the Dearborn.
Group II is superior on the Pintner-Paterson. Group I is
superior on the Kuhlmann-Anderson. Part II of this study will
be published in October in the Journal of Negro Education.

470. Long, H. H. Test results of third grade Negro children selected
on the basis of socioeconomic status: II. Journal of Negro Education, 1935, 4, 523-552.

The present investigation is concerned with test analysis and
with group comparisons. The following tests were selected:
Stanford-Binet; Pintner-Paterson Short Performance Scale;
Dearborn "A" Intelligence; Kuhlmann-Anderson Intelligence;
New Stanford Reading (Paragraph Meaning and Word Meaning);
New Stanford Arithmetic (Reasoning and Computation). 200 third
grade children were selected and divided into two groups of 100
each on the basis of socioeconomic status. Group I is below
the norm for colored people in Washington in socioeconomic
status, while Group II is above the norm by about 15 IQ points.

The correlations among the eight tests were factorized. The consistency of intelligence and achievement among themselves, and the inconsistency of the signs of certain factors operating between achievement and intelligence tests, are the most significant features. There is a tendency indicated in the groups for intelligence and achievement to vary inversely. The mutual inhibition in Group I suggests the possibility that environment and miseducation may account for the difference in terms. It is essential to study the consistency of the factors before combining tests into a composite battery. If the factor patterns are reliable, the Kuhlmann-Anderson Test is the most consistent measure of general ability for both groups.

471. Long, P. A. and Anthony, J. J. The measurement of mental retardation by a culture-specific test. Psychology in the Schools, 1974, 11 (3), 310-312.

The relationship between scores obtained by black students on the Wechsler Intelligence Scale for Children (WISC) and the Black Intelligence Test for Cultural Homogeneity (BITCH) is studied to determine if black students placed in an educable mentally retarded (EMR) program on the basis of WISC Full Scale IQ scores as the primary criterion measures will be ruled out when tested on the culture-specific BITCH test. Subjects were 30 black students enrolled in the EMR program at Gainsville High School. Results suggest that black EMR students obtain similar scores on the WISC and the BITCH and that students who exhibit retarded intellectual development will score poorly on test instruments regardless of the cultural specificity.

472. Lovinger, R. J., et al. Factor analysis of intellectual performance in Disadvantaged Negro adolescents. Paper presented at the Annual Meeting of the American Educational Research Association, February 1966. Also, see ERIC Abstracts, No. ED-096-345, 1966.

The Wechsler Intelligence Scale for Children (WISC) and the Metropolitan Achievement Test (MAT) were administered to seventh graders in a New York City school located in a depressed area with a Negro population approaching 100%. Full scale and subtest scores were analyzed. A factor analysis of the WISC, MAT, and the two scales combined was conducted using an oblique rotation. Data from this analysis are presented and compared to those obtained in a 1959 investigation using the original WISC standardized population. The hypotheses that the present sample has a basically different intellectual structure from that of the normative group was not supported. The effects of disadvantage seem to be evident in the pattern of high and low subtest means, in which the lowest means are on two subtests (Information and Vocabulary) which are both highly open to cultural and educational influence, and also the best subtests for predicting the academic performance of the group.

473. Lysiak, F. and Evans, C. L. Kindergarten -- Fun and games or readiness for first grade: A comparison of seven kindergarten curricula. Paper presented at the Annual Meeting of the American Educational Research Association, March 1976. Also, see ERIC Abstracts, No. ED-121-803, 1976.

Results from this two-year study of seven kindergarten curricula in 1973-74 support the hypothesis that structured programs produce greater cognitive gains for disadvantaged children. The study also suggests that a structured program may be more beneficial for high socioeconomic children. The six curricula described and evaluated are: Lippincott's Beginning Program, Alpha Time, Getting a Head Start, Follow Through Model, Regular Kindergarten Program (Fort Worth Independent School District), and Bilingual Model. The Lippincott's Beginning to Read, Write, and Listen Program (a highly structured language-based program) was found to be most effective for low socioeconomic status (SES), high SES, and Anglo and black children. Program effects were similar for middle SES children in the four curricula examined. The effects of half-day vs. full-day sessions were not supportive of full-day programs for middle SES children either year. High SES students were not in full-day programs the first year of this study; however, the second year of this study full-day programs were found to be more advantageous to high SES children in the Lippincott curricula and the Fort Worth Independent School District continuum. The first year evaluation supported full-day programs for low SES children. Only full-day programs were provided for low SES children during the second year of this study.

474. McAlpin, A. S. Changes in the intelligence quotients of Negro children. Journal of Negro Education, 1932, 1, 44-48.

All of the children in the 3A and 5A grades of the colored schools of the District of Columbia were given the Kuhlmann-Anderson Test in an effort to determine how the IQ averages of the pupils varied with length of residence in the District. The 2A children born in the District have an average IQ of 98.1. The 3A children born outside the District have an average IQ of 92.1. Of those 5A children born in the District, the median IQ was 95.1, while that of the 5A children born outside the District was 89.7. The higher median IQ for the children born in the District is believed to be due to the favorable environment enjoyed there. This statement, the author points out, is in accord with the point of view that "capacities need appropriate stimulation in order that consequent abilities may be realized."

475. McCord, W. M. and Demerath, N. J. Negro versus white intelligence: A continuing controversy. Harvard Educational Review, 1958, 28, 120-135.

The argument of McGurk in support of the innate intellectual inferiority of the Negro, as developed in the September 21, 1956 issue of U. S. News and World Report, is examined criti-

cally and the conclusion is found to be undemonstrated. Analysis of data of a new study of a Massachusetts sample of 562
white and 50 Negro boys, predominantly lower and middle class,
revealed no significant differences in Kuhlmann-Anderson
Test scores. Additionally, scores on Stanford-Binet of 217
white and 21 Negroes in the same group were not significantly
different. All subjects attended urban, integrated schools.
In a further comparative study of 30 matched pairs of Negroes
and whites, equated on the basis of social class, father's
occupation, nationality, generation of entry to America, personality and emotional climate of the home, no significant
differences in intelligence appeared.

476. McCormack, M. K., Scarrsal, S., Katz, S., Thompson, W., Plesky,
H., and Barker, W. Physical and intellectual development of black
children with and without sickle cell trait. Behavior Genetics,
1975, 5 (1), 103.

477. McGurk, F. C. J. Comparative test scores of Negro and white
school children in Richmond, Virginia. Journal of Educational Psychology, 1943, 34, 473-484.

The Chicago Non-Verbal Examination, the Myers Mental Measure,
and the Otis Self-Administering Test of Mental Ability, were
administered to a representative tenth of the school population of Richmond. Significant differences were found between
white and Negro scores in all three tests at all ages and at
all grades. Whatever the causes of white superiority in these
tests, the clinical psychologist working with the groups
studied should be aware of the differences. Norms are being
calculated for use with Negroes, so as to permit classification of an individual in relation to others of his own
race, culture and opportunity. These standards will probably
change as the Negro's lot is improved and he absorbs more of
the white man's culture.

478. McGurk, F. C. J. On white and Negro test performance and socioeconomic factors. Journal of Abnormal and Social Psychology, 1953,
48, 448-450.

The attempt to explain Negro test score inferiority on the
basis of the Negro inability to handle culturally weighted
test material, or on the basis of the Negro's lower socioeconomic status, is challenged. The data presented do not
support either of these explanations.

479. McGurk, F. C. J. Psychological test score differences and the
"Culture Hypothesis." Mankind Quarterly, 1961, 1, 165-175.

480. McHugh, A. F. H-T-P proportion and perspective in Negro,
Puerto Rican and white children. Journal of Clinical Psychology,
1963, 19 (3), 312-313.

A comparison study of H-T-P size and placement for 46 Negro,
38 Puerto Rican, and 46 whites. Negroes drew the house

closer to the left margin, and the person narrower and farther
from the right margin than did the white subjects. Puerto
Ricans drew the persons shorter than the white subjects.

481. McIntosh, E. I., Adams, J., and Weade, B. L. Ethnic background,
measured intelligence and adaptive behavior scores in mentally retarded children. American Journal of Mental Deficiency, n.d., 78 (1),
1-6.

> The degree to which classification of levels of mental retard-
> ation based upon a measure of adaptive behavior (the Vineland
> Social Maturity Scale) differed from the classification based
> upon IQ, for Negro and Caucasian children, was assessed. The
> Negro group scored lower on IQ, but the groups did not differ
> on deviation social quotient (DSQ). The distribution of levels
> of impairment based upon IQ but not for that based upon DSQ.
> On the basis of IQ, more Negro than Caucasian children were
> classified as "borderline" or above. This effect was not
> found for DSQ. The relative utility of the two types of
> classification, which may well vary as a function of ethnic
> background and the purpose of the classification, awaits
> further research.

482. McNamara, J. R. and Porterfield, C. L. Level of information
about the human figure and their characteristic relationship to
human figure drawings in young disadvantaged children. Developmental Psychology, 1969, 1 (6, Part 1), 669-672.

> Related information concerning discrete parts of the human
> figure to Koppitz Human Figure Drawing (HFD) scores in 58
> Negro Head Start children. Information measured at the levels
> of matching, expression, reception and incompletion was sig-
> nificantly correlated with the subjects' drawing scores. Dif-
> ferences in the degree of correct information about parts of
> the human figure were also found. An analysis comparing the
> HFD and information level scores of 20 of the Head Start sub-
> jects with those of a no-preschool group matched for age, sex
> and IQ indicated no significant differences on all measures
> except the incompletion level. The higher scores of the Head
> Start subjects on the incompletion variable were attributed
> to their exposure to certain program activities, i.e.,
> perceptual-motor training, rather than to preschool in general.

483. McNamara, J. R., Porterfield, C. L., and Miller, L. E. The
relationship of the Wechsler Preschool and Primary Scale of Intelligence with the Coloured Progressive Matrices and the Bender-Gestalt
Test. Journal of Clinical Psychology, 1969, 25 (1), 65-68.

> The Wechsler Preschool and Primary Scale of Intelligence (WPPSI),
> the Coloured Progressive Matrices (CPM), and the Bender-Gestalt
> (BG), were administered to 42 Negro boys and girls. An analysis
> of the results indicated many significant relationships. In
> general, the results suggest that the BG is highly related to
> the performance areas of the WPPSI and may be more appropriately
> interchanged than the CPM for obtaining estimates of WPPSI
> Full Scale IQs.

484. McPartland, J. The relative influence of school and of classroom desegregation on the academic achievement of ninth grade Negro
students. Journal of Social Issues, 1969, 25 (3), 93-102.

> Using information on ninth grade Negro students in the Metro-
> politan Northeast (N=5,075) from the U. S. Office of Education's
> Educational Opportunities Survey, this study explores the rela-
> tive influence of classroom desegregation and school desegrega-
> tion on academic performance. Controlling for family background
> differences, Negro student achievement within predominantly
> Negro schools and within predominantly white schools is posi-
> tively associated with the proportion of their classmates who
> are white. This relationship remains when differences in the
> student's program of instruction and track level are taken
> into account. Negro students who remained in segregated
> classes exhibited no apparent benefit from attendance at de-
> segregated schools. It is only for Negro students in mostly
> white classes that increases in the percentage of white enroll-
> ment in their school accompany increases in their average ver-
> bal achievement. Reprinted by permission.

485. MacCoby, E. E., Dowley, E. M., Hagen, J. W., and Degerman, R.
Activity level and intellectual functioning in normal preschool
children. Child Development, 1965, 36 (3), 761-770.

> The ability to inhibit motor movement is distinguished from a
> more generalized low activity level. It is argued that the
> former should be functional for problem solving, while the
> latter should not. With a sample of 42 nursery school chil-
> dren, measures were taken of activity level during free play,
> of inhibition of motor movement, of IQ, and of performance
> on the Children's Embedded Figures Test. Scores on inhibition
> of movement proved to be positively correlated with the mea-
> sures of intellectual ability, while general activity scores
> were not.

486. Manheim, H. L. and Cummins, A. Selected musical traits among
Spanish, Negro, and Anglo-American girls. Sociology and Social
Research, 1960, 45 (1), 56-64.

> A study of ethnic differences in certain musical aptitudes is
> reported. Approximately 700 high school girls of three ethnic
> categories (Spanish, Negro and Anglo) supplied information
> about their musical environment, were tested for musical
> rhythm aptitude, and were measured in rhythm achievement.
> A positive relationship was found to exist between the extent
> of the subject's musical environment and her musical rhythm
> aptitude for the lower division girls. The same results
> concern the relationship between the extent of musical environ-
> ment and musical rhythm achievement for all subjects, and the
> relationship between rhythm aptitude and achievement for the
> upper division girls. The extent of environment for the
> three ethnic categories, in order of decreasing rank, was
> Negro, Anglo, Spanish. Differences between the scores were
> significant for the lower division but not for the upper

division subjects. Rhythm aptitude and rhythm achievement scores varied significantly, with Anglos being the highest and Negroes the lowest.

487. Marshall, M. S. and Bentler, P. M. IQ increases of disadvantaged minority-group children following innovative enrichment programs. Psychological Reports, 1971, 29, 805-806.

IQs of 11 disadvantaged Negro 4-year-olds enrolled in a 9-month innovative enrichment program increased by a mean of 23.5 points on the Peabody Picture Vocabulary Test, Form A, in one school year.

488. Massari, D. J. The relation of reflection-impulsivity to field dependence-independence and internal-external control in children. Journal of Genetic Psychology, 1975, 126 (First Half), 61-67.

The relation of reflection-impulsivity to field dependence-independence and internal-external control was studied in first and third grade black children who were administered Kagan's Matching Familiar Figures Test, Karp and Kondstadt's Children's Embedded Figures Test (CEFT), and Shore, Milgram and Malasky's Locus of Control Interview (LCI). It was hypothesized that reflective children would be (a) more field-independent, and (b) more internal than their impulsive counterparts. The first hypothesis was supported and discussed in terms of task demands of the CEFT. The failure to find strong support for the second hypothesis was attributed to the generalized nature of the LCI.

489. Massari, D. J. and Schack, M. L. Discrimination learning by reflective and impulsive children as a function of reinforcement schedule. Developmental Psychology, 1972, 6 (1), 183.

Classified 28 lower class black male first graders as impulsive or reflective using J. Kagan's Matching Familiar Figures Test. Subjects were then administered a two-choice discrimination learning task under conditions of 70% positive and 30% negative, or 70% negative and 30% positive social reinforcement. Based on the hypothesis that impulsive children are more concerned with speed of responses, and reflective children are more concerned with accuracy, it was predicted that: (a) the negative conditions would lead to better performance of both groups; (b) reflective subjects would perform better than impulsive subjects in both conditions; and (c) impulsive subjects in the negative condition would perform better than impulsive subjects in the positive condition. Results upport the predictions; however, impulsive subjects in the negative condition performed similarly to reflective subjects in the positive condition. The influence of feedback on response style and the interaction between reinforcement effectiveness and socioeconomic status are discussed.

490. Meeker, M. M. and Meeker, R. Strategies for assessing intellectual patterns in black, Anglo and Mexican-American boys -- or any
other children -- and implications for education. Journal of School
Psychology, 1973, 11 (4), 341-350.

> Used a technique derived from Guilford's Structure of Intellect
> (SOI) model to analyze Stanford-Binet item responses of 245
> 4- to 5- and 7- to 9-year-old Mexican-American, Anglo-American,
> and Afro-American boys from lower socioeconomic backgrounds.
> The SOI model conceptualizes three dimensions of intellectual
> abilities in terms of operations, content, and processes.
> Each of the major SOI dimensions' interactive effects were
> analyzed for each subject group. Results are discussed in
> terms of specific abilities (e.g., figural intelligence)
> emphasized in the SOI model. It is suggested that intellectual
> ability can be taught provided appropriate curriculums are
> available, and that SOI ability assessments are more valuable
> than traditional IQ scores.

491. Meers, D. R. Psychoanalytic research and intellectual functioning of ghetto reared black children. Psychoanalytic Study of
the Child, 1973, 28, 395-417.

> Discusses the issue of intelligence and extends to clinical
> and social issues that have been highlighted by research.
> Psychoanalytic literature views intelligence as an ego function,
> more genetically than culturally derived. Two early studies
> illuminate the correlation between nurture and intelligence.
> It is questioned whether the limited intellectual functioning
> of the disadvantaged black child is a psychiatric symptom de-
> riving from the disadvantages of his early years. Cases
> examined include an alert 5-year-old girl who had been raped
> by an adult in her home, and a 5-year-old boy whose chronic
> anxiety was related to his mother's deterioration on heroin.
> It is concluded that their treatment suggests both they and
> their families pay a terrible price for society's indifference
> and the subculture's incapacity to protect them.

492. Meissner, J. A. Use of relational concepts by inner city
children. Journal of Educational Psychology, 1975, 67 (1), 22-29.

> The comprehension and communication of a set of 10 relational
> concepts were studied, using 54 second grade and 38 fourth
> grade black inner city children as subjects. Contrary to the
> observations of sociolinguists and several studies of black
> children's speech, but in accordance with previous psycho-
> linguistic research using white and Mexican-American children,
> concept comprehension was significantly easier than communi-
> cation. Age was an important factor in communication ability,
> with the fourth grade speakers communicating significantly
> more concepts correctly and using a previous exposure to the
> comprehension version of the concepts to communicate more
> effectively. There were no novel expressions of concepts,
> and communication was relatively inefficient, with many
> ambiguous concept descriptions and ineffective questioning.
> Implications for education of inner city children are discussed.

493. Mensing, P. M. and Traxler, A. J. Social class differences in free recall of categorized and uncategorized lists in black children. Journal of Educational Psychology, 1973, 65 (3), 378-382.

Assessed differences in the cognitive abilities of black children from two socioeconomic groups, using A. R. Jensen's theoretical model of intelligence. Black fifth grade children, 30 lower class and 20 middle class, were randomly assigned to one of two free recall tasks, a Level I task using 20 unrelated items, and a Level II task using 20 items in four categories. All subjects were given an IQ test and the Raven Coloured Progressive Matrices. Results indicate significant socioeconomic differences in IQ and progressive matrices scores, but no significant socioeconomic differences in the Level I and Level II analyses. These findings are discussed within Jensen's theoretical framework.

494. Mercer, J. R. Cultural diversity, mental retardation, and assessment: The case for nonlabeling. Paper presented at the Fourth International Congress of the International Association for the Scientific Study of Mental Deficiency, Washington, D. C., August 22-27, 1976. 17 pp. Also, see ERIC Abstracts, No. ED-133-404, 1976.

The System of Multicultural Pluralistic Assessment (SOMPA) is designed for use in a culturally diverse society. The system was developed on 700 English-speaking Caucasian children (hereafter called Anglos) from the Anglo core culture, 700 black children, and 700 Latino children (90% were of Mexican-American heritage) 5 through 11 years of age. The SOMPA is a system of assessment which triangulates the evaluation process. It looks at the child through a medical model and screens for possible anomalies indicated by the health history, performance on the physical dexterity battery, or tests of vision or hearing. Using a social system model, it looks at the child's performances in family roles, nonacademic school roles, peer group roles, community roles, earner/consumer roles, self-maintenance roles, and academic school roles. Using a pluralistic model, it evaluates the child's performance relative to others from the same sociocultural background and makes inferences about the child's estimated learning potential. Through this process, it is hoped that the non-Anglo child whose potential may be masked by the distance between the child's location in sociocultural space and the culture of the school will be identified.

495. Mercer, J. R. Institutionalized Anglocentrism: Labeling mental retardates in the public schools. In P. Orleans and W. R. Ellis, Jr. (Eds.), Race, Change and Urban Society, pp. 311-338. Beverly Hills, California: Sage Publications, 1971.

In California in 1966, twice as many children with Spanish surnames and 2-1/2 times as many Negro children per capita were in special education classes, usually classified as mentally retarded. The preponderance of Mexican-American and Negro children in classes for the educable mentally retarded

does not appear to be the result of overreferral from teachers
and principals but rather of the clinical testing process
itself. In general, there have been three different approaches
to resolving the issues raised in cross-cultural intelligence
testing: attempts to develop culture-free tests, modifying
existing tests for cross-cultural applications, and develop-
ping culture-specific tests. A fourth approach which tends
to reduce the ethnocentrism of present testing procedures is
pluralistic evaluation. This modifies the normative framework
by which the meaning of a particular score is interpreted,
rather than making changes in the form and content of the test
itself. In a pluralistic evaluation procedure, a person is
evaluated as intellectually subnormal only when he scores in
the lowest 3.0% of his own sociocultural group on a standardized test.

496. Mercer, J. R. Sociocultural factors in educational labeling.
In M. J. Begab and S. A. Richardson (Eds.), The Mentally Retarded
and Society: A Social Science Perspective, pp. 141-157. Baltimore,
Maryland: University Park, 1975.

Reports on the current status of a project designed to develop
a multicultural, pluralistic method of educational assessment
with which to evaluate the child as a multidimensional person
undergoing socialization within a particular sociocultural
setting. Stepwise multiple correlations, using the full WISC-R
as the dependent variable for 1,924 black, Chicano/Latino,
and Anglo-American 5- to 11-year-olds, and sociocultural and
socialization factors as independent variables, suggest that
both achievement and aptitude can be estimated with the same
standardized instrument by employing different sets of pluralistic norms.

497. Mermelstein, E. and Shulman, L. S. Lack of formal schooling
and the acquisition of conservation. Child Development, 1967, 38,
39-52.

The performances of Negro 6- and 9-year-old children from Prince
Edward County, Virginia, a community which had been without
public schools for four years, on a series of Piagetian conservation tasks, were compared with those of Negro children
from a community which had had regular schooling. Three
techniques of questioning the children were experimentally
varied. Findings revealed generally no significant differences
attributable to effects of nonschooling, except within one questioning condition. Differences between verbal and nonverbal
tasks were found to be highly significant. Implications for
the Piagetian theory of cognitive development and for the
methodology of conservation experiments are discussed.

498. Milgram, N. A. IQ constancy in disadvantaged Negro children.
Psychological Reports, 1971, 29 (1), 319-326.

Administered annually the Stanford-Binet Intelligence Scale
and the Peabody Picture Vocabulary Test to 27 male and 32 female

Negro children in a longitudinal study from ages 3 to 8. It
was found that: (a) mean Binet IQ was relatively stable, while
Peabody IQ rose appreciably; (b) the magnitude of the correlation between earlier and later IQ scores was a function of the
interval between test-retest and age on the initial comparison
test; (c) ratings on test-taking behavior yielded significant
sex differences and age trends; (d) ratings specific to formal
test performance were significantly correlated with IQ scores
of tests taken concurrent to the ratings and of tests taken
one or more years later; and (e) these ratings did not, however,
enhance in multiple regression the correlation which obtained
for predictor and criterion IQ scores alone.

499. Milgram, N. A. and Ozer, M. N. Peabody Picture Vocabulary
Test scores of preschool children. Psychological Reports, 1967, 20
(3, Part 1), 779-784.

Two groups of preschool Negro children of poor parents were
administered the PPVT, Stanford-Binet, and other linguistic
and perceptual-motor measures. Since the PPVT score was consistently lower than the Stanford-Binet, it is concluded that
this test may be more susceptible to environmental impoverishment than the Stanford-Binet. Substandard performance on the
PPVT is discussed in terms of: (a) cumulative deficiency in
storage and/or retrieval of verbal terms; and (b) an ineffi-
ciency in sustaining the correct mental set required in the
multiple choice format of the PPVT.

500. Miller, L. P. (Ed.). The testing of black students: A sympo-
sium. Symposium Proceedings from the Annual Meeting of the American
Educational Research Association (Chicago, Illinois: April 1973).
Also, see ERIC Abstracts, No. ED-099-400, 1974. 124 pp.

The controversial and complex issues regarding the effects of
educational and psychological testing on the education of
minority group children in America are discussed. Although the
focus is primarily on black students, the issues discussed
are equally valid for all minority populations in the American
public schools. The articles in the book cover psychometric
issues of bias and prediction, social and educational problems
revolving around or directly attributable to testing, alternative multicultural models of testing, and strategies for testing in the future. Articles included are: (1) Some Points
of Confusion in Discussing the Testing of Black Students; (2)
The Problem of Match and Mismatch in Testing Black children;
(3) Psychometric Barriers to Higher Education; (4) Situational
Effects in Testing; (5) Grouping for Instruction; (6) The
Testing of Black Students: Dilemmas for Test Publishers;
(7) Research, Education, and Public Policy: Heredity vs.
Environment in Negro Intelligence; (8) Latent Functions of
Intelligence Testing in the Public Schools; and (9) Testing
the Black Minority: Strategies and Problems.

501. Minuchin, P. Correlates of curiosity and exploratory behavior
in preschool disadvantaged children. Child Development, 1971, 42 (3),
939-950.

> Attempted to develop measures of curiosity and exploration
> applicable to preschool children, and to assess the relation-
> ship between curiosity and other aspects of functioning. Sub-
> jects were 18 4-year-old Negro children in Head Start programs.
> Data were obtained from preschool observations, teacher rank-
> ings and individual sessions. Measures of curiosity were
> intercorrelated and suggested consistent reaction patterns.
> Exploratory behavior was related to differentiation of self-
> image, expectations of coherence and support in the environ-
> ment, and concept formation. Data point to a "developmental
> high risk" group within the disadvantaged preschool population.

502. Mitchell, N. B. and Pollack, R. H. Block design performance
as a function of hue and race. Journal of Experimental Child
Psychology, 1974, 17 (3), 377-382.

> Presented the block design subtest of the Wechsler Intelligence
> Scale for Children in two forms -- the standard red/white and
> an alternative blue/yellow -- to two groups of fourth and fifth
> grade children. 20 black and 20 white children performed the
> red/white task with no significant differences between their
> scores. Another 20 black and 20 white children performed the
> blue/yellow task showing a significant interracial difference.
> Within the groups of black children there was also a signifi-
> cant difference between the red/white design scores and the
> blue/yellow design scores. It is proposed that genetically
> determined differences in the pigmentation of the fundus
> oculi account for these results.

503. Morgan, H. Towards a theory of selected knowledge acquisition
patterns among black children. Paper presented at the National Conference on the Black Family in America: Black Youth (Louisville,
Kentucky, March 5, 1976). 40 pp. Also, see ERIC Abstracts, No.
ED-127-380, 1976.

> The goal of this paper is to combine selected research litera-
> ture concerned with early and advanced sensorimotor development
> in black children, and the institutional management of their
> natural precocity. The first section briefly reviews selected
> literature about sensorimotor development in black children.
> The second section discusses the current use of medication.
> The last section discusses specific implications of selected
> knowledge acquisition patterns of black children. It is con-
> cluded that there seem to be four alternative courses of
> action which school personnel are likely to put into motion
> in dealing with black children who are too active to learn
> comfortably in the established school order. Rather than re-
> examine modes of teaching/learning styles for possible modifi-
> cation, the education establishment prefers to: (a) assign
> children to special learning centers where only minimal learn-
> ing is expected; (b) prescribe drugs to render children affect-

less; (c) complete separate children from their school environment by suspension; or (d) don't do anything: keep things the way they are. These courses of action are demanding and hurtful. The fifth is to apply a humanistic, open individualized learning situation for all students.

504. Morrison, C., Harris, A. J., and Auerbach, I. T. The reading performance of disadvantaged early and non-early readers from grades 1 through 3. Journal of Educational Research, 1971, 65, 23-26.

This study was undertaken to determine the advantages or disadvantages of early reading ability among black, disadvantaged children entering first grade in the New York public schools. Children who were identified as having some word knowledge ability were compared with non-early readers, both matched and unmatched. Post-test comparisons were made at the end of the first three grades. Results indicate that approximately 5% of the population sampled did have some word recognition ability and that they were found to be superior to non-early readers, both matched and unmatched, at each testing interval. The study supports the point of view that early reading is not detrimental to long range achievement.

505. Murnane, R. J. The Impact of School Resources on the Learning of Inner City Children. Cambridge, Massachusetts: Ballinger, 1975. 125 pp.

The nature of the relationships between school resources and the cognitive achievement of children was investigated using 875 inner city black children. The research design focused on individual children, the vital question being whether there are quality differences in the learning environments provided by different classrooms. It was found that there are important differences in the amount of learning which takes place in different classrooms. Furthermore, differences in the quality of classroom environments have a greater effect on children's math achievement than on their reading achievement. Teachers have a critical impact on student achievement, and principals' evaluations of teachers provide valuable information about their performance in teaching reading and math. Black, male teachers were more effective than white or female teachers with the same experience.

506. Murray, W. I. The IQ and social class in the Negro caste. Southwest Journal of Anthropology, 1949, 4, 187-201.

Data obtained from administering five intelligence tests to 401 Negro children showed that there are statistically significant differences in the performance of Negro children in intelligence tests when the children are grouped according to social class.

507. Muzekari, L. H. Relationships between the Goodenough DAM and
Stanford-Binet in Negro and white public school children. Journal
of Clinical Psychology, 1967, 23 (1), 86-87.

       The Goodenough "DAM" and S-B, L and LM, were administered to
       a sample of 41 Negro and 64 white public school children. Sig-
       nificant correlations and no mean differences were found
       between the conventional "DAM" and the S-B, Form L or LM, for
       both Negro and white children. A comparison between the "DAM"
       and the S-B, Form L or LM, utilizing norms developed for scor-
       ing a revised Negro "DAM" resulted in a lower relationship,
       and raised the question of their applicability to similar popu-
       lations as well as to Negroes in general. Reprinted by permission.

508. Nash, L. B. and Seitz, V. Long-term motivational-cognitive
effects of day care: Final report. Washington, D. C.: Children's
Bureau (DHEW), 1975, Report No. OCD-CB-292. 86 pp.   Also, see
ERIC Abstracts, No. ED-119-805, 1975.

       This longitudinal study examined the effects of one year of
       full-day Head Start day care experiences on the long-term
       motivational and cognitive changes in 29 low income black
       children aged 51-61 months. The children were separated into
       two groups: one attended a full-day kindergarten similar to
       Head Start; and the other was sent to half-day public kinder-
       garten. A control group, composed of 20 children who attended
       private nursery school and subsequently attended kindergartens
       in their own neighborhoods, was also used. During the day
       care program and through the middle of the first grade year,
       data were collected in seven time periods for three areas of
       motivational/cognitive interaction: (a) changes in the rela-
       tionship between personal interaction variables; (b) changes in
       intrinsic need to interact effectively and competently with
       the environment; and (c) changes in the impulsivity/reflectivity
       dimension. Comparison of the data from the two experimental
       groups showed little indication that the kindergarten program
       had produced significant effects; the small effects shown
       late in the year would have required an extension of the program
       for verification. However, there were no indications of fade-
       out effects of Head Start for either group. In addition, the
       disadvantaged groups performed comparably to the economically
       advantaged group except on tests which depended on high verbal
       ability.

509. Newland, T. E. and Lawrence, W. C. Chicago non-verbal examination results on an East Tennessee Negro population. Journal of Clinical Psychology, 1953, 9, 44-46.

       A partial saturation sample testing of 1,140 East Tennessee
       Negro school children aged 6 through 14 by means of the
       Chicago Non-Verbal Examination yielded these results: (a) At
       all age levels, these Negro children scored not less than the
       equivalent of two years below the respective age norms for
       this Test. At age 11 thru 14, the disparity increased to
       three or more years. (b) At the 6- and 7-year levels, the

test results lacked completely or largely in discriminability.
(c) Limited discriminability between the 13- and 14-year levels
is indicated. (d) Taking all levels combined, no significant
sex differences were found.

510. Nieman, R. H. and Gastright, J. F. The effects of a three-year
inter-racial preschool program on cognitive and social development
(IPSIP). Paper presented at the Annual Meeting of the American Educational Research Association (59th, Chicago, Illinois, April 1974).
Also, see ERIC Abstracts, No. ED-096-366, 1974.

The Impact of a Preschool Interracial Program (IPSIP) project,
funded under Title III of the 1965 Elementary Secondary Education Act, was designed to test the hypothesis that intervening
with sufficient impact in the early lives of environmentally
deprived children will produce a significant, lasting effect
on their cognitive and social development. The IPSIP program
involved the comparison of two treatment groups with a control
group. Group 1 received a full-time classroom program and the
parent education program. Group 2 received only the parent
education program, and Group 3 served as a control group for
the other groups. Each group contained both economically
advantaged and disadvantaged children and similar racial
balances. The IPSIP classroom curriculum provided a planned
sequence of learning events designed to impact the cognitive,
social, and physical motor development of children. The parent
education program provided for involving parents in the education of their children. The program provided for instruction
in, and practice of behaviors which support learning. Children
for the project were located in a changing community in
northeastern Cincinnati. Most of the 223 children began the
project at age 3 and continued through age 5.

511. Oakland, T. D., King, J. D., White, L. A., and Eckman, R. A
comparison of performance on the WPPSI, WISC and S-B with preschool
children: Comparison studies. Journal of School Psychology, 1971,
9 (2), 144-149.

Analyzed data from two studies on a comparison of performance
on the Wechsler Preschool and Primary Scale of Intelligence
(WPPSI), WISC, and Stanford-Binet Intelligence Scale (S-B) with
preschool children. Subjects were 29 Negro Head Start students
and 24 Caucasian kindergartners. Negro subjects obtained
lower mean IQ, supporting results from other studies on a
tendency of lower socioeconomic status (SES) Negro children
to perform below the mean on the WISC. The three tests did not
appear to be interchangeable, as the WISC and the S-B tended
to yield a higher IQ than the WPPSI with lower SES Negro children. Results with the Caucasian subjects suggest that the
WPPSI more clearly approximates the S-B than the WISC. The
S-B appeared to be more closely associated with abilities
measured by the Verbal scores of the WPPSI and WISC than with
their Performance scores.

512. O'Keefe, R., et al. Influence of age, sex and ethnic origin
on Goodenough-Harris Drawing Test performances by disadvantaged
preschool children. Perceptual and Motor Skills, 1971, 33 (3, Part 1),
708-710.

> Administered the Goodenough-Harris Drawing Test to 120 54- to
> 72-month-olds from eight Head Start centers. 40 subjects were
> selected from each of three age groups, with equal numbers of
> males and females, whites and blacks, in each. Age, sex and
> ethnic group membership influenced performances. On Man and
> Woman drawings combined, performances of girls were signifi-
> cantly higher than boys, white subjects scored significantly
> higher than black subjects, and older subjects scored signifi-
> cantly higher than younger subjects. No significant differ-
> ences for these factors were found when performance on the Man
> and Woman drawings were considered separately.

513. Olim, E. G. Maternal language styles and children's cognitive
behavior. Journal of Special Education, 1940, 4 (1), 53-68.

> Studied the language styles of 163 black mothers from three
> socioeconomic levels and the relationship between the mothers'
> language and their 4-year-old children's cognitive behavior as
> measured by the Stanford-Binet Intelligence Scale, the Sigel
> Conceptual Sorting Task for Children, and a block sorting
> task. Statistically significant social class differences in
> maternal language were found. However, social class per se was
> not as predictive of the child's cognitive performance as the
> mother's language, especially her use of abstract language.
> Mothers who tended to use elaborate language tended to have
> children who were superior on concept sorting tasks. The
> mother's language was a better predictor of the child's cogni-
> tive performance than either the mother's verbal IQ or the
> child's IQ. Results are discussed as supporting the view
> that (a) a method of enhancing cognitive development is to
> expand preschool linguistic environment, and (b) the age for
> entering school should be reduced to the early critical years
> of cognitive development.

514. Olim, E. G., Hess, R. D., and Shipman, V. C. Role of mothers'
language styles in mediating their preschool children's cognitive
development. School Review, 1967, 75 (4), 414-424.

> A study of the role of mothers' language in mediating the
> potential educability of preschool children. The research
> group consisted of 163 nonworking, urban Negro mothers and
> their 4-year-old children, selected from four socioeconomic
> status groups: upper-middle, upper-lower, lower-lower intact
> families, and lower-lower ADC (Aid for Dependent Children)
> families. The major assumptions of the study are presented.
> Three types of maternal approach to control are discussed:
> (1) the use of inhibitory techniques; (2) input control tech-
> niques; and (3) internalizing techniques. It was hypothesized
> that related to these would be different types of maternal
> appeal used as a basis for disciplinary or control maneuvers:

(a) a status-normative orientation; (b) a personal-subjective
orientation; and (c) a cognitive-rational orientation. It was
further hypothesized that the first orientation would be related
to restricted code and communication, whereas the second two
would be related to elaborated code and communication. The
following empirical hypotheses were confirmed by r'al analysis
of mothers' and children's behavior in a wide variety of tasks:
(i) mothers high in status-normative orientation tended to be
low in personal-subjective and cognitive-rational orientations;
(ii) mothers high in the use of imperatives (commands) in
mother-child interaction tended to be low in giving instructions to their children; (iii) personal-subjective and cognitive-
rational orientations were positively related to instructive
behavior and status-normative orientation was +r'ed with impera-
tive behavior; (iv) mothers tending to a status-normative
orientation and a preference for imperatives over instructions
tended to be restricted in their language, whereas mothers
with a personal-subjective or cognitive-rational orientation
tended to manifest elaborated language styles; (v) the children
of mothers who predominantly used status-normative control
techniques generally performed at a lower level on cognitive
tasks; (vi) high language elaboration of mothers was +r'ed with
superior cognitive performance of their children and restricted
maternal language was associated with inferior children's performance; (vii) mothers who were oriented toward status-normative
control and use of imperatives, and whose language was restricted,
tended to be from among the lower SES groups whereas the opposite
type of mother was likely to be from the middle class group.
The results point to the desirability of changing the behavior
and orientations of mothers with restricted language styles
and argue for the view that "sizeable and long-lasting benefits from intervention must involve social reform as well as
attention to the individual victims of social deprivation and
cultural disadvantage."

515. Olivier, K. and Barclay, A. Stanford-Binet and Goodenough-
Harris test performances of Head Start children. Psychological
Reports, 1967, 20, 1175-1179.

The characteristics of revised Stanford-Binet (S-B) and Goodenough-Harris protocols (GHDT) were investigated for 188 culturally disadvantaged children. These children scored in the
low normal level of intelligence. The S-B and the GHDT did
not correlate highly.

516. Olmsted, P., Parks, C., and Rickel, A. The development of
classification skills in the preschool child. International Review
of Education, 1970, 16 (1), 67-80.

Presents a theoretical discussion of classificatory skills
along the lines outlined by Piaget, and reports on an empirical
investigation of the theoretical issues. Subjects were low
economic class Negro children whose classification skills
were assessed with the Object-Picture Categorization Test.
Results show that there was a significant increase in skills

after training when compared with a control group. Results are
discussed in relation to curriculum, and game-type exercises
are listed.

517. Olmsted, P. and Sigel, I. E. The generality of color form
preference as a function of materials and task requirements among
lower class Negro children. Child Development, 1970, 41 (4), 1025-
1032.

Investigated the generality of color-form preferences by
administering several color-form tasks to the same group of
subjects. These tasks employed geometrics, familiar objects,
and pictures of these objects as stimuli; and sorting, categorizing, and matching-to-standard as procedures. It was hypothesized that preferences for individual subjects would be
task specific. 41 lower class black boys and 34 girls 61
to 76 months old served as subjects. Results indicate that
the predominant mode of response varied with the tasks employed.
Color-form preferences by age, sex and school yielded no significant difference. Results also demonstrate the substantial
role played by particular tasks in eliciting responses. It
is concluded that generalizations regarding color form dominance cannot be made for this population since preferences
are task specific.

518. Olson, A. V. and Rosen, C. L. A comparison of reading interests
of two populations of ninth grade students. Adolescence, 1966, 1
(4), 321-326.

140 Negro and 124 Caucasian ninth graders were asked to indicate reading interests on a questionnaire. Significant differences between the racial groups are noted.

519. Osborne, R. T. Racial differences in mental growth and school
achievement: A longitudinal study. Psychological Reports, 1960,
7, 233-239.

The California Achievement and Mental Maturity Tests were
administered to 815 white children and 446 Negro children in
1954, 1956 and 1958, when the children were in grades 6, 8
and 10, respectively. Longitudinal comparisons of arithmetic
skills (Reasoning and Fundamentals), of reading skills (Vocabulary and Comprehension), and of mental maturity, were made.
Reading and arithmetic achievement differences between the
white and Negro groups increased progressively from the 6th
to the 10th grade with the greatest difference found on non-
cultural test questions. For the Negro group, achievement
and mental maturity growth became negatively accelerated or
leveled off in the 14 to 16 age range. At the latest testing,
the regression effect tended to reduce the range of variability
of mental maturity scores for both groups.

520. Overton, W. F., Wagner, J. L., and Dolinsky, H. Social class differences and task variables in the development of multiplicative classification. Child Development, 1971, 42 (6), 1951-1958.

Administered to 96 4- to 5-, 6- to 7-, and 8- to 9-year-old lower class black and middle class white children two forms of a matrix-completion task. One form contained three-dimensional objects; the second form contained two-dimensional pictorial representations of the same objects. The study was conducted to explore the role of this task variable, socio-economic class, and age in the development of multiplicative classificatory skills. Although no differences were found for the two matrix forms, results indicate significant age and age-by-social class effects. Lower and middle class groups performed equally at 4- to 5- and 6- to 7-years of age. At 8-9 years, however, the lower class performed more poorly than the middle class group. There was no improvement for the lower class group between 6-7 and 8-9 years of age. Results are discussed in terms of the development and activation of cognitive structures.

521. Palmer, F. H. Socioeconomic status and intellective performance among Negro preschool boys. Developmental Psychology, 1970, 3 (1), 1-9.

Tested the assumption from studies of Negro elementary school children that differences in intellective performance are a function of the operation of socioeconomic status at earlier stages of development of the Negro child. With sampling pro-cedures and adaptation to the testing situation highly con-trolled, no differences were found by socioeconomic status among 240 Negro children up to age 3.8 years, and 70 matched controls when measures assessing a variety of intellective behaviors were used.

522. Pasamanick, B. and Knoblock, H. The contribution of some organic factors to school retardation in Negro children. Journal of Negro Education, 1958, 27, 4-9.

The large number of organically damaged Negro children will create additional problems in school desegregation. Studies show that inadequate prenatal nutrition, brain injuries to the fetus and neofetus, have a higher incidence among Negroes than among whites. There is a 50% greater risk for pre-maturity for Negro infants. There is a similar association for prematures and the organically injured in the low socio-economic classes of whites.

523. Pavlos, A. J. Sex differences among rural Negro children on the Wechsler Intelligence Scale for Children. Proceedings of the West Virginia Academy of Science, 1961, 33, 109-114.

29 Negro girls and 29 Negro boys between the ages of 11 and 14-1/2 were tested on the WISC. Girls scored statistically significantly higher than boys on the picture completion and

block design subtests. Boys scored higher on picture arrangements and information, as well as VIQ and FSIQ.

524. Peterson, J. Comparisons of white and Negro children in the
rational learning test. Twenty-Seventh Yearbook of the National
Society for the Study of Education, 1928, Part I, 333-341.

>   This study attacks the problem of racial differences in
>   ability through the use of a nonverbal instrument (the rational
>   learning test) which apparently depends very little upon facts
>   or skills accumulated through schooling or through the social
>   milieu. The test was applied in 1920-21 to all children of
>   8, 9 and 10 in three white and three Negro schools in Nash-
>   ville, and to most of the children of these ages in a fourth
>   white school. In 1923-24 it was also applied to 69 white and
>   46 Negro 12-year-olds selected irrespective of grade. The
>   latter group was weighted a little in favor of the Negroes,
>   since some of the accelerated white pupils were omitted from
>   the group due to an error of a principal. In the 1920-21
>   comparison, grouping the three ages together, the whites show
>   a superiority of 2.37 white quartile deviations on time
>   score, 1.23 white quartile deviations on repetition score,
>   and 1.47 white quartile deviations on error scores. In the
>   1923-24 comparison, the difference between the medians of
>   the whites and of the Negroes was, for time, 20.0 times the
>   probable error of the difference; for repetitions, .61 times
>   its probable error, and for errors, 3.0 times its probable
>   error. Measured in terms of white quartile deviations, the
>   differences were 1.19, 0.18, and 0.92 respectively. The
>   differences reported above are about as large as differences
>   which have been found between Negroes and whites upon verbal
>   tests.

525. Peterson, J. and Lanier, L. H. Studies in the comparative
abilities of whites and Negroes. Mental Measurement Monograph,
1929, (5), pp. vi + 156.

>   Comparative tests of 12-year-old white and Negro children.
>   A battery of tests was used as a basis of comparison, as
>   follows: Binet Group Test, Myers Mental Measure, International
>   Group Mental Tests, ingenuity tests, and Yerkes Point Scale.
>   White and Negro children in Nashville, Chicago and New York
>   were tested. Results: (a) There is a tendency for Negroes
>   of the highest intellectual ability to migrate to the Northern
>   and Eastern states. (b) Whites surpass in the ingenuity tests,
>   although the differences are on the whole statistically un-
>   reliable. The average differences of the group tests were
>   2.82 times greater than those of the ingenuity tests. This
>   is probably a measure of culture. As to speed of reaction
>   the whites, both of Nashville and New York, surpass markedly
>   and reliably the Negroes.

>   In Part II, comparisons of certain mental abilities in white
>   and Negro adults were made. Psychological tests used were:
>   (a) general ability tests, (b) mechanical ability tests,

(c) musical ability tests, and (d) will-temperament tests.
White adults are reliably superior over Negro adults in all
group intelligence tests. No sex differences were established.
Whites excel Negroes in all the Seashore tests, except rhythm.
The will-temperament tests are unsuited as race-tests. White
women have greater head length and width, on the average, than
the Negro women.

526. Peterson, J. and Telford, C. W. Results of group and of individual tests applied to practically pure-blood Negro children on St.
Helena Island. Journal of Comparative Psychology, 1930, 11, 115-144.

The authors administered certain standardized group tests and
five individual tests -- Rational Learning, three Pintner-
Paterson performance tests, and the Porteus Mental Maze. Results by the group tests -- Otis Primary, Haggerty Delta I,
Goodenough Draw-A-Man Picture Test, Otis S.-A. Intermediate,
and the Digit-Symbol and the Symbol-Digit tests -- show enormous differences, due, to a large extent, to inadequate training and background of the children. The individual tests results, analyzed in considerable detail as to reliability and
to the size of differences by different tests given in terms
of standard scores (therefore directly comparable), show that
in Rational Learning there is a reliable difference between
the median of the Island Negroes and that of Nashville whites
of equal age. This difference amounts of 1.87 probable errors
of the whites' distribution (P.E.$_w$). There is also a reliable
but smaller difference (1 P.E.$_n$) between the medians of the
Island Negroes and of Nashville Negroes of the same age; but
industrial school children did not excell the other Island
Negroes. The Two-Figure Form Board and the Healy Puzzle "A"
also made large and reliable differences between the Island
Negroes and the whites of equal age tested by Pintner in Ohio,
differences of 2.45 P.E.$_w$ and 1.72 P.E.$_w$, respectively; but
since these tests were less reliable than the Rational Learning
problem (.51 and .22, respectively, as compared with .56) the
corrected difference between race medians by these tests
was over 3 P.E.$_w$. The Mare and Foal test revealed no race
differences. No reliability of this test was available or
obtained. Of the performance test and the Porteus Maze, only
the Mare and the Foal showed a reliable difference between the
Penn School and other Island children. Of the three individual
tests given twice, Rational Learning showed the least practice
effect and also the greatest reliability. Obviously the
larger differences found by the performance tests between the
racial medians and also between those of the Penn School and
other Island Negro children are to a large extend due to
measuring cultural factors. The authors do not pretend to
measure pure innate differences with any test.

527. Phillips, L. W. and Bianchi, W. B. Desegretation, reading
achievement, and problem behavior in two elementary schools. Urban
Education, 1975, 9 (4), 325-339. Also, see ERIC Abstracts, No.
EJ-113-448, January 1975.

> Desegregated students showed greater gains in reading achievement
> at the end of 7 months than segregated students; however, these
> differences may be due to qualitative differences in reading
> instruction and do disappear after 24 months. Black students'
> IQs increased under conditions of desegregation while students
> in the control school lost ground. The only differences in
> the amount of problem behavior were a reduction in the social
> and emotional areas among the girls.

528. Phillips, R. H. The use of behavior modification to improve
self-esteem in low income elementary school children. Available from:
Xerox University Microfilms, P. O. Box 1764, Ann Arbor, Michigan
48106 (Order No. 75-18,920; microfilm or xerography). Also, see
ERIC Abstracts, No. ED-124-654#, 1975.

> The purpose of this study was to determine the effects of
> behavior modification on enhancing the self-esteem of low-
> income black and Puerto Rican elementary school children.
> Social reinforcement in the form of teacher praise was given
> to students who made any legitimate positive statements about
> themselves. The reinforcement was designed to increase the
> number of positive self-referent statements verbalized by the
> students. The Coppersmith Self-Esteem Inventory was adminis-
> tered to see if the experimental procedures were effective
> in improving self-esteem. A total of 30 children selected
> from 10 classes in the third, fourth and fifth grades, in a
> low-income New York elementary school, were used in this study.
> The children were black and Puerto Rican low-income students
> ranging in age from 8 to 11. Ten of the 30 children (5 boys
> and 5 girls) were placed in each of the three treatment groups:
> the experimental group (those receiving praise); the control
> group (those receiving no praise, but in the same classrooms);
> and the inventory group (those in different classrooms). In
> a 7-week study, it was found that a behavior modification pro-
> gram was effective in significantly improving self-esteem.
> The use of praise was effective in increasing the number of
> positive self-referent verbalizations.

529. Plaut, R. L. Variables affecting the scholastic achievement
of Negro children in non-segregated schools. Social Problems, 1955,
2 (4), 207-211.

> The following variables influence favorably or unfavorably
> (a) scholastic difficulties facing Negro children in moving
> from segregated to non-segregated schools, and (b) the time
> necessary for the achievement of scholastic adjustment; are
> described and an appropriate degree of importance assigned to
> each: (1) intellectual ability and emotional stability; (2)
> age of the student; (3) the Negro family's attitudes toward
> whites and toward integrated schools; (4) the community climate

(established lines of communication between Negroes and whites);
and (5) relative quality of instruction and curricular strength
in the formerly segregated and newly integrated schools, and
the degree of integration on the faculty level. Most students
who will catch up at all will do it by the end of their first
year in the new school situation. Some never will, but, then,
neither do some white students. The achievement problems
involved in the changeover are not racial but intellectual,
emotional, education, and socioeconomic. Students with enough
of these variable factors in their favor will catch up fast
enough; those with too many against them, like their less
advantaged white counterparts, will lag behind under any system.
Reprinted by permission.

530. Politzer, R. L. and Hoover, M. R. Teachers' and Pupils' attitudes
toward black English speech varieties and black pupils' achievement.
Research and Development Memorandum, No. 145. Washington, D. C.:
National Institute of Education (DHEW), June 1976. 62 pp. Also,
see ERIC Abstracts, No. ED-128-527, 1976.

The main purpose of this study is to measure the attitudes
of teachers toward speech varieties used by speakers of black
English and to determine whether there is any evidence that
those attitudes are linked to pupils' classroom performance
in reading. Also investigated is whether exposure to information about and experience with varieties of black English
will bring about a change in the attitudes of teachers, and
whether teachers tend to transmit their own attitudes to
pupils. The research was conducted in grades 4-6 in three
sites with a total of 456 pupils and 37 teachers. Among the
main conclusions of the study are the following: (a) that
teachers and pupils tend to agree in their attitudes toward
black speech varieties on certain crucial attitude dimensions,
such as the greater likelihood of the Standard Black English
(SBE) speaker's success in school; (b) the exposure to new
information appears to have no significant effect on apparently
well-established attitudinal characteristics; and (c) that
teacher attitudes have little documentable effect on actual
reading gains made by the pupil, but appear to have some
relation to the grades assigned by the teachers. It is concluded that teacher attitudes do have an impact on pupils --
on their achievement and perhaps most directly on their attitudes -- but the nature of the impact is influenced by many
factors.

531. Price, J. St. C. Negro-white differences in intelligence.
Opportunity, 1929, 7, 341-343.

From birth and during early infancy, Negroes lag behind
whites in weight; but toward the beginning of school age, they
move up and eventually overtake and exceed the whites, maintaining this lead until about the middle of adolescence, when
they again fall behind. This difference of growth, during
school age especially, may explain some of the obtained differences in achievement.

532. Quay, L. C. Language dialect, age and intelligence-test
performance in disadvantaged black children. Child Development,
1974, 45 (2), 463-468.

> The effects of administering the Stanford-Binet in Negro non-
> standard dialect were compared. Subjects were 104 third and
> sixth grade disadvantaged black children. Children from each
> grade were randomly placed by sex into one of two conditions
> of test administration: nonstandard dialect or standard
> English. A 2 (dialect condition) x 2 (sex of subject) x 2 (age
> level) analysis of variance of IQ scores yielded no signifi-
> cant effect of dialect condition or sex. There was a signifi-
> cant age effect, the third grade children making higher IQ
> scores than sixth grade children. There were no significant
> interactions. Comparisons of item difficulty yielded no con-
> sistent differences between nonstandard dialect and standard
> English test administration.

533. Quay, L. C. Language dialect, reinforcement, and the intelligence-
test performance of Negro children. Child Development, 1971, 42 (1),
5-15.

> The Stanford-Binet was administered to 100 4-year-old Negro
> children from Project Head Start under two conditions of lang-
> uage (standard English and Negro dialect) and two conditions
> of reinforcement (praise and candy). No reliable IQ differences
> among the groups and no significant interactions occurred.
> Differences in performance on individual Stanford-Binet items
> were negligible. The findings raised questions concerning the
> existence of motivational and language differences in young
> Negro children who are provided experiences designed to bring
> them into the mainstream culture. Reprinted by permission.

534. Ramirez, M. and Price-Williams, D. R. Cognitive styles of
children of three ethnic groups in the United States. Journal of
Cross-Cultural Psychology, 1974, 5 (2), 212-219.

> Administered the rod-and-frame test to 60 Anglo-Americans,
> 60 Mexican-Americans, and 60 black fourth graders attending
> Catholic parochial schools. Results show that blacks and
> Mexican-Americans scored in a significantly more field-
> dependent direction than Anglo-Americans. Females in all
> three groups were more field-dependent than males. Results
> confirm previous findings that members of groups which empha-
> size group identity and respect for family and religious
> authority, and which are characterized by shared-function
> family and friendship groups, tend to be field-dependent in
> cognitive style. In contrast, members of groups which encour-
> age questioning of convention and individual identity, and
> which are characterized by formally organized family and friend-
> ship groups, tend to be more field-independent.

535. Rapp, M. Sex differences in variability on the Wechsler
Ingelligence Scale for Children. See ERIC Abstracts, No. ED-132-164,
n.d. 9 pp.

> Both sides of a long standing and apparently still heated
> argument are reviewed and presented. Are males more variable
> in intelligence than females? In an attempt to answer the
> question the author employed data from a longitudinal growth
> study. Results indicated that sex differences in variability
> on individual subtests of the Wechsler Intelligence Scale for
> Children (WISC), Verbal IQ, Performance IQ and Total IQ were
> neither significant nor even consistent for both black and white
> subjects over the five-year period in which they were tested.
> Males and females had proportionally equal numbers scoring
> highest on individual subtests. However, in spite of a smaller
> sample size, males most often achieved the lowest subtest
> scores. Reviewing past research and his own work, the author
> hypothesized that the intelligence of males is not normally
> distributed, but slightly skewed towards the lower levels.

536. Ratusnik, D. L. and Koenigsknecht, R. A. Drawing test performance of black and white preschoolers as a function of biracial testing. Paper presented at the Annual Meeting of the American Educational Research Association (Washington, D. C.: March 30-April 3,
1975). Also, see ERIC Abstracts, No. ED-106-340, April 1975.

> Six speech and language clinicians, 3 black and 3 white,
> administered the Goodenough Drawing Test (1926) to 144 pre-
> schoolers. The four groups, lower socioeconomic black and
> white and middle socioeconomic black and white, were equally
> divided by sex. The biracial clinical setting was shown to
> influence test scores in black preschool age children. Although
> not statistically significant, marginally higher test scores
> were achieved in the same-race clinical setting by white pre-
> schoolers. Sex differences in the direction of higher scores
> for girls were noted in white but not black preschool chil-
> dren.

537. Ratusnik, D. L. and Koenigsknecht, R. A. Normative study of
the Goodenough Drawing Test and the Columbia Mental Maturity Scale
in a metropolitan setting. Perceptual and Motor Skills, 1975, 40
(3), 835-838.

> Found that the performance of 144 4- to 5-year-old black and
> white preschoolers on Goodenough Draw-A-Man Test and the Columbia
> Mental Maturity Scale was influenced by socioeconomic back-
> ground rather than race. While no overall difference in IQ
> was noted between the two tests, analysis displayed uniformly
> somewhat lower scores by blacks on the Draw-A-Man Test.

538. Reschly, D. J. and Jipson, F. J. Ethnicity, geographic locale,
age, sex, and urban-rural residence as variables in the prevalence of
mild retardation. American Journal of Mental Deficiency, 1976, 81 (2),
154-161.

> In this mental retardation prevalence study, the Wechsler Intelli-
> gence Scale for Children (revised) was administered to 950 of a

random sample of 1,040 children in Pima County, Arizona. The
sample was stratified for ethnicity (Anglo, N=252; black, N=235;
Mexican-American, N=223; Papago Indian, N=240), urban-rural
residence (urban, N=245; rural, N=230), sex (male, N=468;
female, N=482), and grade level (first, third, fifth, seventh,
ninth). Scores on Verbal, Performance, and Full-Scale tests
(cutoff points of 69 and 75) were used in comparisons of mild
retardation prevalence. This prevalence was significantly related to ethnicity and geographic locale. Sex, urban/rural
residence, and grade level were not related to prevalence.
The study finds that manipulating cutoff points and type of
intellectual measure used changed the disporportionate number
of non-Anglo children in classes for the mildly retarded. Five
tables. Reprinted by permission

539. Richmond, B. O. Creative and cognitive abilities of white and
Negro children. Journal of Negro Education, 1971, 40 (2), 111-116.

An attempt to ascertain both the cognitive and creative output
of white and Negro children in order to understand better the
need for educational experiences appropriate to their current
level of functioning. Subjects were 34 Negro and 36 white children in eighth grade classes that were segregated at the time
research was conducted. All subjects resided in rural areas
in northeast Georgia; thus their cultural background can be
properly designated as southern rural. The test battery included the Lorge-Thorndike Tests (Level 4), and Torrance Tests
of Creative Thinking, Verbal and Figural, Form B. It was predicted and found that white students achieved significantly
higher than Negro students on both verbal and non-verbal measures of intelligence. The second hypothesis, that Negro
students would score lower on creativity factors, was supported,
but only in part. There were no significant differences between white and Negro students on verbal originality and Negroes
scored higher on figural elaboration. It is obvious that measures of creativity do provide the educator with data on the
child that are not obtained through the traditional measures
of intelligence. It appears that a more comprehensive understanding of creativity together with the implementation of
educational practices to enhance creative expression can be
useful in providing meaningful educational experiences to the
disadvantaged child. Reprinted by permission.

540. Rieber, M. and Womack, M. The intelligence of preschool children as related to ethnic and demographic variables. Exceptional
Children, 1968, 34 (8), 609-614.

A group of 568 Negro, Latin-American, and Anglo preschool
children from families with incomes in the lowest 20% for the
community were given the Peabody Picture Vocabulary Test (PPVT).
The average IQ for Anglos was 85, for Negroes 69, and for
Latins 50.3. Children who scored in the lowest quartile were
compared with those in the highest on a number of economic
and family variables. Income and educational level of parents,
size of family, and maternal employment, were found to differ

significantly for the two groups. Approximately one-fourth
were retested after five weeks in a Head Start Preschool Program, and all three groups showed significant improvement.

541. Riley, R. T. and Denmark, F. L.   Field independence and measures
of intelligence: Some reconsiderations.   Social Behavior and Personality, 1974, 2 (1), 25-29.

A field study was conducted in a suburban elementary school to
ascertain the relationship between the Children's Embedded
Figures Test (CEFT), a measure of field independence, and
tests of verbal ability and general intelligence for lower class
black subjects.   A correlational analysis revealed strong interrelationships between these tests contrary to the previous findings of Witkin and his associates.   Grade level and sex interacted to produce different correlational structures for each
condition.   These results question the assertion that field
independence varies independently of intelligence of subjects
regardless of age, sex and social class.

542. Ringenbach, S. E., Houtz, J. C. and Feldhusen, J. F.   Development of a new measure of problem solving abilities of disadvantaged
children.   Proceedings of the American Psychological Association,
1972, 7 (Part 1), 55-56.

Describes the rationale and guidelines used in the construction of the Purdue Elementary Problem Solving Inventory.
Developmental data obtained from Negro, Caucasian and Spanish-
American second, fourth and sixth graders from different socioeconomic backgrounds are also reported.   The inventory includes
a slide presentation of cartoon drawings depicting children in
various real-life, problematic situations, a test booklet,
and an audio-tape of directions, picture descriptions, and item
alternatives.   Reading requirements are minimized.   Reliability
of the inventory is .79.   Analyses of variance demonstrate
that grade level, ethnic origin, and socioeconomic status,
all significantly affect subjects' performance on the inventory.

543. Robinson, M. L. and Meenes, M.   The relationship between test
intelligence of third grade Negro children and the occupations of
their parents.   Journal of Negro Education, 1947, 16, 136-141.

An analysis was made of the IQs and parental occupations of 444
third grade Negro children attending Washington, D. C. schools
in 1938-39, and 491 similar cases in 1945-46.   Both groups had
been given the Kuhlman-Anderson Intelligence Test.   Parental
occupation was determined from teachers' roll books and analyzed according to the Census Bureau occupational classification.   It was discovered that contrary to the findings with
white American children, only a slight relationship existed
between IQ of child and occupation of parent for Negro children.   However, this relationship was greater for the 1945-46
group than for the earlier one.   Correlations of .78 and .64
were found for average IQ and the presence of a radio in the
home, and average IQ and average rent of the community,

respectively. These findings are explained on the basis of cultural factors which influence the IQ.

544. Roen, S. R. Personality and Negro-white intelligence. Journal of Abnormal and Social Psychology, 1960, 61, 148-150.

The hypothesis tested was confirmed: The Negro group scored lower on the ACB (Army Classification Battery) than did the whites; the Negro group manifested a greater lack of self-confidence than did the whites. Research should be done on why Negroes seemed to incorporate intellectually defeating personality traits that play a major role in their inability to score on measures of intelligence.

545. Rohwer, W. D. and Ammon, M. S. Elaboration training and paired-associate learning efficiency in children. Journal of Educational Psychology, 1971, 62 (5), 376-383.

Assigned 60 high socioeconomic status (SES) white and 60 low SES black second graders to three treatment conditions: training, practice and control. In the training condition, subjects were instructed in verbal and visual methods of elaborating noun pairs to increase their efficiency in learning paired associates. Treatment effects were assessed in terms of performance on two post-test paired associate tasks: an aural list consisting of 25 noun pairs presented aurally; and a mixed list, consisting of 25 noun pairs presented both aurally and visually in five different ways. Results reveal a positive effect of elaboration training for both samples, but the effect was confined to the aural list for the high SES whites and to the mixed list for the low SES blacks.

546. Rohwer, W. D. and Harris, W. J. Media effects on prose learning in two populations of children. Journal of Educational Psychology, 1975, 67, 651-657.

Prose learning in high socioeconomic status (SES) white and low SES black fourth grade children was assessed as a function of presentation media, test-item structure, and response methods. Presentation conditions included both single media -- oral, print, and pictures -- and combined media. The learning of intra- and intersentence relations was tested by means of assertion-verification, short-answer, and free recall methods. For the low SES black children, performance in the combined media conditions, especially in oral plus pictures, was superior to that in single-media conditions. Among high SES white subjects, combinations of media were of little benefit.

547. Rohwer, W. D. and Matz, R. D. Improving aural comprehension in white and black children: Pictures versus prints. Journal of Experimental Child Psychology, 1975, 19 (1), 23-36.

The improvement of aural comprehension was examined in white and black children. A total of 128 fourth grade children verified assertions about three prose passages they had heard. Half

of the children were white, from high status families, and
half were black from low status families. Within each sample,
an independent group design was used to appraise the effect
of two presentation conditions under each of two conditions
of testing. Oral renditions of each passage were accompanied
by either pictoral illustrations of text information or printed
versions of the text. Results confirm the hypothesis that
pictorial augmentation is more effective than print in paired-
associate learning.

548. Rosenthal, R., Boratz, S. S., and Hall, C. M. Teacher behavior,
teacher expectations, and gains in pupils' rated creativity. Journal
of Genetic Psychology, 1974, 124 (First Half), 115-121.

The effects of teacher expectations and behavior upon pupils'
creative performance in a ghetto school are discussed. Teachers'
positive and negative inputs and interactions with 416 pupils
and behavioral antecedents were examined. Within each of the
classrooms of a predominantly black inner city school, approximately one-fifth of the children were designated to their
teachers as showing unusual potential for gains in creativity.
Those fifth graders who had been expected to bloom in creativity
also showed significant effects of teachers' expectancies upon
their IQ scores. In general, greater gains in creativity scores
were made by children whose teachers behaved in a more motivated,
more child centered, more professional, and more encouraging
manner. Consistent with the results of other research employing black students, teachers tended to become relatively more
negative toward those students of whom they had been led to
expect more. The method for scoring youngsters' creativity
by teachers was deemed to be a good one.

549. Rotenberg, M. Conceptual and methodological notes on affective
and cognitive role taking (sympathy and empathy): An illustrative
experiment with delinquent and nondelinquent boys. Journal of Genetic
Psychology, 1974, 125 (2), 177-185.

The ambiguity and inconsistency permeating the operational
definitions and empirical measures of empathy and sympathy
are briefly reviewed. The terms "affective role-taking" and
"cognitive role-taking" dispositions are assessed separately
on the same subjects. Preliminary findings comparing delinquents and nondelinquents suggest that the delinquents are in
no way deficient in cognitive role-taking skills, while they
are significantly lower than nondelinquents in affective role-
taking. Unexpected findings indicate that black delinquents
perceive their past relations with home and peers in significantly warmer terms than do white delinquents. The generality
of theoretical formulations concerning the relations between
socialization processes and aggression or delinquency are
seriously questioned. (Modified.)

550. Rowe, G. D. Educational outcomes associated with ethnic changes in school populations. Paper presented at the Annual Meeting of the American Education Research Association (Washington, D. C.: April 1, 1975). 27 pp. Also, see ERIC Abstracts, No. ED-111-894, 1975.

This document examines the data on changes in the ethnic composition of the schools in Milwaukee, and relates them to student achievement. A consideration of the relationship of ethnicity and academic achievement is said to entail six questions as follows: how ethnic proportions of pupils have changed over a 10-year period; their patterns of achievement in reading and math during an 8-year period; the relationship between percent of minorities in school and reading/math achievement; whether the strength of the relationship changes with an increase in proportion of minority pupils; whether the rate of change in ethnicity affects the proportion of the relationship; and, the extent to which open enrollment serves as voluntary desegregation or resegregation. Minority subgroups included American Indian, black, Asian, and Spanish-surnamed children. Findings of the study noted an increase in the number of minority pupils with a decrease of non-minority pupils in the 10-year period. Open enrollment is said to have had a slight effect in increasing segregation. Although achievement in reading and math are said to have decreased, a reduced rate of decrease had been found. A double proportion of minority students in the 8-year period had not been found to increase the strength of the relationship between proportion of minority students and achievement, and rate of change in ethnicity not found to show a stable relationship with the variable of student achievement.

551. Russell, J. J. Mental elaboration and cognitive performance. Journal of Negro Education, 1974, 43 (2), 202-211.

The joint effects of training and inducing black children to use deliberately a general mental elaboration system and an organization device (peg word list) similar to that used in commercial memory texts in learning paired-associates word lists were evaluated. Subjects were in grades 4, 6 and 8, and the peg system is a systemization and/or organizational device for facilitating individual learning performance. Results generally support the hypothesis which posits that learning efficiency improves as the learner elaborates on raw materials presented to him. Students can be trained and induced to use a mental elaboration system to facilitate recall performance on a paired-associates task, especially at grades 4 and 6. Eighth graders, although seemingly using an elaborate mode, tended to have developed their own systems for processing materials. Subjects instructed to use imagery recalled significantly more response nouns than subjects not so instructed, as indicated in the cues' main effect, and there were significant effects for the grades variable.

552. Ryckman, D. B. A comparison of information processing abilities of middle and lower class Negro kindergarten boys. Exceptional Children, 1967, 33 (8), 545-552.

Fifty middle class and fifty lower class Negro kindergarten boys were administered a battery of eight instruments designed to assess specific information processing abilities. An analysis of 19 variables produced five reasonably meaningful components, with a general language ability component the most significant. When class groups were compared, this component discriminated most significantly between the groups. Implications for educational definition, diagnosis, and program planning are discussed.

553. Samuel, W., et al. Motivation, race, social class, and IQ. Journal of Educational Psychology, 1976, 68 (3), 273-285.

Administered the Performance subscales of the WISC to 208 male and 208 female junior and senior high school students (aged 12-16 years) to test the prediction that if performance responded to the manipulation of the testee's motivation state, the size of interracial differences in mean IQ would be more flexible than was suggested by A. R. Jensen's (1969) review of the literature. The variables of test atmosphere (evaluative or gamelike), tester expectation (high or low), race of tester (black or white), and race of subject (black or white) were manipulated. The pattern of mean IQ scores as well as self-ratings of mood indicated that test performance was optimal at moderate levels of motivational arousal. A replication of the experiment employing 208 male subjects increased cell sizes to the point that socioeconomic status could be treated as an independent variable. Results suggested that interracial differences in mean IQ might be erased depending upon the social psychological characteristics of the test setting and the socioeconomic background of the testee.

554. Samunda, R. J. From ethnocentrism to a multi-cultural perspective in educational testing. Journal of Afro-American Issues, 1975, 3 (1), 4-18.

In the literature dealing with educational testing, three models to explain how scoring of minorities have prevailed -- the genetically deficient, the culturally deprived, and the culturally different. The author discusses each of these explanations and then suggests that standardized testing will continue to record how scores for minorities and should be discarded. Because of a set of assumptions about the universality of the population's experiences and values, standardized tests have not erased obstacles to advancement, as some initially intended they whould, but have confirmed them in the case of minorities. The author suggests instead that a student's "functioning level" should be discovered and then his weaknesses, once revealed, should be remedied by programmes fitted to his needs. "If comparisons must be made they must be within the cultural and

socioeconomic group structure of each individual", but to
ignore the facts of cultural differences is to operate a
socially-loaded selection process.

555. Sattler, J. M. and Kuncik, T. M. Ethnicity, socioeconomic
status, and pattern of WISC scores as variables that affect psychologists' estimates of effective intelligence. Journal of Clinical Psychology, 1976, 32 (2), 362-366.

   110 psychologists estimated "true IQs" or "effective intelligence" from WISC profiles that varied for ethnicity (black,
   Mexican-American, or white), social class (lower or middle),
   profile (3 scatter patterns), and direction of Verbal-Performance
   scale discrepancy. Psychologists gave higher IQ estimates to
   black and Mexican-American children's profiles than to the same
   profiles of white children. Social class was not a significant
   factor. Profiles with much scatter received higher IQs than
   profiles with limited scatter. The pattern of subtest scores
   also affected estimates, while the direction of the Verbal-
   Performance discrepancy was not significant. Finally, the
   WISC was judged to be more valid for white than for black
   and Mexican-American children.

556. Scarr, S. and Weinberg, R. A. IQ test performance of black
children adopted by white families. American Psychologist, 1976, 31,
726-739.

   139 black interracial subjects adopted by advantaged white
   families were studied. The socially classified black adoptees,
   whose natural parents were educationally average, scored above
   the IQ and the school achievement mean of the white population.
   Biological children of the adoptive parents scored higher.
   Genetic and environmental determinants of differences among
   the black/interracial adoptees were largely confounded. The
   high IQ scores of the socially classified black adoptees indicate malleability for IQ under rearing conditions that are
   relevant to the tests and the schools.

557. Schaefer, E. S. A home tutoring program. Children, March-
April 1969, 16 (2), 59-61.

   An experimental group of 31 children under two years of age
   and a control group of 33 children of the same age were
   selected from two lower socioeconomic neighborhoods in Washington, D. C. All children were Negro males. College graduates
   were recruited as tutors, and an educational program was designed to develop positive relationships with the child and
   his family and to provide verbal stimulation and complex
   experiences. Intelligence tests were administered to the
   children in both groups at ages 14, 21, 27 and 36 months. Findings indicate that the distribution of IQ scores for the experimental and control groups differed greatly, the lowest IQ
   socres of an experimental infant at 36 months being equal to
   the mean IQ for the control group. Analyses of the extensive
   data collected on the experimental groups at 36 months revealed

significant correlations between methods of child care and the
child's behavior and mental test scores. Three clusters of
interrelated variables were isolated from the tutor's observations and labeled "child neglect," "maternal hostile uninvolvement," and "child hostile maladjustment." Child neglect correlated highly with maternal hostile uninvolvement. Both child
neglect and maternal hostile uninvolvement correlated significantly with hostile maladjustment of the child. The tutors'
observations of child neglect, of maternal hostile uninvolvement,
and of child maladjustment correlated significantly with the
mental testers' independent blind ratings of low task-oriented
behavior and low mental test scores on the part of the child,
and these clusters also correlated highly with one another.
These data suggest that the quality of early maternal care has
a significant effect upon a child's adjustment, task-oriented
behavior, and mental test scores at 36 months.

558. Schultz, R. E. A comparison of Negro pupils' ranking high
with those ranking low in educational achievement. Journal of Educational Sociology, 1958, 31, 265-270.

The results of the study were based upon 50 ninth grade Negro
pupils who scored highest, and 50 who scored lowest, on a
standardized achievement test in one Florida county. Results
of the study are analyzed, implications are discussed and
conclusions drawn.

559. Scott, R. First to ninth grade IQ changes of northern Negro
students. Psychology in the Schools, 1966, 3 (2), 159-160.

Analyzes the impact of northern environment on the patterning
of Negro IQ. The results indicate that there was a tendency
to lose rather than gain in performance on the two different
administrations of intelligence tests. The failure to demonstrate gain (as found in earlier studies of this nature) was
attributed to the change in social conditions.

560. Scott, R. Social class, race, seriating and reading readiness:
A study of their relationship at the kindergarten level. Journal of
Genetic Psychology, 1969, 115 (1), 87-96.

Piaget and Inhelder have suggested that the growth of young
children's logic is characterized by a close interaction of
language (classification) and perceptual (seriation) functions.
This article reports the correlation of kindergarten children's
scores on an experimental seriation test and the Metropolitan
Reading Readiness Test (MRRT). Results support the Piaget-
Inhelder view that there is a close relationship between seriation scores and attainments on both the Reading Readiness and
Number Readiness subtests of the MRRT. The data indicate
that disadvantaged Negro and white kindergarten children are
as severely handicapped on perceptual as on verbal items.
Findings indicate that effective early intellectual enrichment
should consist of both language and perceptual tasks.

561. Scott, R. and Kobes, D. A. The influence of family size on learning readiness patterns of socioeconomically disadvantaged preschool blacks. Journal of Clinical Psychology, 1975, 31 (1), 85–88.

> Preschool readiness measures were secured on 35 pairs of disadvantaged 2- to 3-year-old lower socioeconomic status (SES) black children, who represented large and small families, to determine the impact of family size on readiness profiles. The findings reveal that blacks from small families achieved significantly higher scores on three of the nine skill areas: visual memory, expressive language, and expressive concepts. The results are reviewed in the context of Inhelder-Piaget formulations that concern the early growth of the intellect, which provide a possible explanation of how intrafamily dynamics may depress the learning of black lower SES preschool children. It is suggested that replication and longitudinal studies are needed to ascertain better the long-term social and educational implications of these findings.

562. Scott, R. and Smith, J. E. Ethnic and demographic variables and achievement scores of preschool children. Psychology in the Schools, 1972, 9 (2), 174–182.

> Studied the relationship between mother's verbal IQ, level of education, certain family environmental process variables (FEPV), and intellectual development of preschool disadvantaged children. Subjects were 28 Afro-American (CA=30.6 months) and 10 Anglo-American (CA=30.1 months) in a Head Start program. Among the findings were that FEPV and gain scores on the Iowa Tests of Preschool Development are useful in identifying children who can profit from a cognitive-enrichment program, and material IQ and education are not useful in predicting success in the program.

563. Scrofani, P. J., Suziedelis, A., and Shore, M. F. Conceptual ability in black and white children of different social classes: An experimental test of Jensen's hypothesis. American Journal of Orthopsychiatry, 1973, 43 (4), 541–553.

> Tested A. Jensen's 1969 theory of inherent conceptual ability differences between groups of different socioeconomic status (SES). 382 fourth graders of all SES levels were trained in concept formation. A significant number of low SES subjects were able to achieve middle class performance levels in conceptual tasks. Ability to profit from training was related to the developmental measures of cognition. No sex, age or racial differences were found.

564. Segalla, F. L. Writing vocabularies of Negro and white children. School Review, 1934, 42, 772–779.

> From a study of the vocabularies of colored and white children in the Phillips and Fenger high schools, Chicago, the author found no appreciable difference.

565. Seitz, V. Integrated versus segregated school attendance and
immediate recall for a standard and nonstandard test. Developmental
Psychology, 1975, 11 (2), 217-223.

   Imitative recall was examined for sentences conforming to the
   grammatical rules of standard English versus those suggested
   for nonstandard (black) English in black and white children
   attending segregated and integrated schools. Low income black
   children showed better recall than middle income white children
   for nonstandard sentences, and poorer recall for standard
   sentences. School integration influenced the performance of
   low income black children. Those who attended an integrated
   school were both better on standard, and poor on nonstandard,
   sentences than those who had attended a segregated school.
   For middle income children, both black and white, there were
   no evident linguistic effects of integration. Although dialect
   clearly affects recall, the results do not support a conception
   of black dialect as a separate linguistic system with totally
   consistent rules.

566. Sekra, F. and Arnoult, J. F. Negro intellectual assessment with
three instruments contrasting Caucasian and Negro norms. Journal of
Learning Disabilities, 1968, 1 (10), 564-569.

   Compared the Stanford-Binet (S-B), 1969 Revision (Form L-M),
   the WISC, and the Columbia Mental Maturity Scale (CMMS) intelligence scores of 30 rural and 30 urban Negro subjects divided
   into three groups of 20 each from the second, fifth and eighth
   grades. Both Caucasian and Negro norms of the S-B were used
   to study the need for further standardization of Negro subjects
   on the WISC and CMMS. Results show significant correlations
   between the WISC and the S-B (Caucasian norms), with relatively
   lower correlation between the CMMS and the WISC. When the S-B
   (Negro norms) were compared to all other instrument scores,
   they yielded significantly higher MAs, indicating that neither
   the WISC nor the CMMS is giving an adequate indication of
   intellectual functioning for Negroes. It is concluded that
   "future studies should be made regarding the validity of the
   CMMS and the WISC scores when assessing members of the Negro
   population."

567. Semler, I. J. and Iscoe, I. Comparative and developmental study
of the learning abilities of Negro and white children under four
conditions. Journal of Educational Psychology, 1963, 54 (1), 38-44.

   Subjects were 135 Negro and 141 whites, ages 5 through 9 years.
   Object pairs and picture pairs of these same objects in conceptually similar or dissimilar sets were the four experimental
   conditions for comparing paired associate learning. Despite
   sign, lower FS WISC IQ scores, the ANDUA showed that the differences in paired associate learning favoring white subjects
   at younger age levels disappeared by 9, with no race difference when the age factor was disregarded. Race differences in
   IQ were greatest at 5 years; however, negligible correlations
   were obtained between learning and IQ for both races. Asso-

ciating object pairs in conceptually similar sets was easiest,
and picture pairs in dissimilar sets most difficult, for both
races.

568. Semler, I. J. and Iscoe, I. Structure of intelligence in Negro
and white children. Journal of Educational Psychology, 1966, 57 (6),
326-336.

Performance levels on the WISC and on the Progressive Matrices
(PM) and the factorial structures of the WISC were compared for
white and Negro children. WISCs were administered individually
to 141 white and 134 Negro subjects ranging from 5 to 9 years
of age. The 7-, 8-, and 9-year-old subjects were also given
the PM as a group test. White subjects had higher WISC Full
Scale IQs than Negroes at all age levels (p<.001) and higher PM
total scores at the 7-year level (p<.05), but not at the 8-
and 9-year levels. While the white and Negro WISC intercorrelation matrices appeared to be similar, a multivariate analysis
of variance showed heterogeneous dispersions (p<.001) and mean
vectors (p<.001). Since the multivariate analysis indicated
statistically dissimilar WISC structures for the white and
Negro samples, separate factor analyses were computed to explore the nature of the differences. The PM intercorrelation
matrices for whites and Negroes were highly similar.

569. Sewell, T. E. and Severson, R. A. Intelligence and achievement
in first grade black children. Journal of Consulting and Clinical
Psychology, 1975, 43 (1), 112.

The relationship between IQ, as measured by the Wechsler
Intelligence Scale for Children (WISC), and academic achievement in regularly placed first grade black children, was investigated. 84 black children (43 boys, 41 girls) randomly
selected and ranging in age from 5 years and 10 months to 7
years and 5 months were administered seven subtests of the
WISC, and achievement was measured by the word reading and
arithmetic subtests of the Stanford Achievement Test. The
obtained mean IQ of 86, while lower than the postulated mean
of 100 for a normative white sample, is consistent with standard deviation differences in IQs between blacks and whites.
Correlations between IQ and achievement were significant,
although lower than the reported average coefficient. The
pattern of results generates the suspicion that this sample
differs from the WISC normative population. Until possible
sources of differences are identified, the individual subtests
of the WISC must be used with caution for diagnostic or predictive purposes.

570. Sewell, T. E. and Severson, R. A. Learning ability and intelligence as cognitive predictors of achievement in first grade black
children. Journal of Educational Psychology, 1974, 66 (6), 948-955.

The relationship between achievement and variables associated
with learning ability was examined to determine their predictive
effectiveness. 62 first grade black children were individually

tested on the Wechsler Intelligence Scale for Children and
tasks from the following learning assessment strategies: (a)
learning potential strategy format using Raven's Coloured Progressive Matrices in a pretest, coaching, post-test format;
(b) diagnostic teaching; and (c) paired-associated learning
under three conditions designed to facilitate learning. IQ
correlated moderately with achievement. Diagnostic teaching
generally exceeded IQ in predictive effectiveness. Prospects
for a more precise determination of the learning potential
in young children are discussed.

571. Sheehan, D. S. and Marcus, M. The effects of teacher race and
student race on vocabularly and mathematics achievement. Journal of
Educational Research, 1977, 70 (3), 123-126.

Evidence exists to support the contention that matching teachers
and students on the basis of race would result in increased
student performance. A study was conducted to investigate
these interactions, using 319 first grade teachers and 4,139
first graders. The racial composition of the teachers was
approximately one-third black and two-thirds white; that of
the pupils was about one-half black and one-half white.
Measures used were the Metropolitan Readiness Tests and Iowa
Tests of Basic Skills. Matching students with teachers on
the basis of race was ineffectual in terms of improving resi-
dual gain scores in mathematics and vocabulary. In addition,
overall, white teachers were more effective than black teachers.
Yet, at least in the area of vocabulary achievement, and with
teachers having less than five years experience, the reverse
was true. Because the variables considered did not account
for an appreciable proportion of the total variance in the
mathematics and vocabulary scores, a new approach for matching
students with teachers is suggested.

572. Sheikh, A. A. and Twerski, M. Future-time perspective in
Negro and white adolescents. Perceptual and Motor Skills, 1974, 39
(1, Part 1), 308.

The future time perspective, as measured through TAT stories,
was compared in Negro and white high school students of lower
socioeconomic class. A comparison of the total scores yielded
no significant differences. The total scores on the three
Thompson cards were compared with the total scores on the
three Murray cards separately for white and Negro subjects.
The white group showed a significantly different response
pattern on the Murray administration and the Thompson, with
future time extension constricted on the latter. The Negro
subjects' responses to the two TAT administrations did not
differ. Possible reasons for the results are discussed.

573. Shure, M. B., Spivack, G., and Jaeger, M. Problem-solving
thinking and adjustment among disadvantaged preschool children. Child
Development, 1971, 42, 1791-1803.

The relationship between school behavior adjustment of 4-year-
old disadvantaged children and real-life problem-solving thinking

was studied. The latter includes three parameters of thought
-- conceptualization of solutions to typical peer and authority
problems, consequential thinking, and causal thinking. Resulting data show that the ability to conceptualize alternative
solutions to problems was the only parameter directly related
to teacher-rated judgments of classroom behavior but that all
parameters were significantly interrelated. Implications are
that increasing a child's ability to think in terms of alternative
solutions to real-life problems could supplement a primary
preventive mental health program.

574. Sigel, I. E., Anderson, L. M., and Shapiro, H. Categorization
behavior of lower and middle class Negro preschool children: Differences in dealing with representation of familiar objects. Journal
of Negro Education, 1966, 35, 218-229.

24 socioeconomically disadvantaged, and 20 middle class, Negro
preschool boys and girls were presented three sorting tasks
made up of 12 familiar items. The tasks varied in their mode
of presentation, i.e., actual objects, colored pictures comparable in size to the actual items, and black and white pictures also comparable in size to the actual. Lower class
children differed from their middle class peers in their
ability to group only the colored and black and white pictures.
Differences between the two groups were found in the types
of categories employed, lower class children showing preference
for grouping based on use and interdependence of items, in
contrast to middle class children who preferred to classify
on the basis of common physical attributes. This is true
irrespective of mode of presentation. It is concluded that
lower class children have not yet acquired adequate representation of familiar objects. Implications for education are
presented.

575. Silverstein, A. B. Factor structure of the Wechsler Intelligence Scale for Children for three ethnic groups. Journal of Educational Psychology, 1973, 65 (3), 408-410.

Correlations among the Wechsler Intelligence Scale for Children (WISC) were factored for groups of Anglo, black and
Chicano public school children, and two factors (Verbal Comprehension and Perceptual Organization) were found for each
group. The results of two methods of assessing factorial
invariance suggest that the WISC measures the same abilities
in children of all three groups.

576. Sitkei, E. G. and Meyers, C. E. Comparative structure of
intellect in middle and lower class 4-year-olds of two ethnic groups.
Developmental Psychology, 1969, 1 (5), 592-604.

Hypothesized greater status and ethnic differences for semantic
than for other ability factors for lower status and Negro
subjects. Six ability hypotheses implicit in a 22-test
battery were determined for four subgroups of middle and
lower SES Negro and white children (N=100). Obtained factor

structure showed no qualitative difference among groups but
confirmed and enlarged the structure of intellect patterns
established in previous work. Significant differences in
mean factor scores confirmed hypotheses of status and ethnic
difference only for cognitive semantics. Divergent semantic,
figural, and memory factors did not differ.

577. Smith, M. S. and Bissell, J. S. The impact of Head Start:
The Westinghouse-Ohio Head Start evaluation. Harvard Educational
Review, 1970, 40 (1), 51-104; Reply, 104-129.

The Westinghouse-Ohio national evaluation of Head Start and
the various criticisms it has evoked from both social scientists and statisticians are discussed in the context of the
history of Head Start. Serious questions are raised about the
sampling procedures used in the study and the results of a
re-analysis using different procedures are presented which
suggest that some full-year Head Start Centers were effective,
particularly those with black children in urban areas. Stratified random sampling might have confirmed this; many kinds of
centers were almost unrepresented in the sample, particularly
the full-year centers vs. the summer centers. The re-analysis
shows that the first grade children who participated in full-
year Head Start programs perform significantly better than
controls on the Metropolitan Readiness Test. Second grade
Head Start children from urban black centers were also superior
to the control children on the Stanford Achievement Test and
the Illinois Test of Psycholinguistic Abilities. It is suggested
that disadvantaged children benefit less from their public
school experience than do middle class children. The rate
of achievement of disadvantaged children varies according to
the modal level of their class. The policy implications of
these findings are assessed and some suggestions are offered
regarding the form and place of program evaluation in making
public policy. Three clear implications emerge: (a) Careful
and valid evaluations are extremely difficult to conduct
under the best of conditions. (b) The failure of the
Westinghouse-Ohio Study to successfully match Head Start children and control children suggests that ex post facto studies
of voluntary social action programs are doomed to failure
before they begin. (c) Issue is taken with the Office of
Economic Opportunity notion that "overall evaluations" of
programs such as Head Start, Job Corps, etc., can be used to
provide information about the relative effectiveness of the
various programs. The most useful information evaluations
can provide are concerned with how social action programs
should be carried out, not whether they should exist. Victor G.
Cicirelli, John W. Evans, and Jeffry S. Schiller (University
of Wisconsin, Madison and Office of Economic Opportunity, Washington, D. C.), The Impact of Head Start: A Reply to the Report
Analysis, dispute both the criticism of the Westinghouse methodology and the re-analysis of the data. It is argued that this
re-analysis ignored the bulk of the Westinghouse data, that
it is based on a statistically incorrect procedure, and that
it produces results essentially similar to those reported by

Westinghouse. Careful examination shows that the Westinghouse
evidence indicates that the Head Start program has had a small
impact on some of the children in some portions of the sample
on one of the cognitive measures used, but not on the other
measures. The Westinghouse findings may be unpleasant, but
they cannot be rejected on factual evidence. Agreement is
voiced with the statement that such evaluations are difficult
to conduct. No attack on the idea and purpose of Head Start
was intended; the study was merely a frank recognition of
certain shortcomings. Reprinted by permission.

578. Solomon, D., Hirsch, J. G., Sheinfeld, D. R., and Jackson, J. C.
Family characteristics and elementary school achievement in an urban
ghetto. Journal of Consulting and Clinical Psychology, 1972, 39 (3),
462-466.

Investigated the relationships of sex, father absence, family
size, and birth order, to factor scores representing "general
academic achievement" in a sample of 149 urban black ghetto
fifth graders. Significant main effects were found for sex
(with girls showing higher achievement levels than boys) and
family size (with the highest achievement in small families).
A significant birth order x family size interaction was found:
Firstborn subjects did best in small families; lastborn subjects did best in intermediate (4 to 5 children) families;
and there was no birth order differentiation in large families.
No significant effect on achievement was found for father
absence.

579. Solomon, D., Houlihan, K. A., and Parelius, R. J. Intellectual
achievement responsibility in Negro and white children. Psychological Reports, 1969, 24, 479-483.

Related children's intellectual achievement responsibility
scores to sex, school grade (fourth vs. sixth), socioeconomic
status, and race. Subjects were 137 white and 125 Negro children. Only sex showed significant main effects: Girls scored
higher than boys in acceptance of internal responsibility
overall for positive outcomes. The possibility that situational effects may account for discrepancies between these
race and class results and those obtained with other locus
of control measures was considered.

580. Southern, M. L. and Plant, W. T. Differential cognitive
development within and between racial and ethnic groups of disadvantaged preschool and kindergarten children. Journal of Genetic
Psychology, 1971, 119 (2), 259-266.

Administered (a) the Information and Comprehension subtests
of the Wechsler Preschool and Primary Scale of Intelligence,
and (b) the Vocal Encoding and Auditory Vocal Automatic subtests of the Illinois Test of Psycholinguistic Abilities,
to disadvantaged children in a special preschool program and
kindergarten. Subjects included 438 Mexican-Americans, 85
Negroes, and 92 Anglo-Americans. Different patterns of spe-

cific cognitive and language skills were found within and
between racial ethnic groups. Results support previous findings that disadvantaged children possess deficits in general
intellectual and language abilities.

581. Sperrazzo, G. and Wilkins, W. L. Racial differences on progressive matrices. Journal of Consulting Psychology, 1959, 23, 273-
274.

The authors acknowledge Jensen's (Journal of Consulting Psychology, 1959, 23, 272) correction of their statistical error
and go on to carry out the analyses he suggested. These show
that white children of middle and upper socioeconomic groups
tend to score higher on the Progressive Matrices than do Negro
children in the same groups. The difference in the lower
socioeconomic level is not significant. The authors point
out that socioeconomic strata are probably not comparable
between races.

582. Spilerman, S. Raising academic motivation in lower class
adolescents: A convergence of two research traditions. Discussion
papers 75-70. Washington, D. C.: Office of Economic Opportunity,
August 1970. Also, see ERIC Abstracts, No. ED-133-396, 1970.

Two research traditions in the study of learning and motivation
are integrated for the study of adolescent behavior. One is
concerned primarily with the normal functioning of adolescent
society, the other with the design of reward structures to
foster academic achievement. The literature covering the use
of material incentives for motivating children and the importance of peer group organization in adolescent culture is
surveyed. It is argued that these two considerations are
especially relevant to lower class adolescents, and the
likely impact of a reward structure based upon an amalgam of
these themes is explored. Specifically, it is suggested here
that combining material inducements for achievement with a
reward structure organized around peer groups can provide an
effective strategy for motivating lower class adolescents
toward academic goals.

583. Starkman, S., Butkovich, C., and Murray, T. The relationship
among measures of cognitive development, learning proficiency,
academic achievement, and IQ for seventh grade, low socioeconomic
status black males. Journal of Experimental Education, 1976, 45
(2), 52-56.

Examined the degree of relationship among measures of learning proficiency; cognitive development (following Piaget);
school achievement in reading, mathematics, and spelling;
and IQ among 79 low socioeconomic status black males attending
the seventh grade in an inner city school. The following
hypotheses were tested: (a) There would be a positive and
significant relationship between measures of learning proficiency or cognitive growth and school achievement; (b) learning and cognitive variables would fall into a common factorial

domain; and (c) the latter two variables would hold a reciprocal relationship within that domain. Hypothesis (a) was
not supported, while (b) and (c) were supported. The latter
two results support A. R. Jensen's (see PA, Vol. 43:9740)
2-level theory of learning. These findings and between-
pupil differences in cognitive development are discussed.

584. Steg, D. R., et al. Deviation-amplification: Two case studies
in cognitive development, a seven-year report (1969-1976). The
Netherlands: Bernard Van Leer Foundation, The Hague, September 6,
1976. Also, see ERIC Abstracts, No. ED-134-326, 1976.

Findings of a longitudinal study of early intervention are
presented in this report of two case studies of low socioeconomic status black children. A girl and boy, approximately
three years old when first enrolled in the educational day
care program, exhibited severe behavior problems. Intellectual, emotional, psycholinguistic and perceptual functioning
were retarded. The focus of the preschool program was on
the acquisition of skills leading to reading, typing and number
concepts, with the relationship of intellectual development
to affective and social development also considered. Special
use was made of the "talking typewriter" and "talking page."
Remarkable progress in overall development was shown by both
children in preschool and continued throughout the period
under study, to age nine. Test data is given for the 7-year
period. Achievements in cognitive development of the two
children indicate the same kind of exponential curve, growing
slowly at first, then rapidly, in a basic pattern of escala-
tion. The talking typewriter is seen as a tool whereby the
learner can begin to develop attitudes about learning and
substantial cognitive skills through which he can realize
that he plays a significant role in controlling his environment. In each of these case histories, increasing confidence
seemed to alleviate a particular problem: the girl's chaotic
classroom behavior began to be self-directed into constructive
activity; and the boy's inwardly directed active imagination
began to turn outward in a positive way.

585. Stein, N. L. and Mandler, J. M. Development of detection and
recognition of orientation of geometric and real figures. Child
Development, 1975, 46 (2), 379-388.

Tested 80 black and white kindergartners and second graders
for accuracy of detection and recognition of orientation and
location changes in pictures of real-world and geometric
figures. No differences were found in accuracy of recognition between the two kinds of pictures, but patterns of
verbalization differed on specific transformations. Although
differences in accuracy were found between kindergarten and
second grade on an initial recognition task, practice on a
matching-to-sample task eliminated differences on a second
recognition task. Few ethnic differences were found on
accuracy of recognition, but significant differences were
found in amount of verbal output on specific transformations.

For both groups, mention of orientation changes was markedly reduced when location changes were present.

586. Stradford, G. T. Problems of bright and dull Negro children. Smith College Studies in Social Work, 1943, 14, 241.

587. Strickland, S. P. Can slum children learn? American Education, 1971, 7 (6), 3-7.

Various educational intervention strategies for disadvantaged children have sometimes been based more on hope than on scientific evidence. A University of Wisconsin project in Milwaukee supported by the Social and Rehabilitation Service of the Department of Health, Education and Welfare provides hard data to support the belief that, under the right circumstances, intervention can be successful even in the most difficult situations. The project suggests that some factors affecting learning capacity and intelligence quotients which could be considered matters of inheritance are instead matters of environment. The project's implications relate to several educational concerns from compensatory education to mental retardation. The majority of children reared by economically disadvantaged families develop and learn in a relatively normal fashion. Surveys begun in 1964 in a slum area of Milwaukee found that maternal intelligence was the most reliable single indicator of the level and character of intellectual development of the children. It was found that the mentally retarded mother creates a social environment for her offspring that is distinctly different. A compensatory program has resulted in the marked acceleration in a range of intellectual skills. The children in the experimental group are learning at a rate in excess of the norm for their age peers generally.

588. Stuempfig, D. W. and Maehr, M. L. Persistence as a function of conceptual structure and quality of feedback. Child Development, 1970, 41 (4), 1183-1190.

Attempted to determine how 76 white and 8 black high school students of varying conceptual structure (measured by a sentence completion test) would respond to personal and impersonal feedback on a performance task. It was predicted that, whereas abstract subjects would show no difference in motivation under the two feedback conditions, concrete subjects would show increased motivation when administered personal feedback. These predictions were confirmed and it is suggested that the Conceptual Systems Theory may provide a logical basis for interpreting empirical findings related to social class differences in responding to performance feedback.

589. Sturges, J. An evaluation of the New Orleans Education Improvement Project. New York: Ford Foundation; and Atlanta, Georgia: Southern Association of Colleges and Schools, March 1971. 94 pp. Also, see ERIC Abstracts, No. ED-111-909, 1971.

This report describes and evaluates a five-year program to improve the educational opportunities for underprivileged

children using instructional efforts that included school
community interaction, teacher aides, small group instruction,
a variety of instructional aids, and educational consultants.
The project is said to place top priority on language arts,
especially reading. Information and data used in evaluation
utilized both quantitative and qualitative measures such as
standardized achievement tests, questionnaires, and interviews.
The instructional improvement efforts are said to have resulted in significantly higher achievement of children enrolled
in the target schools. Those children enrolled in preschool
experiences sponsored by the project also had a higher degree
of achievement in elementary school than did comparable children
not provided such preschool experiences. Positive influences
on teacher attitudes and performance are reported. The overall
evaluation is stated to be positive but more systematic efforts
to evaluate the impact of the project desirable.

590. Sullivan, A. R. The influence of social processes on the
learning abilities of Afro-American school children: Some educational implications. Journal of Negro Education, 1972, 41 (2),
127-136.

    Assigned 120 Afro-American males, selected from a larger pool
    of 290 enrolled in Kindergarten and third and sixth grades, to
    three levels of socioeconomic status and two stimulus condi-
    tions on a paired-associate task: (a) concrete dialectic
    where actual objects were presented, and abstract dialectic
    where pictures of objects were presented. The Deprivation
    Index was used as a measure of social process. Results of
    an analysis of variance indicate differences in favor of
    Grade 6 (.01 level), high social process (.05 level), and
    the concrete task (.01 level). It is concluded that educa-
    tional programming should include the variables identified
    in this study.

591. Swan, R. W. and Stavros, H. Child rearing practices associated with the development of cognitive skills of children in low
socioeconomic areas. Early Child Development and Care, 1973, 2 (1),
23-38.

    Studied one child from each of 26 families (12 females and
    14 males -- all black) during the summer between completion
    of kindergarten and entry into first grade. Despite low
    socioeconomic status, subjects exhibited effective learning
    patterns. Parents were evaluated in relation to four dimen-
    sions: parental philosophy and values, perception of the
    child, feelings of competence, and verbal interaction. In
    these families, parents maintained a helpful and encouraging
    attitude toward their children as curious adventurers,
    creative, and independent learners, and often interacted with
    them in situations which were non-conflictual, thus providing
    a rich verbal environment. This research adds to our knowledge
    about atypical parent-child interaction in low socioeconomic
    areas, which leads to effective learning, and may be helpful
    in planning optimal care for disadvantaged children.

592. Taft, R. Selective recall and memory distortion of favorable and unfavorable material. Journal of Abnormal and Social Psychology, 1954, 49, 23-28.

An experiment has been described in which the recall of meaningful material by Negro and white delinquent boys (30 subjects in each racial group) has been compared. In an immediate recall series, the Negro subjects recalled more items favorable and unfavorable to Negroes than did the white subjects. In a delayed recall series the Negro subjects were even more superior in the recall of favorable items, but not in the recall of unfavorable items. There were no significant differences between the groups in the number of distortions of favorable or unfavorable items, but on the whole the white subjects distorted more items.

593. Teahan, J. E. and Drews, E. M. A comparison of Northern and Southern Negro children on the WISC. Journal of Consulting Psychology, 1962, 26 (3), 292.

The southern group is particularly deficient on performance rather than on verbal subtests. Northerners do somewhat better on nonverbal tests.

594. Tehan, S. An exploratory study concerning the effects of race upon school achievement. Connecticut College Psychology Journal, 1965, 2, 13-23.

Results of an exploratory study to determine whether or not a significant difference existed in school performance between Negroes and whites in the New London school system. Hypotheses were: (a) if a difference did exist, it would involve higher scores for the whites; (b) the difference would not appear immediately (first grade). A sample of 73 pairs of children was matched for sex and IQ. The hypotheses were confirmed. A significant difference was found at the seventh and eighth grades only.

595. Thelen, M. H. The effect of subject's race, model race and vicarious praise on vicarious learning. Child Development, 1971, 42 (3), 972-977.

Showed 64 Negro and Caucasian kindergartners and first graders films of a Negro or white model, who was either praised or not praised for performing specific aggressive behavior. Caucasian subjects imitated the Negro model more than the Caucasian model. Subjects who observed a Caucasian model recalled more of the model's motor behavior than subjects who observed a Negro model. Negro subjects who observed a model who was not praised recalled more of the model's motor behavior than Negro subjects who observed a praised model, and more than Caucasian subjects who observed a model who was not praised.

596.   Theman, V. and Witty, P.   Case studies and genetic records of
two gifted Negroes.   Journal of Psychology, 1943, 15, 165-181.

    Studies were made of two gifted Negroes from childhood to
    early adulthood.   Subject B, a girl, had a Stanford-Binet IQ
    of 200 and had a generally superior family background.   Her
    social adjustment and health were good.   Reading was her favor-
    ite activity, with novels, short stories and scientific books
    preferred.   Although her high school record was excellent, her
    college record suffered from a certain amount of indifference
    on her part and a fear of failure.   Subject E, a boy of Stanford-
    Binet IQ 163, had a superior family background, was socially
    well adjusted, and maintained a record of scholastic achieve-
    ment equal to his superior mental status, receiving his Ph.D.
    degree at the age of 18.   At the present time he is doing
    advanced research in mathematics.

597.   Thompson, C. H.   The educational achievements of Negro children.
American Academy of Political and Social Science Annals, 1928, 140
(229), 193-208.

    A study of J. F. Peterson shows that Negroes are lower than
    whites in scores on achievement tests in Nashville, Hamilton
    County and Shelby County.   By applying an index of efficiency
    of the schools it is discovered that these differences in the
    schools correspond to the differences in achievements of the
    pupils.   The V. M. Sims measurement of socioeconomic status,
    when applied to the Nashville schools and used in a second study
    by Peterson, shows that the white and Negro school rank in
    socioeconomic status in the same order as they rank on the
    achievement tests.   Virginia schools used in a survey of
    achievement, when ranked in efficiency, stand in the order
    of city white schools, city Negro, rural white, rural Negro.
    The educational achievements of the children rank in the same
    order.   These facts indicate that environment is a more logi-
    cal interpretation of differences in mental and school achieve-
    ment between whites and Negroes than is mental capacity.

598.   Tomlinson, H.   Differences between preschool Negro children
and their older siblings on the Stanford-Binet scale.   Journal of
Negro Education, 1944, 13, 474-479.

    75 pairs of Negro siblings in the age range of 4 to 9 years
    were given both forms (L & M) of the 1937 Stanford-Binet exam-
    ination.   Age differences between siblings ranged from 9 months
    to 5 years, 2 months.   The mean IQ for composite L & M IQs
    was 10.4 points below the general norm for white children,
    with variability also considered reduced.   The significantly
    higher IQ for the younger Negro children indicated that IQ
    decreases with age.   The inter-sibling correlation of IQs
    was .26 and is of the same order as found for similar homo-
    geneous groups.   Correlation of the Sins index of socioeconomic
    status and IQ suggested an increasing relationship between
    environmental factors and test performance with increase in
    age.

599. Torrance, E. P. Are the Torrance tests of creative thinking biased against or in favor of "disadvantaged" groups? Gifted Child Quarterly, 1971, 15 (2), 75-80.

The Torrance Tests of Creative Thinking have demonstrated their ability to identify creativity among children from disadvantaged or culturally different groups. The stimulus items used for the tests are objects and designs that are either common or uncommon for all children. Only slight differences have been found between black and white groups and between middle and low income groups. Even these differences disappeared in some experiments where rapport was established and the testing atmosphere relaxed. The results of several studies with the Torrance Tests demonstrate that minority group children have the ability to create, if they are given the opportunity at school and home.

600. Torrance, E. P. Current research on the nature of creative talent. Journal of Counseling Psychology, 1959, 6, 309-316.

Centers for research in creativity are noted, indicating the researchers and the nature of their studies. The Minnesota studies of creativity are described in greater detail, including those concerned with the measurement and identification of creative work, the relation of creative thinking and school learning, and the factors which appear to hinder the development of creativity.

601. Torrance, E. P. Non-test indicators of creative talent among disadvantaged children. Gifted Child Quarterly, 1973, 17 (1), 3-9.

Many contemporary writers have criticized the use of tests for low income and ethnically different children. However, the Torrance Test of Creative Thinking has shown black and low-income children scoring higher on some areas than white and middle- or high-income children. In addition, there are several non-test indicators of creativity including checklists, biographical inventories, and observational measures.

602. Vega, M. and Powell, A. The effects of practice on Bender-Gestalt performance of culturally disadvantaged children. Florida Journal of Educational Research, 1970, 12 (1), 45-49.

Administered the Bender-Gestalt Test to two groups of 25 disadvantaged Negro children (mean age = 5.8 years) before and after 33 practice sessions with graphic perceptual-motor tasks. Although both groups scored lower than the established norm, experimental subjects performed significantly better than controls (p<.05). No significant t differences were found between groups on post-practice Peabody Picture Vocabulary Test scores, indicating that the gains made by experimental subjects were not related to greater verbal intelligence or understanding of test directions. It is concluded that the generally lower performance of culturally disadvantaged children is partially caused by lack of previous experience, and that this factor should be considered when evaluating test results.

603. Viteles, M. S. The mental status of the Negro. American
Academy of Political and Social Science Annals, 1928, 140 (229),
166-177.

This paper surveys results of typical studies of Negro-white
differences in mentality measured by psychological tests.
Earlier tests are reviewed: Strong's (1913) showing twice as
many Negro children retarded in mental age as white children,
while almost three times as many whites as Negroes have mental
ages above their chronological ages; Phillipp (1912-14) who
found retardation in Negroes, when examining paired groups,
but much less than did Strong; and Ferguson (1916-20) who
found performance of Negro children only 75% as efficient
as that of whites, except in the cancellation-test where
Negroes scored higher than whites. Arlitt (1922), studying
the IQ of the two races, finds a drop in the score with advancing age, Negro children aged 5 to 7 having a slightly higher
average while those of 8 to 15 have a lower rating. The
relative superiority of Negroes at a lower chronological age
is shown by Murdock (1920). The army tests are quoted showing
lower average score and average mental age for Negroes in 90,000
white and 20,000 Negro cases. Analysis reveals differentiation between southern and northern Negroes as marked as between
whites and the total Negro group. Viteles reviews findings
of Derrick, Pressey, Teter, Schwegler and Winn, annulling
racial differences when considered in connection with special
abilities in rote memory and in concrete problems as opposed
to abstract ones. Crane's (1923) investigations on impulsive-
ness, improvidence and immorality of the Negro are considered
and quoted as showing that volition tends to be a simpler
process among blacks than among whites and one in which
intelligence plays a minor role in inhibition. Viteles
summarizes the results of findings under eight headings.
Despite overlapping between the two races there is a higher
proportion of Negro inferior scores and smaller proportion
of superior test scores among Negroes than whites: the difference between groups increases with age; selection of Negroes
and whites reduces the difference between the two races;
weighting of educational differences reduces the inferiority
of Negro scores; increase in white blood reduces the amount
of Negro inferiority; in testing specific mental abilities
of qualitative differences are suggested; experiments on
temperamental differences are extremely meager. Reuter regards as scientifically worthless the customary proofs of
racial inequality, and Herskovits doubts the value of the basic
hypothesis of white superiority. Yerkes and Freeman adopt
the view of Negro intelligence inferiority while admitting
considerable overlapping between the groups.

604. Vroegh, K. and Handrich, M. The validity of the Howard Maze
Test as a measure of stimulus-seeking in preschool children. Educational and Psychological Measurement, 1969, 29 (2), 495-502.

The Howard Maze Test for Children and the Goodenough-Harris
Draw-A-Man Test were administered to 31 disadvantaged Negro

and 42 Caucasian advantaged 4- and 5-year-olds. Teachers rated each child for "stimulus seeking". IQ was unrelated to Maze and Draw-A-Man scores. Advantaged children had higher stimulus-seeking scores than did the disadvantaged. Correlations of Maze scores with stimulus-seeking ratings were low.

605. Wagner, B., et al. Parent and child -- What's the score? Parental preparation of learning environments for delayed and non-delayed infants. See ERIC Abstracts, No. Ed-114-211, April 1975. 14 pp.

This study was designed to assess the needs of parents in preparing home learning environments for their young children. Subjects included 30 families (10 Anglo, 10 black, and 10 Chicano) with children from birth to 3 years of age. Data on approximately half of the families have been analyzed and are discussed. Half of the subject population had children identified as developmentally delayed/high risk. These children were matched with normal (non-delayed) children in the same ethnic group. Data were collected through videotapes of the child's daily activities, of the parent and child handling new materials, and of sequenced activities based on Piagetian developmental tasks designed to evaluate the child's developmental level. After the completion of the videotape series, parents' knowledge of child development and of how home environments may be prepared for the optimal development of children was assessed by use of a parent questionnaire. An observation instrument was then used to determine the parents' performance in actually preparing appropriate learning environments for their children. Preliminary results indicated that parents of all three ethnic groups had significantly higher knowledge scores than performance scores in the preparation of their children's learning environments.

606. Walla, R. T. and Rude, S. H. Exploration and learning-to-learn in disadvantaged preschoolers. Child Study Journal, 1975, 5, 177-191.

After learning a simple two-choice discrimination problem, Head Start subjects responded to six nondifferentially reinforced trials and 6 extinction trials. A learning effect was evident with regard to both problem solution and decision time. Specific exploration was evident. Children explored a novel object even after learning that the familiar object was associated with reward. Reward sequences did not effect response selection but did increase response latency on initial nondifferentially reinforced trials.

607. Wang, M. C., Resnick, L. B., and Boozer, R. F. The sequence of development of some early mathematics behaviors. Child Development, 1971, 42 (6), 1767-1778.

Administered to 78 black and white kindergarten subjects a battery of tests, each assessing ability to perform a specific task involving counting, use of numerals, or comparisons of

set size. Test scores were subjected to scalograms analysis
in order to test hypotheses concerning sequences of acquisition
of these behaviors. Results suggest: (a) a reliable sequence
of skills in using numerals; (b) the dependence of learning
numerals upon prior acquisition of counting skills for sets
of the size represented; (c) acquisition of numeral reading
for small sets before learning to count larger sets; and (d)
the independence of counting and 1:1 correspondence operations
in young children. Implications of these findings for design-
ing an introductory mathematics curriculum are discussed.

608. Warden, P. G. and Prawat, R. S. Convergent and divergent
thinking in black and white children of high and low socioeconomic
status. Psychological Reports, 1975, 36 (3), 715-718.

Administered two tests of divergent thinking ability and
three tests of convergent thinking ability to 354 eighth
graders, categorized as to race (black vs. white) and socioeconomic status (high vs. low). Consistent with previous
studies, and with W. D. Rohwer's (1971) theory, neither
ethnic nor social class differences were obtained for the
divergent thinking test; both ethnicity and social class
constituted significant sources of variance for the convergent thinking measures, with white and high status subjects
performing significantly better than black and low status
subjects on all three convergent thinking measures.

609. Wasserman, H. L. A comparative study of school performance
among boys from broken and intact black families. Journal of Negro
Education, 1972, 41 (2), 137-141.

The school achievement of two samples of boys were compared:
In one set of families the father was present, in the other one
he was absent; ΣN=117 black lower class families living in a
low-income housing development with at least one son in school
between ages 10 and 16. The father-absent category was defined
as "absence of the boy's natural father as a result of marital
disruption without any M replacement during the most recent
three-year period." 45 fathers were present, 46 were absent,
and 26 were put into a mixed category. Data here presented
refer to the two 'pure' groups alone. The mothers of the boys
were interviewed and school performance was analyzed from
the records via a school achievement index. Presence or
absence of father failed to discriminate between boys who did
better or worse. Boys under 12 were more likely to perform
at the higher levels in age appropriate classes than boys
who are age 12 or over. 65.1% of those under 12 vs. 85.1% of
those 12 years and over performed at a level less than 6 on
the School Achievement Index used. It is suggested that the
explanation for low school performance of lower class black
boys be sought elsewhere and not in whether the father is
present in the home or not. The lower class black boy exists
in an unrewarding, frustrating society and is thus extremely
vulnerable. Reprinted by permission.

610. Watts, G. New evidence in the argument about race and intelligence: How about it, Jensen? World Medicine (London), 1974, 9 (13), 77.

    Evidence refuting connections between race and intelligence
    quotient (IQ) gathered from a sample of 85 children who had
    been in residential nursery groups for at least six months is
    presented. 39 had two white parents, 22 had two black, and
    the remaining 24 were racially mixed. Tests designed to mea-
    sure nonverbal intelligence and language comprehension and
    expression were administered. Results show that mean IQs of
    the different racial groups are not significantly different.

611. Weiner, B. and Peter, N. A cognitive developmental analysis of
achievement and moral judgments. Developmental Psychology, 1973, 9
(3), 290-309.

    Negro and Caucasian 4- to 18-year-olds (N=300) made moral and
    achievement evaluative judgments in 16 situations. The situa-
    tions differed according to the intent (effort) and ability
    of the person being judged and in the objective consequences
    of the behavior. Analyses of variance reveal that the three
    evaluative dimensions of intent, ability and outcome were
    used systematically in both achievement and moral appraisals.
    Further, there were highly significant age trends. In both
    the achievement and the moral conditions, subjective intent
    replaced objective outcome as the main determinant of judg-
    ment. However, after the age of 12 years, in the achievement
    context, objective outcome again became the more important
    determinant of evaluation. It is contended that society
    reinforces this more "primitive" developmental stage. The
    sequence of evaluative stages in the moral and achievement
    situations was identical across racial and sex groupings. Data
    strongly support the position that achievement strivings are
    maintained primarily by social reward, while moral behavior
    is controlled primarily by social punishment.

612. Welcher, D. W., Wessel, K. W., Mellits, E. D., and Hardy, J. B.
The Bender-Gestalt Test as an indicator of neurological impairment
in young inner city children. Perceptual and Motor Skills, 1974,
38 (3, Part 1), 899-910.

    The Bender-Gestalt Test was examined as an indicator of neurolo-
    gical impairment in young inner city children (7 to 8 years old).
    The black and white, 7- to 8-year-old, inner city children in
    the Johns Hopkins collaborative perinatal study obtained
    generally higher error scores on the Bender-Gestalt Test
    than Koppitz' norms. They also performed less well on the
    Wechsler Intelligence Scale for Children, Wide Range Achieve-
    ment Tests, and the Gray Oral Reading Tests than the standard-
    ized populations for each test. Contrary to expectations, no
    significant relationship was found between high Bender error
    scores and neurological status or reading ability. Thus the
    Bender at 7 years was not a good predictor of neurological
    abnormalities in these young inner city children.

613. Whiteman, M. and Peisach, E. Perceptual and sensorimotor
supports for conservation tasks. Developmental Psychology, 1970,
2 (2), 247-256.

Administered tasks progressively incorporating perceptual
cues and sensorimotor experience designed to compensate for
underlying deficits to 32 kindergarten and 31 third grade, low
socioeconomic status Negro children. The situational supports
were compensatory for cognitive inadequacies only on the
number conservation items, the older subjects improving on
both judgment and explained judgment scores, the younger subjects only on the judgment score. There was evidence for
differential effectiveness of type of support on number conservation tasks. Perceptual cues were of greater assistance
to the older subjects and sensorimotor experiences of greater
assistance to the younger.

614. Wikerson, D. Racial differences in scholastic achievement.
Journal of Negro Education, 1934, 3, 453.

Keeping the limitations of the available information ever in
mind, the author compares the relative scholastic achievement
of Negro and white children in the elementary and high schools
of the same system. He has critically evaluated the findings
and technique of these studies and reached the following conclusions: In segregated school systems particularly, Negro
children in general have a lower school achievement than white
children in the same grades in the same system. Second, in
both races there are individuals falling in the upper and
lower quartiles of scholastic achievement. The major causes
of race differences in school achievement are thought to be
race differences in home and school environment. The last
section of this article deals with the limitations in techniques.

615. Wilcox, R. Further ado about Negro music ability. Journal of
Negro Education, 1971, 40 (4), 361-364.

Presents and discusses data from the Seashore Test of Musical
Talents (STMT) for 200 inner city sixth grade Negro pupils.
The data "clearly show the deficiency exhibited by these inner
city children in tested musical ability by contrasting their
performance to the published norms." Data also suggest a
general decline with increasing age in the sixth grade. It
is considered to be significant that these data are congruent
with data regarding intellectual decline. The validity of the
STMT is discussed, and it is noted that "what the test actually
measures are certain of the perceptual processes related to
the hearing and making of music." It is concluded that a need
exists to redirect the research effort toward clarifying the
relationship between measured musical perceptual ability and
more complex aesthetic and creative abilities involved in
music production.

616. Wilcox, R. Music ability among Negro grade school pupils: Or,
I got rhythm? Perceptual and Motor Skills, 1969, 29 (1), 167-168.

   200 "inner city" Negro sixth graders were found to be markedly
   deficient when they averaged at the 20th percentile on the six
   subscales of the Seashore Test of Musical Talents. Analysis
   indicated that 25% of subjects scored at or below the 5th percentile and that they were significantly more variable on
   loudness, rhythm, time, and tonal memory, and significantly
   less variable on pitch. If these data indicate a generalized
   deficiency among Negro pupils, then intensified training programs for developing music ability need to be initiated; if
   they suggest the inappropriateness of certain standardized
   testing programs, then they support the need to develop relevant testing materials for "inner city" children.

617. Willard, L. S. A comparison of culture fair test scores with
group and individual intelligence test scores of disadvantaged Negro
children. Journal of Learning Disabilities, 1968, 1 (10), 584-589.

   Comparison of responses of 89 sixth grade Negro subjects on
   the Cattell Culture Fair Intelligence (CCFI) Test and the
   Academic Promise Tests (APT) shows that subjects' WISC IQ,
   estimated from the total score on the APT, is only, on the
   average, three points lower than on the Cattell. When 83 other
   Negro subjects from special classes for the mentally retarded
   were compared on the Stanford-Binet Intelligence Scale and
   the CCFI Test, the mean score on the CCFI Test was 1.9 higher
   than on the Stanford-Binet. Results suggest: (a) Negro
   children are not at any appreciable disadvantage in taking
   the APT or the Stanford-Binet in preference to the CCFI Test;
   (b) the APT are a more effective measure for predicting
   school achievement and lend themselves to more effective
   qualitative analysis than the CCFI Test; and (c) nonverbal
   IQ is of no major advantage in the school situation. It is
   concluded that the bright Negro child does well on either a
   culture fair or the usual ability and intelligence tests,
   while those who are less well endowed do poorly on either type.

618. Willerman, L., Naylor, A. F., and Myrianthopoulous, N. C.
Intellectual development of children from interracial matings.
Science, 1970, 170 (3964), 1329-1331.

   Reports that interracial offspring of 61 white mothers obtained
   significantly higher IQ socres at 4 years of age than interracial offspring of 27 Negro mothers, suggesting that environmental factors play an important role in the lower intellectual performance of Negro children.

619. Willerman, L., Naylor, A. F., and Myrianthopoulous, N. C.
Intellectual development of children from interracial matings: Performance in infancy and at 4 years. Behavior Genetics, 1974, 4 (1),
83-90.

   Psychological tests at 8 months and at 4 years of age were
   administered to 129 children of interracial (Negro-white)

matings. These interracial children were divided into two
groups, depending on whether the mother was the white or the
Negro partner. Stanford-Binet IQs of the 4-year-old children
of white mothers averaged approximately nine points higher
than those with Negro mothers. The only behavioral difference
on the Bayley Scales of Infant Development at eight months
of age was in favor of the children of Negro mothers. The
results support the hypothesis that postnatal environmental
factors make a very substantial contribution to racial differences in intelligence test performance.

620. Williams, J., Williams, D. V., and Blumberg, E. L. Visual
and aural learning in urban children. Journal of Educational Psychology, 1973, 64 (3), 353-359.

Gave 320 white children (Experiment I) in Grades 2, 4, 6, 8,
and 10 from two school settings (middle class and lower class)
and 96 black children (Experiment II) in Grades 2, 4, and 6,
from the same school settings, paried-associate noun lists.
Visual presentation was superior to aural presentation overall,
the middle class subjects' performance was superior, but
there was a complex interaction indicating no social class
differences in the fourth and sixth grades. Experiment III
with 192 white first through fourth graders (middle class and
lower class settings) als included pictorial presentation and
corroborated the findings.

621. Willis, L. J. A comparative study of the reading achievements
of white and Negro children. Peabody Journal of Education, 1939,
17, 166-171.

112 Negro and an equal number of white children were used in
the study. The groups were subjected to an intelligence test,
a standard reading test, and a questionnaire. An audiometer,
a telebinocular, the Ophtalm-O-Graph, and the Metron-O-Scope
were also used to secure data. The scores made by the white
children averaged higher than those made by the Negro children.
The writer holds that further study must be given to implied
curriculum problems and to remedial programs.

622. Willows, D. M. Reading between the lines: Selective attention
in good and poor readers. Child Development, 1974, 45 (2), 408-415.

This research compared the abilities of good and poor readers
to attend selectively in a reading situation. 26 blocks of
subjects (sixth grade boys) matched on age and IQ, participated in the test phase of the experiment. Each block consisted
of four subjects -- two good readers and two poor readers.
One good and one poor reader from each block were randomly
assigned to selective and control reading conditions, respectively. In the control condition, the reading passages were
simply double spaced and typed in black. In the selective
reading condition, the same black passages were employed,
but red words were typed between the lines. The most interesting finding of the research was that, relative to control

performance, good readers in the selective reading condition made more comprehension errors that were intrusions from the red lines than did poor readers. These results were interpreted as lending support to an analysis by synthesis model of reading for meaning.

623. Winkler, D. R. Unequal achievement and the schools. Integrated Education, 1976, 14 (1), 24-26.

Data obtained from 388 blacks and 385 whites in the secondary schools of a large, urban school district in 1964-1965 consisted of longitudinal records of student test scores obtained from school records, measures of home environment obtained through student quesionnaires, longitudinal records of school inputs obtained from teacher personnel files and school budgets, and longitudinal records of school peer group composition. The results show that part of the racial difference in performance on achievement tests is due to the unequal school environments to which blacks and whites are exposed over their school years and to variations in the productivity of school resources between the races. While the school environment clearly contributes most toward explaining the racial achievement gap, the influence of the home environment may be understated by the measures used to assess that environment. The findings not only indicate that increasing school inputs results in higher achievement, but also that racial and social class integration may bring about a reduction in the racial achievement gap.

624. Witty, P. A. and Jenkins, M. D. The case of "B" -- A gifted Negro girl. Journal of Social Psychology, 1935, 6, 117-124.

This child, found in the elementary schools of Chicago, obtained an uncorrected IQ on the Stanford-Binet of 187; Otis, Army Alpha and McCall Multi-Mental gave IQ values of 180, 185 and 170. She is advanced approximately 1-1/2 grades in school over the norm for her age, and showed an educational age on the New Stanford Achievement Test of 14-9 years at a chronological age of 9-4 years. A short account of the child's interests and adjustment is presented.

625. Witty, P. A. and Jenkins, M. D. The educational achievements of a group of gifted Negro children. Journal of Educational Psychology, 1934, 25, 585-597.

The mean age of the group studied is 9-10; the mean Stanford-Binet IQ is 148.9; the mean EQ is 133.7; and the mean AQ is 91. The conclusions are limited to this group and to those from a strictly comparable milieu. "Gifted Negro children may be found with about equal frequency at every grade- and age-level in the elementary school." They "demonstrate greatest educational superiority in those highly 'verbal' subjects which appear not to depend greatly on school experience."

626. Witty, P. A. and Jenkins, M. D. Intra-race testing and Negro
intelligence. Journal of Psychology, 1936, 1, 179-192.

In a critical survey of the literature, these writers examine
the hypothesis that the American Negro is inherently inferior
in intelligence (based upon poor average test performance of
Negroes than of contiguous whites) in the light of two corol-
laries: (1) "that Negro individuals with the largest amount
of white ancestry should stand higher, other things being equal,
than individuals with total or large amounts of Negro ancestry,"
and (2) "Negroes making the highest test scores should be
those who emanate from admixtures, predominantly white."
Preponderant evidence was found to be negative for the first
corollary. Corollary 2 appeared untenable when 2/3 of the
Negro children (Chicago) in the superior group (IQ 120 or
above) were shown to have come from "pure" or predominantly
Negro ancestry. These writers conclude, tentatively, that the
differences found for average test scores must be attributed
to some factor other than inheritable intelligence.

627. Witty, P. A. and Moore, D. Interest in reading the comics
among Negro children. Journal of Educational Psychology, 1945, 36,
303-308.

Through interviews and questionnaires, data were collected
regarding 207 Negro children's interest in the comics, as
evidenced by the extent to which these are read and by the
expressed preference for specific titles. When this material
was compared with previously published reports of white children, the amount of reading of newspaper comic strips was
found similar for the two groups. However, the Negroes reported an average of 8 comic magazines read regularly, 4
often and 5 sometimes, as contrasted with 3 regularly, 3 often
and 6 sometimes for the white group. The author believes
that the Negro pupils' excessive interest in comic magazines
is largely due to the lack of good reading matter available
for these children.

628. Witty, P. A. and Theman, V. A follow-up study of the educational attainment of gifted Negroes. Journal of Educational Psychology, 1943, 34, 35-47.

Negro youth whose IQs ranged from 120 to 200 in 1934 were re-
studied in 1940 by achievement tests, questionnaires and
school records. Their educational attainment was above average
but lower than has been found for other gifted groups. Interest
in school was as great or greater than that of superior white
pupils. School marks and rank in class were similar for this
and other gifted groups. The authors regard the general level
of attainment as gratifying in view of the very meager opportunities open to some of the individuals studied.

629. Wohlford, P. and Stern, H. W. Reaching the hard-to-reach: The
use of participant group methods with mothers of culturally disadvantaged preschool children. Presented at the American Orthopsychia-
tric Association, Chicago, March 1968. 7 pp.

> Conflicting values from home and from a program such as Head
> Start may cause a child to become emotionally disturbed.
> This paper reports a project involving 13 Negro mothers whose
> children attended a preschool day care program. The mothers
> attended six weekly meetings whose purpose was evaluation of
> and, where necessary, intervention in detrimental parent-
> child interactions. The first part of each meeting entailed
> the discussion and demonstration of things parents can do to
> expand their child's cognitive world, build his verbal power,
> and enhance his prereading skills. The second part of the
> meeting used the T-group method of small-group participation
> to discuss aspects of the mother-child interaction.
>
> The mothers were concerned about their competency as mothers.
> Group leaders felt that many mothers were hostile toward their
> children and failed to interact with them in any way that
> would build cognitive skills. Many mothers identified with
> their children to the point where the boundary between mother
> and child disappeared. This group experience demonstrated
> the diagnostic-evaluative function that the T-group method
> could serve. The same method might be used with culturally
> deprived parents for more educative therapeutic goals.

630. Woods, R. C. and Martin, L. R. Testing in musical education.
Educational Psychology Measurements, 1943, 3, 29-42.

> 578 pupils in the sixth grade of Cabell County, West Virginia
> were administered the Kwalwasser-Dyhema Music Ability Test.
> Negroes were found superior to the white children, and girls
> superior to boys. The type of community in which the chil-
> dren lived seemed to have a direct bearing on the scores.
> Children most retarded in school showed the poorest results,
> and children who had had previous training averaged a higher
> score than those who had not had training.

631. Woods, W. A. and Toal, R. Subtest disparity of Negro and white
groups matched for IQs on the Revised Beta Test. Journal of Consulting Psychology, 1957, 21, 136-138.

> In a study of matched groups of Negro and white adolescents
> on the Revised Beta Test, among the findings was the fact that
> Negroes did better on some subtests and whites did better on
> others. "Whites perform better on Subtests 3 (Detection of
> Errors), 4 (Paper Form Board), and 5 (Drawing Completion).
> All of these differences exceed a 95 in 100 chance expectancy.
> Negroes perform better than whites on Subtests 2 (Digit Symbol),
> and 6 (Visual Comparison). These differences also exceed
> those expected by chance at the 95% level." One interpreta-
> tion of these findings is that "it appears that Negroes, when
> compared with whites of 'equal ability,' are most deficient

in culturally loaded items and in items which require ability
to visualize spatially. They seem superior to whites in items
requiring perceptual speed and accuracy."

632. Wright, L. S. Conduct problem or learning disability? Journal
of Special Education, 1974, 8 (4), 331-336.

47 third grade males identified by their teacher as having
conduct problems were administered a battery of tests (e.g.,
the Wepman Auditory Discrimination Test, the Illinois Test
of Psycholinguistic Abilities, and the WISC Vocabulary subtest)
to determine (a) how many had reading problems and central
processing dysfunctions; and (b) the correlations between
their reading performance and central information-processing
abilities, race, social class, and maternal employment. 24
subjects had both reading problems and central processing dysfunctions; however, factors related to the family and community
were more closely related to reading performance than to measures of specific central information-processing abilities,
per se. Results suggest that remediation for this type of
child should consider not only factors within the child but
the family and community as well.

633. Yando, R., Ziegler, E., and Gates, M. The influence of Negro
and white teachers rated as effective or noneffective on the performance of Negro and white lower class children. Developmental
Psychology, 1971, 5 (2), 290-299.

Tested 72 Negro and 72 Caucasian lower class children on
social approach and avoidance tendencies, curiosity and
intelligence. Three Negro and three Caucasian teachers
judged as effective, and three Negro and three Caucasian
teachers rated as noneffective, served as examiners. It
was found that the performance of children was influenced
by individual variations in the personal characteristics of
the adults with whom they were interacting rather than the
adults' race. This influence was relatively constant for
both Negro and Caucasian children.

634. Yater, A. C., Boyd, M., and Barclay, A. A comparative study
of WPPSI and WISC performances of disadvantaged children. Journal
of Clinical Psychology, 1975, 31 (1), 78-80.

The Wechsler Preschool and Primary Scale of Intelligence (WPPSI)
and Wechsler Intelligence Scale for Children (WISC) performances of black, disadvantaged children, both male and female,
were investigated. The findings are: (a) that there are no
sex differences for either the WPPSI or the WISC; (b) that
the WPPSI consistently overestimated the Verbal and Full
Scale IQ obtained from the WISC; and (c) that there are no
significant WPPSI-WISC differences for Performance and Full
Scale IQ.

635. Young, P. C. Intelligence and suggestibility in whites and
Negroes. Journal of Comparative Psychology, 1929, 9, 339-359.

   323 white and 314 Negro children, 9 and 10 years of age, of
   the third grade and above, were given the National Intelligence
   Test (Scale A) and a number of tests devised by the author.
   The average score of the white children on the intelligence
   test was 72. The average score of the Negroes was 40. The
   median for the whites was 75, as contrasted with 35 for the
   Negroes. Among whites the correlation of intelligence with
   each of the suggestibility tests was positive but low or
   medium. The correlation between intelligence and suggestibility
   was shown to be smaller among the Negroes than among the whites.
   "A clear-cut increase of intelligence with age in both whites
   and Negroes, and an equally noticeable decrease of intelligence as we go from white children to light Negroes, and then
   to dark Negroes, are apparent." The author thinks it important that experiments should mention whether they are working
   with "light, dark or miscellaneous groups of Negroes."

636. Zimet, S. G. and Camp, B. W. Favorite books of first graders
from city and suburb. Elementary School Journal, 1974, 75 (3),
191-196. Also, see ERIC Abstracts, No. EJ-107-795, 1974.

   Describes a study of library-book preferences for black inner
   city and white, middle class suburban first graders. Similarities and differences are noted. Findings showed a marked
   disparity between the story content of first grade reading
   textbooks and content of preferred library books. Includes
   lists of 14 most popular books from each school.

637. Zoloth, B. S. Relative test performances over time of black,
Spanish, and Anglo students: A case study. Discussion papers.
Washington, D. C.: Office of Economic Opportunity, January 1975.
34 pp. Also, see ERIC Abstracts, No. ED-105-062, 1975.

   The major issue investigated in this paper is whether or not
   any change appears over a five-year period in the differences
   in performances between minority and non-minority students in
   that district. Since the relative performance advantage of
   non-minority students is frequently ascribed to their better
   backgrounds, socioeconomic factors are held constant. The
   data used consist of test scores obtained for each student
   in the third, fifth, and seventh grades, plus a measure of
   the socioeconomic status of that student's family. Multiple
   regression analysis is used. The study concludes that the
   test scores of minority students relative to those of non-
   minority students do not appear to change much over time.
   Although Anglo students score higher than black or Spanish
   students, socioeconomic factors, while accounting for a
   significant portion of test-score differences, do not account
   for all racial/ethnic differences. The persistence of significant test-performance differences between Anglos and minorities
   over time leads one to conclude that the school system described in this study succeeded in maintaining the relative

performance position of the three major racial/ethnic groups
but did not substantially succeed in eliminating the performance deficiency exhibited by minority students.

638. Zucker, J. S. and Stricker, G. Impulsivity-reflectivity in
preschool Head Start and middle class children. Journal of Learning
Disabilities, 1968, 1 (10), 578-584.

> Determined differences between lower class Negro and middle
> class white children in perceptual tempo, and investigated
> the adequacy of J. Ragan's Matching Familiar Figures Test
> (MFFT) for children two years younger than those used by
> Ragan. Based on previous findings that culturally deprived
> children fail more frequently in school and have more diffi-
> culty learning to read, it was hypothesized that 30 preschool
> lower class (LC) Negro subjects would have shorter latencies
> and more mean errors on the MFF Test than 30 middle class (MC)
> white subjects. Results, based on t scores between the means
> of the two groups, show that: (a) for comparison of girls or
> boys, the only significant difference was between LC and MC
> girls on errors with all other differences in the predicted
> direction; (b) for overall comparisons, LC subjects made
> problem solving decisions significantly faster than MC sub-
> jects, and also made significantly more errors; and (c) boys
> of both groups are not significantly different from girls of
> both groups. Results suggest that the MFF technique is
> appropriate for preschool subjects, although perhaps it is
> too difficult in its present form.

639. Zunich, M. Perceptions of Indian, Mexican, Negro and white
children concerning the development of responsibility. Perceptual
and Motor Skills, 1971, 32 (3), 796-798.

> Tested the hypothesis that children's perceptions concerning
> the development of responsibility are independent of race.
> Subjects were 564 sixth grade black, white, American Indian
> and Mexican-American children, who were administered the
> Children's Responsibility Inventory. Data failed to support
> this hypothesis, suggesting that children's perceptions of
> responsibility are dependent upon race.

4

PERSONALITY DEVELOPMENT

640. Abel, T. M. Dominant behavior of institutionalized subnormal Negro girls: An experimental study. American Journal of Mental Deficiency, 1943, 47, 429-436.

> Groups consisting of a Negro girl and one or two white girls were asked to reach a common decision about some problems (ranking of objects in order of preference, deciding the price of something, and estimating quantity) presented to them. It was found that the Negro girls imposed their judgment upon the white girls about twice as often as did the white girls on their Negro partners. This dominance was shown regardless of CA, IQ, period of institutionalization or leadership ability of the members comprising the pairs and trios.

641. Abel, T. M. Negro-white interpersonal relationships among institutionalized subnormal girls. American Journal of Mental Deficiency, 1942, 46, 325-339.

> As a result of observations carried on during the course of eight months in an institution for mental defectives where there is no segregation of Negroes and whites, the following conclusions were reached: even though they are in a ten to one minority, Negro girls of 14 years or over show marked aggressiveness toward white girls of equivalent intelligence levels, have a strong sexual attraction for them and become their leaders. The aggressive behavior of the Negro girls can be explained on the basis of their being placed in a setting in which the caste-like system functions much less rigidly than it does in the community, so that these Negroes have a means of expressing their pent-up feelings of frustration. They also develop an attitude of superiority toward white girls who are no longer in a position socially more favorable than their own. The Negro girls are sexually attractive to white girls and succeed in becoming their leaders because the white girls interpret

the Negro aggression and dominance as "maleness," also, their
uninhibited emotional expressions and some of their physical
characteristics (dark skin and odor) seem to enhance the sex
attraction of the Negro girls.

642. Abel, T. M., Piotrowski, Z., and Stone, G. Responses of Negro
and white morons to the Rorschach Test. American Journal of Mental
Deficiency, 1944, 48, 253-257.

The Rorschach Test was administered to Negro and white adolescent subnormal girls and boys matched for CA, IQ and length of
institutionalization. The only difference between responses
of the Negro and white groups (both sexes) concerned the number
of human movement responses. The Negroes (55 subjects) gave
52 such responses and the whites (52 subjects), gave 33. The
performance of the Negro girls on the test was more flexible
and more expansive than that of the white girls. White girls
were more restricted in response and showed signs of anxiety
and negativism. The performance of Negro and white boys was
usually intermediate between that of the white and Negro girls.

643. Abney, V. Effects of school desegregation on black students.
Smith College Studies in Social Work, 1975, 46 (1), 16.

The experience of integration for black students was examined,
to test the hypothesis that blacks suffer primarily from anger
towards society rather than from low self-esteem. The literature on the psychological and educational effects of integration and on the many ways blacks deal with their anger at
racism is reviewed, and it is concluded that desegregation
does have psychological effects. However, these effects
rarely render the black person incapacitated and helpless
over a long period of time. It is suggested that the possible
psychological consequences to black students be considered
whenever a plan of desegregation is formulated and prior to
its implementation. It is recommended that qualified mental
health professionals in the community be used to evaluate
both the mental and physical health of students, and that
parents and teachers be encouraged to offer continuous support
and be attuned to the various ways in which tension and anxiety
manifest themselves in adolescents and latency aged children.

644. Abramson, P. R. The Holtzman Inkblot Test, violent aggression
in fantasy in black preschool age children. Journal of Community
Psychology, 1974, 2 (2), 139-140.

Scored the child doll play responses of 67 male and 56 female
preschool age black children for violently aggressive fantasies.
After classifying subjects according to whether they expressed
a violent aggressive fantasy, a 2 x 2 analysis of variance
(presence of violent aggression in fantasy by sex of the child)
was computed for 22 Holtzman Inkblot Test variables. Results
indicate that subjects who projected violence in fantasy had
higher balance scores. In addition, the data indicate two
significant trends: subjects who projected violence in fantasy
had lower reaction times and higher shading scores.

645. Abramson, P. R. and Abramson, S. D. A factorial study of a
multidimensional approach to aggressive behavior in black preschool
children. Journal of Genetic Psychology, 1974, 125 (1), 31-36.

> A multidimensional aggression scale developed by P. Abramson,
> et. al. (1972), containing 34 variables of aggression was used
> to score the doll-play responses of 123 black preschool age
> children. Six factors were extracted on the basis of the amount
> of total variance contributed by each factor and the number
> of loadings exceeding .50. To assist in verbal reference
> these factors were labeled as follows: Factor 1, Violent
> Aggression Toward the Family; Factor 2, Violent Aggression
> by the Family; Factor 3, Aggression by the Self; Factor 4,
> Aggression Directed Toward the Self; Factor 5, Assertion
> Directed Toward Others; and Factor 6, Assertion Directed
> Toward the Family. The data support the contention that
> aggression can be conceptualized along several dimensions.

646. Adams, R. L. and Phillips, B. N. Motivational and achievement
differences among children of various ordinal birth positions. Child
Development, 1972, 43 (1), 155-164.

> A two-year study investigated consistent motivation, achieve-
> ment, and intellectual differences with two groups of Mexican,
> Anglo and Black fourth and fifth graders: firstborn and
> only children (N=135), and later born (N=235). Firstborns
> were significantly higher than later borns on four measures
> of intellectual and academic performance, and on one measure
> of school motivation. With one exception, dependent measure
> represented an average of four scores separately obtained
> during the Fall and Spring semesters of two consecutive years.
> When differences in level of motivation between the two groups
> were controlled, all of the previously found differences be-
> tween firstborn and later born disappeared, adding empirical
> support to W. D. Altus' theoretical explanation of the birth-
> order effect.

647. Adams, W. A. Methods for the study of personality in Negro
society: Part 2. Psychological aspects of the orientation of Negro
children. Proceedings of the Third Biennial Meeting of the Society
for Research in Child Development, 1939, 34-46.

> A psychosocial analysis of an individual assigned to a parti-
> cular Negro personality type. The nature of the social adjust-
> ment effected is related to the several causative factors.
> There is appended a discussion of the values influencing
> adjustment in Negro society, and of the mechanisms whereby
> orientation is accomplished.

648. Adkins, D. C., Payne, F. D., and Ballif, B. L. Motivation
factor scores and response set scores for ten ethnic-cultural groups
of preschool children. American Educational Research Journal, 1972,
9 (4), 557-572.

> Administered a test of motivation to achieve in school (Gump-
> cookies) to 10 "ethnic-cultural" groups of preschool children.

The tests consist of 75 dichotomous items, for each of which a
single alternative is keyed as indicative of greater motivation.
Children who are uncertain of answers to items report to response sets, which may depend upon position of the answer or
the order in which it is presented. Such response sets do
not systematically affect total score but may distort scores
on separate factors determined by ordinary methods. A new
method of factor analysis that yields factors uncorrelated
with response sets was applied to data for a total group of
1,813 children. Scores were compared on such factors and of
total scores for the 10 groups: Mormons, Catholics, Jews,
Puerto Ricans, urban Negroes, rural Caucasians, "Hawaiians,"
West Coast Orientals, Mexican-Americans, and American Indians.
Response-set scores were also compared for the eight largest
groups.

649. Anderson, W. E. The personality characteristics of 153 Negro
pupils, Dunbar High School, Okmulgee, Oklahoma. Journal of Negro
Education, 1947, 16, 44-48.

In order to determine their personality characteristics, 153
pupils currently enrolled at the Dunbar High School, Okmulgee,
Oklahoma, were given: (1) the Higher Form A of the Otis
Self-Administering Test of Mental Ability; (2) the California
Test of Mental Maturity, Advanced Series, Grade A Adult; and
(3) the California Test of Personality, Secondary Series,
Form A. On the Otis, 69% had IQs in excess of 100; 20% fell
between 90 and 99; and 10% ranged between 80 and 89. No sex
differences were found. The correlation between the Otis and
Mental Maturity tests was .917 ± .07. Pupils at the Dunbar
School have not achieved satisfactory personality adjustment
since they were exceeded by 70% of the normative group on
the California Test of Personality. Self adjustment was
poorer than social adjustment. It was concluded that this
particular high school is not meeting the personality needs
of its students.

650. Armstrong, C. P. and Gregor, A. J. Integrated schools and
Negro character development. Psychiatry, 1964, 27 (1), 69-72.

The defense system of the Negro (NE) psychotic often manifests
itself in a syndrome characterized by color denial and orientation toward the white culture. Color bias permeates the
entire preference system of the NE subculture. As long as
the NE child is insulated in an all-NE environment, however,
psychic tensions are minimized. K. Clarke's studies indicate
that NE children in a racially insultated school situation
have a more positive conception of their own group and a
more substantial sense of self than those in a biracial school
situation. The disposition to delusional defenses is precon-
ditioned by the circumstances attending primary socialization, when the NE child fails to establish an adequate
identity relationship with the adult members of his family.
In biracial schools, the NE child must adjust to membership
in a group where he is accorded inferior status because of

distinctive social visibility. Factors which foster the orientation toward the white culture include: (a) emphasis on white
aesthetic norms and attendant value ascriptions and on negative
stereotypes for the group adjudged inferior; (b) limited or
absent opportunities to identify with authority figures; and
(c) opportunities to perceive manifest non-white group deficiencies in performance. Reprinted by permission.

651. Atwood, J. H., Wyatt, D. W., Davis, V. J., and Walker, I. D.
Thus By Their Destiny: The Personality Development of Negro Youth
in Three Communities. Washington, D. C.: American Youth Commission
of the American Council on Education, 1941.

This booklet presents three brief community studies prepared
for the purpose of giving an understanding of Negro youth.
The independent surveys are of widely separated and very
differently organized communities: Milton, Pennsylvania (6
pages); Greensboro, North Carolina (58 pages); and Galesburg,
Illinois (27 pages). The preface and conclusion are contributed by R. L. Sutherland, who points up the general interpretation that "frustration over minority racial status is
real and corroding, penetrating all aspects of life and
conditioning personality, though not always in the same way
or with the same results. . . . The main basis of frustration is 'economic'." These general findings confirm those
of the other, more intensive studies of the American Youth
Commission and contribute further details concerning Negro
life in small, "liberal" communities of the North (Milton
and Galesburg) and an upper middle class group in the progressive South (Greensboro).

652. August, G. J. and Felker, D. W. Role of affective meaningfulness and self-concept in the verbal learning styles of white and
black children. Journal of Educational Psychology, 1977, 69 (3),
253-260.

The roles of affective meaningfulness and self-concept in
the verbal learning styles of white and black children were
assessed. Both white and black fifth grade children, representing two levels of social class and two levels of self-
concept, recalled (multi-trial free recall format) nouns
which they had pre-rated for likability. While self-concept
failed to have any noticeable influence on the total sample,
it interacted significantly with race. True to prediction,
the high self-concept white children recalled positively
rated words more readily than negatively rated words, while
their low self-concept peers manifested no memory predilection.
Although the low self-concept black children also reflected
no preference for their affective evaluations, the high self-
concept blacks showed a greater propensity to recall their
negatively rated words. Social class had a negligible
influence on the affective learning styles of the children.

653. Ausubel, D. P. Ego development among segregated Negro children. Mental Hygiene, New York, 1958, 42, 362-369.

In the Harlem Negro community, the negative aspects of membership in a "stigmatized" racial group are in part compensated
by ego supporting attitudes existent in the home. (Modified.)

654. Ball, J. C. Comparison of MMPI profile differences among
Negro and white adolescents. Journal of Clinical Psychology, 1960,
16, 304-307.

Subjects were 31 Negro and 169 white ninth grade students.
The MMPI record suggested a high incidence of neurotic tendencies among the Negro boys, as well as withdrawal and intro-
version among the girls. The Si scale was strongly emphasized
on the profiles of the Negro girls, and the D scale was prominent among the Negro boys. Personality differences between
the whites and Negroes were considered also in relation to
age, intelligence, family background, SES, and academic and
educational achievement. (Modified.)

655. Ballard, B. and Keller, H. R. Development of racial awareness: Task consistency, reliability and validity. Journal of
Genetic Psychology, 1976, 129, 3-11.

6 racial awareness tasks plus 1 validity check were administered
to comparable ratios of 85 male-female and black-white 3- to
7-year-olds to determine the differential S variable effects
for and interrelationships among these 6 measures. The 6
racial awareness measures had low correlations with one another.
The implications that these tasks may not all be measuring the
same constructs is discussed.

656. Banks, S. L. Blacks in a multi-ethnic social studies curriculum: A critical assessment. Journal of Negro Education, 1975, 44
(1), 82-89.

Discusses the negative effect on the self-concept of black
children of the continuing neglect of black history and
culture in multi-ethnic curricula. It is argued that textbooks convey fallacious images. Curriculum guides suggest
that black history is separate from American history. Schools
and colleges do not seriously consider the culture and history
of blacks. It is proposed that administrators, curriculum
workers, the mass media, and teachers attempt to correct
fallacies related to identity problems of blacks. Essentials
for a multi-ethnic curriculum are: (a) sensitization and
training of various personnel with respect to minorities,
(b) multi-ethnic materials, (c) biracial staffs, and (d) cooperation between the school and the entire community.

657. Banks, W. Drugs, hyperactivity, and black school children.
Journal of Negro Education, 1976, 45 (2), 150–160.

Notes that a school system that is short of funds and long on
active and aggressive black youngsters might bypass the necessary neurological and psychological examinations to determine
hyperkinesis.

658. Banks, W. C. White preference in blacks: A paradigm in search
of a phenomenon. Psychological Bulletin, 1976, 83, 1179–1186.

A review of the most prominent studies reveals that the predominant pattern of choice behavior among blacks toward white
and black stimulus alternatives has conformed to simple chance.

659. Baron, R. M., Bass, A. R., and Vietze, P. M. Type and frequency
of praise as determinants of favorability of self-image: An experiment in a field situation. Journal of Personality, 1971, 39 (4),
493–511.

Ascertained the effects of variations in type (person vs.
achievement oriented) and frequency (75% vs. 25%) of priase
on favorableness of self-image and task performance for 28
black female 16- to 21-year-old trainees. Subjects were given
the Tennessee Self-Concept Scale and the Interpersonal Perception Questionnaire before and after the experiment. It
was found that: (a) lower frequencies of praise produced
more positive self-evaluations than high frequencies, and
(b) person oriented praise was more effective than achievement
praise in enhancing self-evaluation. No significant effects
were found for the accuracy-type tasks (word recognition,
visual perceptiveness). On the task which involved a
simple, speeded response (manual dexterity), there were significant effects.

660. Baron, R. M., Cowan, G., Ganz, R. L., and McDonald, M. Interaction of locus of control and type of performance feedback: Considerations of external validity. Journal of Personality and
Social Psychology, 1974, 30 (2), 285–292.

Conducted two studies with 85 white male 10- and 11-year-olds,
85 black male 10- and 11-year-olds, and 72 white male undergraduates to establish the generality of R. M. Baron and
R. L. Ganz' (see IV-10) finding of a significant Locus of
Control x Type of Performance Feedback interaction. Locus
of Control was assessed by administering Crandall's Intellectual Achievement Responsibility Questionnaire to the children
and the Rotter Internal-External Control Scale to the adults.
Study #2 (with adults) also used a different problem-solving
task and new procedures for operationalizing the Type of Feedback variable. The superior performance of internals to
externals under a condition of self-discovery success (intrin-
sic feedback), as opposed to the superior performance of
externals to internals when unverifiable verbal praise was

used (extrinsic feedback), was found for lower class white as
well as for lower class black 10- and 11-year-olds and for
adults. Taken together, these studies provide strong evidence
of the generality and usefulness of the Personality x Treatment
interaction design in the area of locus of control.

661. Baron, R. M. and Ganz, R. L. Effects of locus of control and
type of feedback on the task performance of lower class black children. Journal of Personality and Social Psychology, 1972, 21 (1),
124-130.

    Administered the Intellectual Achievement Responsibility Ques-
    tionnaire (IARQ) to 60 black male fifth graders from two inner
    city elementary schools. Subjects' knowledge of success on a
    discrimination task was acquired by self-discovery (intrinsic
    reinforcement) or by examiner's personal praise (extrinsic
    reinforcement). A combined condition consisting of both
    intrinsic and extrinsic feedback was also used. Results
    indicate that, as hypothesized, internally oriented subjects,
    as measured by the IARQ, made significantly more "correct"
    responses in the condition of intrinsic reinforcement than
    externally oriented subjects, while the reverse was true in
    the condition of extrinsic reinforcement. Locus of control
    did not differentiate performance effects under the combined
    condition. Implications for elucidating possible differen-
    tial motivational bases for the performance of internals and
    externals is discussed.

662. Battle, E. S. and Rotter, J. B. Children's feelings of personal
control as related to social class and ethnic group. Journal of
Personality, 1963, 31 (4), 482-490.

    This study explores the interaction of class and ethnic group
    with internal vs. external control of reinforcements. "To
    assess this characteristic, a newly developed cartoon test
    was given to 80 Negro and white school children, and a ques-
    tionnaire scale of 1/2 of the subjects. The relationship of
    test scores to sex, age, social class, ethnic group, and
    behavior on line matching tasks was investigated." (Modified.)

663. Baugh, B. D. and Prytula, R. E. DAPs of black and white
juvenile incarcerates. Journal of Abnormal Child Psychology, 1974,
2 (3), 229-238.

    Two groups of male juvenile incarcerates were separated on
    the basis of race, matched in terms of age, recidivism, and
    intelligence test scores, and given the Draw-A-Person Test
    (DAP). Figures drawn were male and female. The drawings
    were scored on 14 emotional indicators. The results of the
    present study offer little consistent or conclusive support
    for the hypothesis that differences influenced by race can
    be found in the projective drawings of black and white subjects.
    The commonly held impression that there are more incidences
    of neurotic or psychotic features in the projective tests
    of black subjects, and that the projective drawings of black

subjects are generally inferior to the projective drawings
of white subjects, were not supported by the present study.

664. Beckham, A. S. Albinism in Negro children. Journal of Genetic
Psychology, 1946, 69, 199-215.

The writer interviewed and gave psychological examinations to
14 Negro albino boys and 28 girls. It was concluded that: (a)
Many Negro albinos, even at an early age, develop a feeling
of insecurity in their homes and in society generally because
of the discrimination against them and feelings of being different. (b) Psychological and psychiatric treatment are often
necessary to help them face their problems. (c) Albinos
have acute visual problems. (d) The intelligence of albinos
is about the same as their nonalbino siblings. (e) Physical development of the albinos seems somewhat retarded as regards
beginning of walking and talking. (f) There is need of better
understanding of the albinos' problems in the schools and
at home.

665. Beglis, J. F. and Sheikh, A. A. Development of the self-
concept in black and white children. Journal of Negro Education,
1974, 43 (1), 104-110.

A comparison of the self-concept of Negro and white children
is made, controlling for the socioeconomic level, and the
variables of race, sex and age are studied as they relate
to the frequency with which a child uses certain descriptive
content categories to describe himself. It is evident that
the age of the subject is the primary determiner in the
development of the self-concept, while the main effect of
race on self-concept is that Negro subjects use more identification or "census type" responses and less competence, task
achievement responses, than the white subjects. The importance of the sex variable is shown to be relatively unimportant.

666. Bergelson, A. An intercomparison of self, man, and woman
drawings made by culturally deprived Negro children. Child Study
Center Bulletin, 1967, 3 (1), 16-18.

In order to determine whether deprived Negro children draw
more complete self-drawings than man or woman drawings, such
drawings were obtained from 21 male and 23 female 4.6- to
5.6-year-old Negro children who were eligible for compensatory education programs. "The data showed that the girls
demonstrated significant differences between more complete
man drawings than self-drawings. The boys drew a significantly greater number of more complete woman drawings than
self-drawings. No significant differences were present between the girls' woman drawing and their self-drawing scores,
and the boys' man drawings and their self-drawing scores."
Further investigation seems warranted.

667. Betts, F. M., III. Free schools and self-concept in adolescents.
Journal of Negro Education, 1975, 44 (4), 454-467.

The effect of a "free" school program on black students' self-
concept was measured using a semantic differential. The
majority of the indicators support the conclusion that students
at the West Philadelphia Community Free School demonstrate
a significantly higher "concept of self". The only major
contraindication relates to attitude toward achievement in
school. Although it was anticipated that the role of teachers
in the free school would be more clearly indicated in the test
results, this was not the case. It is suggested that small
school unit size, ungraded student groupings, and narrative
evaluation rather than numerical grades are key correlates to
achievement in this student population. It is recommended
that the random nature of the selection process should be
preserved to eliminate gang "turf" problems. Genuine policy
making power vested in a parent community board proved to
be a highly effective means of developing adult commitment to
the school.

668. Bewley, K. Self-esteem: The alternative to genetic inferiority.
The Negro Educational Review, 1977, 28 (2), 95-99.

The findings of this study based on a sample of 51 second and
third grade children of two elementary schools in Texas were
supportive of statements made by Shirley Samuels in a study
of the self-concepts of kindergarten children. Samuels found
that there was no significant difference between black and
white children in self-concept. Rather there was a significant
difference (p=.01) in self-concept between children of middle
class and lower class homes with middle class children of
both races having higher self-concepts. This study has inferred that black children, at an early age, have adequate to
above-adequate feelings of self despite the fact that their
teachers are generally less accepting of their behavioral
characteristics as compared with their white counterparts.
It would appear that teachers usually measure the black
child against white, middle class standards. There should
be encouragement taken in the evidence that black children
have sufficient positive feelings of self needed to deal with
the complexities of today's world.

If compensatory education has failed, possibly the failure
has been through the failure to educate teachers in the
necessity of dealing with the individual child in a manner
commensurate with his needs. Research is revealing a gradual
cessation of comparison of races and a trend toward the investigation of economic and social conditions as a cause for
inadequacy.

669. Blackwell, J., et al. Effects of early childhood multicultural
experiences on black preschool children's attitudes toward themselves
and whites. Paper presented at the Annual Meeting of the American
Educational Research Association. San Francisco, California: April 19-
23, 1976. Also, see ERIC Abstracts, No. ED-125-777, 1976.

This study examines the effects of social studies experiences
on the attitudes of young black children towards themselves
and whites. Subjects were 54 children, 4 years of age, representing a low socioeconomic population. The children were
divided into three groups of 18 each. Group 1 read and discussed selected multi-ethnic social studies materials. Group 2
read and discussed these selections and received field-trip
experiences based upon these readings. Group 3 received
traditional preschool experiences. All groups received a
20-item attitude pretest and post-test. IQ did not differ
significantly between groups. Based upon the results of
Hartley's F test, a one-way analysis of covariance showed
significant differences among treatment groups. Using a
two-sample t-test, the results of the study indicated that
Groups 1 and 3 and 2 and 3 differed significantly in attitude. No significant differences were found in attitude
change between groups 1 and 2.

670. Bloom, R. Dimensions of mental health in adolescent boys.
Journal of Clinical Psychology, 1970, 26 (1), 35-38.

Data on 2,200 white and Negro tenth grade boys were factor
analyzed. Eight factors accounted for 45% of the variance.
Each of these factors was identified and explained: negative
affective states, positive self-evaluation, physical correlates of anxiety, test anxiety, alienation from society,
aggressive impulses, guilt and general anxiety, and negative
self-evaluations. It is suggested that there is difficulty
in trying to identify any single factor or combination of
factors as an optimal index of adolescent adjustment.

671. Bolling, J. L. The changing self-concept of black children:
The black identity test. Journal of the National Medical Association, 1974, 66 (1), 28-31.

Validity statistics on The Black Identity Test, a modified
Draw-A-Person test using crayons, was presented on the basis
of findings from students between the ages of 3 and 17 years
old. Four items in black children were chosen as reflective
of ethnic identification: hair features, physical features,
dress, and skin color response. When the test was given to
four groups of children, the differences in identity score
obtained by different ethnic groups points to the validity
of the procedure as a means of differentiating the groups
according to the content of their drawing. Black subjects
obtained the highest scores, followed by black Puerto Ricans,
white Puerto Ricans, and whites. Results also indicated:
(a) the test has no value below the 5-year- level; (b) black
identification increases with age; and (c) there are clear
sex differences in the degree of black identification.

672. Borowitz, G. Clinical observations of ghetto four-year-olds:
Organization, involvement, interpersonal responsiveness, and psychosexual content of play. Journal of Youth and Adolescence, 1972, 1
(1), 59-79.

> This study attempted to refine the assessment of the effectance
> of four-year-old children through observation of their play.
> Two scales were developed; the first scale defined organiza-
> tion, involvement, and interpersonal responsiveness in play
> while the second operationally defined psychosexual content
> of play. The results confirmed the validity and reliability
> of the instruments (which are reprinted in an Appendix) as
> measures of children's effectance and their capacity as learners.

673. Borowitz, G. Play in the study of personality development of
black ghetto four-year-olds. See ERIC Abstracts, No. ED-103-540,
1970. 69 pp.

> In this study of the personality development of four-year-old
> children, we first attempted to evaluate the personalities
> of the children attending our research preschool in order to,
> on the basis of our clinical evaluations, discover a number
> of factors which would permit us to group the children. We
> then studied their families to see if we could find specific
> and perhaps unique correlations between the children's person-
> alities and the familial milieu. Our preschool nursery
> operated in four converted apartments of a public housing
> development on the near West side of Chicago, an area that
> had been exclusively black for many years. After watching
> the children in a classroom and observing them in free play,
> we decided to group the children into three categories on
> the basis of our clinical assessment of each child's competence,
> i.e., highly, moderately, or low competent. Our clinical
> background suggested that play interviews are most effective
> in assessing four-year-old children. On the basis of a semi-
> structured play interview, we were able to divide the children
> into three competence groupings. We examined the factors
> within the play interviews which contributed to our competence
> judgments and found it useful to consider three particular
> aspects of the child's play: organization, interpersonal
> skills, and content themes.

674. Boyd, G. F. The levels of aspiration of white and Negro children in a non-segregated elementary school. Journal of Social
Psychology, 1952, 36, 191-196.

> The levels of aspiration of white and Negro children of
> matched intelligence were determined by using target and
> arithmetic tests and by interviews. Results "seem to indicate"
> that the Negro group had a higher level of aspiration" and
> "higher verbalized ambitions than the white group."

675. Brody, E. B. Color and identify conflict in young boys. Psychiatry, 1963, 26, 188-201.

The role of mother-child interaction in the development of color identity conflict was investigated for 11 white boys and their mothers and 19 Negro boys and their mothers. The age range of the boys was from 6 to 10 years. Each mother was interviewed twice, one being an unstructured interview and the other relating to her attitudes toward race and color and her attempts to train her son in these respects. The boys were seen for two sessions of directed play in which white and Negro male hand puppets were used according to a predetermined scheme. The results of the study are presented and discussed according to the group of mothers and sons without color conflict and those with color conflict.

676. Brook, J. S., Whiteman, M., and Peisach, E. M. Aspiration levels of and for children: Age, sex, race and socioeconomic correlates. Journal of Genetic Psychology, 1974, 124 (1), 3-16.

Sutdied 165 fifth and 127 first grade children and their parents to examine correlates of the child's own occupational aspirations and of his parents' aspirations for him. The parents' educational and occupational aspirations for the child were related to: (a) socioeconomic status (SES), (b) race in the educational area only, and (c) sex. The correlations between the parents' and the child's aspirations were highest for the fifth grade subjects, for the white parents irrespective of SES, and for the black parents of the higher SES level.

677. Brown, R. G. A comparison of the vocational aspirations of paired sixth grade white and Negro children who attend segregated schools. Journal of Educational Research, 1965, 58 (9), 402-404.

The subjects were two groups of sixth graders who had similar economic status, regional environment and intelligence quotients, and attended white or Negro segregated schools. The questionnaire embedded on a single question concerning the student's vocational ambition. It was found that the choices of the Negro children ranked higher than those of the whites. Generally, the occupational ambitions of both groups were higher than the occupations held by their fathers. (Modified.)

678. Brown, N. W. Personality characteristics of black adolescents. See ERIC Abstracts, No. Ed-121-879, n.d. 14 pp.

446 poor black urban and rural adolescents ages 15-18 enrolled in a summer poverty-work program are administered Gough's Adjective Checklist (ACL) and Holland's Vocational Preference Inventory (VPI) to determine their personality profile, to ascertain differences between this group and blacks attending colleges, and to study what implications for programming can be determined from VPI and ACL profiles. Significant sex differences are found on 12 to 24 ACL scales, with black

females tending to score higher on all differing scales. A
factor analysis of ACL scores yields two significant factors:
that of ego structure and characteristic approach to life. A
comparison of the sample VPI scores with black college students'
scores indicate significant differences on most of the 11 VPI
scales. Results indicate that the poor, black adolescent's
perception of himself is one of self-depreciation. However,
this does not mean that this population possesses a low self-
concept since they may think they are worthwhile individuals
but do not perceive themselves as competent or effective.
The fact that they remain in school and actively seek work
in the summer poverty program reinforces the hypothesis that
they are trying to become effective and competent in their
own lives according to society's dictates.

679. Bruch, M. A., Kunce, J. T., and Eggeman, D. F. Parental devaluation: A protection of self-esteem. Journal of Counseling
Psychology, 1972, 19 (6), 555-558.

    Measured the self-esteem and parental esteem of 159 male
    high school students, using the Interpersonal Differentiation
    Test to assess relationships to age and three cultural classi-
    fications: advantaged whites, disadvantaged whites, and
    disadvantaged blacks. Disadvantaged subjects had signifi-
    cantly higher self-esteem scores. Older subjects had signi-
    ficantly lower father esteem scores. Culture and age were
    not significantly related to esteem for mother scores. In-
    creased discrepancies were noted between self- and parental-
    esteem scores for the two disadvantaged groups in comparison
    to the nondisadvantaged. These findings point to the complexi-
    ties involved in interpreting self-esteem scores without
    consideration of other factors.

680. Buck, M. R. and Austrin, H. R. Factors related to school
achievement in an economically disadvantaged group. Child Development, 1971, 42, 1813-1826.

    50 matched pairs of eighth grade, economically disadvantaged,
    Afro-American students, categorized as adequate achievers or
    underachievers, were administered a measure of internal-
    external control of reinforcements and rated by teachers.
    Maternal attitudes were ascertained from questionnaires and
    interviews. Adequate achievers were found to be more internal
    than underachievers, and rated as more positive and less
    deviant in classroom behavior. Mothers of adequate achievers
    tended to report fewer negative responses and to rate their
    children as more competent. The mothers did not differ in
    minimal standards or in attainment values. Findings were
    discussed in the light of social-learning theory.

681. Burback, H. J. and Wagoner, J. L. Dimensions of powerlessness
among black and white high school students. Journal of Negro Education, 1974, 43 (4), 419-428.

    To examine empirically the structure of the powerlessness
    construct and to compare the factorial structure of the

concept across racial groups of high school students, a scale
was developed and applied to black and white students. Factor
analysis of the data delineated the most meaningful dimensions
of the scale and determined the degree of structural similarity across samples of black and white students. The results suggest that powerlessness can be meaningfully interpreted as a general concept for the total sample and for
black and white subsamples as well, making it possible and
useful to make cross racial comparisons at the level of
general feelings of powerlessness. However, with respect to
the factorial structure of the individual dimensions of
powerlessness, it was established that comparisons across
individual factors are not justified. Further research on
the structure of powerlessness is suggested.

682. Burback, H. J. and Bridgemon, B. Dimensions of self-concept
among black and white fifth grade children. Journal of Negro
Education, 1976, 45 (5), 448-458.

Findings support the view that there are racial differences
in the reported self-attitudes of fifth grade children and
offer clues as to the nature of these differences.

683. Carpenter, T. R. and Busse, T. V. Development of self-concept
in Negro and white welfare children. Child Development, 1969, 40
(3), 935-939.

Administered 80 children of welfare mothers a measure of
self-concept. Subjects were equally divided as to sex, race
and grade (first or fifth). Results show that girls are more
negative in self-concept than boys, and fifth graders are
more negative than first graders. No overall race difference was found. Results suggest that Negroes do not become
increasingly more negative in their self-concepts from first
to fifth grade than do whites of equivalent social status.

684. Chang, T. S. The self-concept of children in ethnic groups:
Black American and Korean American. Elementary School Journal,
1975, 76 (1), 52-58.

Compared the self-concepts of 144 Black American and 151
Korean American intermediate grade children. Subjects responded to the Piers-Harris Children's Self-Concept Scale,
an 80-item scale consisting of several clusters of yes-no
statements on: (a) behavior, (b) intellectual and school
status, (c) physical appearance, (d) anxiety, (e) popularity,
and (f) happiness and satisfaction. Black Americans had
significantly higher mean scores on (c) and (e). Korean
Americans had significantly higher scores on (a), (b), and
(f). Both groups indicated significantly lower self-concepts
with grade progress in (b), (c), and (d). For both groups,
significant differences were found between the sexes with
respect to (d) with the females indicating less anxiety than
males. The mean scores of both groups were higher than the

mean of the norm with Korean Americans exceeding Black Americans. The former subjects' higher level of school achievement
was reflected in their higher scores on the testing instrument.

685. Cicirelli, V. G. Relationship of socioeconomic status and
ethnicity to primary grade children's self-concept. Psychology in
the Schools, 1977, 14 (2), 213-215.

Evidence regarding the controversy about the relationship
of socioeconomic status (SES) and ethnicity to self-concept
is provided. Subjects were 345 first, second, and third grade
children of low SES (180 were black) attending inner city
schools in a large metropolitan area. The Purdue Self-Concept
Scale was the measure of self-concept. There was a decline
in Self-concept with grade level (p=.01), and blacks scored
higher than whites (p=.01). An analysis of black second
grade children's scores indicated that the race difference
was due to the high scores of those with welfare status.
Low expectations resulting from SES and ethnic segregation,
effects of the black pride movement, and defensiveness are
considered as possible explanations.

686. Coles, R. Like it is in the alley. Daedalus, 1968, 97 (4),
1315-1330.

This article describes life in a northern ghetto (Boston)
for 9-year-old Peter and his mother. Peter is a grim and
unhappy child. He does not trust white people, his family,
or his neighbors. He has learned to be careful and calculating. He finds school meaningless. Though his teachers may
not know it, Peter is a good sociologist, political scientist,
and student of urban affairs. In Peter's world, disease and
pain are taken for granted; until he met Dr. Coles, Peter
had never seen a doctor or dentist. Peter's father died
prematurely, probably for lack of medical attention. Peter
and his mother do not take advantage of the free medical care
provided by the city hospital; the hospital is located far
from their neighborhood, carfare is expensive, and they would
have to wait a long time for their turn. Dr. Coles took Peter
to a children's hospital which led to the following: a pair
of glasses; a prolonged bout of dental work; antibiotic treatment for skin lesions; a thorough cardiac work-up, with the
subsequent diagnosis of rheumatic heart disease; and a conference between Peter's mother and a nutritionist. Peter's
mother is a pragmatist and a Christian. She has mixed feelings about having left Alabama for ghetto life in Boston. For
her children she envisions more of the same, but she does
hope that life might be a little better for them.

687. Comer, J. P. Black children in a racist society. Current,
1974, 162, 53-56.

The problem for black parents of developing psychologically
secure children in a racist society is discussed. It is felt

that blacks often feel rejected and are denied both an adequate
income and respect by a white society and thus are confused
as to what values they wish to give their children. It is
concluded that this problem must be resolved at a group,
family and personal level so that black children may acquire
a positive racial identity.

688. Comer, J. P. and Poussaint, A. F. Black Child Care: How to
Bring Up a Healthy Black Child in America -- A Guide to Emotional
and Psychological Development. New York: Simon and Schuster, 1975.
408 pp.

   Child care and child development from the perspective of black
   parents and black children is discussed in a question/answer
   format. The subjects cover the developmental years from
   infancy to adolescence. Special concern is given to questions
   about race discrimination, a dominant white majority, and
   the black experience awaiting the child.

689. Cummings, S. An appraisal of some recent evidence dealing
with the mental health of black children and adolescents, and its
implications for school psychologists and guidance counselors.
Psychology in the Schools, 1975, 12 (2), 234-238.

   Psychological processes among black children are studied from
   a perspective of familiarity with black culture and the circumstances of the black experience in America. Recent
   studies argue that the traditional literature dealing with
   personality formation and self-conceptions among black youth
   assumes that whites serve as significant others for blacks;
   some scholars disagree, and suggest that if this is so, a
   desire to "be white" is not necessarily pathological in
   nature, leading to delusions in identity and distortions
   in self-conception. Some scholars have identified serious
   biases in the psychological orientation of the social pathology
   model when it is used to conceptualize the thought and behavior of black children within the framework of the pathology
   viewpoint. It is felt that such a premise fails to recognize
   the subcultural perspective. It is recommended that guidance
   counselors and school psychologists examine their own
   orientations towards the mental health of black children.
   Assistance and guidance based on faulty cultural and analytical
   assumptions are judged to be destined for failure.

690. Dai, B. Some problems of personality development among Negro
children. Proceedings of the Institute of Child Research, Clinic,
Woods Schools, 1945, 12, 67-105.

   In this study the problems of personality development among
   Negro children are approached from the sociopsychiatric point
   of view. Some of the problems and the effects of these problems upon personality development are discussed. Data were
   obtained from 80 Negro youths ranging in age from 17 to 25
   years. For the purpose of discussion the problems of person-

ality development among Negro children are divided into two
categories: (1) problems that Negro children share with
whites, and (2) problems more or less peculiar to Negro children.

691. Daniell, R. P. Personality differences between delinquent and
non-delinquent Negro boys. Journal of Negro Education, 1932, 1, 381.

692. Davids, A. Self-concept and mother concept in black and white
preschool children. Child Psychiatry and Human Development, 1973,
4 (1), 30-43.

   Utilizing objective psychological assessment instruments and
   projective techniques, measures of self-concept and mother
   concept were obtained from black children and white children.
   Subjects were 42 3- to 6-year-old children, all attending
   either a day care center or a nursery school. No significant
   differences were found between the self-concepts and mother
   concepts of the two groups. As predicted, there was significant positive association between the self-concept and the
   mother concept in both groups. Consideration was given to
   contradictions between the present findings, plus some from
   other studies, and certain views presented in the older
   psychological literature. The need for longitudinal studies
   of self-esteem is emphasized.

693. Davis, A. Racial status and personality development. Science
Monitor, New York, 1943, 57, 354-362.

   This analysis of the personality formation of Negro children
   in the South bears out the theory that personality is not
   inherited; it is learned. The fact that personality, disposition and character form a learned pattern of behavior means
   that there can be no racial "inheritance" of personality.
   People are not born with their personalities; they acquire
   them by experience in a social environment. Finally, it is
   evident that there are no racial types of personality because
   within each race there are several social strata, each of
   which has a different culture, and each of which teaches
   different kinds of behavior and psychological goals to its
   members.

694. Davis, A. and Dollard, J. Children of Bondage: The Personality
Development of Negro Youth in the Urban South. Washington, D. C.:
American Council on Education, 1940.

   Against a background of material obtained from systematic
   interviews of 200 Negro adolescents in New Orleans and
   Natchez, an attempt is made to describe the development of
   personalities and the processes of socialization of eight
   selected adolescents representing various social levels.
   The individual case histories are given in detail and discussed to show the effects of caste and class in the formation
   of the personality and in the development of behavior patterns,
   social life, and emotional attitudes. The last four chapters
   constitute a general presentation of material to portray the

emotional significance of lower caste status, the meaningfulness of social class, and the problems of child training and
of education in relationship to social class.

695. Davis, A. and Dollard, J. Children of Bondage: The Personality
Development of Negro Youth in the Urban South. New York: Harper
Torchbooks, 1964.

A reprint from the original published in 1940.

696. Davis, T. E. Some racial attitudes of Negro college and grade
school students. Journal of Negro Education, 1937, 6, 157-165.

The racial attitudes of 232 Negro college and grade school
students (Nashville) were studied by means of the Robinson
tests (standardization incomplete). Attitudes of the college
students toward (1) Negro traits; (2) Negro business; (3) Negro
professions; (4) Negro ministry; (5) Negro industry; and (6)
Negro militancy were measured by the attitudes test. The
attitudes of grade school students were measured by the "What-I-
Think" test. The author makes no claim that the results are
scientifically valid or reliable, since "they represent phases
of behavior which themselves are invalid and unreliable."
It is only when there is an agreement between these attitudes
and the socio-economic relations of the Negroes that the test
results are worthy of consideration. The general conclusions
are based upon the consistency with which all groups mark the
test and the universality of the attitudes. The results of
the two tests "clearly indicate the adverse attitudes all
of the students had about Negro business" (and professions)
and point out the necessity of changing such attitudes through
Negro education.

697. DeBlassie, R. R. and Healy, G. W. Self-concept: A Comparison
of Spanish-American, Negro, and Anglo Adolescents Across Ethnic,
Sex, and Socioeconomic Variables. Clearinghouse on Rural Education
and Small Schools, New Mexico State University, Box 3-AP, Las Cruces,
New Mexico 88001, March 1970. 19 pp.

Social and cultural factors are believed to play an extensive
role in the development of self-concept. However, there is
substantial disagreement concerning the extent of their
influence. The objectives of this study were: (a) to determine the differences in self-concept among black, Anglo, and
Spanish American youths; and (b) to measure the influence
on these differences of ethnic group membership, socioeconomic
position, sex, and the interaction of these variables. Two
ninth grade groups of students in New Mexico public schools
were given the Tennessee Self-Concept Scale and accompanying
questionnaire. The scale assessed subjects on 14 different
components of self-concept, including personal, family and
social self, and self-criticism. The questionnaire yielded
information on ethnic membership, socioeconomic position, and
father's occupation and educational attainment. None of the
variables were singularly influential in the development of

an individual's global self-concept. However, sex, socioeconomic position, and ethnic group membership influenced specific dimensions of self-esteem. Subjects from lower social
classes did not exhibit a sense of adequacy and worth in social
interaction comparable to that of subjects from upper social
classes. As socioeconomic class position increased, the level
of satisfaction with self-perception increased. Ethnic group
membership was also an influential variable: although Spanish
American students were more satisfied with self-perception,
they had more defensive distortion. Further research could
include the application of this study in other settings.

698. Dielman, T. E., Barton, K., and Cattell, R. B. Prediction of
objective motivation test scores in adolescence from family demographic variables. Psychological Reports, 1973, 32 (3, Part 1),
873-874.

Administered the School Motivation Analysis Test (SMAT) to
298 junior high school students for whom information concerning sex, race, number of sisters and brothers, and father's
education was available. These variables were employed as
predictors of the test scores. All correlations were low,
but sex of child and father's education were most consistently
related to SMAT scores.

699. Dill, J. R., et al. Sex-role preference in black preschool
children using a modification of the IT Scale for Children. Perceptual
and Motor Skills, 1975, 42 (3), 823-828.

Used the facial features of the "IT" figure in the IT Scale for
Children to measure sex-role preferences of 46 male and 47
female black 4- to 6-year-olds. Data show that the majority
identified "IT" as their own sex. Significant differences
were obtained between the present sample of black males and
those in a comparison sample. No differences existed between
the present sample and the original normative white male
sample. Black females in the present sample were as feminine
as both the black and white comparison samples. Results indicate that the facial features version is appropriate when using
the IT Scale. Black subjects seemed to manifest sex-role
preference similar to their white peers, although females'
scores were more variable. Previous assumptions regarding the
socialization of sex-role behavior of black children are
challengeable and must be considered.

700. Dillard, J. M. Relationship between career maturity and self-
concepts of suburban and urban middle- and urban lower-class pre-
adolescent black males. Journal of Vocational Behavior, 1976, 9
(3), 311-320.

Investigated the relationship between career maturity and
self-concepts of 252 sixth grade black males. Student samples
were drawn from (a) the suburban middle class, (b) the urban
middle class, and (c) the urban lower class in 42 schools in
three New York state counties. The Attitude scale of the

Career Maturity Inventory and the Coopersmith Self-Esteem
Inventory were used to assess the association of career
maturity and self-concepts. Results indicate relatively weak
positive relationships between career maturity and self-concepts.
Significant career maturity differences were found; however,
self-concepts of the three groups were not significantly
different. Of the set of independent variables predicting
and estimating variance accounted for (socioeconomic status,
family intactness, place of residence, and reading), socioeconomic status had strongest predictive effect on career
maturity. It is suggested that researchers examine elementary
school black students' career development in view of the group
with whom they identify most.

701. Dillard, J. M. Socioeconomic background and the career maturity
of black youths. Vocational Guidance Quarterly, 1976, 25 (1), 65-70.

Studied the relationship of career maturity to reading achievement and socioeconomic status (SES). Subjects were 252 sixth
grade suburban and urban black males in New York State. Hollingshead's Two Factor Index of Social Position determined
middle or lower SES; the Career Maturity Inventory-Attitude
Scale (CMI) assessed career maturity; and the Stanford Achievement Test, the Metropolitan Achievement Test, and the Iowa
Test of Basic Skills measured reading skill levels. Statistical analyses, including simple correlations, analysis of
variance, and analysis of covariance, showed: (a) a low positive correlation overall between SES and CMI; (b) significantly higher reading levels for subjects of middle than of
lower SES; and (c) a significant relationship between SES
and career maturity even when CMI scores were controlled for
reading ability levels. Overall, reading achievement appears
less related to career maturity than SES variables such as
cultural and socialization factors. Counselors should help
students explore attitudes and values before the end of high
school and should develop career programs that involve students'
families.

702. Dimond, R. E. and Hellkamp, D. T. Race, sex, ordinal position
of birth, and self-disclosure in high school students. Psychological
Reports, 1969, 25 (1), 235-238.

Administered the S. M. Jourard and P. Lasakow Self-Disclosure
Questionnaire to 120 high school students to examine relationships of birth order, race and sex, to self-disclosure. Results indicated that later borns disclosed more than firstborns, whites disclosed more than Negroes, and mother was
the favorite target person. Further, firstborn Negroes disclosed less than any other group, females disclosed most to
mother and female friend, while males disclosed least to
female friend, firstborns disclosed most to mother, and
whites more to father than Negroes. Results are discussed
in relation to possible child-rearing practices affecting
the meaningfulness of interpersonal relationships established
by the various birth ranks.

703. Dmitruk, V. M. Delay of gratification as a function of incentive
preference and race of experimenter. Developmental Psychology, 1974,
10 (2), 302.

> Delay of gratification was studied as a function of incentive
> preference and race of experimenter. Strickland reported that
> black children were less likely to delay gratification than
> were white children on the basis of the results of a study
> employing a single, arbitrarily selected incentive. In the
> present study, 218 children, black and white and of both
> sexes, were shown 14 incentive items arranged on two tables.
> One of the tables held an assortment of 10 "expensive" incen-
> tives, and the other table 4 "inexpensive" objects. If a
> child indicated a preference for one of the "expensive" items,
> he or she was given the option of either waiting three weeks
> to obtain the preferred incentive or receiving any of the
> "inexpensive" items at the end of the school day. It was
> found that the black and white subjects differed with respect
> to their preferences for expensive incentive objects. Ana-
> lysis of delay data did not yield any statistically reliable
> difference between the black and white subjects in ability
> to delay gratification. These results were compared with
> Strickland's; it is concluded that her results may have been
> a function of greater appeal of the incentive used with the
> white subjects.

704. Dukes, L. W. The experience of being-me for black adolescent
males: A phenomenological investigation of black identity. Available
from: Xerox University Microfilms, P. O. Box 1764, Ann Arbor,
Michigan 48106 (Order No. 75-4084; microfilm or xerography).   Also,
see ERIC Abstracts, No. ED-124-635, 1974.   292 pp.

> The purpose of this study was to explore the experience of
> black identity and arrive at a more comprehensive understand-
> ing of the meaning, structure and situational components of
> black identity from a phenomenological descriptive approach.
> The principal criteria for choosing subjects were that they
> were black adolescent males between the ages of 16 and 18
> and able to provide full descriptions of their experiences
> of being-me and not being-me. Recorded interviews were used
> to obtain the data. The interviews were structured in such a
> way which allowed the phenomenon to reveal itself through
> a detailed situational analysis. Findings which emerged
> in the analysis of the data show clearly that black adoles-
> cents experience the process of identity on two levels simul-
> taneously, one being typical to all adolescents while the
> other is unique to the black experience. The results also
> support the theory that the process of black identity is
> experienced within the black community. Given the freedom
> to choose any situation that the subjects had experienced
> being-me and not being-me, most of the subjects chose situa-
> tions which took place within a black environment. Those
> choosing situations that were in white groups, discussed
> them in terms of their reactions to being with members of
> the dominant culture. The information was always volunteered
> by subjects as a factor in their not being themselves.

705. Engle, T. L. Meanness in the primary grades. Elementary School
Journal, 1946, 46, 337-341.

"Meanness" on the part of other pupils seemed to be experienced
more by boys than girls, by urban children rather than rural
children, and particularly by Negro children. A significant
relationship was found between the greater overt expression
of meanness and inner feelings of lacking affection among
adults and children in the Negro group. The information
was collected by means of a questionnaire sent to the pupils
themselves.

706. Engle, T. L. Personality adjustments of children belonging
to two minority groups. Journal of Educational Psychology, 1945,
36, 543-560.

A group of 101 Amish children, and a group of 107 Negro children, as well as 168 children belonging in neither of these
minority groups, were given the California Test of Personality,
Prin. Form A. Comparisons among the groups were made for
the test as a whole, for subsections and for particular
items. In general, differences in favor of the nonminority
control group were found in self-, social and total adjustment,
although there was an exception in the area of Amish boys.
The handicap of belonging to a minority group appeared to
be somewhat greater for girls than for boys. Significant
contrast between the experimental and control groups was
shown in the case of specific test items. No detailed personality patterns were found to be characteristic of both
minority groups.

707. Epstein, R. and Komorita, S. S. Self-esteem, success-failure,
and locus of control in Negro children. Developmental Psychology,
1970, 4 (1, Part 1), 2-8.

Evaluated personality and situational parameters related to
internal-external control by investigating self-esteem and
success-failure treatments. A 3 x 2 factorial design was
employed with 20 fourth through sixth grade Negro boys in
each of six experimental conditions. Results confirm the
predictions that: (a) failure rather than success experiences
were attributed to external causes, and (b) high self-esteem
subjects were more internal than low or moderate esteem subjects. Results imply that the belief in one's powerlessness,
arising from membership in a stigmatized minority group, may
be cushioned by a positive self-concept.

708. Epstein, Y. M., Krupat, E., and Obudho, C. Clean is beautiful:
Identification and preference as a function of race and cleanliness.
Journal of Social Issues, 1976, 32 (2), 109-118.

White and black children of both sexes in grades 2-4 of a
New York City public school indicated their preferences for
four photographs varying in cleanliness and race. Results
indicate that cleanliness is a more potent determinant of
preferences than is the race of the stimulus person.

709. Farley, F. H. and Sewell, T. Attribution and achievement
motivation differences between delinquent and non-delinquent black
adolescents. Adolescence, 1975, 10 (39), 391-397.

> Notes that motivational, personality, and social-psychological
> differences between delinquent and non-delinquent youth have
> been extensively studied, but no significant attention has
> been paid to differences between black delinquent and non-
> delinquent youths. A study was conducted using 27 delinquent
> and 28 non-delinquent male and female black high school
> sophomores, all of whom were of low socioeconomic status
> and from the same school. The measures used were Rotter's
> Internal-External Locus of Control Scale and F. H. Farley's
> (1968) Motivation Scale. Results do not support the notion
> that delinquents are more external in perceived locus of
> control than non-delinquents, at least for black adolescents.
> Thus, data limit the generality of this particular attribu-
> tion hypothesis of white adolescents. The notion that delin-
> quents may be lower in achievement motivation than non-
> delinquents received no support.

710. Farley, F. H. and Sewell, T. Test of an arousal theory of
delinquency: Stimulation-seeking in delinquent and non-delinquent
adolescents. Criminal Justice and Behavior, 1976, 3 (4), 315-320.

> Hypothesized, based on a theoretical analysis of delinquency,
> that adjudicated delinquents would exhibit significantly
> more stimulation-seeking than non-delinquents matched on
> age, sex, race, and socioeconomic status. Stimulation-
> seeking in 32 delinquent and 32 non-delinquent black adoles-
> cents matched on these variables was compared using the
> Sensation-Seeking Scale. Findings that delinquents were
> significantly higher in stimulation-seeking than the non-
> delinquents confirm the hypothesis. Discussion centers on
> comparison with data for white adolescents and on the direc-
> tion future tests of the theoretical analysis should take.

711. Fodor, E. M. Moral judgment in Negro and white adolescents.
Journal of Social Psychology, 1969, 79, 289-291.

> Compared were 25 Negro and 25 white male adolescents in moral
> judgment as assessed by the Kohlberg Interview. Moral judg-
> ment scores were found to be significantly different between
> the two groups. The relationship between moral judgment
> and the parent behavior dimensions of the Cornell Parent
> Behavior Description were also examined.

712. Font, M. M. "Normal" white and colored children: Comparative
study. Delaware State Medical Journal, 1935, 7, 111.

713. Fox, A., et al. In-school Neighborhood Youth Corps: 14-/15-
year old black teenage girl project, Memphis, Tennessee. Final report.
Washington, D. C.: Manpower Administration (DOL), Office of Research
and Development, December 31, 1973. 175 pp.   Also, see ERIC Abstracts,
No. ED-096-375, 1973.   Also, available from: National Technical
Information Service, Springfield, Virginia 22151.

    This study analyzes the effects on 14- and 15-year-old black
teenage girls of entering and participating in a specially
designed work program. The girls were provided with supports
in their work settings, well-defined tasks, supervisors as
well as regularly scheduled peer interaction groups led by a
young black woman considered to be an appropriate role model.
The entire process of recruitment, selection, and certification
was conducted by the Memphis In-school Neighborhood Youth Corps
office. Two kinds of data were collected: (1) personality
assessment on the experimental group and on the two control
groups, and (2) external source data, consisting of school
grades, school absences and tardiness, juvenile court contacts,
known pregnancies, and on-job performance evaluations. The
selected experimental group were given work assignments as
assistants to teachers and leaders in afterschool day care
centers in poverty neighborhoods. They were directed by job
supervisors in each center, and participated in regular
discussion-interaction groups. In brief, the youth employment program, supported by peer interaction groups, produced
positive outcomes for those included in it. At the same
time, those who were not included in the program (or who
dropped out) showed negative changes in school grades and
self-concepts, as well as an increased perception of themselves
as being at the mercy of chance or luck rather than controlling
their own destinies.

714. Frazier, E. F. Negro Youth at the Crossways. Washington, D. C.:
American Council on Education, 1940.

    This is one of a series of studies undertaken by the American
Youth Commission of the American Council on Education in a
survey of the personality development of Negro youth as
affected by their membership in a minority racial group and
as manifested in different parts of the country. The present
study is concerned with Negro youth of the borderline states
and is based on data secured principally from the Negro communities of Washington, D. C. and Louisville, Kentucky. The
general features of the Negro community of the border states
are described, and the experiences of 268 young people who
live in this comparatively isolated world are analyzed. Interview material is organized in relation to the family, the
neighborhood, the school, the church, job hunting, and social
movements and ideologies. Following the analysis, two systematic and complete case studies are presented, one a middle
class Negro boy, the other of a lower class Negro girl. The
first case is discussed from a psychiatric point of view by
H. S. Sullivan. Additional statements and materials are
presented in appendices.

715. Frazier, E. F. Negro Youth at the Crossways. New York: Schocken
Books, Inc., 1967. xxxv + 300 pp.

The paperback edition of a 1940 study sponsored by the American
Council on Education, in II Parts and 9 Chapters, preceded
by introduction to the 1967 edition by St. Clair Drake,
Author's Acknowledgements, and Introduction by the Author.

I -- "Factors Affecting the Personality of Negro Youth" -- contains: (1) The Negro Community -- an examination of the character of the Negro population in the border states from the old
South and its relations with the white world, based on talks
with 123 Negro boys and 145 girls. (2) The Role of the Family
-- deals with the socialization of the Negro child in lower
class, middle class and upper class Negro families in the
South and the District of Columbia. (3) Neighborhood Contacts
-- studies the Negro adolescent's relationship with his neighborhood and background under reference to the three classes
and finds that lower class Negro children are more exposed
to the hostility of the white community than either middle
class or upper class children. (4) The School -- describes
the views of Negro school children on the quality of their
education. It is found that the schools have influenced the
outlook and interests of the more fortunate social group and
have expressed impatience with Negro youth who had had no
cultural background or economic advantages. There are great
cultural and economic difficulties within the Negro community.
The Negro schools in the border states are found to have a
high degree of efficiency which has made Negro youth dissatis-
fied with their inferior social status. (5) The Church -- is
concerned with the attitudes of Negro youth in the three classes
toward religion and the Church and finds that the majority
of Negro youth of all classes believe that God is white.
(6) Seeking Employment -- describes hopes for and attitudes
toward employment in the three different classes of Negro
youth. All classes agreed that Negroes do not have equal
chances with whites for jobs, whatever their qualifications.
Many of the middle class youths are ambitious and hope to rise
above their present status. Upper class Negro youths do not
feel that they have to use the same techniques as lower and
middle class youths in order to survive. (7) Social Movements
and Ideologies -- attempts to analyze the ways in which Negro
youths are influenced in their conceptions of themselves as
Negroes, in their attitudes toward whites, and in their
aspirations and outlook on life by various social movements
and ideas that are current in the Negro community. Data indicate that social movements in the strict meaning of the term
exercise practically no influence on the personality of Negro
youth.

II -- "Two Negro Youth--Warren and Almina" -- includes: Introduction to Part II, which presents remarks on the selection
of two Negro youngsters' case histories. (8) Warren Wall --
describes the case of the Wall family and their son Warren.
(9) Almina Small -- presents the case of the Small family

and their daughter Almina. Comments by both families and youths are cited to study how being a Negro has influenced the personality of these two youngsters. Summary and Conclusion -- points out that Negro youth is shaped in subtle ways by ideas current in the Negro community. 3 Appendices, and a joint name and subject index. Reprinted by permission.

716. Friend, R. M. and Neale, J. M. Children's perception of success and failure: An attributional analysis of the effects of race and social class. Developmental Psychology, 1972, 7 (2), 124-28.

Tested 120 fifth graders equally divided into four groups on the basis of race (black or white) and social class (moderate or low) to determine their perceptions of the causes of their performance on an achievement task. Following a brief reading test, prearranged feedback (success, failure, or no information) was provided; and subjects evaluated the importance of ability, effort, task difficulty, and luck in relation to their performance. White subjects judged that ability and effort were relatively more important for their performance than task difficulty and luck, while the reverse was true for the blacks.

717. Gable, R. K. and Minton, H. L. Social class, race and junior high school students' belief in personal control. Psychological Reports, 1971, 29 (3, Part 2), 1188-1190.

Administered Battle and Rotter's Children's Picture Test of Internal-External Control to 20 male and 20 female eighth graders from each of two schools in a poverty and blue collar neighborhood. Significant differences were found on internal-external control between schools, but not for social class or race. Economic and cultural differences between schools are examined.

718. Gaier, E. L. and Wombach, H. S. Self-evaluation of personality assets and liabilities of southern white and Negro students. Journal of Social Psychology, 1960, 51, 135-143.

Subjects were 223 white and 221 Negro undergraduates. They listed what they considered their greatest personality assets and liabilities. White males showed significantly fewer socially oriented responses than both white females and Negro males and females in the assets listed. No significant differences in responses to the liabilities listed were found among the four groups. (Modified.)

719. Gardner, G. E. Aggression and violence -- The enemies of precision learning in children. American Journal of Psychiatry, 1971, 128 (4), 445-450.

In a diagnostically classifiable and identifiable group of children, learning ability can be considered to have been induced by experiential factors; interpersonal relationships and milieu events that make it impossible for the child to learn. Most of the children in this group are black or the

children of the lowest white group in the inner cities. A life-
long expectation of aggression, violence, exclusion, derogation,
and defeat pervade their environment. A learning disability
can develop as a response to a chronic state of severe and
inordinate anxiety within the child. This anxiety is the
fear of aggressive acts directed at the child and the fear
of not being able to control his own aggressive impulses.
The control of both fear and aggression required in the
exercise of the learning drive in problem-solving involves
both a needful amount of inner control in the learner and
a needful amount of external control by the teacher. The
child suffering from a learning disability caused by an excess
of traumatic events is unable to control his inner fear and
perceives the outer control of the teacher as aggressive.

720. Garrett, A. M. and Willoughby, R. H. Personal orientation and
reactions to success and failure in urban black children. Developmental Psychology, 1972, 7 (1), 92.

Administered the Intellectual Achievement Responsibility
Questionnaire to 82 female and 80 male black fifth and sixth
graders. Subjects scoring as internal or external were then
given the experience of success or failure on an anagrams task
or a control copying task. Subsequently, all subjects were
given 65 trials on a concept-discrimination task. Fifth grade
girls scored higher on internal orientation than the white
female standardization sample (p>.01). I+ scores (responsibility for success) were higher for the fifth grade boys and
girls than the standardization sample (p>.01). I- scores
(responsibility for failures) were below those of the standardization sample for the sixth graders (p>.025). A significant
Orientation x Treatment interaction was found (p>.01); externals
performed better than internals following failure, and internals
performed better after success. Results are discussed in terms
of achievement motivation.

721. Gibby, R. G. and Gabler, R. The self-concept of Negro and
white children. Journal of Clinical Psychology, 1967, 23 (2),
144-148.

56 Negro and 59 white sixth grade students were administered
the California Test of Mental Maturity and the Gibby Intelligence Rating Schedule (IRS). On the IRS each subject made
judgments on how intelligent he believed himself to be, how
intelligent his mother, father, teachers and friends believed
him to be, and how intelligent he would like to be. The results support the hypothesis that Negro and white children
differ significantly in self-concept as measured by self-
ratings of intelligence, with Negro children achieving significantly greater discrepancies between their actual IQ scores
and their ratings of the self scale than the white children.
A number of other findings are noted and discussed in relation
to social class theory. Magnitude and direction of the differences between Negro and white subjects seemed to be dependent
on the sex and IQ level of the children.

722. Goff, R. M. Problems and emotional difficulties of Negro
children due to race. Journal of Negro Education, 1950, 19, 152-158.

    150 Negro children (10 to 12 years of age) of both sexes were
    interviewed in regard to discriminatory evidences surrounding
    the fact that they were Negroes. Their reports were then
    analyzed under several categories of reaction and emotional
    responses. 57% resented the discriminatory experience; 38%
    felt inferior; 37% were fearful; and the remainder were indif-
    ferent. 57% had some urge to fight or argue, but only 17%
    actually carried out their impulses with action. Withdrawal
    was the customary pattern.

723. Goldman, R. K. and Mercer, B. Self-esteem and self-differen-
tiation: A comparison between black and white children in follow
through and non-follow through classes. Educational Research Quarterly,
1976, 1 (3), 43-49.

    A sample of 213 black and white kindergarten children was used
    to compare follow through with non-follow through students with
    regard to self-esteem and self-differentiation as measured
    by a human figure drawing. The children were instructed to
    draw both a black and white child in counterbalanced sequence
    and the comparison between the drawings formed the bases for
    judgments. Follow through children were not significantly
    different from their counterparts in either self-esteem or
    self-differentiation. However, black youngsters, regardless
    of program setting, had significantly more indices of emotional
    problems while white youngsters, also regardless of program
    setting, drew both races in a significantly more differen-
    tiated manner, a finding which may have been influenced by
    the restricted socioeconomic range of the school population.

724. Goldstein, H. S. and Gershansky, I. Psychological differentiation in clinic children. Perceptual and Motor Skills, 1976, 42 (3,
Part 2), 1159-1162.

    In a clinic population the relationship between children's
    perceptual differentiation as measured by the rod-and-frame
    test (RFT) and their self-concept differentiation as evidenced
    in their human figure drawings (Draw-A-Person Test, scored
    using a Body Sophistication Scale) was studied. In addition,
    the WISC Vocabulary Subtest was employed. Subjects were 140
    black and 38 white 8- to 15-year-olds making an initial visit
    to a child guidance clinic. The relationship between perceptual
    differentiation and self-concept differentiation was signifi-
    cantly positive only for white females with a father present.
    Vocabulary and RFT were positively correlated for the black
    and white subjects while vocabulary and the body-sophistication
    scores were significantly related for black males and white
    females with a father present. Differentiation may then
    appear in a variety of patterns in different populations.

725. Graham, T. F. Doll play phantasies of Negro and white primary
school children. Journal of Clinical Psychology, 1955, 11, 29-33.

    To illustrate the value of doll play techniques for studying
    the development of racial attitudes in children, the doll
    play around a stage set of home and family is compared for
    Negro children and for white children varying in sex, grade
    and general ability. The technique is able to reflect the
    presence of individual and group differences. The reliability
    of the observers of the play was evaluated.

726. Gray, S. The wishes of Negro school children. Journal of
Genetic Psychology, 1944, 64, 225-237.

    820 Negro children in Grades I-IV in southern schools were
    rated as to SES and asked to name the one thing in the world
    they would like to have more than anything else. Except for
    increases in interest in bicycles and education and decrease
    in interest in automobiles and toys, there seems to be little
    relationship between wishes and CA or grade placement. The
    only significant sex differences were where girls wished for
    pianos and watches, and in general, for things concerning
    home, while boys were more interested in travel and conveyance.
    There were no differences in wishes by the different economic
    groups. Comparing these results with those in a similar study
    by Boyton of white children, Gray found that, although there
    are some differences, the two groups are basically similar
    and show a lack of relationship between interests and the
    four factors studied -- CA, grade placement, sex, and economic
    status. He concludes: "It would seem that one is led to view
    that a child's interests are dependent upon the particular
    experiences through which he as an individual has gone through."

727. Grossack, M. M. Some personality characteristics of southern
Negro students. Journal of Social Psychology, 1957, 46, 125-131.

    Scores on the Edwards Personel Preference Schedule show that
    personality characteristics of southern Negro students differ
    from those of students in general. (Modified.)

728. Grossman, F., Retish, P. M. Classroom counseling: An approach
to improve student self-concept. Counseling and Values, 1976, 21
(1), 64-66.

    This article concerns itself with the problems of integrating
    into the curriculum a program designed to raise the self-
    concept of lower socioeconomic status black students.

729. Gruen, G. E., Korte, J. R., and Baum, J. F. Group measure of
locus of control. Developmental Psychology, 1974, 10 (5), 683-686.

    Gave the Gruen, Korte, Stephens Internal-External Scale, a
    new measure of locus of control designed for use with children
    of differing socioeconomic and ethnic status, to a total of
    1,100 black, white and Spanish, moderately disadvantaged

children from grades 2, 4, and 6. The white children were
compared to a sample of 155 affluent white children. As
predicted, older children made more internal responses than
younger children, and the affluent children made more internal
responses than the disadvantaged. Also, white children made
more internal responses than either black or Spanish children.
Among black subjects there was a significant sex difference,
females being more internal than males. Further analyses
with another sample of 50 white second graders revealed that
the locus of control scores were significantly related to
grade point averages, but not significantly related to
scores on the Otis-Lennon Mental Ability Test or the Crandall
Social Desirability Scale. The scores on the measures of
locus of control were generally skewed toward the internal
end of the scale but were discriminative at the second grade
level. Internal consistency and test-retest reliability
estimates for Gruen, Korte, Stephens Internal-External scores
were moderately high.

730. Guggenheim, F. Self-esteem and achievement expectations for
white and Negro children. Journal of Projective Techniques and
Personality Assessment, 1969, 33 (1), 63-71.

Investigated the relationship of self-esteem, achievement
expectations, and discrepancies between achievement expectations and actual achievement for Negro and white pupils using
an initial sample of 162 subjects and a final sample of 56.
Negroes had significantly greater discrepancies between their
expectations for achievement and their actual achievement
than whites. No relationship was found between ethnic background and discrepancies between expectations for achievement
and actual achievement as a result of receiving increasing
amounts of information concerning actual performance on an
achievement task. An interrelationship was found between self-
esteem, expectations for achievement, and actual achievement
discrepancies, and experience with the achievement task.

731. Gurin, P., Gurin, G., Lao, R. C., and Beattie, M. Internal-
external control in the motivational dynamics of Negro youth. Journal of Social Issues, 1969, 25 (3), 29-53.

This paper delineates two differentiations in the concept of
internal-external control of reinforcement that are particularly relevant for understanding the motivational dynamics
of people disadvantaged by minority or economic status. One
is the distinction between the belief that internal or external
control operated generally in our society and the feelings
about one's control or lack of control in one's personal
life situation. The other is the distinction between a
belief in external control when the external factors are
structured as "fate" and "chance", and when they are seen
as systematic societal barriers and constraints. Data are
presented from two studies of Negro youth suggesting that
both distinctions are necessary in the prediction of performance and aspiration. Whereas individual aspiration and per-

formance were positively related to the belief in one's
personal control, they were, if anything, negatively related
to the generalized belief in control. The externally, rather
than internally oriented Negro youth showed more "effective"
individual aspirations for non-traditional occupations, and
collective attempts to reduce barriers to Negro achievement.
Reprinted by permission.

732. Guttentag, M. and Klein, I. The relationship between inner
versus outer locus of control and achievement in black middle school
children. Educational and Psychological Measurement, 1976, 36 (4),
1101-1109.

Minority children's expectancies account for a large proportion
of the variance in their achievement. This study examined
the relationship between each of several dimensions of the
expectancies of 980 black urban 5th-8th graders and their
school achievement. The study was designed to reveal whether
these subjects showed the differentiated expectancies (e.g.,
individual vs. system blame) and racial militancy which
characterize minority adolescents. Subjects did not show
this expectancy differentiation, and they did not discriminate between racial and nonracial items. Two important factors
were found: General Personal Efficacy, and Interpersonal
Control.

733. Halpern, F. Self-perception of black children and the civil
rights movement. American Journal of Orthopsychiatry, 1970, 40
(3), 520-526.

Describes black parents' identification with or rejection of
the civil rights movement as a source of confusion to their
children, especially the middle class child whose father has
"made it". For all black children, the movement provides a
channel through which to express positive or negative feelings
for the parents.

734. Hammer, E. F. Frustration-aggression hypothesis extended to
socio-racial areas: Comparison of Negro and white children's H-T-Ps.
Psychiatric Quarterly, 1953, 27, 597-607.

For the child of the Negro race, the outer white world is
often disappointing, frustrating and threatening. A comparison
of the relative degrees of aggression in Negro and white children should therefore be useful in further study of the hypothesis that frustration leads to aggression and hostility. The
author has studied aggression and hostility in 148 Negro school
children and 252 white school children, utilizing the free-
hand drawing of a house, tree and person. The 400 H-T-Ps were
put into random order of Negroes and whites by grade level,
and rated by six judges on a scale of aggression from zero
(no apparent aggression) to 2 (severe aggression). The mean
aggression and hostility rating for the white children was
.308, while the mean hostility rating for the Negro children
was .823. A score of 1 represented mild aggression; the Negro
children proved to be close to this point, while the white

children were closer to the point of no aggression. No consistent trends were apprent in the hostility index of the
Negro and white children when broken down by grades. A
striking number of children made drawings conspicuously too
large for the page, without adequate space framing them.
Buck writes that such drawings tend to indicate a great frustration produced by a restraining environment, and feelings
of hostility and desire to react aggressively. It was found
that 10.3% of the white children presented such drawings,
while 28.3% of the Negro children did so. All six clinician-
judges were placed in rank order in regard to the degree of
hostility they manifested in interpersonal relationships as
judged by the supervisor. A comparison was made of this rank
order with the rank order of hostility they saw in the H-T-P
drawings of the 400 subjects. In 4 cases the rank order was
the same in each instance. The 2 ranking 2nd and 3rd in hostility seen in drawings were ranked in reverse order by the
supervisor. In spite of these differences in perception
of hostility in the H-T-Ps, the judges showed a reasonably
high correlation in their judgments. If it is assumed that
the Negro child suffers more frustration than the white
child, the frustration-aggression hypothesis when extended to
social-racial areas receives support from this study. The
study suggests also that the clinician must be cautious when
interpreting the projective protocols of a Negro subject. He
must keep in mind the problems peculiar to the subject's race,
while at the same time keeping faith with the concept of a
baseline representing an optimum state of personality adjustment.

735. Hammer, E. F. Negro and white children's personality adjustment as revealed by a comparison of their drawings (H-T-P). Journal
of Clinical Psychology, 1953, 9, 7-10.

To determine if Negro children were less well adjusted than
white children, adjustment ratings obtained from H-T-Ps of
148 Negro and 252 white children from grades 1 to 8 in the
same community were compared. The ratings of adjustment were
less good for the Negro children at all ages; they tended
to keep the same poor adjustment rating throughout grade
school, whereas the adjustment ratings of the white children
became steadily worse as age increased. The average Negro
first grade child rating was close to borderline psychotic;
the average rating for this group never dropped below the
severely neurotic category. The average first grade white
child rating was mildly neurotic; the average ratings for
this group increased until they were slightly above the
neurotic category.

736. Hardy, R. C. A developmental study of relationships between
birth order and leadership style for two distinctly different American groups. Journal of Social Psychology, 1972, 87 (1), 147-148.

Administered F. Fiedler's Least Preferred Co-worker (LPC)
Scale to 66 white, middle class undergraduates and 106 black

lower middle class fifth and sixth graders. A Birth Order
(firstborn and later born) x LPC (high and low) contingency
table was constructed for each population. Chi-square values
for both populations indicate that firstborns were more task-
oriented, and later borns were more relation-oriented.

737. Harris, S. and Braun, J. R. Self-esteem and racial preference
in black children. Proceedings of the Annual Convention of the American Psychological Association, 1971, 6 (Part 1), 259-260.

Investigated the interrelation of self-esteem and racial
preference in Negro children from an inner city and suburban
school. The Piers-Harris Children's Self-Concept Scale was
administered to measure self-esteem, and a variation of the
Clark and Clark Dolls Test was used to assess racial preferences. Subjects who made more Negro preference choices had
higher self-concept scores than those who made fewer Negro
preference choices. No significant sex or social class differences were found. A majority of the Negro children preferred the black doll.

738. Hartnagel, T. F. Father absence and self-conception among
lower class white and Negro boys. Social Problems, 1970, 18 (2),
152-163.

Explored the effects of fatherlessness and race on the self-
conceptions of lower class adolescent males using the orientation of symbolic interactionism and the semantic differential
for measurement. A distinction was made between actual and
normative self, and the categories of white and black, father-
absent and father-present boys were examined. All categories
exhibited significant differences between actual and normative
self, but the magnitude of differences varied among categories:
black father-absent boys had smaller differences than white
father-absent boys; there was no difference between white
and black father-present boys. The smaller difference of the
black father-absent boys was the result of their more potent
actual self-conceptions. Several interpretations of these
results are discussed.

739. Hauser, S. T. Black and White Identity Formation: Studies in
the Psychosocial Development of Lower Socioeconomic Class Adolescent
Boys. New York: Wiley-Interscience, 1971. xv + 160 pp.

Most clinical and research studies of personality development
in adolescence have been restricted to white, middle class
subjects. An attempt is made to clarify the relationship
between patterns of identity formation and sociocultural
context through a longitudinal study of non-middle class
white and black youth. New Haven junior and senior high
school guidance counselors and assistant principals selected
for interviews and tests students who were male, entering their
sophomore year of high school, from a lower socioeconomic class
family (Hollingshead index), and neither delinquent, predelinquent, nor college-bound. Thus sex and social class were held

constant, with race the contrast characteristic. A sample of
11 Negro, 11 white, and 1 Puerto Rican boy was seen initially; subjects were then interviewed and tested twice each
year until graduation. Methodologically, a major purpose of
the research was the formulation of an operational definition
of ego development, based on the discussions of Erikson and
of other students of identity problems; from this, several
variants of ego identity formation were given empirical definitions. The instrument used for measuring the modes of identity
formation was a specially designed Q-sort technique. Q-sort
data were supplemented by clinical evidnece of identity formation. Findings revealed unanticipated and striking differences between two of the racial groups. Of particular interest
is the unremitting pattern of identity foreclosure of black
adolescents -- a variant with crucial consequences for continued ego development. Rather than manifesting change with
further experience and education, the Negro patterns emphasized
fixed self-images, unchanging in their content or integration
with one another. The results indicate diminished psychological
growth for black adolescent boys of lower socioeconomic class
at the time of the study (1962-1967). Recent rapid changes
in black-white relations may, perhaps, have influenced identity
formation patterns since the conclusion of this study.

740. Hauser, S. T. Black and white identity development: Aspects
and perspectives. Journal of Youth and Adolescence, 1972, 1 (2), 113-
130.

Constructed empirical definitions and five variants of identity
formation using a technique for studying multiple self-images,
and applied the method to 22 black and white lower socioeconomic class male adolescents. Subjects were tested and
given in-depth interviews twice a year for the last three
years of high school. Results disclose that the subjects
had emphatically different patterns of identity formation.
Blacks were characterized by unchanging configurations of
self-images. Both the content of their self-definitions and
the interrelations for these self-definitions remained strik-
ingly stable over time. Whites displayed a progressive integration of different self-images and stabilization of the content
of these images. The patterns displayed by the blacks were
consistent with the definition of identity foreclosure, a
disruption in ego identity development. The whites' patterns,
however, were consistent with progressive identity formation.
Sociocultural as well as cognitive aspects of racial differences in identity development are discussed in conclusion.

741. Hayes, E. J., Hill, J., and Young, H. Superfly, The Mack, black
youth, and counselors. School Counselor, 1975, 22 (3), 174-179.

Discusses the need for counselors to become aware of the
negative influences of recent "blaxploitation" (the exploitation of blacks) films on the self-concept development, aggressive behavior, and motivational levels of black youth. Examples
of intervention strategies which counselors can employ within
the school and community are included.

742. Healey, G. W. and Deblassie, R. R. A comparison of Negro, Anglo,
and Spanish-American adolescents' self-concepts. Adolescence, 1974,
9 (33), 15-24.

> Negro, Anglo, and Spanish-American adolescents' self-concepts
> were compared to determine: (a) if differences in self-concepts
> exist, and (b) the extent to which these differences were in-
> fluenced by ethnic group membership, socioeconomic position
> or sex, or the interaction among these variables. Subjects
> were 630 ninth grade students in the South Central New
> Mexico public school system. Four data indexes were used:
> scores on the Tennessee Self-Concept Scale (TSCS); the Hol-
> lingshead Two Factor Index of Social Position (ISP); ethnic
> group membership; and sex. Of the 14 measures of self-concept
> assessed, the total positive score was among 8 measures un-
> affected by the independent variables. The ethnic variables
> affected four measures: self-criticism, defensive-positive,
> self-satisfaction, and moral-ethical self. Socioeconomic
> position affected two of the measures -- social self and self-
> satisfaction. Sex differences significantly affected the
> physical self-measure.

743. Henderson, G. G. The academic self-concept of black female
children within differential school settings. Journal of Afro-
American Issues, 1974, 2 (3), 248-266.   Also, see ERIC Abstracts,
No. EJ-106-751, Summer 1974.

> Investigates the relationship between school climate and the
> black females' academic self-concept in different elementary
> school settings and to determine which of the social-psychological
> variables comprising school climate most strongly affect the
> academic self-concept of the black female.

744. Henderson, N. B., Goffeney, B., and Butler, B. V. Do Negro
children project a self-image of helplessness and inadequacy in
drawing a person? Proceedings of the 77th Annual Convention of the
American Psychological Association, 1969, 4 (Part 1), 437-438.

> Compared 232 7-year-old Negroes with 466 white children to
> determine if the Negro group produced less complete human
> figure drawings. The mean total score for the Negroes was
> significantly higher. They drew significantly (p>.01) more
> complete faces, but significantly (p>.01) fewer arm-hand items
> than the white children. Because of the small difference in
> total score and the superiority of each group on different
> parts of the examination, and because previous results are
> impressionistic and limited in sample, caution is suggested
> in drawing social and psychological inferences about impover-
> ished environments from projective test results.

745. Henderson, N. B., et al. Sex of person drawn by Japanese,
Navajo, American white and Negro seven-year-olds. Journal of Personality Assessment, 1971, 35 (3), 261-264.

> Compared Navajo, Japanese, American white and Negro 7-year-old
> drawings for proportions of self-sex to opposite-sex figures

drawn. When the sexes were pooled across the four races, Chi-
square showed a highly significant difference between the
sexes in the proportions of self-sex figures drawn. Girls
drew self-sex more frequently than boys. However, both boys
and girls drew their own sex more frequently than the opposite.
The tendency to draw self-sex was strongest among the Japanese.

746. Hendrix, S. and Dokecki, P. R. The personal-social competence
development of low-income children. St. Ann, Missouri: National
Coordination Center for Early Childhood Education; and Washington,
D. C.: Office of Education (DHEW), May 1973. Also, wee ERIC
Abstracts, No. ED-129-399, 1973.

This paper is a preliminary report of a project designed to
determine the family and other environmental factors which
are associated with effective functioning in children from
low income environments. The purpose of the project was to
determine the strengths in poverty situations which should be
capitalized on in developing educational programs and to learn
more about children's coping and adaptive mechanisms in general.
A total of 143 low income black children served as subjects
in the pilot study. The Stanford-Binet was administered to
each child. The attitudinal variables of need for achievement, delay of gratification, reflectivity and internal-
external control were assessed using individually administered tests and an experimental choice situation. Behavioral
adjustment was measured through behavior ratings by classroom teachers. Results indicated that the measure of need
achievement showed no relationship to other attidudinal
variables, behavioral adjustment, chronological age, or mental
age. The motor inhibition test of impulsivity was significantly related to mental age, but showed no relationship to
chronological age, behavioral adjustment, or the measures of
attitudinal development. The negative internal control sub-
scale was associated with chronological age only. No significant relationships were found for the positive internal
control dimensions or delay of gratification.

747. Hindelang, M. J. Educational and occupational aspirations
among working class Negro, Mexican-American and white elementary
school children. Journal of Negro Education, 1970, 39 (4), 351-353.

Used a pretested interview schedule in interviewing 187 grade
4, 5, and 6 working class pupils from a West Coast community
of 95,000. The racial breakdown of the sample was 68 Negroes
(N), 74 Mexican-Americans (MA), and 45 whites (W), and the
racial composition of the interviewers was fixed in the same
proportion. Subjects were asked how much longer they would
like to go to school, how far in school they thought their
parents and teachers wanted them to go, and what they wanted
to do when they grew up. The N subsample had the highest
educational aspirations, followed by the W, and finally the
MA subsamples. When educational aspiration is held constant,
W and MA pupils are found to aspire to higher educational
categories. It is suggested that Negro students may be preparing themselves for job discrimination in the future.

748. Hindman, B. M. The emotional problems of Negro high school youth which are related to segregation and discrimination in a southern urban community. Journal of Educational Sociology, 1953, 27, 115-127.

This investigation studied the nature of the relationship between experiences involving contact with members of the white race and feelings of hostility or resentment, or other emotionalized attitudes, on a group of Negro high school youth. In this area Negroes comprised approximately 17% of the total population. All eleventh grade Negro high school students were used. Detailed discussion of the study and analysis of the data along with seven tables are given.

749. Hirsch, J. G., Borowitz, G. H., and Costello, J. Individual differences in ghetto 4-year-olds. Archives of General Psychiatry, 1970, 22 (3), 268-276.

To provide better understanding of people living in black inner city neighborhoods, pilot studies have been made focusing on academic achievement during preschool years. Such a study is described involving individual play sessions with 4-year-old socially disadvantaged children during their first preenrollment visit to preschool. Subjects were observed by psychiatrists and rated on a scale (described in this study) covering variables including speech and play behavior, relationship of subject to interviewer, psychosexual content of play, and a general developmental assessment. 1-1/2 years later, subjects' case histories were given to independent judges who again rated the subjects on the same scale. Results suggest useful directions for preventive programs with children and families. The usefulness of a developmental framework for preschool program planning is also discussed.

750. Hughes, J. H. and Thompson, G. G. A comparison of the value systems of southern Negro and northern white youth. Journal of Educational Psychology, 1954, 45, 300-309.

Following a method developed by R. White, a value analysis was made for 88 essays written by school pupils. Northern white children in a nonsegregated school, and southern Negro children in a segregated school, tended to place a similar amount of emphasis on the great majority of values. Knowledge, achievement and economic values were equally valued. White groups put significantly greater emphasis on happiness, security and independence, and a lower value emphasis on justice and group unity. Negro pupils were strongly critical of segregation and were concerned with social justice in this connection.

751. Hunt, L. L. and Hunt, J. G. Race and the father-son connection: The conditional relevance of father absence for the orientations and identities of adolescent boys. Social Problems, 1975, 23 (1), 35-52.

Examined interview data from 445 paid male black and white juniors and seniors in high school to determine the effects

of father presence/father absence on personal identity and
attitudes toward conventional success goals in early adulthood. Results indicate that father absence has quite different consequences by race, with father absence being associated
with damaging effects only among white males. By contrast,
father absence seems to have some slightly positive effects
on black males. This pattern of "costs" for whites and "gains"
for blacks is general across social class levels. The lack
of evidence of detrimental effects of father absence among
black males raises questions about the role of the black family
in sustaining intergenerational patterns of racial inequality.

752. Hurlock, E. B. The will-temperament of white and Negro children. Journal of Genetic Psychology, 1930, 38, 91-100.

110 white and 101 Negro boys from the seventh and eighth grades
in a New York school were examined. Higher scores were made
by whites on speed of decision and movement and volitional
perseveration, by Negroes on self-confidence, finality of
judgment, motor inhibition, and coordination of impulses, with
no advantage to either on freedom from load. Other tests
were omitted as unsuitable with children. In nearly all
cases the differences found were not statistically significant.

753. Jensen, A. R. Personality and scholastic achievement in three
ethnic groups. British Journal of Educational Psychology, 1973, 43
(2), 115-125.

Examined scores on the Junior Eysenck Personality Inventory
(JEPI) of Caucasian, Negro and Mexican-American 9- to 13-year-
olds (N=2,221) in relation to measures of intelligence and
home environment as predictors of scholastic achievement. The
JEPI scales showed quite low but significant and systematic
correlations with achievement (as measured by the Stanford
Achievement Test). Extroversion (E) correlated positively
with Neuroticism (N), and the Lie (L) scale correlated negatively with achievement. The independent contributions of
E, N and L to achievement variance over the variance accounted
for by the ability and background measures were negligible.
However, the three JEPI scales combined in a multiple regression equation along with measures of intelligence and home
background independently contributed a small share of the
predicted part of the scholastic achievement variance. No
appreciable or systematic age or ethnic differences were found
in this relationship, although there were significant age
and ethnic group differences in mean scores on the JEPI scales.

754. Jensen, G. F. Inner containment and delinquency. Journal of
Criminal Law and Criminology, 1973, 64 (4), 464-470.

A basic inner containment -- the inner ability of a person
to direct himself or the inner strengths which help him to
resist deflection from conventional norms -- is delineated,
the minimum test requirements of the hypothesis outlined, and

the hypothesis tested with a sample of black and white male adolescents. Results of a survey of 1,001 black, and 1,588 white, subjects indicate that elements of inner containment account for some variation in delinquency under similar socio-economic conditions and among boys who fall in similar varia-tions in inner containment within the controls may be due to other adversities and aspects of the social environment which were not held constant. Discussion does not include recom-mendations for treatment or prevention.

755. Johnson, D. W. Freedom School effectiveness: Changes in atti-tudes of Negro children. Journal of Applied Behavioral Science, 1966, 2 (3), 325-330.

A report of the effects of teaching Negro history to a small group of Negro subjects between the ages of 8 and 13. The Freedom School was instituted out of concern for the Negro's negative self-attitudes and their effects on his attitudes toward society, maturation, motivations, and aspirations. Inter-views, four months apart, were used to determine changes in super-ego strength, self-confidence, and attitudes toward Negroes and toward civil rights. Selected factors of Cattell's Child Personality Questionnaire and an attitude questionnaire were used. To control for effects of the first interview, a con-trol group received the second but not the first interview. Negro interviewers were used. The statistical norms for Cattell's questionnaire were used as a control, comparing the subjects with the $\overline{X}$ U.S. child. Findings are given as tenta-tive evidence that teaching Negro history and culture can be effective in raising the attitudes of Negroes toward Negroes. Reprinted by permission.

756. Junker, B. H. Methods for the study of personality in Negro society: Part I. Negro personality in the social context. Proceed-ings of the Third Biennial Meeting of the Society for Research in Child Development, 1939, 26-34.

A preliminary report of research on the effects of minority racial status upon the personality development of Negro youth. Principles for classification and interpretation of Negro personality types are illustrated in a social analysis of personality development and adjustment of one particular social type.

757. Karoly, P. Comparison of "psychological styles" in delinquent and nondelinquent females. Psychological Reports, 1975, 36 (2), 567-570.

16 black and 16 white female delinquents and 36 black and 31 white high school females were compared on Rotter's Interper-sonal Trust Scale, the Sensation-Seeking Scale, and the Rathus Assertiveness Schedule. Expected differences for groups and race failed to emerge. Results are discussed in terms of the need to enlarge upon traditional views of adolescent psycho-pathology and to seek improved modes of assessing lower-class clients.

758. Kline, H. K. An exploration of racism in ego ideal formation. Smith College Studies in Social Work, 1970, 40 (3), 211-235.

15 Negro and 15 white children, ages 5 through 7, whose parents consented to their participation in a study, were interviewed concerning components believed to comprise the ego ideal. Subjects were presented first with a doll of their own race and then with a doll of the opposite race and asked to judge whether each doll would achieve the child's standards or which would exceed in attainment. Findings showed both groups expressed positive views about prospects for dolls of both races, suggesting that idealizing operations of children may be uncontaminated by racial influences.

759. Kokonis, N. D. Three wishes of black American children: Psychological implications. Perceptual and Motor Skills, 1974, 38 (3, Part 2), 1335-1338.

The wishes of black American children, 7 to 12 years old (63 boys, 74 girls), were investigated to obtain normative data and to compare these children with other cultural groups. Subjects wished for material things more often than anything else; boys tended to wish for money and material things more strongly than girls; and girls were more interested in personal attributes and skills than boys. No developmental trends were noted. Findings were compared with those of studies dealing with white American and Greek and Greek-American children, emphasizing psychosocial change in human development.

760. Kubie, L. S. The ontogeny of racial prejudice. Journal of Nervous and Mental Diseases, 1965, 141 (3), 265-273.

Thesis is developed that prejudice against other has its roots in three phases of infantile experience: (1) the child's oscillation between a secret, guilty pride and an inversion toward the body, (2) his inability to conceive of himself as ever growing into adulthood, and (3) his inacceptance of the anastomic differences between the sexes.

761. Kuhlman, T. L. and Bieliauskas, V. J. A comparison of black and white adolescents on the H-T-P. Journal of Clinical Psychology, 1976, 32 (3), 728-731.

This study attempted to remedy the inadequate control procedures of Hammer's research and to answer the logical question as to applicability of the H-T-P scoring norms to black subjects.

762. Kumar, S., et al. Anxiety, self-concept, and personal and social adjustments in children with sickle cell anemia. Journal of Pediatrics, 1976, 88 (5), 859-863.

763. Kuzma, K. J. and Stern, C. The effects of three preschool intervention programs on the development of autonomy in Mexican-American
and Negro children. Journal of Special Education, 1972, 6 (3), 197–
205.

     Assigned 42 Mexican-American and 35 Negro children in nine
     Head Start classes to either an autonomy, language, or control
     group to determine (a) the effects of a 7-week summer program
     upon the development of autonomy, and (b) whether the instruc-
     tional treatments produced significantly different changes
     in autonomy or cognitive ability as a function of ethnicity.
     Scores on the Cincinnati Autonomy Test Battery increased for
     all children, with Mexican-American children showing signifi-
     cant gains on 9 and Negro children on 5 of the 11 autonomy
     measures. Using the Peabody Picture Vocabulary Test as a
     measure of mental functioning, results indicate that IQ scores
     increased significantly (p<.01) for children receiving either
     the language or autonomy curriculum.

764. Lambert, N. M. and Nicoll, R. C. Dimensions of adaptive behavior of retarded and nonretarded public school children. American
Journal of Mental Deficiency, 1976, 81 (2), 135–146.

     Investigated the psychometric properties of the Adaptive Be-
     havior Scales, Public School Revision, by administering the
     instrument fo 2,618 7- to 13-year-olds. The sample included
     white, black, and Spanish-surname groups from regular and
     special education classes. Factor analyses of domain scores
     indicated four dimensions of adaptive behavior: Functional
     Autonomy, Interpersonal Adjustment, Social Responsibility,
     and Intrapersonal Adjustment. Comparison of factor structure
     across school classification and age groups revealed the same
     four dimensions for all groups. Implications for the assess-
     ment of adaptive behavior are discussed, and the correspondence
     between the present behavioral objectives and those defined
     by investigators studying effective school behavior is noted.

765. Lane, E. A. Childhood characteristics of black college graduates reared in poverty. Developmental Psychology, 1973, 8 (1),
42–45.

     Studied records of IQ scores obtained in grades 2, 6, and 8 by
     22 black college graduates from poverty backgrounds. Subjects'
     scores were compared to three control groups: school norms,
     siblings (N=45), and classmates matched for sex, age and
     second grade IQ level. Subjects' second grade scores were
     below national averages and showed no differences from the
     three control groups. By eighth grade, however, subjects'
     scores were significantly higher than all three controls.
     School progress, birth order, family stability and family
     composition are also examined.

766. Larson, R. and Olson, J. L. A method of identifying culturally deprived kindergarten children. Exceptional Children, 1963, 30 (3), 130-134.

This article describes one system of identifying factors thought to be significant to the education of culturally deprived children. They are factors which can be described in terms of behavioral characteristics appropriate to curriculum planning.

767. Lavach, J. F. and Lanier, H. B. The motive to avoid success in 7th, 8th, 9th, and 10th grade high achieving girls. Journal of Educational Research, 1975, 68 (6), 216-218.

The hypothesis that a motive to avoid success (M-S) exists in high achieving 7th, 8th, 9th, and 10th grade girls was investigated. 85 black and white subjects responded to verbal Thematic Apperception Test (TAT)-like stimuli. Scores, treated by Chi-square, supported the hypothesis that M-S is prevalent in high achieving girls and is positively correlated with increasing grade level. The M-S was not found to be correlated with race.

768. Lefebvre, A. Self-concept of American Negro and white children. Acta Psychologica Taiwanica, 1973, 15, 25-30.

Hypothesized that urban black children have a lower self-concept than their white counterparts. 40 black male seventh and eighth graders from an all-black parochial school, and 40 white male seventh and eighth graders from an all-white parochial school, were matched in terms of age, IQ, and socio-economic status. Both groups were administered the Tennessee Self-Concept Scale. Blacks scored significantly lower than whites on total scores and the following scales: Behavior, Physical Self, Personal Self, Moral-Ethical Self, Identity and Self-Satisfaction. Scores on the other subscales were all in the expected direction.

769. Lerner, R. M. and Buehrig, C. J. The development of racial attitudes in young black and white children. Journal of Genetic Psychology, 1975, 127 (1), 45-54.

Assessed racial attitude development in four groups of black and white children (374-, 385-, 406-, and 41, 7-year-olds) using a structured, open-ended interview employing black and white dolls as stimuli. The majority of statements made at each age level by both black and white subjects were meaningful, as opposed to irrelevant, and black and white at all age levels described both the black and white stimuli with responses that were preponderantly concrete, neutral in evaluative connotation, and nonpejorative. Findings contradict the results of racial attitude studies using forced-choice methods. The discrepant depictions of racial attitude structure in young children found by these two methods are discussed.

770. Lewald, J. Emotional differences in white and colored inmates in an institution for mental defectives. Proceedings of the American Association on Mental Deficiency, 1937, 42, 91-94.

> In an institution for mental defectives caring for both colored and white boys and girls, colored girls offer the greatest problem in maintaining order, and colored boys seem more prone to disturbance than white boys. Since behavior pattern is tied up with the emotions, a study was made of the emotional responses of 48 subjects to five sets of sensory stimuli. The method of paired comparisons was used. The scores showed lack of correlation with mental age, but socially adjusted children scored higher as a rule than those with a low sense of social value. The author hopes that further study of emotional responses to ordinary stimuli will lead to more accurate measurement of the social adjustability of individuals in order to attain suggestions regarding the course to pursue in character training.

771. Lewandowski, N. G., Saccuzzo, D. P., and Lewandowski, D. G. The WISC as a measure of personality types. Journal of Clinical Psychology, 1977, 33 (1), 285-291.

> Attempted to provide evidence for the utility of the WISC to identify a specific group of individuals. 80 incarcerated juvenile offenders in the 70-79 IQ range were separated according to race and sex and their differential WISC patterns studied. Results focus on the efficiency of each of Wechsler's hypotheses for the adolescent sociopath. Post-hoc analysis provided tentative additional signs by which to identify juvenile offenders in the 70-79 IQ range. Consistencies between results of the present analysis and previous studies are noted. The clear pattern that emerged strongly supports the potential of the WISC as a measure of personality types.

772. Littlefield, R. P. Self-disclosures among some Negro, white and Mexican-American adolescents. Journal of Counseling Psychology, 1974, 21 (2), 133-136.

> Differences in self-disclosure existing among male and female samples of black, white and Mexican-American ninth grade students with respect to the sex of the discloser, and amount and direction of the disclosure, were observed. Rivenbark's revision of Jourard's self-disclosure questionnaire was administered to 300 ninth graders in the rural South and Southwest: 100 blacks, 100 whites, and 100 Mexican-Americans. Each group was composed of an equal number of males and females. Females reported more disclosure than males; when sexes were pooled, the white subjects reported the greatest amount of disclosure, the Mexican-American group the least; males favored the mother as the target of most disclosure, whereas for all groups the least favored target of self-disclosure was the father.

773. Long, B. H. and Henderson, E. H. Social schemata of school
beginners: Some demographic correlates. Merrill-Palmer Quarterly,
1970, 16 (4), 305-324.

   A non-verbal method was applied to an investigation of the
   self-social concepts of 192 rural southern school beginners,
   selected on the basis of sex, race, and socioeconomic class.
   Negroes were found to have a lower self-esteem and less preference for father. Lower class children placed the self
   closer to mother, teacher, and friend; boys, closer to father.
   Girls showed a greater preference for teacher; boys for father.
   A race by class interaction was found for social dependency
   and distance from teacher. Results were interpreted in terms
   of experiential sources of the child's social schemata.
   Reprinted by permission.

774. McAdoo, H. P. An assessment of racial attitudes and self-
concepts in urban black children. Final report. Washington, D. C.:
Children's Bureau (DHEW), 1973. 82 pp. Also, see ERIC Abstracts,
No. ED-114-437, 1973.

   This study compares information about the attitudes of black
   children in a predominantly black urban community with that
   from a previous study on Mississippi and Michigan children in
   which no difference in race attitudes and no relationship
   between racial attitudes and self-concept were found. The
   report studies a sample of 4- and 5-year-old black children,
   testing them on two occasions a year apart with the stated
   intent of assessing the impact of three demographic settings
   (an integrated northern area, an all-black rural southern area,
   and an all-black urban mid-Atlantic area) on self-concept,
   racial attitudes, and self-identification. Self-concept and
   IQ were found to be positively related at the retesting. The
   D. C. children had good positive self-concepts and showed
   positive changes in self-concept and IQ at the retesting.
   It is suggested that the black child feels better about himself when he is surrounded by those of a similar group
   membership.

775. McAdoo, H. P. A reexamination of the relationship between
self-concept and race attitudes of young black children. Paper
presented at The Demythologizing the Inner City Black Child Conference (Atlanta, Georgia, March 25, 1976). Also, see ERIC Abstracts,
No. ED-122-968, 1976.

   Relationships between race attitudes and self-concept were
   examined in black preschool children in three demographic
   areas: (1) a Mississippi rural town, (2) a Michigan urban
   setting, and (3) a mid-Atlantic urban setting. Data were
   collected on racial attitude, self-concept, and educational
   aspiration. The children were retested one year later in the
   Mid-Atlantic sample and five years later in the two other
   areas. Positive self-concepts were found in all groups, and
   self-concepts became more positive over time. The children
   were all able to make correct self racial identifications.
   The racial attitude responses indicated a moderate majority

group preference at the first testing but at the end of five
years, the children had markedly (.01) modified their race
attitudes and were own-group oriented. The northern children
had the greatest change in attitude toward their own racial
group. There was agreement in the occupational aspirations
held by the children, their parents, and their teachers in
the southern sample but not in the northern sample. A linear
relationship between self-concept and racial attitude was not
found, providing support for discarding the self-hatred hypothesis that implies that white-orientation in black children
is significantly related to self-hatred.

776. McAdoo, J. L. The relationship between observed paternal
attitudes, behavior and self-esteem of black preschool children.
Rockville, Maryland: National Institute of Mental Health (DHEW),
1976. 28 pp. Also, Paper presented at the Annual Meeting of the
Association of Black Psychologists (Chicago, Illinois, August 2,
1976). Also, see ERIC Abstracts, No. ED-130-793, 1976.

This study examines the relationship between observed behaviors and attitudes of black fathers and the association of
these paternal measures with the self-identity of their
preschool children. 21 working and middle class suburban
black families were studied. Four black male interviewers
were trained to collect the parent-child interaction in two
interviews. Verbal and nonverbal interactions between the
father and child were recorded. Results indicated that the
fathers of this study exhibited a warm nurturant attitude in
their verbal interactions with their children. The fathers of
boys were more nurturant than the fathers of girls. There
were very few restrictive kinds of father-child interaction.
Fathers interacted verbally more with their sons and more
non-verbally with their daughters. The children in this
sample had high self-concept scores. The fathers' attitudes
toward child-rearing practices seemed to fall into the
moderately strict categories. These findings contradict the
stereotype of black fathers as well as the findings of a number
of past studies.

777. McCormick, C. H. and Karabinus, R. A. Relationship of ethnic
groups' self-esteem and anxiety to school success. Educational and
Psychological Measurement, 1976, 36 (4), 1093-1100.

Studied differences in measures of self-esteem (Self-Esteem
Inventory) and anxiety (Test Anxiety Scale for Children and
General Anxiety Scale for Children) among 1,235 white, black
and Spanish-surname, 4th, 5th, and 6th graders. Subjects had
been divided by placing high or low on scores on tests of
reading achievement, arithmetic achievement, and scholastic
aptitude. In contrast to previous findings by A. H. Frerichs
(see PA, Vol. 47:7723), no self-esteem differences were noted
in high vs. low reading achievement groups of black children.
Self-esteem and anxiety differences between subsamples of
high vs. low achievement and of high vs. low scholastic aptitude were inconsistent across ethnic groups. Sample charac-

teristics, differences in conditions for instrument administration, and varying child/adult relationships are suggested as possible sources of influences upon the findings.

778. McCullers, J. C. and Plant, W. T. Personality and social development: Cultural influences. Review of Educational Research, 1964, 34 (5), 599-610.

Two types of research are considered: the culturally deprived child, and personality changes in college-age adults. The first section is concerned with research on minority ethnic groups, particularly Negro. The second section is concerned with the effects of college experience upon personality. It is suggested that there is a faster than average rate of personality change among brighter young adults.

779. McDonald, R. L. and Gynther, M. D. Relationship of self and ideal self-descriptions with sex, race and class in southern adolescents. Journal of Personality and Social Psychology, 1965, 1 (1), 85-88.

The effect of sex, race and social class was evaluated on the self and ideal self-concept as determined by the Interpersonal Checklist. Subjects were 261 Negro and 211 white high school seniors who attended segregated urban high schools. Social class was determined by parental occupation. Sex and race influenced the results, but class did not have any effect. Negro subjects obtained higher dominance and love scores than whites for self-ratings, but lower scores on ideal descriptions. Males' self- and idea-self-ratings yielded higher scores on the love variable. There was less discrepancy between ideal and self-ratings of: (a) Negroes compared with whites; (b) males compared with females on dominance; and (c) females compared with males on love. (Modified.)

780. McNabb, D. R. Delinquent acting-out and the task of sexual identification in black male adolescents: A replication study. Smith College Studies in Social Work, 1973, 44 (1), 23-24.

Previous research using white male adolescents was replicated in an experiment on delinquent acting-out and the task of sexual identification among black male adolescents to test the finding that acting-out behavior is associated with high levels of unconscious femininity and conscious masculinity. Subjects were between 14 and 16 years of age and were residents of a rehabilitative institution following adjudication for a variety of offenses. The measure of unconscious femininity was the Gough Femininity Scale, the scores furnishing a basis for assignment of each subject to one of four sex-role categories: MM--high unconscious masculinity and high conscious masculinity; MF--high unconscious masculinity and high conscious femininity; FM--high unconscious femininity and high conscious masculinity; and FF--high unconscious femininity and high conscious femininity. Unlike previous results, the relative proportions of black subjects were evenly distributed

throughout all sex-role categories, rather than heavily weighted
in the FM category. This suggests that the relationship between delinquent acting-out and the task of sexual identification may not be as important in the etiology of delinquency
among blacks as among whites.

781. Madge, N. J. Context and the expressed ethnic preferences of
infant school children. Journal of Child Psychology and Psychiatry
and Allied Disciplines, 1976, 17 (4), 337-344.

Studied 44 black and white 6- to 7-year-olds to test the hypothesis that children may not be consistent in their ethnic
"attitudes" between test situations where choice behavior is
controlled by different variables. Subjects completed a
photographs test in which they chose, from 15 pairs of photographs, the individual they liked best; a sorting test, in
which subjects were asked to group the pictures according to
whether they belonged together or were the same; and a stories
test, where subjects responded to a story in which a black
child received adult approval while a white child received
disapproval or vice versa. In the photographs test there was
a significant difference between black and white subjects in
their frequencies of preference for white figures. However,
there was no difference between the two subject groups in
the proportion of in-group choices made in the stories test;
yet when responses of the two stories were analyzed separately
there was a marked tendency, particularly by black children,
to prefer the "approved" figures independent of their skin
color. Sociometric data revealed that both racial groups
chose more friends of their own skin color.

782. Mann, L. Effects of a commitment warning in children's decision behavior. Journal of Personality and Social Psychology, 1971,
17 (1), 74-80.

Conducted three studies with 104 preschool children in the
United States and Australia to determine whether a commitment
warning (admonition that a decision will be binding) would
influence behavior on immediate and on unrelated decisions.
In comparison with subjects in the noncommitment condition,
commitment subjects took longer to announce their choice
of a gift toy and showed greater willingness to make some
sort of decision on an unrelated problem. Contrary to expectation, the commitment warning did not produce an increase
in postdecisional bolstering. 5-year-olds tended to show
more mature decisioning than 4-year-olds. Negro and white
United States children were very similar to Australian children in their responses. Findings suggest that even in young
children, issuing a commitment warning initiates a psychological set to approach decisions problems carefully and decisively.

783. Marks, E. S. Factors in the personality development of Negro
children. Psychological Bulletin, 1938, 35, 711.

784. Marmorale, A. M. and Brown, F. Comparison of Bender-Gestalt
and WISC correlations for Puerto Rican, white and Negro children.
Journal of Clinical Psychology, 1975, 31 (3), 465-468.

    Obtained correlations between Bender-Gestalt scores and WISC
    IQs for three ethnic groups of 123 Puerto Rican, 82 white,
    and 61 black children in the first grade. The Bender-Gestalt
    Test did not show any significant relationship with the WISC
    scores of the Puerto Rican children. Significant correla-
    tions between the Bender-Gestalt and all the WISC scores
    were found for the black group. For the white subjects, the
    relationship between the WISC and Bender-Gestalt was signifi-
    cant but only for the Performance and Full Scale scores. The
    absence of a significant correlation between the Bender and
    the WISC Verbal IQ in these children is attributed to the
    relative superiority of their Verbal scores.

785. Martin, J. Self-perceptions of the school-age unwed mother.
Smith College Studies in Social Work, 1974, 45 (1), 31-32.

    The perceptions of the school-age unwed mother who chooses
    to keep her baby were examined. The perceptions of a group
    of black school-age unwed mothers in regard to significant
    relationships, their pregnancy-motherhood experience, and
    attitudes toward counseling, were explored. Data were col-
    lected through semistructured interviews. More positive
    responses to the pregnancy-motherhood experiences occurred
    among the prenatal subjects. Both prenatal and postnatal
    subjects denied extensive life changes or problems related
    to the experience. Most of the subjects did not view them-
    selves as in need of counseling.

786. Marx, R. W. and Winne, P. H. Self-concept and achievement:
Implications for educational programs. Integrated Education, 1975,
73, 30-31.

    Research examining relationships between academic achieve-
    ment in the basic skills and self-concept has been presented
    in a form that suggests causality. Most researchers believe
    self-concept to be a fundamental determinant of academic
    performance. To test this theory, 38 fifth graders and 60
    sixth graders from a predominantly black school were strati-
    fied by classroom. In both grades, girls had higher achieve-
    ment scores, but boys scored significantly higher on self-
    concept. It was clear that children who scored higher on
    either of the two achievement measures tended to have poorer
    social self-concepts. The study suggests that programs to
    bolster academic achievement by enhancing self-concept may
    be misdirected.

787. Massey, G. C., Scott, M. V., and Dornbusch, S. M. Racism without racists: Institutional racism in urban schools. Black Scholar,
1975, 7 (3), 10-19.

    A survey of students in eight San Francisco high schools, in-
    cluding 209 black, 133 Spanish-surname, 184 other white, and

183 Asian-American students, was conducted to tap students'
perceptions of themselves and their academic environment.
Despite their extremely low grades and achievement scores,
blacks were not found to suffer from extremely low self-
concepts. Black students consider learning school subjects
more important than do other groups of students. Social influences from parents do not explain differences between
blacks and other groups in school performance, nor do blacks
have lower aspirations; blacks aspired to be doctors, lawyers
and other professionals just as often as did white students,
Chicanos. The ethnic groups who were doing less well in
school, saw teachers as more friendly and warm than did
the other ethnic groups. The academic standards and evaluation system found in the schools did affect the students'
assessment of their effort and achievement. Students in
every ethnic group were allowed to misinterpret feedback on
their level of effort and achievement. Blacks are most hurt
by this distorted system of evaluation.

788. Milgram, N. A. Locus of control in Negro and white children
at four age levels. Psychological Reports, 1971, 29 (2), 459-465.

Administered Bailer's Locus of Control Scale for Children,
Raven's Coloured Progressive Matrices, and a measure of occupational aspiration to male and female, Caucasian and Negro,
1st, 4th, 7th, and 10th graders (N=80). Scholastic achievement was assessed with either the Otis-Lennon Mental Ability
Test or the Metropolitan Readiness Tests. Age-related pro-
gressions, but not sex or ethnic differences, were obtained
on Bailer's scale. Test-retest correlations of locus of control were not significant, despite the minimal shift in score
by individual, because of the narrow range of scores at these
grade levels. The absence of significant relationships between
locus of control and measures of scholastic achievement, nonverbal intelligence, and occupational aspiration is discussed.

789. Milgram, N. A., Shore, M. F., Riedel, W. W., and Malasky, C.
Level of aspiration and locus of control in disadvantaged children.
Psychological Reports, 1970, 27 (2), 343-350.

Compared culturally disadvantaged and advantaged six-year-
old subjects on level of aspiration and locus of control.
No differences between disadvantaged Negro and white subjects
were found on either measure, but disadvantaged subjects in
general were characterized by higher and less accurate levels
of aspiration on specific performance tasks and by less
internal locus of control.

790. Miller, T. W. Cultural dimensions related to parental verbali-
zations and self-concept in the child. Journal of Social Psychology,
1972, 87 (1), 153-154.

Studied parental verbalization and self-concept in the child
using a stratified random sampling of 200 eighth graders and
their mothers in a large metropolitan area in the United States.

Results suggest verbal styles of responding differ between black inner city and white suburban mothers with higher levels of descriptiveness apparent with the latter group. Self-concept in the child was highly related to parental form of appraisal in the inner city sample only. Speculations regarding the observed differences are presented.

791. Miller, T. W. Effects of maternal age, education and employment status on the self-esteem of the child. Journal of Social Psychology, 1975, 95 (First Half), 141-142.

The effects of maternal age, education and employment status on self-esteem of the child were examined. An all-black inner city sample, and an all-white suburban sample of eighth grade children and their mothers were chosen from a random selection of schools in six school districts. The self-esteem inventory was administered to each child, and demographic data were obtained from each mother. Self-esteem of inner city males was affected by the amount of the mother's formal education, but this was not significant for the inner city female sample. Mother's employment status had less of an effect on the self-esteem of suburban children.

792. Milner, D. Children and Race. Penguin Paperbacks, 1975. 281 pp.

This volume, in seven chapters, reviews and assesses the major research related to racial attitudinal development in children. The author, a British psychologist, provides an important expansion to the knowledge in this area by presenting the extant research conducted on black and white British children, a topic that will be appreciated by most American readers. The volume's organization provides a creditable, if nor praiseworthy, approach to understanding the development of racial attitudes. Chapter 1, "Prejudice and Psychology," traces the historical origins of racial attitudes in terms of both societal trends and social science thought. Chapter 2, "The Socialization of Attitudes and Identity," examines theories, constructs, and empirical findings pertinent to the developmental phenomena of learning racial attitudes. The third chapter, "Children's Racial Attitudes," analyzes the contribution of global social influences on the development of racial attitudes. Chapter 4, "Racism and Black British Children," examines racial attitudes and identification in minority group British children. The remaining 3 chapters -- "Black Identity and Mental Health," "Education and Black Children," and "Education Against Prejudice" -- provide an enriching expansion and application of the empirical studies of racial attitude development. The two appendices contain brief, yet helpful, listings of educational resource materials about nonwhite groups that can be obtained in England. For its compact size, this volume is a wealthy sourcebook for the reader interested in children's racial attitudes. Perhaps the most salient feature of the book is its discussion of racial attitudinal development in both white and nonwhite British children that is interwoven with the more

widely known American studies. The author's patient and careful description of the British sociocultural milieu and its
impact on children of various racial groups is an important
addition to the literature. This book would be suitable
to a broad readership -- psychologists, educators, social
workers, and policy planners will enjoy this very readable
volume. The use of the book as collateral reading in both
undergraduate and graduate child development courses would
also be appropriate.

793. Milner, E. Some hypotheses concerning the influence of segregation on Negro personality development. Psychiatry, 1953, 16, 291-
297.

On the basis of extensive observations, several hypotheses
are discussed concerning the comparative influence upon the
Negro personality of legal versus tacit segregation. The
author hopes to stimulate a systematic investigation of this
sociopsychological problem.

794. Minigione, A. D. Need for achievement in Negro and white children. Journal of Consulting Psychology, 1965, 29 (2), 108-111.

Need for achievement (nAch) was defined as concern with achieving high standards of excellent. (nAch was measured by stories
told or written in response to line drawings.) Two studies
were done comparing nAch of Negro and white children in rural
central North Carolina. In both studies white subjects scored
significantly higher than Negro subjects, and nAch scores increased significantly with age.

In Study #2, Negro girls scored significantly higher than Negro
boys. In Study #1, Negro subjects had more hostile non-nAch
themes, but there was no meaningful pattern on non-nAch themes
in the second study. (Modified.)

795. Moore, C. L. The racial preference and attitude of preschool
black children. Journal of Genetic Psychology, 1976, 129, 37-44.

42 black subjects were assigned to three black female and three
white female examiners who administered a preference measure
which was a variant of the Clark Doll Test. Although black
males preferred the black model, they viewed the black model
negatively and the white model positively. Black females
preferred the black model and viewed her positively. Choices
made by the children were not influenced by the race of the
examiner.

796. Moses, E. G., Zirkel, P. A., and Greene, J. F. Measuring the
self-concept of minority group pupils. Journal of Negro Education,
1973, 42 (1), 93-98.

The results of self-report instruments in the measurement of
the effect of ethnic group membership upon self-concept of
disadvantaged students was undertaken. The effects of minority

membership across the two instruments was analyzed. The 42-
item Coopersmith Self-Esteem Inventory (CSEI) was chosen as
the self-report instrument. Subjects consisted of 120 students
in elementary schools in a large Connecticut city. Subjects
were to be evenly distributed according to sex, socioeconomic
factors, and IQ. It appears that ethnic group membership had
a significant effect on the self-report results of the self-
concept of the disadvantaged pupils. The self-concept level
of Puerto Rican pupils was significantly lower than that of
Negro and white pupils. Implications and limitations of this
experimental situation are discussed.

797. Mussen, P. H. Differences between the TAT responses of Negro
and white boys. Journal of Consulting Psychology, 1953, 17, 373-376.

The TAT protocols of 50 white and 50 Negro lower class boys
were analyzed and scored in terms of 50 categories of need
and pressure. Significant differences included the following:
Negro boys' stories showed more aggressive pressure from the
environment, mild verbal aggression from heroes; they displayed
less interest in having friendly relations with others, and
relative indifference to achievement.

The white boys suffered more from feelings of rejection, showed
more extreme hostility, saw others as rejecting them, were
interested in establishing friendly relations, and had the
desire to achieve something credible. Dynamic interpretation
of these stories, like similar projective material, can be
meaningful only when the cultural background of the subjects
is considered.

798. Nelson, J. C. Interests of disadvantaged and advantaged Negro
and white first graders. Journal of Negro Education, 1968, 37 (2),
168-173.

Reports the results of a survey of identity subjects of high
interest level for six-year-old culturally deprived Negro
children. An identical survey of advantaged Negro children,
deprived white children, and advantaged whites was conducted
to see if differences existed along racial, economic or sex
lines. Results indicate that at age six aspirations in all
groups are similar although differences begin to appear.

799. Newman, I., et al. Matching factors of vocational interests
by grade, sex, and race. See ERIC Abstracts, No. ED-110-483, 1974.
14 pp.

Vocational interests among eighth and ninth grade students
were examined and factor structures by grade, sex, and race
were compared. The Ohio Vocational Interest Survey (OVIS)
was the only inventory given. Results indicate that: (a)
eighth and ninth grade students have similar interest patterns;
(b) black and white eighth and ninth grade students have similar interest patterns; and (c) male and female eighth and ninth
grade students have similar interest patterns except for on

the artistic dimension. Possible implications of this study
are that similar interests for both eighth and ninth graders
may be indicative of a more stable interest pattern among
junior high school students than many theorists have assumed,
that OVIS can be used effectively to measure similar interests
of both black and white students, and that OVIS, since it is
not a sex-restrictive instrument, can be a useful test with
both men and women.

800. Nolle, D. B. Changes in black sons and daughters: A panel
analysis of black adolescents' orientations toward their parents.
Journal of Marriage and the Family, 1972, 34 (3), 443-447.

Although there have been a large number of studies analyzing
black adolescents' experiences in their family, no major study
has focused on an assessment of potentially dynamic aspects
of black adolescent/parent relationships through repeated
measurements of the same individuals over time. In an analysis
of 278 southern, urban black adolescents, this study examined
these adolescents' perceived orientations toward their parents
on closeness, openness, respect and susceptibility to moral
influence over a 3-year period. This study found very few
differences over time in perceived orientations. Nevertheless
one result replicated itself three times: differences in perceived closeness to the father over time appeared among working
class sons, working class daughters, and middle class daughters.
Aspects of role theory were used to explain these results. At
this point it is possible to conjecture that less positive perceptions of the father over time might generate less positive
self-images for the adolescent which, in turn, might generate
less favorable exchanges between the adolescent and his father.
Reprinted by permission.

801. Oldham, E. V. The socioeconomic status and personality of
Negro adolescent girls. Journal of Negro Education, 1935, 4, 514-522.

This study attempts to discover the relationship between socioeconomic status of Negro adolescent girls and certain personality
traits which are observable in the teacher-student relationship.
The study was conducted in four public schools in the "near"
South Side of Chicago. Schools were chosen to represent different social levels; 319 cases were studied. In addition to
a battery of intelligence tests and personality tests and
socioeconomic status, a schedule for directed observation of
behavior was used. More than half of the pupils showed no
outstanding behavior and were therefore not rated by the teachers. Only a small percentage showed overt reactions which
were instances of anti-social traits. A larger percentage of
"non-conformists" showed outstanding favorable behavior. There
was found to be nearly as much unfavorable behavior at the high
level as at the low, but fewer individuals were involved at
the high level. The coefficients of correlation are low and
indicate no significant relationship.

802. Page, W. F. Self-esteem and internal versus external control
among black youth in a summer aviation program. Journal of Psychology,
1975, 89 (Second Half), 307-311.

Changes in self-esteem and belief in internal versus external
control of reinforcement (skill versus chance) were investigated among 24 black male and female youth in an aviation program. Subjects were aged 12 through 19, from diverse backgrounds and geographical locations. Age, socioeconomic status,
geographic location and achievement in flight training were
varied. Results showed significant gains in self-esteem by
subjects under 16 years of age and subjects from middle income
families. There was no significant change in belief in internal
versus external control among any of the subgroups.

803. Palermo, D. S. Racial comparisons and additional normative
data on the Children's Manifest Anxiety Scale. Child Development,
1959, 30, 53-57.

Subjects were 136 Negro and 394 white children from segregated
schools, and retest data on 99 Negroes and 371 whites from
mixed schools. Data showed that Negro subjects scored significantly higher on both parts of the test, and girls scored
higher than boys. (Modified.)

804. Pavendstedt, E., M.D. Overview of the North Point project. In
E. Pavendstedt (Ed.), The Drifters: Children of Disorganized Lower
Class Families, pp. 33-44. Boston: Little, Brown and Company, 1967.

The 1955-1965 North Point (Boston) project for slum children
began with home visits by one full-time worker assisted by
consultants in child psychiatry, psychology, and social work.
Between 1957 and 1959 the staff was increased, and referrals
were solicited from the Department of Public Welfare. Multi-
disciplinary personnel were used. During these two phases
children were tested, and mental health work was undertaken
with them. Many adult traits can be linked to early emotional
deprivation. In order to alleviate this process in children
it was essential to move them at the earliest possible age
into an environment where there were trustworthy, responsive
adults. Between 1960 and 1965, a demonstration project was
undertaken to build on any achievements for strengthening
adaptive functions which would be helpful in middle class
schools, to dispel the fear and suspicion of authority figures,
and to buttress the usual development of children between 3 and
5. Referrals and selection procedures, staff work, and test
results are described. Most of the children tested had average
intellectual potential. Only a few showed either higher or
lower potentials. For many of the children everyday functioning was below the level attained on formal testing. However,
there was deviant instability of test function in items involving language and thought. Cognitive process was literal, un-
imaginative, and poorly organized. Attempted mastery of fear
through flight, manifested by general evasiveness toward outside objects and people, was a common adaptation to environmental stimuli.

805. Peatman, J. G. and Greenspan, I. An analysis of results
obtained from a questionnaire regarding superstitious beliefs of
elementary school children. Journal of Abnormal and Social Psychology, 1936, 30, 502-507.

> Results obtained from a questionnaire designed to furnish
> information about the superstitious beliefs of elementary
> school children were summarized and analyzed in relation to
> the 431 Negro children's differences in sex, age, school grade
> and birthplace. 50% of the group indicated that they believed
> at least one-half of the 35 superstitious statements to be
> true. The girls exceeded the boys in the average frequency
> of superstitious responses. The mean differences in the fre-
> quency of superstitious responses for the various age groups
> were not very great, and in no case was a difference found
> to be statistically significant. The lower the school grade,
> the greater the average frequency of superstitious responses.
> Whether the subjects had or had not been born in New York
> City, or whether they were born in the Old South, made no
> significant difference in the frequency of superstitious res-
> ponses.

806. Pehazur, L. and Wheeler, L. Locus of perceived control and
need achievement. Perceptual and Motor Skills, 1971, 33 (3, Part 2),
1281-1282.

> Administered the Children's Locus of Control Scale and the
> Graphic Express Scale to 45 black, 8 Puerto Rican, and 23
> Jewish fifth and sixth graders. Black and Puerto Rican sub-
> jects indicated more perceived external control than the
> Jewish subjects, and this was related to low need achievement.
> When the black and Puerto Rican subjects read a story making
> perceived internal control more salient, measurements indi-
> cated an increase in both need achievement and internal control.

807. Petersen, A. C. and Kellam, S. G. The measurement of psycholo-
gical well-being: A multi-media approach. Paper presented at the
Annual Meeting of the American Educational Research Association (60th,
San Francisco, California, April 19-23, 1976). 21 pp. Also, see
ERIC Abstracts, No. ED-124-569, 1976.

> This paper presents data on a follow-up study of a project in
> the 1960's: a classroom assessment and intervention program
> directed at mental health for all the first grade classrooms
> of Woodlawn, a black poor community on Chicago's South Side.
> Now, ten years later, the mental health of these adolescents
> as well as the mental health, structure, and process of the
> family, are being studied. The general research objective is
> to learn what early and concurrent factors predict good versus
> poor functioning at adolescence. The study reported here
> focuses primarily on the "How I Feel" instrument constructed
> to measure self-reported psychological well-being in adoles-
> cence. To circumvent the generally poor reading skills of the
> population, the test items are presented on a tape accompanied
> by a single answer booklet in which answers are reported. The

tapes were produced by a black actor. Items were developed
for the usual clinical components of psychopathology: anxiety,
depression, anger and aggression, bizarre-peculiar-paranoia,
obsessions, and compulsions, fears and phobias, mania and
grandiosity, plus a global psychopathology construct. Results
of the various statistical analyses and reliability and validity
data are included. The results show great potential for
affective measurement in school settings.

808. Phillips, B. N. School-related aspirations of children with
different socio-cultural backgrounds. Journal of Negro Education,
1972, 41 (1), 48-52.

Studies of educational aspirations of Negro parents and children show inconsistencies, and an analysis of the literature
in the area suggests that this occurs because measures of
aspirations which reflect hopes and desires give results
differing from those which reflect expectations. Thus, it
would appear that Negroes hope for and desire, but do not
expect to achieve, as high a level of educational attainment
as middle class whites. In this study, the focus is on children's aspirational reactions to social and academic opportunities in the classroom. 30 items from the 198-item Children's School Quesionnaire were administered to subjects in
the fourth grade in four different elementary schools, each
representing a homogeneous socio-cultural subgroup; namely,
middle class white (N=76), upper lower-class white (N=95),
Mexican-American (N=73), and Negro (N=87). These items represent achievement opportunities in the classroom, and in indicating his own status in relation to them, the child reveals
something about his school related aspirations, especially
his hopes and desires in contrast to expectations, and subgroup
comparisons can be made. Results show that Negroes generally
have the highest hopes and desires for school achievement, both
social and academic. Differences between middle and upper
lower-class whites are similar to those between Negroes and
Mexican-Americans, with middle class whites and Negroes
having the higher aspirations. In general, white children have
higher school expectations, leading to stronger achievement-
related motives, and more achievement-oriented behaviors,
while nonwhite children desire and hope for school success
at least as much as white children but do not have the means
to achieve success, and thus are exposed to additional sources
of school stress. Comparing school aspirations to the degree
of success/failure in school, the discrepancy is largest among
Negroes, followed by Mexican-Americans, lower class whites,
and middle class whites. The stress potential of such discrepancies is therefore greatest for Negroes and least for middle
class whites, so that if school stress is a major source of
school anxiety, Negroes ought to be the most school anxious,
followed by the Mexican-Americans, lower class whites, with
middle class whites being the least school anxious -- a conclusion supported by other studies. Reprinted by permission.

809. Portnoy, B. and Stacey, C. L. A comparative study of Negro
and white subnormals on the Children's Form of the Rosenzweig P-F
Test. American Journal of Mental Deficiency, 1954, 59, 272-278.

> 30 institutionalized subnormal white, and 30 institutionalized
> subnormal Negro children were tested with the Children's Form
> of the Rosenzweig Picture-Frustration (P-F) Test. The follow-
> ing results were obtained: (a) for all groups, the Extrapuni-
> tive type of response predominated consistently; and (b) the
> study of trends revealed that all four subnormal groups be-
> came less Extrapunitive, more Impunitive, and more obstacle-
> dominant. The Negro female group became less need persistent.

810. Poussaint, A. F. and Atkinson, C. O. Negro youth and psychological motivation. In A. C. Ornstein (Ed.), Educating the Disadvantaged: School Year 1968-1969, pp. 57-70. New York: AMS Press, 1970.

> The study of motivation of black youths must consider the
> individual's self-concept, his patterned needs, and the rewards
> which society offers for performance in any of its institu-
> tional areas. The first two motivational factors are internal.
> The third factor is external. In order to determine an optimal
> meshing of these factors and effectively formulate action pro-
> grams, the relationship between the motivation of black youths
> and their behavior must be explored. The individual's self-
> concept is developed by anticipating and assuming the atti-
> tudes and definitions of others toward him, and is controlled
> through the adoption of community attitudes, norms, and values.
> For the black youth, a negative self-concept results from con-
> tact with a devaluating, discriminating society. Furthermore,
> he learns that, for him, the fulfillment of socially endorsed
> needs results in inconsistently conferred rewards. Thus, the
> fulfillment of patterned needs -- achievement, aspiration,
> approval -- will often be frustrated or assume directions not
> sanctioned by society. Aspirations are a manifestation of the
> achievement motive. Black youths typically have high aspira-
> tions in regard to education and occupation, yet these aspira-
> tions are not translated into appropriate behavior. Low self-
> esteem is not generally associated with high achievement.
> However, the needs for self-assertion and aggression are stronger
> motivators of behavior than are predispositions related to
> self-concept. A sense of control over the environment indicates
> that fulfillment of these needs, and this sense is lower for
> black youths than for whites. Needs for approval, not often
> met in black children through the established institutional
> channels, may be met outside these legitimate institutional
> areas. Consequently, for black youths patterned needs and
> societal rewards, external motivation factors, are weak moti-
> vators of behavior since they are discriminatorily and incon-
> sistently given.

811. Powell, E. R. and White, W. F. Affect structure and achievement in a select sample of rural Negro children. Journal of Negro Education, 1972, 41 (1), 53-56.

Administered the Children's Personality Questionnaire, 3 forms of "Cloze" Tests on third grade reading materials, the Metropolitan Achievement Tests, and a semantic differential scale, to 101 male and female Negro fifth grade children in a southern rural community. Subjects were identified as deprived by the Poverty Index. Results were factor analyzed using principal components with unities in the diagonal, and factors with a latent root greater than one rotated to a verimax solution. Four factors were labeled ideal self, intellectual power, submissive, and being good, happy and fair.

812. Prendergast, P., Zdep, S. M., and Sepulveda, P. Self-image among a national probability sample of girls. Child Study Journal, 1974, 4 (3), 103-114.

Self-esteem and -concept were studied as part of a larger study on attitudes of young American females. The relation of self-image to race, social class, urbanicity and age was studied among a nationally representative sample of more than 1,800 girls aged 9 to 17. As part of a larger personal interview, a total of six questions dealing with ability, appearance and interpersonal relations were asked. On all of the items black girls rated themselves higher than white girls rated themselves. Significant differences on the basis of the other variables were not found. The results were discussed in terms of increasing racial pride and social defensiveness.

813. Price, A. C. A Rorschach study of the development of personality structure in white and Negro children in a southeastern community. Genetic Psychology Monographs, 1962, 65, 3-52.

Subjects were 180 school children in Florida, half of whom were white, and half of whom were Negro. Ages were 6, 10 and 14 years. Significant racial differences in personality were projected on the Rorschach Test. In order to apply the Rorschach Test to children, one has to be aware of developmental differences among children of varying ages, between children of different races, and between children and adults.

814. Price-Williams, D. R. and Ramirez, M. Ethnic differences in delay of gratification. Journal of Social Psychology, 1974, 93 (2), 23-30.

Ethnic differences in delay of gratification were investigated. The sample consisted of 60 Anglos, blacks and Mexican-Americans, respectively. Results showed that at the fourth grade level, black and Mexican-American children were more prone than Anglo children to accept the immediate gratification rather than choose the later and bigger reward. No sex differences within each ethnic group were found, with the exception of the Mexican-American group, for one out of the three conditions tested.

The factor of mistrust in the promises of the investigators
was noticeable in the black children, despite the fact that
they were tested by a black investigator.

815. Radin, N. Material warmth, achievement motivation, and cognitive functioning in lower class preschool children. Child Development,
1971, 42 (5), 1560-1565.

Observed 52 black and white lower class mothers interacting
with their 4-year-old children at home. Maternal behaviors
reflective of warmth were tallied and correlated with the
child's IQ, the tester's rating of his motivation, and the
teacher's rating of his behavior in school. Maternal warmth
correlated significantly and positively with initial IQ, IQ
gain in preschool, teacher ratings of the child's academic
motivation, and tester ratings of his motivation in the testing situation. Partial correlations suggest that motivation
to achieve is one intervening variable between maternal behavior and cognitive development, but not the only one.

816. Ramirez, M. and Price-Williams, D. R. Achievement motivation
in children of three ethnic groups in the United States. Journal of
Cross-Cultural Psychology, 1976, 7 (1), 49-60.

Asked 30 male and 30 female fourth graders from each of three
ethnic groups in the United States (Anglos, blacks, and
Mexican-Americans) to tell a story to match drawings depicting persons in a setting related to education. Stories were
scored for need achievement (nAch) and family achievement
(oriented toward achievement goals from which the family
would benefit or that would gain recognition from family
members). Results show that Mexican-Americans and blacks
scored higher on family achievement than did Anglo subjects.
Anglos, however, scored higher on nAch. On those cards depicting parental figures, however, Mexican-Americans and
Blacks tended to score higher on nAch than Anglos. Females
in all three ethnic groups scored lower on nAch but higher
on family achievement than males. It is concluded that contextual conditions are most important in expression of achievement motivation and that the particular form in which achievement is expressed is determined by the definition that culture
gives to it.

817. Richmond, B. O. and Vance, J. J. Cooperative-competitive game
strategy and personality characteristics of black and white children.
Interpersonal Development (Basel), 1975, 5 (2), 78-85.

Social interaction expressed in either a cooperative or competitive mode was examined as a function of personality, racial, or
biological sex factors. 240 elementary school children were
administered the Arrow-Dot Test and the Circle Matrix Board,
a game technique to measure the cooperative/competitive behavior of children. It was found that sex and racial differences were related to personality styles. Black children were
more successful in employing cooperative game strategies than

white children. Some personality characteristics of black
and white children were found to be more likely to occur with
cooperative than competitive behavior.

818. Richmond, B. O. and White, W. F. Sociometric predictors of
the self-concept among fifth and sixth grade children. Journal of
Educational Research, 1971, 64 (9), 425-429.

Isolated factors of self-esteem and of peer ratings to determine significant relationships between derived factors. 204
elementary pupils were selected from two metropolitan areas.
Approximately one-half were black disadvantaged pupils; the
remainder were white with above average cultural advantages.
The Coopersmith Self-Esteem Inventory (SEI) and a Semantic
Differential (SD) were administered to all subjects. From a
factor analysis of responses to the SEI, four factors of self-
esteem and a lie scale emerged. Three SD factors were obtained
from a factor analysis of the peer ratings. One significant
canonical correlation (.325 p>.01) resulted from the correlation of the three SD factor scores with the scores on the
five SEI factors. "Activity" dominated the relationship
between peer feelings and self-concept dimensions.

819. Roberts, A., Mosley, K. Y., and Chamberlain, M. W. Age differences in racial self-identity of young black girls. Psychological
Reports, 1975, 37 (3), 1263-1266.

The Clark and Clark doll procedure was modified to assess
racial self-identity in young black girls. Two groups of
black children (3 to 4 and 6 to 7 years old) were shown three
dolls that differed in skin color and/or hair style. They were
asked which doll looked like them, which doll was prettiest,
and which doll was ugliest. Although the majority of both
groups identified with the black dolls, the older children
displayed a more accurate racial self-identity. The children
differed significantly in their perception of the ugliest
doll: the younger group selected the black doll wearing an
Afro while the older group selected the white doll. These
results were discussed in terms of the role of greater experience with blacks and whites and a possible overreaction to
the "Black is Beautiful" feeling on the part of the older
group.

820. Roberts, S. O. Some mental and emotional health needs of Negro
children and youth. Journal of Negro Education, 1950, 19, 351-371.

There is a relationship between a "healthy society" and an
integrated, normal personality. The ameliorative measures
and programs advanced in this connection include education in
the broadest sense, legislation, and the provision of various
psychological facilities and services. The removal of want
or fear provides "increased opportunity for the type of family
life which fosters better mental health and meets more fully
the emotional and mental health needs of the developing child."
This continuation of a segregated pattern of life is antitheti-
cal to these aims.

821. Rohrer, G. K. Racial and ethnic identification and preference
in young children. <u>Young Children</u>, 1977, <u>32</u> (2), 24-33. Also, see
ERIC Abstracts, No. EJ-155-622, 1977.

> This study investigated racial and ethnic identification and
> preference in 4-year-old children as related to racial/ethnic
> group membership, sex of the subject, and degree of racial/
> ethnic contact in the subject's preschool class.

822. Rosser, P. L. Mental health of black children. Paper presented
at the Annual Meeting of the American Psychological Association (84th,
Washington, D. C., September 7, 1976). Also, see ERIC Abstracts,
No. ED-130-779, 1976.

> This paper argues that the mental health needs of black children
> and families have never been properly assessed. Central to
> black mental health has been the notion of cultural normality
> and deviance and the related questions of adjustment and malad-
> justment. Research is needed in three areas: (1) the black
> family, (2) schools, and (3) tests and measurements. There
> has been little research on the life histories or social
> factors of black children and families who succeed despite
> racism and poverty. Coping strategies for child rearing need
> investigation in order to factor out those that do and those
> that do not lead to the development of healthy children.
> School is the next most important socializing force impacting
> on the black child. However, a preponderance of educational
> philosophy is based on the Anglo-Saxon ideal instead of on the
> black child's needs. Future research needs to focus on what
> is wrong with this system for the black child. Part of accepted
> educational philosophy is a belief in tests and measurements.
> Intelligence testing, especially, has had devastating effect
> on black children. An IQ test alone will not differentiate
> between pathology and cultural difference. Clearly, a new
> direction in the study of black mental health is needed -- it
> must involve blacks at all levels of research.

823. Rychlak, J. F. Affective assessment, intelligence, social
class, and racial learning style. <u>Journal of Personality and Social
Psychology</u>, 1975, <u>32</u>, 989-995.

> Subjects were 160 seventh grade children drawn from both a
> lower and middle socioeconomic community. After prerating
> words for reinforcement value, unmixed lists were constructed
> and subjects put through an individual free-recall learning
> procedure. The lower class subjects were retested in a mixed-
> lists, free-recall format approximately three months later.
> It was found that blacks as a group and as a subgroup within
> the lower socioeconomic level clearly reflect the positive
> reinforcement value effect to a greater extent than whites.
> The influence of affective assessment is also more apparent
> at the lower than at the middle socioeconomic level. Intel-
> ligence does not affect these findings in any systematic fashion.

824. Samuels, S. C. An investigation into the self-concepts of
lower and middle class black and white kindergarten children. Journal
of Negro Education, 1973, 42 (4), 467-472.

> Administered two child self-concept tests (Clark U-Scale and
> Brown Test) during the first month of school to 93 of 417
> kindergartners, boys and girls, from white and black lower
> and middle class families in a New York City suburb. Results
> indicate (p>.05) that black middle class children had higher
> self-concepts than black lower class children on both tests,
> while white middle class children had higher self-concepts
> than white lower class children on the Clark U-Scale only.
> Mother's church attendance and community group involvement
> were significantly related (p>.01) to self-concept for lower
> class, but not for middle class children.

825. Santrock, J. W., et. al. Effects of social comparison on
aggression and regression in groups of young children. Child Development, 1976, 47 (3), 831-837. Also, see ERIC Abstracts, No. EJ-157-
280, 1976.

> The influence of negative, equal, and positive social compari-
> son and of nonsocial comparison upon 4- and 5-year-old black
> children's subsequent aggressive and regressive behavior in
> 3-member groups was investigated.

826. Schack, M. L. and Massari, D. J. Effects of temporal aids and
frustration on delay of gratification. Developmental Psychology, 1973,
8 (2), 168-171.

> Examined the effects of temporal aids and frustration level on
> the voluntary delay behavior of 60 lower class, black, first
> grade children. Three types of temporal aids (sand glass timer
> plus instructions about its relevance; timer without instruc-
> tions; and no timer control) and low frustration levels (visual
> presence or absence of rewards) were compared. In general,
> subjects waited longer when rewards were absent. However, sub-
> jects in the toys-present time-instructions group waited longer
> than subjects in the other toys-present group, and did not
> differ from subjects in the toys-absent groups. Results are
> discussed in terms of the facilitatory effect on waiting of
> the perception of a decrease in temporal distance from a goal.

827. Schwartz, M. and Baden, M. A. Female adolescent self-concept:
An examination of the relative influence of peers and adults. Youth
and Society, 1973, 5 (1), 115-128.

> The relative influence of peers and adults on female adoles-
> cent self-concept was studied. Data were obtained by adminis-
> tering a 7-page semantic differential test to girls in two
> high schools. Data were viewed in terms of the differential
> impact on self-descriptions made by perceived descriptions of
> the self made by parents, siblings and teachers. Three hypo-
> theses were posed concerning the generation gap, deviancy
> and alienation. It is concluded that adolescents are

not socio-psychologically cut off from adults. Adults are
more significant for blacks than for whites. It also appears
that white youth experiencing heavy self-involvement with
peers, and moderate involvement with adults, may be potentially deviant. Male values are also compared and contrasted
to these results according to racial and economic background.

828. Scott, M. B. Wishing will make it so. Mental Retardation, 1975,
13 (1), 27.

Considers the economically disadvantaged black child who
obviously exaggerates his means in the presence of teacher
and peers, and compares such a child to the retarded student.
Reasons for the "lying" are traced to varying concepts of
the truth among cultures and to the perceptions, judgments,
and values of the disadvantaged child which often differ
from those of mainstream society. It is recommended that
teachers of the disadvantaged acquire greater knowledge of
subcultures.

829. Segal, S. M. and DuCette, J. Locus of control and premarital
high school pregnancy. Psychological Reports, 1973, 33 (3), 887-890.

The relationship between premarital pregnancy and locus of
control was assessed for 165 female, junior and senior high
school subjects from two metropolitan high schools -- one
middle class white and one lower class black. No significant
differences between the two schools in mean locus of control
scores was found. Significant differences indicated that
within the white middle class school, pregnant girls tended
to score external and non-pregnant girls tended to score internal. In the black lower class school, the opposite tended
to be true -- pregnant girls tended towards internality and
non-pregnant girls towards externality. These seeming differences were not inconsistent, and internally oriented girls in
both environments were perceiving their environments accurately.

830. Shade, B. J. The modal personality of urban black middle class
elementary school children. Journal of Psychology, 1976, 92, 267-275.

Scores for 120, 6- to 8-year-old subjects on 13 traits were
determined using the Early School Personality Questionnaire.
Subjects' scores differed from expected scores on four factors,
that is, blacks were more reserved, critical, and detached
from their school environment; more emotionally stable, mature,
and capable of facing reality; more obedient, accommodating,
and docile; yet more shrewd, calculating, and canny.

831. Shannon, B. E. The impact of racism on personality development.
Social Casework, 1973, 54 (9), 519-525.

Discusses the importance of circumstantial uniqueness, or con-
tinual victimization by racist strategies, as a factor in black
personality development. Personality factors such as dependency,
self-image, passivity and aggressiveness, manipulation, and

depression and despair versus hope are detailed. Suggestions are offered for more effective diagnostic assessments and treatment plans. Diagnostic evaluation of a black client should include the assessment of trust levels, problem-solving patterns, the degree of future orientation, and the quality of the client's self-image.

832. Shaw, M. E. The self-image of black and white pupils in an integrated school. Journal of Personality, 1974, 42 (1), 12-22.

Two studies were conducted on the self-image of black and white pupils in a recently integrated southern school to determine whether there were differences between disadvantaged (black) and advantaged (white) pupils, and whether these differences changed during the academic year. The first study was implemented during the first full school year after the schools had been integrated, and the second one was carried out the following year. Self-perceptions were measured by the Harvey Self-Image Scale. Data consistent across both studies show that: (a) boys saw themselves significantly less sociable but more independent than did girls; (b) blacks perceived themselves as significantly more independent and hostile than did whites; (c) sociability generally increased, whereas achievement orientation decreased as a function of grade level; (d) blacks either decreased in sociability or showed no change, whereas whites either showed no change or increased in sociability; and (e) during the school years, pupils in grades two and three decreased in hostility, those in grades four and five showed no change, and pupils in grade six increased in perceived hostility.

833. Simon, R. J. An assessment of racial awareness, preference, and self-identity among white and adopted non-white children. Social Problems, 1974, 22 (1), 43-57.

Reports levels of racial awareness, racial preference, and racial identities among non-white children (American, Negro, Korean, and American Indian), who have been adopted by white families, and among their white siblings who were born into those families. All respondents were children 3-8 years old. The basic object of this research was to determine how similar or different are the reactions of these children compared to those of the same sex, age range, and race who have been reared in typical families. The major findings were that black children reared in multiracial families did not acquire the ambivalence toward their own race that has been reported among all other groups of young black children, and that there are no significant differences in the racial attitudes of any of the categories of children.

834. Simpkins, G., Gunnings, T., and Kearney, A. The black six-hour retarded child. Journal of Nonwhite Concerns in Personnel and Guidance, 1973, 2 (1), 29-34.

Suggests that the apparently "retarded" performance of many black children on standardized ability tests may be the child's

way of adapting to a hostile, racist and white-oriented educational and assessment system. Black children may often act out
the retarded role in what is actually a self-fulfilling prophecy. The ways in which current educational criteria and
programs in effect develop "retarded" children are discussed.
Recommendations for eliminating the syndrome of the child who
is considered retarded during the six-hour school day are
presented.

835. Smith, D. F. Adolescent suicide: A problem for teachers?
Phi Delta Kappan, 1976, 57 (8), 539-542.   Also, see ERIC Abstracts,
No. EJ-138-015, 1976.

Discusses the increasing frequency of suicide among teenagers
and young adults, and the role the teacher can take in recognizing early distress signals.

836. Smith, P. M. Jr. Personal and social adjustment of Negro
children in rural and urban areas in the South. Rural Sociology,
1961, 26 (1), 73-77.

A study developed on the theory that Negro children's personality characteristics are the same regardless of whether they
lived in an urban or a rural area. Data was assembled from
150 students, randomly selected, in the eleventh and twelfth
grades of schools located in a rural and urban area of North
Carolina. The California Test of Personality (secondary grades
9 to college, 1953 revision) was used to measure patterns of
personal and social adjustment. Analysis of data in terms of
(a) percentiles (above 75th, 75th to 25th, below 25th); (b)
$\bar{X}$ scores; and (3) T-tests of significance. It was found that
the nomenclature of the community made no clear distinction
in the personal and social adjustment patterns of Negro youth.
The test did isolate traits of behavior which were different
in the two groups. These were: nervous symptoms, community
relations, feelings of belonging and social skills. Reprinted
by permission.

837. Soares, A. T. and Soares, L. M. Self-perceptions of culturally
disadvantaged children. In A. C. Ornstein (Ed.), Educating the Disadvantaged: School Year 1968-1969, pp. 3-20. New York: AMS Press,
1970.

The expectations and opinions of others influence an individual's
self-perception. Negative self-attitudes are likely to develop
if an individual is constantly devaluated by society and its
institutions. This is often true of disadvantaged children,
yet the negative self-concepts of such youths are not a foregone
conclusion. Recent research indicates that the insulation of
segregated schools fosters more positive self-images. The
present study was formulated to determine the direction and
intensity of self-perceptions of disadvantaged children in
comparison with the self-perceptions of more advantaged children. Tests were administered to approximately 500 students
in two urban elementary schools -- one consisting of children
from an advantaged area, the other of disadvantaged children.

The grade levels involved (four through eight) are crucial
in developing a positive self-concept in regard to educational
success. The self-perceptions of the disadvantaged group
were not only positive, but higher than those of the advantaged children. Both groups attended neighborhood schools.
Children were exposed only to others of similar background,
and the more advantaged students were probably subjected to
greater pressures. Self-concepts probably diminish when disadvantaged children join an integrated school system. Lower
self-concepts were found among middle class male children,
possibly reflecting the greater pressures to which they are
subjected during the early middle childhood years. Disadvantaged female children had lower self-esteem than their male
counterparts; the males receive more attention and affection
in matriarchal disadvantaged families. Despite differences
by sex, both disadvantaged and advantaged elementary school
children indicate positive self-concepts. The challenge to
educators is to maintain the positive self-images of disadvantaged children, especially when entry to integrated high
schools initiates increased competition and greater pressures
to achieve.

838. Solkoff, N. Reactions to frustration in Negro and white children. Journal of Negro Education, 1969, 38 (4), 412-418.

The results of several studies have suggested that in a variety
of situations, adult Negroes or whites will respond differently
in the presence of a white experimenter than they will with a
Negro experimenter. This study addresses itself to the question: How is the performance of Negro and white children on
a perceptual-motor task affected by Negro and white frustrators?
Consistent with previous findings based upon all white children, the performance of the boys in the present study was
significantly worse than the girls' performance following all
conditions of frustration. However, both white and Negro boys
showed extreme post-frustration impairment only in the presence
of a Negro experimentor. An important finding of the present
study was the absence of racial differences in response to
frustration. In spite of the fact that Negro children suffer
more environmentally induced frustration than do white children, their subsequent behavior did not show greater signs of
disruption or disorganization. In addition, Negro children
showed no more overt signs of aggressive behavior than did
the whites.

839. Stabler, J. R., Johnson, E. E., and Jordon, S. E. The measurement of children's self-concepts as related to racial memberships.
Child Development, 1971, 42 (6), 2094-2097.

Asked 60 black and white preschool children to guess which
of two boxes, one painted white and one painted black, and each
containing tape recorder speakers, had broadcast self-concept
statements, e.g., "I am good," and "I am bad". Though the 32
statements were actually broadcast with equal intensity from
both speakers, white subjects reported that they heard more

positive than negative statements originating from the white
box; and black subjects reported hearing more negative statements originating from the white box than did white subjects.
Results are related to the influence of attitudes toward color
on development of self and other perception.

840. St. John, N. The elementary classroom as a frog pond: Self-
concept, sense of control and social context. Social Forces, 1971,
49 (4), 581-594.

The J. S. Coleman finding in "Equality of Educational Opportunity,
Department of Health, Education and Welfare, 1966" that self-
concept falls but sense of control rises with school percentage
white, is replicated with a sample of black and white sixth
graders in classrooms of various socioeconomic status (SES)
and racial mixtures. Correlational, cross-tabular, and regression analyses indicate that high achievement relative to classmates, contributes most to raising an individual's self-concept
and sense of control. Class and SES contribute negatively
to self-concept and positively to sense of control. With
other variables controlled, class percentage white shows a
small but significant relationship in these same directions
on both variables for whites, but not for blacks. When previous school percentage white is added to the equation, it
shows a significant positive relationship to black self-concept,
and also raises the negative beta for class percentage white
to significant level. The positive contribution to black
self-concept of previous integration experience, suggesting
that long-term benefits of a "big pond" outweigh its short-
term hazards. Reprinted by permission.

841. Strickland, B. R. Aspiration responses among Negro and white
adolescents. Journal of Personality and Social Psychology, 1971, 19
(3), 315-320.

Administered the Rotter Level of Aspiration Board Test to 20
male and 20 female ninth graders from each of three groups:
(a) low socioeconomic black, (b) low socioeconomic white, and
(c) high socioeconomic white. Level of aspiration was related
to sex, with lower class black and middle class white males
giving higher aspiration estimates than their female counterparts. Frequency of shifts in expectancy following performance
was different across groups, with lower class black females
giving the highest and middle class white males the least
number of shifts. Unusual shifts were related to race, with
white subjects giving less erratic responses than the black
subjects. Implications of results are discussed in regard
to minority group membership and expectancy of success.

842. Strickland, B. R. Delay of gratification as a function of race
of the experimenter. Journal of Personality and Social Psychology,
1972, 22 (1), 108-112.

Offered a total of 300 black and white sixth graders one
45-r.p.m. record as an immediate reward for completing S. Nowicki

and B. Strickland's Locus of Control Scale, or three records
if they would wait for either a black or white male experimenter to return three weeks later. About 80% of the white
subjects chose the delayed, more valuable reward, regardless
of the race of the experimenter. 33% of the black subjects
chose the delayed reward from the white experimenter, and 56%
from the black experimenter. Black subjects were more likely
to be assessed as external than whites. While no relationship
was found between locus of control and delay behavior among
blacks, internal white subjects chose more delayed rewards
than external white subjects. Results are discussed in terms
of the mistrust of the white experimenter on the part of the
black subjects.

843. Strodtbeck, F. L., Short, J. F. Jr., and Kolegar, E. The analysis of self-descriptions by members of delinquent gangs. Sociological
Quarterly, 1962, 3 (4), 331-356.

A study of the self-descriptions of 25 members of a delinquent
gang of Negro boys in Chicago and 23 non-gang boys who served
as controls. A paired comparison instrument using 14 adjectives, some salient to lower class, some to middle class, and
some to adolescents in general, was administered. The attempt
was made to ascertain the relationship between the behavior
and self-descriptions of the boys in the peer-group context.
Contrary to expectations, the self-descriptions of the gang
boys were not more similar to those of the non-gang members;
rather, the reverse was found. The attitudes expressed in
the self-descriptions were broken down so that 2 polar types
were isolated: the 'cool aggressives' who favored the adjectives 'troublesome,' 'cool,' 'tough,' and 'mean' and the 'scouts'
who favored 'religious,' 'polite,' 'loyal,' 'helpful,' 'smart,'
'clean,' and 'obedient.' Behavior differences between these
2 types were found to be insignificant. Thus, it is seen that
"the scout and cool aggressive constellations of self-description
are not deep-seated personality characteristics. . . . The
scouts and cool aggressives identifications seem not to be
badges by which the boys are known to one another; they seem
to be less conscious adjustments to the group environment."
Hence differential self-descriptions are not associated with
differential delinquent behavior and the use of self-descriptions
is not of any predictive value. Reprinted by permission.

844. Strom, R. and Greathouse, B. Play and maternal self-concept.
Theory Into Practice, 1974, 13 (4), 297-301.

Describes a program to elevate child self-concept and achievement by training the mother as a teacher. Assessment is individualized for each mother-child dyad using the Parent As A
Teacher (PAAT) Inventory. A 30-hour program of mother-child
play seeks to: (a) enhance mother and child self-concept;
(b) increase the quantity and quality of interaction; (c)
improve the child's oral comprehension and verbal facility;
(d) aid the mother's development of the child's affect; and
(e) internalize the teacher role of the mother. An 8-week

treatment of 12 black inner city mother-preschool child dyads
resulted in significant pre-/post-PAAT gains in mother self-
concept as teacher and in knowledge of the teaching-learning
process (p<.005), children's self-concept as learners (p<.005),
and vocabulary (p<.01). Most preschool programs remove children
from low income homes to schools at increasingly early ages.
Joint effort by the school and the home is considered a more
logical approach.

845. Suggs, R. C. An identity group experience: Changing priorities.
Journal of Non-White Concerns in Personnel and Guidance. 1975, 3 (2),
75-81.

Discusses the development of black youths' individual identity
and role and suggests a model for group counseling to be used
with minority group members. Literature on the identity crisis
of ethnic adolescents is reviewed and the bond between group
and individual identity is stressed. A 10-session group counseling program is outlined in which group members are encouraged
to discuss their concerns about identity, being a black in
America, their feelings of control over their destiny, and
their areas of personal conflict.

846. Sutherland, R. I. Color, Class, and Personality. Washington,
D. C.: American Council on Education (744 Jackson Place), n.d.
xxiii + 136 pp.

Dr. Sutherland served as Associate Director of the Commission
in charge of studies of Negro youth, and this volume is the
seventh and last published study of a series of carefully
planned and executed researches, all of them attempting to
answer the question, "How does the fact of being born a Negro
affect the developing personality of a boy or girl?" This
volume summarizes the chief findings of the entire project
and suggests their implications for our national life. Part I
deals with things as they are now in terms of attitudes,
dreams and desires of Negro youth. Part II portrays changes
to be made if we wish to solve the problems of Negro youth.
Dr. Sutherland pulls no punches, and throughout the book
quotes pertinent snatches of case studies or interviews that
give a realistic atmosphere to his writing and help us to
appreciate the viewpoint of the Negro youth. This series,
and especially the last volume, has won a high place in the
literature on the Negro.

847. Sweet, J. R. and Thornburg, K. R. Preschoolers' self and
social identity within the family structure. Journal of Negro Education, 1971, 40 (1), 22-27.

Focused on the young child's comprehension of the family
structure. The instrument was administered to 60 black and
60 white 3- to 5-year-old subjects. The first task required
that the subject exhibit some ability to identify himself
before he was expected to indicate his understanding of familial labels. Subjects identified first with the members of the

same sex and race. The findings were in agreement with previous studies. The succeeding tasks were administered and
determined the subject's ability to understand and verbalize
his knowledge of the family. Age was a significant factor:
5-year-old subjects scored higher than 4-year-old subjects;
and those who were 4 years old scored higher than 3-year-olds.
At each age level, white subjects scored significantly higher
than black subjects on familial tasks. There was no significant difference between boys and girls in the performance
scores for this concept.

848. Symonds, M. Disadvantaged children growing in a climate of
hopelessness and despair. American Journal of Psychoanalysis, 1968,
28 (1), 15-24.

This article focuses on the 20% of the nation's children who
are growing up in poverty. Three major effects of poverty
on the personality are identified: hardening, feelings of
insecurity, and feelings of inferiority. The hardening
process produces a child who moves away from others emotionally.
Insecurity causes a child to move toward others, and feelings
of inferiority lead him to being aggressive toward others.
Crowded living conditions, under which most disadvantaged
children live, increase the hardening process. Under crowded
conditions violence, irritation, and annoyance are the ordinary methods of communication between parents and children,
and between parents. In such a climate children grow up dis-
illusioned, pessimistic, and resentful. School is the major
constructive escape route from the ghetto. Other routes
include arts, athletics, religion, and politics. However,
positive moves are required to interest children in constructive escape routes.

849. Taylor, R. L. Psychosocial development among black children
and youth: A reexamination. American Journal of Orthopsychiatry,
1976, 46 (1), 4-19.

The fundamental assumptions and empirical evidence on which
conventional view of the nature and meaning of black self-
esteem are based are examined. A review of the literature
reveals that a number of these assumptions and conclusions
have been drawn from rather weak empirical data. Results of
recent investigations, suggesting alternative interpretations
and conclusions regarding the level and quality of black
self-esteem, are presented. The development of self-esteem
and personality among black children and youth is considered,
focusing on several significant monographs.

850. Teahan, J. E. and Podany, E. C. Some effects of films of
successful blacks on racial self-concept. International Journal
of Social Psychiatry, 1974, 20 (3-4), 274-280.

Personal success achieved by six black and six white men was
depicted in 12 short films shown to 53 black male high school
students. Scores on two measures of racial self-concept were

obtained before and after the film series and were compared
with the scores of 56 black students who had not seen the
films. From trends in the data, it is inferred that attitudes
toward blacks were not altered by the film series. More
favorable attitudes toward whites were observed in experimental
subjects of higher socioeconomic class, while less favorable
attitudes toward whites typified lower class experimentals.

851. Teicher, J. D. Some observations on identity problems in
children of Negro-white marriages. Journal of Nervous and Mental
Disease, 1968, 146 (3), 249-256.

Reports studies indicating that the quest for identity of
the child of a Negro-white marriage is even more difficult
than that of the Negro child in this country. In "addition
to the devaluation of 'black', there are likely to be resentment of siblings whose racial characteristics are different."

852. Teplin, L. A. A comparison of racial/ethnic preferences among
Anglo, black and Latino children. American Journal of Orthopsychiatry,
1976, 46 (4), 702-709.

Used a photo-choice method to compare racial/ethnic group
preferences of 398 third and fourth grade black, Anglo-, and
Latin-American children, focusing on the latter relatively
little-studied group. While both black and Anglo-American
children chose ingroup photos, Latin-American children preferred pictures of Anglo-Americans. A comparison is made
between these findings and those of studies ten years ago
which focused on black children.

853. Thompson, C. H. and Knox, E. O. Bibliography (of Negro Education). Journal of Negro Education, 1937, 6, 217-224.

Contains notations on the following masters' theses of psycho-
logical interest: Hodges, A. B., Racial differences in the
eidetic imagery of preschool children, Texas, 1936; Mason, A. E.,
Source of moral judgments of children in Harriet Beecher Stowe
School, Cincinnati, 1936; Sellers, J. B., Personality of ser-
vants, with special reference to the Negro, Fisk, 1936;
Young, H. L., A study of the mental and physical traits of
Negro children in the Fields Special School, Temple, 1936.

854. Trowbridge, N., Trowbridge, Lambert, and Trowbridge, Lisa.
Self-concept and socioeconomic status. Child Study Journal, 1972,
2 (3), 123-143.

Administered the Coopersmith Self-Esteem Inventory to 1,662
third to eighth graders with low socioeconomic status (SES),
and 2,127 with middle SES. Scores were analyzed according to
SES, race (black vs. white), population density (rural vs.
urban), age, and sex. The SES factor accounted for most of
the variance (p>.05), with higher self-concept scores for
subjects who were low in SES, black, and/or from rural areas.
Sex and age were not significant factors. Further analysis

reveals that low SES subjects scored higher on general self, social self-peers, and school academic items, while middle SES subjects scored higher on items concerning home and parents. The sampling procedure used is described, and implications of findings for educators are discussed.

855. Verinis, J. S. Maternal and child pathology in an urban ghetto. Journal of Clinical Psychology, 1976, 32 (1), 13-15.

A group of 80 black, urban ghetto mothers, 40 with a behaviorally disturbed child and 40 with no disturbed child identified, was evaluated by the MMPI. The literature reports a relationship between maternal pathology and child disturbance for middle and working class families. The present study, however, showed no such relationship between these two variables in ghetto families.

856. Vershure, B. Black is beautiful: A reexamination of racial self-identification. Perceptual and Motor Skills, 1976, 43 (3, Part 1), 842.

Administered the Draw-A-Person test to 50 black and 50 white lower class 9- to 11-year-olds. Results show that when given a neutral color paper and an assortment of crayons black subjects most often drew black persons. It was also found that all subjects described their persons on an adjective checklist as having equally favorable status, physical, and personal characteristics. Blacks also described their persons as being significantly harder workers, more attractive, admired, dependable, and having longer and curlier hair than did white subjects. Results are interpreted in light of methodological improvements and heightened racial consciousness in the black community.

857. Von Raffler-Engel, W. The non-verbal behavior of children in a listening situation: Theoretical implications and practical applications. Paper presented at the 25th Annual Meeting of the American Anthropological Association (Washington, D. C., 1976). Also, see ERIC Abstracts, No. ED-132-233, 1976.

The present paper is part of a long-range research project in Developmental Kinesics. The gist of the project is empirical: the object is to find out what happens rather than look for anything in particular or test a hypothesis. The methodology for the analysis is ethological in approach. Empirical observations are carefully described. Subsequently, attempts are made to classify these observations according to the structure which emerges from the data, and to discern possible causes and effects. This specific paper presents the results of the sub-project dealing with Black Kinesics. Ten hours of live video tape were recorded. The subjects were 36 black children, ranging from 3 to 18 years of age. All children were healthy, of good intelligence, residents of Nashville, Tennessee, and from three different social backgrounds: professional, skilled and unskilled labor. Subjects were told stories by

an adult and were asked to retell the story to other subjects.
Interactants were randomly mixed and grouped according to
age, sex, sibling status, and socioeconomic status. Most subjects appeared in three situations -- as hearer to adult
speaker, as speaker to another child, and as hearer to a child.
The story teller and all the children were black, as were all
the technicians on the television crew who did the taping.
Observations made as a result of the project show that the
child's non-verbal behavior follows a developmental curve
depending on age and that there are striking differences in
behavior according to sex.

858. Ward, S. H. and Braun, J. Self-esteem and racial preference
in black children. American Journal of Orthopsychiatry, 1972, 42
(4), 644-647.

In the 1950's and early 1960's, studies of racial preference
of children consistently showed black children choosing white
models and rejecting black models. In the present study with
60 black 7- to 8-year-olds growing up since 1963, a significant positive relationship was found between scores on the
Piers-Harris Children's Self-Concept Scale and preference
for a black puppet over a white one. Findings are interpreted as a reflection of a more accepting incorporation of
racial identity and pride within the child's self-concept.

859. Washington, K. R. The effects of systematic reinforcement
and a self-awareness program on the self-concept of black preschool
children. Child Study Journal, 1976, 6 (4), 199-208.

This study assesses the effect of an intervention program
on the self-concepts of black preschool children as well as
investigating whether the treatment would have an impact on
the children's perceived teacher perceptions. Subjects were
52 black preschool children.

860. Webster, S. W. and Kroger, M. N. A comparative study of
selected perceptions and feelings of Negro adolescents with and
without white friends in integrated urban high schools. Journal
of Negro Education, 1966, 35 (1), 55-61.

Three types of perceptions regarding the ways in which Negro
adolescents attending urban high schools and having white
friends differ from those who have no white friends are explored. Since Negroes as a group tend to have lower levels
of self-esteem than do members of the dominant group, i.e.,
whites, those Negro adolescents who have white friends would
have a more favorable perception of themselves. Seven hypotheses are presented: (1) Negroes with white friends will
have higher scores on a measure of personal independence than
their peers without such friendships; (2) Negro adolescents
with white friends will display higher social competence,
intellectual esteem, physical esteem, and total self-concept
scores than those without white friends; (3) Negro adolescents
with white friends will report higher vocational aspirations,

levels of desired vocational attainment, and perceptions of
potential for later occupational attainment than those without
white friends. (4) Negro subjects reporting friendships with
whites as contrasted with those who do not will predict for
themselves higher levels of future social acceptance by
society; (5) they will score lower on a measure of ethnic
concern or anxiety; (6) they will score lower on group-esteem;
and (7) Negro subjects reporting no friendships with whites
will report greater preference for associations with Negroes
than will their compeers with such friends. 312 Negro adolescents, 144 male, 168 female, in three integrated high schools
in the San Francisco Bay Area School District were investigated via questionnaires. The results were: (a) Self as an
Individual Perception: Of the four hypothesis involving the
self-concept propositions, three were supported at acceptable
levels. The physical esteem dimensions of the self-concept
failed to produce the predicted difference. (b) Self as a
Negro Perception: The obtained ratio was in the predicted
direction. (c) Feelings about Negroes as a Group Perception:
No significant difference between the two groups was found
regarding their levels of esteem for Negroes as a group.
Hypothesis (7) was confirmed.

861. Wellman, B. Social identities in black and white. Sociological Inquiry, 1971, 41 (1), 57-66.

The theoretical usefulness of a convergence of symbolic
interactionism with urban sociology is discussed in reference
to the social identities of a group of black and white adolescents. Empirical data derived from a questionnaire survey
among ninth grade students in Pittsburgh high schools (N=1,266
black and 1,198 white sutdents) demonstrate the saliency of
racial identity among blacks who are of different socioeconomic
statuses and who are attending schools of various racial mixtures. Racial identity is far more salient for blacks than
for whites, but even for blacks a number of other identities
are seen to be more employed; of particular importance was
the situational factor of school racial mixture. The data
showed that as race becomes incongruent with social setting,
identification in terms of race increases. When race becomes
important for social actions, then it assumes far greater
prominence as a social identity. The notion of a "standard
package of identities" is developed and the utility of such
a model for understanding group differentiation and intergroup linkages is explored. The "standard package" facilitates
the maintenance of inter-categorical and inter-group linkages
by providing that within every category or group there are
likely to be individuals with social identities similar to
those held by members of one's own categories or groups. Thus
the study of social identities becomes a means of understanding the diverse attachments that are formed in a social system
and, in particular, in the urban social system, with its
size, density, and heterogeneity. 5 tables.

862. Wells, T. T. The effects of discrimination upon motivation and achievement of black children in urban ghetto schools. American Behavioral Scientist, 1969, 12 (4), 26-33.

    Problems of motivation, ambition, and success of the Negro child in the school situation are discussed with specific focus on (1) inadequate motivation to pursue a long-range educational career and poor estimate of self; (2) antagonism toward the school and the teacher. Black ghetto children see themselves as members of an outgroup in relation to the total society. To counteract this, a very positive support is needed, but is seldom provided by experiences in school. The school system in cities across the U. S. makes several invalid assumptions about Negro pupils entering school: (a) that most of the children have completed a program of "reading readiness" during the kindergarten year; (b) that the children possess auditory discrimination skill, correct pronunciation, a fairly long attention span, knowledge and familiarity with "syntactical regularities of a language," familiarity with the world around them, a sense of time and how to relate events sequentially by memory. In the black culture, mastery of these skills is not necessary, hence few children possess them when they enter school. Another assumption is that black children expect approval for success. The series of IQ and achievement tests given to gauge a child's intellectual potential also place the black child at a disadvantage. Various works on urban ghetto schools are discussed and excerpts from them are quoted to support the contention that it is the school system which causes black children to fail in education. Schools produce dropouts. There must be a change within the make-up of the school system itself in the way it handles disadvantaged children who come into the school situation deficient in certain language skills and school techniques. This would include training teachers, informing them about disadvantaged groups and the various forms of discrimination and urging them to respect the black subculture. Textbooks need to be overhauled to present black people in a positive light. The best, rather than the worst teachers must be recruited for the ghettos.

863. White, W. F. and Richmond, B. O. Perception of self and of peers by economically deprived black and advantaged white fifth graders. Perceptual and Motor Skills, 1970, 30 (2), 533-534.

    Neither the concept of self nor the feelings about peers appeared to be different between 98 economically deprived black and 111 advantaged white fifth graders. Subjects were administered the Self-Esteem Inventory and 12 bipolar adjectives of Osgood's Semantic Differential. Although the sample was small and the reading ability of some of the subjects was poor, both groups perceived the connotative meaning of "activity" as the primary characteristic of importance.

864. Wilking, V. N. and Paoli, C. The hallucinatory experience:
An attempt at a psychodynamic classification and reconsideration of
its diagnostic significance. Journal of the American Academy of
Child Psychiatry, 1966, 5 (3), 431-440.

The occurrence of hallucinatory phenomena in poor SES Negro
and Puerto Rican children is not unusual and reflects developmental failure related to specific environmental factors,
inside and out of the home. Non-schizophrenic hallucinatory
experiences are expressions of fear, wishes, conflicts and
defense against them, typical of the specific child and his
own intrapsychic dynamics. Hallucinatory experiences are
classified on the basis of courses of stress which may inter-
fere with developmental processes and their dynamic significance. (Modified.)

865. Williams, J. E., Best, D. L., and Boswell, D. A. The measurement of children's racial attitudes in the early school years. Child
Development, 1975, 46 (2), 494-500.

The Preschool Racial Attitude Measure II (PRAM II) is a procedure for assessing the attitudes of preliterate children
toward light-skinned (Euro-American) and dark-skinned (Afro-
American) human figures. PRAM II is also appropriate to the
test-taking ability of children in the early school grades.
In Study 1, 458 first-fourth graders in an integrated public
school were administered PRAM II by Euro- and Afro-American
examiners. Among Euro-American subjects, it was found that
pro-Euro/anti-Afro (E+/A-) bias reached a peak at the second
grade level and subsequently declined. Afro-American subjects
also displayed evidence of E+/A- bias, but to a lesser degree,
and with no appreciable age trends being observed. Evidence
regarding race-of-examiner effects was inconclusive. Study 2
established the representative nature of the data by comparing
the PRAM II scores of the second graders in Study 1 with the
mean scores of 255 second graders in other geographical locations.

866. Williams, J. E., Boswell, D. A., and Best, D. L. Evaluative
responses of preschool children to the colors white and black. Child
Development, 1975, 46 (2), 501-508.

Summarizes previous findings with the Color Meaning Test I
(CMT I), describes the revised CMT II, and discusses theories
of the development of color and race bias in young children.
CMT II data are reported for 160 Euro-American and 160 Afro-
American 40- to 91-month-olds who were tested by Euro- and
Afro-American examiners. Analyses of the white-black color
meaning scores indicated satisfactory internal consistence
(r=.63). A tendency to evaluate the color white more positively than the color black was found among the Euro- and
Afro-American subjects. The scores varied systematically with
race of subject, but not with sex of subject or race of examiner.
It is concluded that CMT II provides a reliable index of white-
black color bias and that it and its companion procedure, the

Preschool Racial Attitude Measure II, provide useful techniques
for the study of color and race bias in preliterate children.
Theoretically, it is proposed that pro-white/anti-black color
bias may be related to the child's status as a diurnal animal
and, hence, to his experiences with the light of day and dark
of night.

867. Willis, F. N. and Hofmann, G. E. Development of tactile patterns
in relation to age, sex, and race. Developmental Psychology, 1976,
11 (6), 866.

An investigation of the development of tactile patterns in
relation to age, sex, and race is presented. Over 1,000 primary
school children ranging from kindergarten through sixth grade
were observed in school cafeteria queues for the frequency
of body areas touched and used to touch. It was found that
touch was more frequent in same-sex pairs than in different-
sex pairs and that the percentage of touches between the four
racial combinations was as follows: Black to black, 61.1%;
black to white, 40.1%; white to white, 40%; and white to
black, 20.9%. With regard to body area touched, hand to
hand touches were frequent between two females and never observed
in male to male interactions. It is noted that sexual and
racial segregation begins early in primary school and it is
suggested that sexual taboos and racial discrimination are
important in the reduction of touch in primary school children.
It is concluded that statements about touch in Americans must
be qualified for racial groups.

868. Zytkoskee, A., Strickland, B. R., and Watson, J. Delay of
gratification and internal versus external control among adolescents of low socioeconomic status. Developmental Psychology, 1971,
4 (1, Part 1), 93-98.

Compared the responses of 76 Negro and 56 white ninth grade
adolescents of low socioeconomic status concerning belief
in internal versus external control of reinforcement and delay
of gratification under high- and low-status conditions. Negro
subjects were significantly more likely to be external and
less likely to delay gratification than their white counterparts. A Sex x Race interaction approached significance,
with the difference between Negro and white males in both
internality-externality and delay of reinforcement. No
relationship was found between internal-external control or
the status conditions and delay behavior.

5

SOCIAL DEVELOPMENT

869. Abicht, M. Black children and their environment. College Student Journal, 1976, 10 (2), 142-152.

Discusses how the behavior of black children is influenced by their environment. In the educational environment, reasons for black children's underachievement are sought in their achievement motivation, expectation, delay of gratification, language factors, independence, and discipline. Since the schools are geared toward white middle class values and role models, black children find less encouragement, and indeed, often expect to fail. Their intelligence is questioned on the basis of the white man's intelligence tests. The social environment with its assumptions of broken families among blacks makes it hard for black children to form a positive self-concept. The implications of an autonomous black culture or black subculture are discussed. With respect to the influence of the economic environment, some facts illustrate that the material conditions of many black children are not conducive to their development. As long as these basic conditions are not improved, the fate of the black child cannot be expected to improve.

870. Aiello, J. R. and Jones, S. E. Field study of the proxemic behavior of young school children in three subcultural groups. Journal of Personality and Social Psychology, 1971, 19 (3), 351-356.

Observed the proxemic relationships of 210 interacting pairs of black, Puerto Rican, and white first and second graders in school playgrounds. Interaction distance and directness of shoulder orientation (axis) were recorded. Middle class white subjects stood farther apart than lower class blacks and Puerto Ricans. Sex differences among white subjects in distance scores and culture and sex differences in axis scores were also found. Results suggest that proxemic patterns are acquired early in life and support the contention that differences between the dominant culture and other groups in the use of space are basic, with the qualification that sex roles may also influence proxemic behavior.

871. Alam, B. A. Perception of opportunity and occupational expectation: A racial comparison of rural youth. Proceedings of the
Southwestern Sociological Association, 1968, 19, 69-72.

> An abstract of a report on a survey designed to determine
> the role of the racial factor in determining perceptions of
> opportunity and occupational expectations. Data were obtained
> from a 1966 study (no reference given) of white and Negro
> high school sophomores living in low income rural areas of
> Texas. Three hypotheses were proposed: (1) Negro youth have
> a greater awareness of limited occupational opportunity;
> (2) they have lower levels of occupational expectation; and
> (3) there exists a positive relationship between perception
> of opportunity and occupational expectations for both racial
> groups. From data presented in four tables, it is concluded
> that hypotheses (1) and (3) are supported by the findings,
> while there is no conclusive evidence about the second.

872. Allen, W. R. The family antecedents of adolescent mobility
aspirations. Journal of Afro-American Issues, 1976, 4 (3 and 4),
295-314. Also, see ERIC Abstracts, No. EJ-154-389, 1976.

> The results of this research study illustrate the dynamics
> which underlie the formation of black and white adolescent
> mobility aspirations with regard to expected educational and
> occupational attainment and actual educational and occupational
> attainment.

873. Alman, E. The child of the American poor. In M. Cowles (Ed.),
Perspectives in the Education of Disadvantaged Children, pp. 5-31.
Cleveland: The World Publishing Company, 1967.

> This general essay concentrates on the socialization process
> of the children of the poor. After a brief definition of
> these children in terms of their general physical deprivations
> and a few brief comments on location -- rural, urban, and
> ethnic -- the author examines the effects of the isolation
> of the poor brought about by their inability to pay for living
> in the nonpoor society, the general uneasiness among the nonpoor,
> and the reluctance of the nonpoor to have any contact with
> the poor. The total disparity between the image of America
> and the reality of the world of the poor is shown in a number
> of areas. The poor child's birth in a public hospital ward
> falls outside the American ideal of private medical care. His
> existence as a child of the poor is met by negative attitudes of
> social planners and welfare critics. The mother to whom he
> is attached is a nonmother in the American sense of meeting
> the needs of her family with poise and efficiency. The ideal
> American father is visible, powerful, wise, moderate, loving,
> and protective. His counterpart among the nonpoor provides
> a reasonable duplicate of the model. When the material and
> social advantages available in the mainstream elude the poor,
> the parents are ineffective in meeting the needs of the child
> in the American way, and this inadequacy is communicated to
> the child.

The education of the child of the poor is middle class in
content and triggers an adolescent "tuning out". His maturing
years are characterized by the realization of his low market
value in the dominant society. He is adjudged mature when
he ceases to show signs of discontent and appears to be making
the best of it. The author underline public responsibility
to examine government welfare poverty, policies which arbi-
trarily displace the poor, and the industrial system within
which the underclass has been generated.

874. Anonymous. The position of the Negro in the American social
order. Journal of Negro Education, 1939, 8, 261-616.

This is the eighth in a series of yearbook numbers of the
Journal of Negro Education, each of which presents a rather
comprehensive study of some particular aspect or problem in
the education of Negroes. In this yearbook Professor Allison
Davis of Dillard University contributes an article on the
socialization of the American Negro child and adolescent.
Paul B. Cornely and Virginia M. Alexander of Howard University
discuss the health status of the Negro in the United States,
and Professor E. Franklin Frazier discusses the present
status of the Negro family in the United States. Associate
Professor Doxey A. Wilkerson of Howard University writes on
vocational education, guidance, and placement of Negroes in
the United States. Other articles deal with the present
industrial, economic, and cultural status of Negroes and
with the probable status of Negroes in the United States in
1950.

875. Avila, D., Gordon, I. J., and Curran, R. Behavioral changes
in culturally disadvantaged children as the result of tutoring.
Psychological Reports, 1968, 22, 389-390.

Subjects from a disadvantaged population manifested improved
classroom behavior as the result of being involved in moderately or highly structured, skill-centered tutoring sessions.
This appears to conflict with educational philosophies that
advocate unstructured pupil-centered learning situations.

876. Axelrad, S. Negro and white male institutionalized delinquents. American Journal of Sociology, 1952, 57, 569-574.

300 Negro and white delinquents in the same institution were
compared to determine whether the courts were committing
Negro and white children on the same basis and whether the
two groups differed in family constellations. The study
discloses that Negro children are committed younger, for
less serious offenses, with fewer previous court appearances,
and with less prior institutionalization. Negro children came
from more unstable homes and from homes with a different kind
of family pathology from that of the white delinquents.

877. Banks, S. L. and Harris, J. L. Blacks and handicapped students
in our public schools: A Bicentennial challenge. Negro History
Bulletin, 1976, 39 (4), 580-581. Also, see ERIC Abstracts, No.
EJ-142-184, 1976.

   Notes that exclusion from school is based on many grounds:
   mental retardation, emotional disturbances, hyperactivity,
   or inability to pass a standardized test. Socioeconomic and
   racial factors are also considerations.

878. Banks, W. C. and Rompf, W. J. Evaluative bias and preference
behavior in black and white children. Child Development, 1973, 44
(4), 776-783.

   In an attempt to reexamine the phenomenon of "self-rejection"
   in blacks, 34 black and 34 white 6- to 8-year-olds were asked
   to view the performance of two players (one black, one white)
   in a ball tossing game. Each subject was in the presence of
   an examiner who was either black or white. Each game consisted
   of 5 trials; the performance outcome of each trial was controlled. Consistent with past research, white subjects showed
   preference for the white player by rewarding him more for his
   performance and by more often selecting him as overall "winner".
   Although black children showed preference for the white player
   in rewarding him more, those same subjects showed preference
   for the black player by choosing him more often as overall
   winner. No consistent white preference in blacks was found
   to support an interpretation of global "self-rejection".
   Instead, black subjects showed preference for whites and
   blacks as a function of the expressive task within which they
   were asked to make evaluations.

879. Barber, J., Garner, N. M., and Richardson, L. C. A follow-up
study of black unwed mothers. Smith College Studies in Social Work,
1973, 44 (1), 25-26.

   The attitudes and ways of life of young black unwed mothers
   who received service from the Baltimore Family and Children's
   Society are reviewed. Included were the girls having premarital conception, whether or not it ended in legitimate or illegitimate birth, and married women who conceived a child with
   a man other than the husband. Data were gathered principally
   by interview and questionnaire. All girls reported difficulty
   in separating the Society worker from the school counselor
   or from other social workers. The girls came from lower
   socioeconomic class families. Contrary to popular belief,
   the majority came from stable, two-parent homes and did not
   receive public assistance. The girls were not very dependent
   pre-Oedipal functioning individuals. Most had stable relationships with their families. The putative fathers played
   very important roles with the mothers and their babies.

880. Barry, T. E. and Hansen, R. W. How race affects children's TV
commercials. Journal of Advertising Research, 1973, 13 (5), 63-67.

Despite the current advertising interest in children, there is
little research devoted to black children in TV advertising. Data
were obtained from questionnaires given to two classes of 30 second grade students from Dallas suburbs; one class was all black,
the other all white. Each group of students was shown two 60-
second color TV commercials. Both commercials were about break-
fast cereals. Immediately after viewing the commercials, the
children responded to a 12-item questionnaire, which tested 2
hypotheses: (1) that racial differences do not affect advertising
recall of children; and (2) that racial differences do not affect
advertising preference responses of children. Results supported
the first hypothesis and rejected the second. Specifically, black
children's stated preferences are influenced positively by the
presence of a black character in a commercial; white children's
preferences seem not to be influenced either way by the presence
of a black character in a commercial. Several limitations of
the study are enumerated; more research is suggested. However,
the present findings do provide a basis for the idea the advertising should give serious consideration to the inclusion of black
actors in advertising directed toward children. "Today's children are tomorrow's consumers."

881. Bartel, H. W., Bartel, N. R., and Grill, J. J. A sociometric
view of some integrated open classrooms. Journal of Social Issues, 1973,
29 (4), 159-173.

The effects of interracial association on tolerance and increased
interracial acceptance were investigated in integrated open classrooms. A 16-item sociometric device was administered to 160
children in kindergarten through grade four. Four items dealt
with each of the following areas of evaluation: Positive Social
(PS), Positive Intellectual (PI), Negative Social (NS), and Negative Intellectual (NI). Indications were that black children selected more black children overall; white children selected more
black children on NS and NI items, more whites on PS and PI. On
PS and PI items, both groups tended to select members of their own
race; on NS and NI items, both tended to select black children.

882. Baughman, E. E. and Dahlstrom, W. G. Negro and White Children:
A Psychological Study in the Rural South. New York: Academic Press,
1968 (Second Printing, 1969). xxiii + 572 pp.

While exploding urban ghettos have seized the headlines in
recent years, 20% of Negro Americans are still rural Southern-
ers. Ghettos themselves are symptoms of the corrosive poverty
and inadequacy of rural life, however, so that programs must
extend beyond them to achieve solutions to social problems.
This in-depth study of children in the rural South compares
black and white children in "Millfield," an unorganized, un-
incorporated community in North Carolina, where people depend
on the land (tobacco) and the mills (textiles, hosiery) for
their livelihood. Many white families are poor and Negro

families, poorer. The youth seek their futures elsewhere and
migration is forced rather than voluntary for the Negro. Although the black population outnumbers the white, the minority
group controls the power structure, and options for blacks are
few. Among the areas studied are what personal qualities children of elementary school age develop in a segregated society,
and what characteristics develop as they grow older. Psychological instrumentation -- intellective and personality tests,
interviews, questionnaires, and ratings -- provide the analysis
of data. Findings in general show the damaging effects of
cultural isolation, prolonged economic deprivation, and racial
discrimination on Millfield's children.

883. Bauman, R. (Ed). Black Girls at Play: Folkloric Perspectives
on Child Development. Washington, D. C.: National Institute of
Education (DHEW), 1975. 101 pp. Also, available from: Information
Division, Southwest Educational Development Laboratory, 211 East 7th
Street, Austin, Texas 78701. Also, see ERIC Abstracts, No. ED-131-917.

This document brings together two preliminary reports on field
research undertaken as part of the Children's Folklore Program of the Southwest Educational Development Laboratory.
This research is an inquiry into the nature and function of
the traditional, expressive activities of black, Mexican-
American and Anglo children, of both sexes, between the ages
of 5 and 9 years. The principal goal of the research is to
delineate developmental trends in children's folklore, with
particular reference to similarities and differences in reper-
toire, acquisition, use, and function, across sex and ethnic
lines. The two papers presented here are concerned with the
folklore of black girls. The first study explores the culture-
specific functions and implications for socialization of a
range of folklore and other play forms characteristic of
black girls from 5 to 9. The second paper examines the proxemic
structure of a series of handclaps, ring plays and line plans,
and demonstrates that implications of increasing proxemic
complexity upon the sequence in which the forms are acquired
in the course of development, and the sequence in which they
are played on specific occasions.

884. Baumrind, D. An exploratory study of socialization effects on
black children: Some black-white comparisons. Child Development,
1972, 43, 261-267.

In a recent study of current patterns of parental authority
and their effects on the behavior of preschool children, the
data for the 16 black children and their families were analyzed
separately since it was thought that the effect of a given
pattern of parental variables might be affected by the larger
social context in which the family operates. The major conclusion from this exploratory analysis was that if the black
families were viewed by white norms they appeared authoritarian, but that, unlike their white counterparts, the most
authoritarian of these families produced the most self-
assertive and independent girls.

885. Beckham, A. S. A study of race attitudes in Negro children of adolescent age. Journal of Abnormal and Social Psychology, 1934, 29, 18-29.

Several persons in this study have not faced any humiliation based on race prejudice. Of those who have had such humiliating experiences, the average age for the first experience was 11 for both the delinquent boys and the non-delinquent boys and girls. The average age at which adults received a first humiliation was 12. The most common effect of the adults and the non-delinquent children was resentfulness; of the delinquent boys the most frequent effect was mixed emotional states as sadness, regret, fear, pain, etc. The most frequent changes brought about within the individuals, based on this humiliation, was for the adults the actual attempt in their own way to put into effect a program that would enlighten other races on the futility of race prejudice. With the non-delinquent children, the desire for personal achievement is foremost. Delinquent boys became aloof and antagonistic. The most frequent occurrences that caused a first racial humiliation was, for all three groups, a disagreeable personal experience rather than a group experience.

886. Bell, R. R. Lower class Negro mothers' aspirations for their children. Social Forces, 1965, 43 (4), 493-500.

Data presented from 202 interviews offer support for the hypothesis that it is possible to distinguish different subgroups along the Negro lower class continuum. Support for the hypothesis was given by differences in variables that help distinguish socioeconomic class levels as well as in differences between the mother subgroups in aspirations for their children. Data also provide some support for H. Rodman's concept of "lower class value stretch". The differences found between the Negro mother subgroups regarding aspirations suggest a range of beliefs and values in the Negro lower class. The findings also offer support for Rodman's suggestion that general social values have less exclusive force in the lower class and also indicate that the closer the mother is to the bottom of the lower class range the greater the deviation of her stated aspirations from those values.

887. Bender, L. Behavior problems in Negro children. Psychiatry, 1939, 2, 213-228.

Of 7,000 children observed during the past 15 years by the Psychiatric Division of Bellevue Hospital, 1,100 were Negroes, more than half of these were seen during the past three years, a rate of increase duplicated in other children's agencies. The author then cites various sociological, medical, and psychological studies bearing upon Negro questions, and gives a qualitative report of the Bellevue physical, psychometric, and mental examinations and of the case history material obtained on these children. Summarizing statements are: there are no essential differences between the white and Negro races in

mental and nervous disease, including mental deficiency and
syphilis; a proportionately greater number of Negroes require
public care; poor physical conditions, sexual delinquency, and
similar problems are traceable to the socioeconomic background;
the greater variation in cranial contours in Negroes does not
seem to be associated with changes in brain functions; specific behavior reaction patterns occur in Negro children, particularly blocking, mutism, catalepsy, negativism, and sleepiness,
apparently in direct response to emotional conflicts and difficult situations; racial conflicts find ready expression among
Negro children; asocial or neurotic behavior problems arise
from special family situations and from a combination of warm
human relationships and poorly crystallized family constellations.

888. Bennett, P. D. and Lundgren, D. C. Racial composition of
day care centers and the racial attitudes and self-concepts of young
black and white children. Journal of Intergroup Relations, 1976,
5 (1), 3-14. Also, see ERIC Abstracts, No. EJ-140-505, 1976.

The effects on young children's racial attitudes and self-
concepts of school situations in which both teachers and children were integrated, in comparison with semi-integrated
(children only) and segregated school situations were examined.
42 black and 42 white 4-year-old boys were sampled from fully
integrated, semi-integrated, and segregated day care centers.
Subjects were individually tested with a racial attitudes and
a self-concept measure. For both measures, differences between
racial attitudes and self-concept as a function of race of
child or racial composition of center were found to be nonsignificant. However, for the racial attitude scores, a trend
was obtained in the predicted direction. In particular, white
subjects from the fully integrated settings tended to exhibit
less pro-white/anti-black bias than white subjects from segregated and semi-integrated settings. Also, more black subjects
from segregated and semi-integrated settings rejected their
racial group identity than did white subjects from these types
of settings. However, in the fully integrated settings, a
roughly equivalent proportion of black and white subjects
were accepting of their racial group identity. Except for
black subjects from segregated settings, subjects who identified themselves correctly with respect to race had significantly
more favorable attitudes toward their own race than did those
who misidentified themselves.

889. Berger, A. S. and Simon, W. Black families and the Moynihan
Report: A research evaluation. Social Problems, 1974, 22 (2), 145-
161. Also, see ERIC Abstracts, No. EJ-120-218, 1974.

Examines the joint effects of race, gender, social class, and
family organization on a number of indicators of family interaction, anti-social behavior patterns, educational aspirations,
and gender role concepts, using data collected from a random
sample of the 14- to 18-year-old population of Illinois.

890. Bernstein, M. E. and Di Vesta, F. J. The formation and reversal of an attitude as functions of assumed self-concept, race and
socioeconomic class. Child Development, 1971, 42 (5), 1417-1431.

Studied racial attitudes in 112 black and white fifth-sixth
grade males from a school in a lower socioeconomic urban area
and in 28 white fifth-sixth grade males from a school in an
adjoining upper-middle socioeconomic area. Each subject
learned a favorable or unfavorable attitude about a stimulus
depicting either a white or a black boy in one phase, and
reversed it in the second phase of the experiment. A positive
(favorable) attitude was developed by indicating that favorable
(pleasant) words were "right" or that unfavorable words were
"wrong". The procedures were reversed in developing an unfavorable attitude. Favorable attitudes were learned more
easily than unfavorable ones, and fewer errors were made in
acquiring attitudes about the stimulus depicting the white
than the black boy. The positive attitude was more resistant
to change than was the negative attitude. Congruency between
contingencies or reinforcement in the formation and reversal
stages were found to inhibit the reversal of an attitude.

891. Best, D. L., Smith, S. C., Graves, D. J., and Williams, J. E.
The modification of racial bias in preschool children. Journal of
Experimental Child Psychology, 1975, 20 (2), 193-205.

Conducted two experiments to study previous reports of a pro-
Euro-American-anti-Afro-American racial bias in preschool
children of both races. An attempt to modify this bias using
the Preschool Racial Attitude Measure II (PRAM) is reported.
Experiment I involved 39 Euro- and Afro-American preschool
children and employed operant learning principles to modify
the bias via a teaching machine procedure which provided
reinforcement for pro-Afro/Anti-Euro (E+/A-) responses. Following training, subjects showed a reduction in E+/A- bias on
a test procedure not associated with the training. Follow-up
testing of 30 subjects one year after the post-test revealed
a tendency for the E+ bias to be partially reestablished.
Experiment II involved 70 Euro-American kindergarten children
and was concerned with the modification of E+/A- bias via a
classroom curriculum procedure and the possible influence of
the race of the teacher. The experimental curriculum, designed
to develop positive associations to dark-skinned persons and
to the colors black and brown, had no effect on E+/A- bias,
nor was the race of teacher a variable of significance.

892. Biller, H. B. A note on father absence and masculine development in lower class Negro and white boys. Child Development, 1968,
39 (3), 1003-1006.

Explored the relation of father absence and socio-cultural
background to masculine development. Subjects were 29 6-year-
old lower class Negro and white boys. In terms of projective
sex role orientation (Brown's IT Scale), white father-present

boys were the most masculine; there was no significant difference between white father-absent and Negro father-present boys;
and the Negro father-absent boys were the least masculine.
No significant differences relating to either direct sex role
preference or teacher's ratings of masculinity on a multidimensional scale were found. The results suggested that
underlying sex role orientation is more influenced by father
availability and family background than are more manifest
aspects of masculinity.

893. Billingsley, A. and Giovannoni, J. M. Children of the Storm:
Black Children and American Child Welfare. New York: Harcourt
Brace Jovanovich, 1972. 263 pp.

The system of child welfare services in this country is failing black children as a result of racism. The kinds of services developed are not sufficient for the special situation
of black children, and black children are not treated equitably.
At the national level, the distribution of services to black
children has barely changed in the last 50 years. Previous
efforts to overcome discrimination against black children
have failed because they were not sufficiently radical.
Changes in the structure and operation of the major institutions of the larger society are needed, as well as local,
community-based institutions managed by members of the black
community.

894. Black, M. H. Characteristics of the Culturally Disadvantaged
Child. New York: Syracuse University Urban Teacher Preparation
Program (mimeographed), n.d. 6 pp.

Discusses the following questions: (a) Who is the educationally
or culturally disadvantaged child? and (b) What are the characteristics of the culturally disadvantaged child? Factors oper-
ative include the following: (1) language; (2) learning
patterns; (3) readiness for instruction; and (4) school behavior. Characteristics of disadvantaged areas are presented.

895. Blakely, K. B. and Somerville, A. W. An investigation of the
preference for racial identification terms among Negro and Caucasian
children. Journal of Negro Education, 1970, 39 (4), 314-319.

400 children, grades 1-12, participated in this study in May,
1968. All schools involved serve a mixed, low middle and middle
class socioeconomic area in California. Subjects above grade 3
completed a questionnaire in their classroom setting by indicating their preference among the racial names "Negro," "Black,"
"Colored," and "Afro-American," and between "white," and "Caucasian." Preferences of subjects in grades 1-3 were obtained
on an individual basis. All subjects indicated a desire to
avoid using terms pertaining to color when designating the
Negro race; less than 1/4 of the total sample selected either
"colored" or "black". This tendency toward the Caucasian
race is not as apparent. Data also show that children learn
the correct racial designation for the Negro race prior to

learning the proper anthropological designation for the Caucasian race.

896. Bloom, R. D. Dimensions of adjustment in adolescent boys:
Negro-white comparisons. Journal of School Psychology, 1968-69, 7
(3), 63-69.

> Performed separate factor analyses on the responses of a random
> sample of 30 white and Negro adolescent boys to 40 closed end
> questions dealing with adjustment states. There was apparent
> overlap between the two factor structures. For both samples,
> the following factors were tentatively identified: global
> distress, aggressive impulses, physical distress, social isola-
> tion, optimism versus pessimism, test anxiety, general anxiety,
> and guilt reactions. While there was comparability between the
> two factor structures, the factors extracted for the Negro
> sample exhibited less coherency and organization.

897. Bloom, R., Deutsch, M., and Whiteman, M. Race and social class
as separate factors related to social environment. The American Journal of Sociology, 1965, 70 (4), 471-476.

> A survey of race and class as separate factors determining
> social environment. The sample consisted of approximately
> equal numbers of Negro and white children, and their parents.
> Of 11 dependent variables evaluated (e.g., parental educational
> aspirations for child), eight showed stronger relationship with
> class than with race. The conclusion is that social class may
> be more potent a variable than race in predicting environmental
> and attitudinal factors.

898. Boesel, D. The liberal society, black youths, and the ghetto
riots. Psychiatry, 1970, 33 (2), 265-281.

> The ghetto riots that swept the country between 1964 and 1968
> together constituted the most massive black revolt in American
> history to date. This paper summarizes similar events of years
> past, drawing parallels and differences between today and
> yesterday in the history of black revolt in America. An analy-
> sis is given, explaining the short-lived character of early
> black insurrections in the context of unified white (elite)
> repressive processes. Following the New Deal, the coherence
> and unity of purpose of the elites began to erode, and the
> subsequent alterations in economic and social patterns also
> altered the system of racial controls within which blacks
> moved. These changes, affecting particularly the younger
> blacks in the Fifties and early Sixties, have established the
> conditions for revolt and have put black youths in the fore-
> front of the ghetto riots. The ramifications of these changes
> are discussed, emphasizing their impact on the new generation
> of black youths. A case history is provided of the Plainfield,
> New Jersey, riot in which black youths, in a display of collec-
> tive rationality rarely seen in other urban disorders, ini-
> tiated, and within limits, controlled and exploited for political
> ends the threat and the fact of black rebellion. In general,

there appears to be more deliberateness in riot actions
than is immediately evident. Past grievances are very much
present and connected to the action; often in the midst of
the rioting, meetings between young blacks and public authorities
are held; demands are articulated and sometimes acted upon;
efforts to work out a "truce" proceed from both sides. Overall
control of the black community is absent, but that is part of
the major point: breaking white control over the ghetto is a
central aim in itself, and even though black control can rarely
be established, the simple fact of taking possession of the
streets is a cause for great celebration. The riots of the
past constitute a rudimentary exercise of black power and may
be giving way to more disciplined means of asserting black
claims.

899. Boone, S. L. Language, cognition, and social factors in the regulation of aggressive behavior: A study of black, Puerto Rican, and
white children, 1975. 147 pp. Available from: Xerox University Microfilms, Post Office Box 1764, Ann Arbor, Michigan 48106: Order No. 76-
1102; microfilm or xerography. Also, see ERIC Abstracts, No. 124-626.

The purpose of this study was to investigate the Language
Aggression Hypothesis. This hypothesis suggests that measurable
high language proficiency is associated with low observable
aggression and low language proficiency is associated with high
observable aggression. Consideration was also given to qualitative differences in aggressive behaviors as a function of
family income, race, age, number of parents in household, and
school membership. Further data on differences in free speech
and its relationship to the former variable were treated. The
subjects were 55 black, 25 Puerto Rican, and 50 white male
fourth, fifth and sixth graders selected from schools within
the Newark public school system. Aggression was measured
using an adaptation of the physical and verbal categories
employed by Walter Pearce and Dahms. The vocabulary subtest
of the WISC, Metropolitan Reading Test (Elementary Form), and
measures of free speech were used to measure language proficiency of subjects. The results reported suggest that the
language, cognitive and social factors considered in this
study may, indeed, play an important role in regulating the
aggressive behavior displayed in the classroom among black,
Puerto Rican, and white children. Further, it appears that
when these factors interact, these interactions can often
explain a significant proportion of the variation of aggression.

900. Boone, W. H. Problems of adjustment of Negro students at a
white school. Journal of Negro Education, 1947, 11, 476-483.

Adjustment problems of economic, social, academic, and mental
health nature are discussed.

901. Boswell, D. A. and Williams, J. E. Correlates of race and
color bias among preschool children. Psychological Reports, 1975,
36 (1), 147-154.

The relationship of individual differences in racial bias and
white-black color bias to preschool Euro-American children's
general responses to light and darkness, and to certain material
attitudes and personality traits is examined. Using the preschool Racial Attitude Measure II and Color Meaning Test II,
procedures developed by Williams and his associates, significant correlations were found between the child's white-black
color bias and race bias and reports of aversive experience
with darkness. There was also a significant correlation between the racial attitudes of mothers and their child. Findings with a behavioral measure of dark avoidance and measures
of the mother's anxiety and authoritarianism are inconclusive.
Results are discussed in terms of their implications for the
development of race and color bias in preschool children.

902. Boxhill, C. J., Kalarickal, T. V., and Curcio, M. Certain
expressed moral beliefs of three groups of early adolescent boys.
National Catholic Guidance Conference Journal, 1969, 14 (1), 21-24.

Subjects were 63 Negro, 68 Puerto Rican, and 51 white eighth
grade boys from Catholic schools of the East and Central
Harlem whose families were in upper-low and lower-low socioeconomic levels. The instrument used was Isler's revision
of the Havighurst and Taba Student Belief Inventory. Whites
scored higher on honesty and responsibility than did the other
two groups. No significant difference was found in regard
to friendliness, loyalty, and moral courage among any of
the groups.

903. Bradfield, R. H., et al. Project B.E.A.M.: An experiment in
intervention. Journal of Negro Education, 1975, 44 (1), 34-41.

Describes an intervention program used to improve the academic
and social behavior of delinquent and predelinquent black
adolescents in grades 7 and 8 of a ghetto junior high school.
The program included a tutorial reading program, biweekly group
counseling, and cultural enrichment. TOTE (a performance-
demonstrated instructional management system) and cash-
redeemable tokens were used to facilitate reading progress.
Cash was given for attendance at the group counseling sessions, led by more advanced black students. Change in reading
scores (measured by the Gilmore Oral Reading Test), teacher
evaluations, and change in probationary status suggest that
appropriate intervention programs can solve problem behavior.

904. Brenman, M. Minority-group membership and religious, psychosexual, and social patterns in a group of middle class Negro girls.
Journal of Social Psychology, 1940, 12, 179-196.

A group of middle class Negro girls showed, in intensive interviewing, both a greater religiosity and greater religious

conflict than a comparable group of whites. Age appears to
be more important than race in determining psychosexual attitudes and practices, there being greater intragroup resem-
blances among 18-year-olds, for example, than among Negro
girls or white girls taken as a group without regard to age.
Negro girls showed ambivalent attitudes toward white esthetic
standards of male attractiveness.

905. Brenman, M. The relationship between minority-group membership
and group identification in a group of urban middle class Negro girls.
Journal of Social Psychology, 1940, 11, 171-197.

Intensive interviews with 25 Negro girls showed three types
of "defense" against problems of racial awareness: (1) conscious rejection of racial identification; (2) keen awareness
accompanied by deep anxiety feelings; and (3) keen awareness
accompanied by rebellion and in-group pride. Most subjects
present a mixture of all three types.

906. Brenman, M. Urban lower class Negro girls. Psychiatry, 1943,
6, 307-324.

Observations are reported on a group of lower class urban
Negro girls covering their reactions to minority group membership, interracial attitudes, sexual behavior and morality
standards. The conclusion is offered that the adjustment
of a member of a minority group is always conditioned by the
interplay of the normal strivings of the person and the psychological strength of the barriers to the "forbidden areas".

907. Breyer, N. L. and May, J. G. Effect of sex and race of the
observer and model on imitative learning. Psychological Reports,
1970, 27 (2), 639-646.

Investigated the effects of sex and race of observer and
model characteristics, verbal, motor and total numbers of
imitative responses, within a 2 x 2 x 2 x 2 x 3 x 4 repeated
measures design which also assessed the effects of idio-
syncratic model effects within each model characteristic.
Subjects were 96 Negro and white male and female 60- to 72-
month-old children. Data collectors were 24 18- to 26-year-
old adults, representing each race-sex combination. Analysis
of the verbal imitation data indicate that Negro females
imitated more than Negro males while white males imitated
more than white females. Analysis of the motor and total
imitation resulted in similar significant effects. In both
cases, a significant race of subject effect and an interaction effect between race of subject, sex of model (M) and
exposure trials are reported. An analysis of the motor
imitation yielded a significant race of subject (S) by team
of model effect and a four-way interaction between sex of S,
sex and race of M, and exposure trials.

908. Brigham, J. C. Views of black and white children concerning
the distribution of personality characteristics. Journal of Personality, 1974, 42 (1), 144-158.

White and black school children in grades four through twelve
in two segregated schools in the Deep South were asked whether
each of 50 "stereotype relevant" traits was more characteristic of whites, of Negroes, or whether no difference between
races existed. Within race agreement on direction of trait
attributions increased with age in both samples, but whites
showed more agreement than blacks at all grade levels. The
trait attribution patterns of these children do not support
the commonly held notion that southern white children will
adopt a purely pro-white orientation, and that black children
will tend to support such an orientation. Rather, both samples
showed a significant tendency to attribute favorable traits
to their own race, but this tendency was significantly greater
within the black sample than within the white sample. Encouraging findings are the widespread use of the no-difference
response category and the very high agreement between races
as to the favorability of these 50 traits.

909. Brisbane, F. The causes and consequences of alcohol abuse
among black youth. Journal of Afro-American Issues, 1976, 4 (1),
241-254.

Explores the potential causes of abusive use of alcohol among
young blacks, focusing on the black family, with emphasis given
to the children, their peers, their communities, and the conditions that influence their lifestyles and drinking patterns.
The data includes interviews with 13 males, aged 8-13 years,
and 9 females, aged 13-15 years, and questionnaire data from
27 males, aged 16-23 years.

910. Broderick, C. B. Social heterosexual development among urban
Negroes and whites. Journal of Marriage and the Family, 1965, 27
(2), 200-203.

A questionnaire and derived index of social heterosexuality
which allowed for interracial comparisons by sex and age of
pre and early adolescents was developed. The greatest difference between the races occurred at 10 to 13. At these
ages, the white children showed the traditional pattern: girls
were far more romantically oriented than boys although at about
the same level in terms of actual heterosexual interaction.
Negro boys showed a high pre-adolescent heterosexual interest
and involvement together with an apparent progressive dis-
enchantment with marriage. Findings suggest that social
heterosexual development in the Negro subculture differs
markedly from that in the dominant culture. (Modified.)

911. Brody, E. B. Minority Group Adolescents in the United States.
Williams and Wilkins, 1968. vii + 243 pp.

A collection of contributed essays on problems of the American
Negro, the Puerto-Rican-American, Mexican-American, Chinese,
Japanese and Indian-American youth. There is an interesting
chapter on the middle class adolescent psychiatric inpatient
as a member of a minority group. The editor has contributed
an introductory statement summarizing the dimension of prejudice and marginality, social change, and socialization during
adolescence; his concluding chapter on minority group status
and behavioral disorganization is thought-provoking. In
general, the essays are background and orienting in character,
as well as problem-definitional; they are, however, adequately
based on social data. The book will be useful to many professionals, and holds much of interest for the general reader
as well. It is especially timely, in that it draws attention
to a number of minority groups which are too frequently over-
looked.

912. Brooks, M. S. and Hawley, J. B. Differentials in misperceptions
of racial attitudes by 36 black and 334 white Carbondale High School
male students. (No published information from Sociological Abstracts.)

The three basic hypotheses underlying the research are: (1) that
people have exaggerated ideas concerning how favorably members
of 'each' race (black and white) rate their own race in comparison to the 'other' race; (2) that the misperception of this
differential is greater than the differential between actual
ratings of the two races; and (3) that both of these misperceptions are greater for the other race than for one's own race.
Racial 'attitudes' were obtained by an anonymous, long, structured questionnaire submitted to Carbondale High School students
during a special 'home room' period on May 27, 1968. Of the
469 questionnaires returned, 21% were completely discarded and
one or more sections of an additional 22% were also eliminated.
There is strong reason to believe that, by and large, the
responses which were not discarded were conscientiously answered.
The responses of both blacks and whites very strongly support
hypothesis (1). Hypothesis (2) is strongly supported by responses of the blacks; the mean difference being 1.5 points,
but is only weakly supported by responses of the whites, the
mean difference being a negligible .3 of a point. Hypothesis
(3) is firmly supported by the differences for all four racial
combinations, the differences being .9 and 1.6 for ratings by
blacks and 1.8 and .8 for corresponding ratings by whites.
The 4th hypothesis, "the difference in the perceived ratings
of the two races exceeds the difference in the actual ratings
of the two races to a greater degree in the favorable direction
when each race estimates the ratings of the other race than
when each race estimates the ratings of its own race," was
also supported by the data, the difference being .7 of a point
when blacks were rating and .8 of a point when whites were
rating. The probable unrepresentativeness of the 21% of cases
discarded because of unacceptable quality responses is con-

sidered the most serious weakness of the data. Nevertheless,
indications that these respondents on the average had more
extreme racial attitudes than the other students make probable
that the differences found would have been greater than reported
herein, not smaller, had all students fully cooperated. A
general conclusion would appear to be that both blacks and
whites believe that the degree of prejudice -- rating one's
own race favorably and the other race unfavorably -- is greater
for both races than is actually the case and that the perceptions of racial attitudes held by members of the other race
are more inaccurate than the perceptions of attitudes held by
members of one's own race. Also, it would appear that the
misperceptions held by blacks tend to be greater than the misperceptions held by whites.

913. Brown, J. V., Bakeman, R., Snyder, P. A., Fredrickson, W. T.,
Morgan, S. T., and Hepler, R. Interactions of black inner city
mothers with their newborn infants. Child Development, 1975, 46,
677-686.

Interactions of 45 black inner city mothers with their healthy
full-term newborn infants were observed during a bottle feeding on the third day after birth. An exhaustive catalogue of
some 100 mother and infant behaviors was used to describe
objectively the interactions of mothers and infants. In addition to being observed with their mothers, infants were examined with the Rosenblith scale. The infants' birth weights,
birth order, and sex and maternal medication were found to
affect the infants' behaviors and/or patterns of mother-
infant interactions.

914. Bullock, H. A. (Ed.). Proceedings of the Eleventh Educational
Conference: Crime and delinquency of Texas Negro youth growing out
of the present economic and social change. Bulletin of Prairie View
Normal and Industrial College, 1940, 32, 1-76.

A survey is first given of the characteristics of the delinquents and of their criminal records, with a comparison to
data from the nation as a whole. A contrast is then made
between delinquent and non-delinquent groups: of family
background, of economic status, and of educational accomplish-
ments. Attitudes of Texas Negro citizens toward the problem
of crime are discussed. Finally, suggestions are given for
the amelioration of the present situation.

915. Bullock, R. W. A study of the occupational choices of Negro
high school boys. Crisis, 1930, 37, 301-322.

916. Bunton, P. L. and Weissbach, T. A. Attitudes toward blackness
of black preschool children attending community controlled or public
schools. Journal of Social Psychology, 1974, 92 (1), 53-59.

Attitudes toward backness of black preschool children attending a pro-black community controlled or public schools were
studied. Two groups of black children were asked to indicate
their preferences for different race dolls. It was hypothesized

that children not exposed to the community schools program
would prefer less frequently and identify less with dolls
of their own race than children who were exposed to the
program. Data support the hypothesis -- children exposed
to the program gave more pro-black responses after exposure
than before, and gave more pro-black responses than a control
group.

917. Busk, P. L., Ford, R. C., and Schulman, J. L. Effects of
school's racial composition on the self-concept of black and white
students. Journal of Educational Research, 1973, 67 (2), 57-63.

Self-esteem and self-concept of ability of black and white
students attending integrated and segregated schools were
investigated. A total of 696 subjects in 6th, 7th, and 8th
grades from six parochial elementary schools (2 all-black,
3 integrated, and 1 all-white) in similar socioeconomic sections
of Chicago were administered the Coopersmith Self-Esteem Inventory (CSEI), the I See Myself rating scale, and Brookover's Self-
concept of Ability measure (SCA). A multivariate analysis of
variance performed on the test battery scores yielded significant differences for type of school on the Self-esteem measure
and the rating scale, and for grades on both the SCA measure
and the peer and school subscales of the CSEI, but did not
yield significant differences for any of the interactions.

918. Busse, T. V., et al. Environmentally enriched classrooms
and the cognitive and perceptual development of Negro preschool
children. Journal of Educational Psychology, 1972, 63 (1), 15-21.

Evaluated the effects of placing additional equipment in preschool classrooms on the cognitive and perceptual development
of 123 Negro preschool children. Subjects were randomized
into 6 experimental and 6 control classes. Pre- and post-tests
of the Stanford-Binet IQ, Wechsler Preschool and Primary Scale
of Intelligence Performance IQ, and four subtests of the
Illinois Test of Psycholinguistic Abilities were administered.
Both desirable and undesirable effects resulted from the
environmental enrichment. Results suggest that certain claims
about the cognitive and perceptual value of play materials
should be reconsidered.

919. Busse, T. V. and Busse, P. Negro parental behavior and social
class variables. Journal of Genetic Psychology, 1972, 120 (2), 287-
294.

Rated the observed child-rearing behavior of 48 mothers and
48 fathers from a Negro community to social class variables.
The parental behaviors were derived from a parent autonomy-
fostering behavior, sufficiency of orientation, and number
of words. Fathers' education was positively associated with
their amount of expressed love and number of words and was
negatively associated with their smiling behavior. Fathers'
occupation was positively related to the mother's autonomy-
fostering behavior.

920. Busse, T. V., Ree, M., and Gutride, M. Environmentally enriched
classrooms and the play behavior of Negro preschool children. Urban
Education, 1970, 5, 128-140.

> Two Head Start classrooms in each of six areas of a large city
> were paired for physical facilities and equipment. Each class-
> room was located in a different Head Start center, but paired
> classrooms were never more than three blocks apart. The chil-
> dren used in this study were randomly selected from the total
> group. Complete data was obtained for 20 experimental boys,
> 17 control boys, 18 experimental girls, and 19 control girls.
> After the initial registration was completed, one classroom
> from each pair was randomly selected and "enriched". A
> sample of the materials placed in the enriched classrooms
> included a tape recorder and tapes, a Polaroid camera, book
> sets, rubber farm animals, sound cylinders, magnets, wooden
> puzzles, a shape-sorting box, prisms, rhythm band instruments,
> record sets, Negro dolls, Negro community workers (rubber
> figures), and Negro puppets. Taken as a whole, the findings
> show that the enrichment significantly altered the classroom
> environment in the experimental classes. In particular, the
> play behavior of the experimental boys was more cooperative
> than that of the control boys. It would thus seem that the
> social development of boys, but not girls, can be helped by
> the enrichment of the play materials available in their pre-
> school classrooms.

921. Caffrey, B. and Jones, C. Racial attitudes of Southern high
school seniors: A complex picture. Journal of Social Psychology,
1969, 79 (2), 293-294.

> A Likert-type Negro Attitudes Test (NAT) was given to high
> school seniors in two Southern schools. One school was in
> a rural area, near a large university; the other was in a
> textile-mill city noted for its conservatism. Parental
> occupations (professional, academic-professional, non-
> professional) were not related to NAT scores. A 2 x 2 x 2
> analysis of variance revealed that NAT scores were related to
> school area, sex of respondent, and educational level of
> parents, but in a complex manner. Boys, in general, obtained
> higher (prejudice) scores than girls (p<.01). A significant
> (p<.02) triple interaction was found, as girls in the college
> area school whose parents had not attended college obtained
> a high mean score, while boys in the mill town whose parents
> had attended college obtained a low mean score. The data
> reflect the complex nature of racial attitudes in the South.

922. Cahill, I. D. Child-rearing practices in lower socioeconomic
ethnic groups. In R. Dentler, B. Mackler, and M. E. Warshauer (Eds.),
The Urban R's, pp. 268-287. New York: Frederick A. Praeger, 1967.

> When the child-rearing practices of poor Puerto Rican, Negro,
> and Caucasian mothers were compared, more similarities than
> differences were found. This supports the assumption that
> there is such a thing as a culture or subculture of poverty.

More important, it supports the assumption that social class
exerts a stronger influence than ethnogeny does upon child-
rearing practices as a whole. On the other hand, though
subtle differences in culture make it difficult to evaluate
the relative influences of each, the evidence for ethnogeny
is overwhelming. Still, the practices that are different
are important ones. 40% of these were variables relating to
basic training procedures, such as weaning and toilet training.
These variables were related to each other and to more than
60% of the other Chi-square significant variables. Variables
such as aggression, dependency, and anxiety about sex proved
to be affected more by ethnogeny than class. These variables
are also important in the socialization and enculturation
process. The mothers' responses to dependency were the most
significant of the variables which were positive when the
Chi-square was applied. This suggests that this variable is
a key to cultural differences, at least as far as these three
ethnic groups are concerned. There is no tolerance of nudity
or sex behavior. Immediate obedience is expected, and aggression toward parents is not tolerated. Physical punishment is
swift and severe with means of control being object-oriented.
Withdrawal of love is never used. Aggression for self-
protection and independence are valued, except among Puerto
Ricans. The study demolishes the validity of many stereotypes of the lower class family.

923. Caliver, A. The Negro child in the world chaos. Journal of
Educational Sociology, 1943, 17, 230-237.

In dealing with the problem of the Negro child, the home life
appears to be a most important factor in its normal development.
The needs of Negro children are outlined, and the opportunities
for securing these needs are contrasted with the opportunities
of white children. Some progress in Negro schools is indicated,
but a list of deficiencies which handicap the development of
Negro children is given. This article is designed to give the
reader a clearer understanding of the personality defects of
Negro children by showing the excessive handicaps which they
are subjected to in their home and school life.

924. Campbell, J. D. and Yarrow, M. R. Personal and situational
variables in adaptation to change. Journal of Social Issues, 1958,
14 (1), 29-46.

Evidence suggests that desegregation holds the greatest initial
hazards for Negro girls. The Negro girls come to desgregation
weighted with feelings of self-rejection and the recognition
of the favored social and power positions of the white girls.
Since they tend to internalize their feelings there is relatively little opportunity for these girls to work through
their tensions to an adequate resolution. Despite these
handicaps to adequate adaptation Negro girls begin to experience equalitarian living with white children. In several
ways the learned social values and norms and the self-pictures
of boys facilitate adjustment to intergroup relations in a

fashion that does not hold for the girls. The greater tolerance
of aggression and its ambiguity, discussed above, is an example.
The boys, too, have the advantage in the adult role models
available to them. The not to dissimilar occupational roles
of lower class white and Negro males may further strengthen
a feeling of equal status in adult identification of the boys.
Three illustrative case studies are included. Reprinted by permission.

925. Campbell, J. D., Yarrow, L. J., and Yarrow, M. R. A study of
adaptation to a new social situation. Journal of Social Issues, 1958,
14 (1), 3-7.

A study of adjustment of Negro and white children and Negro
and white leaders to an integrated camp setting is reported
in the following papers. These chapters are oriented around
the following major areas of analysis: (a) the effectiveness
of an imposed situation in bringing about individual conformity
to new norms; (b) the interaction of situational requirements
and personal differences, conceptualized as differences both
in socialization experiences and in other personality characteristics; (c) the nature of the stimulus situation, an attempt at
dealing more systematically and specifically with structural
and psychological situational variables, and (d) the role of
the adult leader in social change as an influence agent and
on object of influence.

926. Canady, H. G., Buxton, C., and Gilliland, A. R. A scale for
the measurement of the social environment of the Negro youth. Journal
of Negro Education, 1942, 11, 4-14.

The authors present an inventory, designed especially for
Negro youth of high school age, which purports to measure the
intellectually stimulating value of the environment furnished
by the home, community and other influences. Comparisons are
made between this scale and others and some preliminary data
are given from which tentative conclusions are drawn. A distinction is drawn between the dynamics of environmental forces
and the maternal and non-maternal possession in the home,
the former sharing a higher correlation with intelligence
scores.

927. Cantor, G. N. and Paternite, C. E. A follow-up study of race
awareness using a conflict paradigm. Child Development, 1973, 44
(4), 859-861.

Attempted to replicate G. N. Cantor's pattern of results
from an earlier conflict paradigm finding which suggested
the presence of negative attitudes toward blacks in early
elementary school aged white children. Subjects were 60
second and third graders. The previous results were not reproduced; subjects took significantly longer to choose a boy
they thought "would do a bad thing" than one they thought
"would do a good thing", regardless of the racial make-up
of the picture pairs (white-white, black-black) constitut-
ing the choices provided them. A tendency to choose white

for "good" and black for "bad" when white-black pairs were
involved -- clearly in evidence in the earlier experiment --
was not apparent in the present case.

928. Cantor, G. N. Sex and race effects in the conformity behavior of
upper-elementary-school-aged children. Iowa Testing Programs Occasional Papers No. 16, 1975. 24 pp. Also, see ERIC Abstracts, No.
ED-115-658, 1975.

In two studies, children rated infant pictures on an "unhappy-
happy" scale after being told how adolescent male models (black
or white) had allegedly rated them. The subjects in Experiment 1 were black and white females and males (ages 9-12 years)
attending inner city schools in Des Moines, Iowa. Those in
Experiment 2 were white females and males (ages 10-11 years)
attending school in a predominantly white, middle class,
university community (Iowa City). In both experiments, the
subjects as a total group were significantly affected by the
models' ratings. In Experiment 1, girls conformed more than
did boys; there was no sex difference in Experiment 2. With
regard to race, only one obtained effect is of any direct
interest (in Experiment 1, black subjects conformed more to
white than to black models). The results suggest that social-
class differences may now exist in the conformity behavior of
the sexes. The general absence of race effects is viewed as
encouraging, from an equalitarian standpoint.

929. Carpenter, C. M., Rahm, E., Kirkendall, L. A., and Winchester,
M. E. An experiment in venereal disease education in Negro schools.
American Journal of Syphilis, Gonorrhea, and Venereal Disease, 1945,
29, 392-402.

"A survey of the knowledge of venereal disease possessed by
students in seven Negro schools comprising 1,119 pupils ranging
in age from 12 to 18 years demonstrated their paucity of accurate
information. This was generally true regardless of age." The
display of simply worded posters in school lavatories, the
use of venereal disease pamphlets, or class discussions resulted in gains in information varying from 20 to 300 percent.

930. Carringer, D. and Wilson, C. S. The effects of sex, socioeconomic class, experimenter race, and kind of verbal reinforcement
on the performances of black children. Journal of Negro Education,
1974, 43 (2), 212-220.

The effects of sex, socioeconomic class, experimenter race,
and kind of verbal reinforcement on the performance of middle
class and lower class black second graders were investigated
in two experiments. Findings indicate that children are not
responsive to the different semantic nuances connoted by praise
and correctness reinforcers. The fact that middle class blacks
were significantly more responsive, regardless of kind of reinforcer, suggests that higher motivation of these subjects is
the critical factor rather than intellectual ability. Data
do not show any significant effects of sex except in second

order interactions. The contention that the experimenter's
race affects performance, especially in lower class black
children and in black girls, was strongly supported. This
finding is at variance with the general finding that black
experimenters are generally more effective than white examiners
with black male children in performance tasks.

931. Carroll, R. E. Relations of social environment to the moral
ideology and the personal aspirations of Negro boys and girls. School
Review, 1945, 53, 30–38.

> Responses were obtained from 298 Negro adolescents of lower
> and middle class status concerning their moral concepts and
> their notions of the person they would like most to resemble.
> When grouped according to McDougall's four levels of moral
> development, the reasons given for the wrongfulness of
> cheating, lying and stealing in the case of the middle class
> group are predominantly at the level of "social approval",
> while in the lower class they are mainly at the second level
> of moral development, namely, "rewards or punishments". The
> ratings of the "ideal self" held by lower class adolescents
> falls most frequently (71% of the cases) in the "glamorous
> adult" category; and while this is also true of the middle
> class group (38%), many of the latter select "successful adults"
> or "family members". Middle class adolescents stress moral,
> altruistic and intellectual qualities in their ideal, while
> those of the lower class emphasize physical beauty, personality
> and fame. This study supports the view "that environment
> conditions the moral and social values of middle and lower
> class adolescents."

932. Carter, D. E., DeTine, S. L., Spero, J. B., and Forrest, W.
Peer acceptance and school–related variables in an integrated junior
high school. Journal of Educational Psychology, 1975, 67 (2), 267–273.

> Interracial peer acceptance at the junior high school level
> was related to 9 predictor variables: grade point average
> (GPA), IQ, attendance, self–concept of academic ability, sex,
> race, age, years in the school, and classroom racial composi-
> tion. 322 seventh and eighth grade students from predominantly
> lower–middle class backgrounds were administered modified
> Syracuse Scales of Human Relations, measuring academic and
> social acceptance. Analysis of variance results show that
> white subjects slightly preferred whites for the satisfaction
> of their academic and social needs. However, with stepwise
> multiple regression analysis, race was not a significant pre-
> dictor variable for academic or social acceptance by white
> subjects. GPA and sex were the most prominent predictors of
> acceptance. Black subjects accepted both black peers and
> white peers equally for academic interaction but preferred
> blacks for social interaction. Race was a significant predictor
> variable for academic and social acceptance by black subjects.
> However, race was secondary to GPA and/or sex for academic
> acceptance by black females and black males.

933. Cawley, J. F., Burrow, W. H., and Goodstein, H. A. Performance
of Head Start and non-Head Start participants at first grade. Journal of Negro Education, 1970, 29 (2), 124-131.

Society has great expectations for preschool intervention
programs for disadvantaged children. However, simple exposure to preschool will not guarantee substantial results.
Active participation in a system of successful education is
more fundamental; Head Start should be only one part of this
system. This study compares the developmental status of
participants and nonparticipants in Head Start. Three samples
of first grade children, two of which participated in Head
Start, were identified. Initial comparisons were based upon
data from the cumulative files of the cooperating school
system. Tests administered to the three groups midway through
kindergarten did not indicate significant differences of
selected developmental characteristics. Furthermore, no
significant differences were found through the more comprehensive testing administered in first grade. The differences
that were found were attributable to the previous exposure
of one Head Start group to testing. However, although the
Head Start groups did not achieve significantly higher results
than the nonparticipants, the overall developmental pattern
of all three groups was replete with deficits. Total language
scores and visual perception measures, for example, indicated
a nine-month to one-year inadequacy. Head Start programs
cannot compensate for these deficiencies. The general curriculum approach to Head Start does not yield significant results. More comprehensive intervention strategies, beginning
at an earlier age, are needed.

934. Childers, A. T. Some notes on sex mores among Negro children.
American Journal of Orthopsychiatry, 1936, 6, 442-448.

The writer has found Negro children of the lower class excep-
tionally free from restraint in telling of their sex lives.
Living in homes where both parents work, they begin sex play
as they do any other childish game of spontaneous origin,
frequently at 5 or 6 years of age. In this setting perver-
sions are extremely rare. The sex act is accepted casually,
assuming approximately the significance of good fellowship.
No discrimination against illegitimacy is found. Sex dreams
are usually frank and not particularly symbolic. Brother-
sister incest does not appear, but children of the same family
cooperate. Venereal disease is little feared, and illegitimate pregnancy is viewed with slight concern. Two case summaries
of psychotic breakdowns are presented to illustrate what may
happen when social and moral censorship is applied too strictly
to children in whom the sex appetite has been developed.

935. Chimezie, A. Transracial adoption of black children. Social
Work, 1975, 20 (4), 296-301.

Discusses the controversy about the transracial adoption of
black children by white parents. The argument for transracial

adoption appears to be based on two reasons: that the black
community cannot provide the needed black adoptive parents
and that raising black children in a white home will be better
than raising them in an institution or foster home. The limitations of current data on the adoption rates of blacks by blacks
are examined, and it is suggested that the benefits of adopting
a black child at a younger age by white parents do not necessarily outweigh the disadvantages of later adoptive failures.
The issue of right of choice is discussed, and it is noted
that no black consensus has been reached on the question of
black adoption. The psychosexual needs of the child are
discussed in relation to whether transracial adoption would
fulfill both the child's present and future needs. It is concluded that (a) transracial adoption may harm the black child
in that he may lose his sense of black identity and the ability
to relate to other blacks, and (b) until empirical studies
are made of the adult personalities of white-raised blacks,
placements of black children should not proceed as though
transracial adoption had already been found to be beneficial.

936. Clark, K. B. and Clark, M. K. The development of consciousness
of self and the emergence of racial identification in Negro preschool
children. Journal of Social Psychology, 1939, 10, 591-599.

The authors modified the Horowitz picture technique by showing
to 150 Negro children between 3 and 5 years old, cards illus-
trating white and Negro children, animals, and asking: "Which
is you?" It was found that the majority of children at all
ages studied made the correct identification.

937. Clark, K. B. and Clark, M. K. Emotional factors in racial identification and preference in Negro children. Journal of Negro Education, 1950, 19, 341-350.

160 Southern and Northern Negro children from 5 to 7 years
of age were asked to color a picture of the opposite sex
with a free range of colors permitted. Pretesting on non-
human objects was first done to assure stability of color to
objects concept relationship. Rejection of the brown color
(choosing white) or escapist tendencies (non-realistic colors)
was most marked in the dark children, but appeared in all
skin color groups and at all ages. Escapist responses were
greater among Northern children and at age 5. However, by
age 7 unrealistic tendencies had virtually disappeared. This
suggests that by age 7 realistic self-identification is possible
and that emotional conflict in regard to status is already
present since many of them show a clear-cut preference for
white.

938. Clark, K. B. and Clark, M. K. Segregation as a factor in the
racial identification of Negro preschool children. Journal of Experimental Education, 1939, 8, 161-163.

In this study, children were asked to show the experimenter
which one of a series of drawings of white and colored boys,
animals, and a clown they considered to be themselves. In

general, the tendency to identify with either the colored or
the white boy approximated a chance frequency among Negro
children in nursery schools where there were both white and
colored children in a semi-segregated group and even more so
in an all-Negro nursery school. A further analysis is made
of the age at which the subjects in the three groups ceased
identifying themselves in terms of animals or clowns. Effect
of degree of skin color of the Negroes on identification is
also considered.

939. Clark, K. B. and Clark, M. K. Skin color as a factor in racial
identification of Negro preschool children. Journal of Social Psychology, 1940, 11, 159-169.

In a continuation of a previously-reported experiment (Journal
of Social Psychology, 1939, 10, 591-599), it was found that
36.5% of light-colored Negro children; 52.6% of medium-colored
children; and 56.4% of dark children identified themselves
with a picture of a colored child; between the light and dark
groups CR = 3.15. This seems to establish skin color as an
important factor in the genesis of consciousness of self and
racial identification.

940. Clark, R. M. The dance party as a socialization mechanism
for black urban pre-adolescents and adolescents. Sociology and
Social Research, 1974, 58 (2), 145-154.

The dance party as a mechanism for the socialization of urban
black youth, and in relation to the interpretation of cere-
monies and rituals by Ban Gennep is described and analyzed.
The dance party serves as an arena for black cultural growth,
offering an introduction to black unity and an introduction
to ways of acting as an adult through social interaction and
a spirit of community.

941. Cohen, D. K. Policy for the public schools: Compensation and
integration. Harvard Educational Review, 1968, 38 (1), 114-137.

The leading public policy question in urban education appears to
be whether to take students and school attendance patterns as
they are and seek to improve Negro achievement by improving
educational quality in the existing schools, or to desegre-
gate schools and thus improve educational opportunities for
Negro students. Although there is a general view in the government that school segregation is harmful to Negro children,
Title I of the 1965 Elementary and Secondary Education Act
provides unprecedented funds to improve education in the
existing segregated schools. The arguments for assigning
high priority to compensation and low priority to desegregation
are expounded. Programs of compensatory education typically
proceed on the assumption that children who experience academic
retardation do so mainly because their preparation for school
is seriously deficient. However, evidence has shown that
compensatory programs isolated by race and socioeconomic class
have resulted in no substantial or lasting improvement in

students' academic competence. Two basic problems are advanced
to account for this failure: (1) compensatory programs mis-
conceive the sources of academic failure, locating them exclusively in individual children's "cultural deprivation",
and (2) there has not been a clear definition of compensation
or of the required changes in the schools' programs. It is
pointed out that in addition to the negative effects of
attending schools whose populations are lower class, Negro
students suffer from the special effect of the racial composition of their schools. However, the idea that the only major
barrier to effective learning lies in the students' cultural
deprivation is naive. The student body is the immediate
medium in which instruction and learning occurs; its educational strength or weakness can facilitate or impede intellectual growth. The More Effective Schools Program in New York
City is described, and stated to be the only compensatory
program to have made serious efforts in this direction. Both
drastic reductions in pupil-teacher ratios and improvement of
teacher quality and working conditions are necessary conditions of effective compensation. Basic objections to a policy
of segregated compensation are expressed: though there is
direct and indirect evidence that integration will improve
achievement, there is little such evidence for segregated
compensation; and there is direct evidence that compensatory
programs will compound other major educational problems. Survey
data show that the Negro students who attended schools with
whites exhibited about 50% of the academic disadvantage of
those Negroes who attended school only with Negroes. Further,
crucial outcomes of education are not restricted to the
development of academic competence: there is good evidence
that racial composition of schools shapes the racial preferences
and interracial behavior of both children and adults. Compensatory programs institutionalize segregation and therefore
compound racism in a number of important ways. "A policy of
segregated compensation can promise only the continuation of
a segregated, closed and inferior system of education for
Negro Americans." Reprinted by permission.

942. Cohen, E. G. Modifying the effects of social structure. _Ameri-_
can Behavioral Scientist, 1973, 16 (6), 861–879.

Means of modifying effects of interracial imbalance in the
social structure are examined within the framework of altering the school structure to foster and reinforce equal status
behavior. Interracial interaction disability is described
on the basis of a controlled laboratory setting, and translation of research to a field setting is reported. Attempts to
modify racial imbalance include an experimental summer school
program in which treatment groups received either expectation
training or an alternative treatment designed to produce interracial cooperation. Findings suggest different approaches to
conventional school organization and practice at three levels:
(1) A direct attack on expectations for black competence held
by both blacks and whites; (2) An attack on classroom social
structure to prevent a single status order based on perceived

academic ability and use of group, rather than individual,
accountability; and (3) A change in the power and authority
structure of the school to produce racial balance among adults
as well as children.

943. Comer, J. P. and Poussaint, A. F. Black Child Care: How to
Bring Up A Healthy Black Child in America. A Guide to Emotional
and Psychological Development. 408 pp.   Available from:
Simon & Schuster, Inc. Rockefeller Center, 630 Fifth Avenue, New
York, New York 10020. 1975.

This book is designed to serve as a practical reference guide
for parents. The bulk of it is devoted to a stage-by-stage
study of the black child's development from infancy through
adolescence with special emphasis on the role of parents and
teachers of school age children. The book begins with a brief
summary of the historical experience of black youth in America.
A question-and-answer format is used throughout the book.
Most child care books are considered to be geared toward the
middle income white family, and few discuss race-related issues
of child rearing and low income children and families. Because race-related and income-related issues are said to cause
special problems, it is held essential that an approach to
child rearing that takes these important factors into consideration be available. Among the topics discussed are how children
mature and how that growth affects their emotional, psychological, and social development. The intent is to share with the
parent some of the latest findings and thinking in the child
development field. Knowing the causes of black family problems
and what can be done about them, as well as having an awareness of black family and community strengths, can affect how
black mothers and fathers think about themselves and, in turn,
influence the kind of care they give their young. It can also
affect, it is stated, how white teachers and others view black
youth.

944. Cook, H. and Smothergill, D. W. Racial and sex determinants
of imitative performance and knowledge in young children. Journal
of Educational Psychology, 1973, 65 (2), 211-215.

154 low socioeconomic white and black preschoolers observed
a white or black young adult model choose one of two pictures
in a series of 12 pairs. Subsequently, observers (Os) chose
(imitative performance) from the same pictures, then, under an
incentive condition they recalled the model's choice (imitative
knowledge). Results indicate that imitation performance was
significantly higher when the model was white, regardless of
race or sex of the O, and when the model was the same sex
as the O. In imitative knowledge, black Os (regardless of
sex) recalled significantly more with female than with male
models; whereas for white Os, no significant difference was
obtained.

945. Cosby, A. G. and Picou, J. S. Structural models and occupational aspirations: Black-white variations among Deep-South adolescents. Journal of Vocational Behavior, 1973, 3 (1), 1-14.

Applied multivariate techniques for attribute data and the backward elimination procedure developed in regression analysis in an analysis of the occupational aspirations of Deep-South adolescents. Examination of models constructed revealed that: (a) social class indicators accounted for largest effect estimates; (b) residence was associated with a smaller, yet statistically significant, portion of variation; and (c) effect of race was negligible when controls were applied. Application of the most efficient model to black and white subsamples revealed race variations in both composite effect estimates and rank order effect estimates. Findings are discussed in terms of a developmental model of occupational choice.

946. Costello, J. Effects of pretesting and examiner characteristics on test performance of young disadvantaged children. Proceedings of the Annual Convention of the American Psychological Association, 1970, 5 (Part 1), 309-310.

Reports the effects of pretesting, race of examiner, and familiarity of examiner on the Stanford-Binet and Peabody Picture Vocabulary Test scores of 62 preschool black children. Test conditions were carefully controlled for validation not under study. None of the three variables had an effect on test performance. These nonsignificant findings raise questions of significance for decision-making, i.e., Is the general atmosphere of testing more powerful than any one variable, or are there unique interactions among variables which may potentiate or neutralize the negative impact of any one examiner variable?

947. Criswell, J. H. Racial cleavage in Negro-white groups. Sociometry, 1937, 1, 81-89.

950 children in a Brooklyn, New York public school, with a 75% Negro population were tested by Moreno's sociometric test and interview, to determine with which two classmates each would like to sit, and why. The white children were largely of Italian parentage. 30 classes from nine grades were tested. The intelligence of the group was low-average. The results indicate that sexual cleavage is far greater than that on racial lines. Further analysis was made within the boys' and girls' groups. In general, a decrease of interracial choices is found with increasing age; girls' groups show variable cleavage, colored girls withdrawing more; boys develop equal cleavage or groups where one has more prestige; there is never complete cleavage. Some other findings: where whites are a very small minority their self-preference tends to be unusually high before and unusually low after reaching the fifth grade; white girls forming a small majority show increased self-preference; Negro girls below 12 do not separate from the whites; it is probable that when whites

reach a concentration of 58%, Negroes show a loss of self-
preference. A tentative explanation of racial group formation
is offered; it is to be checked by further studies.

948. Cross, A. The black experience: Its importance in the
treatment of black clients. Child Welfare, 1974, 53 (3), 158-166.

A 10-month participant-observation experience at a Los Angeles
area home for 15 black adolescent delinquent girls ages 13 to
17 made obvious the need for programs and services that are
specific to the problems of black adolescent delinquent girls.
Black girls cannot "make it" in white placements because of
the differences in background and ethnicity. Several concepts
must be incorporated into the program's framework. The first
concept is acceptance from certain people having the qualities
required to meet the girls' special needs. Second, the girls
must be treated as though they were deprived, not depraved.
And third, understanding of expressive mechanisms used by
the girl is essential in distinguishing adaptive behavior from
incorrigibility or mental imbalance.

949. Cross, John F. and Cross, Jane. Age, sex, race, and the perception of facial beauty. Developmental Psychology, 1971, 5 (3), 433-439.

Studied the preference judgments of 300 subjects of both
sexes and two races at 4 age levels from 7 years to adult
for 72 portrait photographs of persons of three similar
age levels and of both sexes and races. Subjects rated the
perceived beauty of the preferred faces on a 7-point scale.
Age, sex, and race of judge and of face were analyzed to identify
sources of variation in the ratings. Age of judge effects and
their interactions were not significant. Females down-rated
adult male faces. Blacks gave higher ratings than whites,
with white males down-rating females and white females down-
rating males. Female faces and adolescent faces received
higher ratings than other sex and age groups.

950. Cummings, S. and Mercy, J. The determinants of children's
attitudes toward their future: The relative impact of sex role
socialization, minority status, and class position. Paper presented
at the Annual Meeting of the Southern Sociological Association, 1976.
18 pp.

Sixth grade students of selected schools in the five largest
cities in Connecticut were tested to determine the impact of
sex role socialization, minority status, and class position
on future orientations as opposed to aspirations. Some sample
questions are given, along with results and corresponding
tables. The data suggest that the majority of sixth graders
are aware of general sexual, racial, and class restrictions.

951. D'Andrade, R. G. Father absence, identifcation, and identity.
Ethos, 1973, 1 (4), 440-455.

Studied the effects of father absence during early and late
childhood on sex role identification. A sample of 121 children

ranging in age from 5 to 14.9 years was drawn from 58 black
working class households. Households were divided for analysis
into categories based on timing and length of paternal absence.
Subjects' patterns of sex identification and sex identity were
measured by the Franck Test, by verbal self-descriptions and
by a role preference task. It was found that subjects who
did not have a father present during the first three years of
life exhibited a feminine response pattern on the Franck Test.
It appeared that paternal absence influenced conscious sex
role identity through the indirect processes of reciprocal
role learning and perception of sex role advantages and disadvantages. It is concluded that household composition has
an important effect on development of sex role identities and
sex role preferences.

952. Daniell, R. P. A psychological study of delinquent and non-
delinquent Negro boys. Teachers College Contribution to Education,
1932, (546).

Compared three groups of Negro boys (100 boys in a reform
school, 80 behavior-problem boys in a public school, 120 non-
problem boys in a public school). Seven tests were administered: Haggerty Intelligence; Delta II; Mathews Questionnaire;
Character sketches I and II (Maller); Sweet's Personal Attitude Test for Younger Boys; Ethical Judgment Test; Maller Test
of Sports and Hobbies (trustworthiness). The groups were
all from the fifth grade, ages varying from 9 to 16 years;
IQ averaged 75, 86, and 94 respectively. Significant differences between the groups were found with the trustworthiness
test, Mathews Questionnaire, and the character sketches. "Data
show that delinquents differ from non-delinquents . . . chiefly
in degree rather than kind." The bibliography contains 46
titles. (Modified.)

953. Datta, L., Schaeffer, E., and Davis, M. Sex and scholastic
aptitude as variables in teachers' ratings of the adjustment and
classroom behavior of Negro and other seventh grade students. Journal of Educational Psychology, 1968, 59, 94-101.

Both ethnic group and sex were significantly related to teachers' descriptions of the classroom behavior of 153 seventh
grade students; girls and other subjects were described more
favorably than boys and Negroes on 75% of 64 behavioral rating
scales. There were no interactions of ethnic group and sex.
Comparisons of IQ equivalent subgroups showed, however, that
the effect of ethnic group tended to be contingent on scholastic aptitude and was not dependent on sex; higher-IQ
Negro subjects were described as favorably as were higher-IQ
other subjects, but the lower-IQ Negro pupil was more likely
than the lower-IQ other child to be described as maladjusted,
verbally aggressive, and low in task orientation. Boys,
regardless of IQ or ethnic group, were described less favorably than girls.

954.   Davis, A.   The socialization of the American Negro child and
adolescent.   Journal of Negro Education, 1939, 8, 264-275.

The problem of socialization of the Negro is defined in the
light of recent social and anthropological research studies.
With illegitimate births 7.5 times the white rate and juvenile
delinquency 255 times the white rate as "symptoms" explorations
are sought in the high percentages (50 to 66) of broken homes,
in the caste system, and in home training.   In suggesting
plans for solving the problem of socialization, the author
concludes that "until we know a great deal more about the
training experiences of specific individuals in lower class
positions, we shall not find a scientific or useful method
for dealing with the problems of illegitimacy, delinquency
and retardation among Negro adolescents."

955.   Davis, A. and Havighurst, R. J.   Social class and color differences in child rearing.   American Sociological Review, 1946, 11, 698-
710.

"The study consisted of holding guided interviews with mothers
of young children, recording their responses on a schedule,
and making a statistical analysis of the data from the sche-
dules.   There were 50 mothers in each of four groups: white
middle class, white lower class, Negro middle class, and Negro
lower class."   All were residents of Chicago; most had children in nursery schools.   Five women were trained in several
sessions with the authors for the taking of the interview,
which consisted of three main parts: (a) data on child rearing; (b) the mother's expectations and regimen for the child;
and (c) socioeconomic data.   The conclusions were as follows:
(1) there are significant class and color differences in child
rearing practices; (2) middle class parents, regardless of
color, are more rigorous in their training for feeding and
cleanliness and expect their children to take responsibilities
earlier; (3) Negroes are more permissive than whites in feeding and weaning, but more rigorous in toilet training; (4)
class differences were more conspicuous than color differences.
There is discussion of the results in relation to two interacting components in personality formation, the cultural and
the individual habit systems.

956.   Deitz, G. E.   The influence of social class, sex and delinquency-
nondelinquency on adolescent values.   Journal of Genetic Psychology,
1972, 121 (1), 119-126.

Solicited value preferences from 280 male and 281 female 12-
to 18-year-olds in three groups: middle class whites, lower
class blacks, and juvenile delinquents of both races.   Subjects were given the following open-ended instructions: "Write
down as many personal qualities as you can think of that you
regard as important for people to have."   Where delinquents
valued traits underlying the making of a favorable social
impression, nondelinquents valued traits concerned with
social responsibility.   Males focused slightly more upon

physical attractiveness, and females upon traits functioning
in interpersonal relationships. The middle class was distinguished from the lower class in their preference for the
possession of intelligence and ambition.

957. DeJung, J. E. and Edmonson, B. Measurement of Social Incompetency in Adolescents. Final Report. Washington, D. C.: Division of Research and Demonstration Grants, Social and Rehabilitative
Service (DHEW), 1972. 211 pp. Also, see ERIC Abstracts, No. ED-
107-694, 1972.

Project activities involved: (1) examination of exploratory
measures of social incompetency of junior high school adolescents; (2) development and trial of educational units designed
in response to problems in black urban schools; and (3) a
compilation and review of cross-sectional Test of Social
Interference (TSI) data. Extensive test data was obtained
from junior high school students and teachers in two white
semi-rural and two predominantly black urban schools. Examination of teacher "labelling" of students as socially incomp-
etent (SI) using behavior descriptions and checklist responses
revealed considerable individual arbiter idiosyncrasy. In
the semi-urban schools, means for students consensually identified as SI were lower on all experimental tests, outside
school activity reports, and home interview ratings and also
lower with respect to academic and socioeconomic measures.
In the urban schools, behavior problem students scored lower
on nearly all measures of social awareness, school attitudes,
self-concepts, social relations with respect to various groups,
classroom teacher ratings and interview reports, and school
record comments and file data. Statistical analysis revealed
a general nonrelatedness among sets of variables and lack of
simplified factor structure.

958. Diggs, M. H. The problems and needs of Negro youth as revealed
by delinquency and crime statistics. Journal of Negro Education,
1940, 9, 311-320.

The comparatively high incidence of juvenile delinquency
among Negroes is caused by extensive family disorganization;
absence of community controls; absence of parental controls;
inferior and unsavory home conditions and social environment;
lack of recreation; and economic and social inferiority. The
juvenile court should play a part in the treatment of the
individual case as it actually does in some districts. Educational agencies should meet fundamental human needs more
adequately rather than mere academic traditions.

959. Dion, K. L. and Miller, N. Determinants of task related
self-evaluations in black children. Journal of Experimental Social
Psychology, 1973, 9 (5), 466-479.

Assessed self-evaluations of performance on an ambiguous
task by 56 black males in grades 5 through 8 as a function
of experimental variation in prior social reinforcement and

subjective privacy of self-evaluation. In the private self-
evaluation conditions, subjects given disapproval-oriented
reinforcements were less self-approving and less positive
overall in evaluating their own performance than those
receiving approval-oriented reinforcements. Moreover, they
exhibited lower levels of aspiration on a subsequent ring-
toss task, subjects whose self-evaluations were public rather
than private, failed to exhibit these effects. Results provide support of I. Katz' theoretical model of academic motivation among minority children.

960. Doke, L. A. and Risley, T. R.   Some discriminative properties
of race and sex for children from an all-Negro neighborhood. Child
Development, 1972, 43 (2), 677-681.

Six 4- to 6-year-old, and six 9- to 12-year-old Negro children
served in a comparison of the discriminative control exerted
by sex and race aspects of other children. For all subjects,
base lines were established in which color photoslides of a
Negro girl and a Caucasian boy differentially controlled
responding on two push buttons. Responses during test
probes picturing Negro boys and Caucasian girls, as well as
different Negro girls and Caucasian boys, indicate predominant
control by the stimulus dimension of sex for the younger subjects, but less predictable stimulus control for the older
subjects.

961. Doland, D. J. and Adelberg, K.   The learning of sharing behavior. Child Development, 1967, 38 (3), 695-700.

Sharing behavior was studied in two groups of preschool age
children, one consisting of 10 boys and 10 girls, all white,
at a private nursery school, and the other of 9 boys and 7
girls, the majority Negro, at a child welfare center for
dependent and neglected children. In the pre-training situation, 50% of nursery school children shared, as contrasted
with 12% of welfare center children. Among initial nonsharers
a higher percentage of nursery school children learned to
share following specially devised learning trials using the
incentive of social reinforcement. Categorization by sex
revealed that the poorer learning performance of the welfare-
center children was more characteristic of boys than girls.
A newly devised technique for studying children's sharing
behavior is described in detail.

962. Doll, P. A., Fagot, H. J., and Himbert, J. D.   Experimenter
effect on sex-role preference among black and white lower class
male children. Psychological Reports, 1971, 29 (3, Part 2), 1295-
1301.

Administered the IT Scale for Children to 120 white and 120
black lower class male children at 6-, 9-, and 12-year-old
age levels. Neither sex of examiner nor the age and race of
subject had any main effects on sex-role preference scores,
but there were significant interactions between sex of examiner, race of subject, and administration method.

963. Donohue, T. R. Black children's perceptions of favorite TV
characters as models of antisocial behavior. Journal of Broadcasting,
1975, 19 (2), 153-167.

The relationship between TV violence and childhood socialization has received a great deal of attention, while the relationship between TV and other cultural and social values has been
relatively neglected. A study was conducted to determine the
extent to which TV characters serve as behavioral models for
black children, as against other models available. Five hypotheses were explored. It is expected that: (1) there would
obtain a preference for violent over nonviolent characters;
(2) there would be a higher incidence of violent responses
among males than females; (3) black children would report more
violent responses than white children; (4) younger children
would be more likely to report violent responses than older
children; and (5) TV character and child's response would show
a higher correlation than either parental and child response
or best friend and child response. Verbal data were collected
from 247 1st, 2nd, and 3rd grade children attending two randomly
selected, predominantly black, St. Louis schools. Background
data were elicited, including age, sex, number of TV sets in
home, favorite programs, and favorite characters. Open-ended
questions elicited responses to four situations, each conflictual. Children were asked for their response, that of their
favorite character, the morally correct response, and that of
their best friend. The data support hypotheses concerning
male preference for violent programming and violent characters,
while no choice differences for females emerged. Two trends
surfaced in regard to behavioral responses: younger males
adopted more violent responses and children responded more in
terms of their favorite character than parental value choices.
However, correlational findings were insignificant. Reprinted
by permission.

964. Dunn, J. R. and Lupfer, M. A comparison of black and white
boys' performance in self-paced reactive sports activities. Journal
of Applied Social Psychology, 1974, 4 (1), 24-35.

Results of competition in reactive and self-paced athletics
by boys of both races is reported. Support is provided for
Worthy and Markle's thesis that whites excel at self-paced
and blacks at reactive sports activities, by assessing the
performance of 55 white and 122 black fourth grade boys playing
a modified soccer game. The research also explored the relationships between several dimensions of socialization and
relative performance on the self-paced-reactive dimension.
Two significant correlations emerged: Regardless of their own
racial identity, boys who excelled at the self-paced activity
tended to have several younger siblings and attended schools
with a sizeable representation of white students. Subsequent
interviews revealed that black and white boys did not differ
in their preference for self-paced and reactive sports activities. Other differences in socialization and in inherited
characteristics are also discussed.

965. Eaton, W. O. and Clore, G. L. Interracial imitation at a summer camp. Journal of Personality and Social Psychology, 1975, 32 (6), 1099-1105.

Collected imitation data at week-long summer camp sessions involving prolonged and intimate contact between black children and white children of equal status. As part of an initiation ceremony, 57 black and 55 white 8- to 12-year-olds observed the behavior of unfamiliar black adult and white adult models responding to the commands of an Indian Chief. In three separate camp sessions, the proportions of responses imitative of racially different models were 0.40, 0.42, and 0.37 for campers observed on the first day; and 0.52, 0.49, and 0.53 for those observed on the fifth day. The overall difference between low and high contact groups was significant (p.<.05). A separate-sample pretest-posttest design ruled out threats to the internal validity of the study, and the observation of behavior in a naturalistic context enhanced the ecological validity. It is concluded that interracial contact effects were not limited to changes in behavior among the children themselves but generalized to unfamiliar adults encountered in the same setting.

966. Edmiston, R. W. and McBain, L. C. Social and economic background affects school achievement. School and Society, 1945, 61, 190-191.

150 ninth grade Negro pupils in the Dunbar High School, Dayton, Ohio, were given intelligence and general achievement tests, and social and economic background inventories. Positive partial correlations were obtained on (a) the relationship between social background scores and achievement, with the influence of economic background and intelligence removed, and (b) the relationship between economic background scores and achievement, with the influence of social background and intelligence removed.

967. Elder, G. H. Jr. Intergroup attitudes and social ascent among Negro boys. American Journal of Sociology, 1971, 76 (4), 673-697.

Over the years two conflicting appeals have been directed toward black youth: (a) the achievement of racial equality through integration; and (b) black power or solidarity. On this basis, it was assumed that integrationists among Negroes would have greater interracial experience and be less handicapped by environmental and personal limitations to achievement than Negro boys in the other groups. This hypothesis was tested in a sample of 286 black male high school students from Richmond, California. Cross-tabulation of attitudes toward black solidarity and racial integration generated four attitude groups: (1) support for only integration (integrationist); (2) black solidarity (nationalist); (3) endorsement of both causes (pluralist); and (4) endorsement of neither (uncommitted). The four groups were relatively similar on father's occupational status and father absence from the home.

Boys who identified with either or both racial integration and
black solidarity tested substantially higher on IQ than the
uncommitted. Nationalists were more likely than other boys
to have been suspended from school 3 or more times, and they
also ranked highest on interpersonal conflict and punishment
by school officials and police. Intergroup distance on estrange-
ment from school was most pronounced among the nationalists and
the integrationists. The uncommitted closely resembled the
nationalists on degree of ·dissatisfaction with school, but
they, as well as those who favored integration, were less
inclined to act out their frustrations in the classroom. The
pluralists, by comparison, differed primarily on their lower
expectations regarding future achievement, were more aware of
racial discrimination and more likely to anticipate failure
to achieve their aspirations. The nationalists were more
limited in achievement opportunity or prospects than the
integrationists; they had less confidence in parental support,
received lower grades in school and were less satisfied with
school. The uncommitted also perceived limited opportunity,
but differed regarding relative incompetence, expressed by a
low average IQ, family dependence, and fatalism. Reprinted by
permission.

968. Ellis, R. R. Looking toward desired behaviors in teachers of
the disadvantaged. Urban Education, 1965, 1 (2), 117-126.

In studies of disadvantaged children conducted by the Institute for Developmental Studies, certain characteristics were
discovered which affect a child's learning capacity, e.g.,
poor development of visual and auditory discriminations and
nondevelopment of language. His home life offers no incentive
for learning and provides an independence inconsistent with
school situations. Difficulties arise when an essentially
middle class teacher imposes her set of standards on a
lower class child; she must understand his weaknesses and
limitations as well as his assets.

969. Entwisle, D. R. and Webster, M. Jr. Expectations in mixed
racial groups. Sociology of Education, 1974, 47 (3), 301-318.

How the status characteristics of adults and children affect
adults' ability to raise a child's expectations of his own
performance at school-like tasks was studied. White adults
are effective at raising expectations of white children or
black children in mixed racial work groups; black adults are
effective with black children but not apparently with white
children in mixed groups. These results, both consistent
and inconsistent with previous findings for homogeneous
groups, are interpreted in light of the children's relative
position in socioeconomic status with respect to members of
their own race. Unlike most research related to the effects
of desegregation, both black children's and white children's
reactions to black adults are examined.

970. Epstein, R. and Komorita, S. S. Prejudice among Negro children
as related to parental ethnocentrism and punitiveness. Journal of
Personality and Social Psychology, 1966, 4 (6), 643-647.

        The relationship of parental punitiveness and the perceptions
        of parental social attitudes to the social distance attitudes
        of Negro children were investigated. (Modified.)

971. Erickson, E. L., Bryan, C. E., and Walker, L. The educability
of dominant groups. Phi Delta Kappan, 1972, 53 (5), 319-321.

        The terms used in relation to poor youth have changed in recent
        years. The term "culturally deprived" became "culturally dis-
        advantaged" on the theory that black children come from a cul-
        ture just as everybody else does, and it is as important
        for educators to learn about lower class culture as it is
        for lower class children to learn to compete in terms of the
        middle class culture. Eventually, the term "educational dis-
        advantage" began to be used, and a major justification of
        school desegregation plans has been the findings of some
        studies that the academic achievement of lower class black
        children has approached middle class norms in desegregated
        schools. However, it must be realized that many whites are
        lower class and have the same kinds of problems as have black
        students. Studies by Ray Rist have shown that children are
        divided by class by teachers and labeled fast learners and
        slow learners according to class origin. These definitions
        are picked up by the children with regard to each other and
        internalized with regard to themselves; thus school not only
        mirrors the inequalities of the larger society but signifi-
        cantly contributes to maintaining them.

972. Estvan, F. J. The relationship of nursery school children's
social perception to sex, race, social status and age. Journal of
Genetic Psychology, 1965, 107, 295-308.

        In a study of social perception of 78 Negro and Caucasian
        preschool children, the author concludes that: "The evidence
        indicates that nursery school children's social perception is
        related to sex, race, and social status. Differences are
        evident in each group comparison. They appear in each compo-
        nent of social perception, the greatest number falling in the
        realm of values and attitudes; the fewest, in awareness of a
        space-time setting or field."

973. Ewing, D. B. The relations among anomie, dogmatism, and
selected personal-social factors in asocial adolescent boys. Journal
of Social Issues, 1971, 27 (4), 159-169.

        Studied black, Mexican, and white American high school boys to
        examine relations between observed asocial behavior and anomie,
        dogmatism, and selected personal-social variables. Hypotheses
        were predicted on the assumptions that belief systems of
        anomic adolescent boys would center about a dim world view,
        indicating closed-mindedness (dogmatism); and that such boys

would be more likely than their counterparts to pursue illegitimate goals in order to reduce their anomic condition.
The study investigates whether boys who exhibit observed
asocial school behavior also manifest high anomie, dogmatism,
and self-reported asociality (tested pre-delinquency).

974. Fodor, E. M. Moral judgment in Negro and white adolescents.
Journal of Social Psychology, 1969, 79 (2), 289-291.

25 Negro and 25 white male adolescents were administered the
Kohlberg Interview Schedule in order to assess level of moral
judgment, and also the Cornell Parent Behavior Description.
Data analysis revealed no difference in level of moral judgment by race. When Moral Judgment scores for all 50 subjects
were examined in terms of amount of education received by the
mother, analysis disclosed that those boys whose mothers
had completed the twelfth grade or had attended college received significantly higher scores than did those whose mothers
did not complete high school. The only parent behavior dimension which exhibited any relation to level of moral judgment
was that of Instrumental Companionship. Those subjects whose
questionnaire responses placed them above the median on
Instrumental Companionship received significantly lower Moral
Judgment scores than did those falling below the median on
this dimension.

975. Fox, D. J. and Jordan, V. B. Racial preference and identification of black, American Chinese and white children. Genetic Psychology Monographs, 1973, 88 (Second Half), 229-286.

The current validity of the Clark and Clark findings of black
children's negative racial preference and identification was
assessed and Clark's paradigm was extended to American Chinese
and white children in order to generate a tri-racial group
comparison of racial preference, identification and awareness.
The Clarks' test of racial preference and identification was
administered to 360 black, 360 American Chinese, and 654 white
children who ranged in age from 5 through 7 and attended integrated or segregated schools in New York City. The findings
revealed that a majority of black children preferred and
identified with their own racial group, reflecting a significant reversal of the pattern observed by the Clarks. In
fact, the pattern of own-race preference and identification
manifested by black children was similar to that shown by
white children, while American Chinese children demonstrated
significantly less own-race preference and identification
than either black or white children. On the racial awareness and identification scores, significant relationships
between age and type of school were observed among some of
the racial groups. For black children, skin color was significantly related to both preference and identification, with
light skinned black children manifesting less own-race preference and identification than either medium or dark skinned
black children. No relationship between black and American
Chinese children's own-race preference or identification and
academic achievement in school was observed.

976. Frazier, E. F. Children in black and mulatto families. American Journal of Sociology, 1933, 39, 12-29.

Basing his work on an analysis of the 1910 and 1920 statistics for children in over 13,000 Negro families in three cities and three rural counties in the South, the author studied the mooted question of the hereditary inferiority of the mulatto. On the whole, the mulattoes have a smaller proportion of families without children and there is on the average a larger number of children in the mulatto families. Further analysis of the 1910 statistics for the number of children born and living in 10,921 families showed: (a) mulattoes and blacks had about the same proportion of families in which no children were born; (b) on the whole, the mulattoes and blacks in the same community had the same average number of children born; (c) a larger proportion of black families had one or more children dead; (d) the blacks had lost on the average a larger number of children; (e) the mulattoes had about 7% more of all their children living than the blacks. Differences in the socioeconomic status of these two groups as reflected in literacy and home-ownership seemed to point to cultural rather than biological causes for the differences between them.

977. Frazier, E. F. Ethnic family patterns: The Negro family in the United States. American Journal of Sociology, 1948, 53, 435-438.

Loss of African cultural heritage and the requirements of slavery caused the Negro family to develop as a natural organization with the mother as head. After emancipation the family tended to assume an institutional character among those elements which had taken over the familial mores of the whites and those who had become homeowners. Urbanization especially since World War I, has caused considerable disorganization since the family which evolved among Negroes could not function efficiently in the city. Important differences in the organization of family and its approximating to the American pattern are related to the energy class structure.

978. Frazier, E. F. The Negro family and Negro youth. Journal of Negro Education, 1940, 9, 290-299.

The efficacy of the Negro family as a socializing agency is a complex problem. In addition to the differences in the economic and social states of the Negro in various areas, there are even greater differences in the larger social organization which affect the development and states of the Negro family.

979. Frazier, E. F. Problems and needs of Negro children and youth resulting from family disorganization. Journal of Negro Education, 1950, 19, 269-277.

The Negro father has failed to assume his role in family life so that nearly a fifth of the Negro children must depend upon the mother for economic support. Of greater importance yet,

however, is the absence of masculine identification and of
family traditions. Their lack hampers the establishment of
a code of behavior; and discipline is inconsistent if not
entirely absent. The mobility of the Negro further adds to
family disorganization. The lack of socializing influence
on the part of the family sets the potential for juvenile
delinquency, since community institutions such as the school,
religion, etc., do not have the organizing and identification
values that they do for children from normal family homes.

980. Freeman, H. R., Schockett, M. R., and Freeman, E. B. Effects
of gender and race on sex-role preferences of fifth grade children.
Journal of Social Psychology, 1975, 95 (First Half), 105-108.

The effects of gender and race on sex-role preferences of fifth
grade children were examined. 29 white and 14 black fifth
grade American students categorized 15 words as either masculine or feminine items. The subjects then rated the degree
to which they liked each item. Results show that girls significantly preferred items associated with their own sex,
whereas boys were more ambiguous in their choices. Furthermore, girls assigned significantly less value to masculine
items than boys assigned to feminine items. No significant
effect due to race was found.

981. Frumkin, R. M. and Brandyburg, M. S. Expected versus actual
social behavior of Negro adolescent girls in a southern rural community. Journal of Negro Education, 1954, 23, 197-200.

Very little difference was found between actual behavior of
girls and expected behavior of parents and community. Significant differences did occur in two areas: (a) kissing and
petting with boys; and (b) going to juke joints. Auther felt
these activities resulted because of a lack of recreational
programs for adolescents. (Modified.)

982. Fulcher, D. and Perry, D. G. Cooperation and competition in
interethnic evaluation in preschool children. Psychological Reports,
1973, 33 (3), 795-800.

Factors which have been successful in altering interethnic
perception in adults were studied to determine if they might
be applied successfully to changing interethnic evaluations
in very young children. White preschoolers in Queensland
were administered a pretest of attraction towards black
aboriginal children. Children classified as high, medium or
low in prejudice either cooperated or competed with a black
picture playmate (or were assigned to a control group). Results from a post experimental test of attraction indicated
that children cooperating with their black partner significantly decreased their prejudice. There were no differences
attributable to levels of initial attitude.

983.   Furstenberg, F. F. Jr.   Premarital pregnancy among black teenagers.   Trans-Action, 1970, 7 (7), 52-55.

> The issue whether there is "a culture of poverty" or whether
> poor people are different is examined through data on black
> unmarried pregnant girls admitted for prenatal services to
> Sinai Hospital during 1966-1968.   The feelings and reactions
> of these girls to the discovery that they were pregnant were
> studied.   One girl in seven indicated that she was happy
> about becoming pregnant.   65% reported that they were both
> unhappy and incredulous.   Their most common explanation was
> that they thought the pregnancy would upset their parents.
> They did seem to be more positive about being pregnant when
> they thought that their close friends approved of their preg-
> nancy.   But this association was not very high.   The closer
> a girl was to marriage, the happier she was about the preg-
> nancy.   More than 33% of the girls planned to marry the father
> of the child.   But many girls said they wanted to postpone
> marriage because they felt that at the present time it offered
> them so little.   Many stated that they would have used birth
> control, had it been available to them.   Over 90% said that
> they did not "know enough about birth control."   95% of the
> mothers were "very sure" that they would like their daughters
> to be in a "medical program which would provide different
> methods of birth control."   Most girls who are in a birth
> control counseling program by Sinai Hospital for pregnant
> girls and who remain sexually active after their child is
> born, are using contraception regularly.   Repeat pregnancy
> is being significantly reduced among them as a result.   Reprinted
> by permission.

984.   Gabbard, A. V. and Coleman, A. L.   Occupational and educational
goals of low income children in Kentucky, 1969 and 1975.   Washington,
D. C.:   Department of Agriculture, Report No. RS-49, May 1976.   Also,
see ERIC Abstracts, No. ED-127-079, 1976.

> Changes in the occupational and educational aspirations and
> expectations of fifth and sixth grade children over a 6-year
> period were studied.   In 1969, a questionnaire was administered
> to 355 students from four rural mountain schools and three
> urban schools in low income areas in three Kentucky counties.
> In 1975, 199 students from the same rural mountain schools
> and 292 from three Fayette County schools serving low income
> areas were given the same questionnaire.   Both years, the urban
> sample was half black and half white, whereas the rural Appa-
> lachian sample was all white.   The questionnaire consisted
> of questions about the students' aspirations and expectations,
> influence of various people on their future plans, and their
> parents' influence on their educational goals.   Some findings
> were: expectations were lower than aspirations both years;
> in 1969 only 27.8% of the black males and 25.0% of the white
> urban males aspired to profession-technical jobs, while in
> 1975, 58.7% and 46.3% respectively did; in 1975 black urban
> males projected higher career and educational goals than in
> 1969; white rural boys projected much lower goals in 1975;
> in 1975 females still projected higher educational and occupa-

tional status levels than did the boys; and black girls indicated higher parental aims, up from 74% to 82%.

985. Gable, P. and Heckel, R. V. The effect of race and apparent
reward magnitude in modeling behavior in black and white children.
Journal of Clinical Psychology, 1974, 30 (2), 223-225.

The effect of race and apparent reward magnitude on modeling
behavior was studied in black and white children, 8-12 years
old. Control subjects showed a reliable tendency to choose
the larger of two boxes when they were presented. When a
model (M) was present, a majority of subjects imitated and
chose the same boxes as the M. Neither race of the subject
or the M nor box color appeared to affect significantly the
subject's choice. On the basis of findings concerning the
tendency to imitate and the significance of the magnitude of
reward, it may be assumed the subjects were uncertain whether
to choose an object associated with a high reward value because
of its size or whether to choose based on cues from the Ms.
A further clarification of the color factor might be provided
by having all subjects each view two films, one that used a
black model and one that used a white model. This would provide the effect of determining a preferred model in a choice
situation.

986. Gaier, E. L. Adolescence: The current imbroglio. Adolescence,
1969, 4 (13), 89-110.

An essay on the conflicts of adolescence including Negro-white
and rural-urban contrasts.

987. Gerson, W. M. Mass media socialization behavior: Negro-
white differences. Social Forces, 1966, 45 (1), 40-50.

A comparative analysis of differences between 351 Negro and
272 white adolescents in their uses of the media as an agency
of socialization. Two socialization behaviors were measured:
(1) media reinforcement; and (2) media norm acquiring. Data
indicate that more Negro than white adolescents were media
socializers. The interpretation suggests that many Negro
adolescents use the mass media to learn how to behave like
whites (behave in socially acceptable ways). (Modified.)

988. Gist, N. P. and Bennett, W. Jr. Aspirations of Negro and white
students. Social Forces, 1963, 42 (1), 40-48.

Occupational and educational aspirations of 873 Negro (N) and
white (W) high school subjects were studied and compared. The
plans (or 'realistic' expectations) of the subjects were also
investigated. No difference was found between N and W aspirations or plans for occupation or education, per se. But N's
revealed higher mobility aspirations than W's, as measured over
a revised North-Hatt scale. N girls showed particularly high
mobility aspirations. An extension of the study examined
social influences on educational and occupational aspirations,

and found, as predicted, evidence of strong maternal influence
among N's. Actual maternal influence was not as strong among
W's, but both W and N samples reported high attempted maternal
influence. The N's reported fathers, in general, more influential than mothers. Chi-square tests were applied to all relevant comparisons, and percentage tables are presented. Reprinted
by permission.

989. Gitter, A. G., Mostofsky, D. I., and Satow, Y. The effect of
skin color and physiognomy on racial misidentification. Journal of
Social Psychology, 1972, 88 (1), 139-143.

Examined the effects of race, sex, and age of black and white
4- to 6-year-olds (N=80) on racial misidentification. Subjects
were shown six slides of dolls differing in skin color (light,
medium and dark) and anthropologically-based physiognomy
(white, mulatto, and black). Race and sex effects were significant for both color and physiognomic misidentification.

990. Gitter, A. G. and Quincy, A. J. Race and sex differences among
children in perception of emotion. CRC Report, Boston University,
1968, 27, 26.

Utilized a 2 x 2 x 2 factorial design to investigate the
effects of race of expressor (3 Negro and 3 white adults),
and race and sex of perceiver (40 white and 40 Negro 4- to
6-year-old males and females) on perception of emotion (POE)
in children. Perception of anger, happiness, surprise, and
pain was analyzed in terms of three scores as dependent
variables (DVs): (a) overall accuracy scores; (b) correct
perception of individual emotions scores; and (c) erroneous
perception of individual emotion scores. Results indicate insignificant main and interaction effects for all of the DVs.
Theoretical implications of the impact of cultural forces on
POE are discussed.

991. Gitter, A. G., Satow, Y., and White, A. Racial misidentification, skin color, and physiognomy. CRC Reports, Boston University,
1968, 33, 24.

Examined the effects of race, sex, and age of 80 4- to 6-year-
old Negro and white children on racial misidentification. Both
skin color and physiognomy of stimuli (9 male and 9 female
dolls) were varied. Race and sex effects were significant for
both color and physiognomic misidentification.

992. Glazer, N. Y. and Creedon, C. F. (Eds.). Children and Poverty:
Some Sociological and Psychological Perspectives. Chicago: Rand
McNally and Company, 1968. 328 pp.

This book explores the relationship between social institutions
and social and psychological characteristics of poor children.
Part I discusses concepts which are useful in understanding
the current interest in poverty. Questions are raised about
the theoretical models of man underlying current social science
theory. Professor Robert K. Merton's article on relative depri-

vation aids in understanding the relationship between the
civil rights movement and the elimination of poverty. In
Part II the poor present their life experiences in Harlem,
Mississippi, and other locales. Part III evaluates contemporary perspectives on poverty and specifies the distinguishing characteristics of the poor. S. M. Miller's article
develops a typology of the lower class which identifies
four groups: the stable poor, the strained, the copers, and
the unstable. Roy Lubove explores the assumption of social
workers that poverty is due to individual character defects.
Part IV discusses the impact of poverty on the personality
systems of children, their ability to learn, and their capacity to engage in demanding tasks. Part V examines American
institutional arrangements which lock children out of the social
mainstream. Social-psychological effects of major institutions on poor children are considered.

993. Globetti, G. A comparative study of white and Negro teenage
drinking in two Mississippi communities. Phylon, 1967, 28 (2), 131-
138.

Questionnaire responses anonymously supplied by 314 white and
214 Negro high school students indicated a pervasive normative
pattern concerning the use of intoxicants by adolescents. Both
subgroups were influenced similarly by community of residence,
sex, school grade, socioeconomic status, and religious behavior. However, adult Negroes exerted a greater control than
whites over the drinking behavior of their youth. This sample
does not fit the stereotype of lower class Negro drinking
habits. Further study is required for the middle class Negro.

994. Goff, R. M. Some educational implications of the influence of
rejection on aspiration levels of minority group children. Journal of
Exceptional Education, 1954, 23, 179-183.

Social pressure of rejection as it acts as a barrier to effective intellectual and social functioning was studied by interviews with 120 children in two age groups, 6- to 8-year-olds,
and 12- to 14-year-olds. Questions centered around successes or
failures in competitive out-of-school games and sports, ranking
self in relation to in-school academic performance; ambitions,
aspirations and major wishes. Trends revealed feelings of
confidence expressed, positive attitudes of competence, ambition directed toward occupations which yield economic returns,
wishes in terms of further self-enhancement.

995. Gold, A. R. and St. Ange, M. C. Development of sex-role
stereotypes in black and white elementary school girls. Developmental
Psychology, 1974, 10 (3), 461.

Examined the effect of race on degree of stereotyping. 20
first and 20 third grade girls (half from each grade were
black and half were white) answered 20 questions about characteristics usually considered typical of one or the other
of the sexes. Both races gave equally stereotyped responses

to questions about children, but blacks gave fewer stereotyped responses than whites to questions about adults. The
bearing of the results on theories of the development of
sex-role stereotypes is discussed.

996. Goodman, M. E. The education of children and youth to live
in a multi-racial society. Journal of Negro Education, 1951, 19,
399-407.

In a study of 100 nursery children four years of age it was
found that Negro children were more often highly sensitized
to race than white children and furthermore their reactions
differed qualitatively. This was determined through interviews, observations and projective tests. Older and brighter
children of either group tend to be more alert to racial
differences and show a greater readiness for social contact.
Degree of pigmentation was strongly associated with race
awareness. The solution to the discrimination problem is
education for human race relations which should consist
of a uniform and permissive teacher in a flexible curriculum, the teaching of objective and rational thought patterns,
and the utilization of social and psychological insights.

997. Goodman, M. E. Evidence concerning the genesis of interracial
attitudes. American Anthropologist, 1946, 48, 624-630.

White and Negro children of a Boston nursery school were
studied with reference to racial self-identification and
distinction in sociocultural patterns with reference to
race. Negroes made fewer identification of themselves in dolls
than whites and showed aesthetic preference for white characteristics. Though more than half of all children distinguished dolls on the basis of color, children at this age
did not consider color a bar to social intercourse. Children
with personal tension tended to utilize the racial channels
as a basis for aggression.

998. Goodman, M. E. Race Awareness in Young Children. Cambridge,
Massachusetts: Addison Wesley Press, 1952. viii + 280 pp.

The personal and social background of 103 colored and white
nursery school children is described. Even before five years
of age, the personalities of Negro children may be affected
by the discrimination of our society. "We have observed
higher levels of activity, emotionality, sensitiveness, gre-
gariousness, competitiveness" among them and an absence of
lethargy and apathy that is supposed to be characteristic
of adults. The author concludes that to create an America
for everybody, more people must be concerned with teaching
democracy to young children. Means of showing children that
color and race can be talked about openly and rationally,
and suggestions for helping victims to meet prejudice are
outlined.

999. Gottfried, N. W. and Seay, B. Early social behavior: Age and
sex baseline data from a hidden population. Journal of Genetic Psychology, 1974, 125 (1), 61-69.

    The influences of age and sex on early social behavior were
    investigated. 37 children aged 3 to 5 in a day care setting,
    and 16 5-year-olds in a Head Start center, were from an
    impoverished, rural background. Most of the subjects were
    black. With the use of a standard observational category
    system, individuals were observed while in a 15-minute play
    session in three child groups homogeneous as to age and sex.
    Results for 14 object-directed and nine peer social categories
    indicate males and older children engage more frequently
    in peer social activity. However, no pattern of age or
    sex effects was found for object directed behavior. Of
    special importance were the higher scores for verbalization
    for boys in both samples.

1000. Gottlieb, D. Poor youth do want to be middle class but it's
not easy. The Personnel and Guidance Journal, 1967, 46, 116-122.

    This paper explores certain goals and values held by poor
    youth and identifies some of the factors that appear to aid
    or block the goal attainment process. From a sample of 1,327
    male adolescents (Caucasian and Negro) between the ages of
    16-18 who were enrolled in the Job Corps, data were obtained
    that suggest that these youth aspire to a style of life that
    resembles that of the middle class. Perceptions and comments
    of these youth do not tend to support the proposition that
    the lower class culture has a built-in set of values that
    discourage social mobility. Rather it would appear that
    lower class parents, while having the desire to have their
    children succeed, lack the abilities important to facilitate
    movement into more advantageous social positions.

1001. Gray, S. The vocational preferences of Negro school children.
Journal of Genetic Psychology, 1944, 64, 239-247.

    The subjects of this study were 797 Negro children enrolled
    in the first six grades in elementary schools in Tennessee
    and North Carolina. The four outstanding vocational pre-
    ferences of the boys were: doctor, farmer, carpenter and
    teacher. The occupational choice of teacher gained with
    age of pupil. Other occupations listed by the boys repre-
    sented fairly wide fields of interest, mostly not higher than
    the skilled-labor level. Teaching, nursing, beauty-parlor
    work and domestic service accounted for four-fifths of the
    occupational choices of the girls.

1002. Greenberg, E. S. Black children and the political system.
Public Opinion Quarterly, 1970, 34 (3), 333-345.

    Accumulated literature on the political socialization of
    children indicates the existence of a homogeneous, consensual,
    and supportive socialization process in the United States.

Social reality since 1965 shows a contradictory picture of
social conflict in American cities. This study examines the
possibility of a difference in the socialization of black
and white children, posits a divergent model of development,
and uses public schools in Philadelphia and Pittsburgh as the
source of data. In both cities, an elementary school and a
junior high school representing black lower class, black middle
class, white lower class, and white middle class were selected
on the basis of neighborhood characteristics as the determination of social class. Children were sampled from grades 3, 5,
7, and 9 by a questionnaire dealing with the child's orientation to abstract items. A small but significant difference
was shown between the white and black child's support of the
political system; black children became less supportive of the
system as they grew older, confirming the hypothesis of a
divergent model for the two racial groups. Disaffection was
particularly strong for black, lower class males. The results of this study challenge the assumptions of persistence
in political socialization and its use to stabilize and maintain the current political system. The acquisition of and
change in attitudes is not homogeneous in groups defined by
race.

1003. Greenberg, E. S. Children and government: A comparison
across racial lines. Midwest Journal of Political Science, 1970,
14 (2), 249-275.

The socialization of black and white children to governmental
orientations, i.e., children's evaluation of government and
judgments as to their own relationship to it, were studied
via a questionnaire survey among 980 children in grades 3
through 9. Aspects measured were: attitude of good-will
toward the government, perception of government's paternalism-
benevolence, distinctions in attitudes and perceptions regarding different levels of government (Federal, state, city),
and seeing oneself as a subject of government vs. a participant in government. Both black and white children fail to
see government very clearly in the lower grades. The greatest racial disparities appear in children's assessment of
government benevolence. Black children show serious declines
between the third and seventh grades but then rally during
the junior high school years. These patterns are most accentuated regarding the national government, especially among
the most perceptive black children. Environment and political events seem to have a great impact of children's political orientations. Awareness of the deprivation around them
but later information about favorable government activities
seems to account for the pattern of decline and recovery.
4 tables; 8 figures. Reprinted by permission.

1004. Greenberg, E. S. Children and the political community: A comparison across racial lines. Canadian Journal of Political Science,
1969, 2 (4), 471-492.

An analysis of black and white children's orientations toward
the American political community. Data were collected in Phila-

delphia in the Spring of 1968. As predicted, black and white children differ significantly in the development of both cognitive and affective orientations. While all children basically conform to the "center-periphery" pattern of cognitive development, black children progress more slowly, and further, see the local community as particularly salient. Children of the two races differ as well in their regard for the United States. While white children maintain consistently high support through the grades, black children manifest a decline in affect for America as they grow older. The data suggest that as the black child moves from the third through the ninth grade he simultaneously increases the accuracy of his cognitions of the political community and decreases the levels of his affect. He moves from an orientation that is very favorable with respect to a vague and diffuse community, to a more accurate perception of the nature of the political communities of which he is a member, but with increasing levels of disaffection. In effect, cognition and affect for the political community move in opposite directions. Reprinted by permission.

1005. Greenberg, E. S. Orientations of black and white children to political authority figures. Social Science Quarterly, 1970, 51 (3), 561-571.

Lack of research is noted in the political socialization literature in general and the child-authority literature in particular regarding American subcultures. Previous research suggests three dominant themes: (1) Young children in Western democracies idealize authority figures. (2) Idealization can be traced to feelings of anxiety and helplessness in young children and their consequent need to see authority positively. (3) Idealization of authority figures is the mechanism by which the child first forms stable links to the political system. The political socialization patterns of black and white children regarding authority figures are compared in this context. 980 public school students from grades 3, 5, 7, and 9 in Philadelphia were given a questionnaire. Findings show that both black and white children are likely to be highly supportive of authority figures in the lower grades, but this support suffers serious erosion in the upper grades. The policeman had a relatively much stronger position than the President among younger children of both races. Black and white children above grade 3 sharply diverged: black children declined in affect for the President much more quickly than white children, but by grade 9 were overtaken by their white peers. The frequency of hostility expressed toward President L. B. Johnson was shocking. Black children beyond grade 3 showed an unambiguous decline in role-related judgments regarding both the President and the policeman. White students by comparison maintained a substantial appreciation for the role attributes of the President. Data support the vulnerability-idealization hypothesis in previous literature and suggest that maturing black children come to perceive the President as a kind of benign grandfather figure. The initial attachment of the black child to the police becomes eroded rapidly after grade 3. Longitudinal data are needed. Reprinted by permission.

1006. Greenberg, E. S. The political Socialization of black children."
In E. S. Greenberg (Ed.), Political Socialization, pp. 178-190. New
York: Atherton, 1970.

    The black child lags behind his white counterpart in his ability
    to identify the American political community and relate the
    various levels. Children of both races learn first about the
    neighborhood, then the city, then the state, then the nation,
    as suggested by Piaget. Black children move through this
    general process at a much slower rate and retain strong cogni-
    tive ties to the local community. This finding of a study made
    in Philadelphia in 1968 is important because the older black
    child manifests growing disaffection for the local level of
    political organization. In general, the black child experiences
    an erosion of his early positive diffuse support for most of
    the elements of the political system. Lower class children are
    far less supportive than those of the middle class. Older
    black children seem to gain a renewed sense that the national
    government is important, helpful, and benevolent, but by
    the ninth grade the black child's assessment of America,
    state and local government, and the police suffers serious
    damage. While this is generally true for white children, too,
    the trends are clearly more pronounced for blacks.

1007. Greene, J. F. and Zirkel, P. A. The validation of a scale
designed to measure cultural attitudes. See ERIC Abstracts, No.
ED-117-246, 1975. 12 pp.

    This document comprises two papers. The stated purpose of the
    first paper was to describe the development of the "Cultural
    Attitude Scales" (CAS), a pictorial measure designed to assess
    attitudes toward the black, Puerto Rican, and Anglo-American
    cultures. The development of the CAS encompassed: (a) the
    derivation of an item pool from interviews and discussions
    with parents, pupils, and teachers of each of the target
    cultural groups; (b) systematic selections by a group of
    adolescent student judges representing each of the target
    cultures; and (c) item analysis based on the responses of
    336 students in the elementary grades representing these
    three cultures. The end product was a scale of 15 pictorial
    items for each of the three cultures with Likert-type response
    options in the form of faces. The stated purpose of the
    second paper was to report a study designed to determine
    the reliability and validity of the CAS using a sample of
    330 Anglo-American, black American, and Puerto Rican pupils
    in grades 1-6. Evidence of construct validity was revealed
    in the pattern of the mean scores for each cultural group
    in the same sample of pupils. Evidence of criterion validity
    was revealed in terms of its statistically significant rela-
    tionship to the results of a teacher rating scale (r=.32 to
    .46).

1008. Greenwald, H. and Oppenheim, D. Reported magnitude of self-
misidentification among Negro children, artifact? Journal of Personality and Social Psychology, 1968, 8, 49-52.

        Methodological aspects of previous racial doll studies
        prompted a replication with certain changes: white as well
        as Negro children were given a choice of three.

1009. Gregg, H. D. Non-academic and academic interests of Negro
high school students in mixed and separate schools. Journal of Negro
Education, 1938, 7, 41-47.

        A questionnaire study of 2,127 Negro students in 42 Ohio
        schools indicated that the development of interests depends
        to a certain extent upon whether a mixed or colored insti-
        tution is attended. Interests and the percentage of boys and
        girls in both schools engaged by them are listed.

1010. Gross, D. A developmental program in the black community: A
critical appraisal. Journal of Black Studies, 1975, 127-135.

        In a southern U. S. city a Federally funded summer program
        was established to develop a sense of awareness, organization
        and application to the environment for seventh and eighth
        grade black students from a lower income neighborhood. Occu-
        pational therapy objectives were to provide for individual
        success, peer group interaction, and community exploration.
        It was found that individualized, sexually differentiated
        activities conducted within a small group context were most
        successful and popular with participants. Changes in group
        participants were evidenced via decisions to enter college
        as opposed to obtaining only a high school degree, awareness
        of a greater variety of vocational and educational alterna-
        tives available, and positive group cohesion developing within
        each group.

1011. Grossack, M. M. Attitudes toward desegregation of southern
white and Negro children. Journal of Social Psychology, 1957, 46,
299-306.

        Subjects were 136 Negro and 90 white ninth and tenth graders
        in Little Rock, Arkansas, tested in December 1954 and January
        1955. An open-ended questionnaire was given. It showed
        Negro children more favorable to desegregation than whites,
        with a definite white minority favoring desegregation. Both
        groups see adults favoring segregation. (Modified.)

1012. Grow, L. J. and Shapiro, D. Adoption of black children by
white parents. Child Welfare, 1975, 54 (1), 57-59.

        A three-year study of adoption of black or part-black children
        by white parents is reported. The study focused on 125 chil-
        dren who were at least six years of age at the time of follow-
        up and who had been in their adoptive homes at least three
        years. The data collected cover a wide range of topics about

the child, the family and the neighborhood, general social
attitudes and attitudes on racial issues. The child's behavior and adjustment are emphasized, with attention to her
or his racial awareness and sense of identity. The predominant picture that emerges is that of healthy and well adjusted children, aware of their heritage, living with parents
who were highly satisfied with their adoption experience.
However, 27 cases or 23% were identified as presenting
serious difficulties. The success rate of 77 is approximately the same as that of a number of studies that have
examined conventional white infant adoption as well as adoption of older children and other racial groups.

1013. Grow, L. J. and Shapiro, D. Black Children-White Parents: A
Study of Transracial Adoption. Child Welfare League of America, 1975.
vii + 239 pp. Also: Transracial Adoption Today: Views of Adoptive
Parents and Social Workers. Child Welfare League of America, 1975.
v + 91 pp.

Transracial adoption, the placement of black children in
white adoptive homes, is a social phenomenon generally preci-
pitated by the climate of the civil rights movement of the
1960s. These monographs are separate reports of two related
research projects aimed at studying transracial adoption.
Black Children-White Parents: A Study of Transracial Adoption
is a descriptive outcome study of 125 black or part-black
children, at least 6 years of age who had lived in white
adoptive homes for at least 3 years. Noting the children's
adjustment at home, in school, and in the community as well
as the children's awareness of their racial heritage, Grow
and Shapiro studied families in six communities around the
country and in Montreal. The collected data included joint
and individual interviews with the parents, personality
test results for the adoptees, extensive parent and teacher
questionnaires, and interviewer ratings. Indicating that
the large majority of adoptions in their study were apparently
successful, the authors conclude that "we should not reject
the alternative of adoption of black children by white parents."
The first study was conceived at a time when transracial
adoption was an increasingly vigorous trend; Transracial
Adoption Today: Views of Adoptive Parents and Social Workers,
by the same authors, is a report of a substudy of "current"
transracial adoption placement, a practice which, as a result
of strong criticism, has declined considerably. The second
study focuses on the experiences of 38 sets of prospective
adoptive parents with social agencies and on their social
workers' perceptions of the placement procedures. In addition, transracial adoption attitudes and opinions of professional adoption staff members in the various agencies were
gathered. The second monograph will be particularly useful
to personnel in adoption agencies and public officials who
demand a data base before implementing changes in their adoption practices -- pre- and post-placement. Grow and Shapiro
have presented an extensive amount of interview data in a
clear, highly readable format. Effectively organized into

chapters with appropriate subheadings, the two monographs
are written in a lucid, interesting style. Using many tables
to document their findings, the authors develop their conclusions based on a logical presentation of the data. The
reader is warned of methodological flaws in the studies and
the need to restrain from inappropriate generalizations. For
the reader who is less interested in the detailed analyses,
excellent summaries are provided. These important works will
be valuable sources to a wide range of professionals interested
in the highly controversial phenomenon of transracial adoption. While many questions remain about the long-range impact
of transracial adoption on the psychological development
of the black children and their identity, as well as on the
families and society at large, Grow and Shapiro have provided us with an initial description of the placement of
black children in white family settings.

1014. Hale, M. L. Black adolescent females' perceptions of feminity.
Smith College Studies in Social Work, 1974, 45 (1), 29-30.

How black adolescent females perceive feminine behavior was
examined. Nine black adolescent females participated in a
series of eight group discussions which focused on what it
means to be a black female. The findings were assessed on
the basis of the discussion material supplemented by a sentence completion questionnaire administered to the participants. The major finding was that the girls exhibited positive attitudes about being black females and did perceive
themselves as feminine although they differed on what constituted feminine behavior. As the group was fairly homogeneous,
the findings suggest that the differences in their definitions of feminine behavior might be related closely to their
family's individual input.

1015. Hall, V. C. and Turner, R. R. Comparison of imitation scores
between two lower class groups and the effects of two warm-up conditions on imitation of the same groups. Child Development, 1971, 42
(6), 1735-1750.

Administered a test devised and used by H. Osser, M. Wang,
and F. Zaid, designed to measure speech imitation and comprehension abilities, to 16 lower class Negro (NLC) and 16
lower class Caucasian (CLC) kindergarten boys. One-half of
the subjects received feedback during warm-up designed to
define "exact imitation". Errors were classified as: (a)
omissions of inflections and words; (b) changes in tense and
number; (c) morphological errors; (d) word substitutions;
(e) importation of words; and (f) transposition of word
order. The CLC and NLC groups were not significantly different in any of the three general measures of deviation
from standard English. The NLC subjects did give significantly more examples of three of five known Negro dialect
deviations. The warm-up had no effect on imitation, nor
was there any evidence found which indicated that accurate
imitation necessarily resulted in accurate comprehension.

The CLC subjects did perform better (p<.10) on the comprehension task.

1016. Hampe, G. D. Adolescent drinking in two rural areas of Mississippi: 1964 and 1975. Paper presented at the Annual Meeting of the
Rural Sociological Society (New York, New York, August 26-29, 1976).
33 pp.   Also, see ERIC Abstracts, No. ED-127-083, August 1976.

The study examined the increase of drinking from 1964 to 1975
among teenagers enrolled in two high schools in different
sociocultural rural areas of Mississippi. The sample was
composed of students in two high schools located in a "wet"
county and a "dry" county. A questionnaire was administered
to 525 students in 1964 and 793 in 1975. Both years, participation was voluntary and respondents completed the quesionnaire in small groups of 25 to 40. The dependent variable,
"drinker", was considered to be a regular user of alcoholic
beverages. Three types of independent variables were used
to measure the amount of change by social categories of
adolescent drinkers: socio-demographic factors (sex, race,
age, and socioeconomic status), religiosity, and parental
and peer influences. Findings included: 60% of the respondents in 1975 were classified as "drinkers" compared to 37.5%
in 1964, and increase of 22.5%; increase in the proportion
of drinkers occurred by sex, race, age, socioeconomic status,
religious behavior, parental attitudes, and peer influence;
the largest increases were for whites, males, and those in
the youngest age group; and religious attitudes and peer influence remained very good predictors of adolescent drinking.

1017. Harnischfeger, A., et al. Early Childhood Socialization and
Social Class Environment. Washington, D. C.: National Institute of
Education (DHEW), 1975. 144 pp.   Also, see ERIC Abstracts, No.
ED-135-457, 1975.

This report of family social class influences on children's
characteristics is based on data from a longitudinal study
of more than 1,000 children, black and white, of various
social backgrounds. The sample was originally selected for
another study (the St. Louis Baby Study) giving only secondary
consideration to social factors. It includes a large number
of lower class black families and is not considered to be
representative of the general American urban population. Data
were collected from the mother, as general family informant
and personal respondent, and from the child. Data on child
and family cover the period from birth through the first year
of school. Child characteristics include physical characteristics, scores on developmental measures, and scores on the
Peabody Picture Vocabulary Test. Family factors include:
family income, parental authority and role, number of siblings
and size of household, paternal stability, maternal employment and age, parental education, and housing. Changes in
maternal attitudes are also examined. The report differen-
tiates between social class (its primary concern) and social
status, attempting to keep parental occupational level, educa-

tion and source of income conceptually distinct. The bulk
of the volume consists of charts, tables and other background
materials. Appendices include materials from an earlier
report dealing with social class configurations of early
childhood socialization.

1018. Harris, H. Development of moral attitudes in white and Negro
boys. Developmental Psychology, 1970, 2 (3), 376-383.

White and Negro boys of four social class levels were compared in maturity of moral attitudes. A Piaget-type interview
was individually administered to 200 9-1/2- to 11-1/2- to 2-
year-old subjects, equally distributed in an eight-cell 2 x 2
analysis of variance design. The interview yielded five
moral attitude scores for each subject. The WISC Vocabulary
Test was also administered. The hypotheses tested were that
maturity of moral attitudes was positively related to: (a)
social class, (b) white race, and (c) vocabulary skills.
Results of (a) were supported on all five subtests (p<.01
on four and p<.05 on one), while (b) was supported on only
two subtests (p<.05 on both). The hypothesis relating to
(c) was supported (p<.01). Complex interrelationships on
the three variables are suggested.

1019. Havelick, R. J. Jr. and Vane, J. R. Race, competency, and
level of achievement: Relationship to modeling in elementary school
children. Journal of Psychology, 1974, 87 (First Half), 53-58.

White and Negro boys observed white and black female models
under two conditions of competency. Results showed that the
high competency model was imitated significantly more than
the low competency model, but the amount of modeling across
all conditions was low. Subjects with school records of
average or below average achievement modeled significantly
more than subjects with records of average or above average
achievement. Questioning revealed that subjects correctly
perceived the competency of the models. White subjects rated
Negro and white models equally competent. Negro subjects
rated the Negro model as significantly more competent, but
imitated the white model significantly more. The prediction
that subjects of the same race as the model would imitate
more than subjects of a race different from the model was
not confirmed.

1020. Heacock, D. R. The black slum child and the problem of aggression. American Journal of Psychoanalysis, 1976, 36 (3), 219-226.

Discusses antecedent conditions of aggression expressed by
black children in urban ghettos. Important factors include
frustration and violence at home, decreased living space,
experience of racial antagonism and discrimination, abuse
at school, constant exposure to danger on the streets, and
the high incidence of deaths caused by fires, crime, and violence within the ghetto. It is suggested that much of the
aggression expressed by the black slum child can be viewed

as an adaptive response to his environment. The clinical history of a black ghetto boy is used to illustrate the significance of these factors in the development of aggressive behavior patterns and the effect of the black slum child's aggression on the psychotherapeutic relationship itself, especially with a white therapist.

1021. Helgerson, E. The relative significance of race, sex and facial expression in choice of playmate by the preschool child. Journal of Negro Education, 1943, 12, 617-622.

Negro and white children in several nursery schools in Minneapolis were presented with eight photographs of children paired in three different groupings for race, sex and facial expression (sober or laughing) and were asked in each case to point out which child of the pair they would choose for a playmate. The sex factor was of greatest significance in choice of a playmate and race second. Children of preschool and kindergarten age chose their own sex more frequently than the opposite sex. Older groups favored an opposite-sex playmate slightly more than the younger group. There was also a decided tendency for the older white children to choose colored playmates less frequently than did the younger children. Facial expression was of little significance although there was a tendency for the younger children to prefer the laughing picture.

1022. Helper, M. M. and Quinlivan, M. J. Age and reinforcement value of sex-role labels in girls. Developmental Psychology, 1973, 8 (1), 142.

In a verbal operant conditioning paradigm with sex-role attributes as reinforcers, black and white first grade (N=40) and fourth grade (N=40) lower class females were shown pictures of animals and were asked questions to be answered by naming one of the animals. After baseline (no reinforcement), one predetermined animal choice was reinforced by examiner's statement, "Girls say that," or "Boys say that." Results support the hypotheses defined as (a) responses defined as feminine would increase in frequency over baseline in both grades; and (b) for first graders only, the decline in response frequency for "Boys say that" would be significantly different from the increase in frequency for "Girls say that".

1023. Henderson, D. H. and Washington, A. G. Cultural differences and the education of black children: An alternative model for program development. Journal of Negro Education, 1975, 44 (3), 353-360.

Presents views of some black social scientists that school behavioral problems of black American children result from conflicts between school and community social control processes (SCP) because of insensitivity to the distinctiveness of black culture. It is proposed that parents become significant within school SCP, and facilitating inter-related activities is suggested.

1024. Henderson, E. H. and Long, B. H. Personal-social correlates of academic success among disadvantaged school beginners. Journal of School Psychology, 1971, 9 (2), 101-113.

A fair proportion of rural southern Negro children do not attain literacy in the primary grades and are educationally handicapped thereafter. Moreover, the usual standardized readiness and IQ tests have proven poor predictors for this group. A study investigated the personal-social character-istics of successful first graders among a sample of these children. The subjects were divided into successful readers, promoted nonreaders, and repeaters. Inasmuch as 56 of the 95 subjects failed to learn to read in the first grade, this study illustrates clearly the extent of the early educational difficulties among Negro children in the rural South. A major implication of the study's findings is that the personal-social correlates of academic success among school beginners involve complex patterns of self-other orientations. The repeaters were found to be shy with the teacher and other children, and presumably express a frightened or hostile withdrawal. Significant changes toward greater academic success for these children could probably only be achieved by warm teacher-pupil relationships and a great deal of individual attention. The picture emerging of the promoted nonreaders suggests an immature overdependent child with a "good child" facade. These children need to be stimulated to act in an exploratory, individual, and self-directed manner. The readers show themselves to be confident enough to move away from their parents as they enter school.

1025. Henderson, R. D. School climate in white and black elementary schools: A comparative study. Urban Education, 1975, 9 (4), 380-399.

An attempt is made to examine school climate differences between white and black elementary schools. A social-psychological frame of reference was utilized. School climate was measured by scales and factors developed from a student questionnaire administered at 16 schools (N=2,743). High achievement level was defined by a score at or above 50, and SES was classified with 49 as the high/low boundary. Data were obtained from a nonrandom sample of 10 white and 6 black urban elementary schools. Design for the study was a 3-way MANOVA with two levels of race, SES, and achievement. Results indicated that black and white schools differed on scales and four factors. Seven scales were considered: reported student press for competition or individual perform-ance; importance of student self-identity or role; academic norms of the school; sense of control; self-concept of aca-demic ability; perceived expectations and evaluations; and reported teacher press for competition or individual perform-ance. Further inquiry into those measures which are differ-ent between races may provide insight into the achievement differential between black and white schools. Reprinted by permission.

1026. Hepler, R. and Stabler, J. R. Children's perception of the
origin of personal evaluations: Broadcast simultaneously from a
white box and a black box. Psychology, 1976, 13 (2), 26-28.

> Conducted an experiment with black and white colored "talk-
> ing boxes" from which positive and negative statements re-
> flecting appraisals of individual subjects were broadcast
> (e.g., "You are a good-looking boy (girl)." "You are a
> winner." "You're stupid." "You are a loser.") 10 positive
> and 10 negative statements were recorded by a Euro-American
> adult male who was not identifiable as to race or sex by
> two samples of children. Subjects were 15 female and 15
> male black and 15 female and 15 male white second graders.
> More positive than negative statements were perceived as
> originating from the white box. The race variable approached
> significance, and inspection of the group means indicated a
> greater tendency for blacks than whites to associate negative
> statements with the white box.

1027. Hess, R. D. The transmission of cognitive strategies in
poor families: The socialization of apathy and underachievement. In
V. L. Allen (Ed.), Psychological Factors in Poverty, pp. 73-92. Chicago: Markham Publishing Company, 1970.

> In the following observations about the impact of poverty
> upon children, the central themes are: first, that children
> in poor families acquire patterns of learning and of rela-
> tionships to authority which are maladaptive for later expe-
> rience in the classroom; second, that these learning styles
> and authority orientations are acquired in the preschool
> years primarily through experience with the environment, of
> which the mother and other family members are the primary
> points of contact; and third, that the patterns of socializa-
> tion in the home are rooted in the social and cultural matrix
> of which the family is a part, and are not amenable to sign-
> ficant remedy without some change in the social structure of
> the community. These themes are considered in the context
> of an inquiry into the relationship between social structure
> and thought, with particular emphasis upon the functional
> connections between the social and cultural conditions in
> which the poor live, the socializing behavior of parents,
> and the consequent educability of young children. These con-
> nections between social structure and individual behavior
> may usefully be considered in terms of: (a) the nature of
> the physical and social environment, (b) the effects of this
> environment upon the adults who interact with small children,
> and (c) the behavioral outcomes that emerge in the child in
> his school achievement and his pattern of interaction with
> the school, its rules, and its representatives. In order to
> give some focus to the discussion, and to the project which
> is described, these comments are applied particularly to urban
> working-class populations.

1028. Hetherington, E. M. Effects of paternal absence on sex-typed
behaviors in Negro and white pre-adolescent males. Journal of Personality and Social Psychology, 1966, 4 (1), 87-91.

    Investigates the effects of race, father absence, and time
    of departure of the father on sex-typed behavior of pre-
    adolescent males. (Modified.)

1029. Hobart, C. W. Underachievement among minority group students:
An analysis and a proposal. Phylon, 1963, 24 (2), 184-196.

    There are four main dimensions to the situation of the minority
    group (Puerto Rican, Negro, Mexican) child: (1) a damaged
    self-concept; (2) inadequate motivation; (3) an unawareness
    of employment opportunities to which he might aspire and for
    which he could train; and (4) resistance by peers and the
    community to self-advancement. This results in significant
    differences in the mean number of school years completed by
    adults of 25+ years of age. According to 1957 Bureau of
    Census figures, 41.1% of white males have graduated from high
    school, while 16.3% of non-white males have finished. 45.1%
    of the white, female population have graduated from high
    school, while 19.3% of non-white females have done the same.
    A program eliminating these four main obstacles to minority
    group advancement would provide for: (a) special attention
    by teachers and the school to bright, minority group students;
    (b) special enrichment plans involving trips to museums, uni-
    versities, industries, etc.; (c) special classroom instruction
    in typewriting; (d) current events materials; and (e) photo-
    graphic equipment to record class events and experiences. The
    families of the youths chosen should be brought together, to
    form a group which can overcome the hostility of the general
    community. The best time to institute such a program is at
    the junior high school level. Reprinted by permission.

1030. Holloway, R. G. and Berreman, J. V. The educational and occupational aspirations and plans of Negro and white elementary school
students. Pacific Sociological Review, 1959, 2 (2), 56-60.

    Difficulties in the interpretation of many studies of aspira-
    tion level suggest the following alternative hypotheses: (1)
    if aspiration level reflects the varying values of class sub-
    cultures, then (a) aspiration level should vary with class,
    and (b) aspiration level should not differ significantly be-
    tween similarly socialized Negroes and whites when class is
    constant. (2) On the other hand, if there is a tendency in
    the face of reality considerations simply to scale down uni-
    formly high aspirations, then (a) aspirations, when measured
    independently of plans, should not differ by race or class,
    (b) there should be no difference between aspirations and
    plans in the white middle class, (c) the Negro middle class,
    and the lower class of both races, should show plans signi-
    ficantly lower than aspirations, and (d) there should be a
    greater difference between plans and aspirations in the Negro
    lower class than in either the Negro middle class or the

white lower class. Data on occupational and educational
aspirations and plans obtained from 313 Negro and white
male pupils in 6th, 7th and 8th grades in three Pacific
Northwest elementary schools gave results as follows: educational aspirations of both classes and both races were
high and essentially equal. Lower class subjects plan
lower than they aspire, but this is not significantly more
true of the Negroes than of the whites. White middle
class occupational aspirations are significantly higher
than those of white and Negro lower class subjects, while
occupational plans do not differ significantly from aspirations in any of the four race-class categories. Results
do not clearly support one and reject the other information
of previous aspiration level researches. Occupational data
point one way while educational data point the other. For
future research, however, the inclination is to look on
plans rather than abstract wishes as a more significant
measure of achievement orientation. Reprinted by permission.

1031. Holmberg, M. C. Social interchanges in the 2nd and 3rd years.
Paper presented at the Biennial Southeastern Conference on Human
Development (4th, Nashville, Tennessee, April 15-17, 1976). 15 pp.
Also, see ERIC Abstracts, No. ED-131-940, 1976.

This study examines the development of cooperative and
negative behavior in a setting in which children of varied
ages had regular opportunities for social encounters. Subjects were 16 children, half 16-19 months, half 28-32 months.
Each child was observed 30 minutes per day for five days.
Behaviors were recorded continuously. A narrative written
record was made distinguishing child and adult interchanges
and specifying who initiated the interchanges. Results
centered around the following questions: (1) How do children in the middle of their second and third years differ
in their social initiations to peers and adults? (2) How
does the age of the peer in the dyad affect these developmental findings? (3) How does the course or dynamics of
the interchange relate to the age of the child? Behaviors
were organized into two broad categories: prosocial and
negative. More prosocial than negative social initiations
were observed. More negative behaviors were observed toward
peers than adults. Older children showed more prosocial
than negative behavior to other 2-1/2-year-old peers.
Younger children showed no reliable difference in type
of behavior initiated to other 1-1/2-year-old peers. In
summary, a basic finding was that the other person in the
dyad was a critical component in the social system.

1032. Horton, C. P., et al. Attitudes of black teenagers and their
mothers toward selected contemporary issues. Journal of Afro-
American Issues, 1976, 4 (1), 172-192. Also, see ERIC Abstracts,
No. EJ-149-136, 1976.

The purpose of this study was to assess the extent to which
a "generation gap" exists in a sample of black adolescents

and their mothers and the extent to which adolescents'
attitudes were related to the time (in terms of adjacent
two-year periods) at which they were measured. The attitudes and opinions of the two generations on the issues
of premarital sex and drug usage were measured using a
comprehensive interview.

1033. Hughes, J. H. and Thompson, G. G. A comparison of the value
systems of southern Negro and northern white youth. Journal of
Educational Psychology, 1954, 45, 300-309.

Following the method developed by R. White, a value-analysis
was made for 88 essays written by school pupils. Northern
white children in a non-segregated school and southern Negro
children in a segregated school tended to place a similar
amount of emphasis on the great majority of values. Knowledge, achievement and economic value were prized highly
and equally by the two groups. As compared with the Negroes,
the white pupils put significantly greater emphasis on
happiness, security and independence and a much lower value-
emphasis on justice and group unity. Negro pupils were
strongly critical of segregation, and were concerned with
social justice in this connection.

1034. Hughes, R. E. and Works, E. The self-concepts of black
students in a predominantly white and in a predominantly black
high school. Sociology and Social Research, 1974, 59 (1), 50-54.

The self-concepts of black students in a predominantly
white and in a predominantly black high school are compared.
The data show that the self-concepts of the black males
in the predominantly black school were more positive than
those of their counterparts in the predominantly white
school, but there was no significant difference for the
black females. There was no significant difference between
the sexes in the predominantly black schools, but there
were slight consistent sexual differences in the predominantly white school in the direction of more positive self-
concepts for females. The findings indicate the possibility that black attendance at a predominantly white school
can have more damaging consequences for some aspects of
the self-concept than black attendance at a predominantly
black school. Results are discussed.

1035. Hunt, D. E. and Hardt, R. H. The effect of upward bound
programs on the attitudes, motivation, and academic achievement
of Negro students. Journal of Social Issues, 1969, 25 (3), 117-128.

Data collected from a national sample of Upward Bound (UB,
a pre-college enrichment program sponsored by the Office
of Economic Opportunity for high school students from low
income families) students were examined to determine whether
the programs produced differential effects among Negro and
white participants. N=213 Negro students and 90 white
students from 21 target programs. A longitudinal analysis

of students who participated in UB programs for two consecutive summers revealed that significant positive changes
occurred in several measures of attitude and motivation,
e.g., feelings of self-esteem and internal control. The
patterns of changes were quite similar for Negro and white
students. When changes in high school grades of UB students
were compared with those of a control group of non-UB high
school students, no significant impact of UB programs could
be detected. However, while both white UB students and
their controls maintained stable grades, both Negro UB
students and their controls showed a decline in grades
over this 18-month period. The findings suggest that while
programs such as Upward Bound can produce significant changes
among Negro and white students in attitude believed relevant
to college success, the alteration of patterns of academic
performance will require innovative programs which represent a continued cumulative effort. Reprinted by permission.

1036. Hutton, J. B. Relationship between teacher judgment,
screening test data and academic performance for disadvantaged
children. Training School Bulletin, 1972, 68, 197-201.

Significant correlations were obtained between three screening tests, teacher judgment ratings and first-grade academic
performance measures for 108 disadvantaged children attending a Head Start project. The results suggested that more
attention be given to teacher judgment measures as means
for screening Head Start children who are most likely to
encounter difficulty in meeting first-grade expectations.

1037. Hyte, C. Occupational interests of Negro high school boys.
School Review, 1936, 44, 34-40.

86.6% of a Negro high school population of 1,248 intend to
finish high school; 69.5% expect to attend college; 68.6%
claimed to have made a definite occupational choice, three-
fourths in the professions. A scatter of remaining choices
is given, also reasons for making choice, agencies influencing choice, and occupations of fathers (12% were professional).

1038. Iscoe, I., Williams, M., and Harvey, J. Age, intelligence
and sex as variables in the conformity behavior of Negro and white
children. Child Development, 1964, 35, 451-460.

Negro and white children at ages 7, 9, 12, and 15 years
were subjected to simulated group pressures. Two criteria
of conformity were employed in a multiple regression technique. The main effect variables of sex, age, race, and
IQ plus simple interactions accounted for 36% of the
variance on Criterion 1 and 26% on Criterion 2. Age and
race were significant main effect variables. Negro females
conformed less than white females. IQ was not a significant variable. The two criteria correlated .76. The

importance of criterion specificity was emphasized. Results were discussed in terms of differential cultural
roles, and the regression analysis model was recommended
for investigation of the relation between personality factors and conformity behavior.

1039. Jacobson, C. K. Separatism, Integrationism and Avoidance
Among Black, White and Latin Adolescents: A Longitudinal Analysis.
Washington, D. C.: National Institute of Education (DHEW), May
1976; and Milwaukee: Language and Area Center for Latin America,
Wisconsin University, May 1976. Also, see ERIC Abstracts, No.
ED-127-398, 1976. 63 pp.

The racial attitudes of junior and senior high school students in Milwaukee were examined for students in integrated
and segregated schools. Black, white, and Latin students
in selected public schools were interviewed in the Spring
of 1974 and reinterviewed in the Spring of 1975. Approach/
avoidance and integration/separatism dimensions emerged
from a factor analysis of racial attitude items. The
dimensions indicate that student reactions to intergroup
school experiences are complex. The social correlates of
both dimensions are presented and the implications of the
two dimensions for continued research on race and ethnic
relations are discussed. Black students in all-black schools
scored more on the avoidance end of the approach/avoidance
dimension, while black students in integrated schools scored
on the approach end. However, the black students in the
all-black schools tended to score on the integration end
of the integration/separatism dimension, while the black
students in the all-black schools tended to score on the
separatism end. The attitudes of the students in the all-
black schools changed towards those in the integrated
schools during the year between interviews. Reasons for
the changes are suggested and partially tested.

1040. Janney, F., Mallory, S., Rositto, R., and Simon, J. Conformity as a function of race and age. Psychological Reports, 1969, 25
(2), 591-597.

Studied the conformity behavior of 16 black and 16 white
male subjects, ages 7 and 11, using the "Asch technique"
in same race and opposite race, 3-member confederate groups.
Data showed that conformity was not a function of the race
of subjects or the confederates. Age of subjects was a significant factor, conformity decreasing as age increased.

1041. Jenkins, W. W. An experimental study of the relationship
of legitimate and illegitimate birth status to school and personal
and social adjustment of Negro children. American Journal of Sociology, 1958, 64 (2), 169-173.

An attempt to determine whether legitimate and illegitimate
Negro children of similar economic status differed significantly in adjustment. For this study, 'adjustment' was

defined as consisting of IQ, age-grade placement, school
absences, teacher's ratings, cumulative grade scores, and
scores on the California Test of Personality. Findings
indicate that the legitimate children rated higher in every
area except one, though significance was reached only on
teacher's ratings and IQ-age correlation; younger illegitimate children rated consistently higher than the older
group, when compared to legitimate children. The results
suggest that birth status may affect the adjustment of
Negro children. Reprinted by permission.

1042. Johnson, C. L. Attitudes toward premarital sex and family
planning for single-never-pregnant teenage girls. Adolescence, 1974,
9 (34), 255-262.

Attitudes of black low income females toward premarital sex
and family planning for single, never pregnant teenagers
were examined via questionnaire. Findings support Vincent's
hypothesis of normative contradiction and reveal that
single and separated respondents approved of premarital sex
and family planning for such teenagers and disapproved of
illegitimacy. This suggests that for groups characterized
by these normative contradictions, illegitimacy rates will
probably decrease as effective contraceptive methods become
accessible to them. In addition, findings indicate that
while married respondents disapproved of premarital sex for
adolescent girls, they disapproved of illegitimacy and
approved of family planning. In terms of a decrease in the
incidence of adolescent pregnancies and births (legitimate
and illegitimate), it appears that program planning and
development for single, never pregnant teenage girls should
be directed more at attitudes toward family planning than
by actual or presumed attitudes towards premarital sex.

1043. Johnson, C. S. Growing Up in the Black Belt: Negro Youth
in the Rural South. Washington, D. C.: American Youth Commission,
American Council on Education, 1941. 360 pp.

The establishment of a more satisfactory relationship between
the Negro and white in this country probably constitutes
the most significant problem which faces the American student of sociality. That such a problem exists is obvious
notwithstanding the ostrich-like attitude maintained by many.
Moreover, if a solution worthy of our civilization is desired, the future modus vivendi of the two races should
not be left to chance but should be the outcome of careful
and dispassionate study. A noteworthy contribution on this
point is made by Johnson in the inquiry on Negro youths
here reported. The investigation was conducted in eight
representative counties of the South, and a sample of over
2,000 youths received a series of personality tests. About
20% of these persons and over 900 families altogether
were interviewed further. The results of this investigation are presented in detail and effectively introduced
by a chapter in which the "profiles" of 10 representative

or typical youths are fully described. The main findings
reveal again that among the factors that hinder the material
and spiritual progress of the Negro the most important
derives from the lack of rapport between the Negro and white,
a situation which inspires the Negro with antagonistic
emotions from fear to hatred towards the white. While
these findings are not surprising they serve to impress
one with the gravity of the problem. However, this work
deserves careful study not only for the results obtained
but also because of the author's methodologic approach
to his study which delineates with a precision not always
achieved for other groups the development of the personality
of the Negro.

1044. Johnson, N. J., Gilbert, N., and Wyer, R. Quality education
and integration: An exploratory study. Phylon, 1967, 28 (3), 221-
229.

The proposition that predominantly Negro high schools in
which the students have a middle class orientation can
provide a high quality education (as measured by their
subsequent performance in college) is explored. Data was
collected on the percentage of Negro students attending
high schools in Metropolitan Chicago from a report in the
Chicago Daily News (1965). The first term grades of 121
Negro and 250 white freshmen students at the University
of Illinois, Chicago Circle, were obtained and tabulated
as a function of the percentage of Negro students in the
high schools they attended. The results suggest the possibility of four theoretical high school settings: (a) predominantly white (70-100%) high school where the students
have a middle class orientation; both Negroes and whites
from this setting performed well in college. (b) Racially
mixed (30-70% in either direction) school where the students
have a lower class orientation; both Negro and white students from this setting did poorly in college. (c) Predominantly Negro (70-100%) school where students have a
lower class orientation; both Negroes and whites from this
setting also performed poorly in college. (d) Predominantly
Negro (70-100%) school where students have a middle class
orientation; both Negro and white students from this setting performed better than those from setting (b) and setting
(c). It is theorized that a middle class orientation and
a lack of interracial conflict facilitated the educational
experience in settings (a) and (d). Further study is needed
to verify the existence of the four settings and their
effects on education. Reprinted by permission.

1045. Johnson, S. B. The effects of tactile communication in
sport on changes in interpersonal relationships between black and
white children. See ERIC Abstracts, No. ED-096-296, August 1973.

This study determines the effects of tactile communication
in sport on changes in interpersonal relationships between
black and white children. The experimental design consisted

of three treatment groups each emphasizing tactile, cooperative, or individual experiences in physical education.
The control group participated in tactile, cooperative, and
individual activities. Subjects, consisting of 235 elementary school children representing four integrated, self-
contained, third-grade classes in two schools, were pretested
by a sociometric rating scale to determine their interpersonal
relationship status with other children. After participating in a 6-week sports unit, the subjects were post-tested
on the same sociometric rating scale. Results indicated
that there is a statistically significant change in a
positive direction in interpersonal relationships of black
children who experience tactile communication with white
children in sport and that there is not a statistically
significant change in a positive direction in interpersonal
relationships of white children who experience tactile
communication with black children in sport.

1046. Johnson, S. R. The role of black glamorous figures in the
ego-ideal formation of black youth. Smith College Studies in Social
Work, 1974, 45 (1), 30-31.

Black television figures as a source of idealization for
black youth were investigated. Male and female youths were
surveyed in a partially structured interview. It was found
that a significant percentage of the idealized figures
chosen were glamorous and black. The black television
figures were chosen mainly because they are comical. Among
females, there was a high percentage of cross-sexual ideal
choices, particularly black television figures, and glamorous figures seemed idealized most between the ages of 8 and
14 years, with a decline of glamorous figure idealization
as age increased.

1047. Jones, F. N. and Arrington, M. G. The explanations of physical phenomena given by white and Negro children. Comparative Psychology Monographs, 1945, 18 (5), 1-43.

Written explanations of 10 physical demonstrations obtained
from 134 white and 161 Negro children in grades 3, 4, 5 and
7 of the public schools of Tuscaloosa, Alabama, were scored
quantitatively for accuracy, and then divided into three
categories: material, non-material, and omitted and "don't
know." In comparison with the white children, the Negroes
were retarded in school grade, in quantitative score on
the test, and in development along the direction of the
age trends within subcategories under the "material" head-
ing. Very few answers from either the white or the Negro
children were classifiable as non-material. It is concluded
that : "(1) In view of the inequalities in scholastic and
other opportunities for our two groups, the differences
obtained were (a) less striking than the similarities, and
(b) readily attributable to environmental causes; and (2)
The Negro children do not tend to be superstitious or supernatural in their approach to concrete situations, either as

compared to the white sample, or in absolute number of
responses."

1048. Jones, J. D., Erickson, E. L., and Crowell, R. Increasing
the gap between whites and blacks: Tracking as a contributory
source. Education and Urban Society, 1972, 4 (3), 339-349.

There are several issues concerning the reasons for and the
consequences of tracking in school. One of the main issues
concerns the mobility of students once they are placed in
tracks. Proponents often argue that the placing of children
into lower tracks does not academically impede them, and
that there is a high degree of mobility likely, with many
students moving up. Opponents of tracking content that to
place a child in an academic track is to fix that student's
level of performance. The primary data reported come from
subpoenaed school records and the court testimony of school
officials. They are utilized to assess placement and mobility
during the junior high school years. The data also consist
of the track placement of one cohort of students over a
three-year period in one of the school system's junior high
schools. Court testimony of school officials indicated
that there was a high degree of mobility of both black
and white students among academic, general and basic tracks.
However, it also appears that certain effects of school
tracking may not be realized when mobility is viewed in
terms of individual mobility instead of in terms of group
mobility. While the tracking system operates primarily in
a downward fashion for both racial groups, it has more of
a negative impact on black children. If equality of educational opportunity is to be achieved, blacks as a group
should experience upward mobility or less downward mobility
than whites; as it is blacks as a group are not only experiencing downward mobility, they are moving downward in
larger porportion than the white group, thereby increasing
the gap between them and white students in the tracking
system studied.

1049. Jones, R. L. Delivery of special services to young black
children. Journal of Non-White Concerns in Personnel and Guidance,
1973, 1 (2), 61-68.

Argues that in planning special services for retarded, disadvantaged, or deprived black children, little attention
has been given to the effects of these labels on the self-
concepts and expecations of the children, and that many
positive aspects of young black children's cognitive,
affective, and life circumstances have not been fully
recognized. Data on these issues are presented and the
need to adjust the current deficiency-oriented view of
black children is emphasized.

1050. Jordan, M. F., Golden, J. F., and Bender, L. D. Aspirations
and Capabilities of Rural Youth. Bulletin 722, Agricultural Experiment Station, University of Arkansas Division of Agriculture, May
1967. 50 pp.

    A battery of tests and questionnaires was administered to
    44 Negro and 121 white senior high school boys in Little
    River and Sevier Counties, Arkansas. A multiple regression
    model was used to test the importance of each variable or
    group of variables under consideration. Data analysis
    indicates the following conclusions: (a) five variables
    significantly related to occupational aspirations are
    mechanical interest, scientific interest, ascendance,
    social class value orientation, and the number of years
    of education and training planned after high school; (b)
    information readily available from school records and inter-
    views was not significantly related to occupational aspira-
    tions; (c) the level of occupational aspirations of the
    senior boys in these two low income counties was similar
    to that of similar groups in high income, more urban areas
    in Michigan; (d) five variables found to be significantly
    related to capabilities are reading speed, reading compre-
    hension, age, race, and the student's estimate of his
    ability for his chosen occupation; (e) reading speed, ascend-
    ance, and sociability were found to be significantly related
    to the discrepancy between aspirations and capabilities;
    (f) the incidence of higher mean discrepancy scores in
    the larger schools may be attributable to their guidance
    and counseling programs and their more adequate basic
    school curricula; (g) wide discrepancies were found between
    the occupational plans of the students and the projected
    U.S. needs for 1970 in some occupational categories; (h)
    education and training programs and occupational informa-
    tion services should consider the inclusion of remedial
    and/or developmental reading in the elementary and secondary
    school curricula, the development of an occupational infor-
    mation unit in each department in the high schools, the
    establishment of guidance services, the development of
    special training programs for students with low capabili-
    ties, and the collection and utilization of test and back-
    ground information in the counseling of program participants.

1051. Kalsie, S., Kalsim, B., and Pargament, R. B. H. Children's
social distance constructs: A developmental study. Proceedings
of the Annual Convention of the American Psychological Association,
1971, 6 (11), 151-152.

    Developmental changes in children's concepts of the normative
    and personal social distance between the sexes and the races
    were assessed with a nonverbal measure for 4,167 black and
    white boys and girls in grades 1-12. Subjects made judgments
    concerning the appropriate distances in race and/or sex
    should be placed from one another, and judgments concerning
    the appropriate distances between the races increased with
    age. Black girls' self-other distances from white and black
    female stimuli changed markedly with age.

1052. Kamii, C. K. and Radin, N. L. Class differences in the socialization practices of Negro mothers. Journal of Marriage and the Family, 1967, 29 (2), 302-310.

Investigates class differences in the socialization practices of Negro mothers in the context of their child rearing goals. Direct observation of mother-child interactions in the homes and a card-sorting method of studying child-rearing goals led to the conclusion that middle and lower-lower class Negro mothers do not differ in their goals, but do in their socialization practices. The relationship of these practices to the development of anaclitic identification, internal controls, and subsequent conformity to society's norms is discussed along with the implication of these conclusions for education.

1053. Kaplan, R. M. and Goldman, R. D. Interracial perception among black, white and Mexican-American high school students. Journal of Personality and Social Psychology, 1973, 23 (3), 383-389.

Interracial perceptions among black, white and Mexican-American high school students are discussed. Results of a survey indicate that black subjects perceived both their white and Mexican-American classmates as dissimilar to themselves, but the Mexican-American subjects did not demonstrate differential perception between themselves and the other two groups. All three groups had relatively vertical perception of how black and Mexican-American students would respond to the questionnaire. Blacks and Mexican-Americans were substantially inaccurate in their perceptions of whites. Data suggests that blacks and Mexican-Americans are more aware of each other's personality characteristics than they are of the characteristics of white students.

1054. Katz, I. Conflict and Harmony in an Adolescent Interracial Group. New York: New York University Press, 1955. iii + 47 pp.

This report is the first of a new research series. This represents a new and promising, although expensive for the purchaser, approach to the publishing of research. Much constructive thought has gone into the physical design of the monograph. The author participated as an observer in an adolescent interracial group created to present plays about racial prejudice to groups in the community. The 39 Negro and white high school students involved seemed to be aware that they were participating in an interracial group with a purpose. Through observations, the recording of social contacts, conversations with the adolescents involved and weekly interviews with the adult leaders, information was obtained about the workings of the group and the interactions taking place within the group. In individual interviews, attitudes of the Negro members were explored in terms of their positive or negative identification with their "own-race." For both Negro and white members of the group, information was obtained relevant to feelings about

the "other-race" and motivational factors in interracial
friendships. Emotional conflicts arising from discrepancies
between behavior norms of the interracial group and norms
of the Negro or white community in which the adolescent
lived were examined. In addition, the author obtained
Rorschach and TAT (condensed version) protocols for 26
members of the group. The author, in Part I, describes the
group and presents anecdotal material with which he analyzes
factors underlying tensions within the group. In Part II,
he discusses racial interactions in the group. Of particular importance is his discussion of the "relation between
degree of intimacy of Negroes and whites and their opinions
about each other" in which, particularly for the white
group, "interracial intimacy was more closely associated
with expressions of negative than of positive sentiments."
Motivational aspects of interracial contacts are then
further discussed along with problems of community disapproval.

1055. Katz, I., Henchy, T., and Allen, H. Effects of race of tester,
approval-disapproval, and need on Negro children's learning. Journal of Personality and Social Psychology, 1968, 8 (1), 38-42.

In this experiment, 148 Negro boys, ages 7 to 10, from low
income neighborhoods in a large northern city were administered individually a social desirability questionnaire and
then a verbal learning task by white and Negro examiners.
Each subject received either approval or disapproval on the
learning task. Subjects performed better on a verbal learning
task with Negro examiners than with white examiners, and
when given approval rather than disapproval. In addition,
the strength of the child's need for approval influences
his reactions to the first two variables in combination.
In order to understand the effects of positive and negative
social reinforcement on verbal learning in Negro pupils,
it is necessary to take into account the need-state of
the individual child and the racial identity of the adult
reinforcer.

1056. Katz, P. A. Perception of racial cues in preschool children:
A new look. Developmental Psychology, 1973, 8 (2), 295-299.

Tested the prediction that young children would experience
more difficulty in learning to discriminate faces of another
race than those of their own. 192 black and white nursery
and kindergarten children were administered a two-choice
discrimination-learning task employing pairs of either
brown, pink-tan, or green faces which varied in shade.
The effect of treatment was significant, and the major
prediction was confirmed for both age groups. Additional
findings reveal that discrimination-learning performance
with racial stimuli was related to a number of factors
including developmental level, race of the subject, and
race of the examiner.

1057. Katz, P. A. Stimulus predifferentiation and modification
of children's racial attitudes. Child Development, 1973, 44 (2),
232-237.

> Tested the prediction that increased perceptual differen-
> tiation of other-group faces could reduce prejudicial atti-
> tudes. Subjects were 96 black and white second and sixth
> grade children who previously obtained high prejudice
> scores on two racial attitude measures (a projective
> prejudice test, and a social distance index). Subjects
> were randomly assigned to one of three training conditions:
> (a) learning distinctive names for photographs of other-
> race faces; (b) making same-different judgments of facial
> pairs; or (c) observing the faces without labels. Race
> of examiner was varied within each group. Attitude tests
> were subsequently readministered and findings confirm the
> hypothesis. Post-test prejudice scores of the labeling
> and perceptual training groups were lower than those of
> the control subjects. Additionally, data show that this
> treatment effect was influenced by both developmental
> level and race of examiner.

1058. Katz, P. A., Johnson, J., and Parker, D. Racial attitudes
and perception in black and white urban school children. Proceedings of the Annual Convention of the American Psychological Association, 1970, 5, 311-312.

> In Experiment I, a battery of tests designed to assess
> racial attitudes was administered to 480 second, fourth
> and sixth graders. Tests with evident social desirability
> responses showed a decline in prejudice attitudes with
> age. In contrast, projective tests revealed racial atti-
> tudes to be constant across age groups. In Experiment II,
> second, fourth, and sixth graders viewed slides of facial
> pairs varying systematically along a number of attributes,
> including color and shade. Subjects assessed the similarity
> of the two faces by means of a continuous motoric scale.
> Results indicate that color was a more dominant cue with
> black examiners. Additionally, an interaction between
> perceptual ratings and ages was obtained with a white exam-
> iner, whereby younger subjects viewed other-race pairs as
> more distinctive, while older subjects judged other-race
> stimuli as more similar.

1059. Katz, P. A., Sohn, M., and Zalk, S. R. Perceptual concomi-
tants of racial attitudes in urban grade-school children. Developmental Psychology, 1975, 11 (2), 135-144.

> Children's racial attitudes and their concomitant perceptual
> responses were investigated in a two-part study using black
> and white children at two racially integrated urban elemen-
> tary schools. In the first phase, a battery of attitude
> tests was administered to second, fourth, and sixth grade
> children. In the second phase, children (classified into
> high and low prejudice groups on the basis of attitude

scores) judged the similarity of pictures of facial pairs.
Stimuli varied as to color (black or white, purple or green),
shade, expression and hair type. Findings indicate that the
various ways of assessing racial attitudes of children were
not equivalent. Some instruments were strongly affected by
developmental and racial factors, whereas others were not.
Correlations between indices were low. Findings on Phase Two
indicate that racial attitudes do have perceptual correlates,
particularly for white children. Race related cues were
accentuated by high prejudice children, whereas non-race
related ones were less salient.

1060. Katz, P. A. and Zalk, S. R. Doll preference: An index of
racial attitudes? Journal of Educational Psychology, 1974, 66 (5),
663-668.

Administered a doll choice task to 96 white and 96 black
nursery and kindergarten children by same- and other-race
examiners. In contrast to earlier studies, male and female
dolls were presented which differed in skin color, not hair
or eye color. The strong preference for white dolls found
by previous investigators was not obtained. Young children
exhibited a slight preference for other-race dolls, although
gender cues were more significant determinants of choice
behavior than were skin color cues. Children's responses
were, in part, a function of examiner's race. Stronger
preferences for same-race dolls were exhibited in the presence of a same-race examiner.

1061. Kee, M. E. W. Many faces: Partners in power. Negro History
Bulletin, 1976, 39 (4), 562-566. Also, see ERIC Abstracts, No.
EJ-142-181, 1976.

Describes an experiment in mutual growth between blacks and
whites in its account of a successful counseling program, a
pilot educational experiment in the early education of inner
city children.

1062. Keig, N. G. The occupational aspirations and labor force
experience of Negro youth. American Journal of Economics and Sociology, 1969, 28 (2), 113-130.

The occupational aspirations and labor force experiences
of 124 Negro youths in a medium size southern city reveals
the gap that exists between the promises and the reality
of civil and economic democracy for Negroes. These Negro
youths were interviewed at the time of their graduation from
an all-Negro high school in 1964. Less than 50% were living
with both parents, the median number of children in the
families was 5.7, and the median years of school completed
by fathers was 7.1 years. The parents were employed primarily
as laborers, private household workers, and as cooks, wait-
resses, and kitchen helpers. The largest number of seniors
(73) expressed interest in professional and managerial occupations, the second largest number (31) in clerical, craft,

and service occupations requiring additional training, and
the third largest number (18) did not know what they wanted
to do. A further analysis of their occupational goals,
however, revealed that the students were traditionally
oriented. They had selected occupations that traditionally
have been opened to Negroes -- teaching, cosmetology, social
work. Only 8 wanted to become engineers, 4 technicians,
and 3 business managers. Furthermore, of the 65 students
who planned to continue their education in the Fall of 1964,
only 1 had selected integrated formerly all-white institutions. Those students who planned to work felt that they
could only get jobs similar to those held by their parents.
In 1966, a follow-up survey was made of the educational
and work experiences of the 82 students who lived in the
city at the time of graduation. Of these students, 27 were
enrolled in college, 26 were working, and 14 were in the
armed forces. Although some of the youths had changed their
occupational goals, few had selected occupations previously
closed to Negroes in this community. With a few exceptions,
the students enrolled in college were attending all-Negro
institutions. Students who were working or had worked
during this two-year period found jobs for the most part in
the traditional service occupations open to Negroes. Although many of the students felt that the Civil Rights Act
had opened new economic opportunities for Negroes, these
students felt that they lacked the educational qualifications
that the opening economic opportunities required. They
wanted more, not less, manpower training programs. Negro
youth seemingly are caught by the hold of the tradition
that gave Negroes limited opportunities and the pull of
the economic opportunities implicit in the Civil Rights
Act of 1964. Reprinted by permission.

1063. Kell, L. and Herr, E. Reaching low income students in home
economics classes. Marriage, Family, and Living, 1963, 25, 214-218.

Although this paper seems primarily directed toward practice
rather than research people, its findings may be of interest
to researchers concerned with poverty and the development of
lower class adolescents. The subjects included 45 lower class
adolescent girls, equally divided among Negroes, Mexicans,
and whites. Data were gathered through interviews which
included an incomplete sentence blank and the girls' spontaneous "wishes" in addition to general exploration of their
family situations. Their responses are discussed with
emphasis on their home deprivation, aspirations, and wishes.
It is noted that, among their wishes, personal aspirations
and better family relationships are mentioned more frequently
than material goods or school attainment. Comparisons are
offered between the three subgroups, including the observation that school attainment was mentioned most often by the
Negroes, personal aspirations by the white girls, and better
family relations by the Mexicans. The latter seems to be
attributable at least as much to a cultural pattern as to a
relatively deficit in this area among the Mexican girls.

1064. Keller, S. The social world of the urban slum child: Some
early findings. American Journal of Orthopsychiatry, 1963, 33 (5),
823-831.

> This paper compares selected aspects of the after school and
> home activities of a sample of poor Negro and Caucasian chil-
> dren currently attending first and fifth grades in New York
> City Schools. Discussion centers upon factors that distinguish
> family life, self-image, and recreational activities of these
> children with those of their middle class peers, with whom
> they must compete in school.

1065. Kellogg, W. N. and Eagleson, B. M. The growth of social perception in different racial groups. Journal of Educational Psychology, 1931, 22 (5), 367-375.

> Following the procedure used by G. S. Gates for measuring
> growth of facial perception in white children, 232 Negroes,
> aged 3 to 14 years, were tested for ability to interpret
> facial expression as an index to social perception. Six
> pictures of the Ruchmick Series were presented one at a time
> to each subject who recorded his interpretation of the emo-
> tion represented. A rough relationship appeared between
> social perception ratings and the teacher's intelligence
> rating of the individuals. Negro girls appeared superior
> to Negro boys. In general there was a similarity in the
> findings for the two groups and neither race nor social
> status seemed to affect ability to interpret facial expres-
> sion.

1066. Kempler, B. and Shatzer, C. Attributions of helpful and
blameworthy behavior by black and white boys and girls. Perceptual
and Motor Skills, 1976, 42 (3, Part 1), 795-800.

> 30 black and 30 white boys and girls, aged 5, 8 and 11 years,
> were shown four pictures depicting conflict and four pictures
> depicting cooperation between a black and a white figure.
> Subjects were instructed to tell stories that included the
> attribution of helpfulness and blameworthy behavior to one
> of the two figures. No age trends were found, and helpful-
> ness was attributed on a racial basis; however, females,
> particularly white females, blamed their own race, while
> males did not make racially-based blame attributions. The
> traditional female sex-role of accepting blame in resolving
> conflict situations may be involved. Methodologically,
> studies of racial attitudes should concentrate on specific
> attributions in emotionally arousing situations.

1067. Kentucky University, Lexington, Agricultural Experiment Station;
Southern Regional Committee for Family Life. Research Report -- Base-
line and Experimental Phases, Influences on Occupational Goals of
Young People in Three Southern Subcultures. 338 pp. Information
Series 1, Southern Regional Research Project S-63, June 1974. Avail-
able from: Department of Sociology, S-205D Agricultural Science
Building, North, University of Kentucky, Lexington, Kentucky 40506

(Attention: Dr. A. Lee Coleman). Also, see ERIC Abstracts, No. ED-100-545, 1974.

The educational and occupational aspirations and expectations of 1,412 low-income youths were analyzed and compared to those their parents had for them according to such variables as social, racial, and cultural factors. Youths were from three low-income subcultures (urban Negro, rural Negro, and Appalachian rural white) in the Southeast. The 6-year study consisted of: (a) planning and pretesting, (b) a baseline study of fifth and sixth graders and their mothers, (c) preliminary analysis of baseline data, (d) a follow-up (before) study of a subsample followed by a series of three lesson-discussions for the mothers on "Helping your Child Plan for Education and Career," (e) an after interview of mothers, children, and a control sample from the baseline study, (f) an analysis of before and after data, and (g) an experimental program during the children's junior high or mid-adolescent years. Data from the children were obtained by self-administered questionnaires; mothers were interviewed. This report discusses: theoretical and research background, variables and their measures as operationalized in the study, design and methodology, the sample's characteristics, baseline findings, and the experimental phase. A summary and interpretation are also given.

1068. Koch, H. L. The social distance between certain racial, nationality and skin pigmentation groups in selected populations of American school children. Journal of Genetic Psychology, 1946 63, 6 -95.

Several hundred children mostly from mixed Negro-white schools, were asked to indicate their preference for classmates by the method of paired companions. Students from all-white and partly Italian schools were used as control and check groups. Whites showed an increasing preference for whites from the second grade on. Negroes showed the same trend in their attitudes toward Negro classmates. By the eighth grade, race preference percentage scores showed a J-shaped distribution. The results are further broken down to show relations of preference to sex, skin color and size of minority group.

1069. Koch, H. L. A study of some factors conditioning the social distance between the sexes. Journal of Social Psychology, 1944, 20, 79-107.

By the method of paired comparisons, children (both Negro and white) from nursery school to high school indicated their preference in association among their classmates. In general, the individuals stated preference for members of their own sex. The distance between sexes first increased and then decreased with grade and age. The data are analyzed in detail with respect to age, grade, sex, and race.

1070. Koslin, S. C., Amarel, M., and Ames, N. The effects of race
in peer evaluation and preference in primary grade children: An
exploratory study. Journal of Negro Education, 1970, 39 (4), 346-350.

      Explored the use of children's preference for sketches of
      classrooms which differ in racial composition as a measure
      of school related racial attitudes in the primary grades.
      120 grade 1 and 2 children from three elementary schools in
      a middle-sized Eastern city served as subjects. One school
      was all white, one all Negro, and the third one-half white
      and one-half Negro. Pairs of sketches depicting classroom
      scenes, differing only in racial composition, were used.
      In individual interviews subjects were shown the pictures
      one pair at a time. No questions indicating preference
      were asked. The white subjects showed an overwhelming pre-
      ference for the white classrooms. The Negro subjects were
      divided in their preferences.

1071. Krystall, E. R., Friedman, N., Howze, G., and Epps, E. C.
Attitudes toward integration and black consciousness: Southern
Negro high school seniors and their mothers. Phylon, 1970, 31 (2),
104-113.

      The concern is with the black integration vs. the black con-
      sciousness debate in the Negro community. Data were collected
      from 240 mothers or female guardians of 166 students who
      were interviewed as part of the 1967 Tuskegee Area Study,
      which is an annual social survey carried on by junior and
      senior social science majors at Tuskegee Institute. Atti-
      tudes toward integration were assessed through questions
      concerning feelings about integration in housing and schools,
      intermarriage, and civil rights participation. Black con-
      sciousness was assessed through questions concerning feel-
      ings toward black power, Stokely Carmichael, Africa, violence,
      group labels, and the Afro hair style. Data show that black
      consciousness is not as prevalent in the sample as is pro-
      integration sympathy. It was also found that seniors have
      more black consciousness than do their mothers, that they
      are more likely to have heard of black power, and that they
      tend to think it means black supremacy. They are a bit
      more willing than their mothers to join a black power move-
      ment and much more willing to give it active rather than
      financial support. They are more likely than their mothers
      to think demonstrations will cease to be nonviolent.
      Mothers were pro-integrationist, but not pro-black conscious-
      ness. Students were both pro-integration and pro-black
      consciousness. A typology was constructed based on the
      assumption that these two concepts are not psychological
      opposites. A person who favors integration and has black
      consciousness is called a cultural pluralist under this
      typology. One who favors integration and does not have black
      consciousness is called an assimilationist. These two
      categories typify the majority of the respondents here
      studied. It is expected that the distribution of the types
      will change with shifts in the course of the civil and
      human rights movements. 6 tables. Reprinted by permission.

1072. Kuvlesky, W. P. and Dietrich, K. T. Southern black youths' orientations toward military service: A metropolitan-nonmetropolitan comparison. Journal of Political and Military Sociology, 1973, 1 (1), 105-120.

  98 black high school sophomores in selected nonmetropolitan East Texas counties and 111 black sophomores from a Houston, Texas high school (all were aged 15-16) were interviewed in the Spring of 1966 and given an anonymous self-administered questionnaire. The following hypotheses served as a guide for the analysis of the data: (a) nonmetropolitan black boys have more positive orientations toward military service than metropolitan blacks; (b) lower class metropolitan boys with high occupational aspirations have more positive orientations toward military service than other metropolitan youth. The specific orientations examined are desire to enter the military, anticipation of military service, certainty of this expectation, and general attitude towards participation in the military. Findings did not support the above hypotheses. In general, all of the nonmetropolitan and metropolitan boys were favorably inclined towards military service, and lower class black youth with high aspirations were not more favorably inclined toward participation in the military than other black youth. None of the three independent variables used (place of residence, SES, and level of status aspiration), when used alone or in combination, appear to explain the variation in black youths' military service projections and attitudes. Inferences are drawn and suggestions for future study are offered. 8 tables. Reprinted by permission.

1073. Kuvlesky, W. P., and Lever, M. Occupational goals, expectations, and anticipatory goal deflection experienced by Negro girls residing in low-income rural and urban places. Proceedings of the Southwestern Sociological Association, 1967, 18, 76-79.

  An attempt was made to test the validity of S. M. Lipset's contention that rural youth have lower occupational aspirations than do urban youth as it applies to Negro girls. A comparative analysis was made of the occupational orientations of 99 rural Negro high school sophomores from three rural East Texas counties, and 170 urban Negro females, a 50% sample of sophomore girls from a Negro high school in Houston. Open-end questions were used to elicit both occupational goals and expectations. Responses were scaled hierarchically, employing a modification of the census scheme. Over 75% both desired and expected white-collar employment. Over 60% of the urban and 50% of the rural girls desired professional employment. 14% of the rural and almost none of the urban girls desired blue-collar employment. Almost 30% of the rural as compared to 20% of the urban girls anticipated goal deflection, most notable being the anticipated deflection of rural girls from high white collar to blue collar. Greater percentages of all girls expected to be housewives than so desired. While highly similar in both goal and expectation profile, the two groups

differed most regarding expectations. Support is offered
R. K. Merton's proposition that high success goals are
universal in U.S. society and Lipset's contention concerning
rural/urban differences in occupational aspirations receives
its first empirical support regarding Negro females. Reprinted
by permission.

1074. Kuvlesky, W. P. and Pelham, J. T. Place of residence projections of rural youth: A racial comparison. Social Science
Quarterly, 1970, 51 (1), 166-176.

Very little information exists about place of residence
projections of rural youths. Evidence does indicate that,
regardless of region, females are more inclined to hold
urban residence goals than males and that in the South,
black youths are more apt to desire urban status than white
youths. To further investigate place of residence projections, a study of 484 high school sophomores was conducted
in three East Texas counties. The specific purpose of the
study was to obtain detailed information about a wide range
of status projections held by rural youths living in economically deprived areas. The results indicate that black
youths aspire to live in large cities in much greater proportions than white youths. Conversely, the white youths
more often desired to live in the country and in small
cities. Generally speaking, few youths of any race-sex
type desired to live in a small town or on a farm. In
general, the findings on residence expectations were similar
to those for aspirations. One exception to this general
statement is that black male youths expected urban status
more frequently than black female youths. There is a need
to test these propositions through future research including
more diverse populations. The great concern evolving among
government policy makers and among the general public about
the increased crowding of low-income populations into the
urban centers and about mass depletion of populations in
many areas will make accurate information on place of residence desires and intentions of youths highly desirable.

1075. Ladner, J. A. Labelling black children: Social-psychological
implications. Journal of Afro-American Issues, 1975, 3 (1), 43-50.

Labelling is a form of control and also a way of justifying
continued discrimination against blacks: it begins at school
and takes on a deterministic quality as the child grows into
adulthood. Stereotypes about the black family, and about
black maleness and femaleness as well as negative judgments
on black culture in general have generated for most black
children situations in which resisting the labelling produces "aggressive, hostile and mistrusting responses," while
accepting it is also very damaging. Attempts to intervene
in this process, such as Head Start, while helpful in some
ways, have generally stressed the need to overcome, rather
than function in, the black child's environment. Therefore,
the proposals of Jay Chunn (1972) are adopted by Ladner as
preferable and these aim to stress certain attributes which

low-income black children need within their community, such
as creativity, resourcefulness, resiliency, aggressiveness
and astuteness. Further discussion of labelling, particularly
within the context of the currently fashionable white view
that blacks are culturally deprived can be found in the
article by Donald Henderson in the same issue of Journal of
Afro-American Issues.

1076. Landreth, C. and Johnson, B. Young children's responses to
a picture and inset test designed to reveal reactions to persons
of different skin color. Child Development, 1953, 24, 63-80.

    Reactions to people of white, brown and black skin color
    were studied in 228 children, using a picture and inset
    test which required the child to complete a picture using
    one of a pair of insets. Results indicate different res-
    ponses to skin color in white upper class and lower class
    children and Negro lower class children, the latter seemingly
    responding to skin color in terms of a value judgment.
    "Patterns of response to persons of different skin colors
    are early as three years and become accentuated during the
    succeeding two years."

1077. Landreth, C. and Platt, E. F. A problem in factorial design:
The development of a picture and inset test for determining young
children's responses to persons of different skin color. Journal
of Educational Psychology, 1951, 42, 385-398.

    The authors repeat the experimental design of study now in
    progress. A picture inset test, including pictures of persons
    with white, brown, or black colored skin is being given to
    576 children in California and Alabama. This population
    includes equal and adequate samples of white and colored
    children, three years and five years old of upper, lower
    and unidentified socioeconomic status. The factors of per-
    severation and right-hand choice are held constant by ran-
    domized or systematized order of presentation. It is be-
    lieved that with irrelevant influences minimized, differ-
    ent responses of the several groups may be properly inter-
    preted in terms of native, developmental, and experimental
    factors.

1078. Lane, J., et al. The Status of Minority Children in Idaho,
1974. Volume III. Boise, Idaho: Idaho State Economic Opportunity
Office; and Western Interstate Commission for Higher Education,
June 4, 1974. See ERIC Abstracts, No. ED-101-841, 1974. 55 pp.

    This paper presents a study designed to develop a better
    understanding of the needs of minority families with pre-
    school children in Idaho. The project had three aims: to
    determine the general needs of families, to find which ser-
    vices were known and utilized, and to identify services
    adequately meeting needs. Four minority populations were
    included in the study: Mexican-Americans, Migrant, American
    Indian, and Black. A personal interview was conducted with

each subject family utilizing a structured questionnaire.
In assessing the need of minority families, six areas were
considered: social environment (i.e., housing, income),
educational attainment, language skills, health care, child
care, and nutrition. Analysis of the data revealed that:
(a) general socioeconomic conditions of the minorities
were below the general population of the state; (b) child
care arrangements were generally made by utilizing an immediate family member or friend; (c) immunization data was
difficult to assess; and (d) low consumption of fruits and
vegetables by each group. The areas which warrant improvements include: migrant and Indian housing, family health
care and immunization, child care facilities, nutrition
information and a public assistance program which more adequately meets each family's needs.

1079. Lapouse, R. and Monk, M. A. Behavior deviations in a representative sample of children: Variation by sex, age, race, social
class and family size. American Journal of Orthopsychiatry, 1964,
34, 436-446.

Responses to a structured interview by mothers of a nonpsy-
chiatric sample of 482 children, aged 6-12, were used to
disclose the differential risk of deviation from prevailing
patterns in subgroups divided according to sex, age, race,
social class and family size. Deviant behavior was reported
most in younger children, Negro children, and boys. Presence or absence of siblings seemed unimportant. There is
support for the thesis that "deviant behavior occurs as a
transient developmental phenomenon in school-aged children.

1080. Larkin, R. W. Class, race, sex, and preadolescent attitudes.
California Journal of Educational Research, 1972, 23 (5), 213-223.

Present results of a survey disputing the view that social
disadvantagement and attitudinal deficits can explain failure in school. 1,750 fourth, fifth and sixth graders (lower,
middle, and upper-middle class) in California public schools
were administered a test battery to obtain demographic data
and to measure attitudes of self-esteem, school orientation,
peer group orientation, and orientation to family authority.
61% were white, 20% black, 17% Mexican-American, and 2%
Oriental. No significant relationships were found between
socioeconomic background and any of the four attitudes. Results indicate greater differences in attitudes between boys
and girls than between racial, ethnic, and social class groups.
Self-esteem of girls was negatively affected in families that
gave boys a higher status.

1081. Laurence, J. E. White socialization: Black reality. Psychiatry, Washington, D. C., 1970, 33 (2), 174-194.

Asserts that political socialization is a process beginning
in childhood, and a number of definitions are discussed. 178
black and 821 white children from 5th, 6th and 8th grade
integrated classes filled in a questionnaire in March, 1968.
Feelings of general efficacy within the politicsl system

and information on politics are constant among younger black
and white subjects, but older black subjects had less information and felt less efficacious than whites. A number of
specific variables are questioned including feelings for
minority groups, responses to black power, trust of police-
men, and the Vietnam war. Attempts to increase political
socialization of blacks is seen to be futile as long as
what is taught is in contrast to the reality of their lives.
Two suggestions for reducing polarization and immunizing
conflict between the races are: (a) intensifying efforts
for socialization of white children in the area of racial
realizations, and (b) changing attitudes of black children
by changing the reality of their circumstances.

1082. Lefebvre, A. and Bohn, M. J. Occupational prestige as seen
by disadvantaged black children. Developmental Psychology, 1971,
4 (2), 173-177.

Studies developmental and differential aspects of occupational
prestige among 300 disadvantaged Negro children in grades 4-8.
Subjects ranked 12 occupations representative of high and
low socioeconomic levels. There was high agreement in the
rankings among the grades (p<.81), and between boys and girls
(p<.81). In comparison with the general population, the
subjects' rankings also showed high similarity at all grade
levels (p<.75). By the 4th grade, disadvantaged subjects
of both sexes show a high level of awareness of adult,
standard concepts of occupational prestige.

1083. Lessler, K. and Fox, R. E. An evaluation of a Head Start
program in a low population area. Journal of Negro Education,
1969, 38 (1), 46-54.

This study of the results of an eight-week Head Start program showed increased sensitivity and receptivity to the
spoken word by both Negro and white children in the segregated program. Some verbal skills, such as fluency and
clarity, were also significantly improved by the program.
Enthusiasm for school was generated and children who initially were uncomfortable with adults became less so. The
ncessary follow-up educational programs required to capitalize
on these gains must be investigated.

1084. Levin, H. and Wardwell, E. The research uses of doll play.
Psychological Bulletin, 1962, 59 (1), 27-56.

Besides methodological studies the findings in five areas
of investigation which have used doll play were summarized:
aggression, stereotyping, doll preference, effect of separation from parents, and prejudice. Although certain groups
of studies give interrelated results the use of this research
tool has been so varied that the overall impression is of
many disparate findings, in spite of the basic similarity
of method. (Modified.)

1085. Lewis, C. and Biber, B. Reactions of Negro children toward
Negro and white teachers. Journal of Experimental Education, 1951,
20, 97-104.

This study reports an investigation of 51 Negro children's
responses to varying pictures of Negro and white teachers.
It was found that Negro children with Negro teachers showed
a slight preference for pictures of Negro teachers and Negro
children with white teachers showed a marked preference for
pictures of white teachers. All of the children were positively influenced in their choices by the pleasantness or
unpleasantness of the faces. Girls seemed more ready than
boys to accept the Negro teachers.

1086. Lewis, R. G. and St. John, N. H. Contributions of cross
racial friendship to minority group achievement in desegregated
classrooms. Sociometry, 1974, 37 (1), 79-91.

Hypothesized that growth in achievement for desegregated
black pupils would be facilitated by acceptance into the
majority group peer structure, using path analysis of longitudinal data. Subjects were 154 black sixth graders in 22
majority-white classrooms. The model was to some degree
validated. Previous desegregation experience contributed
to popularity with whites, contributed to sixth-grade
achievement measured by GPA but not by Metropolitan Achievement Test reading scores. Two social mechanisms are identified that may explain the effect of popularity on achievement: the social facilitation of acceptance into the
majority group peer structure, and the normative influence
of association with achievement-oriented peers.

1087. Lewis, V. V. Rural social services for Negro children. The
Child (U.S. Children's Bureau), 1941, 5, 228-232.

In order to do social work with Negro children, child welfare workers need a special facility which results from
acquaintance with the fields of anthropology and sociology
in addition to training in technical social work, especially
among the "folk Negroes." It is also pointed out that
social workers who develop the facility to work with other
races and in strange or different cultures increase the
value of their services. The Special Demonstration Units
of the Children's Bureau and the Special Consultation Service
to the States are described with reference to the development
of adequate social services to meet the needs of the Negro
children.

1088. Lewit, D. W. and Abner, E. V. Black-white semantic differences and interracial communication. Journal of Applied Social Psychology, 1971, 1 (3), 263-277.

In Phase I, black and white adolescent males made semantic
differential ratings of 14 concepts representing a wide range
of values. Mother, father, girls, TV. God, police and next

yielded profiles significantly different for two racial
groups. In Phase II, 28 blacks and 28 whites each attempted
to decode the profiles of one black and one white other. For
combined racial groups accuracy was greater when other was
semantically similar. Disregarding semantic similarity,
accuracy was greater when the other was semantically similar.
Disregarding semantic similarity, accuracy was greater when
the other was of the same race. Semantic similarity made
little difference, however, when both encoder and decoder
were black. Whites excelled in decoding the profiles of
other whites where concepts were commonly encoded by both
racial groups, while blacks were more accurate interracially
where concepts were differentially encoded by the two racial
groups. Results are related to the assumption of a standard
set of meanings for whites and two standard-nonstandard dual
systems for blacks.

1089. Lightfoot, S. L. Socialization and Education of young black
girls in school. Teachers College Record, 1976, 78 (2), 239-262.

The treatment of black girls in the social sciences literature is characterized by contradictory imagery, strong stereotyping, and lack of attention. Two sources of information
in the literature concern the teacher's relationship with
young girls and the teacher's characteristic interactions
with black children. These studies reveal sexism and
racism in the schools. Strategies for documenting classroom
life should emphasize the characteristics and structure of
the environment, the roles and relationships of people, and
the social and cognitive meanings of interactions. They
should deal with children's roles as assertive beings in
their environment and should emphasize peer interactions.
There is a need for longitudinal study as well as research
in other social settings -- playground, home, and church.

1090. Likover, B. The effects of black history on an interracial
group of children. Children, 1970, 17, 177-182.

This study assessed how the racial prejudices of an interracial group of children were affected by the presentation
of a black history program within a day camp setting. The
naive subjects (N=26; 16 white, 10 black) were 6 to 7 years
old and from comparable middle class socioeconomic backgrounds.
Two non-interacting groups (N=13) were formed by stratified
random assignment. The experimental group received exposure
to a black history program emphasizing the affective and
cognitive components of racial prejudice. This group also
received the day camp's usual program of activities as did
the control group. Effects were measured by an interaction
scale, daily reports, and reports of concepts expressed at
home. Descriptive statistics showed an increase in racial
interaction, an increase in counter-racial affect, and a
decrease in black subjects' interaction with the group
observer. Little racial interaction was found with the
control group. Racially prejudiced statements were expressed
by this group as opposed to the experimental group.

1091. Lipscomb, L. W. Socialization factors in the development of
black children's racial self-esteem. Paper presented at the Annual
Meeting of the American Sociological Association (San Francisco,
California, August 25-29, 1975). Also, see ERIC Abstracts, No.
ED-123-508, 1975. 25 pp.

> Recent studies on racial self-esteem show a reversal in the
> tendency for black children to have negative self-concepts.
> This research explored the causal explanations for such a
> reversal by investigating the process by which social status,
> parental attitudes, and socialization practices influence the
> development of black children's racial preferences and stereo-
> types. Data were obtained from interviews with 60 black mothers
> of 5- or 6-year-old children, and from a race awareness
> test of the children in the home. The theoretical model
> predicted that the SES variables (mother's occupation,
> mother's education, and family income) affects two family
> relationship variables (mother's racial attitudes, and
> mother's socialization practices such as presence of black
> cultural objects and teaching of blacks' treatment in society)
> which in turn affects the child's racial self-esteem (mea-
> sures of child's own race preference and racial stereotypes).
> It was further hypothesized that the socialization variables
> would be the most effective predictors of children's racial
> self-esteem and act as mediators of the socioeconomic and
> attitudinal variables. The underlying theoretical model
> was supported. It was also found that the socialization
> variables were the most effective predictors of children's
> racial self-esteem. It was found, however, that not all
> of the effects on the child's racial self-esttem were mediated
> through socialization.

1092. Litcher, J. H., Johnson, D. W., and Ryan, F. L. Use of pictures of multiethnic interaction to change attitudes of white elementary students towards blacks. Psychological Reports, 1973, 33
(2), 367-372.

> The use of pictures of multiethnic interaction in changing
> the attitudes of white elementary school students towards
> blacks was investigated. Several pictures portraying varied
> mixed racial groups of children in either a middle class
> suburban or a lower class inner city setting were used
> as part of a one-month long curriculum unit. White second
> graders in a midwestern metropolitan area were subjects.
> Results indicate that the attitudes towards blacks were
> not affected by the curriculum unit.

1093. Long, S. Political alienation among black and white adolescents: A test of the social deprivation and political reality
models. American Politics Quarterly, 1976, 4 (3), 267-304.

> "Political alienation" is conceptualized here as an inter-
> related cluster of feelings including personal political
> inefficacy, political distrust, discontent with systematic
> policy outputs, and estrangement or apartness from the poli-

tical system. A social deprivation model (based on the
notion that persons deprived of opportunity and denied
respect will have low feelings of political trust) and an
alternative political reality model (based on the assumptions
that blacks have less ability to influence political leaders,
less reason to trust them, and that black children are aware
of this situation) are described and compared. Data derived
from a questionnaire survey of 970 St. Louis high school
students do not indicate the hypothesized correlations between
black students and (1) perceived social deprivation, (2) low
self-competence, or (3) political alienation. A third model,
integrating the social deprivation and political reality
explanations of political explanation, also fails to be
supported by a path analysis of the survey data. Although
the political reality model appears to be the strongest,
problems of definition and direction of causality are
inherent in all three.

1094. Longabaugh, R. Mother behavior as a variable moderating
the effects of father absence. Ethos, 1973, 1 (4), 456-465.

Tested the hypotheses that father-absent boys have a more
feminine semantic style than father-present boys, and that
father absent homes have a higher rate of mother-son interaction than father-present homes. 51 mother-child dyads
were selected for study from a group of black, lower class
households. Children ranged in age from 5 to 12 years, and
18 were from households in which the father had been absent
for at least two years prior to the study. Mother-child
interactions were observed and coded with a resource process
coding system, and each child was administered a modified
semantic differential test. No significant relationship
was found between father's absence and masculinity of semantic
style of either sons or daughters. Father absence was related to alterations of behavior of mothers toward sons.
It is concluded that increased mother-son interaction
moderates the impact of father absence on the femininity
of the son's semantic style.

1095. Lott, A. J. and Lott, B. E. Negro and White Youth. New York:
Holt, Rinehart, and Winston, 1963. iv + 236 pp.

This very timely work appears at an appropriate period to
shed some necessary light on the values and goals of Negro
and white youth in regard to their educational and vocational
plans. Fayette County, Kentucky, which includes the city
of Lexington, was the area from which the sample of Negro
and white youth was drawn. The Negro sample in the investigation consisted of 166 seniors, 23 of whom were from a
county high school and 93 from a city school. The 185
white seniors investigated came from two predominantly white
schools, the county school contributing 79 subjects and the
city school, 106. The data-gathering devices consisted of
the Goal Preference Inventory, the Modified Form of the
Study of Values, the Background and Outlook Questionnaire,

a Leadership Pool, and a Test of Insight, all of which are
exhibited in the appendix of the volume. In additiona, all
but two of the 30 white and 28 Negro leaders as determined
by the Leadership Poll were subjected to an interview schedule
to obtain information on their attitudes toward education,
their dominant values, and their preferences for achievement
and ways of living. The carefully documented interpretations
of the results include some intriguing findings as well as
several expected conclusions. Of the latter type, it is
not surprising to learn that the Negro student is less likely
to be from a home with both natural parents and to associate
himself with working-class status, while middle-class status
is largely white. More unexpected is the finding that,
despite the separation of the groups in their living conditions, schooling, churches, and recreation, the Negroes and
whites share basic agreement in values as found in their
evaluations of the relative desirability of religious, social,
theoretical, political, esthetic, and economic goals. The
Negro youth has a realistic picture of his status and opportunities and hopes to see changes for the better in personal
advancement, which includes expectations of leaving Kentucky
and the South. In contrast, the white youth does not show
strong desires to leave his home community. Furthermore, the
white leader is more concerned than his Negro counterpart
with questions pertaining to the maintenance and control
of those with power in order to preserve the status quo.
The Negro female leaders are concerned with respectability,
financial security, and service. The white female leaders,
on the other hand, are more interested in their families,
the attainment of knowledge, religious satisfaction, creativity, and happiness. These are but a few of the findings
to be discussed in this valuable research report. The
authors have employed sound methodological procedures in
their study of some of the psychological factors affecting
Negro-white educational problems. They present findings
which offer a challenge that professional educators involved
in school integration will have to face if progress in this
area is to be achieved.

1096. Lowe, E. T. and Taylor, W. L. Trends in Black School Segre-
gation, 1970-1974. Volume I. Washington, D. C.: Center for
National Policy Review; and National Institute of Education (DHEW),
January 1977. See ERIC Abstracts, No. ED-135-900, 1977. 434 pp.

As a statistical tabulation based on raw data collected by
the Office of Civil Rights of the Department of Health,
Education and Welfare (DHEW), this report presents tables
of data which illustrate trends in black school segregation
from 1970-1974. The statistics provide a detailed profile
of the pattern of black enrollment in schools with various
porportions of minority students (American Indian, Asian
American, Spanish Surnamed American, and others). They show
the number and percentage of black students and the number
and percent of the district's schools at each level of
segregation or integration each year. Statistics have been

gathered for all 50 states according to five regions: northeast, border, south, mid-west, west. Alaska and Hawaii have
been excluded. The detailed statistical profiles of 204
school districts with more than 20,000 students enrolled
permit examination of trends in middle size cities and a
number of major suburban and metropolitan school systems as
well as the 100 largest systems (the only ones on which DHEW
data was previously available). A short introduction provides historical background and analyses of school segregation.

1097. Lowe, J., Childers, W., Doucet, W., and Dilettuso, J. The
effects of using a mod versus a traditional approach in communications with juvenile delinquents. Journal of Research in Crime and
Delinquency, 1974, 11 (1), 56-62.

A study was done to ascertain the differing responses of
institutionalized juvenile delinquents to young adult
interviewers using differing strategies of communications.
One pair of interviewers used a traditional approach in
which they asked straightforward questions using middle
class language while being well-groomed and dressed in a
suit and tie. The other pair assumed a mod appearance
with beard, long hair, sport clothes and used the language
of the subculture. 20 boys (10 white, 10 black) were
interviewed by both the mod and traditional pairs of interviewers. Data indicated that institutionalized juvenile
delinquents respond more freely to persons who attempted
to relate to the youth life style and who have acquired
and used skills that facilitate good communication.

1098. Luchterhand, E. and Weller, L. Effects of class, race, sex,
and educational status on patterns of aggression of lower class
youth. Journal of Youth and Adolescence, 1976, 5 (1), 59-71.

Patterns of aggression in urban center youth were investigated with respect to the influence of social class, race,
sex, and education status, with a random sample of 1,844
13- to 19-year-olds in Bridgeport and New Haven, Connecticut.
Responses to open and closed ended questions were measured
for degree of aggression with expectations that: (1) youth
from the lower class would be more aggressive, (2) blacks
would be more aggressive than whites, and (3) boys would
be more aggressive than girls. Race emerged as the most
important discriminator for exhibition of aggression. Blacks
were less aggressive than whites, but when aroused, were
more likely than whites to assult others. 3 tables. Reprinted
by permission.

1099. Mabe, P. A. and Williams, J. E. Relation of racial attitudes
to sociometric choices among second grade children. Psychological
Reports, 1975, 37 (2), 547-554.

Investigated the relationship of racial attitudes to interpersonal choice behavior among 32 Euro-American and 20 Afro-
American second graders who comprised two intact classrooms

in an integrated public school. Subjects were administered
the revised Preschool Racial Attitude Measure (PRAM II) and
a sociometric procedure which asked them to choose classmates
as associates for three different activities. For all subjects a correlation of 0.52 was obtained between the degree
of pro-Euro/anti-Afro bias displayed on PRAM II and the frequency of choice of Euro-American associates. There was
some evidence of less racial bias and less frequent choice
of Euro-associates in the racially balanced classroom than
in the classroom which was predominantly Euro-American. It
is concluded that the validity of the PRAM II procedure as a
method for assessing racial attitudes in young children was
supported.

1100. Macke, A. and Morgan, W. R. Mother's employment and daughter's
work orientation: A test of alternative socialization processes
for blacks and whites. Washington, D. C.: Public Health Service
(DHEW), 1975. See ERIC Abstracts, No. ED-117-228, 1975. 37 pp.

This study successively tests simple modeling, normative
influence, and conditional positive modeling hypotheses
about the working mother's effect on her daughter's work
orientation. Four hypotheses are postulated and tested
separately by race to examine possible racial differences.
The most complex hypothesis is that if modeling is conditioned
by other characteristics of the mother than those considered,
that modeling will be heightened by the following two characteristics: increasing the work oreintation of girls with
working mothers, and decreasing the work orientation of girls
with nonworking mothers. It is also hypothesized that white
girls' work orientation is more likely than black girls' to
be a function of commitment to the exclusive homemaker role.
Data from a 1973 urban population of black and white high
school girls and a sample of their mothers revealed no evidence of either simple positive modeling or normative influence, but simple negative modeling occurred for black girls
whose mothers worked in blue collar jobs. Conditional positive
modeling is evident for all girls. Findings are contrasted with
those from studies of male achievement socialization, which are
said to stress the importance of direct normative influence.

1101. Mackie, J. B., Maxwell, A., and Rafferty, F. T. Psychological development of culturally disadvantaged Negro kindergarten
children: A study of the selective influence of family and school
variables. American Journal of Orthopsychiatry, 1967, 37 (2),
367-368.

Began as an investigation of the relative merits of various
psychological tests in assessing development among inner
city Negro slum children over a 15-month period. The results indicate that the developmental level of both boys
and girls appeared to be more strongly influenced by certain
characteristics of their families than by preschool enrichment programs or by the character of their formal school
experience.

1102. Maddock, R. C. and Kenny, C. T. Impression formation as a function of age, sex, and race. Journal of Social Psychology, 1973, 89 (2), 233-243.

Varied sex, age (8, 10, and 12 years), and race (black and white) in a study in which subjects formed an impression of a boy who displayed ambivalent behavior. Hypotheses derived from Werner's theory that subjects' impressions would become more differentiated and more integrated as a function of age were confirmed. Among the boys, blacks formed more integrated impressions than whites; there were no racial differences among the girls. Also, subjects who formed more integrated impressions gave less affective judgments on a checklist.

1103. Madsen, M. C. and Shapiro, A. Cooperative and competitive behavior of urban Afro-American, Anglo-American, Mexican-American and Mexican-village children. Developmental Psychology, 1970, 3, 16-20.

Children of three ethnic groups in Los Angeles, California ages 7 to 9, performed on the Cooperation Board developed by Madsen. In Experiment 1, Mexican-American boys were less competitive than Mexican-American girls and Afro- and Anglo-Americans of both sexes. In Experiment II, all three ethnic groups behaved in a highly competitive manner. In Experiment III, the three ethnic groups in Los Angeles behaved in a nonadaptive competitive manner while a sample of village children in Mexico behaved cooperatively.

1104. Malone, C. A., M.D. The psychosocial characteristics of the children from a developmental viewpoint. In Eleanor Pavenstedt (Ed.), The Drifters: Children of Disorganized Lower Class Families, pp. 105-124. Boston: Little, Brown and Company, 1967.

This chapter summarizes children's psychosocial characteristics in relation to environmental influences and developmental processes. Descriptive data from relationship oriented services to the children in the nursery school and to the families in the home are used. The focus is on the influences of deprivation, devaluation, and danger. The children's psychosocial characteristics are discussed in two parts: First, maternal deprivation and external danger are described separately as formative environmental influences. Second, leading features of the youngsters' make-up are discussed as illustrations of the interrelated effects of the three classes of influence.

The author finds that many of the leading characteristics are similar to those reported in other studies of maternal deprivation. Children in multiproblem families grow up in an environment with a strong sense of devaluation. This has far-reaching effects on growth. Since the children are regularly exposed to real dangers in their families and neighborhoods, external danger and survival influence their

growth in a number of ways. Four interrelated sets of
qualities illustrate this influence: danger orientation;
visual and auditory hyperalertness to some stimuli and
hypoalertness to others; the use of many forms of denial;
and areas of precocious ability, as in role reversal with
parents in various practical matters.

1105. Manning, B. A., Pierce-Jones, J., and Parelman, R. L. Cooperative, trusting behavior in a "culturally deprived" mixed ethnic-
group population. Journal of Social Psychology, 1974, 92 (1), 133-
141.

Cooperative, trusting behavior was examined in a culturally
deprived mixed ethnic group population. Subjects were 144
Mexican-American, Negro, and Anglo-American 5- and 6-year-
old Head Start children who took part in a two-person, two-
choice game in which they could cooperate or compete with
another child. The 72 males and 72 females were divided
into similar and dissimilar ethnic group pairs and immediate
and delayed reward groups. Results indicate that for females,
similar ethnic pairs cooperated significantly more than
dissimilar pairs with the exception of Mexican-American,
Negro pairs who maintained a high level of cooperation;
females in the three ethnic groups differed significantly
in their amount of cooperative behavior, with Anglo-Americans
competing the most; and cooperative behavior was not differentially affected by the type of reinforcement used nor did
it increase as a function of trials.

1106. Manzer, C. W. The uniformity and variety of work associations
of Negro boys and girls. Psychological Bulletin, 1934, 31, 627.

1107. Marascuilo, L. A. and Dagenais, F. The meaning of the word
"integration" to seniors in a multi-racial high school. Journal of
Negro Education, 1974, 43 (2), 179-189.

Eight definitions of integration were examined across sex,
race, political preference, religious service attendance,
and socioeconomic status for 449 graduating high school
seniors. Students mainly chose definitions of integration
closest to their own idealistic concept of the free association of people of different races on all levels of contemporary life, along with the open acceptance of another
person and his racial and cultural heritage. The concepts
of equal justice under the law and equal opportunity were
also stressed. Whereas whites and Asians showed no major
disagreement with the dictionary definition of integration,
blacks did not accept it as a reasonable one. Implicit in
this definition is the idea that incorporation into the
larger society requires that minority persons must give up
their own cultural and racial heritage for the values of the
larger society. Finally, youth attributes to the adult community an acceptance of integration under force, while for
itself it believes that integration is voluntary.

1108. Marcus, R., Bispo, E., and Katuna, I. Social change and
curriculum innovation. Journal of Negro Education, 1967, 36 (2),
121-128.

>   The implementation of a new teaching program, entitled "Cul-
>   tural Profiles for All," aimed at raising the interest and
>   participation level of pupils from low socioeconomic groups
>   is presented. The premise of the program is that profile
>   images secured from Negro leadership in the urban community
>   will allow many Negro children living in metropolitan ghettoes
>   to identify with leaders of their own race, providing moti-
>   vation for learning and vocations. Team teaching is used,
>   with two curriculum assistants and the class teachers con-
>   cerned. A concomitant of the program is that it does not
>   only teach students but teachers as well, since too often
>   teachers see only the disadvantaged Negro child but fail to
>   see the successful image. This also leads to the development
>   of appropriate sections on Negro history in the school library.
>   It is suggested that the project be administered as a "pack-
>   age," to be offered on loan to any school desiring or in
>   need of it. The project should be considered the nucleus
>   of an operational plan under which lower socioeconomic groups
>   and higher socioeconomic groups be interchanged systematically
>   over a three-year period between two schools. Additional
>   expansion of the program is also discussed, opening up new
>   overtures to the solution of discrimination. Reprinted by permis-
>   sion.

1109. Marks, E. S. Standardization of a race attitude test for
Negro youth. Journal of Social Psychology, 1943, 18, 245-278.

>   Schedules of Negro attitudes toward whites and toward
>   Negroes were developed. "The Thurstone method of attitude
>   scaling proved of great value in item selection, while use
>   of the Likert method allowed for a considerable simplifi-
>   cation in scoring after the items had been selected. A
>   combination of the two methods plus cluster analysis seems
>   desirable."

1110. Martin, J. H. A model program for educationally deprived
children. New Jersey Community Action Training Institute, 2465
South Broad Street, Trenton, New Jersey 08610, May 1968. 7 pp.

>   This article shows the effect of slums, poverty, and parental
>   attitudes on the intellectual level of Negro children. When
>   the Negro child does not succeed in school, he turns to
>   antisocial activities to prove to himself that he is not a
>   failure. To meet this problem, many elementary schools
>   have put into effect practices that have been successful in
>   Head Start -- small classes, large numbers of nonprofessional
>   teacher aides, new technology, new recognition of the role
>   of medicine in education, a new role for the psychologist,
>   and recognition of the importance of nutrition. More is
>   needed to bring the slum child up to the level of the
>   middle class suburban child. A model program for educationally
>   deprived children is outlined, with the following recommenda-

ions: (1) a change in the attitude of the teacher of slum
children (teacher expectation is the most dynamic factor in
bringing about change); (2) ungrading the elementary schools
and mixing the ages of the children (the grade system does
not allow for individual differences); (3) a change in the
method of operation of the specialists on the staff (a spe-
cialist should not work in isolation, but as part of a diagnostic team); (4) establishment of a true supervisory system in education (superintendents and principals must observe
the instruction process as it relates to the child and then
work with the teacher to diagnose and change the methods
used); (5) provision of part-time jobs for junior and senior
high students; (6) restructuring the system of vocational
education (older students should be given jobs first and
educated in conjunction with work so that the subject matter
is relevant).

1111. Masters, J. C. and Peskay, J. Effects of race, socioeconomic
status, and success or failure upon contingent and noncontingent
self-reinforcement in children. Developmental Psychology, 1972, 7
(2), 139-145.

Gave 112 7- to 9-year-old black and white children from
upper- and lower-socioeconomic status (SES) homes success,
failure, and neutral feedback concerning their performance
on various trials at a game. After each trial they were to
self-dispense rewards in whatever amount they wished (noncontingent) or thought their performance deserved (contingent).
Low SES, success feedback, and noncontingent dispensation
encouraged increased levels of self-gratification. There
was a tendency for black subjects to show greater self-
gratification than white subjects, and a subject's race
entered into several interactions with other variables in
determining the extent of self-gratification. White subjects
showed increased noncontingent self-gratification following
both success ("self-congratulations") and failure ("self-
therapy"), but blacks showed only "self-congratulations."

1112. Mathis, A. and Oyemade, U. J. Ecological influences on
psycho-social development of black children: Interim progress
reports, year II. Washington, D. C.: Office of Human Development
(DHEW), March 1976. See ERIC Abstracts, No. ED-135-901, 1976.   105 pp.

This paper is an interim report of a three-year study to
investigate the relationship between personality and social
development and varying environmental experiences on low
and lower-middle income black preschool children. The subjects are 40 black preschool children between the ages
of three years, nine months and four years, four months,
selected from seven day care centers and classified according to social status based on the educational and occupational
status of their parents. The overall objectives of the
study are to determine preschool behavioral correlates of
personality variables which have been identified as having
developmental significance in relation to academic achieve-

ments of black children, and to ascertain from parental interview and ecological data, major influences of the home and
preschool environments which appear to be correlates and
possible antecedents of black preschool behavior. A further
major objective is to develop a preschool curriculum relevant to normative developmental behaviors of black children.
The purpose of the curriculum is to enhance a more effective
transition from the environment of the preschool child to the
school environment of the larger society. Included in this
report are a review of the recent literature, Year II data
analysis and procedures, and an analysis and interpretation
of data collected on 4-year-old subjects. Summary findings
of pilot studies are included and projections for Year III
data collection, procedures, and analysis are outlined.

1113. Mattick, I. Description of the children. In Eleanor Pavenstedt (Ed.), The Drifters: Children of Disorganized Lower-Class
Families, pp. 53-81. Boston: Little, Brown and Company, 1967.

This chapter presents a summary of child behavior in a
Boston nursery school based on intensive study of each child
as an individual and as a group member. Data were organized
into categories which would yield information about the children
when they first entered nursery school and their progress
over a period of time. Behavioral characteristics studied
include outward appearance, motor abilities, self-image,
coping with daily living, capacity for relationships, and
language and cognitive development. Though the children
displayed many individual characteristics, they shared some
traits. Although age differences were revealed by some
aspects of their behavior and by formal testing, their developmental deviancies were similar regardless of age. Among
the major findings are: (a) the children often used their
bodies for diffuse discharge and avoidance, with little focus
on the pleasures of attaining mastery; (b) their behavior
indicated low self-esteem; (c) their prevalent mode of coping
with daily living was defensive rather than aggressive; (d)
their characteristic relationships to people were need-
oriented, distrustful, shallow, and nonspecific; (e) vocabularies were limited and speech was often incomprehensible;
(f) communication was often effected by means other than
language; (g) they showed marked deviation in cognition
with an overreliance on concrete action and a paucity of
abstract thought; and (h) the capacity of each child to
focus on activities was very limited.

1114. Maynard, P. E. and Hansen, J. C. Vocational maturity among
inner city youths. Journal of Counseling Psychology, 1970, 17, 400-
404.

This study investigates the efficacy of the Vocational
Development Inventory in measuring the vocational maturity
of inner city eighth grade boys. The Vocational Development
Inventory was administered to 180 white and 180 black inner city
boys and 90 white suburban boys. Intelligence test results

were obtained and converted to standardized T scores. The
mean vocational maturity scores indicate large differences
among the samples. However, when intelligence was controlled
by analysis of covariance, the differences were erased. Researchers and counselors must take into account a variety of
intellectual and social variables when working with the
vocational maturity of inner city youth.

1115. Mayo, C. Quality education and integrated education: A
conflict of values. Paper presented at the Eastern Research Institute for Supervision and Curriculum Development (Philadelphia,
Pennsylvania, April 29, 1970). See ERIC Abstracts, No. ED-127-377,
1970. 13 pp.

The thesis of this paper was to question the validity of a
goal of integration achieved through the elimination of
differences. In the course of structured interviews with
mothers enrolling their children for the first time in
Operation Exodus, a black administered and financed school
busing program in Boston, a majority of respondents indicated
they were busing their children out of the ghetto to obtain
quality education, but not necessarily integrated education.
In order to clarify the parents' position as to the value
of quality and integrated education, the parents were reinterviewed at the beginning of the second year of busing for
their children and asked if they would prefer that their
children attend a quality school in their neighborhood if
such a school could be established. Although these parents
still asserted that a desire for integrated education played
in the decision to bus, they endorsed the concept of quality
schooling within the black community to a greater degree than
the parents of new enrollees in the busing program. For
many black parents, quality education and integrated education represented a conflict in values. In relation to this
finding, the issue of matching environments to persons, the
consequences of mismatch, and one example of a strategy based
on awareness of mismatch are discussed.

1116. Meers, D. R. Crucible of ambivalence: Sexual identity in
the ghetto. Clinical Proceedings, 1973, 29 (8), 171-194.

The impact of ghettoization on the informal social institutions and cultural values which shape the child's potential
for psychosexual maturity are examined. Consideration is
given to problems of masculine identity in matrifocal ghetto
families. Ghettoization of black inner city families is
seen as an indirect function of latent male-female ambivalence, and the influence of irrelevant middle class
social institutions, including the family structure and
various community agencies. Psychoanalytic and sociological
data suggest that a ghetto childhood may produce an intense
male-female ambivalence which is part of a dynamic process
through which the biases of the dominant white culture are
reinforced.

1117. Meers, D. R. and Gordon, G. Aggression and ghetto-reared
American Negro children: Structural aspects of the theory of
fusion-defusion. Psychoanalytic Quarterly, 1972, 41 (4), 585-607.

    Presents a psychoanalytic formulation of the theoretical
    structural aspects of aggression in ghetto-reared American
    Negro children. An illustrative case study is included.

1118. Meltzer, H. Nationality preferences and stereotypes of
colored children. Journal of Genetic Psychology, 1939, 54, 403-424.

    The nationality preferences of 364 colored school children
    were secured as well as reasons for these preferences. 1,265
    white school children in the same southern city also indi-
    cated their preference among the same 21 nations and races.
    The Negro was ranked first by the Negro, 20th by the whites.
    Likewise, more favored by Negroes were Japanese, Mexican,
    South American and Chinamen. Less favored by the Negroes
    were German, Pole, Swede, Jew, Scotch and Greek. Negroes
    indicated "intense like" reactions more than "intense dis-
    like" and more "like" than "dislike" reactions. The descrip-
    tive phase (concepts) applied to various groups were definitely
    stereotyped, the six most common offered for any nationality
    including 45-91% of all those submitted. Stereotyping was
    most characteristic of reasons given for unfavorable reac-
    tions.

1119. Miller, J. Jr. A comparison of racial preference in young
black and Mexican-American children: A preliminary view. Sociological Symposium, 1971, 7, 37-48.

    Previous studies have consistently indicated that minority
    children tend to show signs of a negative reaction formation
    to their minority status by preferring the image of the
    dominant race. A study is reported which explored and
    compared the patterns of racial preference of contemporary
    young black and Chicano children aged 5-7 from working class
    backgrounds. The Doll Test by K. Clark and M. Clark was
    applied to 238 black and Mexican-American children from
    Detroit and Los Angeles metropolitan areas. A strong pre-
    ference for white dolls was found at all age levels, but
    with increased age the black children moved from a total
    preference for the white doll to a medium preference for
    the black doll. Thus, age seems to influence these chil-
    dren's preference in a direction that is more supportive
    of their in-group. For the Chicano subjects, however, the
    reverse seems to be true. With increased age, these chil-
    dren showed a weaker preference for the Chicano doll and
    a stronger preference for the doll not of their racial group
    -- the white doll. Chicano girls showed a stronger racial
    preference for their own race than did the black girls; the
    same was true for boys. Black males seem to have the weak-
    est level of racial preference for their own race, with the
    black female next in own-group racial preference. Data con-
    firm earlier research on racial preference among black chil-

dren, but do not confirm the presence of ethnocentric characteristics among Mexican-American children postulated by
some scholars. Implications of these findings for the
school as a developmental socialization system are examined.
Reprinted by permission.

1120. Minuchin, S., et al. The disorganized and disadvantaged
family: Structure and process. In Families of the Slums: An
Exploration of Their Structure and Treatment, pp. 192-243. New
York: Basic Books, Inc., 1967.

This chapter deals with disorganized, low socioeconomic
families with more than one delinquent child. The study
was carried on by psychiatrists at the Wiltwyck School for
Boys in New York. The children relate to their surroundings
in a stereotyped way. This relation includes several factors: a sense of being a passive recipient of stimuli;
aggression without nuances of emotion; a narrow range of
verbal response; and a concomitant inability to focus on
an event so as to store and recover the experience.

The home environments studied are impermanent and unpredict-
able: meals have no set time, order, or place; a shared bed
may be turned over to another child or a visitor; parents'
responses to children's behavior are random, with emphasis
on inhibition rather than guidance. The child becomes impulsive in his responses, searches the reactions of others
for clues to the solution of conflict, and doesn't observe
himself or the characteristics of a situation.

This chapter includes three sections: (1) capacity for self-
observation and communication; (2) socialization of affect,
including modes of family contact; and (3) family structure.

1121. Mock, R. L. and Tuddenham, R. D. Race and conformity among
children. Developmental Psychology, 1971, 4 (3), 349-365.

Examined the relationship between susceptibility to group
pressure and the racial composition of small groups. Subjects were 280 fourth, fifth, and sixth graders, divided
evenly by sex and by race. Subjects in groups of five made
perceptual judgments, using apparatus which in successive
phases of the experimental run distorted to specified degrees the judgments allegedly coming from others in the
group. The racial, but not the sexual, composition of the
groups was systematically varied, as was the examiner's
race. Negro subjects showed more conformity than whites,
and girls more than boys. A white examiner induced more
conformity than did a Negro examiner. Conformity among
Negroes and whites increased as the number of white subjects in the groups increased.

1122. Moore, C. L. and Retish, P. M. Effect of examiner's race on
black children's Wechsler Preschool and Primary Scale of Intelligence
IQ. Developmental Psychology, 1974, 10 (5), 672-676.

> The effect of the examiner's race on low-income preschooler's
> IQ scores was examined by administration of the Wechsler
> Preschool and Primary Scale of Intelligence to 28 black males
> and 14 black females who ranged in age from 47 to 69 months,
> by three black and three white female examiners. Each child
> was tested once by a black examiner and once by a white
> examiner. The main effect of the examiner's race was sig-
> nificant for the Verbal, Performance, and Full Scale IQs.
> The children earned higher mean scores when tested by the
> examiner of similar ethnic origin. A statistically signi-
> ficant administration effect and Administration by Sex effect
> was revealed on the Verbal scale.

1123. Morland, J. K. Racial recognition by nursery school children
in Lynchberg, Virginia. Social Forces, 1958, 37, 132-137.

> 344 white and 110 Negro children in six nursery schools
> were given a picture test designed to measure their ability
> to recognize Negroes and whites. They were found to vary
> in this ability by age and race, but not by sex or by status
> of whites.

1124. Morland, J. K. A comparison of race awareness in northern
and southern children. American Journal of Orthopsychiatry, 1966,
36, 22-31.

> A comparison of northern and southern Negro and white pre-
> school children (41 in each group) on race awareness, using
> a set of photographs, showed racial and regional variations.
> ". . . In both regions Negro subjects preferred and identi-
> fied with the other race, white subjects with their own race.
> Such preference and identification were accentuated in sou-
> thern subjects. These results indicate adjustment problems
> as racial integration proceeds."

1125. Mumbauer, C. C. and Gray, S. W. Resistance to temptation in
young Negro children. Child Development, 1970, 41 (4), 1203-1207.

> Employed a game-like situation to investigate the resistance
> to temptation of 48 female and 48 male disadvantaged 5-year-
> old Negro children. Sex of examiner, sex of subject, and
> father absence or presence were varied. Expectations based
> on potential influences of father absence were not confirmed.
> Boys and girls from father-absent homes did not differ sig-
> nificantly in their resistance to temptation. Boys from
> father-present homes resisted temptation more with a female
> examiner while girls resisted temptation more with a male
> rule giver. Findings are discussed in light of previous
> research by other investigators. A satiation-deprivation
> of social reinforcement explanation is suggested to account
> for the findings.

1126. Mundy, P. The young Negro worker in Washington, D. C. Journal of Negro Education, 1949, 18, 104-113.

    Examination of 2,897 work permits issued after employment
    was secured to Negro boys, 15-17 years old, in 1945-47
    showed that such jobs as messenger, helper, porter, bus-boy,
    dishwasher, and stock boy accounted for 90%. The ratio of
    such jobs to all jobs for white boys was considerably lower,
    and white boys had monopolies in several fields. Vocational
    placement of Negro boys is criticized.

1127. Murray, W. I. A study of an aspect of social sensitivity of
some Negro high school pupils. Journal of Negro Education, 1945, 14,
149-152.

    The Progressive Education Association Scales of Social
    Attitudes, Tests 4.21-4.31, were given to two groups of
    Negro high school students in Gary, Indiana. Both groups
    were markedly liberal on the race variable. Students above
    the 75th percentile on the Otis Classification Test were
    more liberal than those below the 25th percentile. No re-
    lationship was found between liberalism and economic status
    of the family.

1128. Muse, D. Black children's literature: Rebirth of a neglected
genre. The Black Scholar, 1975, 11-15.

    The author hails the renaissance of black children's lit-
    erature, which sends "the legacies and realities of black-
    ness through the universe." The author notes that black
    children's books have been neglected by school textbook
    selection committees and librarians, by teachers and parents,
    and most of all by the young readers themselves. She also
    traces the history of black literature in America, discussing
    many authors and portrayers of black realities, who suffered
    from underexposure to an audience that sorely needed them.

1129. Nalven, F. B. Manifest fears and worries of ghetto vs.
middle class suburban children. Psychological Reports, 1970, 27,
285-286.

    The manifest fears and worries of 101 ghetto fifth and sixth
    graders were compared with those of 150 of their suburban
    counterparts. The major difference was the greater number
    of specific animal fears (including many "rats" and "roaches")
    reported by the ghetto subjects. Suggestions for developing
    relevant curriculum materials were made.

1130. Neale, D. C. and Mussel, B. Effects of big-brother relationships on the school-related attitudes of disadvantaged children.
Journal of Special Education, 1968, 2, 397-404.

    Disadvantaged children (N=87) were compared before and after
    participation in a big-brother program. Reading achievement
    and attitudes toward school, self and others were measured.

Trends in the data supported the view that participation
in the project resulted in improved attitudes toward college
students, going to high schools, and playing with friends,
as well as more favorable self-evaluations and higher aspirations.

1131. Neeley, J. J. Heckel, R. V. and Leichtman, H. M. The effect
of race of model and response consequences to the model on imitation
in children. Journal of Social Psychology, 1973, 89 (2), 225-231.

Assigned 80 Negro boys and girls, ages 3-5, to one of eight
conditions. Race of model (Negro vs. Caucasian), type of
consequence to model (reward vs. punishment), and percent of
rewarded or punished responses (20% vs. 80%) were varied.
Subjects viewed a television tape of a model (M) performing
a simple two-choice discrimination task with either verbal
reward or verbal punishment. After watching M make his
choice subject (S) then made his own choice. When S's
choice was the same as M's, imitative behavior was said to
have occurred. There were significant effects of both race
of M and type of consequence to M. Negro Ss imitated the
Caucasian M more than the Negro M and imitated the rewarded
M more than the punished M. The punished Caucasian M was
imitated at approximately the same level as the rewarded
Negro M. No significant effects of percent of reinforcement
were found. Possible explanations of the experimental results
are discussed.

1132. Nellans, T. A., Reinsel, M., Binder, B., and Burrow, W. H.
Maternal participation in a preschool project for disadvantaged
handicapped children. Training School Bulletin, 1972, 68, 207-211.

10 inner city families with preschool children participated
in a 10-month program to confront issues surrounding the
raising of a handicapped child. Basic principles of early
education were taught to all mothers. Regular opportunities
for group and individual counseling were also provided. Of
the children involved, 7 have gone to public school programs,
2 to day care programs, and 1 has remained for another year.

1133. Nelson, L. and Madsen, M. C. Cooperation and competition
in four-year-olds as a function of reward contingency and subculture.
Developmental Psychology, 1969, 1 (4), 340-344.

36 pairs of 4-year-old subjects played a game which required
cooperative interaction in order to get prizes. There were
6 trials in each of 2 conditions. When it was possible for
both Ss to get prizes on every trial, interaction was cooperative. When it was possible for only 1 S to get a prize
on a trial, interaction was most frequently of a domination-
submission variety where 1 S received only 1 or no prizes.
Subjects were often competitive such that neither S received
a prize, but some pairs reacted to the limitation or reward
with a cooperative, taking-turns interaction. It is suggested that Ss were highly responsive to the cue of limited

reward and relatively insensitive to the necessity of mutual
assistance, and the possibility of sharing by taking turns.
None of the differences between Negro and Caucasian pairs
or between middle class and Project Head Start pairs approached
significance.

1134. Nicholas, K. B., McCarter, R. E., and Heckel, R. V. The
effects of race and sex on the imitation of television models.
Journal of Social Psychology, 1971, 85 (2), 315-316.

Describes an experiment with 60 second graders divided into
four groups according to race (Caucasian or Negro) and sex.
Subjects observed four peer models of both races and sexes
in a TV film. Subjects and model confederates answered 20
questions concurrently, 10 of which were too difficult to
answer without assistance. Results indicate that females
imitated males more often than males modeled females. Caucasian females imitated males of both races frequently;
Negro females imitated Negro males. The significance of TV
as a discriminative cue for modeling behavior is discussed.

1135. Nicholas, K. B., McCarter, R. E., and Heckel, R. V. Imitation of adult and peer television models by white and Negro children. Journal of Social Psychology, 1971, 85 (2), 317-318.

Describes an experiment, with 60 second graders divided into
four groups according to race (Caucasian or Negro) and sex,
which utilized the same materials and procedures used in
another study by the same authors. Subjects observed four
white adults and peers of both sexes in a TV film. Subjects
and model confederates answered 20 questions concurrently,
10 of which were too difficult to answer without assistance.
Results indicate that subjects imitated adults of their sex.
Negro subjects imitated the woman model less than Caucasian
subjects. Peers were not imitated and no sex and race interactions were found.

1136. Oberle, W. H. Role models of black and white rural youth at
two stages of adolescence. Journal of Negro Education, 1974, 43
(2), 234-244.

The types and occupational status of the role models which
black and white rural Texas youth selected as high school
sophomores and at an interview two years later were examined.
Regardless of sex or stage of adolescence, blacks and whites
selected different types of role models. Black males selected
more glamour figures than whites and more direct family related models. Black females selected 26% glamour figures,
as opposed to 6% for white females; two years later, they
chose 16%, as opposed to 4% for whites. Substantial racial
differences also occurred in the occupational status of the
role models of black and white males and females. Again,
such differences were primarily linked to the differential
selection of glamour figures. Occupational role models in
the professional or related areas, however, were equally

popular among black and white females. Implications of findings for educators of blacks are discussed.

1137. Obordo, A. S. Status orientations toward family development:
A racial comparison of adolescent girls from low income rural areas.
Department of Agricultural Economics and Sociology, Texas A & M Uni-
versity, College Station, Texas 77840, January 1968. 99 pp.

This study examines differences in status orientations toward
family development held by Negro and white adolescent girls
and attempts to ascertain whether social class accounted
for these racial differences. Data were obtained from 99
Negro and 134 white girls who were high school sophomores
in three east central Texas rural counties. The majority of
both Negro and white girls expected an average of three children, and both groups wanted husbands with high-prestige
white-collar occupations. The expectations of both groups
were lower than their aspirations. White girls wanted to
marry 1-1/2 years earlier than the Negroes, expected their
husbands to make more money, and planned to work until starting a family. Negroes desired and expected to work after
having children. Even when social class was controlled, the
differences between Negro and white girls remained. Consequently, race does influence a number of status orientations of adolescent girls toward family development. In
some cases racial differences were even greater when only
the lower class groups were considered, indicating that class
may have an effect independent of race on the orientations
studied. Race had little effect on orientation to family
size and desired occupational level of the future husband,
but it was a significant factor in age at marriage, anticipated level of income of husband, and work after marriage.
Race does have an independent effect on aspirations and
expectations. The inculcation of a high success goal is a
dominant feature of American culture, and the Negro in some
respects is becoming assimilated into the social mainstream.

1138. Ogletree, E. Skin color preference of the Negro child. Journal of Social Psychology, 1969, 79 (1), 143-144.

Previous research has shown that in the main preschool and
primary school Negro children tended to reject their own
color, more often than older Negro children. In order to
test these findings, 199 3rd, 4th, and 5th graders (74 Negro
and 45 white), of a nonsegregated public school were given a
skin color preference test. The findings showed: (a) 72% of
the Negro children colored both figures brown; and (b) 75%
of the white children colored both figures white.

1139. Ogletree, E. and Ujlaki, V. E. The effects of ability grouping on inner city children. Illinois Schools Journal, 1970, 50 (1),
1970, 63-70.

Professional educators have long debated the values of
ability grouping of young school students. While it allows

teaching to be aimed at the level of the class as a whole,
at the same time, it creates class distinctions among the
pupils and may lead to feelings of inferiority or superiority.
Moreover, previous studies have shown that the attitudes of
the teachers toward the students' abilities have much to do
with the development of those abilities in the future. In
a situation in which ability grouping is done, the teachers
and administrators are naturally predisposed to match their
expectations to the pupils' assigned class level. The present study was conducted on elementary school students in
Detroit and Chicago while one of the authors was a teacher
in the public school system of one of these cities. A 24-
item questionnaire was given to 175 fifth and sixth graders
aged 11 and 12. The children were in ability groups designated A for high, B for average, and C for low abilities.
The questionnaire showed that a larger number of students in
the B and C groups desired to stay away from school than
those in the A group. Although all of the groups had the
same teachers for the same basic subjects, the responses
indicated that the two lower groups were generally dissatis-
fied with various aspects of their education. The responses
also indicated that all students were well aware of the
status and stigma associated with each group. In support
of this, teachers reported that when a pupil is moved from
a higher group into a lower one, it is a traumatic experience
for both the student and the class.

1140. O'Reilly, A. Racial attitudes of Negro preschoolers. California Journal of Educational Research, 1971, 22 (3), 126-130.

Results indicate that while Negro preschoolers are certainly
aware of sex roles and have a slight tendency to rate the
Negro negatively, they are not as aware of racial differences
as the children in a previous study. There was an equal
association of positive with the Negro and Caucasian figures.
There was more association of negative identification with
the Negro, which may be the result of cultural influences.
However, the difference was not great, which may be associated with the black movement trying to provide a positive
identity for Negroes.

1141. Orum, A. M. and Cohen, R. S. The development of political
orientations among black and white children. American Sociological
Review, 1973, 38 (1), 62-74.

Recent research suggests that, with socioeconomic differences
held constant, black adults are more disaffected and active
politically than their white counterparts; yet, this same
research neglects to specify the timing and location of these
differences. The present study undertakes this task, attempting to discover whether the differences in political orientation between blacks and whites is found among children as
well. The data for the study were collected by means of
self-administered questionnaires completed by 2,365 Illinois
students in 1971. The total sample consisted of approxi-

mately 50% white and 50% black students, with equal numbers
of each sex. The four major dimensions of political orientations used are the affective, behavioral, cognitive, and
evaluative. The results convincingly demonstrate that such
differences are found among very young children as well as
teenagers: e.g., among children who are 9, 10 and 11 years
old, black youngsters are consistently the more cynical and
informed politically. An effort to isolate the general
origins of these differences, moreover, suggests the via-
bility of a subcultural as opposed to a psychodynamic thesis.
The concept of a black subculture, and the evidence for it
in the analysis is promising for the study of the founda-
tions of black youngsters' political beliefs. Reprinted by permission.

1142. Palmer, E. Color prejudice in children as a function of race,
age, and residence neighborhood. Proceedings of the 81st Annual
Convention of the American Psychological Association, Montreal,
Canada, 1973, 8, 226-255.

Divided 80 children into 8 groups according to race (black/
white), age (3-4 / 8-10), and residence neighborhood (racially
mixed/racially segregated). Subjects individually participated in a two-phase, paired comparisons color selection
procedure designed to detect color prejudice. No distinctive preference-prejudice trends emerged as a function of
race and age, but white preschool 3- and 4-year-olds from
racially mixed neighborhoods demonstrated the exact opposite
of prejudice, changing significantly toward black in Phase 2
(person connotation).

1143. Palmer, E. L. The public kindergarten concept as a factor
in racial attitudes. See ERIC Abstracts, No. ED-129-936, 1975. 9 pp.

The question of whether the public kindergarten neighborhood
can effectively assume a meaningful role in the development
of children's racial attitudes is investigated in this study.
Focus centers on the public kindergarten since, in the
absence of racially mixed neighborhoods, it constitutes the
first formal interracial experience for most children. 246
6-year-old children were divided into eight groups on the
basis of race, sex, and public kindergarten experience.
Subjects individually participated in a two-part selection
procedure designed to investigate racial preferences. Children consistently registered strongest preference for same-
race individuals and totally same-race classroom settings.
The study suggests that the racially mixed kindergarten
neighborhood seems to be unable to perform effectively the
social interaction and attitude development functions one
would associate with the racially integrated residence
neighborhood. Until the latter becomes social reality, the
most concerted efforts in racial mixing may have primarily
cosmetic rather than depth effects on children's attitudes.

1144. Palmer, R. J. and Masling, J. Vocabulary for skin color in
Negro and white children. Developmental Psychology, 1969, 1 (4),
396-401.

    Hypothesized that Negro children have larger vocabularies
    for describing skin color than white children. 48 subjects
    (Ss) were used in a 2 x 2 x 2 design based on age, sex, and
    race. The experimental task had the children describe to a
    white interviewer the skin color of 16 bubble gum pictures
    of Negro and white baseball players. To determine vocabulary
    for all colors, Ss also described a series of blue paint
    samples. Results showed that the white Ss had significantly
    greater verbal ability for both the blue paint and baseball
    pictures than the Negro Ss. When a measure of relative
    vocabulary was devised, it was found that all groups of
    the Negro Ss used relatively more words to describe skin
    color than white Ss.

1145. Parish, T. S., Fleetwood, R. S., and Lentz, K. J. Effect of
neutral conditioning on racial attitudes of children. Perceptual
and Motor Skills, 1975, 40 (3), 695-701.

    An experiment to diminish the anti-Afro-American attitudes
    of 73 Euro-American children by repeated association of
    neutral words (unconditioned stimulus) and slides showing
    the color black (conditioned stimulus) is presented. Three
    experimental groups underwent one, four, and eight sessions,
    respectively, with a control group undergoing no sessions.
    Attitudes were subsequently measured by either Williams'
    Preschool Racial Attitude Measure II or Parish's Revised
    PRAM II. While an unweighted means analysis of variance of
    the Revised PRAM II results showed no significant differences
    between the anti-Afro-American attitudes regardless of
    whether the children had received zero, one, four, or eight
    conditioning sessions, the same analysis of the PRAM II re-
    sults showed a significant difference between the mean of
    the group receiving zero or one sessions, and that of the
    group receiving eight sessions. It is concluded that the
    PRAM II is more sensitive to attitude change than the Re-
    vised PRAM II and that racial attitudes of young children
    can be changed by association of a racial group with both
    positive and neutral stimuli.

1146. Patchen, M., Hofmann, G., and Davidson, J. D. Interracial
perceptions among high school students. Sociometry, 1976, 39 (4),
341-354.

    The factor structure of interracial perceptions is analyzed
    for 1,969 black students and 2,292 white students at 11
    high schools in Indianapolis. Black students' perceptions
    of white students showed six factors: norm-violations,
    academic orientation, friendliness to blacks, unfriendli-
    ness to whites, unfriendliness to blacks, and toughness.
    White students' perceptions of blacks showed six factors:
    negative views of blacks, positive views of blacks, unfriend-

liness of blacks to other blacks, physical toughness, help-
fulness, and unfriendliness to whites. Whites showed less
differentiation between positive and negative distinct features of blacks than did blacks for whites, tending to judge
them simply as 'good' or 'bad'. Perceived differences of
behavior appear realistically supported, but perceived differences of motives do not. Reprinted by permission.

1147. Pelham, J. T. An Analysis of Status Consistenty of the Pro-
jected Frames of Reference: A Racial Comparison of Males in Selected
Low-Income Areas of the Rural South. Department of Agricultural
Economics and Sociology, Texas A & M University, College Station,
Tesas 77840, January 1968. 136 pp.

This paper studies the status orientations of youths. Data
were obtained from 192 Negro and 223 white male high school
sophomores in three Texas counties and two Georgia counties
during the Spring of 1966. The major findings of the study
were the following. (1) Large proportions of Negroes and
whites alike experienced inconsistency in their projected
frames of reference. (2) Most of the inconsistency noted
was of a one-rank nature. (3) The frames of reference differed only in that the aspirational frames were slightly
more consistent than the anticipated frames of both races.
(4) Almost all of the consistency observed for both races
occurred at the highest status level. (5) Universally large
proportions of inconsistency for both races were accounted
for by two patterns -- income higher than education and occupation, and occupation lower than education and income. Two
theoretical implications emerge from the study: (a) the
degree to which the goals comprising the projected frames
of reference are integrated is a question of empirical fact;
and (b) the relevance of the theoretical formulations of
socialization and anticipatory socialization (involving subcultural differences) for studies focusing on racial comparisons of social phenomena is questionable.

1148. Peniston, E. Levels of aspiration of black students as a
function of significant others in integrated and segregated schools.
Paper presented at the Annual Meeting of the American Educational
Research Association (Washington, D. C., March 1975). See ERIC
Abstracts, No. ED-103-541, 1974. 51 pp.

The primary purpose of this study was to determine if there
are differences in level of student aspirations between students in segregated and those in integrated schools. There
are other highly related and interacting variables that may
influence levels of aspirations; namely, student performance,
significant others, and significant others' expectations. An
attempt was made to determine the importance of a student con-
stellation of "significant others" is determining both the
quality and scope of his educational performance. The second
purpose of this study was to compare, for substantial lengths
of time, the constellations of "significant others" for black
students in integrated versus segregated schools. Subjects

for this study were 428 black adolescents randomly selected
from public junior high schools in the Oklahoma City and
Boley public school systems. Among the instruments used were
the following: A "Significant Other Measurement" questionnaire developed by Stewart was used to identify those people
the subject considers important to him and those specific
people who expect of him various levels of attainment respective to education. Peniston's "Significant Others' Expectations" was constructed so as to measure the adolescent's
perception of the level of expectations which he perceives
significant others hold for his behavior.

1149. Perkowski, S. Some observations concerning black children
living in a residential care agency. The International Journal of
Social Psychiatry, 1974, 20 (1-2), 89-93.

The focus is on the experience of black children undergoing
residential treatment. The contention is that the treatment
practices developed to meet the needs of white children are not
adequate for blacks. Norwood is a residential care agency
which accepts emotionally disturbed and socially maladjusted
children who are unable to remain in their own or foster
homes for care. The children must be minimally high grade
mentally retarded level; most are in the dull-normal range.
20 black children were in residence at the time of this study
ranging from 8-15 years of age. All of the black children
had experienced the breakup of their homes either through
death or desertion of a parent. 3 children had been previously released only to be returned due to the instability
of their home situations. Black children were more disturbed than a similar group of whites. Black girls in residence were the most disturbed. The blacks in Norwood did
not socialize or form friendships with each other, the staff,
case workers, or anyone in the community. Blacks at Norwood
were taught white culture and could not identify with or
adapt to the black community when they left Norwood. The
black does not know the current jargon or body language
of his group and is not accepted by his peers upon his re-
lease from Norwood. These black children require contacts
with the elements of the black community while they are still
residents of the agency. This suggests a community based
approach to child welfare. Reprinted by permission.

1150. Peters, M. F. Socialization of black children: A critical review of the literature on parent-child relationship and socialization
patterns within the black family. See ERIC Abstracts, No. ED-117-225,
1975. 84 pp.

This review examines some of the basic sociological, psychological, and philosophical issues of childhood socialization,
and briefly discusses some of the significant influences
which impinge upon all children as they grow and develop
within their society, subculture, and family. The stated
purpose of the review is to provide a perspective for examining the basic assumptions which underly current research

on parent-child relationships within the black family. Research in the 70's concerning the socialization of black
children that also addresses various aspects of the influences in the black child's development is also examined.
Research in general is said to be characterized by poor
methodology; to ignore black families; and to concentrate
on the black poor, father-absent families, the mother-child
dyad; and to have an ethnocentric approach. The literature
is seen to be discussed in terms of popular but misleading
assumptions that seem to be explicitly involved when hypotheses are made concerning socialization patterns within
black families. What are stated to be more promising approaches
are also pointed out and two recent research projects are described in detail. In conclusion, the paper suggests a black
child family-society interaction model said to be useful
in the conceptualization of the socialization process, policy
making, and program planning.

1151. Picou, J. S. Black-white variations in a model of the occupational aspiration process. The Journal of Negro Education, 1973,
42 (2), 117-122.

By developing and analyzing a causal model of the occupational aspirations for black and white rural youth, an attempt
is made to expand knowledge about occupational choice. The
causal model relates SES, academic performance, and occupational aspirations consistent with current theoretical and
empirical literature. 915 black and white rural high school
seniors in Louisiana make up the sample. Three SES indicators were used: Father's occupation, family income, and
father's education. Five major findings were: (a) black and
white students had similar occupational aspirations; (b) the
three status indicators had weak direct effects on academic
performance; (c) father's occupation and education showed
the greatest direct effects for white youth while family
income showed the greatest effect for the black; (d) academic
performance had the strongest direct effect on aspiration,
even more so for whites; and (e) this model explained more
variance for the occupational aspirations of white youth.
The process of forming occupational aspirations incorporates
one's personal evaluation of his own competency. Reprinted by
permission.

1152. Picou, J. S., Azuma, H. T., and Cosby, A. G. Status projections of delinquent and non-delinquent lower class black males. L.S.U.
Journal of Sociology, 1971, 1 (1), 4-19.

A report on a comparative analysis of the occupational and
educational projections of lower class delinquent and non-
delinquent black youth residing in a selected area of Louisiana. Data were obtained from group administered questionnaires presented to 141 black ninth grade males and 73 students incarcerated in an all-black juvenile institution in
the Baton Rouge area. A sample of 98 noninstitutionalized
students was also used from high schools within Baton Rouge.
The occupational aspirations of both delinquent and non-

delinquent respondents were found to fall primarily into
three categories -- professional, glamour, and skilled occupations. The distribution of aspirations in both subsamples
were similar. The occupational expectations of the respondents followed a pattern similar to occupational aspirations;
both groups had similar high school occupational aspirations
and expectations. Regarding educational projections, the
educational goals of respondents in both subsamples were
relatively similar. There was a tendency for larger percentages of non-delinquents to have educational projections.
Implications of the findings are discussed. It is concluded
that, overall, the study revealed that lower class black
youth are oriented toward upward social mobility. Reprinted by
permission.

1153. Picou, J. S., Cosby, A. G., Lemke, J. W., and Azuma, H. T.
Occupational choice and perception of attainment blockage: A study
of lower class delinquent and non-delinquent black males. Adolescence, 1974, 9 (34), 289-298.

The types of occupational choices made by southern black
delinquent adolescents were investigated to compare the
occupational projections of delinquent and non-delinquent
males and to determine the degree of perception of a set
of factors as possible blocks to obtaining these occupations.
Findings reveal that both lower class delinquent and non-
delinquent black ninth grade males desire and are optimistic
enough to plan for prestigious occupational placement. Further, respondents maintained an overall awareness concerning
possible blocks to their occupational success. Future research in this area should be designed on a longitudinal
basis to provide information concerning occupational attainment and patterns of adjustment to blockage factors.

1154. Picou, J. S. and Curry, E. W. Athletic success as a facilitator of adolescents' mobility orientations: A black-white comparison.
Paper presented at the Southern Sociological Society Annual Meeting
(Atlanta, Georgia, April 1974). See ERIC Abstracts, No. ED-109-269,
1974. 24 pp.

Past research is held to indicate a consistent relationship
between participation in interscholastic athletics and
educational orientations. This research is said to focus
specifically on the "athletic success." Athletic success
should be a stronger facilitator of the mobility attitudes
of black youth, it is argued, because sports is fast becoming a viable avenue of mobility for blacks in the U.S. The
data for this study come from a statewide probability sample
of Louisiana high school seniors, collected in 1970. Variables incorporated in the analysis include socioeconomic
status, scholastic performance, significant-other influence,
athletic success, and educational aspirations. The results
of a partial correlation and regression analysis are said
to indicate that athletic success is significantly related
to the educational aspirations for only the black respondents. This finding, along with others, is considered to

lead to the conclusion that the student-athlete role provides behaviors that lead to higher-status educational
orientations primarily for black youth: white youths'
aspirations appear to develop more so in terms of relationships posited in current models of status attainment. Some
suggestions are presented which modify achievement models
for black athletes, and several alternative research strategies are outlined.

1155. Pierce-Jones, J., Reid, J. B., and King, F. J. Adolescent
racial and ethnic group differences in social attitudes and adjustment. Psychological Reports, 1959, 5 (3), 549-552.

Hypothesis was that white and Negro adolescents with similar
mental ability levels differed in selected orientation
toward society and its institutions, and in personal social
adjustment. Two self-report instruments were given to 84
Negroes, 84 Anglos and 84 Latin Americans. Negroes score
highest or most negativistic, Anglos lowest. Different
attitudes of these groups are interpreted as culture related.

1156. Piwowar, E. M. Preschooler's response to questions concerning parental roles while enrolled in a 1965 Head Start program of
a settlement house. Child Study Center Bulletin, State University
College, Buffalo, 1966, 2 (5), 110-115.

14 Negro children were individually tested for verbal responses to the questions, "What does a father do?" and "What
does a mother do?" The majority of responses to the mother's
role were positive. Both boys and girls were very close
in their concept and perception of the mother role. The
boys had a larger percentage of negative responses to the
father's role than the girls. The responses of the girls
showed a greater variety than the boys.

1157. Porter, James N. Race, socialization and mobility in educational and early occupational attainment. American Sociological Review, 1974, 39 (3), 303-316.

It is suggested that significant others, such as parents and
peers, relate to a boy on the basis of their perception of
his mental ability and his (and their) origin position in
the stratification system. Data were first collected in
1960 from grade 12 males in a stratified random sample of
American high schools, and a follow-up was conducted in 1965.
It was found that for both blacks and whites, intelligence
is the most important antecedent of significant others'
influence (SOI); but for blacks creativity is of slight
import and SES origin has no significant effect while the
reverse is true for whites. Among both blacks and whites,
ambition does not affect expectations more strongly than
aspirations, suggesting that for blacks, being ambitious
is partly a matter of conforming to (white) middle class
conceptions of self. The educational attainment of both
groups is more strongly affected by intelligence, and occupational attainment for both groups is more strongly affected

by education than by any other variable in the model. It
would appear that the theoretical view of ambition as a direct
expression of a middle class world view is largely incorrect
for whites, but tends to be correct for blacks.

1158. Porter, Judith D. R. Black Child, White Child: The Development of Racial Attitudes. Cambridge: Harvard University Press, 1971.
278 pp.

Two interconnected problems are studied: (1) the effect of
sociocultural factors on the formation and content of preschool
children's racial preferences; and (2) the assimilation of
attitudes and objective factors by the black child that define him as a member of a negatively evaluated social group.
Variations in age, sex, social class, intergroup contact,
shade of skin color, and racial evaluations on components
of self-concept were considered for a group of 400 black
and white children in preschool facilities during 1965 in
Boston. Racial feelings are already present in preschool
children, but not uniformly so for each racial group. Black
children have low self-esteem, and white children are
attracted to the favored white status. The self-esteem of
black children, however, is further defined by a group
identity affected by class identity and a personal identity
more influenced by economic and family stability; i.e., the
black middle class child has more positive personal esteem
and less positive racial esteem than the poorer black child.
These data add a dimension to the consideration of black
self-image and indicate the necessity for including variations in social class and racial attitudes in future studies.
Available literature is assessed, and recommendations for
future research are made. Desegregation was shown to have
no negative effect on black self-esteem, since racial attitudes were not as important in social contacts as other
variables such as age and sex. Recommendations are made
for increased desegregation at the preschool level with a
commitment to integration by policy makers and teachers
trained in the presence and development of racial attitudes
at this early age.

1159. Powell, E. R. and White, W. F. Peer-concept ratings in
rural children. Psychological Reports, 1969, 24 (2), 461-462.

Comparison of peer perceptions of 95 rural Negro and 95 white
elementary level students shows substantial differences
across race in the factor structure on a form of Osgood's
Semantic Differential. Caste, class, race, grade level,
poverty level, or other factors should, in further studies,
be related to the depressed peer evaluation of Negro samples
should this low evaluation reappear.

1160. Pugh, R. W. A comparative study of the adjustment of Negro students in mixed and separate high schools. Journal of Negro Education, 1943, 12, 607-616.

   The Symonds Adjustment Questionnaire was administered to 100 students from mixed schools (black and white students) and 106 students from separate schools (all black) to compare the adjustment of the Negro students in two school situations. To determine the attitudes of Negro students toward Negroes and correlates with their adjustment, a revision of the Baumgardner Scale for the Measurement of Negroes' Self-Respect was administered to 81 students from a separate high school and 41 from a mixed school. Students in mixed schools were better adjusted in their homes and family relationships than those in separate schools. The latter were less satisfied with their administrators and teachers. Separate school students were better adjusted to the school life in their schools. There is a low positive correlation between racial self-respect and the adjustment of the students but no significant difference was found in race pride for the two groups. (Modified.)

1161. Radin, N. and Kamii, C. The child-rearing attitudes of disadvantaged, Negro mothers and some educational implications. Journal of Negro Education, 1965, 34 (2), 138-146.

   The Parental Attitude Research Instrument (PARI), a Likert-type questionnaire, was administered to 64 culturally deprived, Negro mothers and 50 middle class, Caucasian mothers of 3-, 4-, and 5-year-old children. An item analysis was performed in terms of the percentage of mothers in each sample who agreed with each statement. Items revealing the greatest agreement and disagreement between the two groups were identified and analyzed. It was concluded that lower class mothers view the world with profound suspicion. They approve of overprotective behavior regarding external dangers and suppressive behavior regarding internal impulses. Neither approach is conducive to the development of internal controls, which is essential to academic achievement. In addition, their lack of interest in listening to children's problems prevents youngsters from learning to resolve conflicts by verbal means. The role of the school in aiding disadvantaged mothers to foster success in the classroom is discussed. Among the suggestions offered is that educators encourage parents to emphasize the importance of thinking through the causes and consequences of behavior, and to point out alternative ways of responding to problem situations. Reprinted by permission.

1162. Radke, M. J. and Frazer, H. G. Children's perceptions of the social roles of Negroes and whites. Journal of Psychology, 1950, 29, 3-33.

   Studied 90 Negro and 152 white children in kindergarten, first and second grades in Philadelphia public schools,

from residence populations varying from 5 to nearly 100%.
Negroes were tested as to comprehension and interpretation
of social roles of Negroes and whites. Essentially, they
were given colored dolls and asked to tell stories about
them. 38% of the white children and 16% of the colored ascribed to the Negro dolls inferior social roles. The poor
house was typically assigned to the Negro dolls, and the good
to the white, on the part of children of both races. Stereotyping and assumption of inferior roles for the Negro characterized colored as well as white children.

1163. Radke, M. J., Sutherland, J., and Rosenberg, P. Racial attitudes of children. Sociometry, 1950, 13, 154-171.

475 Negro and 48 white children between ages of 7 and 13
were studied for children's evaluation of racial differences. The attraction and repulsion expressed by both Negro
and white children on the questions of friendship are related to perceptions of personality characteristics of each
race. These perceptions, in which the undesirable characters are ascribed to the Negro children and desirable to
the white are consistent with the wish to both Negro and
white children to name white children as friends. Conclusions emphasize early patterning of social perceptions and
reactions to race.

1164. Raths, L. and Schweickart, E. F. Social acceptance within
inter-racial school groups. Educational Research Bulletin, Ohio
State University, 1946, 25, 85-90.

By use of a six-point social acceptance scale designed for
use in upper grades of the elementary school, two fifth grade
sections and two sixth grade sections, each of which included both white and colored children, were studied. Acceptance cut across sex and race. White boys showed a high
social acceptance of Negro boys and white girls showed
positive acceptance of Negro girls. Negro children indicated that they thought white children were "good persons
to have around." Each racial group tended to give higher
acceptance scores to members of the opposite sex who were
of like race but not without exception. The authors interpret their findings as indication that in these classes
"the field is rich for further experimentation in curriculum-
making directed toward closer integration of the racial
group.

1165. Reed, R. J. Ethnicity, social class and out-of-school educational opportunities. Journal of Negro Education, 1975, 44 (3),
316-334.

An examination of the extent to which formal out-of-school
educational opportunities were used by a stratified sample
of eighth grade students randomly selected from the public
schools in one urban center and those of its suburban satel-
lite cities. Students were stratified on the basis of school

location which provided an initial estimation of SES level
and ethnicity -- Asian, black, Mexican, and white Americans.
Out-of-school education opportunities (OSEO) were defined
as formal institutionalized educational services found outside the formal school setting and included private services
(purchases), semi-private services (provided by churches,
clubs, or other groups with perhaps a small fee attached)
and public (free). Questions were formulated to examine
whether: (1) parental knowledge of OSEO and students' use
of OSEO were associated with ethnic group membership and
SES; (2) parental attitude toward the value of education was
related to the students' use of OSEO activies; (3) propinquity
was associated with knowledge of the availability and students'
use of OSEO activities; and (4) students' sex was associated
with knowledge of availability and use of OSEO activities.
Data were collected through the use of questionnaires mailed
to parents and structured parental interviews. The Rund-
quist and Sletto Attitudes toward the Value of Education
Scale, and a self-developed questionnaire and interview
schedule were also used. Methodology used by the U.S. Bureau
of the Census was employed to determine SES. Data were analyzed through the use of multivariate and univariate analysis
of variance and Scheffe's post hoc pairwise contrasts. An
overall alpha of .05 was used to determine statistical significance. Responses were received from 296 parents (56%)
and interviews were conducted on a random sample of 28 parents.
The responding sample included 18.9% Asian-Americans, 21.3%
black Americans, 15.5% Mexican-Americans, and 44.3% white
Americans. Only 1 upper SES Mexican-American was identified
in the responding sample and was not included in the analysis.
Findings revealed that: (a) knowledge of the availability
of OSEO activities is related more to SES than it is to
ethnicity with the possible exception of low SES Asian-
Americans who demonstrate little difference on the dimension
when compared to middle and upper SES groups regardless of
ethnicity; (b) greater use of public OSEO activities were
observed within middle and upper SES ethnic groups -- Asian-
Americans, and to a lesser extent white Americans, used these
services more than black Americans; (c) upper SES groups regardless of ethnicity used private OSEO activities to a
greater extent than did middle or low SES groups; (d) use
of OSEO activities declines with lowering SES levels, however,
Asian-Americans generally excell in the use of OSEO activities within each SES group; (e) no differences were observed
on parental attitude toward the value of education between
ethnic groups of SES levels; (f) significant differences
were observed between SES levels for propinquity as upper
and middle SES groups were located further away from the
OSEO services they used; and (g) only one significant difference was found on the basis of SES: black American females
reported private OSEO activities were less available than
did males. Reprinted by permission.

1166. Reid, I. De A. General characteristics of the Negro youth
population. Journal of Negro Education, 1940, 9, 278-289.

    This paper discusses the following aspects of Negro youth:
    Forces which form the community background; statistics of
    population distributions; health status, including birth,
    sickness and death rates; occupational trends; economic
    characteristics; educational determinants and attitudes
    toward the social situation.

1167. Rice, A. S., Ruiz, R. A., and Padilla, A. M. Person perception, self-identity, and ethnic group preference in Anglo, black
and Chicano preschool and third grade children. Journal of Cross-
Cultural Psychology, 1974, 5 (1), 100-108.

    Presented color photographs of young male adults to 72 pre-
    school and 68 third grade Anglo, black and Chicano children.
    The photographs depicted persons of the same ethnic groups
    as the children. All subjects (Ss) were able to discrimi-
    nate between the photographs of the Anglo and black males
    but the preschool Ss were unable to make the finer distinc-
    tion between the Anglo and Chicano photographs. All Ss
    indicated the appropriate photograph when asked which looked
    most like them. Among the preschool Ss neither the black
    nor the Chicanos expressed significant preferences for their
    own ethnic group, while a significant number of Anglos se-
    lected the Anglo photograph as the one they liked most. At
    the third grade level, only the Chicano subjects displayed
    a strong preference for their own ethnic group.

1168. Richardson, S. A. and Emerson, P. Race and physical handicap
in children's preference for other children. Human Relations, 1970,
23, 31-36.

    The previous study reported by the senior author indicated
    that physical handicap is such a powerful cue in establish-
    ing preference that it almost completely matched the pre-
    ference based upon skin color. This study attempted to
    explore the problem in a situation where skin color was a
    predominant or deciding factor. 199 Negro girls in two
    schools of southern cities were asked to respond to a
    stimuli which showed children with various physical handicaps.
    The subjects were asked to select pictures illustrating chil-
    dren with different skin colors and a variety of physical
    handicaps. Previous research indicated that the Negro girls
    in segregated schools do indeed take skin color into account.
    Their judgments represented that of the dominant white society;
    the researchers conclude that the school setting offers an
    opportunity for influencing the self-respect of Negro girls.

1169. Richardson, S. A. and Royce, J. Race and physical handicap
in children's preference for other children. Child Development, 1968,
39, 467-480.

    The purpose of this study is to determine the relative
    salience of skin color and physical disability in establish-

ing children's preference for other children. The method
employed was to obtain a rank-order preference of drawings
in which skin color and handicap were systematically varied.
Subjects were children aged 10 to 12 from lower income
Negro, white, and Puerto Rican families and from upper
income white Jewish families. Results suggest that, for
all subjects, physical handicap is such a powerful cue in
establishing preference that it largely masks preference
based on skin color. Interpretation of results was aided
by use of sociometric data on race preference.

1170. Rist, R. C. The milieu of a ghetto school as a precipitator
of educational failure. Phylon, 1972, 33 (4), 348-360.

A kindergarten through eighth grade ghetto school was
studied from 1967 to 1970. The principal, teachers, and
staff were black, as were all students. Corporal punishment was administered by the teachers and principal in
blatant disregard of the rules governing the striking of
children. The teachers carried rattan sticks up to five feet
long. In some cases, ability to control the children was a
factor in determining the grade level at which a teacher
taught. Eighth grade students who supervised rooms in
the teacher's absence were permitted to use force, as were
school patrol boys in halls and corridors. The violence
system of the school was a hierarchical one. The violence
within the school reflects the surrounding cultural milieu,
but the presence of violence and control-oriented behavior
reinforces this. Thus, the principal and teachers placed
themselves in the untenable position of reinforcing the
failure and withdrawal of the students. Palliative measures
of restraining the use of violence will not be sufficient
if there is serious intention of improving the education
of black children within the ghetto school. There will have
to be a fundamental shift in how children within the school
are viewed.

1171. Rist, R. C. The Socialization of the Ghetto Child into
the Urban School System. Washington, D. C.: Brueau of Research,
Office of Education (DHEW), June 1970. Also, see ERIC Abstracts,
No. ED-111-898, 1970.   521 pp.

Both participant and non-participant observation were used
to analyze longitudinally a single group of black ghetto
children in their school, homes, and with their friends. A
basic goal of the study is said to consist in accounting for
the educational experience of children over time. Two beginning chapters describe public schools and American society,
and the methodology of the study. A third chapter on the
St. Louis public schools provides a backdrop from which is
analyzed the activities of an individual classroom within
the system. An introduction to the Attucks School follows,
along with a description of its social and cultural milieu.
Four subsequent chapters which follow are said to demonstrate the impact of teachers' expectations, initially based

on a series of subjectively interpreted social criteria for
both the anticipated academic potential and subsequent differential treatment accorded to students perceived as having
dissimilar social status. A final chapter on black children
in a public school provides a summary, conclusions, considerations for innovation (policy and programs), and the
perceptions of low income children. Appendixes and a bibliography are included.

1172. Rist, R. C. Student social class and teacher expectations:
The self-fulfilling prophecy in ghetto education. Harvard Educational
Review, 1970, 40 (3), 411-451.

A major concern has been to analyze the various ways in which
the school experience of the black child is affected by the
impact of social organization developed in the classrooms
by the various teachers. The kindergarten, first and second
grade classrooms observed in consecutive years revealed an
organizational pattern that perpetuated the existing stratified
class patterns of the larger society. For example, the manner
in which the black children were organized beginning with
their kindergarten experience may have had the function of
ensuring that they remained on a similar, if not identical
occupational status level as their parents. The ghetto
school strongly shares in the complicity of maintaining
the organizational perpetuation of poverty and unequal opportunity for blacks in the United States. Reprinted by permission.

1173. Rivera, R. J. and Short, J. F. Jr. Occupational goals: A
comparative analysis. In M. W. Klein (Ed.), Juvenile Gangs in Context, pp. 70-90. Englewood Cliffs, N.J.: Prentice-Hall, Inc., 1967.

This is a report on the status of origin and the occupational
goals of 462 Negro and white gang and nongang adolescents,
interviewed in Chicago by the staff of the Youth Studies
Program. Data indicate that all categories of Negroes rank
below all categories of whites in terms of social status,
and that if social status is to be used as an explanatory
variable in theories of delinquent behavior, then race must
be controlled as a conditional variable whatever the social
level -- community or nation -- at which explanations are
sought. Data analysis of occupational goals reveals the
following: (1) all groups expect to attain positions well
above their present status; (2) within the gang and nongang
categories, racial differences are either less pronounced
or actually reversed; and (3) with race controlled, the expectations of gang boys are lower than those of nongang boys,
considering their status of origin. Variation in occupational
goal levels is found to be related to certain aspects of
local structure of opportunity. In three out of four instances,
boys without fathers or father substitutes are more frequently
oriented toward higher levels of occupational success. In
three out of four comparisons, adolescents who maximize contact with high status adults have higher occupational goals
than their peers. Goals are especially high for those lower

class adolescents whose contacts and orientations are directed
to persons and occupations beyond those represented within the
local community. A review of all variables under consideration
indicates that family organization, as such, is only tenu-
ously related to the types of community-level influences
which the authors take as their central concern. From their
data, the authors make some suggestions for dealing with
the actual and perceptual occupational discrepancies with
which gang boys must deal.

1174. Robins, L. N., Jones, R. S., and Murphy, G. E. School milieu
and school problems of Negro boys. Social Problems, 1966, 13 (4),
428-436.

A test of a hypothesis that the more children having social
characteristics associated with good school performance there
are in a school the better will be the performance of the
remainder of the student body. The study was carried out
on the whole population of Negro boys entering segregated
schools in St. Louis in 1937-38 and attending for six or
more years (N=528). Characteristics found associated with
an absence of academic failures and/or truancy for the population taken as a whole were high IQ, guardian's high status
occupation, birth in a non-southern city (other than St.
Louis), and few changes of address. The presence or absence
of the father was not related. Modal (i.e., nonadvantaged)
children were then defined as children with IQs of 85-109,
who had none of the social characteristics found associated
with superior school performance. The school performance of
these modal children was compared among schools successively
grouped according to the percentage of advantaged male
classmates (classmates who had guardians with high occupational status, northern cities as birthplaces, and only 1
or 2 home addresses). The percentage of classmates with
fathers present was also tried, though it had not been related to performance in the total population. Differences
by two-tailed Chi-square test were not significant, but the
presence in the school of a higher percentage of children
of high SES or born in northern cities was associated with
somewhat fewer academic failures among modal children. The
presence of a higher percentage of children of high SES
and with a father in the home was associated with somewhat
less truancy among modal children. Effects may have been
slight because advantaged Negro children were rare in all
the schools. Reprinted by permission.

1175. Rohwer, W. D. Jr. Learning, race, and school success. Review
of Educational Research, 1971, 41 (3), 191-210.

A consideration of the questions, "Why does school success
depend more directly on ethnicity, socioeconomic status (SES),
and IQ than on the ability to learn?" and "Do intelligence
tests index learning proficiency?" Negro and white children
are compared and it is concluded that the development of
tests to measure learning proficiency and learning style is

crucial for obtaining an understanding of the phenomena en-
compassed by the topic of "Race and School Achievement." A
major objective of curricula in the early years of schooling,
especially for low-SES Negro children, should be to assist
them in mastering elaborative learning skills, i.e., to
actualize children's capacity for imaginative conceptual
activity through concrete and specific instructional programs.
It is hoped that the pursuit of these two aims will help to
increase the degree of school success attained by disadvantaged
children to the level indicated by their basic learning proficiencies.

1176. Rooks, E. and King, K. A study of the marriage role expectations of black adolescents. Adolescence, 1973, 8 (31), 317-324.

Administered the Marriage Role Expectation Inventory and a
personal questionnaire to 112 16- to 19-year-old twelfth
grade black students to ascertain if their marriage role
expectations were of an equalitarian or traditional type.
The Kolmogorov-Smirnov, two-sample, two-tailed test was
used to determine if the expectations were independent of
sex, family structure, family power structure, and social
class. Results indicate that despite social class black
adolescents expect equalitarian marriage roles concerning
authority, housekeeping, and the care of children. (Modified.)

1177. Rosen, C. E. The effects of sociodramatic play on problem-
solving behavior among culturally disadvantaged preschool children.
Child Development, 1974, 45 (4), 920-927. Also, see ERIC Abstracts,
No. EJ-109-767, 1974.

1178. Rosenberg, M. L. An Experiment to Change Attitudes of Power-
lessness Among Low-Income Negro Youth. School of Applied Social
Sciences, Case Western Reserve University, Cleveland, Ohio 44106,
June 1968. 156 pp.

This paper tests the hypothesis that attitudes of powerlessness among low-income Negro youths can be reduced through an
experimental manipulation which reverses the power relationship between a youth and a role partner who would ordinarily
be in the high power role. In addition, it was hypothesized
that there is a correlation between powerlessness and self-
esteem and that therefore attitudes of self-esteem would
also be elevated as a result of the role reversal intervention. An experimental situation was structured in which 56
Negro youths from the Neighborhood Youth Corps were paid for
a six-week period to perform the duties of field instructor
to college graduates who were being trained as youth employment counselors. Attitudinal questionnaires were administered before and after the experimental period to participants and to a control group of 40 similar youths. A second
area of analysis sought to gain a deeper understanding of
the relationship between powerlessness and social aspirations
related to goal-striving behavior.

Among the major findings of the study are the following: (a)
The experimental intervention of role reversal failed to
alter the attitudes of powerlessness. The most plausible explanation is that intervention was not of sufficient magnitude to alter an attitude that was deeply rooted in social
and economic circumstances which were left unaltered. (b) The
hypothesis of an inverse relationship between powerlessness
and self-esteem was refuted by statistical findings. If
current social service approaches continue to expand, unaccom-
panied by major social structural reform, these programs will
probably succeed in intensifying the very strife they seek
to ameliorate. (c) There is a significant degree of association between high aspirations, high expectations, and
low powerlessness -- and the converse is true. (d) Social
workers and others should abandon their misplaced efforts
to motivate low-income Negro youths. Their level of aspiration far outstrips the capacity of the opportunity system
to accommodate these aspirations. However, if opportunities
were opened, the capacity to utilize them would have to be
developed because of deeply entrenched attitudes of powerlessness among Negro youths.

1179. Rosenhan, D. L. Effects of social class and race on responsiveness to approval and disapproval. Journal of Personality and
Social Psychology, 1966, 4 (3), 253-259.

An interaction theory of social class behavior was proposed
in which young lower class children were presumed to be more
alienated and uncomfortable than middle class children with
middle class people and institutions. Hypothesis was, as a
result of alienation, approval should facilitate the performance of lower class children while disapproval should
retard it. Hypothesis was substantiated. Within the lower
class there were no performance differences between Negro
and white subjects, indicating that for young children social
class differences are more potent determiners of behavior
than racial differences.

1180. Rothman, C. Differential vulnerability of WISC subtests to
tester effects. Psychology in the Schools, 1974, 11 (3), 300-302.

A study to determine whether the previously observed vulnerability of WISC subtests to tester effects appeared under
ordinary testing conditions, and which subtests were most
susceptible to these effects is presented. The WISC was
administered to 175 white, black and Puerto Rican children,
aged 8-13, who had been placed in foster care. Subjects
were randomly assigned to one of three trained testers. To
determine the vulnerability of each subtest to tester effects,
multiple correlations were computed between the three testers
as a group and each subtest. Results support the presence
of both general and differential vulnerability of subtests
to tester effects during routine test administration, and
reaffirm the need for more serious consideration of the
tester variable in the evaluation of WISC performance.

1181. Rubin, D. Parental schematic of Negro primary school children.
Psychological Reports, 1969, 25 (1), 60-62.

Used a modified Kuethe Felt Figure Technique to objectively
measure Negro (N=115) and white (N=127) primary school children's placement of self on a field in relation to parental
figures. This study using a more stringent measurement for
achievement than an earlier study by D. Rubin substantiated
earlier findings with white subjects, i.e., placement of
"self" for white subjects is a function of both sex and
achievement. The new findings show that for Negro subjects,
placement of "self" is only a function of achievement.

1182. Rubin, R. H. Adult male absence and the self-attitudes of
black children. Child Study Journal, 1974, 4 (1), 33-46.

Administered a self-concept and background questionnaire to
280 black fifth and sixth graders to investigate the finding that the frequent absence of adult males from the household of lower class blacks results in boys perceiving themselves as less worthwhile persons compared to boys who live
with adult males and to girls who live with and without an
adult male. This is attributed to a lack of male role models
for boys and to negative female attitudes about males. No
support for this hypothesis was found for the subjects. The
availability of male role models outside the home and the
significance of adult males within the home are suggested
as explanations for the nonsignificant results. (Modified.)

1183. Russell, M. J. The socioeconomic background of Negro youth
in California. Journal of Educational Research, 1956, 49, 617-620.

Southern Negro youths were interviewed regarding migration
to other parts of the country. Tenth grade California youths
were also interviewed as to problems associated with migration.

1184. Sachdeva, D. Social class origin and interracial student
attitudes in desegregated schools. Southern Journal of Educational
Research, 1975, 9 (4), 209-222.

Administered a demographic and attitude questionnaire to
1,131 black and white students in a newly integrated junior
high school in Berkeley, California. Subjects were classified into 12 groups according to grade level, socioeconomic
status (determined by census tract data), and race. Social
class origin, race, and grade level did not have any effects
on student responses to 11 of 19 items dealing with work in
school, attitudes toward school, or making new friends. Findings suggest that personal contact explains more changes in
student attitudes than social class origin.

1185. Samph, T. and Sayles, F. Racial Attitude and Cultural Expression Test (RACE): Student questionnaire. Washington, D. C.: National
Institute of Education (DHEW), May 1974. 12 pp. Note: Not available separately from #1186 below. See ERIC Abstracts, No. ED-101-014.

>   Designed to measure the racial attitudes of children, the
>   items of RACE (Racial Attitude and Cultural Expression Test)
>   are founded on a theoretical base established from the liter-
>   ature. Each item is replicated to provide internal consistency
>   checks on each response set. Scoring is done by hand and is
>   assumed to provide interval data. Reading skills are not
>   required for the student to respond. RACE has 12 tasks to
>   be read and described by the teacher. Each task has a picture
>   or group of pictures which the student may arrange in any
>   order he desires in relation to himself. These pictures are
>   of black and white males and females. Test-retest reliability
>   was computed and demonstrated an acceptable level on the
>   variables of Linear Distance, Student Inclusion, Identifica-
>   tion, and Power. Even though selected variables discriminated,
>   overall, the instrument failed to discriminate positive and
>   negative student attitude groups.

1186. Samph, T. and Sayles, F. A Validation Study of RACE (Racial
Attitude and Cultural Expression Test): Final Report. Washington,
D. C.: National Institute of Education (DHEW), May 1974. 87 pp.
See ERIC Abstracts, No. ED-101-013, 1974. Note: For question-
naire, see #1185 above.

>   The intent of this investigation was to perform a validation
>   study to determine whether RACE (Racial Attitude and Cultural
>   Expression Test) differentiates between primary grade students
>   identified as having negative and positive attitudes. Stu-
>   dents were categorized by a combination of administrator,
>   teacher and clinical assessment into a negative or positive
>   racial attitude group. These students were administered
>   RACE to determine whether it could discriminate and whether
>   an acceptable level of reliability was present. The variables
>   of Linear Distance, Student Inclusion, Identification, and
>   Power demonstrated acceptable reliability and discrimination
>   levels. Even though selected variables discriminated, over-
>   all, the instrument failed to discriminate positive and nega-
>   tive student attitude groups.

1187. Santrock, J. W. Paternal absence, sex typing, and identification. Developmental Psychology, 1970, 2 (2), 264-272.

>   The effects of paternal absence, and its relationship to
>   older siblings and a father substitute, on the dependency,
>   aggression, and masculinity-femininity of 60 preschool
>   Negroes were assessed by structured doll-play and maternal
>   interviews. Preschool father-absent (FA) boys were signi-
>   ficantly more feminine, less aggressive, and more dependent
>   than their father-present (FP) counterparts, but no signifi-
>   cant differences occurred between FA and FP preschool girls.
>   The maternal interview proved to be a more discriminative

device than the doll-play interview in revealing sex-typed
behaviors. FA girls with older female siblings only were
significantly more dependent than FP girls with older male
siblings only, and FA girls with older male siblings only
were significantly more aggressive than FA girls with older
female siblings only. FA boys with older male siblings only
were significantly more masculine than FA boys with older
female siblings only. FA boys with a father substitute were
significantly less dependent than FA boys with no father
substitute.

1188. Sappington, A. and Grizzard, R. Self-discrimination responses in black school children. Journal of Personality and Social
Psychology, 1975, 31 (2), 224-231.

Self-discrimination responses in black school children are
examined. Trials of a digit symbol task were administered
to black junior high school subjects in the presence of
either white or black counselors. The task was labeled as
either intellectual or motor skill. In addition, measures
of expectancy, incentive anxiety, hostility, defensiveness
and task satisfaction were obtained. The subjects performed
better in the presence of whites and this results was a
function of task complexity and task labeling. Of several
theories considered, Spence's analysis of the relationship
of drive level to performance can best explain the data.
No source for the increased drive in the presence of whites
was found.

1189. Schab, F. Adolescence in the South: A comparison of black
and white home, school, religion and personal wishes. Adolescence,
1974, 9 (36), 565-568.

A sample of 1,806 high school students from Eastern Tennessee, Georgia, and Western Florida were divided by race and
sex (437 white females, 655 white females, 400 black females,
and 314 black males) and completed an open-ended questionnaire. Each item began with "I wish . . . ," followed by "my
father," "I were more," "my teachers," "I were less," "growing
up," I didn't have to," or "the future." In their responses
sex and race made little difference except when affluence
was involved and here black males wished for more than
their environment was providing. All the subjects wished
for more understanding and consideration. All were not
completely satisfied with themselves.

1190. Schaefer, C. and Brown, S. Investigating ethnic prejudice
among boys in residential treatment. Journal of Social Psychology,
1976, 100 (2), 317-318.

32 black, 11 white, and 10 Hispanic 8- to 13-year-old boys
in a residential treatment center for emotionally disturbed
children rated all the other boys in their cottages using
the Comfortable Interpersonal Distance Scale (CIDS). There
were no significant differences between CIDS scores that

members of each ethnic group gave to their own versus those given to the other groups. Results support the value of the CIDS as a quick, economical means of assessing ethnic prejudice among youth.

1191. Scherer, S. E. Proxemic behavior of primary school children as a function of their socioeconomic class and subculture. Journal of Personality and Social Psychology, 1974, 29 (6), 800-805.

A study of the proxemic behavior of primary school children as a function of their socioeconomic class and subculture is reported. In the first study, pairs of lower class black children and white children were photographed conversing in a school yard, and interaction distances between dyad members were computed. Results indicate no differences between subcultures. In the second study, the effects of subculture and socioeconomic class on interaction distance were explored. Middle class children were found to stand further apart while conversing than were lower class children. There was no difference between blacks and whites.

1192. Schuler, E. A. Attitudes toward racial segregation in Baton Rouge, Louisiana. Journal of Social Psychology, 1943, 18, 33-53.

A series of hypothetical case situations involving racial segregation were described to 357 white and 276 colored eighth grade pupils in Baton Rouge. For each, the subjects were asked to check one of five possible solutions, representing varying attitudes toward the general problem, and to indicate the reasons for their choice. The overall scores for the white children were not significantly different from the Negro scores. Members of each racial group tended to infer advantages in segregation for their own race.

1193. Schuster, J. W. The values of Negro and Caucasian children: Do they differ? Journal of Negro Education, 1968, 37 (1), 90-93.

A study is reported which assessed the values of a total sample of 93 Negro and Caucasian children with the use of the measuring instrument devised by Monroe Rowland in Elementary School Study of Values, San Diego, California: San Diego State College. Parental vocation was used as a variable to determine upper socioeconomic class. Only children of parents who were members of a profession, who operated key managerial positions, or who had a college education were included. Family income was not considered. Analysis of value variance showed that there were no significant differences between the $\overline{X}$ deviations of the female children of either race on any of the values and only 1 significant difference for the male children. This one difference occurred between Caucasian and Negro males in the category 'theoretical values.' Further analysis of the data showed that the three most important variables in the differentiation between the two sexes of both races were the same values in which females score usually higher than males: esthetic,

social, and religious values. In general, a large area of
homogeneity which appears to transcend race is seen to exist.
Even regarding the one observed difference in theoretical
values it may be assumed that with integration a regression
toward the X̄ will occur within a generation. Reprinted by permission.

1194. Sciara, F. J.   Effects of father absence on the educational
achievement of urban black children. Child Study Journal, 1975, 5
(1), 45-55.

In a study of the effects of father absence on educational
achievement, achievement test scores in reading and arithmetic
were collected from 300 children from father absent homes
and 773 children from father present homes, and analyzed
by utilizing the variables of year, sex, family status and
intelligence. Test scores were from fourth grade black
youngsters from eight urban schools in a low income area.
Consistency of the test scores was established over the
two-year period. The analysis of variance revealed significant differences favoring the academic achievement of
both boys and girls from father present homes in the two
test areas. Father absence had a much greater effect on
the achievement of boys and girls whose measured intelligence quotient was above 100.

1195. Sciara, F. J. and Jantz, R. K.   Father absence and its
apparent effect on the reading achievement of black children from
low income families. Journal of Negro Education, 1974, 43 (2),
221-227.

The effect of father absence on the reading achievement of
all black fourth grade children enrolled in eight model
cities schools of a large metropolitan midwestern school
system was examined. For 1,073 children, those from father
present homes achieved significantly higher reading achievement scores than those from father absent homes. Both sexes
were equally affected. When subjects were analyzed by
three various ranges of IQ scores, father absent children
achieved lower reading scores than those from father present homes. Findings are tentative, however, because
several important variables (length of time living in father
absent home and socioeconomic level) were not controlled.
Father presence nonetheless fosters a greater cohesiveness
of family and more family activities offering greater adult-
child verbal interaction and experiential variety than father
absence conditions. All of these characteristics are directly
related to school placement and particularly to reading.

1196. Scott, R.   Home Start: Family centered preschool enrichment
for black and white children. Psychology in the Schools, 1973, 10
(2), 140-146.

Presents some results of a Home Start program designed as a
total milieu effort to shape the interaction of children,
families, and communities into a sequence of experiences

conducive to physical, social, emotional, and cognitive
growth. Subjects were 160 4- to 5-year-old children who
were placed into either the Horizontal Home Start (HHS)
consisting of classroom-centered educational enrichment or
the Vertical Home Start (VHS) consisting of individualized
enrichment. Analysis of the Primary Mental Abilities tests
data indicate that white subjects appeared to profit from
participation from either kind of Home Start program while
black subjects derived cognitive benefits from a more extensive and home-centered program.

1197. Scott, R. Home Start: Follow-up assessment of a family
centered preschool enrichment program. Psychology in the Schools,
1974, 11 (2), 147-149.

Reports a follow-up of a family-centered preschool program.
The white subjects' profile remained stable but the black
subjects' profiles had significant accretional shifts on
the number-facility and spatial relations subtests of the
Primary Mental Abilities Test.

1198. Scott, R. Research and early childhood: The Home Start
Project. Child Welfare, 1974, 53 (2), 112-119.

The Home Start project, an experiment in early intervention
to promote learning in deprived children is discussed. Factors included are parental involvement in Home Start. The
ways that particularly vulnerable families are identified
and referred to community agencies, and longitudinal effects
19 months after termination of the program. The parents of
89 children, 51 black and 38 white applied for Home Start;
all were accepted. 44 children had older siblings who were
used as controls. The tests of Primary Mental Abilities (PMA)
were utilized to assess the impact of Home Start, inasmuch
as this instrument yields not only a total IQ, but four subtest scores that provide a general, but educationally useful,
readiness profile. A follow-up study compared the scores
of the Home Start children and their older siblings 19 months
after similar comparisons were made. Findings revealed that
there was little change in the cognitive profiles of the
white Home Start group and their siblings, while there were
significant shifts in the cognitive profiles of the black
Home Start group.

1199. Seeman, M. Skin color values in three all-Negro school classes.
American Sociological Review, 1946, 11, 315-321.

Skin color ratings were made for 81 children in three all-
Negro classes (3-6). Data were also obtained by sociometric
and interview techniques. There was almost complete absence
of skin color as a verbalized motivation, except in response
to direct questioning, when a preference for light skin was
found. When friendship choice and reputation in the group
were used as measures of the operational importance of skin
color differences, skin color was an important variable in

two of the three classes, lighter color being associated with
greater acceptability and better reputation. There is a discussion regarding skin color as a social value in socialization.

1200. Seeman, M. A situational approach to intragroup Negro attitudes. Sociometry, 1946, 9, 199-206.

79 pupils from two interracial fifth grade classes were given
the Ohio State Social Acceptance Scale. The pupils had previously been rated as to skin color on a six-point scale
from "white" to "very dark brown". Analysis of acceptability
scores shows that skin color is a factor in determining
social acceptability. In general, white skinned children
are less acceptable than those with any brown skin in spite
of the fact that many Negro children apparently desire white
skin. A light brown skin was found to be characteristic of
the children most acceptable to this group.

1201. Seiden, R. H. Why are suicides of young blacks increasing?
HSMHA Health Reports, 1972, 87 (1), 3-8.

In recent years, the suicide rate of 15- to 19-year-old black
females has exceeded that for their white female age peers.
Suicide rates for blacks of both sexes below the age of 35
in New York, Washington, Los Angeles, Chicago, and Atlanta
are higher than for whites. On a national level, mortality
statistics indicate that the suicide rate for black males
and females is now at the highest point in 50 years. Research is needed in such variables as social class, stresses
of urbanization, and militant activities. If the rise in
black suicides is to be explained by the theory of status
integration, the increase would occur largely among middle
class and upwardly mobile members of the population. Conversely, if fatalistic suicides were responsible for the
increased rates, the bulk would occur among the lower class.

1202. Shapiro, B. N. Comprehension of Television Programming De-
signed to Encourage Socially Valued Behavior in Children: Formative
Research on "Sesame Street" Programming with Social and Affective
Goals. New York: Children's Television Workshop; and Amherst:
University Research Council, Massachusetts University, September 22,
1975. 228 pp. Also, see ERIC Abstracts, No. ED-122-863, 1975.

A study assessed children's comprehension of Sesame Street
programming that is designed to encourage socially valued
behavior and whether the children relate the programming to
their own living experiences. Material relating to four
goal areas was tested: (1) entering social groups; (2) coping
with failure; (3) coping with basic emotions; and (4) sex
role stereotyping. Some 73 black, white and Spanish-speaking
children who were enrolled in Head Start Centers in inner
city areas of Springfield and Holyoke, Massachusetts, were
the viewers and respondents in the study. In general, the
children's comprehension of the social goals material was

good. About one-third of the children seemed to be able to
answer open-ended questions about most of the material without
prompting. Another large proportion of the children appeared
to be the least able to recognize the correct answers to questions when they were read lists of multiple choice alternatives which served as prompts. There were no striking differences in the responses of the male vs. female children or the
black vs. white children. All of the children were attentive
or very attentive to the program segments and appeared to
enjoy themselves. Although older children performed significantly better than younger children on some questions, this
finding did not occur consistently.

1203. Shaw, M. E. Changes in sociometric choices following forced
integration of an elementary school. Journal of Social Issues, 1973,
29 (4), 143-157.

The effects of integration on racial tolerance and acceptance
were investigated. Sociometric questionnaires were administered to grade school children, after desegregation. Both
blacks and whites at three grade levels chose significantly
more members of their own race. Interactions increased
significantly with grade level; however, subsequent analysis
revealed that the primary variable determining interracial
interactions is the proportion of blacks to whites in the
classroom. A relatively low proportion of minority members
(black or white) appears to be most effective in improving
interracial relations.

1204. Shaw, M. E. and Schneider, F. W. Negro-white differences in
attribution of responsibility as a function of age. Psychonomic
Science, 1969, 16, 289-291.

An attribution-of-responsibility (AR) questionnaire was
administered to matched samples of Negro and white children
representing four age levels. Ethnic differences were observed in the two youngest groups, whereas there were no
ethnic differences among the older children. In the younger
age groups, Negroes showed a generally less differentiated
pattern of AR than the whites. The results were interpreted
as supporting the hypothesis that a deprived cultural background retards the rate of learning norms concerning responsibility attribution.

1205. Shoffner, S. M. Influences on occupational goals of young
people in the North Carolina appalachian area -- Baseline data and
action program. North Carolina Agricultural Experiment Station
Technical Bulletin No. 233. Washington, D. C.: Department of Agriculture. Also, see ERIC Abstracts, No. ED-133-130, 1975. 93 pp.

The study focused on the level and nature of low-income
youths' ambition to achieve, the factors relating to varying
degrees of ambition, and the extent to which group sessions
with the mothers influenced the children's career thinking
and planning. The study design included a baseline phase

in which a large sample survey provided background information for analysis and for the second phase's design, and an
experimental phase which included group meetings with the
mothers. In the baseline phase, 217 children and their
mothers were drawn from three communities in one county in
the Appalachian region of North Carolina (regional sample
totaled 1,412 mother-child pairs). The experimental group
discussion program was designed to influence information,
attitudes, and aspirations concerning education and occupations among low-income mothers, and indirectly among their
children (seventh and eighth graders) as a result of the
mother's interaction with them. Data were analyzed with
those from the regional sample (rural and urban Negro and
Appalachain white subcultures). Standardized questionnaires
were administered to both mothers and their children before
and after application of the experimental program. Program
content was designed to help mothers understand: their
children's unique interests and abilities, the variety of
work opportunities for their children, the relationship
between education and occupations and between the children's
interests and career possibilities, and their own roles in
motivating their children toward career planning.

1206. Short, J. F. Jr. Comment on Lerman's "Gangs, networks, and
subcultural delinquency." American Journal of Sociology, 1968, 73
(4), 513-514. Reply, 515-517.

Comments on SA 2151/C9561 are presented which raise some
conceptual and methodological questions. P. Lerman's thesis
that "the pair or triad, not the group or gang, is the social
unit most frequently used by subcultural boys in their
deviance," was tested through a survey of Chicago gang and
nongang boys. Data, in one table, illustrate that "there
is less large-group solidarity among Negroes and perhaps
less willingness to report association with a regular group
among Negroes." All of the respondents in this sample were
members of regular groups, but chose to identify themselves
with one or two friends in answer to the survey question.
These data do not deny the gang (regular group) as a setting
for delinquent subcultures; they may, in fact, define its
nature. For it is in the closer relationship among two or
three friends that much of gang life occurs. Reply, Paul
Lerman (Columbia University, New York, New York), notes that
Short's paper ignores the fact observed and stated by Lerman
that many pairs and triads which by word and deed are active
participants in a neighborhood's deviant youth culture are
nevertheless not members of gangs. The main research issue,
according to Lerman, is phrased as follows: "How shall we
conceptualize the placement of pairs and triads within a
delinquent subculture?" It is stated that instead of perceiving the Negro pairs and triads in Short's survey as dispersed
gang boys, it seems more appropriate to accept their own
descriptions of peer life; they probably gang together only
when they have to. On the basis of Short's data, his conclusion is rephrased: "Boys who participate in a deviant youth

culture are either nonmembers, occasional members, or persistent
members of regular groups." Hence, the differences between
the two authors are but on social facts and interpretations
of these facts. Reprinted by permission.

1207. Short, J. F. Jr. Street corner groups and patterns of delinquency: A progress report. American Catholic Sociological Review,
1963, 24 (1), 13-32.

An overview of a large-scale study of 'delinquent gangs'
involving collaboration of the YMCA of Metropolitan Chicago
and a research team under the direction of the author. Detached workers from the YMCA provide entry to the gangs for
the research team and constitute a primary source of data
concerning the boys, individually and collectively. The
research is directed to the examination of recent theories
regarding the impact of the social class structure on adolescent boys. Semantic differential data suggest that Negro
and white lower class gang and nongang boys, and middle
class boys do not differ in their recognition of the moral
validity and the legitimacy of some middle class values.
However, gang boys evaluate illegitimate images more highly
than do other boys, and their behavior is inconsistent with
middle class values. An explanation for this discrepancy
is sought in terms of the operation of 'aleatory' factors
peculiar to lower class settings and group process considerations. Further study is underway concerning these processes
and various elements of competing delinquency theories. Reprinted by permission.

1208. Silverman, I. and Shaw, M. E. Effects of sudden mass school
desegregation in interracial interaction and attitudes in one southern
city. Journal of Social Issues, 1973, 29 (4), 133-142.

The extent to which blacks and whites interacted socially
on school grounds and their attitudes toward each other were
ascertained across time during the first semester of an
investigation program in three secondary schools. Interracial interactions remained sparse throughout the semester,
and over time showed no increases approaching significance
though attitudes did become more tolerant. Several effects
on both variables related to race, sex, and grade level are
reported.

1209. Simon, R. J. An assessment of racial awareness, preference
and self-identity among white and adopted non-white children. Social
Problems, 1974, 22 (1), 43-57.

Levels of racial awareness, racial preferences and racial
identities are reported for non-white children (American,
black, Korean, American-Indian), who have been adopted by
white families. The respondents are all children between
the ages of 3 and 8. The reactions of these children are
compared to those of the same sex, age range, and race who
have been reared in typical family settings. The major
findings are that black children who are reared in the

special setting of multiracial families do not acquire the
ambivalence toward their own race that has been reported
among all other groups of young black children, and that
there are no significant differences in the racial attitudes
of any of the categories of children.

1210. Slaughter, D. T. Parental potency and the achievements of
inner city black children. American Journal of Orthopsychiatry, 1970,
40 (3), 433-440.

Educators, behavioral scientists, clinicians, and parents
have recently focused on the effect of the attitudinal
variable futility, or a sense of powerlessness, on the
achievement of black children. This study explores the
assumption that the sense of impotence and frustration felt
by the inner city black parent contributes significantly to
the low level of achievement performance among ghetto children. The method was to examine the product moment correlation coefficients of the variable, futility, measured
by an educational attitude survey, with inner city black
children's achievements and with other related parental
variables. The initial sample was drawn from 153 children
and mothers enrolled in a Head Start program. The results
indicate that futility, when associated with mothers' attitudes toward the educational system, has little significance for the actual achievements of inner city black
children in the early grades. Futility is, however, a
stable attitudinal disposition of these mothers and is
significantly correlated with their own educational level
and value for school achievement by their children. Con-
ceivably, this variable is important for the continuity
of children's achievements. Parental feelings of potency,
while perhaps necessary, are not sufficient conditions for
higher levels of achievement by black children. Maternal
behaviors which focus upon the teaching and informing or
protective efforts of the mother seem to be of greater significance in the early grades. Futility may be a realistic
attitude within the urban black community. The findings
imply that any efforts aimed only at change of this attitude
may miss the central objective of the educational system --
to teach the children. The second objective is to demonstrate that the children have been taught. Programs for
parental involvement must be developed to support these
objectives. Those designed to make the parents feel more
powerful are insufficient.

1211. Smith, D. H. The street is the community school. Education
and Urban Society, 1969, 1 (4), 363-374.

A description of the exploitation and abuse black people
are subjected to in the inner city by almost all institutions
of society: stores and supermarkets, the school and, worst
of all, the police and the national guard and the armed forces.
But black children learn a whole community culture, mostly
in the street, that serves them as protection against the

aggression of white society. First there is the language.
Beginning with the days of slavery, through the emancipation
and the migration to southern and northern cities, there has
developed a black idiom, with a unique patterning and
sprinkled with African terms, that serves both communicative
and protective needs. Another thing the black inner city
child learns is the facility to tell a convincing lie. Still
another quality learned at the street academy is distrust
of everyone. The street school also develops a brilliant
hustler culture. The final attribute of the ghetto child
is a fierce in-group loyalty. The situation of the blacks
has changed radically since the Summer of 1967, the black
Summer. They have developed a pride in themselves, and
they demand control over their lives. The changed mentality
has taken the school by surprise, and teachers do not know
how to handle the new black pupils. White people instinct-
ively believe that "white is beautiful," a bias that does
not allow for the equal beauty of a pluralistic society.
They must work themselves out of this monistic position
and schools must learn how to teach pupils with a black pride.
Reprinted by permission.

1212. Smith, E. J. Reference group perspectives and the vocational
maturity of lower socioeconomic black youth. Journal of Vocational
Behavior, 1976, 8 (3), 321-336.

A nearly economically homogeneous sample of 188 black high
school seniors of both sexes from a New York metropolitan
area, provided an opportunity for investigating possible in-
group differences in reference group perspectives and vocational maturity among lower socioeconomic black youth. The
Survey of Community Opinions, the Career Maturity Inventory
(both primary instruments here), and the Two-Factor Index
of Social Position were administered. Reference group
perspectives emerged as related to career maturity. Students
evidencing an orientation toward middle class reference group
perspectives obtained higher vocational maturity scores
than those who subscribed to reference perspectives traditionally associated with the lower class. Subjects' sex
and family background were not related to their reference
group perspectives nor to their vocational maturity ratings.
Subjects' post-high school plans (either work or college)
and their views of the U.S. opportunity structure were related
to both their reference group perspectives and career maturity
scores. Black youth from a lower socioeconomic group must
not be treated as a homogeneous group in terms of career
maturity. Reprinted by permission.

1213. Smith, K. B. and Ohlendorf, G. W. Marital and procreative
projections of rural Louisiana youth: A historical comparison.
Paper presented at the Annual Meeting of the Southern Association
of Agricultural Scientists (New Orleans, Louisiana, February 1975).
See ERIC Abstracts, No. ED-101-881, 1975. 46 pp.

Changes in marital and procreative projections among rural
Louisiana high school youth between 1968 and 1972 were examined.

In 1968 a proportionate, stratified, random cluster sampling
technique was employed to secure data on seniors from 13
white and 7 black high schools. In 1972 public school integration and the establishment of private schools prevented
historical comparison of the same schools, but insofar as
was possible an attempt was made to involve the specific
respondents who would have been 1972 seniors in the 20
schools from 1968, corresponding to the racial grouping of
the 1968 sample. In both instances an 18-page version of
the 1968 S-61 Southern Youth Study Questionnaire was group
administered with the exception of one school in the 1972
sample (544 questionnaires were completed in 1968 and 453
in 1972). Data measuring change were analyzed by sex, race,
and residence relative to the following items: (a) Desired
Age at Marriage; (b) Number of Children Desired; (c) Number
of Children Expected; (d) Desire for Wife Working After
Marriage; (e) Expectation for White Working After Marriage;
and (f) Importance of Family and Marriage. Tabular data
constitutes the major portion of this paper, while a brief
narrative describes the research procedure.

1214. Solkoff, N. Race of examiner and performance on the Wechsler
Intelligence Scale for Children: A replication. Perceptual and
Motor Skills, 1974, 39 (3), 1063-1066.

A replication of a previous study undertaken to assess the
relationship between race of examiner and performance on the
Wechsler Intelligence Scale for Children is reported. Findings indicate that, as in the study of a Buffalo, New York
sample of 108 black and white boys and girls, there is no
evidence in the present research, conducted with a St. Louis
sample, that white examiners depress the WISC performance
of black children. Results reveal that where there are
significant race of child-race of examiner interactions,
the black children achieve their highest scores with a
white examiner.

1215. Solomon, D. and Houlihan, K. A. Relationships of parental
behavior to "disadvantaged" children's intrinsic-extrinsic motivation for task striving. Journal of Genetic Psychology, 1972, 120
(2), 257-274.

Assessed the "intrinsic-extrinsic" motivation of 72 Negro
fifth graders by subtracting scores measuring their performance on tasks with "uninvolved" examiners (Es) from scores
on tasks with "involved" Es. Several measures of school
achievement and achievement orientation correlated negatively
with these discrepancy scores. Parent behavior factors
were derived from parent-child interaction measures obtained
in the home. Several mother behavior factors were positively
correlated with girls' striving discrepancy scores in divergent tasks, while several father behavior factors were
positively correlated with boys' discrepancy scores in convergent tasks. It is suggested that results represent the
combined effect of the child's familiarity with the E behavior and the sex-appropriateness of the particular tasks.

1216. Solomon, D., Parelius, R. J., and Busse, T. V. Dimensions
of achievement related behavior among lower class Negro parents.
Genetic Psychology Monographs, 1969, 79 (2), 163-190.

> 72 sets of lower class Negro parents were observed helping
> their fifth grade children with a series of intellectual
> tasks. Measures of behavior, obtained from observers' ratings,
> tallies of nonverbal acts, and analysis of tape recordings,
> were factor analyzed separately for mothers and fathers.
> Mother factors were called: direct, simple participation;
> encouragement of independent achievement efforts; warmth;
> and general interest. Father factors were called: encour-
> agement of independent achievement efforts; general verbal
> participation; geniality; hostility; and interest in situa-
> tions and tasks. Relationships were found between parent
> factor scores and family size, apartment condition, sex of
> child, and birth order of child.

1217. Spencer, M. B. and Horowitz, F. D. Effects of systematic
social and token reinforcement on the modification of racial and
color concept attitudes in black and in white preschool children.
Developmental Psychology, 1973, 9 (2), 246-254.

> Investigated previous findings that preschool children nega-
> tively perceive the color black and black people and posi-
> tively perceive the color white and white people. Subjects
> were 24 black and 24 white Head Start children. Attempts
> to modify this finding were made using black and white
> puppets, contingent reinforcement, color meaning, racial
> attitude, and preference procedures. Subjects were divided
> into groups as to race of subject and race of examiner. Re-
> sults indicate negative attitudes about the color black
> along with black people. An improvement was noted with con-
> tingent reinforcement.

1218. Sprey, J. Sex differences in occupational choice patterns
among Negro adolescents. Social Problems, 1962, 10 (1), 11-22.

> Observed differences between the educational and occupa-
> tional choice patterns of Negro male and female high school
> subjects (Ss) are explained within the framework of the
> theory of anomie. The data -- occupational aspirations,
> expectations, and curricular enrollment figures -- were
> obtained in New Haven, Connecticut, and Harrisburg, Pennsyl-
> vania. Total population: 2,596 Ss of whom 533 Negro. The
> choice pattern of the white Ss was used to evaluate the choice
> differences within the Negro category. Negro males were
> found to differ significantly from white, and from Negro
> females in aspirations and curriculum choice. The factor
> of a southern background was found to affect Negro males
> as a category more negatively than females. It was tenta-
> tively concluded that the condition of anomie in which Negro
> adolescents find themselves affects males, as a category,
> more severely than females, and results in a different mode
> of adjustment for the former. The adjustment is a redefini-
> tion of the male role within the Negro subculture. Reprinted
> by permission.

1219. Stabler, J. R., Johnson, E. E., Berke, M. A., and Baker, R. B.
The relationship between race and perception of racially related
stimuli in preschool children. Child Development, 1969, 40 (4),
1233-1239.

    67 white and Negro preschoolers evaluated 40 assorted objects
    for their positive or negative affect quality by placing the
    objects before a painted smiling or frowning face. Although
    racial differences between groups were predicted, none were
    found. Subjects subsequently made guesses as to which of
    two boxes, a white or black one, contained the different
    objects. Both groups tended to guess that the negatively
    evaluated objects were located in the black box and the
    positively evaluated objects were located in the white box,
    but the effect was more evident for white subjects than
    for Negro subjects. Results were related to the introjec-
    tion of racial stereotypes by children.

1220. Stabler, J. R., et al. Children's evaluation of the colors
black and white and their interracial play behavior. Child Study
Journal, 1976, 6 (4), 191-198. Also, see ERIC Abstracts, No. EJ-
157-306, 1976.

    This study investigated the relationship between children's
    response to the colors black and white and their interracial
    behavior. Subjects were 20 black and white male and female
    preschoolers. The children were observed in a free play
    situation on a playground. Color preference and attitudes
    were measured in three different ways.

1221. Stake, J. E. Effect of achievement on the aspiration behavior of black and white children. Journal of Personality and Social
Psychology, 1973, 25 (2), 187-191.

    Members of five fifth grade classes of a racially inte-
    grated school in California were divided into low-achievement,
    average-achievement, and high-achievement groups on the basis
    of an arithmetic test. Discrepancy scores were obtained
    from subject expectations. The results of the study offer
    further evidence of a strong relationship between achieve-
    ment and aspiration. Failure groups produced very high and
    negative discrepancy scores. Race had no significant effect
    in the study.

1222. Staples, R. To be young, black and oppressed. The Black
Scholar, 1975, 7 (4), 2-9.

    Approximately 54% of the black population is under 24 years
    of age, compared to 42% of the white group. This large
    number of young Afro-Americans is central to the function-
    ing of certain "colonial" institutions, such as the schools,
    the military, and the economy. As in classical colonial
    societies the use of colonized youth seems to increase the
    privileges which accrue to members of the ruling group.
    The official unemployment rate for black male teenagers is

38.1% and for females 41.3%, but the actual rate may be
65%. Black youth now comprise the largest segment of the
industrial reserve army, yet to many low-income black
families the additional income of their children is vital
to their existence. The behavior of many unemployed black
dropouts is harmful to the black community since most victims
of black crime are blacks. While the suicide rate for black
people is generally lower than for whites, the suicide rate
for black youth in large cities is higher than for their white
counterparts.

1223. Starkey, K. and Boyce, J. A. III. Experimenter effect in a
study of racial identification by urban kindergarten children.
Paper presented at the Annual Meeting of the American Educational
Research Association (Washington, D. C., March 30-April 3, 1975).
See ERIC Abstracts, No. ED-107-376, 1975. 14 pp.

A total of 192 kindergarten children were randomly chosen
from an urban school district. The pupils were divided
equally between 5- and 6-year-olds, males and females, and
blacks and whites. The four experimenters -- a black female,
a black male, a white female, and a white male -- presented
five photographs to the children. The number of pictures
correctly identified on a "something like me" basis, were
entered in a 2 x 2 x 2 x 2 x 2 factorial analysis of variance.
The only significant difference (p=.003) was the interaction
between the child's race and the experimenter's sex.

1224. Stephan, W. G. and Kennedy, J. C. An experimental study of
interethnic competition in segregated schools. Journal of School
Psychology, 1975, 13 (3), 234-247.

Decomposed matrix games were used to study interethnic
competition in the ethnic school system of a Southwestern
city. The sample consisted of sixth grade males (N=135)
from segregated schools. In addition to the data from the
matrix games, brief questionnaire measures of internal vs.
external locus of control, self-esteem, and authoritarianism
were also obtained. The results on the game matrices indicated that Anglos competed more and were less trusting than
blacks or Chicanos. Questionnaire results indicated that
blacks were highest on feelings of external control and on
authoritarianism, while Chicanos were lowest in self-esteem.
Cooperative interethnic work groups were suggested as a
means of coping with problems these differences might cause
in integrated schools. Reprinted by permission.

1225. Stevenson, H. W. and Stevenson, N. G. Social interaction
in an interracial nursery school. Genetic Psychology Monograph,
1960, 61, 37-75.

The social behavior of ten 2- and 3-year-old children at an
interracial nursery school was observed. The majority of
the children showed some form of racial awareness. There
were no differences by race on behavioral measures of the

children. Conclusion was that physical difference associated
with race did not influence the type or degree of social interaction the children had with other members of the group. (Modified.)

1226. Stevenson, H. W. and Stewart, E. C. A developmental study of
racial awareness in young children. Child Development, 1958, 29,
399-409.

A series of tests involving discrimination of physical differences between Negroes and whites and attitudes toward
race were presented to 125 white and 100 Negro subjects
between ages of 3 and 7. There was a relationship between
age and the ability to discriminate. White subjects developed this ability at a younger age. (Modified.)

1227. Stinnett, N., Talley, S., and Walters, J. Parent-child
relationships of black and white high school students: A comparison. Journal of Social Psychology, 1973, 91 (2), 349-350.

Compared selected aspects of parent-child relationships
of 167 white and 167 black high school students. Variables
included degree of closeness with fathers and/or mothers
during childhood, source of the most discipline during
childhood, degree of praise received, source of most affection, greatest source of parental influence, and degree of
freedom in talking with parents about problems. Black
subjects experienced closer parent-child relationships than
white subjects even though black subjects were much less
likely to have both parents at home. Results also indicate more mother-oriented environments among black families.

1228. Stroup, A. L. and Robins, L. N. Elementary school predictors
of high school dropout among black males. Sociology of Education,
1972, 45 (2), 212-222.

In a sample of 223 black urban males, elementary school
predictors of high school dropout were analyzed. Of 13
original variables, six produced a multiple correlation
with dropout of .637. School retardation, truancy, early
drinking activity, parental social status and number of
elementary schools attended were most clearly associated
with high school dropout. In the past, large families
with consequent overcrowding, lack of an educational tradition, and broken homes have been cited as reasons for
high school dropouts among slum children. Results here
suggest that early school performance, continuity in the
same school and family atmosphere matter more than these
factors. The variables that were not found important were
variables which the school has no power to influence. The
variables found important suggest activities which the
school system itself might experiment with in hopes of
giving slum children a better chance. Elementary schools
could offer greater incentives to regular attendance, individualized instruction to prevent failure, and could allow

children to stay on in a familiar school when their families move across a school district boundary. Reprinted by permission.

1229. Summers, D. L. and Felker, D. W. Use of the It Scale for Children in assessing sex-role preference in preschool Negro children. Developmental Psychology, 1970, 2 (3), 330-334.

Investigated the effectiveness of the It Scale for Children (ITSC) with 30 preschool lower socioeconomic class Negro children and the validity of the It figure as a projective device. The mean age of the boys was 64.6 months (SD = 8.2) and that of the girls was 63.5 months (SD = 6.2). The It figure was employed as the projective device during one test administration, while a child figure drawn by each subject (S) served as the projective device during a second testing session. Results supported the hypothesis that if the ITSC is a valid projective device, scores obtained with the IT figure and the figure drawn by the child will not differ. Significant differences were found between the present data and data for lower class white children reported by M. Hall and R. A. Keith. Further analysis indicated that the identified sex of the projective figures was not crucial to the projections of the Ss and that Ss can utilize a figure of either sex as an effective projective device.

1230. Swan, R. W. and Stavros, H. Child-rearing practices associated with the development of cognitive skills of children in low socioeconomic areas. Early Child Development and Care, 1973, 2 (1), 23-38.

Studied one child from each of 26 families (12 females and 14 males, all black) during the summer between completion of kindergarten and entry into first grade. Despite low socioeconomic status, subjects exhibited effective learning patterns. Parents were evaluated in relation to four dimensions: parental philosophy and values, perception of the child, feelings of competence, and verbal interaction. In these families, parents maintained a helpful and encouraging attitude toward their children as curious adventurers, creative, and independent learners, and often interacted with them in situations which were nonconflictual, thus providing a rich verbal environment. This research adds to our knowledge about atypical parent-child interaction in low socioeconomic areas which leads to effective learning, and may be helpful in planning optimal care for disadvantaged children.

1231. Tabachnick, B. R. Some correlates of prejudice toward Negroes in elementary age children. Journal of Genetic Psychology, 1962, 100 (2), 193-203.

This study examines satisfaction with self in 10 categories as possible correlates of prejudice toward Negroes in elementary age children. Subjects were 302 children attending the fifth grade in San Francisco area schools. Gener-

ally, children who were more satisfied with themselves tended
to be less prejudiced than children who were less satisfied
with themselves. (Modified.)

1232. Taylor, T. H. Intergroup relations at a cosmopolitan junior
high. Journal of Educational Sociology, 1947, 21, 220-225.

A survey of opinions concerning group status was made among
pupils, parents and teachers of a junior high school in a
poor part of "Plains City." The school population included
Spanish-Americans, Negroes, Japanese-Americans and "Anglos."
Ten questions about equality of treatment and opportunity
and a question concerning what the schools should do, were
asked. Adults were less critical of school training than
children. Children proportionately made more suggestions
for school improvement. On these points there was not significant intergroup differences. There was a general belief
in equality of educational opportunity but of unequal housing
and job opportunity, attributed to poverty or lack of education by the children, and to race by adults. These and
other responses vary by race and nationality of the people.
Antagonism was directed mainly at the Spanish, second at
the Negroes.

1233. Teahan, J. E. The effect of sex and predominant socioeconomic
class school climate on expectations of success among black students.
Journal of Negro Education, 1974, 43 (2), 245-255.

The influence of the predominant socioeconomic class of
students on the expectations of future occupational success
of all other students, regardless of their individual socioeconomic status, was examined in five black schools in the
Catholic school system of a large industrial midwestern city.
Data support the contention that peer influence or the
predominant socioeconomic class of a school, has considerable
impact on many aspects of achievement, including those related to occupational achievement. In primarily middle
class schools, lower class males were elevated in terms of
expected success in contrast to lower class males in predominantly lower class schools. Females face additional
general influences which seem to lower both aspired goals
as well as anticipated occupational achievement. Individual
lower socioeconomic status dampens expected occupational
status, but seems to leave untouched dreams of success when
reality considerations are ignored.

1234. Thelen, M. H. and Fryrear, J. L. Imitation of self-reward
standards by black and white female delinquents. Psychological Reports, 1971, 29 (2), 667-671.

Studied the effects of 40 black and 40 white female 14- to
17-year-old delinquents observing a black or a white male
model who employed liberal or stringent standards of self-
reward even when given explicit normative information.
Subjects imitated the self-reward standard of the model.

There were no differences in imitation as a function of subject's or model's race. Comparison with a comparable recent
study showed that the black male delinquent imitated the white
liberal male model more than the black female delinquents.

1235. Thelen, M. H. and Soltz, W. The effect of vicarious reinforcement on imitation in two social-racial groups. Child Development, 1969, 40 (3), 879-888.

30 4- to 6-year-old boys observed a male model exhibit aggressive behavior. In Experiment I Head Start subjects who observed a model who received considerable verbal positive reinforcement imitated significantly less than subjects who
observed a model who received no reinforcement. Experiment II
replicated certain portions of Experiment I, but with subjects
from a laboratory school. Results showed that subjects who
observed the reinforced model imitated more than subjects who
observed the nonreinforcement model. Subjects in the positive
vicarious reinforcement condition imitated significantly more
than their counterparts from Head Start. Results were discussed in terms of past history of reinforcement for imitation
which may be linked to racial or socioeconomic variables.

1236. Thomas, E. C. and Yamamoto, K. Minority children and their
school-related perceptions. Journal of Experimental Education, 1971,
40, 89-96.

A semantic differential was administered to 300 Negro Americans, 300 Mexican-Americans, and 300 American Indian children
in sixth through eighth grades to study their attitudes to four
curriculum (social studies, language, science, mathematics) and
four people (classmates, parent, teacher, myself) concepts. No
overall sex or grade differences were found, but ethnicity and
concept differences were significant on all three people factors (movement, security, merit) and on both curriculum factors
(vigor, certainty). In addition, there were complex interactions among ethnicity, grade, sex, and concepts. Parent
enjoyed the most favorable rating for each ethnic group, while
teacher was ranked fourth position on two of the three factors.
Generally Negro children provided the most favorable ratings
on people and Indian children the least. Of the curricular
areas, language was rated most vigorous and certain by all
ethnic groups, while social studies generally ranked in fourth
position. When compared with Caucasian middle-school children, these minority children in rather favorable school
environments indicated good school-related attitudes.

1237. Thomas, H. B. The effects of social position, race and sex on
work values of ninth grade students. Journal of Vocational Behavior,
1974, 4 (3), 357-364.

The effects of social class, race and sex on the work values of
ninth grade students in a large metropolitan area were studied.
Measures of work values were obtained using Super's work values
inventory. Factorial analysis of variance and multiple range
tests were employed to determine the differences between and
among variables. Results indicated that the primary differences
were for the dependent variables of race and sex. In general,

low social position black females scored low on the work values
scales.

1238. Thompson, N. L. Jr. and McCandless, B. R. IT score variations
by instructional style. Child Development, 1970, 41 (2), 425-436.

Brown's IT Scale for Children (ITSC) is an instrument widely
used with young children for measuring sex-role preference. The
effects were examined for projective, semi-projective, and objective instructions on I score performance in 72 lower class
Negro and white pre-kindergarten children. Many white girls
responded to masculine cues in the I figure, which was not true
of Negro girls. This may be due to differences in sex-role
prestige in the two subcultures. Lower class Negro boys showed
greater preference for the feminine role as measured under the
semiprojective and objective instructions. The relation of
the ITSC scores and teacher ratings of subjects' behavior supports the hypothesis that the development of sex-role preference
precedes development of sex-role adoption, suggesting that the
development rate may be faster among white boys.

1239. Tolor, A. and Orange, S. An attempt to measure psychological
distance in advantaged and disadvantaged children. Child Development,
1969, 40, 407-420.

The psychological distance of groups of advantaged and disadvantaged children was measured with a psychological distance
board (PDB) and a modified version of the Make-A-Picture Story
(MAPS) technique. The PDB called for subjects (Ss) replacing
combinations of pairs of figures differing in social or non-
social value on a felt-covered board. The MAPS procedure permitted Ss to choose figures and scenes differing in their
advantaged-disadvantaged characterizations and to place them
wherever they preferred. Disadvantaged children are more variable in their distance responses than advantaged children and
consistently place farther apart all classes of social stimuli
but not neutral stimuli. On the MAPS there are again greater
distance responses for disadvantaged children in their placements of disadvantaged figures. The themes of disadvantaged
children's stories, however, are more affiliative, suggesting a
conflict in the establishment of optimal psychological distance.

1240. Trent, R. D. The color of the investigator as a variable in
experimental research with Negro subjects. Journal of Social Psychology, 1954, 40, 281-287.

To investigate the influence of white and Negro experimenters a
motor identification test consisting of three pictures of women,
one white, two Negro, was employed in studying 81 white and
Negro kindergarten children. Both white and Negro children
showed significant differences in the color of mother identification response depending on the race of the experimenter.
The author states "that the shift in the direction of the color
of the investigator should be considered an important variable
in experimentation with Negro subjects."

1241. Trent, R. D. The relation between expressed self-acceptance and expressed attitudes toward Negroes and whites among Negro children. Journal of Genetic Psychology, 1957, 91, 25-31.

A checklist estimated the attitudes and a sentence completion test the degree of self-acceptance of 202 Negro children. There were no significant differences between the children who were most self-accepting and those who were ambivalent; but both groups expressed significantly more positive attitudes toward Negroes and whites than did children who were least accepting.

1242. Tucker, S. Black strategies for change in America. Journal of Negro Education, 1971, 40 (3), 297-311.

Educational change is high on the priority list of black America. With a tragic lack of relevance, the educational system grinds on in most cities in seeming oblivion to the society whose needs it should be serving. Educational change does not take place in a vacuum, and strategies for change must be devised with the social, political, and economic realities which exist clearly in mind. Most black children are victimized by geography and poverty, but conflict over the legal ambiguities of desegregation could easily be immobilizing. Black children carry disadvantages with them to school, and these must be dealt with as much as the educational system itself. Concerned black people should form tactical alliances on specific issues in a pragmatic way. Indigenous leadership is developing in black communities, and its effectiveness is enhanced by a capacity to negotiate.

1243. Tuddenham, R. D., Brooks, J., and Milkovich, L. Mothers' reports of behavior of ten-year-olds: Relationships with sex, ethnicity, and mother's education. Developmental Psychology, 1974, 10 (6), 959-995.

Mothers' description of their 9-, 10-, and 11-year-old children were secured by means of a behavior inventory of 100 items, to be sorted into "true," "not true," and "uncertain" categories. Findings are reported for 2,212 whites, 641 blacks, 117 Orientals, and 79 Chicanos from an urban, largely middle class sample, broken down by ethnicity, sex of child, and in the case of whites and blacks, by education of the mother. Comparisons with 7 other studies, both American and British, show noteworthy agreement in problem prevalence, despite major differences in samples and in methods of investigation.

1244. Turner, S. M. and Forehand, R. Imitative behavior as a function of success-failure and racial-socioeconomic factors. Journal of Applied Social Psychology, 1976, 6 (1), 40-47.

Examined whether success-failure experiences, race, and social class are related to the likelihood that young children will engage in imitative behavior, using 96 economically deprived and nondeprived black and white 6- and 7-year-olds. Blacks imitated significantly more than whites on a preexperimental measure of imitation. Analysis of a difference score between pre- and post-experimental measures of imitation indicated that prior success was associated with less imitation than failure or a neutral condition. In addition, a white model was imitated significantly more than a black model in both the failure and the success con-

ditions, with little difference between models in the neutral
condition. No significant difference was found between the
nondeprived and deprived groups. Results are discussed in
terms of an outer-directedness hypothesis.

1245. U. S. Department of Health, Education and Welfare, Public
Health Service. School Achievement of Children by Demographic and
Socioeconomic Factors. Rockville, Maryland: National Center for
Health Statistics, 1971. 88 pp.

The reading and arithmetic subtests of the Wide Range Achievement Test was given to a probability sample of 7,119 children.
Average achievement ratings were highest among children in
the Midwest and lowest in the South. White children consistently surpassed Negroes in all four geographical regions. The
strongest association was between school achievement and the
socioeconomic status of parents, as measured either by parental
educational level or family income, although the white-Negro
differential was generally maintained for all demographic
and socioeconomic variables. These findings are remarkably
similar to those of the Coleman Report.

1246. Uzell, O. Occupational aspirations of Negro male high school
students. Sociology and Social Research, 1961, 45 (2), 202-204.

The purposes of this study were: (1) to investigate the
occupational aspirations of a selected sample of urban
senior high school youth in eastern North Carolina and to
relate the expressed aspirations to significant social background characteristics; (2) to identify the patterns of
inter-occupational mobility, if any; (3) to determine the
relation between occupations to which the respondents aspire
and the occupations which they expect to enter; (4) to
identify the nature of the difficulty, if any, respondents
should expect to encounter in entering aspired occupations;
and (5) to determine the sources of influence of respondents'
occupational aspirations. Questionnaires and interviews
were used to obtain data from a proportionate random sample
of 301 respondents in 14 schools and the critical ratio
test for significance was used. The two categories used
to categorize respondents for analysis of occupational
aspirations were: (a) respondent's occupational aspirations
were ranked regarding their North-Hatt prestige score, actual
or interpolated; the upper and lower third were compared on
the basis of relevant social background characteristics;
and (b) respondents were categorized regarding their aspirations as compared with their fathers' occupations. It was
found that there is a significant relationship between the
levels of aspiration of Negro male high school students
and the parents' educational level. There was a significant relationship between the levels of aspiration and
success in school. Lack of money and inadequate preparation were mentioned most frequently as difficulties which
respondents expected to encounter in seeking preferred
occupational choices. Reprinted by permission.

1247. Veroff, J. and Peele, S. Initial effects of desegregation on
the achievement motivation of Negro elementary school children. Journal of Social Issues, 1969, 25 (3), 71-91.

> Assessed change, over a one-year period, when a compulsory
> transfer of students occurred to achieve racial balance. Data
> were obtained on children's autonomous and social comparison
> achievement motivations. Results indicate that the transfer
> had a positive effect on autonomous achievement motivation
> of Negro boys, and counteracted a tendency to overaspire in
> levels of social comparison in older boys. Other results:
> school settings where a child has contact with children of
> social status below his when he is in a minority status may
> promote defensive overaspiration over some groups. Sugges-
> tions are made regarding the implications of age, sex and
> race differences in desegregation.

1248. Vriend, T. J. High-performing inner city adolescents assist
low-performing peers in counseling groups. Personnel and Guidance
Journal, 1969, 47, 897-904.

> Operating from the theoretical base that the adolescent
> social system and group procedure could be incorporated
> into strategies for improving the school performance of dis-
> advantaged students, and supervised program of peer leader-
> ship in counseling and study groups was developed for a
> group of inner city high school students. A method of
> training students to be peer leaders in the groups was de-
> veloped, and the effects of the program on the academic
> performance of the selected students were evaluated. In
> the demonstration program, the example of achieving peers
> and the support and reinforcement of a group with similar
> goals provided the impetus for inner city high school juniors
> to develop better classroom skills, higher grades, and higher
> levels of vocational and educational aspirations and expect-
> ations.

1249. Wasik, B. H., Senn, S. K., and Epanchin, A. Cooperation and
sharing behavior among culturally deprived preschool children. Psychonomic Science, 1969, 17 (6), 371-372.

> Paired culturally deprived Negro and white kindergarten
> children (N=12) in like-sex dyads to investigate cooperative
> and sharing behavior. The development of cooperative be-
> havior was demonstrated in a game situation in which subjects
> received a marble for cooperative responses. Selfish be-
> havior was analyzed using two different definitions which
> resulted in varying percents of selfish behavior. Dispari-
> ties are discussed.

1250. Wasserman, S. A. Values of Mexican-American, Negro and Anglo
blue collar and white collar children. Child Development, 1971, 42
(5), 1624-1628.

> Tested a sample of 180 4-year-old Mexican-American, Negro
> and Anglo blue collar and white collar children, using a

picture-type instrument depicting value conflict situations.
Results reveal ethnicity to be significantly (p<.05) related
to "success" and "humanitarian" values as total scores and
to three individual "success" values. The interaction variable, Sex x Socioeconomic Status, was significantly (p<.05)
related to two "humanitarian" values.

1251. Watts, F. P. A comparative clinical study of delinquent and
non-delinquent Negro boys. Journal of Negro Education, 1941, 10,
190-207.

When general intelligence and age are held constant, delinquent Negro boys do not differ significantly in competency
to respond to concrete situations as measured by the Detroit
Manual Ability Task, the Healy Picture Completion II, and
the Minnesota Paper Form Board. Neither are there any significant differences in tendencies toward problem behavior,
emotional stability as measured by the Personal Index,
Woodworth-Mathews Personal Data Sheet, and the Vineland
Social Maturity Scale, respectively. The use of these tests
in prediction relative to delinquency is questioned. The
92 delinquent and 91 non-delinquents did differ in interests,
habits, and a few attitudes as indicated by the results
obtained in an adaptation of the CET Pupil Data Sheet.
Apparently parents of delinquents exercise less control
over their children than do parents of non-delinquents.
The conclusion that delinquent Negro boys are intellectually
and educationally retarded is not supported by the data
presented. Rather, it is indicated that both groups are
retarded.

1252. Weaver, E. K. How do children discover they are Negroes?
Understanding the Child, 1955, 24, 108-112.

Subjects were 100 southern Negro children ages 6 to 13.
They were asked to answer, "When did you first discover
you were Negro?" Thirty typical responses were derived.
(Modified.)

1253. Webster, S. W. Some correlates of reported academically
supportive behaviors of Negro mothers toward their children. Journal of Negro Education, 1965, 34 (2), 114-120.

The problem is given as whether there are significant relationships between designated academically-supportive
behavior of Negro mothers to their children early in
school careers and the self-perceptions and levels of
academic achievement of the children in adolescence. It
is hypothesized that a positive relationship does exist,
regarding self-concepts, aspirations, and perceptions of
future attainments. The research method is presented, followed by discussion and a table presenting findings. It
is concluded that supportive behavior of the mother was
not directly related to high school grades when sex of children was considered; however, it was directly related to

the self-perceptions and aspirations which are associated
with the tendency to achieve high grades. Reprinted by permission.

1254. Weiner, M. J. and Wright, F. E. Effects of undergoing
arbitrary discrimination upon subsequent attitudes toward a minority
group. Journal of Applied Social Psychology, 1973, 3 (1), 94-102.

The effects of undergoing arbitrary discrimination on subsequent attitudes toward a minority group were investigated.
The hypothesis that, in this situation, a child will be
less likely to hold prejudiced beliefs and exhibit discriminatory behavior toward a minority was tested. A third grade
class was randomly divided into orange and green people.
One day, orange children were superior and the green children were inferior. On Day Two, statuses were reversed.
On Day Three and again two weeks later, the experimental
class was significantly more likely to desire a picnic with
a group of black children and held less prejudiced beliefs
when compared to the control. The manipulation did not
affect performance on Days One and Two.

1255. Wellman, B. Crossing social boundaries: Cosmopolitanism
among black and white adolescents. Social Science Quarterly, 1971,
52 (3), 602-604.

Two types of social boundary crossing are presented: attitudinal and spatial cosmopolitanism. The concept of cosmopolitanism is extended beyond its original spatial delineation
by R. Merton to include relationships across any sort of
social boundary. The data analyzed are drawn from a survey
of 1,266 black and 199 white Pittsburgh ninth graders, conducted in 1966. The students' race and SES and the racial
composition of the census tracts in which they reside are
related to measures of spatial and attitudinal cosmopolitanism.
The data are presented in a series of cross-tabulations, with
elaboration. Black respondents are found to be at least as
attitudinally and spatially cosmopolitan as are the whites.
SES is positively related to attitudinal cosmopolitanism.
There is little meaningful relationship between census
tract racial composition and attitudinal cosmopolitanism
for both blacks and whites. Implications of these findings
for changes in blacks' cosmopolitan engagement with the city
are discussed. Evidence is presented to show that blacks
are not as ghetto-bound as has often been proposed. There
is evidence of strong ties of urban black adolescents to
the larger social system of the city. There are strong
underlying commonalities in the cosmopolitanism of both
blacks and whites. There are indications that the spatial
boundaries of the black community are being extended to
include the downtown area, and that their presence there is
becoming defined as legitimate by whites. Reprinted by permission.

1256. White, K. and Knight, J. H.   School desegregation, socioeconomic status, sex, and the aspirations of southern Negro adolescents. Journal of Negro Education, 1973, 42 (1), 71-78.

> The effects of school desegregation on the aspirations of
> Negro adolescents in the South are discussed in relation
> to socioeconomic status (SES) and sex. Unemployed seniors
> from either segregated or desegregated high schools were
> selected. The sample was stratified by sex, 162 each of
> boys and girls. Aspirations were measured by questionnaires
> surveying career and college preferences. It was concluded
> that segregated southern blacks displayed higher aspirations
> in regard to college education. The lower aspirations of
> Negro adolescents in desegregated schools were not related
> to the SES of Negro adolescents. Negro females in desegre-
> gated schools in the South chose college much less frequently
> than their counterparts in segregated schools. Several
> causative interpretations are also offered.

1257. Whitmore, J. R.   "Thinking About My School" (TAMS): The
development of an inventory to measure pupil perception of the
elementary school environment. R & D Memorandum No. 125. Washington, D. C.: National Institute of Education, 1974. 86 pp.   Also,
see ERIC Abstracts, No. ED-100-998, 1974.

> Preliminary research testing the reliability and the validity
> of the "Thinking About My School" (TAMS) instrument is re-
> ported, and extensive data and analyses are included for the
> benefit of those who wish to do further evaluative work. In-
> structions for scoring and appropriate conditions for adminis-
> tering TAMS to students with low reading skills and little
> experience with self-report measures are described. TAMS
> was tried out with approximately 280 students, of whom 64,
> identified as leaders, were studied intensively. The valid-
> ity of these 64 students' scores was tested by means of
> self-concept inventories, measures of power, teacher ratings
> of behavior, sociometrics, formal observations of behavior,
> and academic achievement scores. The 64 student leaders had
> been identified by their teachers as either positive or
> negative in their attitudes toward school. TAMS results
> confirmed the reported differences. However, it appeared
> that conclusions about reliability and validity could not
> be made until the instrument has been used with samples
> from other populations.

1258. Williams, J. A., Bean, F. D., and Curtis, R. L.   The impact
of parental constraints on the development of behavior disorders.
Social Forces, 1970, 49 (2), 283-291.

> On the basis of symbolic interaction theory, it was hypo-
> thesized that either high parental permissiveness or restrict-
> iveness would lead to symptoms of behavior disorders among
> children. This hypothesis was confirmed when tested for a
> sample of 103 black households. The observed association
> was generally unaffected by a number of control variables,

but it was somewhat weaker for families with high occupational prestige, high income, or some high school education.
It is suggested that alternative sources of self-evaluation
are more available to the higher than the lower socioeconomic
status groups and that these have bearing upon the association between permissiveness-restrictiveness and behavior
disorders.

1259. Williams, J. E., Best, D. L., Boswell, D. A., Mattson, L. A.,
and Graves, D. J. Preschool Racial Attitude Measure: II. Educational and Psychological Measurement, 1975, 35 (1), 3-18.

The revised version of the Preschool Racial Attitude Measure
(PRAM II) is described. Standardization data are reported
for 252 Caucasian and 140 Negro children, ranging in age
from 37 to 85 months, who were tested by Caucasian and Negro
examiners. Analysis of the racial attitude scores revealed
that the measure had good internal consistency and satisfactory test-retest reliability. It was demonstrated that
the test may be divided into two equivalent short forms for
the test-retest purposes. Other findings were that the
racial attitude scores were found to vary systematically
with race of subject, but not with sex of subject, IQ, or
age. Evidence regarding race of examiner effects was inconclusive. It was concluded that PRAM II provides a reliable
index of racial attitudes and that the same rationale could
be employed in the assessment of other attitudes at the preschool level. Theories of racial attitude development are
discussed.

1260. Williams, J. E. and Edwards, C. D. An exploratory study of
the modification of color and racial concept attitudes in preschool
children. Child Development, 1969, 40 (3), 737-750.

Employed laboratory reinforcement procedures to weaken the
naturally formed black-white concept attitudes of 84 5-year-
old Caucasian children. Subsequently, some evidence was
found for a reduction in the tendency to attribute negative
adjectives to pictures of Negroes and positive adjectives
to pictures of Caucasians. Findings were viewed as consistent with theory that the color concept attitude acts
as one support for the racial concept attitude.

1261. Williams, J. E. and Rosseau, C. A. Evaluation and identification responses of Negro preschoolers to the colors black and white.
Perceptual and Motor Skills, 1971, 33 (2), 587-599.

Notes that previous studies have demonstrated a tendency
toward the positive evaluation of white and the negative
evaluation of black among Caucasian and Negro college students, and among Caucasian preschoolers. This tendency and
the tendency toward self-identification with these colors
was assessed among 89 Negro 3- to 6-year-olds. Subjects'
responses to procedures employing pictures of two animals,
one colored white and one black, indicate that subjects:

(a) tended to associate positive evaluative adjectives
(e.g., "good") with the white figures and negative evaluative adjectives (e.g., "bad") with the black figures; and
(b) tended to identify with the white figure rather than
the black figure. Findings are interpreted as providing
additional evidence of the cross-racial, cross-cultural
character of the evaluative connotations of white and black.
Possible origins of these meanings, and their relationship
to self-concept development in the Negro child, are discussed.

1262. Williamson, R. C. Social distance and ethnicity: Some subcultural factors among high school students. Urban Education, 1976,
11 (3), 295-312.

A sample of high school students drawn from 14 eastern
Pennsylvania schools -- inner-city ghetto, middle-class and
upper-class suburbs, middle-size cities and semi-rural areas
-- was surveyed. Whites showed less social distance toward
Puerto Ricans than toward blacks, as well as less differentiation between four kinds of interaction -- eating together,
dancing, attending a party, and marriage. Sex (girls are
consistently more tolerant), grade average, and father's
occupation proved to be more predictive for the responses
of whites than for the other two groups. Moreover, the
assignment to either an academic or vocational curriculum
had a marked influence on the social network of students.
Generally, the blacks showed less social distance in mixed
schools than in the two ghetto schools. Despite problems
of sample size, validity, and realibility, the Puerto Rican
sample appeared to be the most tolerant. Social distance,
it is concluded, is affected by the specific social climate
of the school setting, by curriculum, and by social class.

1263. Willis, F. N. and Reeves, D. L. Touch interaction in junior
high students in relation to sex and race. Developmental Psychology,
1976, 12 (1), 91-92. Also, see ERIC Abstracts, No. EJ-138-509, 1976.

The data from this study indicate that black junior high
school students, particularly females, engage in more interpersonal touching in queues than white students, but that
their rate of touching is much less than that observed in
younger children.

1264. Woods, M. B. The unsupervised child of the working mother.
Developmental Psychology, 1972, 6 (1), 14-25.

Studied 108 fifth grade children of employed mothers attending school in the black ghetto of North Philadelphia. The
California Test of Personality, the California Short Form
Test of Mental Maturity, the Iowa Test of Basic Skills, and
the Parent Behavior Inventory, were administered. Other
information was gathered from teachers, schools, and community records. 38 mothers were interviewed. Data reduction included t-tests, Chi-squares, and a cluster analysis.
Results indicate that more girls exhibited impoverished

cognitive development. Full-time employment of the mother
was a (+) influence. Maternal quality mother-child relationships, and maternal attitudes toward employment were also
influential. Findings suggest a two-variable theory as the
explanation of the effects of maternal employment on children.

1265. Wright, G. O. Vocational choices of a selected sample of
Negro pupils. Educational Research Bulletin, 1942, 21, 5-9.

The responses obtained from 114 ninth grade Negro boys and
girls (age range 10-15 years) in Columbis, Ohio to a question about vocational choices revealed the following facts:
The vocational choices of these pupils related to the actual
employment situation in Columbis were patently unrealistic.
By far the largest proportion of choices was professional
and white-collar jobs. When the responses were grouped
according to fathers' occupation, the following indices of
conformity were obtained, with -2 representing absolute
absence of conformity and +2 absolute conformity: pupils
with parents engaged in unskilled work, -1.66; pupils with
parents in skilled work, -.84; and pupils with parents in
the professions, +1.54.

1266. Wubberhorst, J., Gradford, S., and Willis, F. N. Trust in
children as a function of race, sex, and socioeconomic group. Psychological Reports, 1971, 29 (3, Part 2), 1183-1187.

Assessed trust in 880 first thru eighth graders by employing
a method in which subjects might choose to aid or not to
aid a young male examiner who was a stranger to them. Data
show that (a) boys were more likely to trust the examiner,
and (b) blacks were less likely to trust a white examiner
than were white subjects but even less likely to trust a
black examiner. Results are interpreted in relation to
urban crime statistics indicating that the victims of crime
are poor and black and that the criminal is likely to be a
young man.

1267. Wyatt, D. W. Racial handicaps in the Negro delinquent. Pro-
bation, 1943, 21, 112-115.

Comparing two groups of adolescent Negroes, one delinquent
and the other a high school honor group, the author suggests
that delinquency cannot be explained simply in terms of
economic, social or environmental factors.

1268. Youmans, E. G., Grigsby, S. E., and King, H. Social Change,
generation, and race. Rural Sociology, 1969, 34 (3), 305-312.

This paper views the different values held by younger and
older generations of rural American Negroes and whites. It
considers the implications of these values for social change.
Data were obtained from 411 Negro and white high school
seniors in northern Florida, and from their parents. The
white parents had twice as much education as the Negroes.
The median annual income of white families was $3,792 as

The median annual income of white families was $3,792 as
compared with $2,010 for black families. The values held
were measured along three dimensions: achievement orientation, the sociopsychological concept of anomie, and family
identification. No significant generational differences
were found among the whites regarding the first two dimensions. However, the younger generation of Negroes scored
much lower in achievement orientation than their parents.
Negro youths also scored much lower than their parents with
respect to anomie, or alienation. A high score indicates
distress, despondency, despair; thus the youths had more
hope than their parents though they were less confident of
their ability to succeed. Negroes and whites showed substantial generational differences in the family identification category. The adults of both races showed 30 to 40%
more family identification than did their offspring. Within the younger generation, a comparison of the two racial
groups reveals several important differences. Negro youths
had less confidence, greater feelings of despair, and greater
attachment to their families than did the white youngsters.
Similar differences obtained between Negro and white adults
with respect to anomie and family identification, but not
with respect to achievement orientation. Negro adults scored
substantially higher in this category than did the white
adults. From this data the inference is made that young
rural Negroes are well equipped to identify with the aims
of the Negro movement in urban areas, and that their migration to urban centers will probably continue.

1269. Young, M. B. The Negro girl and poverty. The American Child,
1965, 47 (3), 11-13.

The low-income Negro girls are cut off from middle class Negro
girls and from low income whites. The mass media do not
show the low income Negro girl. She often resorts to osten-
tation for recognition. Her educational situation is difficult. Her early recognition of the matriarchal Negro
society presents problems. The Negro girl seeks ways to
cope with the injustices of the larger society. The direction
she takes depends on the guidance she receives.

1270. Zalk, S. R. and Katz, P. A. Katz-Zalk Projective Prejudice
Test: A measure of racial attitudes in children. Available from:
Order Department, American Psychological Association, 1200 Seventeenth
Street, N.W., Washington, D. C. Order No. JSAS MS. 1235, 1976. 37 pp.

A test consisting of slides of ambiguous school situations
was designed for measuring racial attitudes in children. For
each slide, the subject is asked to choose which child initiated or is the recipient of a positive or negative event.
The instrument was standardized on 547 black and white urban,
public school children at the 1st, 2nd, 4th, and 5th grades.
Additional data were collected from the 2nd and 5th grades
of a suburban community. Administration of the test was
counterbalanced for race of examiner. Differences in res-

respect to the Puerto Rican, Anglo-American, and Black-American cultures. They are applicable to programs which propose to enhance ethnic identity or cross-cultural under-standing among any one or more of these three ethnic groups. These modular measures do not require reading ability; rather, they are based upon pictorial stimuli and response options. The directions are particularly appropriate for elementary school programs involving children who may differ culturally and linguistically. The 15 stimuli for each scale are graphic illustrations of the dress, sports, foods, and popular symbols of the Puerto Rican, Anglo-American, and Black-American cultures, respectively. The child indicates his attitude toward each pictorial stimulus by marking one of five faces on a happy-sad Likert-type scale. There is also an alternate response option indi-cating no knowledge of the particular cultural referent. Each scale thus yields two scores: a cultural attitude index and a cultural knowledge index.

1274. Zschock, D. K. Black youth in suburbia. Urban Affairs Quarterly, 1971, 7 (1), 61-74.

Significant numbers of the poor live in suburbs that are generally regarded as sancuaries of the affluent. A series of interviews with black youths in Suffolk County, New York, disclosed an overall unemployment rate of 25%. There are relatively few low-level, entry-level jobs in Suffolk County, and transportation on a regular basis is difficult. The conservatism and apathy of the public is a common theme of black youth dissatisfaction. Black students tend to find themselves assigned to general education courses before they realize that this track militates against entering higher education. Few among the youths inter-viewed had ever talked with a guidance counselor. The youths complained of being intimidated by whites in certain social areas and of being the ones held responsible in sit-uations of racial conflict.

ponse patterns were found as a function of
examiner, race of subject, and in some inst
These differences are discussed, and some p
regard to measurement are noted.

1271. Zalk, S. R., et al. Sex bias in children.
at the Annual Meeting of the American Psychological
Washington, D. C., September 3-7, 1976). See ERIC A
129-441, 1976. 13 pp.

This study investigated children's sex biased
a function of the sex, age, and race of the ch
as a geographical-SES factor. Two attitudes we
on a 55-item questionnaire: Sex Pride (attribu
characteristics to a child of the same sex) and
dice (attributing negative characteristics to a
the other sex). Subjects were 1,169 children (5
656 white) in grades 2 and 5, who were taken fron
lower-middle, upper-lower class urban or a suburb
Gender was divided fairly equally. The children v
in their schools, with examiner race varying equal
each grade level. Results indicated that all chil
to select children of the same sex for the positive
butes, but that both boys and girls selected boys f
negative attributes. Although all Sex Pride scores
with age, this was most exaggerated for the girls f₁
lower-middle, upper-lower class urban environment.

1272. Zimmerman, B. J. and Brody, G. H. Race and modeling
on the interpersonal play patterns of boys. Journal of Educ
Psychology, 1975, 67 (5), 591-598.

Studied the effects of race and modeling cues on the p
patterns of dyads of young boys. 40 white and 38 blacl
fifth graders were observed during play on the basis of
five indices of interaction. Black subjects talked sig:
ficantly less together, faced each other less directly,
interacted at greater interpersonal distances than did w
subjects. Racially mixed dyads were intermediate in soc:
distance, talk, and body axis. Biracial dyads observed
a televised episode of a black male adolescent and a whit
male adolescent play together in a warm or cold fashion.
Post-tests revealed that subjects viewing the warm interaction were more cooperative, played at a closer distance,
faced the other child more directly, gave more eye contact, and talked more frequently than did those who were
exposed to the cold modeling videotape.

1273. Zirkel, P. A. and Greene, J. F. Cultural Attitude Scale
technical report. April, 1974, 58 pp. Report, test booklet(s),
and manual available from: Learning Concepts 2501 N. Lamar, Austin,
Texas 78705. Also, see ERIC Abstracts, ED-102-195, 1974.

The Cultural Attitude Scales represent a modular approach
to the measurement of cultural attitudes and knowledge with

AUTHOR INDEX

SUBJECT INDEX

ABOUT THE COMPILERS

Hector F. Myers is currently Director of Research at the Fanon Research and Development Center and Assistant Professor of Psychology, University of California, Los Angeles.

Phyllis Gabriel Rana is an assistant researcher at the Fanon Research and Development Center. She received her masters in Public Health from the University of California, Los Angeles, and is currently working toward a Ph.D. in the School of Architecture and Urban Planning there.

Marcia Harris is a graduate student in Social Psychology at the University of Michigan. Her major focus of interest has been group identification and sex role of minority women.

SUMMER 83